CW01209172

BANNOCKBURN

BANNOCKBURN
THE TRIUMPH OF ROBERT THE BRUCE

DAVID CORNELL

YALE UNIVERSITY PRESS
NEW HAVEN AND LONDON

Copyright © 2009 David Cornell

All rights reserved. This book may not be reproduced in whole or in part, in any form (beyond that copying permitted by Sections 107 and 108 of the U.S. Copyright Law and except by reviewers for the public press) without written permission from the publishers.

The right of David Cornell to be identified as the author of this Work has been asserted by him.

For information about this and other Yale University Press publications, please contact:

U.S. Office: sales.press@yale.edu   www.yalebooks.com
Europe Office: sales@yaleup.co.uk   www.yaleup.co.uk

Set in Minion by J&L Composition Ltd, Filey, North Yorkshire
Printed in Great Britain by TJ International, Padstow, Cornwall

Library of Congress Control Number: 2009921474

ISBN: 978-0-300-14568-7

A catalogue record for this book is available from the British Library.

10 9 8 7 6 5 4 3 2 1

CONTENTS

List of Illustrations vii
Acknowledgements ix
A Note on the Sources xi
Preface xiii
Maps xix

Part I The Scottish Wars
1. A Battle Won — 3
2. The Wolf in the Fold — 12
3. A Poisoned Chalice — 24

Part II The Power Struggles
4. The Dark Stain of Treachery — 37
5. Bequest of a Warrior-King — 53
6. Lords of War — 69
7. Raised from the Dust — 88

Part III 1314
8. A Tale of Three Castles — 111
9. Tears of a King — 129
10. Baiting the Trap — 149
11. Playing with Fire — 165
12. The Shortest of Nights — 182
13. Flesh and Blood — 196

Part IV The Shockwave
14. One Fleeting Hour — 217
15. The Legacy — 237

Appendix I   24 June 1314: The Field of Battle 255
Appendix II   English Casualties 261
Abbreviations 264
Notes 266
Bibliography 281
Index 285

ILLUSTRATIONS

1 Cambuskenneth Abbey. © Crown Copyright reproduced courtesy of Historic Scotland.
2 Edinburgh Castle. © Crown Copyright reproduced courtesy of Historic Scotland
3 Stirling Castle. West crags. © Crown Copyright reproduced courtesty of Historic Scotland
4 Bothwell Castle. East curtain wall, great hall, chapel and south-east tower. © Crown Copyright reproduced courtesy of Historic Scotland.
5 Bannockburn. Illustration from John of Fordun's *Scotichronicon geminum*, c. 1384. Courtesy of the Master and Fellows of Corpus Christi College, Cambridge.
6 Second Great Seal of Robert I. SCOTLANDSIMAGES.COM © Crown Copyright 2007 The National Archives of Scotland RH17/1/23.
7 Bronze aquamanile of a cavalry soldier. © The Trustees of the British Museum.
8 Chain-mail shirt, fourteenth century. © Museum of London.
9 Sword, fourteenth century. © Museum of London.
10 Carved slab from the Cheapside Cross, thirteenth century. © Museum of London.
11 Pewter badge of an archer, late fourteenth century. © Museum of London.

ACKNOWLEDGEMENTS

I WOULD FIRST LIKE TO THANK THOSE WHOSE EXPERTISE WAS INFLUENTIAL IN THE publication of this book. My agent, Andrew Lownie, provided invaluable guidance from the initial proposal right through to publication. His enthusiasm for the subject matter was also greatly appreciated. At Yale University Press, I would like to thank Heather McCallum not only for commissioning the book but also for being readily available to offer prompt and friendly advice whenever it was needed. In terms of content, I am grateful to Professor Michael Prestwich and Dr Michael Penman for reading an earlier version of the manuscript and for providing a number of valuable comments and references.

I have been fortunate enough to study medieval history, both as an undergraduate and as a postgraduate, at the University of Durham, and I would like to take this opportunity to express my gratitude to those academics from whom I learnt so much, namely, Professor Michael Prestwich, Professor Robin Frame and Dr Richard Britnell. My greatest debt, however, is to Michael Prestwich, who supervised my postgraduate degree and whose expert knowledge of the thirteenth and fourteenth centuries, and in particular of medieval military history, has proved indispensable.

Finally, and most of all, I would like to thank my parents. Throughout my increasingly many years of study they have unfailingly provided their full encouragement and support, without which I would never have had the opportunity to pursue my interests. In many ways this book is as much theirs as it is mine, and it is to my parents that I wish affectionately to dedicate it.

A NOTE ON THE SOURCES

Robert Bruce and Edward II were both the subjects of fourteenth-century works which focused on their lives. *The Bruce*, by John Barbour, was a romance-biography written in verse in the language of Scots during the later part of the century, most probably between 1371 and 1375. Barbour was an educated Scotsman who in 1356 became archdeacon of Aberdeen and who had also studied in England and France. Writing several decades after the events he recounts, and not having been an eyewitness himself, Barbour's account was influenced by the fact that *The Bruce* was written during the reign of Robert II of Scotland, and Barbour was almost certainly writing to please the Stewart king. Barbour did not intend *The Bruce* to be an accurate and faithful chronicle of the period, but a stirring romance centred on the figures of Robert Bruce and James Douglas. Barbour is consequently prone to melodramatic embellishments and his work must be treated with caution. However, he did have access to contemporary chronicles and accounts of the period, and his work does appear to be broadly accurate. As *The Bruce* is the sole authority for many events of Robert Bruce's life, there is little to contradict it and on these occasions it must be taken on trust.

Nor is the *Vita Edwardi Secundi* (*Life of Edward II*), strictly a chronicle. The *Vita* takes the form of a memoir or journal written by an extremely well-connected English secular clerk who lived through the turbulent events of Edward II's reign. It has been proposed that John Walwayn, who was a royal clerk in 1314 and Treasurer in 1318, may have been the author. The *Vita* provides an extremely detailed and often analytical account of Edward's reign. The other two major English chronicles that are invaluable for both this period and the Scottish wars are the *Chronicle of Lanercost* and the *Scalacronica*. The former was written in the Austin priory of Lanercost in Cumberland and was based on a lost Franciscan chronicle. *Lanercost* is a well-informed contemporary account of the period from 1201 to 1346 and is especially valuable for its coverage of events in the north of England, particularly the Scottish wars. The *Scalacronica* was written by the Northumberland knight Thomas Gray of Heton, who was a veteran of the Scottish wars. Gray was captured by the Scots in 1355 and during his imprisonment in Edinburgh Castle he began to write this history of England covering the period from 1066 to 1362. The *Scalacronica* is particularly important because Gray's father, also Thomas, had fought at Bannockburn and had been captured in the battle. A soldier himself, the author of the *Scalacronica* knew of the conflicts of which he was writing.

These four contemporary, or near contemporary, narrative sources form the basis of any account of the Scottish wars in this period. Although there is a range of other chronicles from which information can be drawn, it is these four that provide the foundation for a study of Bannockburn.

PREFACE

Midsummer's Eve, 23 June 1314

NIGHTFALL WAS EMBRACED BY THE SCOTSMEN WITH A PALPABLE SENSE OF RELIEF. It had been a long time in coming. The day had been hot and seemingly endless. Blood had been shed. Men had died. In the brief respite of the night's shrouding darkness, wounds were roughly dressed, meagre rations of food and drink gratefully taken. Too tired to talk, men sank to the ground in exhaustion, their arms heavy with fatigue, legs stiffening with cramp. Many lay full length in the cool softness of the undergrowth and stared blankly at the abyss of blackness above them. No light penetrated the heavy canopy of the wood, neither the sheen of the moon nor the glimmer of a star. Alone with their thoughts, men humbly muttered prayers of thanks that they had survived the day and desperately begged that they would also be spared on the next.

For most of the several thousand Scots encamped in the wooded enclosure of the New Park this, one of the shortest of nights, seemed agonisingly long. Despite their exhaustion few slept. Many believed this to be the last night of their lives. They knew what awaited them outside the confines of the New Park. Somewhere beyond the tree line, hidden from sight by the fragile darkness of the summer night, a formidable army advanced towards them.

For the Scots it was a terrifying prospect. An English host with a Plantagenet king at its head, and confronting an external enemy, had never before been defeated on British soil. The English host heavily outnumbered them. It was better equipped. Sixteen years before, at Falkirk, it had engaged a Scottish army in battle and annihilated it. Now the English sought their destruction. In the heat and dust of a vicious skirmish that afternoon the English had been bloodied yet, physically at least, remained unbowed. Even as the Scots took sanctuary in the New Park, the English remorselessly maintained their advance, thousands of men engaging in a laborious night crossing of the treacherous waters of the Bannock Burn, the valuable warhorses of English knights and men-at-arms slowly being led along the makeshift timber walkways that had been laid upon the soft, peaty earth. No effort was to be spared in bringing the Scots to battle. No time could be lost.

Meanwhile, in the darkened isolation of the New Park, Scotsmen contemplated their own mortality. They commended their lives into the hands of the Lord. They made their peace. Yet this night it was not the Lord who presided over their fate but a man who stood among them. Nor was it only their lives that were in his hands. Upon his actions also rested the immediate future of the Scottish kingdom.

In life few men find themselves empowered with a decision that has the potential to dictate the fate of a nation. To possess such an awesome responsibility is both a privilege and a curse. A correct decision promises unsurpassed success but a wrong one invites catastrophic failure. Such a man holds in his hands the lives of those who follow him. It is his duty to ensure that if they are killed, they will have died in pursuit of something tangible, and their lives will not have been wasted. That man knows he himself will live or die by his decision, that his own life, his own reputation, is at stake. Everything he has ever done, anything he has ever achieved, whatever respect and admiration he has earned – none of it now counts for anything. A single moment will encapsulate his life and it is for this moment that he will be remembered. However hard he might try to believe otherwise, he knows that it has all come down to this – to the making of one torturous decision.

On the night of Midsummer's Eve, 23 June 1314, the weight of this terrible burden fell upon the shoulders of one man. That man was Robert Bruce, the largely self-appointed king of Scotland, and the choice that confronted him was whether or not to give battle to the might of the English host. That Bruce was even considering doing so is remarkable. At noon, less than twelve hours before, he would have found such a thought inconceivable. For seven years Bruce had fought the English, and at the very heart of his skilfully constructed strategy was the need to eliminate the risk of such a set-piece battle. It was a strategy that had proved immensely effective. His success had won him a following so substantial that he could assemble a Scottish army. This army, his whole military strength, now awaited his decision. If Bruce chose to withdraw, his men would obey him; if he should decide to stay, then they would stand and fight beside him. Their lives were his to command.

The brevity of that short midsummer's night lent urgency to the troubled deliberations of Robert Bruce. In the gloom of the New Park his men shifted restlessly around him. Hidden in the expanse of darkness that stretched eastward towards the Forth river, the English host was moving relentlessly towards him. To the north loomed the towering stone crag upon which Stirling Castle was perched, a monolithic silhouette etched even blacker than the night. Within the castle a beleaguered garrison of over one hundred English soldiers commanded by the knight Philip Mowbray waited impatiently for the prolonged siege they had endured to be lifted. It was to relieve the castle that the English host had ostensibly come. An agreement had been reached between Edward Bruce, brother of the Scottish king, and Mowbray that if Stirling Castle was not relieved by Midsummer's Day, then it would be surrendered to the Scots. That deadline was tomorrow.

Robert Bruce was rightly furious with his brother, Edward, for agreeing the pact with Mowbray, which had tied his army down before Stirling Castle. The awful predicament that now confronted Bruce was whether to give battle or retreat. If he was to avoid battle, then he must withdraw his army under cover of night. Time was short. Each moment of indecision drew the Scots closer to battle. The Scottish army crowded within the New Park anxiously awaited an order. They had complete faith in Bruce. Throughout the last seven years he had proved himself to be an extremely capable commander, a gifted strategist and tactician blessed with an innate ability to identify an objective and employ the most efficient means to achieve it. Now, on the night of Midsummer's Eve, his judgement underwent the ultimate test. Bruce made his fateful decision. The Scots would give battle. It was a courageous call – and with hindsight a spectacularly successful one – yet considering the situation in which Bruce found himself that night, with the dreadful risks that defeat entailed, many must have wondered whether his choice was the wrong one. The victory for which Robert Bruce is best remembered was arguably a battle he should never have fought.

This is the bitter irony of Bannockburn: it was a battle that Bruce should have avoided at all costs yet one from which he emerged victorious; it was a battle that the English so desperately wanted and in which they were completely routed. In this can be found the enduring fascination of Bannockburn, an against-the-odds victory to rank among the very finest that history has to offer, a glorious triumph that appeared to defy all logic and convention. It encapsulates the successful resistance of a smaller, weaker nation in the face of a larger, much more powerful neighbour. With the passage of time Bannockburn has increasingly, and quite rightly, taken on the mantle of an heroic victory for the Scottish nation. This triumph, together with its inextricable link to Robert Bruce, one of the greatest of all national icons, has infused the battle with a sense of romance and legend which has taken on epic proportions. Even in our modern society, frequently derided for its lack of awareness with regard to British history, the battle of Bannockburn is one of the few events for which there remains a body of popular knowledge. However, it is this very popularity, this sense of romance and legend, that now threatens to obscure a true understanding of Bannockburn.

How much do we really know about the events that took place during the two midsummer days – Sunday 23 and Monday 24 June 1314 – on which the battle was fought? On what is our knowledge based? The key sources containing details of the engagement comprise a handful of fourteenth-century narrative chronicles which, by their very nature, are vague and fragmentary, and often provide more questions than answers. From these it is possible to gain an idea of the course of the battle, a sense of the broad outline of events, of how the engagement generally unfolded. On the English side a little more can be gleaned from official documents, but those that survive reveal nothing of significance. Any documents of real importance were destroyed in the rout. The handful of chronicles and official documents therefore represent the limit of our knowledge of the two days during which the battle was fought, and it is on the basis of these that most attempts to reconstruct Bannockburn have been founded.

However, the battle of Bannockburn was about much more than just the two days on which it was fought. Frequently it is approached in strictly military terms, with the most thorough studies also encompassing an account of the campaign leading to the engagement. Yet as much as Bannockburn was the product of a series of wars waged between the kingdoms of England and Scotland since 1296, it was also the product of separate political conflicts within each of these kingdoms which had been ongoing since 1306–7. Both of these internal conflicts concerned the Crown; more precisely they focused on the rights and authority of the Crown, and the extent to which these could be exercised.

In Scotland a brutal civil war had been fought over Robert Bruce's usurpation of the Scottish Crown in 1306 and, as a largely self-appointed king, his ensuing attempts to appropriate the power and authority invested in it. The conflict within England had been the result of a series of attempts, from 1307 onwards, by the great lords of the realm, the magnates, to place institutional restraints on the power and authority of the English Crown. The struggle of

Edward II to resist these restraints, together with his inability to recognise and understand the responsibilities that the Crown bestowed upon him, plunged the country into a crisis rapidly descending towards civil war. Bannockburn resulted from the fusing of the Scottish wars with these two separate political conflicts. If we are truly to understand the battle, then it is necessary not only to have an understanding of the wars fought between England and Scotland, but also of the causes and the course of the separate civil conflicts within each of these kingdoms.

It was in the persons of Robert Bruce and Edward II that these conflicts became irrevocably joined. The shadows of these two sharply contrasting men are cast long upon the field of Bannockburn. Both considered Bannockburn not only as an engagement in a national war but as an opportunity to strike a decisive blow in the civil conflicts in which they had become embroiled. In leading into battle their armies of kingdoms they sought to rule with absolute power, each man stood to gain much more than a victory for his respective nation. Their civil conflicts can be studied in a wealth of sources, and it is through these that the road to Bannockburn can be more clearly charted, and the course of the engagement more fully explored.

However, the big question that hangs tantalisingly unanswered over Bannockburn is not so much why the battle occurred or how it unfolded, but rather how it was possible that the battle resulted in such an extraordinarily unlikely outcome. The vastly superior English host was not just defeated, it was comprehensively routed. Should we look to the chronicles for an answer, then we will be disappointed. By the terms of the conventional piety of the period, Scottish victory is ascribed to the justice of the Scottish cause and the divine favour with which the Scots were consequently blessed. Nor do most of the major scholarly works on Bannockburn offer a convincing explanation of the outcome of the battle. They proffer reasons for the English defeat but lack any credible explanation of how the English could have been defeated so thoroughly. Indeed several questions that are fundamental to understanding the outcome of the battle have rarely, if ever, been asked. This is particularly true of the second day of battle, 24 June, for which no attempt has been made to identify features as elementary as the actual duration of the crucial mêlée or the proportions of the two armies that were actively engaged in the fight. Nor has the vital role of the Scottish offensive against the three principal English-held castles of Scotland in 1314 been fully appreciated; without this offensive the battle of Bannockburn would never have taken place. Indeed, in military terms, the real objectives of both the Scottish and English campaigns of 1314 have remained undefined or misrepresented despite their critical importance.

By answering the questions as to why the battle occurred and how it unfolded, it is possible to reach an understanding of how such a severe defeat came to be inflicted upon the superior English host. The dynamics that produced the battle were also critical in deciding its outcome. This is not to claim that Bannockburn was not won on the two days during which it was fought, but rather that several of the factors which made such a comprehensive Scottish victory possible were already in place long before the two armies met on the field of battle.

A battle fought between the armies of two kingdoms is much more than just a military engagement; it becomes a measure of their political and economic strength, a test of their society, a glimpse into their very heart and soul. The battle of Bannockburn has suffered due to the narrow perspective from which it has generally been viewed, an introspective study of the two days on which it was fought. In fact, it can only truly be understood by placing it within its wider context as a phenomenon inextricably linked to the political events within Scotland and England in this period.

Bannockburn, therefore, is certainly deserving of our fresh attention. It was both a great victory for Scotland – arguably the greatest in its history – and one of the most humiliating defeats that England has ever suffered. As such, it remains inscribed in the pantheon of each nation's history, albeit with directly contrasting emotions. Bannockburn was a pivotal event in the shaping of British history: both the battle and its enduring legacy have proved of crucial importance in the forming of national identity in both countries. So much about what we know of the two days on which the battle was fought remains fragmentary and imprecise. However, if we take a new look, and in so doing make use of the wider context in which the fighting took place, it becomes apparent that perhaps we know more about Bannockburn than we think we do, and that its extraordinary outcome was not as unlikely as it may at first appear.

Map 1 Sunday, 23 June

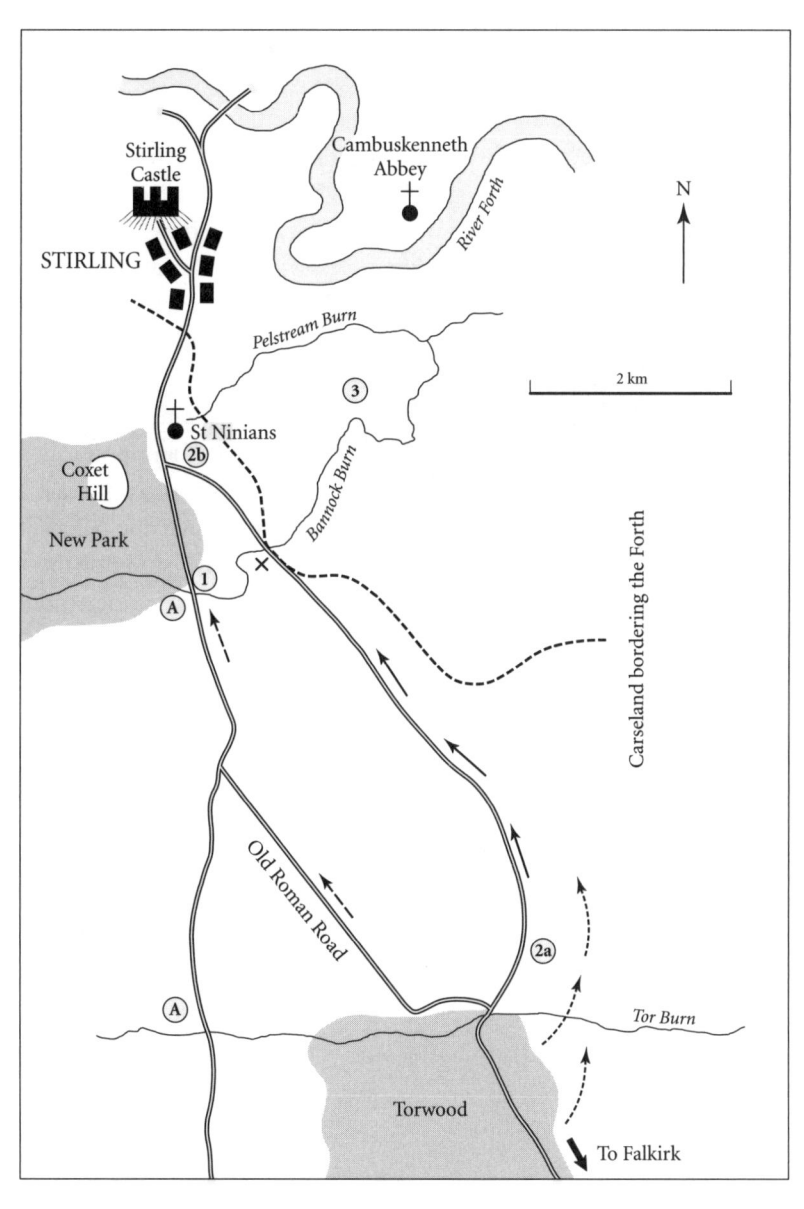

✗	Approximate location of Bannock
------	100 ft contour line
①	Engagement between English vanguard and Scottish rearguard
②a ②b	Alternative sites for engagements between Scottish vanguard and Clifford's division
③	Carse of Balquhiderock. Site where English encamped on night of 23/24 June
◄---	Route taken by English vanguard
◄-----	Initial advance of Clifford's division
◄──	Advance of English host late afternoon/early evening
Ⓐ	Alternative locations of Scottish cavalry trap

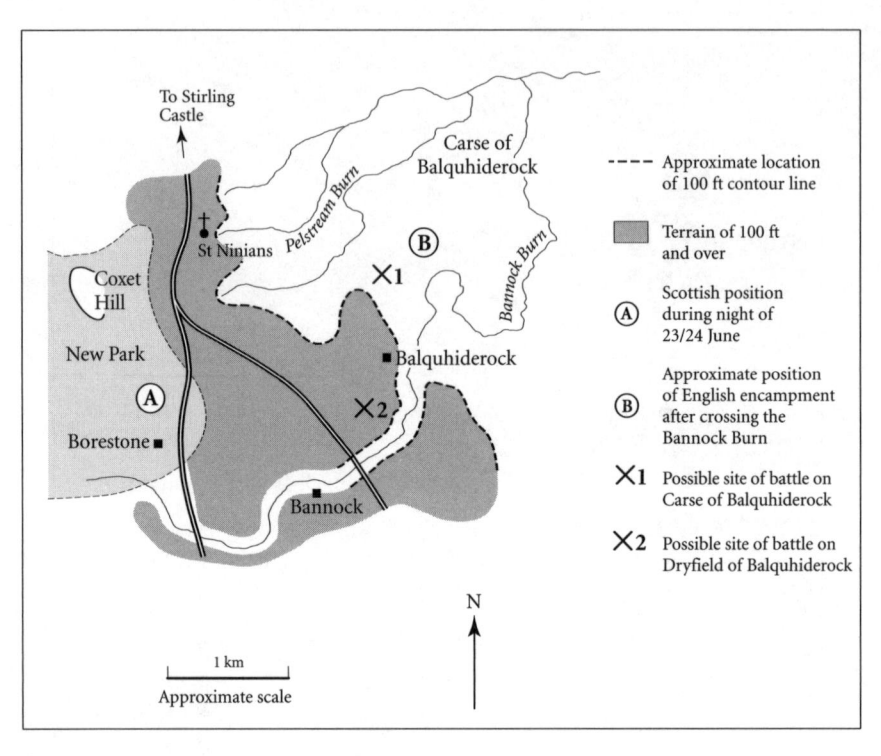

Map 2 Monday, 24 June

Map 3

I

THE SCOTTISH WARS

For as long as a hundred of us remain alive, we will never on any conditions be subjected to the lordship of the English. For we fight not for glory nor riches nor honour, but for freedom alone, which no good man gives up except with his life.

The Declaration of Arbroath

CHAPTER ONE

A BATTLE WON

THE SPECTACLE THAT CONFRONTED ROBERT BRUCE ON THE MORNING OF TUESDAY, 25 June 1314, was so gruesome that it would have lived with him for the rest of his life. Never before had he witnessed the horrific aftermath of a major set-piece battle. It was not an experience he would have wished to repeat.

Brutally spread out before him was a vile panorama of butchery and carnage. Bodies littered the ground: the eviscerated corpses of men bloody and broken, the rotting carcasses of horses already becoming foully swollen and bloated. Severed limbs protruded awkwardly from among dismembered torsos. Entrails and organs lay starkly exposed where they had spilt from horrendous gashes torn into the soft paleness of flesh; the bleached whiteness of bones gleamed where they had burst through the delicate tissue of skin. Faces were contorted in agony, the pain of a violent death set as an unsightly mask. Noses were broken, eye sockets fractured, jaws smashed where fists, elbows and shields had desperately been slammed into snarling faces. Skulls had been caved in by the vicious blows of axes and swords. Razor-sharp iron spearheads and lance tips lay buried deep within the sinews into which they had been ferociously driven.

The barbarity of this repellent scene was exacerbated by the naked state of the corpses, vividly exposing the horrendous wounds that had been inflicted. Immediately the battle had ended, hordes of victorious Scottish foot soldiers had promptly abandoned the pursuit of their defeated enemy and mercilessly clambered over the dead and the dying, ruthlessly stripping them of anything of value. They pulled rings of gold from still-twitching fingers; they tore silver buckles and clasps from clothing; they ripped the very clothes themselves from the warmth of skin that still ran with sweat and blood. Those Englishmen found to be alive were unceremoniously dispatched by the Scots with the peremptory flash of a knife blade and rigorously despoiled of their possessions. Discarded weapons were seized with alacrity, expensively crafted swords and fine-handled daggers were snatched from the ground or pulled out of bodies, and valuable chainmail and armour were roughly manhandled from corpses.

Throughout the hours that followed the rout of the English host, on Monday 24 June, the battlefield had been picked clean as the victorious Scottish foot soldiers, and those men who had guarded the Scottish baggage, indulged in an orgy of plunder. Only with the coming of night had they stopped. Now, in the cold light of morning, men prowled again among the corpses, scouring the dead for a glint of metal, for anything of value that might have been missed the previous day. Randomly they kicked out at lifeless arms and legs, and carelessly turned over bodies in the hope of uncovering something of worth. Swarms of flies rose from the disturbed corpses. Overhead the ragged black wings of carrion birds flapped in the morning sky, raucous cries shrilly piercing the still air as the birds swooped down to partake of the grisly feast below.

After the heady elation of victory the previous day, for Bruce this must have been an incredibly sobering scene. The sight of death was accompanied by its overpowering stench. Corpses were strewn across the field. Devastation surrounded him. Here was the price of the victory he had won. Before him the human cost lay bluntly exposed. As Bruce watched the human scavengers roam among the detritus of battle, the elation of victory within his heart must have been severely tempered by the reek of death which befouled the very air he breathed. It was a battle won, but so many lives had been lost. There was nothing glorious about the field of battle that morning.

As Bruce sombrely regarded the battlefield, a flicker of movement suddenly caught his eye. A figure was walking towards him through the carnage as if an apparition. The man carried no weapon nor wore any armour. As he picked his way forward, his stride was measured but purposeful. Every few steps the man turned his head, anxiously glancing from side to side, desperate to ensure he kept well away from the prowling foot soldiers. It was clear he was not a Scotsman. The clothes he wore, though bloodied and soiled, were those of a man of wealth. His furtive movements were invested with a sense of suppressed urgency. He drew close in some haste. Not once did his pace falter as he made straight for Bruce.

Only as the man came close did Robert Bruce recognise this mysterious figure. He was certainly no apparition. Before Bruce stood Marmaduke Tweng, an English knight of status and considerable renown. Bruce now understood the increasing urgency with which the knight had approached him, for Tweng was an extremely lucrative prize. A knight of Yorkshire, Tweng possessed a significant landed estate in northern England which yielded a comfortable annual income. Unable to escape from the field of battle as the English host broke apart around him, Tweng had hidden among what scant cover he could find. Miraculously he had avoided capture. Divesting his person of everything of value, secreting his expensive armour and chainmail within the thick foliage of a bush, and retaining only the sparsest of garments, Tweng had lain low as the tramping feet of scavenging foot soldiers had passed within inches of his hiding place. Tweng was a veteran of the Scottish wars and knew the grim fate that awaited those found alive on the field of battle. As a prisoner, his ransom would be worth a small fortune to his captor, but he was well aware that the rapacious foot soldiers were as likely to kill him for the clothes on his back, unmindful of the lucrative prize they would be throwing away. Afraid to move, hardly daring to breathe, Tweng had remained concealed throughout the night, his life hanging by the slimmest of threads. When dawn broke and he had spied Bruce upon the battlefield, Tweng realised this was his opportunity. He had waited until Bruce approached closer, then he had made his move.

Surprised as he must have been at the sudden appearance of Tweng, Bruce remained outwardly unperturbed. According to John Barbour in his romance-biography *The Bruce*, Tweng, mindful of his desperate situation, dropped to his knee in a gesture of supplication. 'Welcome, Sir Marmaduke', announced Bruce impassively, 'to whom are you prisoner?' 'To none', replied Tweng, 'but I surrender to you here, to be at your disposal'. It was an offer that Bruce promptly accepted. In his moment of victory Bruce could afford to be magnanimous to those who had fought against him. Not only did Tweng secure his life by surrendering to Bruce but he also avoided the payment of a hefty ransom, for Bruce subsequently allowed him to return freely to England.[1]

Yet Bruce would have seen more than a defeated enemy in Marmaduke Tweng. As he looked upon the bedraggled form before him, as the English knight uttered his words of surrender, Bruce would instantly have been taken back to an earlier war. A vivid flashback of what had gone before would have passed through his mind, a time that Bruce would rather not recall. Memories that were best forgotten would also have stirred uncomfortably within Tweng. This was not the first time he had been a prisoner of the Scots nor was this the first field of carnage from which he had miraculously emerged alive. As Tweng knelt before Bruce in the midst of the butchery of the battlefield, the stench of death heavy in his nostrils, the horror of that earlier battle would have been brought graphically to his mind.

The Scottish wars had been little more than a year old when, on 11 September 1297, an English expeditionary force led by John de Warenne, earl of Surrey, had encountered a Scottish army beside the River Forth at Stirling. The Scots, commanded by William Wallace and Andrew Murray, had occupied the heights of the Abbey Craig on the north bank of the river. A single bridge spanned the Forth and over this the English vanguard crossed. It should never have been ordered to do so. The bridge was barely wide enough to take two horsemen abreast; to advance unsupported on such a narrow front in the face of the enemy was suicidal. Wallace and Murray deliberately waited until the vanguard had crossed before unleashing their troops. The massed ranks of the Scottish army stormed down from the heights of the Abbey Craig and cut the vanguard off from the bridge. While the rest of the English force watched helplessly from the far bank, the vanguard was surrounded and slaughtered.

Tweng had been a commander of the vanguard, mounted on his warhorse. As crowds of Scotsmen closed in around him, he refused to join the foot soldiers of the vanguard who, in their desperation, had cast aside their weapons and thrown themselves into the freezing waters of the Forth. In an act of incredible bravery and bloody-minded defiance, Tweng grasped the reins of his powerful warhorse, bodily pulling it around. Accompanied by a handful of followers, he dug his spurs into the flanks of the animal and charged back towards the north bank of the bridge. Slashing with his sword, violently hitting out with his elbows and knees, Tweng and his companions savagely cut their way through the seething mass of Scottish foot soldiers until at last they gained the bridge. By now it was emptying rapidly as those English stragglers still on it fled for the safety of the south bank. Thundering across the timber planking, Tweng led a headlong sprint which only eased when the frantically clattering hooves dug into the softness of earth once again. Shortly after the desperate crossing by Tweng and his few companions, the bridge broke apart and crashed heavily into the foaming waters of the Forth. Behind them, on the far north bank, the rest of the English vanguard was massacred.[2]

Tweng was the only Englishman to come away from the battle of Stirling Bridge with his reputation enhanced, his heroic escape ensuring that he was forever afterwards associated with that battle. However, this was not the end of his dogged tenacity and courage. The English garrison of Stirling Castle had formed part of the vanguard and had been decimated. Its commander, Richard Waldegrave, a former constable of the Tower of London, had been killed alongside his men during the rout on the far north bank, and the critically important castle was now in grave danger of falling to the Scots.[3] As the surviving English divisions conducted a swift retreat, a scratch force was hastily gathered together and installed within Stirling Castle. Tweng was one of the garrison's three commanders.

For two years Tweng remained a constable of Stirling Castle as the Scottish war continued to rage. In late 1299 the Scots made a concerted attempt to take the castle. By November it had come under siege and was increasingly isolated from the supply of victuals that it so desperately needed. The Scottish leaders based themselves to the south of the castle in the Torwood, William Wallace supervising the siege in person. The Stirling Castle constables eventually surrendered to the Scots and Tweng entered his first, albeit brief, period of captivity. However, they surrendered on condition that the garrison was guaranteed safe passage to England. By 18 January 1300 Tweng and his fellow garrison soldiers had safely arrived in the fortress town of Berwick over eighty miles to the southeast.

The military career of Tweng was consequently one of dubious distinction. At Stirling Bridge and Bannockburn he had been in the thick of devastating routs, and had lived to tell the sorry tale; he had barely escaped both battlefields with his life. His first captor was William Wallace, his second Robert Bruce; mercifully, both of his terms of imprisonment were short-lived. Tweng was a survivor who had lived through the brutal violence of the Scottish wars. As he knelt before Bruce after the battle of Bannockburn, he would have known as well as anyone that the two battles which had nearly cost him his life belonged to two quite distinct phases of the wars. At that moment this would have mattered little to Tweng; the cause of the wars may have differed, but the carnage they produced was just as visceral.

Bruce would have felt the full weight of the history that Tweng personified, for Bruce had also fought in that earlier phase of the wars. As he surveyed the devastation sprawled around him, he too would have been acutely conscious of the difference between the two battles. The mutilated corpses before him belonged to a war that he himself had triggered. However, worse memories hung over Bruce that sombre morning. Tweng only told a fraction of the story. Strewn among the desolation of the battlefield three disfigured corpses exposed the ugly vicissitudes of a history that Bruce would rather have wished to forget.

The maimed body of Robert Clifford could be found where the dead lay thickest. Clifford had been killed in the chaotic heart of the battle on 24 June, struck down as he vociferously urged on his English knights and men-at-arms against the immovable press of the massed ranks of Scottish foot soldiers. An experienced combat commander who had fought throughout the Scottish wars, Clifford died perhaps fittingly, a warrior in the midst of the maelstrom of battle. The manner of his death, however, was of no consolation to his widow or to the hundreds of people to whom he was lord. The scion of a great baronial family of northern England, Robert Clifford was the lord of Westmorland, the seat of his power residing at Brougham Castle. The extensive lands he owned, along with further estates in Yorkshire and Durham, marked Clifford out as one of the most powerful magnates of northern England.

Clifford's northern power-base had led him to occupy several of the highest English offices in the Scottish wars. As well as being appointed marshal of England, Clifford had served as the English captain and chief guardian of Scotland, and had subsequently been the keeper of Scotland south of the Forth. He had been warden of the Scottish lordship of Annandale, while also being charged with holding the critical English-held castles of Dumfries and Lochmaben. In 1298 Clifford had been provided with a vested interest in the English subjugation of Scotland when he was granted the confiscated lands of William Douglas. However, the corpse of Clifford would not have brought these distinguished offices to the mind of Robert Bruce, but instead the occasions when Clifford had directly impinged upon his own life.[4]

The first of these occasions had come in 1297. In June, at the very outset of the popular revolt that led to the battle of Stirling Bridge on 11 September, Clifford was one of two English commanders ordered to 'arrest and imprison' all disturbers of the peace in Scotland. Decisive action was taken the following month when Clifford entered into negotiations with the three self-appointed Guardians of Scotland – one of whom was Robert Bruce. On 7 July, at Irvine, near Kilmarnock, Bruce and his fellow Guardians had briefly surrendered to the English. This humiliating act was compounded by the continued resistance of Wallace and Murray, which would shortly culminate in their shock victory at Stirling Bridge. By then Bruce had reversed his premature act of subservience, but the agreement at Irvine was a sorry episode to which he could only look back with an uncomfortable mixture of shame and regret.[5]

In the wake of the disastrous English defeat at Stirling Bridge, Clifford had conducted two devastating raids into the Bruce lordship of Annandale in an attempt to shore up the English position in Scotland. In July 1298 the English had exacted their revenge. A vast English host, led in person by Edward I, entered Scotland and on 22 July met a Scottish army commanded by Wallace at Falkirk. The small contingent of Scottish cavalry immediately fled, and in a hard-fought engagement the Scottish foot soldiers were eventually annihilated. Clifford was in the thick of the fighting at Falkirk. Although it is extremely doubtful that Bruce fought on the Scottish side, the battle of Falkirk, like Stirling Bridge before it, was not one to which Bruce could look back with anything but sadness and regret.

Bruce would certainly also have retained a vivid recollection of the winter of 1303–4 when Clifford had led an English cavalry raid into Lothian. At Happrew early in 1304, on the edge of Ettrick forest not far from Peebles, Clifford had routed a Scottish force commanded by Wallace. It was an encounter that Bruce would have remembered, as he had participated in that murderous skirmish. Yet Bruce had not fought against Clifford, but Wallace. At Happrew, having previously deserted the Scottish cause, Bruce had fought alongside the English and battled against his Scottish compatriots.[6] Now, as Bruce surveyed the aftermath of Bannockburn, the corpse of Robert Clifford would have revealed to him the mistakes, regrets and trials of his life with the same stark rawness as the wounds that scarred the naked corpses among which the body of Clifford lay.

Not far from Clifford could be found the remains of Giles d'Argentan. An English warrior of immense renown, d'Argentan was so famous that he was popularly regarded as the third best knight in Christendom, surpassed only by Bruce himself and the Holy Roman Emperor, Henry VII. On the field of Bannockburn, at the moment of his death after a lone charge into the Scottish lines, d'Argentan had won himself immortality. But the heroic manner of d'Argentan's death would not have played on the mind of Bruce as he looked down upon the lifeless body. Nor would the corpse of d'Argentan have reminded Bruce of the vicissitudes of his own past, but instead of the spectre of bloody defeat. In 1306 d'Argentan had lost a horse while pursuing Bruce after the skirmish at Methven; it was an engagement in which Bruce had lost almost everything, including his life.[7]

Methven firmly belonged to the same phase of the wars as the battlefield on which Bruce now stood. In 1306, during the dying light of the evening of 19 June, on the slopes of a wooded hill six miles from Perth, Scottish and English forces had clashed in the first engagement of this latest outbreak of war. It was a war that Bruce had triggered by the darkest act of his chequered career and, on that summer's evening, was almost strangled at birth as an English strike force of knights and men-at-arms bloodily crushed the modest army that Bruce had scraped together. It was a nightmarish debacle from which Bruce barely escaped with his life, the flailing hands of his adversaries twice clawing at the reins of his horse as he attempted to flee. In desperation Bruce had turned his mount and crashed through the depths of the darkening wood in headlong flight. The blood of the English strike force was up. In the days following the skirmish at Methven, an English contingent had pursued the fleeing Bruce and his battered band of followers. Amongst these pursuers had been d'Argentan. At Loch Tay the English had briefly caught up with Bruce. In a fleeting skirmish d'Argentan lost a warhorse and Bruce again escaped.

The summer of 1306 had been the bleakest and most desperate period in the life of Robert Bruce, and the corpse of Giles d'Argentan would have recalled to him those dark and frightening days. If the field of carnage at Bannockburn on which the body of d'Argentan lay demonstrated how far Bruce had come since the desperate encounters at Methven and Loch Tay, then it was also a harsh reminder of the grim trail of violence and death that had pervaded the intervening years. The Scottish bodies that had soaked the grass with their blood on the wooded slopes of Methven were as much a part of the war that Bruce had initiated as those among which he now tentatively moved.

If there remained one solace for Bruce as he surveyed the devastation of the battlefield of Bannockburn, it was the knowledge that the most notable casualty of the battle, namely, Gilbert de Clare, earl of Gloucester, the second most powerful magnate of the English realm, no longer lay among the despoiled ranks of the dead. Bruce had ensured that the body of the 23-year-old earl was treated with the utmost respect. The previous day, as soon as it had been located, he had instructed that the corpse be removed from the field of battle and reverentially placed in the sanctuary of a nearby kirk. Trusted soldiers had received strict orders to guard the kirk and no doubt to keep away the acquisitive hands of covetous soldiers. Throughout the night the flickering flames of candles had solemnly lit the body where it was laid out in the silent solitude of the kirk. The soft light that illuminated the smooth features of the young face would have invested it with an even greater impression of youth.[8]

Bruce had treated the body of the earl of Gloucester with such honour not only out of respect for his status but also because he was his brother-in-law, both men being married to daughters of Richard de Burgh, earl of Ulster. The body of Gloucester was a graphic evocation of the high-aristocratic world of which Bruce was very much a part. Bruce was a man of such elevated status that he believed he could seize the Scottish Crown. When he looked down upon the young earl's face, he would also have been mindful of the turbulent political conflict that had convulsed the English realm and provided the vital breathing space allowing him to reclaim his cause from the brink of defeat. The violence with which he had fought back had culminated in the devastation that now surrounded him after victory at Bannockburn.

The mournful vicissitudes of the Scottish wars were present in the personal histories of many more of the corpses strewn across the field. Although slain in the ferocious battle of Bannockburn, many had previously fought throughout the wars. In life, few would have noticed any distinction between these conflicts. No one, however, would have been more aware of these distinctions than Robert Bruce.

When Marmaduke Tweng dropped to his knee in surrender to Robert Bruce and then humbly rose to his feet, this earlier war would have preyed on Bruce. It was a conflict with which Tweng, the most famous survivor of Stirling Bridge, was synonymous. The war that Tweng brought to his mind was a dark tale of terrible misfortune and appalling misjudgement, of vaulting ambition and astounding incompetence. It was a phase of the Scottish wars to which Bannockburn did not belong, but without which it could never have been fought.

CHAPTER TWO

THE WOLF IN THE FOLD

A DECADE BEFORE BANNOCKBURN WAS FOUGHT, DURING THE SPRING AND summer of 1304, a war was about to be brought to a close as an English army laid siege to Stirling Castle. A short distance from the field where that momentous battle was destined to take place stood a sprawling military encampment of tents and temporary wooden huts. Towering over the encampment reared the giant oversize beams of some of the greatest siege engines of the day. Above the engines, dominating the skyline, the battlemented walls of Stirling Castle loomed high upon the ancient volcanic crag on which the castle defiantly stood.[1]

Those present bore witness to one of the most formidable siege trains ever assembled by the medieval English state. It was also one of the most technologically advanced for among the prize possessions of this frightening arsenal were several sophisticated trebuchets operated by counterweights. To see these fearsome weapons in action was an amazing spectacle. A crew of perhaps more than a dozen men laboriously loaded the looping slings of these enormous engines with heavy, rounded stones, and then unleashed them. In a frenzied whipcord of motion, the trebuchets' timber arms snapped upwards, hurling boulders high into the summer sky after which they plummeted down into the battered masonry of Stirling Castle. Indeed, it was such a dramatic spectacle that an oriel window was specially built into a nearby lodging so that the English queen, Margaret of France, and the ladies of the court who were present could watch this brutal display of military power from a position of detached comfort.

For this was not only a siege but also a grandiose parade of English military might, a demonstration intended as a warning to those who might be foolish enough to consider challenging that power. The architect of this display was the great warrior-king of England, Edward I, a hardened veteran approaching sixty-five years of age who had ruled England for more than three decades. To Edward, the political theatre into which he deliberately transformed the siege of Stirling also served as a celebration marking the victorious conclusion to a bitter war waged against Scotland. That the siege was largely symbolic would have mattered little to him. It was certainly of no comfort to the beleaguered Scottish garrison who, for three interminable months, had been pinned behind the castle walls as lethal shards of splintered rock and masonry exploded around them.

In the spring of 1304 the garrison of Stirling formed the last pocket of Scottish resistance in a war that had been contested for the last seven years. The previous year, as Edward I led an army into northern Scotland, he had bypassed Stirling claiming that he wanted the castle to act as a deterrent to those in his army who harboured thoughts of desertion. The campaign of 1303 had proved an unmitigated success, and in early 1304 the formal submission to Edward I of the Scottish lords, the leaders of Scottish resistance, effectively brought the war to a victorious conclusion for both Edward and England.

Three loose ends remained. Two were individuals, namely William Wallace and Simon Fraser, Scottish knights whom Edward I considered to be traitors, and whose pitiless destruction he consequently demanded. The third was the garrison of Stirling Castle. In the spring of 1304 Edward held a Scottish parliament at St Andrews in which Wallace, Fraser and the Stirling garrison were declared outlaws.[2] They were no longer protected by law, their lives effectively considered to be forfeit. The brutal executions that Wallace and Fraser were subsequently to suffer would provide a vivid demonstration of the grisly end awaiting those who had been outlawed. On 20 April the fate of the garrison was sealed when Edward granted away their goods and chattels, dispossessing them of everything they owned. At the outset of the siege the constable of the castle, the Perthshire knight William Oliphant, had refused to surrender without first speaking to the Scottish lord, John de Soules, as Oliphant held the castle 'of the Lion' – of the Scottish Crown. Soules was one of the few lords of Scotland not to have submitted to Edward I, but he was presently in exile in France. Edward bluntly refused to countenance such a delay; he wanted to bring an end to the war. Outlawed and landless, isolated and without hope of relief, the garrison of Stirling Castle, the last forlorn remnants of Scottish resistance in a war already lost, could do nothing but watch the awesome might of the English siege train continue to build up around them.

It was in late April that the siege began in earnest. At the beginning of the month the castle had been cut off from supplies, and the boats retained by the garrison below the castle on the Forth had been seized by English forces. Initial orders for the assembly of the siege train had been issued a month earlier, in March, when the English constable of Edinburgh Castle had been ordered to repair his siege engines and send them to Stirling. English ships from Berwick and Newcastle sailed north with the components of engines stowed within their holds and laid upon their decks. In the fortress town of Berwick the core of the siege train began to take shape, Master Reginald the Engineer receiving two siege engines from Brechin, sixteen beams of another engine called *Forster* and eighteen beams from Aberdeen.

On 21 April 1304, with the siege about to begin, Edward I was still not satisfied. The king ordered that all the iron and great stones stored in Glasgow should immediately be seized and sent to Stirling Castle for the use of his siege engines. He also instructed his son and heir, the future Edward II, to strip as much lead as he could for the siege engines from the roofs of churches in Perth and Dunblane, the only exception being where the roofs covered the altars. Large numbers of workmen were drafted in to undertake work on the engines and prepare for the assault on the castle. Batches of tools were sent north, including 'pickes' and 'stonaxes'. Crossbows were delivered in large quantities, over twenty-four thousand crossbow bolts arriving in one instance alone, while the sheriffs of London, Lincolnshire and Northumberland, and the mayor of Newcastle, were required to provide substantial numbers of bows and enormous quantities of arrows. Cotton thread, sulphur and saltpetre were also delivered, the ingredients necessary for the making of Greek fire. To prepare this volatile, highly flammable liquid fire (the precise mixture of which still eludes historians and chemists to this day), Edward I employed the services of the Burgundian expert Jean de Lamouilly. Launched at the castle by means of siege engines, this Greek fire, most probably contained in earthenware pots, would have exploded with startling ferocity. Its use against Stirling Castle was one of the first instances in which the English deployed what was essentially a gunpowder weapon.

Yet this remained a period in which the science of fortification held sway over that of assault, in which methods of defence were superior to those of attack. Despite the unprecedented array of siege engines, the walls of Stirling Castle remained impervious to the hail of missile fire to which they were subjected. The English built a battering ram, but when brought into action it was found ineffective due to a fault in its construction. Impatient at the lack of success, Edward I rode dangerously close to the walls, his advanced age failing to temper his characteristic boldness. The king became increasingly troubled by the prolonged nature of the siege as it dragged on into summer. But Edward still had one card to play and, in terms of the most sophisticated technology, he had saved the very best until last.

For several weeks a team of fifty men headed by five master carpenters had been working intensively on the construction of the greatest of all English siege engines, a trebuchet of such size and proportion that it dwarfed all others. It was a weapon that was appropriately christened the *Warwolf*. In fact, it was so substantial that it was still not ready when Oliphant finally offered the unconditional surrender of the castle on 20 July. However, Edward was so determined to witness the *Warwolf* in action that he refused to accept the offer of surrender until his gargantuan trebuchet had flexed its timber limbs and pounded Stirling Castle with a further heavy barrage. When the garrison were finally allowed to exit the battered castle, they came before the English king in symbolic humility, barefoot and with ashes on their heads as they pleaded for mercy. According to some accounts, Edward was only prevented from having them disembowelled and hanged by the intervention of his queen; however, it is possible this may have been no more than an act of conventional posturing on the part of the king. Having won widespread admiration for their courageous resistance, the garrison were led off into England and captivity. With the conclusion of the three-month siege of Stirling, the last remnant of Scottish resistance had finally been eliminated.

Of all the siege engines assembled before Stirling Castle, the *Warwolf* was undoubtedly the star of the show, yet it is not the presence even of this imposing weapon that is of most interest. Among the many engines that contributed to the spectacular assault on the last outpost of Scottish resistance were those supplied by the Scottish earl of Carrick. On 16 April 1304, as the siege was about to begin, Edward I had written a letter of thanks to the earl for sending siege engines to Stirling Castle, whilst also requesting that he forward the beam of his great engine if at all possible.[3] The earl of Carrick was Robert Bruce, and it was engines supplied by Bruce that featured in this great English military pageant that hurled death at the courageous Scottish garrison. Indeed, Bruce was there in person. During the siege he quietly slipped away from the besieging army. At Cambuskenneth Abbey, in a bend of the Forth, he met the influential bishop of St Andrews, William Lamberton, and entered into a secret agreement with him. This was the first move in the creation of a network of clandestine alliances orchestrated by Bruce; it was also the first step on the road to a new war.

There is something undeniably distasteful about this scene: Robert Bruce was scheming for his own gain whilst siege engines supplied by him battered the beleaguered Scottish garrison; he was professing allegiance to Edward I while treacherously plotting against him. As one war was ending so Bruce was planting the seeds of another. That he should do so by the banks of the Forth is, however, particularly fitting. So broad was the natural barrier of the Forth and its great estuary that it was known to contemporaries as the 'Scottish Sea'. The origins of the conflict that was now ending lay on the banks of the Forth. Indeed, the very course of that bitter war can be traced by the lives lost beside the hostile waters of the Scottish Sea.[4]

The death of King Alexander III of Scotland on the night of 18 March 1286 was both a personal tragedy and a national disaster. It was a tragedy in that Alexander, having suffered the distress of the loss of his immediate family – his wife, two sons and a daughter all passing away prematurely – had remarried just six months before, and the prospect of a new family lay ahead of him. Furthermore, the desire of Alexander to spend the night with his new French wife, Yolande de Dreux, had led to his tragic death. Perhaps he should have listened to the flurry of wild rumours relating that 18 March was a day laden with evil portents, a gloomy prophecy of the type to which the superstitious medieval mind was so readily receptive. The weather that night was certainly appropriate for a doom-laden scene, with high, howling winds gusting waves of sleet across the ice-cold waters of the Forth. Alexander had spent the day engaged in the business of state at Edinburgh Castle; his new wife was lodged at the royal manor of Kinghorn, twenty miles away on the far north side of the Forth estuary. Disregarding the advice of his counsellors, who urged him not to attempt the journey, Alexander ventured out into the teeth of the storm. The king and his small escort safely crossed the Forth by ferryboat, but as they proceeded along the far bank Alexander became separated from his escort in the appalling conditions. His body was found the next morning. Alexander III lay dead at the bottom of a cliff, his neck broken in the fall. Beside his corpse lapped the implacable waters of the Forth.

As the atrocious weather died down, so the ominous thunderclouds of a political storm began to build up over the kingdom of Scotland. In this sense the personal tragedy of Alexander became a national disaster. Only one direct heir to the Crown of Scotland existed. Margaret, popularly known as the Maid of Norway, was Alexander's granddaughter. Worryingly, she was also a three-year-old child who was notoriously frail and prone to ill-health. The lurking nightmare that haunted medieval kingdoms now crept upon Scotland with alarming reality: the succession of a young child and the minority government this entailed. It is a tribute to the Scottish kingdom's outward display of unity that the government which was now formed remained firmly committed to preserving the interests of the Crown. Six of Scotland's leading men – two earls, two bishops and two barons – comprised the new government, their equal numbers an attempt to make them, the Guardians of Scotland, a representative body. Two problems immediately faced them: the Maid of Norway's uncertain health, and a dubious claim from Alexander's French widow, Yolande, that she was pregnant with the late king's child. This was a not uncommon gambit in cases where such a child stood to inherit a great deal. In this case, any child of Alexander's would take precedence over the Maid in succession to the Scottish Crown.

The Guardians could do little but wait for time to reveal the answers. All the same, they were acutely aware that a minority government was a fragile institution which could fall prey to the ambitions of several powerful Scottish lords, each seeking to advance his own position. These lords were impatient men and it would be more than a decade before the Maid came of age. It was clear to the Guardians that they must shore up the minority government so that it could not be destabilised by the hard-headed ambitions of these lords. The Guardians recognised that the most effective way of empowering their government was to bind the infant Maid to a figure of indisputable authority. For this reason, on 7 August 1286 they sent three envoys to seek the support of the most powerful authoritarian figure they could think of: Edward I.

The Guardians were not to know they had invited a wolf into the fold. During the mid-1280s they had no reason to doubt the intentions or integrity of the English king. In 1286 Edward I was an obvious figure to whom to turn. Alexander III's first wife, Margaret, had been a daughter of Henry III of England, and so a sister of Edward I. Edward himself was the highly respected ruler of one of the greatest kingdoms in medieval Europe, and was widely considered to be the foremost statesman of the age. He had been on crusade in the Holy Land, was instrumental in the development of English law and had first-hand political experience of dealing with his own ambitious magnates. Nor was Edward's ongoing conquest of Wales of any immediate concern to the Scots. There was little resemblance between the two countries; Scotland had a more centralised government, and its largely feudalised aristocracy could trace its origins to the same Anglo-Norman lineage as their English counterparts. Many noblemen possessed lands in both Scotland and England, and so formed a cohesive group of cross-border landholders. In the late thirteenth century the old flashpoints between the two kingdoms appeared very much to be a thing of the past.

To the Guardians there was no reason to think Edward I would bring anything other than security to Scotland. Rather than being seen as a threat, Edward was viewed as the guarantor of the kingdom's stability. The Guardians naturally expected Edward would want something in return, that he would seek an opportunity to advance the interests of the English Crown. To secure the stability of the Scottish kingdom, the Guardians were prepared to accept this. Always alive to such an opportunity, Edward proposed the marriage of his son and heir, Prince Edward, to the Maid, a plan that would accomplish the immediate aims of both Edward and the Guardians. Extensive negotiations based on the eventual marriage of the Maid of Norway to Edward of Caernarfon, the future Edward II, culminated on 18 July 1290 in the Treaty of Birgham. The marriage of these two heirs, neither yet an adult, would provide Scotland with the guarantee of its integrity that the Guardians craved whilst still preserving the kingdom's independence. There would be no union of kingdoms or Crowns; when Edward II succeeded to the throne he would be king of England while the Maid would remain queen of Scotland. The possibility of the heir of this marriage ultimately becoming the ruler of both countries was inherent in the treaty. At the very least the treaty and prospective marriage promised a long and harmonious future between the two kingdoms.

So it was a particularly cruel twist of fate that the frail Maid should die en route to Scotland less than three months after the treaty had been sealed. Four years of negotiations between the two kingdoms vanished in an instant. Suddenly, with no direct heir, the Crown of Scotland was there for the taking. A sense of stability and certainty dissolved into a state of troubled anxiety. At Perth the magnates of Scotland had begun to assemble for the Maid's inauguration at Scone; when they heard the news of her death, the mood changed from respectful ceremony to naked ambition. Several potential claimants for the Crown immediately entered into hasty agreements and sought to strengthen their hand by gathering armed retinues. The Guardians were caught out by the speed of events. A violent civil war loomed ominously on the horizon. In alarm the bishop of St Andrews, William Lamberton, dispatched a letter to Edward I urgently requesting the king of England's intervention. This was just the opportunity for which Edward had been waiting.

Exactly how long Edward had been planning the subjugation of Scotland will never be known. As the projected marriage of his heir and the Maid had been an attempt to initiate a peaceful political penetration of English interests into Scotland, so with her death Edward continued to pursue the power he desired over the kingless nation. It was not until May 1291 that he finally put his plan into action. He eventually responded to the bishop's plea by calling an Anglo-Scottish parliament to the rugged English border castle of Norham, which stood upon the borderline of the Tweed. To assuage any concerns, the king assured the Scottish delegates that by crossing into England to discuss the matter of the Scottish Crown they would in no way be prejudicing the integrity of the Scottish kingdom.

It was a barefaced lie. When the parliament assembled, Edward dropped his bombshell. In a move completely without binding legal precedent, he abruptly demanded that the Scots recognise his feudal suzerainty over the kingdom of Scotland. Edward was claiming that the king of England was effectively the overlord of the king of Scotland, that the kingdom of Scotland was subordinate to that of England. It was a claim so wholly lacking in substance that Edward offered no proof in support of it; instead, he bluntly challenged the Scots to disprove it. The reply they composed in the three weeks' grace that Edward gave to them said the only thing it could say: it unequivocally denied any such claim. Yet Edward was nothing if not tenacious, and he now pressurised the potential claimants to the vacant Crown into recognising his overlordship. Their burning ambition meant they were easy prey. It was a small price to pay for the illustrious prize each so desperately wanted.

Political cunning was backed up by brute force. Edward had not given the Scots three weeks to reply out of the goodness of his heart; this was the length of time it would take to muster the English host he had summoned. On 3 June 1291 an English army duly assembled at Norham, and the following day Edward's mail-clad troops symbolically took possession of the Scottish kingdom by proceeding to occupy the chief royal castles of the realm. In the face of such an overwhelming *fait accompli* there was nothing the Scots could do but relent. However, this was not a wholesale acceptance of English overlordship – Edward's concession, namely, that within two months of the Scottish Crown being awarded he would restore the kingdom and its castles to the new king, was an indication of the lack of direct control he would have. Nevertheless, through a combination of deception and force Edward believed he had successfully pressurised the kingdom of Scotland into recognising the overlordship of the English Crown.

Edward I formally took control of the Scottish government on 11 June, reappointing the Guardians so that they now operated under his own authority. Two days later the Guardians and the magnates of Scotland individually swore their fealty to Edward in a meadow beside the Tweed. Throughout June and July further high-ranking individuals across Scotland were required to swear their fealty. His authority established, Edward now set about presiding over the contest for the Scottish Crown, although in reality the actual decision rested with a court of 104 auditors who sat in judgement on the merits of each claimant's case. Even by the standards of most legal proceedings, this was a long, tedious and extremely protracted affair that was to last from the summer of 1291 until late 1292, and it became popularly known as the Great Cause. It was a contest of litigation that saw some of the finest legal minds in Europe put their skills to the test in pursuit of the ultimate prize – a Crown.

Of the handful of men with a credible claim to the Scottish Crown there were only ever two serious contenders. One was John Balliol, lord of Barnard Castle in County Durham. The other was Robert Bruce, lord of Annandale, grandfather of the victor of Bannockburn and a lord of Scotland whose relentless pursuit of the Crown was to earn him the sobriquet of Robert the Competitor. In 1291, as the Great Cause got underway, the Competitor had reached the remarkable age of eighty-one, yet this did nothing to dampen the fervour with which he fought to obtain the Crown for himself and his heirs. All that separated the Bruces from the kingship of Scotland was the claim of Balliol. The latter, however, presented a formidable obstacle.

The claims of both Balliol and Bruce were based on their descent from Earl Henry of Northumbria, son of David I of Scotland (1124–53). Henry's eldest son, Malcolm IV (1153–65), had died childless and been succeeded by his brother, popularly known as William the Lion (1165–1214). The recently deceased Alexander III (1249–86) was the son of William's own son, Alexander II (1214–49), and therefore William the Lion's grandson. This royal dynasty had ruled Scotland for more than 260 years. The death of the

Maid of Norway had brought an abrupt end to the line of monarchs descended from William the Lion. The strongest claims in 1291 came from those who traced their descent from Earl Henry's third and youngest son, David, earl of Huntingdon, who had died in 1219.

The descendants of Earl David's three daughters were the chief claimants to the Crown in the Great Cause. John Balliol was the grandson of David's eldest daughter, Margaret, while Robert the Competitor was the son of David's second daughter, Isabel. Both men took precedence over another claimant, John Hastings, grandson of David's third daughter, Ada. The Great Cause was contested because no official priority existed among the various rules of succession. Balliol based his claim on primogeniture, that he was descended from the eldest daughter. Robert the Competitor anchored his claim on the rule of proximity, in that he was a generation closer to David than Balliol was, Robert's mother being a daughter of David whereas it was Balliol's grandmother who was another daughter of David. Primogeniture was far from being the sacrosanct rule of succession, but traditionally it bore much greater weight than that of proximity. The Great Cause was undoubtedly an impartial legal contest, and during it the rule of primogeniture eventually prevailed. In late 1292 Robert the Competitor saw that the writing was on the wall and resigned his claim to the Crown to his son and heirs. On 30 November 1292 – St Andrew's Day – at the ancient royal site of Scone, amid scenes of great ceremony, John Balliol was inaugurated as King John of Scotland.

The crisis that had gripped Scotland following the death of Alexander III in 1286 should now have been settled. A new king sat upon the throne of Scotland, a man in good health with a son and heir of his own, a king who had been awarded the Crown by means of a thorough and impartial legal contest, and who had the full support of the Scottish kingdom. Civil war had been successfully avoided. The kingdom of Scotland was now ostensibly in Scottish hands. Edward I had gained his pound of flesh in the oath of fealty that Balliol and his countrymen had sworn before the Great Cause had begun. Should the Scots remain disturbed by this oath, then they could take solace in its imprecise nature, and view it as something vague and loose rather than binding. If by paying it lip service they satisfied the self-esteem of Edward I, then so be it. The last thing they expected was for the king of England to make the weight of this oath emphatically felt.

In this they were sorely mistaken. Edward was only too aware that such an oath could be dismissed as something cosmetic rather than real; what he sought was an oath of substance whereby the subjugation of the Scottish kingdom to the king of England was a matter of indisputable fact. Characteristically, he wasted no time in attempting to make the weight of the oath felt. In 1293 appeals were made to Edward I from nine individuals unhappy with the judgements of the Scottish law courts with regard to their separate cases. Edward demanded to know how the courts had reached their decisions in these cases, and ordered Balliol, King John of Scotland, to appear before him in person to explain them. Balliol refused this summons and bluntly defended the judgements. At stake was not so much a matter of principle but precedent. If Edward's demands were met, then Scottish law would ultimately be subject to English control, and if the king of England controlled Scottish law then effectively he ruled the kingdom. The appeals of these individuals were the means by which Edward sought to make real the authority over Scotland that was implied in the oaths of fealty. Of the nine appellants, three were English subjects, and the evidence strongly suggests that they were encouraged by Edward himself to submit their appeals. Despite his reputation as a great lawgiver, Edward never hesitated to manipulate the law if it suited his own interests.

Relentless in his demands, Edward finally forced Balliol to attend an English parliament later that year. The disdain with which Balliol was treated must have come as a terrible shock to the new king. He was held in contempt of court for his previous refusal to attend. Until amends were made the three chief castles and towns of Scotland – Edinburgh, Roxburgh and Berwick – were to be confiscated by the English, the king of Scotland being treated as if a 'defaulting debtor'.[5] It was all too much for Balliol. Cowed by the severity with which he was treated, his spirit of resistance soon broke and he humbly renewed his submission and homage to the English king. This was the beginning of the end for Balliol. The lords of Scotland, though appalled at his treatment, were troubled by the ease with which he had been broken. It was clear to them that Edward I could not be turned from the authority he sought over Scotland, yet they could not allow the subjugation of the Scottish kingdom. In this head-on collision, war appeared inevitable. To the Scottish lords, it was not a hopeful prospect; led by a king whose mettle they now doubted, and confronted by a much larger and richer kingdom, they knew such a war promised defeat.

The Scottish lords needed a powerful ally to fight England, and it was Edward himself who inadvertently provided one. In 1294 Edward had become embroiled in an argument with the French king, Philip IV. It centred on the contentious issue of the conditions by which the king of England held the duchy of Aquitaine in southwest France. Aquitaine was an English possession, but technically it remained a fief of the French Crown for which the king of England owed homage, and consequently it was a frequent source of bitter dispute. In May, Philip summarily confiscated Aquitaine. In June, Edward responded by declaring his intention of taking an army to France. The English host was to muster on 1 September. In late June, writs of summons were issued by the English Crown to those obliged to provide troops. In an unprecedented move, Edward also issued writs to Balliol, as king of Scotland, to two earls of Scotland and sixteen Scottish barons.

This summons to serve the English king overseas went far beyond what the Scots were prepared to accept. The time had come to make a stand. A precious breathing space was provided when the Welsh, having been armed by the English ahead of their participation in the French campaign, broke out in a revolt of such severity that Edward was compelled to postpone the expedition to France. The English army he had begun to assemble was instead directed against Wales, where it campaigned throughout the winter of 1294/5 as it sought to crush the revolt.

The Scottish lords did not waste the time they had been gifted. A parliament was held at Stirling in July 1295 and a council was appointed to treat with the French. Extreme action may have been taken. According to English sources, the Scottish government was removed from Balliol's control, a radical act in which power was forcibly taken away from the king, and was handed to a council of twelve elected Guardians who immediately entered into discussions with the French. On 23 October 1295 a treaty of mutual offence and defence was concluded between the kingdoms of Scotland and France, and on 23 February 1296 this was formally ratified by the Scottish council. The Scottish host was then summoned. Less than four years after the Great Cause had been peacefully concluded, England and Scotland were at war.

CHAPTER THREE

A POISONED CHALICE

THE RUTHLESS EFFICIENCY WITH WHICH THE WELSH REVOLT WAS CRUSHED BY Edward I in early 1295 should have served as an ominous warning to the Scots. By the mid-1290s the English had developed a well-honed war machine. The campaign of 1294–5 was only the latest in a series of conflicts that had led to the English conquest of Wales. At the head of this war machine was the formidable figure of Edward I. The English king was a veteran campaigner. As well as conquering the Welsh, he had fought in the vicious Barons' Wars of the mid-thirteenth century, and in the 1270s he had been on crusade to the Holy Land where he had campaigned against the Saracens. Whilst in the Levant he had negotiated with the Mongols and had almost been killed by the poisoned dagger of a Saracen assassin. In March 1296 this battle-scarred warrior-king turned his army on the Scots. It was Edward's first campaign in Scotland and he soon made his presence felt.[1]

Berwick was his first objective. The chief trading port of Scotland, Berwick was an increasingly rich and populous town that was the jewel in the kingdom's economic crown. It was also appallingly vulnerable, being situated just across the border from England and protected by nothing more than a ditch and a timber palisade. Upon the approach of the English, the Scots within the town refused to surrender; those inhabitants who bellowed insults at Edward and bared their backsides at him from behind the scant protection of such pitiful defences were either foolish or delusional. The hot-blooded anger that coursed through the veins of Edward Plantagenet was further heightened by a premature naval attack which saw three English ships burnt and a number of crewmen killed. The inhabitants of Berwick were about to feel the full fury of this warrior-king's fearsome wrath.

Berwick was stormed swiftly and viciously on 30 March. English troops broke down the meagre defences as if they were matchwood. The streets of the port literally ran red with blood as rampaging soldiers ran amok through the crowded thoroughfares and alleyways. They lashed out indiscriminately, striking down anyone they came across, clogging the narrow streets with corpses as they remorselessly worked their way through the town. The women they found were allowed to leave, but the men were brutally massacred. Edward had given strict orders that no quarter was to be given to the male population; it was a directive that his soldiers ruthlessly obeyed. According to one chronicler, so many Scotsmen were killed that they 'fell like autumn leaves', one contemporary estimate placing the number massacred at over eleven thousand. The scale of the slaughter was so great that many of the corpses were not buried but cast into the sea or thrown into deep wells and pits. Only a desperate appeal from those clergy present finally persuaded Edward to call off his troops. However, Edward was not driven to such extreme measures only through anger; the horrific magnitude of the bloodshed suggests it was also intended as a brutal warning to the rest of Scotland of what they could expect should they persist in their resistance.[2]

Not only the English were guilty of perpetrating such atrocities. Although those in which the Scots engaged did not equal in scale the English slaughter at Berwick, they were just as indiscriminate and senseless. On Easter Monday, before Berwick had been assaulted by the English, a substantial Scottish force descended on Cumberland and devastated the immediate region, killing the local inhabitants, burning their settlements and driving off livestock. A Scottish force also made an attempt on Carlisle, but the walled fortress town proved too strong. In April, after Berwick had fallen, a Scottish raid targeted Northumberland. Another swathe of devastation was cut through northern England, but again with as little strategic impact as the raid into Cumberland. Indeed, if these senseless Scottish raids achieved anything it was only to raise the anger and determination of King Edward. Knowing that their forces were too inferior to meet the English army in battle, the Scottish lords subsequently sought refuge in the castle of Dunbar. Seduced by the outward defensive strength of the castle, they failed to appreciate that its walls could also serve as a prison to those trapped inside.

In late April Edward dispatched a cavalry force under the command of John de Warenne, earl of Surrey, to take Dunbar. The Scottish lords inside bluntly refused an opportunity to surrender and sent for a relieving force, which duly appeared. Caught between the castle and the relief force, Warenne left a section of his troops to continue the siege and with the remainder he manoeuvred to face the approaching Scots. In a disastrous misinterpretation of this action, the Scots believed the English were in retreat. With a euphoric rush the relieving force broke ranks and charged the English. The Scots were hopelessly routed. The battle of Dunbar may have been little more than an intense skirmish, but it was decisive. Having witnessed the destruction of their relief force from within the castle, the disheartened Scottish lords surrendered the following day. With their capture the Scottish cause imploded. Of the principal castles of Scotland, only Edinburgh offered any resistance; when the English approached Stirling, they found the castle empty except for the porter who tamely handed over the keys.

John Balliol, King of Scotland, was brought before Edward I at Kincardine Castle in July 1296. Pitifully confessing his unlawful rebellion against Edward, Balliol was forced to resign both the kingdom of Scotland and the royal dignity to the king of England. In a highly symbolic physical expression of his abject humiliation, the tabard worn by Balliol, emblazoned with the royal arms of Scotland, was torn from him. It was an act that led to Balliol being derogatorily called 'Toom Tabard', labelling him as an empty, anonymous disgrace. Balliol was sent to the Tower of London and the ceremonial regalia of the Scottish Crown, including the crown itself and the Stone of Destiny upon which its kings were inaugurated, were similarly transported to London under armed guard.[3]

Edward I had required just twenty-one weeks to defeat the Scottish lords and to crush their attempt to assert the right of Scotland to be an independent kingdom. By forcing Balliol to resign the kingdom, Edward had effectively confiscated Scotland like a lord confiscating the land of a rebellious vassal. English control over Scotland was now put on a formal basis. Work began to transform the devastated town of Berwick into the centre of an English administration. Warenne was appointed lieutenant of Scotland and every significant Scottish landholder was required to swear their fealty to Edward I as the lord of Scotland. The enormous list of those who did so, their names still preserved in the famous Ragman Roll, provides an exhaustive catalogue of almost every Scotsman of national, regional and local prominence. As Edward rode south to the border, a later chronicler recounted that he commented pithily, 'When you get rid of shit, you do a good job'.[4] It had all been so easy for

Edward I and the English – too easy. Indeed, the brief conflict of 1296 hardly merits the description of a war compared to what was about to erupt.

Popular disturbances against the new English administration began in the spring of 1297, the first flames of revolt flickering into life in the north of Scotland and the wilds of Galloway. In Lanark the English sheriff was murdered and at Scone an attempt was made on the life of the English justiciar. Both acts were perpetrated by a relatively insignificant Scotsman from a family of knightly status – a man by the name of William Wallace. The flickering flames of revolt soon became a blazing conflagration as Wallace in the south and Andrew Murray to the north led uprisings which gained popular momentum. In August the two rebel leaders joined forces. This revolt spectacularly exploded into a full-blown war beside the Forth, in the shadow of Stirling Castle, as the Scots performed the impossible and defeated an English army in battle.

The battle of Stirling Bridge, though a great Scottish victory, must rank as one of the most inept displays of generalship in English history. Two men were responsible for this: Warenne, the victor of Dunbar, and Hugh Cressingham, the despised English treasurer of Scotland. Warenne and Cressingham had been provided with an expeditionary force and ordered north to put down the Scottish revolt. Upon reaching the Forth at Stirling on 10 September, they made camp. Beneath the castle rock stood the long and narrow timber bridge along which the army would cross. The Scots, under Wallace and Murray, watched warily from the heights of the Abbey Craig on the far north bank. Warenne decided the army would make the crossing the following morning. Incredibly, he overslept. Although the crossing was already well underway, one account claiming five thousand Englishmen were already upon the north bank, a ludicrous order was given for them to be recalled. Having eventually awoken from his slumber, Warenne then wasted more precious time by dubbing new knights, apparently more concerned with pre-battle etiquette than winning the fight itself. When the second crossing finally began the troops were again recalled. Two Scottish lords in English allegiance, who had sought a surrender of the Scottish forces, were seen to be returning and Warenne wished to hear what they had to say. When informed that these lords had proved unsuccessful, Warenne sent his own envoys to speak with the enemy, but inevitably they also returned without success.

As precious time passed, the English troops must have become increasingly aware of the danger their delayed crossing was courting. It was certainly clear to Richard Lundie, a Scottish knight in English allegiance, who urged Warenne to allow him to lead a force across the Forth at a nearby ford and undertake an attack on the Scottish flank, thereby protecting those crossing the bridge. Warenne saw the sense of this; Cressingham saw the cost. The latter objected, declaring that such a delay would increase the expense of the campaign. Astonishingly, Warenne changed his mind and sided with the treasurer, Cressingham. The entire English army would cross the Forth by means of the narrow bridge, in full sight of Wallace and Murray and the Scottish army they commanded.

It was a disaster waiting to happen and the Scots were only too willing to oblige. As the English crossing took place, several thousand Scotsmen swarmed down from the heights of the Abbey Craig and engulfed the leading elements of the English army before they could redeploy. Marmaduke Tweng was in the thick of this escalating disaster, as we have seen; his opinion of the commanders whose incompetence almost cost him his life can only be imagined. Confined by the narrowness of the bridge, unable to advance in aid of their countrymen, the bulk of the English army could only watch in horrified dismay. The bridge was broken down, whether on the orders of Wallace or Warenne it is unclear, but either way the fate of the vanguard was irrevocably sealed. Desperate men threw themselves into the Forth to escape the Scots; some swam to safety, many drowned. The hated Cressingham had crossed with the vanguard and was killed, his bloated corpse later skinned and a strip fashioned into a macabre sword belt for Wallace. Warenne, the chief architect of the disaster, had not made the crossing and survived. On the back of this unexpected victory, Wallace was knighted and appointed sole Guardian of Scotland.[5]

When he heard of the defeat, Edward I was predictably enraged. The battle of Stirling Bridge was a cutting embarrassment to English arms and he was determined to avenge it; in this sense the only decisive outcome of the battle was an intensification of the ferocity with which the war was fought. Edward himself was in Flanders at the time of the defeat and the summons of an army that had been issued in Edward's absence was subsequently cancelled by his direct order. The king did not want another mistake; this time he was going to deal with the Scots in person. His determination to avenge the humiliating defeat was heightened by a savage raid into northern England that Wallace conducted following the battle. The chief towns of Scotland had also fallen to Wallace, but crucially the major castles remained in English hands – Stirling Castle, in which Tweng was based, being among the most important.

Edward ordered the English host to muster at Roxburgh, the site of another vital English-held castle, on 25 June 1298. The army that assembled was formidable. At its peak it totalled around twenty-nine thousand men, comprised of approximately three thousand cavalry and twenty-six thousand foot soldiers, a considerably larger army than that which was to take to the field at Bannockburn. As it crossed the border, the English host systematically devastated the land through which it passed. Wallace, confronted by a force of such overwhelming power, was careful to withdraw his army before it. Denied an enemy to whom they could give battle and from whom they could pillage, the English soon began to run low on provisions. Their campaign threatened to stall completely as they were forced to await the arrival of supply ships at Edinburgh. Then Edward's luck changed; he received intelligence that placed the Scottish army less than twenty miles away at Falkirk.

Edward seized the moment and ordered an immediate advance towards Falkirk. On 22 July battle was met. Upon the approach of the English, Wallace formed his foot soldiers into tight circular defensive formations known as schiltroms, the iron tips of their spears jutting venomously outwards ready to repel the charge of English cavalry. As English knights and men-at-arms roared their war cries and spurred their mounts towards the wall of spears, the small force of cavalry the Scots possessed, formed by the lords of Scotland who had now seen fit to join the cause, faithlessly turned and fled. Wallace and the foot soldiers were left to face the might of the English host alone. Desperately they fought for their lives. It was a close, hard-fought encounter, in which the English struggled to break the tightly packed schiltroms. At length the all-round superiority of the English host prevailed, and when the Scottish formations finally broke a massacre ensued. Wallace managed to escape, but the defeat at Falkirk brought his leadership of the Scottish cause to an end and allowed it to pass into the hands of ambitious lords who thought themselves more suitable for the task. Edward had gained the revenge he sought, but it was by no means the conclusive victory for which he had hoped.[6]

Falkirk, like Stirling Bridge before it, was not a decisive battle. Emphatic victories they may have been, but their impact on the overall course of the war was negligible. Indeed, rather than ending the war, Falkirk signalled the beginning of six years of desultory, drawn-out, low-intensity conflict; years during which the Scots resorted to guerrilla warfare, years that were punctuated by several costly but ultimately unsuccessful English campaigns interspersed with periods of truce. Three engagements in three years – Dunbar, Stirling Bridge and Falkirk – proved to be the exception rather than the rule.

As so often is the case, the war took on a remorseless, apparently endless character, a struggle of attrition that neither side appeared to be capable of winning.

The Scots fought to reassert the independence of their kingdom. To achieve this, their immediate aim was the full restoration of Balliol, formerly King John of Scotland. If English sources are to be believed, then this was the man in whom the Scottish lords had possessed so little faith that they had forcibly removed control of the government from him in 1295. If so, some of the lords now at the forefront of the Scottish cause would have been among those who were influential in making that decision. Why, then, were they now fighting for Balliol? In fact, they were not fighting for Balliol himself but for what he represented, what he symbolised. Balliol had been proclaimed king of Scotland by the Scots, therefore in their eyes he still held the Crown, and it was the restoration of that Crown that they sought. The war the Scots fought was for the return of their king and for the power of the Crown he held to be exercised with its full authority. In the independence of the Scottish Crown lay the independence of the Scottish kingdom.

International pressure now began to focus on the person of Balliol. As the war dragged on, so for Edward I the costs began to spiral and the diplomatic tensions began to build. The Scots still maintained their alliance with Philip IV of France. They also appealed to the papal curia, engaging in a diplomatic offensive aimed at establishing the justice of their cause and the restoration of Balliol. In 1299 the pressure on Edward became so great that he agreed to release Balliol into papal custody. Before the year was out, Balliol had been passed to the French and permitted to reside at his ancestral home in Picardy. By early 1302 English finances were in such a poor state that Edward was forced to conclude a truce with France which was to last for most of the year, a truce in which Scotland was also included. It has been suggested that the Scots were close to success, however a more accurate assessment is that the truce at best offered the prospect of preventing an outright English victory.[7] With characteristic stubbornness Edward refused to buckle, and during the truce he spent what money he had strengthening English-held castles in Scotland. Then on 11 July 1302, right in the middle of the truce, the decisive battle of the war took place.

It was fought not in Scotland between the English and Scots, but at Courtrai in Flanders by the French and the Flemings. In a battle bearing haunting similarities to Bannockburn, the Flemish foot soldiers stood firm against the knights and men-at-arms of France, the elite heavy cavalry of medieval Europe, and won an astounding victory. The French nobility suffered horrendous casualties, the gilded spurs of 500 of those killed being displayed as trophies by the triumphant Flemings.[8] The defeat reverberated throughout Christendom; in Scotland the news was received with dismay, in England it was greeted with joy. The diplomatic tension that had been building against Edward I was suddenly released. Philip IV now had a more pressing concern than his argument with Edward, and in the aftermath of Courtrai he sought a rapprochement with England. On 20 May 1303 a peace was duly concluded between England and France; it was a peace from which Scotland was pointedly excluded. The Franco-Scottish alliance lay in ruins. Freed from French interference, Edward was determined to put an end to the Scottish war.

The truce of 1302 ended in November and an English host had been summoned to march against the Scots in May 1303. In February an English expeditionary force suffered a minor defeat five miles to the south of Edinburgh at Roslin but, although the Scots continued to resist, their willingness to do so was gradually waning. When confronted by a renewed English invasion under Edward I in the summer of 1303, the spirit of the Scottish leaders was finally shattered. Prefabricated timber bridges were shipped north from England to enable a crossing of the Forth, and in a wide-ranging campaign the English advanced as far north as the Moray Firth and entered Aberdeen. As summer turned to autumn Edward did not return to England but remained defiantly in Scotland where he wintered at Dunfermline Abbey. Early in 1304 Robert Clifford, accompanied by Robert Bruce, led the troop of English cavalry that routed a Scottish force commanded by Wallace and Simon Fraser at Happrew, not far from Peebles. It was all too much for the Scottish leaders; that Edward was capable of undertaking such an oppressive and prolonged campaign after seven years of exhaustive warfare emphatically demonstrated both the desire of the English king to win the war and the resources he could still call upon. The Scottish lords had lost the stomach for the fight.

In the first months of 1304 John Comyn, lord of Badenoch, one of the most influential of Scottish lords, entered into negotiations for a conditional surrender on behalf of the Scottish leaders. Comyn was a leading figure in the Scottish resistance. On 9 February he and eleven of his fellow lords surrendered to Edward at Strathord in Perthshire. In March Edward held a Scottish parliament at St Andrews which set out the terms for peace and effectively formalised the English victory. The only loose ends that remained were

Wallace, Fraser and the garrison of Stirling Castle. Edward demanded that all three should be outlawed under Scottish law and the parliament gave its assent. It was now that Edward turned to the last pocket of resistance in the kingdom of Scotland and laid siege to Stirling Castle. After such a costly, interminable war, Edward can hardly be blamed for transforming the siege into a great military spectacle, a celebration of a victory that this time had been well and truly won.

In retrospect Edward must have realised that the twenty-one week conflict of 1296 had been too brief to prove a lasting victory. The Scottish lords had been captured but popular resentment at English oppression had remained strong and found expression in leaders such as Wallace and Murray. The conflict that had followed, enduring from 1297 until 1304, was the true war in which the English had fought to enforce the subjugation of Scotland and the Scots to regain their independence. The defeat suffered by the Scots in 1304 was consequently on a different scale altogether to that of 1296. This time not only had the Scottish lords been beaten but also the Scottish people. The war of 1297 to 1304 had been as much their fight as that of the lords, and it had been lost. With the capitulation of Stirling Castle the door seemingly slammed shut once and for all on an independent kingdom of Scotland.

It was perhaps with relief that Balliol heard news of the Scottish defeat. As the figurehead of a kingdom whose lords may have forcibly stripped him of control of the government, as a king pitifully humiliated by Edward I, a man passed from English to papal to French custody, as a helpless pawn in a game of diplomacy, Balliol may have reflected that the Crown of Scotland had, for him, been a poisoned chalice. The allure of the Crown was intoxicating yet perilous. It was a trap for the unwary. What it beguilingly promised was not necessarily what it delivered. Balliol, his reputation irrevocably shattered, emerged from his tenure of the Crown a broken man. He was to live out the remaining years of his life in the obscurity of exile on the continent. The cruel fate of Balliol served as a stark warning to those ambitious Scottish lords.

Such a man was Robert Bruce. It was a warning he did not heed. The fate of Balliol did nothing to diminish his ambitions, among which possession of the Scottish Crown featured so prominently. It was this ambition, this all-consuming desire to advance his own cause, which was to drive him to dark deeds that would culminate in the horrors of Bannockburn. On the field of battle, amid the corpses, both Bruce and Tweng would have known that Bruce's personal ambition was ultimately responsible for the carnage sprawled around them. If Tweng was a reminder of that earlier war, then Bruce was the driving force behind the war that had followed.

In 1314, at his moment of victory on the field of battle at Bannockburn, Bruce could afford to be magnanimous. Tweng was allowed to leave for England free of ransom and with his costly armour and weapons returned. It was a chivalric gesture by Bruce, which was in keeping with a man considered to rank among the two best knights in Christendom. However, it had not always been that way. There was a darker side to Bruce, a sinister edge, that had developed from the days when success had eluded him. A trail of treachery led to Bannockburn, a trail that snaked its dark path through this earlier war. Due to the unrivalled glory that he reaped from his great victory at Bannockburn, the stigma of this treachery could at last be laid to rest. Yet Bruce was beset by a still darker deed, which even the glory of victory could not completely dispel. It was an act that had triggered a new outbreak of war with England and had plunged Scotland into the horrors of a civil war. It was an act that ultimately led to Bannockburn.

II

THE POWER STRUGGLES

. . . the whole land was much desolated by such a tumult: for every kingdom divided against itself shall be brought to desolation.

Vita Edwardi Secundi

CHAPTER FOUR

THE DARK STAIN OF TREACHERY

IT WAS NEVER MEANT TO END IN MURDER.
To the handful of men who waited outside the Franciscan kirk of the Greyfriars in Dumfries on 10 February 1306, their breath frosting the icy winter air, such a thought was far from their minds. Muffled deep in leathers and furs, they stamped their booted feet hard against the frozen earth. Outwardly their restless movements were attempts to generate some warmth; inwardly they were the product of a gnawing sense of unease. Each man was impatient for the meeting within to finish, for the two protagonists to emerge, for it all to be over. They knew there was no love lost between their lords. The clandestine nature of the meeting was apparent in the small number that waited. Normally the power of a lord was emphasised by the presence of a large retinue; that only three or four men were outside was a measure of the utmost secrecy surrounding the meeting. All were close relatives of those inside. Anxiety and apprehension, as well as the penetrating cold, caused them to shift restlessly, but whatever they feared might occur within the kirk was certainly not murder.

Inside the kirk, Robert Bruce, lord of Annandale and earl of Carrick, and John Comyn, the 'Red Comyn', lord of Badenoch, two of the most powerful of all Scottish magnates, stood face to face before the high altar. Among the stonework there lingered the smell of incense, while the flickering flames of candles created ever-changing patterns across the bulk of their cloaked figures. The brief kiss of greeting they shared was perfunctory and as cold as the thin slab of winter light that shone weakly through the glass windows. There was nothing amicable about their meeting and no attempt was made to hide the fact. It was simply a matter of business.

Words were spoken, their low voices echoing thickly off the walls despite the hushed, guarded tones in which they were delivered. It was Bruce who had asked Comyn to meet him here. He wanted a question answered, a position clarified, so the onus was on him to broach the sensitive subject. The reply Comyn gave was far from what Bruce wanted to hear. Worse, Comyn added something else, uttering words that touched a raw nerve deep within Bruce. A surge of anger was unleashed. There was the sudden flash of a blade. Hot blood spilled onto the cold flagstone floor. Comyn staggered and slumped to the ground in front of the altar, clutching incredulously at where he had been fatally stabbed. A pained cry rang out shattering the reverential silence. Outside the boots stopped stamping. Within seconds they were clattering their way through the kirk. Taking in the shocking sight of his fallen nephew, Robert Comyn was the first to react. He made straight for Bruce but in mid-stride he was sent sprawling to the floor as a sword cleaved his skull, killing him instantly. The vicious blow was delivered by a Yorkshireman, Christopher Seton, Bruce's brother-in-law. In a matter of seconds a place of inviolate sanctity had become a scene of brutal savagery.

Nor was the violence finished. Bruce did not have time for the shock of what he had done to register. He had to take action before there were any repercussions. Leaving John Comyn bleeding to death in the kirk, Bruce and his men made straight for Dumfries Castle where the justices of Edward I were in session. The locals, inhabitants of a town in the heartland of Bruce territory, rallied to his cause. Frantically, the justices barricaded themselves in the great hall, but they promptly surrendered when Bruce threatened to set fire to the castle. Only after he had taken the castle did Bruce learn that John Comyn was still alive, the friars having taken him to the kirk's vestry where they were tending to his fatal injuries and administering the last sacrament. No chances could be taken. Bruce's men, the same who had waited outside the kirk, returned in haste and ruthlessly dispatched Comyn, so finishing the work their lord had begun. This time there could be no turning back for Bruce.[1]

The account given above is perhaps the most plausible of several widely different contemporary versions of the killing of John Comyn, none of which can be fully substantiated. There can be no doubt, however, that the killing of his rival before the high altar of a kirk during the course of a meeting that he himself had arranged was by far the darkest and most inexcusable act in the life of Robert Bruce. It was this 'guilt of homicide' that prevented the author of the *Vita* from praising the later successes of Bruce. Indeed, even his panegyrist, John Barbour, author of *The Bruce*, was unable to gloss over this terrible act, believing it was this that lay behind the great misfortunes subsequently to befall Bruce. Barbour claimed they were the results of divine retribution, but in fact their origin was much more prosaic. By killing his arch-rival, Bruce ruptured the Scottish kingdom along its political fault lines and cracked open the chasm in which lurked the monster of civil war. It was a shocking event which was also to reignite the Scottish wars and ultimately led to the conflict in which an even greater scene of savagery was played out on the field of battle at Bannockburn. The ramifications of the slaying of John Comyn were to be immense.

However, though this was by far the darkest controversial act in the life of Robert Bruce, it was by no means the first. As well as Bruce's guilt of homicide, the *Vita* speaks forebodingly of 'the dark stain of treachery' with which he was tainted.[2] There can be no doubt that Bruce was guilty as charged. By the time the 31-year-old Robert Bruce thrust the blade of his dagger, or sword, into Comyn, he had already committed at least three major acts of treachery. Plunging the blade into Comyn was but the latest act in a series of sinister incidents which were motivated by the ambitions of Bruce and the allure of the poisoned chalice that was the Scottish Crown.

The real venom of Bruce's strike resulted from years of thwarted ambition, mistakes, frustrations and personal enmity, from pent-up exasperation at his inability to achieve his aims. Behind the blow that claimed the life of Comyn lay the failure of Bruce to realise his goals. His grandfather Robert the Competitor had died in 1295 and so did not live to witness his grandson murder a fellow Scottish lord in the sanctuary of a kirk. The act would undoubtedly have appalled him. Yet it was the Competitor who had infused his grandson with the insatiable desire that lay behind his acts of treachery and the fatal strike. In this sense the murder of Comyn was about more than just thwarted ambition; in the shadows of the kirk, Bruce was confronted by the past failures of his life.

Robert Bruce's grandfather did indeed shape his life. In his youth the presence of the Competitor was so strong that it must always have remained with him. By birth one of the great lords of Scotland, the Competitor, the fifth Robert Bruce of Annandale, was a man with the blood of Scottish kings running through his veins. A handsome man, a gifted speaker and a generous host, he had moved effortlessly among the high aristocracy into which he was born. His entrance onto the great political stage of England was secured by marriage to Isabel de Clare, a daughter of the earl of Gloucester, one of the greatest of English magnates. The Competitor fought in the Barons' Wars of the mid-thirteenth century, and was captured at Lewes in Sussex in 1264 whilst fighting alongside Henry III of England and the king's heir, the future Edward I. In 1270, though in his fifties, the Competitor went on a crusade to the Holy Land and shortly after his safe return arranged the marriage of his son, the sixth Robert Bruce of Annandale, to Marjorie, the widowed daughter of the late earl of Carrick. On 11 July 1274 this marriage produced its first child with the birth of Robert Bruce himself.[3]

When the Great Cause began in 1291, Bruce was seventeen. At such an impressionable age he could not fail to have been enthralled by his elderly grandfather. As a boy he would almost certainly have listened with rapture as the Competitor regaled him with stories of his life, of the kings, queens and princes he had met, of the exotic lands through which he had travelled, no doubt recounting the drama of the battle at Lewes in which he had fought and been captured. As they ate and drank in the tapestry-draped great hall of Lochmaben Castle, the fortified caput of the lordship of Annandale, the Competitor would have stressed the pedigree of the Bruces of Annandale, emphasising the royal heritage of the family and its elevated position among the high aristocracy of Scotland. This was the world into which the Competitor had been born and now, by means of his artful eloquence, he must have made it come alive for Bruce.

As he watched his grandfather fervently argue his claim to the Crown before the auditors who presided over the Great Cause, the prospect of ultimately becoming king of Scotland must have played vividly in the mind of Bruce. Should the Competitor prevail, then Bruce would one day be king. It was an intoxicating vision that lay tantalisingly close to becoming a reality. That the Bruce claim was only beaten by that of John Balliol emphasised how close the teenage Bruce had come to one day inheriting the Crown. In November 1292 the Competitor resigned his claim to his son and his heirs, and stepped down from the running.

There was no shame in his defeat. In the last great challenge of his life, the Competitor had expended every legitimate means in his attempt to secure the Crown. Before the Great Cause his graciousness had earned him the popular epithet of Robert the Noble, and it was with the grace of such nobility that he accepted defeat. The Competitor died on Good Friday, 1295. Had he lived another year he would have watched with astonishment as Scotland and England went to war and his erstwhile rival, Balliol, was stripped of the Crown. It was perhaps just as well that he did not live to see the year that followed. In 1297 Robert Bruce was to commit his first act of treachery. The tenacity with which his grandfather had fought for the Crown had earned him the sobriquet of the Competitor, but it was a tenacity that had never stepped outside the bounds of law. His grandson was to show no such restraint.

The popular rebellion of 1297 provided Bruce with the occasion for his treachery. To suppress the outbreaks of revolt in Lanark and Galloway, and to prevent it from spreading, Edward I had turned to those influential Scots who were in his allegiance. Among these were the Bruces of Annandale. When war had broken out in 1296 they, like many other cross-border landholding Scots, had put their own interests first and refused to join their rebellious countrymen. There was certainly no incentive for the Bruces to fight for John Balliol. Indeed, during 1296 Robert Bruce had remained in Carlisle where his father was keeper of the castle for Edward I.

They were both still in Carlisle in early 1297 when Edward ordered that Robert Bruce ride to Annandale and raise the knights of his father's lordship to fight in defence of the English Crown. Bruce duly arrived in Annandale in May and called the knights together. However, rather than requisitioning them to fight on behalf of Edward, Bruce passionately exhorted them to fight against the English and embrace the Scottish cause. In a startling act of premeditated treachery, Bruce had defected to the Scots. This was a personal betrayal of his father as well as the breaking of the oath of allegiance he had sworn to Edward I. His duplicity was further exacerbated by the fact that, prior to leaving Carlisle, the bishop of the town, John de Halghton, had insisted that Bruce swear a special oath of allegiance. After his defection Bruce attempted to argue that this oath was invalid, claiming he had been forced to accede to it under duress.[4] What the oath does demonstrate, however, is that there were doubts about his allegiance even before he departed for Scotland. There should not have been any.

In 1297 there was no logical reason whatsoever for Bruce to defect to the Scots. The brief war of 1296 had immeasurably strengthened the position of the Bruces. By refusing to join the Scottish resistance and remaining loyal to the English Crown, the Bruces had been amply rewarded by Edward I. In stark contrast to their defeated peers who were incarcerated in English castles, they enjoyed the political kudos that came with the favour of the English king. The substantial estates they possessed in England were secure and their Scottish estates, briefly lost due to their support of the English, were soon returned to them by Edward. There could be no doubt about it: 1296 had been a very good year for the Bruces.

The position in which Robert Bruce found himself in early 1297 was also one of great promise. He possessed the earldom of Carrick, which had passed to him in 1292, and he had married well, his wife being the daughter of the Scottish earl of Mar. The marriage had already produced a daughter, Marjorie, who in 1297 was no more than an infant. This, then, was Robert Bruce on the eve of his first act of treachery: a young man of twenty-two, in the prime of his life, with a wife and a child; as earl of Carrick he was a first-rank magnate of Scotland; his father was the lord of Annandale; both men enjoyed the trust and patronage of the English king. By the summer, Bruce had recklessly thrown all of this away.

What was his motivation? Why were there doubts about his allegiance whilst he was still in Carlisle? Barbour recounts that when Bruce exhorted the knights of Annandale to join him, he declared, 'No man holds his own flesh and blood in hatred and I am no exception. I must join my own people [of Carrick] and the nation in which I was born.' Walter of Guisborough, an English chronicler, similarly voiced the opinion that Bruce defected to the Scots simply because he was a Scotsman.[5] Clearly, Bruce was influenced by his Scottish antecedents. Whereas his father came from an Anglo-Norman family, his mother, as the daughter of a late earl of Carrick, brought with her a Gaelic lineage. Carrick itself was a rugged region of western Scotland with firm links to Ireland, and Bruce was most probably born in Carrick. As well as having the conventional education of an Anglo-Norman nobleman, Bruce was consequently exposed also to Gaelic culture; he may well have had a Gaelic foster-brother, which would indicate that he spent some of his youth in a Gaelic household.[6]

Yet this cannot have been his prime motivation. There is little evidence of patriotic sentiment in his stance the previous year. Bruce had too much to lose to risk it all for patriotism, especially because the latter had still to develop fully as a concept in the late thirteenth century. Indeed, many of his contemporaries gave scant credence to the belief that the defection of Bruce was impelled by a sense of patriotism. From the moment Bruce switched sides, whispers could be heard that he aimed for the Crown. There can be no doubt that it would have exercised a profound influence on his thinking. Nor was Bruce alone in having such thoughts. In late 1296, following the Scottish defeat at Dunbar and the deposition of Balliol, Bruce's father had approached Edward I and broached the delicate subject of the recently vacated Scottish Crown. His request was simple: as the inheritor of the claim that had finished second only to Balliol in the Great Cause, he asked that he be crowned king in place of Balliol. The caustic reply of Edward I was typically blunt: 'Have we nothing to do but win kingdoms for you?'[7]

Edward was in no mood to countenance the inauguration of another Scottish king. He was still seething about the war he had been compelled to fight and was glad to see the back of Scotland. His embittered reply was an unguarded, throwaway remark, bred out of anger and resentment. Yet, as is the nature of such a remark, it also contained a hard kernel of truth. No king of Scotland was going to be appointed and the country would be run by an English administration. The legal route to the Crown which the Competitor had pursued was firmly closed. Edward was not going to appoint a king of Scotland unless his hand was somehow forced. If the Bruces still coveted the Crown, then they would have to win it for themselves.

Clearly, this was not what Edward meant, but it was a conclusion that could easily be inferred from his retort. To Bruce himself, when told of Edward's reply, it may well have had the same unintentional resonance as the infamous outburst of Henry II when he had railed against Thomas Becket the previous century. The knights of Henry II had interpreted his explosion of anger as an order to kill Becket. Similarly, Bruce inferred he would have to win the Crown for himself. The prospect was certainly tempting. When the popular revolt broke out in 1297 the vast majority of Scottish lords were imprisoned in England. The two most powerful figures still at liberty in Scotland were Robert Wishart, bishop of Glasgow, and James the Stewart, both of whom had supported the Competitor in the Great Cause. Balliol had been stripped of the kingship and was being held in custody in London. The Crown, so it seemed, lay tantalisingly vacant. The circumstances were too enticing for Bruce to resist. Bruce did not defect to the Scots, therefore, primarily out of patriotism, but to try and gain the Crown.

From the start Bruce's campaign did not go well. The knights of Annandale refused to respond to his exhortations; their lord, his father, was still in allegiance to the English. A more favourable response was gained from the men of his own earldom of Carrick, and Bruce was welcomed with open arms by Wishart and James the Stewart. The three men were quick to appoint themselves as spokesmen for the revolt and as de facto Guardians. While William Wallace and Andrew Murray led the uprising, they remained in the background attempting to pull the political strings. Their commitment, however, remained doubtful. When confronted by Robert Clifford and Henry Percy at Irvine in July 1297, they entered into talks that culminated in an embarrassing climb-down by the de facto Guardians.[8] Bruce was almost certainly not present at the battle of Stirling Bridge in September 1297, nor is it likely that he participated in the crushing Scottish defeat at Falkirk in July 1298; the unsubstantiated allegation, first advanced by Fordun, that Bruce fought on the English side at Falkirk is scarcely credible. Of the two battles, the latter was to prove of more importance for Bruce. Following the defeat at Falkirk, Wallace vacated his position of sole Guardian, and Bruce replaced him as one of two joint Guardians. The man with whom he shared office was John Comyn.

It was a relationship that was doomed from the start. Their partnership was riven with enmity and distrust. Both men were from families of the high aristocracy, both vied to exert their preeminence in Scotland, and both had a vested interest in the Crown. Comyn, a nephew of Balliol, had been a chief supporter of the latter during the Great Cause. He had fought against Edward I in 1296 and had been a prisoner of the English king until early 1298. Arguably, Comyn also had a valid claim to the Crown.[9] Rumours that Bruce sought the Crown would have heightened the brittle tension between the two implacable rivals. Neither man wished to work with the other, but neither would relinquish his position of authority. They were trapped in a volatile and fractious partnership in which the cracks soon began to show. When these eventually ruptured they did so in spectacular style.

In August 1299 an English spy reported with alacrity on a meeting between the Scottish leaders which had taken place at Peebles. Passions had run high. An argument had broken out over an attempt to confiscate the lands of William Wallace who, it was alleged, had left the kingdom without the approval of the Guardians. Angry words were exchanged, which rapidly escalated to a situation in which physical blows were dealt. Daggers were drawn. Comyn leapt at Bruce and grabbed him by the throat. Comyn's cousin, the earl of Buchan, seized Wishart and bellowed that treason was being committed. A timely intervention by the Stewart and other bystanders was all that prevented this vicious scuffle from developing into a disastrous fight. To keep the peace between the two men, the bishop of St Andrews, William Lamberton, was appointed as a third Guardian.[10] Yet this did nothing to quell the intense rivalry and hostility that festered between Bruce and Comyn.

To find himself embroiled in such a malicious internecine conflict was certainly not what Bruce had envisaged when he deserted Edward I in 1297. Bruce had plenty of time to reflect on this when he and his men were encamped in the Torwood in late 1299, impatiently awaiting the capitulation of Stirling Castle. Its eventual surrender, in which Marmaduke Tweng was briefly captured, did nothing to assuage his growing disillusionment. After the fall of Stirling Castle, Scottish attacks centred on the southwest of Scotland, bringing the war to Bruce's own ancestral lands. In the bitter cold of winter, Bruce led a failed attempt to recapture Lochmaben Castle. This was the castle in which his grandfather, the Competitor, had lived during the last years of his life and in which he had died. To find that he was reduced to this, to attacking a castle that belonged to his father, was a measure of the hopelessness of Bruce's position. It was as if the bitter winds that lacerated the rugged landscape of Annandale carried away with them any last lingering traces of the optimism that had once burnt bright within him. On 10 May 1300, in a parliament held at Rutherglen, Bruce resigned his office of Guardian. Ingram de Umfraville, a partisan of Comyn, took his place.

Having endured three years of desultory warfare, Bruce at last realised that he had been fighting the wrong war. The conflict in which he was engaged was for the restoration of Balliol as king of Scotland. William Wallace had consistently fought in the name of Balliol. Those appointed Guardians – including Bruce – had formally exercised their authority in the name of King John. International pressure centred upon the person of Balliol, and from 1299 documents and letters generated by the papal curia increasingly referred to Balliol as king of Scotland.[11] Rumours that diplomatic pressure on Edward in 1301 forced him to consider the possibility of restoring Balliol as king would have emphatically brought home to Bruce just how misguided his defection had been. He had cornered himself into a no-win situation: if the Scots should emerge victorious, then Balliol would regain the Crown; should Edward I win, then Bruce would be severely punished by him for his duplicity. The recognition of his desperate position provoked Bruce into undertaking his second act of treachery.

Early in 1302 Bruce voluntarily surrendered to John de St John, the English warden of Annandale and Galloway, and submitted to Edward I. It was an act of treachery as startling as that of 1297, for in the first months of 1302 the Scots were in their most advantageous position since the beginning of the wars. That Bruce chose this moment to desert the Scottish cause flatly contradicts any notions of patriotism. It was, however, a piece of brilliant timing; Edward I was under tremendous international political and financial pressure and so was eager to grasp at any opportunity that could be to his advantage. Bruce knew he was dealing from a position of relative strength and he exploited this to the full by skilfully extracting himself from his desperate situation without suffering any punishment or censure from the notoriously unforgiving Edward. This time Bruce was careful to ensure he gained this assurance from Edward in writing before he deserted the Scots.[12] By the end of February 1302 Robert Bruce was firmly back in allegiance to the English Crown.

His turnaround was complete. Whatever the satisfaction of avoiding the harsh reprisals of Edward I, however, it cannot have been with anything other than bitterness and regret that Bruce endured the last two years of the war. In 1297 he had made the mistake of thinking that the Crown was there for the taking. He had believed he could somehow win that Crown by assuming the leadership of a country at war. What he thought he saw in 1297 was an opportunity, but he had no idea how to exploit it. His time in the wilderness of Scottish resistance had taught him that instinctive and unplanned actions could be the downfall of a man, and that a seismic shift in the faction-riven power-politics of Scotland would be required for him to become king. The Robert Bruce who submitted to Edward I in 1302 was of a different calibre to the naive and opportunistic Robert Bruce who had deserted Edward five years before. Calculating, cynical and realistic, the older, more experienced Robert Bruce was now a clearsighted 27-year-old who saw the intractable obstacles that stood between him and the Crown. Above all he understood that overtures to nascent patriotism were worthless without the requisite political support.

Bruce played out the last two years of the war as a halfhearted enemy of his former comrades. During 1303 he served as sheriff of Lanark and Ayr for Edward I, and participated in the English campaign of 1303; in 1304 he rode among the cavalry force commanded by Robert Clifford that routed Wallace at Happrew near Peebles, and in the same year he sent siege engines to Stirling Castle at Edward I's request for the great showpiece siege. It was also in 1304 that Bruce's father died. His inheritance included not only the claim to the Crown but also the lordship of Annandale and a substantial swathe of English estates, including a house in London and the manor of Tottenham. This advantageous position had been further enhanced in 1302 when, his first wife having died, Bruce married Elizabeth de Burgh, daughter of Richard de Burgh, the powerful earl of Ulster and a close ally of the English king. Robert's brother, Edward Bruce, had served in the English contingent of the future Edward II during the campaign of 1303–4, and another brother, Alexander, was a recent graduate of Cambridge. Yet despite this, it was during the siege of Stirling Castle in 1304 that Bruce slipped away from the English camp and secretly met with William Lamberton, bishop of St Andrews, at

Cambuskenneth Abbey. This was the beginning of Bruce's third act of treachery, and the trail of duplicity it generated can be traced from Cambuskenneth to that fateful meeting with Comyn in the kirk of the Greyfriars at Dumfries two years later in February 1306.

His killing of Comyn does not appear to have been planned.[13] A flashpoint sparked by the incredible intensity of the moment and the palpable friction between two implacable rivals, it was almost certainly an emotional reaction. Violence had flared between them before. Bruce most probably harboured no murderous intent when he requested Comyn meet him. Rather, it is the meeting itself that is disturbingly sinister. Why were two bitter rivals convening in such secrecy? What did Bruce find so pressing that he felt the need to speak to Comyn about it face to face? Barbour recounts that Bruce killed Comyn because he suspected the latter had betrayed him to Edward I. If so, what had Bruce done that would allow Comyn to betray him? And if Bruce had committed treachery against Edward, why might he have entrusted the fact to his deadliest rival? The answers can be found not in Bruce's instinctive character but in the calculating and measured political brain that had been forged during those hard, disillusioning years between 1297 and 1302.

At Cambuskenneth Abbey, Bruce had entered into a clandestine agreement with Bishop Lamberton. On 11 July 1304 the two men put their seals to a written document in which they entered into a secret bond of mutual support against all potential enemies; should one of them default, the penalty was the extremely substantial sum of £10,000. This was a bond that overrode their allegiance to Edward I and as such it was effectively an act of treason.[14] The alliance they entered into could, if discovered, potentially destroy them. Why were they prepared to take such an enormous risk? What was the purpose of the bond? For Lamberton it was simple; he sought to regain an independent Scotland. A figure without strong partisan sympathies, Lamberton had supported the restoration of Balliol as king throughout the war. Now, in the immediate aftermath of defeat, he was prepared to pursue any means by which independence could be achieved. Bruce offered him a chance to regain Scottish independence. The price Lamberton would have to pay was not specified but, considering the scope of Bruce's ambitions, it might well have been a tacit agreement to support Bruce should he make a bid for the Crown.

Naturally the bond was not this explicit; it was already a sufficiently dubious and treasonable document. It is clear from later events, however, that this may well have been the understanding implicit in the bond. Bruce was putting into practice the hard lessons he had learnt. Even before Stirling Castle was surrendered in 1304, he was beginning to construct a network of alliances which could potentially provide him with the political support he would need to take the Crown. Bruce ruthlessly exploited the political vacuum left by the defeat of the Scots in 1304: John Balliol was a spent force, a succession of Guardians had proved unable to secure Scotland its independence, and the will to fight had gradually been bled out of the Scots. A new impetus was desperately needed and it was this that Bruce offered. In the dark days of defeat Bruce held out a light of hope. It was a blunt quid pro quo: influential Scottish lords wanted an independent Scotland; Bruce ultimately harboured a desire for the Crown. This was the foundation upon which Bruce began to build his network of alliances.

John Comyn was a key political figure in Scotland. A firm adherent of Balliol, and lord of Badenoch since the death of his father in 1303, Comyn wielded considerable power and influence. It was essential for Bruce to get him on board. Any talks between the two were bound to be fragile at best, yet despite this the basis of an understanding appears to have been reached by 1306. The precise details remain unknown – it is doubtful it was committed to writing – though in outline it must have been similar to Bruce's previous bond agreed with Lamberton in 1304. It is likely that Robert Wishart, the pro-Bruce bishop of Glasgow, was another link in this secretive network. There is the possibility that it was spread even wider. When William Wallace was captured in 1305 a number of letters were found on his person, papers that purportedly detailed agreements between Wallace and several Scottish magnates. It has been observed that from the time of Wallace's capture there was a noticeable cooling off in the attitude of Edward I to Bruce. If there was an agreement between Bruce and Wallace, however, then it was so vague and ambiguous that Edward did not feel compelled to take immediate action.[15]

What is evident is that Bruce had taken on the mantle of the conspirator. Moving furtively among the shadows of Scottish defeat, he set about constructing a series of Scottish political alliances while ostensibly remaining loyal to Edward I. It was a dangerous, excruciatingly perilous strategy. The threat of being spied upon must have haunted his every cautious move. Discovery could well result in death. The capture of Wallace in the midst of the plotting must have sent a shiver down Bruce's spine. Wallace was hung, disembowelled and beheaded, his heart and entrails burnt, his butchered torso cut into quarters and his head gruesomely set on a spike upon London

Bridge. Bruce was in no doubt that the grisly fate of Wallace could so easily be his own.

It was with long-suffering patience that Bruce tended to these alliances. In 1297 his treachery had been abrupt and impetuous; by 1304 he had learnt the virtue, if also the frustration, of patience. Although his agreement with Lamberton was concluded in July 1304, he made no move that year. As the days and months slipped into 1305, still no action was taken, his nerve holding despite the capture and brutal execution of Wallace. As 1305 became 1306 still nothing happened. When Bruce arranged to meet Comyn in February 1306, almost two years had passed since his bond with Lamberton. Bruce appears to have been waiting for the optimum time to strike. He may well have been waiting in expectation of the death of the ageing Edward I.[16] There were other crucial factors he also had to take into account. One of the most pressing was John Comyn.

The arrangement with Comyn was the most fragile of his alliances. Because of their loose association, there can have been little trust between them. The agreement that existed between Bruce and Lamberton was deliberately vague, its true import remaining implicit, and the one agreed between Bruce and Comyn would have been broadly similar. There would have been a tacit acknowledgement of what each man sought to gain. This ambiguity, an uncertain, perhaps tentative understanding, was almost certainly the reason for their fateful meeting. If Bruce believed Comyn had betrayed him to Edward I, then he must have feared that their secret understanding had been revealed to the king. In the stillness of the kirk of the Greyfriars their uncertain alliance spectacularly disintegrated. A surge of violent anger coursed through Bruce. His hand flew to the hilt of his bladed weapon. Viciously he struck out at his greatest rival and fatally stabbed him.

Bruce's killing of Comyn was like an explosive release of years of embittered frustration and personal enmity. As soon as he realised the enormity of what he had done, the world must have seemed to close in on him. The network of alliances he had so patiently constructed would collapse. Bruce knew there would be an instant clamour for his arrest and execution from the many relatives and allies of Comyn. The wrath of Edward I would inevitably follow. Bruce was a wanted man. There was only one possible way out – the immediate seizure of the Crown.

Although Bruce's network of alliances was significantly damaged, he still possessed influential allies. In the desperate weeks that followed it was Wishart, the bishop of Glasgow, who proved to be of vital importance to him.

Far from excommunicating Bruce for killing Comyn – and before the very altar of a kirk – Wishart readily absolved Bruce of the crime and provided him with the royal banner of the last Scottish king which the bishop had hidden. He also gave Bruce clothes suitable for the royal dignity of a monarch. It may even have been Wishart who actually encouraged him to take the Crown. Bruce himself issued an eleventh-hour plea to Edward I, stating that the English king should recognise him as king of Scotland or he would defend himself 'with the longest stick that he had'.[17] Castles in the southwest of Scotland were seized by partisans of Bruce, while he himself rode through Rutherglen and Glasgow acting as if he were king, receiving the fealty of individuals and exercising the right of a king to mobilise the men of the region. On 25 March 1306 he was at the ancient royal site of Scone. Six weeks after Comyn had been killed, Robert Bruce was inaugurated as king of Scotland.

Few men of influence were present. Wishart, despite the central role he played in organising the inauguration, was most probably not present, nor, at first, was Lamberton. The only bishop definitely in attendance was the bishop of Moray. Only three earls – Atholl, Malcolm and Lennox – looked on. The event by no means suggested the popular acclamation of a new king. Tremendous effort went into ensuring that the traditional ceremony was followed but not only the great men of Scotland were notable by their absence. The regalia of the Scottish Crown, in particular the crown itself and the Stone of Destiny upon which its kings were inaugurated, had been taken to London a decade earlier. Bruce had to make do with substitutes. An incoming king was traditionally led to the Stone of Destiny by the earl of Fife. The earl himself was held in England, but the late arrival of his aunt, Isabel, led to the farce of a second inauguration taking place two days after the first, on Palm Sunday. Further formality was lent to this second ceremony by the appearance of Lamberton who said mass.[18]

Yet as Bruce sat on the substitute stone with a replacement crown upon his head, his heart must have been extremely heavy. This was not the moment of which he had dreamt. Like the stone and the crown, the whole event was appallingly makeshift. Those present were so desperate to invest it with a sense of traditional propriety precisely because they knew that in truth this was a crude usurpation of the Crown. Anyone wishing to dispute the accession of Bruce did not have far to look; arrayed against him were many vociferous opponents. Scots associated with Comyn sought vengeance for his murder. Supporters of Balliol opposed Bruce for his blatant usurpation of the Crown. Edward I wanted him both for the murder and usurpation and also for the breaking of his oath of allegiance for a second time. All shared a visceral desire to see Bruce destroyed. Bruce himself must have realised that his kingship was as artificial as the cold metal of the replacement crown which touched his temples with such a biting chill.

By late March an English strike force was already in Scotland. It was led by the future earl of Pembroke, Aymer de Valence, an experienced combat commander and brother-in-law of the murdered Comyn. Valence wasted little time in getting rid of the few vestiges of support that Bruce possessed. Wishart was captured and Lamberton surrendered. The castles occupied by the supporters of Bruce were quickly taken. Before midsummer, Valence had seized and occupied the strategic walled town of Perth. Back in England, Edward I had set in motion the assembly of a substantial host which would shortly march on Scotland. If Bruce was to have any chance of clawing back his rapidly diminishing authority, he realised he would have to take on and defeat the initial English strike force before the arrival of the main host. Victory at Stirling Bridge had won Wallace a great popular following, and Bruce now sought a similar triumph.

Robert Bruce gathered his troops and on 19 June approached the walls of Perth. In an attempt to draw the English into the field he resorted to chivalric convention and challenged Valence to bring his men out and fight. Valence refused. Some accounts relate that Valence agreed to meet the Scots in battle the following day. Denied an immediate engagement, Bruce led his men to Methven, six miles from Perth, and made camp on a wooded hilltop. A third of his force left the camp to forage for food while the rest laid out bedding for the night. In an appalling lack of foresight no watch was maintained on Perth. It was a fatal mistake.

The English waited for vespers. Within the walls, knights and men-at-arms mounted their destriers, or chargers, and made the final adjustments to their armour and weapons. As dusk fell a town gate was heaved open. The strike force thundered out and made straight for Methven. Valence and his mounted troops were upon the Scots almost before they knew what was happening. Bruce and his men snatched what weapons and armour they could. Then the English were among them. Bruce's men were caught in a bewildering storm of movement and noise. Lances speared through unprotected skin and bone, rearing horses trampled men underfoot. The initial charge over, swords rasped from scabbards and horses were wheeled around as English knights and men-at-arms set about the flailing Scots with merciless abandon. Twice English hands snatched at the reins of Bruce's mount, and twice they were brusquely dislodged. But it was soon clear the fight was lost. Bellowing at his men to retreat, Bruce turned his mount from the escalating rout and, crashing through the undergrowth, plunged into the depths of the wood. Many of his men were not so fortunate. It is a measure of the desperate position in which Bruce found himself that, when he had challenged Valence outside the walls of Perth, his followers had covered their blazons with white surcoats in order to hide their identities. In the deepening dusk of Methven these white-coated figures now fled like wraiths into the woods; for those unable to escape, the surcoats became blood-soaked shrouds.[19]

Methven was a minor engagement, but it was decisive. The force that Bruce commanded represented all of those willing to support him, and they had been decimated. Any lingering vestiges of power that Bruce possessed had been broken. At Loch Tay his dwindling band of followers fought off an English pursuit. An ambush at Dalry was carried out by axe-wielding Scotsmen, the enormous blades of their weapons curving in great arching blows as they savagely ripped open horses, inflicting horrific, gaping wounds. Those who survived fled westward with Bruce. Blood-stained, their faces streaked with sweat and dirt, their weapons blunted and armour dented, they doggedly pressed on, seeking refuge in the wild fastness of Scotland. The man who led them was not a king but a hunted fugitive wanted for murder.

The killing of Comyn had brought an English army to Scotland and shattered the peace which had existed since the Scottish surrender in 1304. It was also to provide the spark that ultimately reignited the Scottish wars, yet in late 1306 the long-term renewal of the wars seemed extremely remote. The consequence of Bruce's murder of Comyn was not a Scottish uprising against English rule but a desire for the perpetrator of the crime to be destroyed, a desire shared by both the English and many influential Scots. To large numbers of his countrymen Bruce was both a murderer and a usurper. Bruce did not now face a war for the independence of Scotland but a power struggle to assert his extremely tenuous hold on the Crown. It was to be a bitter struggle which was to culminate eight years later on the field of battle at Bannockburn.

CHAPTER FIVE

BEQUEST OF A WARRIOR-KING

EDWARD I REACTED TO THE MURDER OF COMYN FIRST WITH DISBELIEF, AND THEN with mounting fury.[1] The dispatch of an English strike force and the raising of an army failed to sate his anger. So determined was Edward to ensure Bruce was destroyed that the old warrior-king decided to hold the greatest chivalric event of his long reign. On the feast of Pentecost, 22 May 1306, teeming crowds lined the narrow streets of London, jostling one another in their eagerness to glimpse the resplendent procession of armour-clad esquires and the bright, dazzling array of heraldic devices. The short route from the Temple Church to Westminster Abbey was ablaze with colour and rang with noise. Basking in the adulation, the esquires held their heads high as they made their way towards the abbey.

Nearby, at the royal palace of Westminster, within the privacy of the chapel, the cacophony diminished, failing to carry into the reverential stillness. Standing in the chapel was a handful of the most important lords of the English realm. Dominating them was the king. Edward I was advanced in years, his tall frame increasingly sparse, yet his potent aura of power and authority remained. In his hand he held the royal sword. At his feet knelt his son and heir, Edward of Caernarfon, Prince of Wales. The king, his demeanour solemn, extended his arm and touched the shoulders of the prince with the gleaming sword blade. Slowly, encumbered by the weight of his exquisite armour, the prince rose to his feet. He remained unnaturally still as the king moved towards him and fastened a sword belt around his waist. The king stepped back. Beside the prince stood Henry de Lacy, earl of Lincoln, and Humphrey de Bohun, earl of Hereford. Both now bent low as they attached the prince's spurs. With the final symbols of knighthood in place, Edward of Caernarfon became a knight of the English realm.

Now it was the duty of the prince to knight the great multitude of esquires who made their way to Westminster Abbey. An edict declaring that all eligible esquires should be in attendance had elicited such an enormous response that 267 esquires had descended upon London. The Abbey Church was so overcrowded that a warhorse was required to drive a path through to the altar. Taking centre stage, the prince proudly conferred the honour of knighthood with a touch of his sword as the esquires slowly came forward in pairs. Tall, powerfully built and strikingly handsome, the prince was the very image of a king-in-waiting. Those esquires he knighted were men of his own generation and in their hands rested the fate of Plantagenet England. As he presided over the spectacular ceremony, the prince must have felt the promise of that future closer than ever before.

Nor was this the end of the day's celebrations. Beneath the magnificent vaulted timber roof of Westminster Hall a sumptuous feast was held in honour of those who had been knighted. It was by far the most extravagant event of Edward I's reign. No expense had been spared. The hall was bedecked in colour, the walls awash with tapestries and silks, the cavernous room filled with the music and singing of eighty minstrels. On the vast trestle tables which ran the length of the hall, course after course of the most fabulous food was served, to the delight of those present. Copious measures of wine were poured. Talk and laughter drowned out the music. The prince was in his element, indulging in the food and drink, delighting in the entertainment having personally handpicked the minstrels. In its excess the feast was redolent of the prince's own pleasure-seeking court. But this was not yet his court. Although the prince had taken centre stage throughout the day, the king was firmly in control. Edward I remained aloof from the revelry surrounding him. He bided his time, for the feast had an ulterior, more sinister motive; he was about to ensure that the serious business of the Scottish war would be passed to this new, younger generation.

At last the moment arrived for which he had waited. Abruptly the music ceased. Servants entered the hall bearing an enormous dish upon which were two swans entwined beneath a fine net of gold. Gasps of astonishment faded to a hushed silence as the old king stood up. Raising himself to his full height, Edward stared out across the sea of expectant faces. He spoke, his voice deep and clear, echoing through the hall. With heartfelt passion he swore upon the swans that he would avenge the death of John Comyn and exact vengeance upon the treacherous Scots. It was an emphatic demonstration of his commitment to their destruction. Now Edward I asked his son and heir to match that commitment. Before the crowded hall the king asked the prince to swear a vow that should he, the king, die before he had exacted vengeance, then the prince would commit himself to taking it on his behalf. Caught up in the sheer intensity of the moment, his spirit perhaps emboldened by the food and drink, the prince rose to his feet and publicly vowed that he would not sleep two nights in the same place until he had reached Scotland, where he would fulfill his father's vow for revenge. In response, those attending the feast similarly swore a medley of vows to exact vengeance.[2]

Edward I can be excused if his mouth twisted into a wry grin of satisfaction. The Feast of the Swans was a carefully disguised and expertly stage-managed political vehicle designed by him to commit his heir to the destruction of Bruce and his Scottish adherents. By exacting this vow, the king believed he had ensured the destruction of Bruce even from beyond the grave. He had committed a younger generation to a war that he feared he might not live long enough to win himself. The knights who were so quick to volunteer such bold promises amidst the seductive splendours of a glorious feast in Westminster Hall could not know of the horror to which they had bound themselves. They were not to know that, in less than a decade, their blood would flow as freely as the wine did that night. For many of those present it was a vow that would be fulfilled when they took to the field at Bannockburn.

For Edward the Feast of the Swans had achieved its purpose, but the fact that he had felt compelled to engineer a commitment from the prince hints at his deep misgivings about the suitability of his heir as a future king. Edward should not have had to go to such extraordinary lengths to ensure that the prince would continue to prosecute the Scottish war and attempt to destroy Robert Bruce. The military strength of a kingdom, its willingness and ability to fight its enemies, was invested in the person of the king. It was the king who raised armies, who appointed commanders, and who led his subjects on campaign and in battle. If Edward I should die before Bruce was defeated, then the subsequent course of the Scottish wars would largely be dictated by the character of the prince. However, his was a character about which the king had grave misgivings. Yet if the prince sought a role model for the ideal warrior-king then he need not have looked any further than his father, Edward I himself.

A tall, imposing man, standing literally head and shoulders above many of his contemporaries, Edward 'Longshanks' had the physique to match his formidable reputation. Edward was a king of the old school; a warrior, a statesman, a lawgiver. He equated to the greatest of the Anglo-Norman kings of England, those hard-headed, iron-willed men who had forged a kingdom by fighting to protect and extend their lands, subduing and harnessing the support of their powerful magnates, subjecting their people to the early English systems of law and order. Such kings did not expect or need the love of their subjects. A great king became great by doing exactly what his subjects expected of him: he simply got the job done. This was the secret to Edward's long and successful reign. As an uncompromising, hard-hearted ruler, his subjects occasionally disagreed with him, but ultimately they still respected him.[3]

It was not only external threats against which kings had to guard. For more than two centuries, clashes had occurred between English kings and their magnates, the latter always seeking to enhance their power, the former jealously guarding their rights. Ever since King John had attached his seal to the Magna Carta in 1215 this ceaseless power struggle had provided English politics with a volatile undercurrent. In the mid-thirteenth century, civil war had erupted and Edward I had been in the thick of it. Then a young prince in his twenties, Edward had fought alongside his father, Henry III, in the Barons' Wars of mid-century. Opposing the reform movement of his uncle, Simon de Montfort, Edward had fought in the battles of Lewes and Evesham. At Lewes he had been captured along with his father Henry III; at Evesham he had witnessed the horrific mutilation of his uncle's corpse upon the field of battle. The bitter wars had provided Edward with a brutal lesson that the power of the Crown was not inviolate and that its authority had to be constantly defended. Inevitably, Edward encountered his own problems as king, the worst political crisis of his reign coming in 1297 when heavy expenditure on wars in Scotland, France and Wales resulted in a powerful bloc of opposition led by the earls of Norfolk and Hereford. Their grievances were set out in a document, the Remonstrances, and civil war loomed. Edward managed to defuse the situation, even persuading the two earls to participate in the Falkirk campaign of 1298. A compromise was agreed, but Edward followed the precedent set by King John in 1215 by accepting the need for reform in the midst of the crisis and then, when the immediate trouble had passed, brusquely ignoring the promises he had made.[4] No king would willingly accept terms diminishing and limiting his authority and that of the Crown. If the storms of kingship were to be weathered, if external enemies were to be defeated and internal threats suppressed, then the Crown had to be held by a strong-minded and aggressive king. What troubled Edward I was that the prince appeared to lack almost all the qualities required of a successful king.

Superficially, these troubling deficiencies were masked by the prince's striking appearance. The *Vita* describes him as 'tall and strong, a fine figure of a handsome man', the English chronicler Thomas Gray declaring that 'physically, he was one of the strongest men in the realm'. Barbour similarly recounts that 'he was the strongest man of any that you could find in any country'. A more physically powerful figure even than his father, contemporaries sensed his potential, the *Vita* lamenting with hindsight that if the prince had devoted himself to feats of arms he would have 'raised England aloft; his name would have resounded throughout the land. What hopes he raised as Prince of Wales! How they were dashed when he became king!'[5]

Born at Caernarfon Castle on 25 April 1284, Prince Edward became heir to the Crown four months later upon the death of his ten-year-old brother, Alphonso. Edward spent little time with his parents, and his mother, Eleanor of Castile, died whilst he was still an infant. But Edward I, mindful as ever of the dignity of the Crown, did ensure that the prince was provided with a household befitting the heir to one of the great realms of Christendom. At the age of five this included seven knights, nine sergeants-at-arms and a body of huntsmen and hounds. In 1288–9, when the prince was not yet six, the annual expenses of this household already totalled more than £2,000. His education followed that of every young nobleman: the prince would have learned to ride almost as soon as he could walk; he would have undergone hours of training in the use of lance and sword; innumerable hunts would have perfected his horsemanship; aspiring tales of chivalry, the legendary romances of Arthur and Roland, would have imbued the brutal business of war with a gloss of mythic glory. From 1295 the prince's tutor, his *magister*, was Guy de Ferre, an experienced and trusted knight whose royal service stretched back to the reign of the prince's grandfather, Henry III. Ferre would have taught the prince the workings of the military camp and of the court, and have provided instruction in military affairs and politics. The prince himself owned several books including a Latin prayer book, a romance inherited from his late mother, a history of England and a life of St Edward the Confessor, the latter written in French. Although possession is not proof of literacy, it is fair to assume the prince was literate in both Latin and French.[6]

Like all noble households his was peripatetic, travelling throughout the kingdom on an almost ceaseless circuit. It was not a lifestyle that bred stability, and the desire of the prince for a regular home manifested itself in the fondness he attached to the royal manor of Langley in Hertfordshire. His household wintered here in 1292–3, the harsh weather precluding any movement along England's mud-clogged roads. In 1291 the great hall at Langley had been decorated with strong martial overtones, the likenesses of fifty-two different shields painted upon the walls, vibrant images that were complemented by a vivid scene depicting four fully armoured knights on their way to participate in a tournament. There can be little doubt that the king, his father, had ordered this scheme of decoration, commissioning paintings that conveyed the virtues of knighthood and the strong martial culture of chivalry. Edward I was determined to mould his heir into a man worthy of the English Crown.

The real interests of the prince, however, lay outside the great hall. The royal manor of Langley was a sprawling estate consisting of 120 acres of arable land, 8 acres of parkland, meadows and pastures, and well tended gardens in which grew an abundance of fruits and vines. Through the estate wound the course of the scenic River Grade with two water mills built upon its banks and two small islands breaking its flow.[7] The delights of the countryside enthralled the young prince. Living in a household dominated by the heavy themes of war and politics, the prince found Langley to be a great playground where he could indulge in whatever pursuit he chose. It was probably here that the prince developed a passion for rustic pursuits such as ditching, thatching and hedging, while his love of water found expression in his fondness for boating and swimming.[8]

Edward I was appalled to find his son engaging in such pastimes. They were the interests and skills expected of peasants, not of a future king. Edward had formed an alarming sense that the prince did not possess the mettle of an iron-willed warrior-king. Instead, it was clear that his interests lay outside the arenas of war and politics. The painted walls of Langley had failed to infuse him with the required martial spirit. But all was not lost. The ongoing Scottish wars provided the king with the ideal opportunity for immersing the prince in the brutal business of war. The king believed that exposure to the conflicts north of the border could be the making of the prince.

In 1300, at the age of sixteen, the prince participated in his first campaign. The objective of the English was the Scottish castle of Caerlaverock. The king split the host into four divisions, one of which the prince commanded, although in practice real power resided in the figure of John de St John, a veteran of the Scottish wars. A five-day siege of Caerlaverock was the main focus of the campaign. Although a siege engine eventually brought about the fall of the castle, the English siege camp provided a glorious roll call of the most famous knights of the realm, their banners flying above their extravagant tents and hastily constructed but elegant timber houses. The chivalric ethos of the siege is exemplified in the contemporary poem, the 'Song of Caerlaverock', which provides an overwhelmingly romanticised account of the event. It was a campaign in which the prince would have learnt little about the brutality of warfare, although some of the captured garrison may have been hanged.[9]

A more ambitious campaign was undertaken the following year. Two armies were to enter Scotland, the king commanding one to the east, the prince leading a larger one to the west although the earl of Lincoln, Henry de Lacy, directed its operations. The army led by the prince was to attack the position of strength that the Scots had built up in the southwest, Edward I declaring that he desired the 'chief honour of taming the Scots to fall to his son'. The Scots, however, deliberately avoided the English, whose only notable action was an entry into Ayr and the capture of Robert Bruce's castle of Turnberry. The king and the prince wintered together at Linlithgow before a temporary truce with the Scots halted the war in January 1302.[10]

When aged nineteen, the prince also participated in the campaign of 1303–4 which ultimately led to the defeat of the Scots. The king remained in Scotland from the summer of 1303 until the summer of 1304, driving his army as far north as Aberdeen and dominating the landscape by seizing castles and burning villages. These tactics were repeated throughout Scotland by several English forces, one of which the prince commanded. He would certainly have looked the part. A record survives of the items prepared for him in the campaign of 1303, a dazzling array of equipment which included: the construction of a three-posted portable chamber; forty-two banners of sindon emblazoned with the arms of the prince; thirty-six banners, a dozen each depicting the arms of St Edward, St Edmund and St George; several swords with scabbards and embroidered belts; copper-gilt crests painted with the arms of the prince; three bacinets for his personal use; two caps of iron, one with a crest; and two war helms, one of which was equipped with a visor. Riding at the head of his troops, wreaking a path of destruction as he ranged through Strathearn and the north-east of Scotland, the prince would have cut a formidable figure in his gleaming armour, advancing beneath a brilliant sea of streaming heraldic banners.[11]

In the winter of 1303 the business of state took precedence over warfare. On Christmas Day the powerful men seated around the prince's table in the town of Perth included the earls of Lancaster, Warwick, Ulster, Atholl and Strathearn. His dinner guest on 22 February 1304 was John Comyn, the Scottish lord who had just negotiated the Scottish surrender and who would later be killed by Bruce.[12] The prince was still in Scotland in the spring when he was instructed by the king to order his soldiers to strip lead from the roofs of all the churches in Perth and Dunblane to equip the siege engines that were intended to batter Stirling Castle into submission. By the time the war was brought to a close in the summer of 1304, the twenty-year-old prince was experienced in warfare and had held positions of command. The Scottish campaigns had provided him with every chance of moulding his character into that required of a strong and successful future king. Yet the performance of the prince in these campaigns did nothing to assuage Edward I's deep misgivings. Indeed, if anything, it only appears to have confirmed them.

Although the prince had spent increasing amounts of time in the company of his father, the king was extremely reluctant to provide his heir with the offices and responsibilities that were his due. On 7 February 1301 the prince, then almost seventeen, was formally granted the royal lands in Wales and Chester. The king himself had received these lands when he was fourteen. The prince was almost twenty-two when he was granted the lands of Gascony, the grant prompted by the need to provide him with a substantial endowment for his projected marriage to Isabella of France. The king himself had been only ten when he had been granted Gascony. Edward I denied the prince important military commands which were critical in providing a future king with invaluable experience. When the offices of lieutenant of Gascony and lieutenant of Scotland became vacant in the early fourteenth century, the king appointed his nephew, John of Brittany, earl of Richmond, and not the prince. The failure of Edward to appoint the prince as lieutenant of Scotland in 1305 is particularly striking; so low was the king's opinion of his heir that he did not even trust him to oversee a beaten country.[13]

By a stroke of bitter irony, a further attempt by Edward I to remould the character of his heir led to the prince being introduced to a young Gascon esquire by the name of Piers Gaveston. Theirs was a relationship that would ultimately tear the realm apart. Arnaud, Gaveston's father, had served Edward I for more than two decades before settling in England in 1297. Both Gaveston and his father had fought for Edward in Flanders that year, and it is likely that Gaveston was among the English host that annihilated the Scots at Falkirk in 1298. Gaveston had served in the Caerlaverock campaign of 1300 and by the end of the year had been transferred from the king's household to that of the prince. Edward I was so impressed with the martial aptitude and chivalrous valour of Gaveston that he believed the young Gascon would provide an ideal role model for the impressionable prince. It was a decision that would backfire spectacularly.

The prince was immediately captivated by Gaveston. The Gascon was witty and charming, no doubt full of tales recounting his military service and his life overseas. That Gaveston had also lost his mother when still a boy can only have strengthened the affinity between the two young men. But above all the prince must have been drawn to Gaveston because he realised that the Gascon had won the elusive approval of the king, an accolade the prince himself so desperately craved. Gaveston was equally taken by the prince, delighting in his affable charm and ready geniality. The prince was certainly a good friend to have. He was well-educated, quick in speech and able to converse knowledgeably on a wide range of subjects. Thomas Gray believed that 'he was generous, and genial well beyond measure to those whom he loved, and very affable to his close companions'.[14]

Nor did it take long for Gaveston to be seduced by the hedonism of the prince's splendid household. A lion was now a permanent feature of this household, which, together with its cart and keeper, travelled with the prince throughout the English realm. The prince's taste for expensive jewels led to a number of lavish purchases, the most expensive being a great ruby which he presented as a New Year's gift to his stepmother, Queen Margaret. The prince possessed a collection of sumptuous clothes and was enthralled by the entertainments of minstrels and fools.[15] As a young man from a relatively poor background, Gaveston could not help but indulge himself in this extravagant materialism. The emotional attachment of the two men surpassed the bounds of friendship. Speculation remains rife that a homosexual relationship existed between them. If so, contemporaries never explicitly described it as such; the punishment for homosexuality frequently being death, this should not be surprising. A different theory is that the prince effectively adopted Gaveston as his brother. Whether the undoubted love that existed between the two young men was sexual or fraternal, the exact nature of their relationship is to some extent immaterial. What is important is the fact that the heir to the Crown and a formerly impoverished Gascon esquire had become dangerously inseparable.

Yet despite the materialism of the prince's household there was a serious edge to his character. A lion may have accompanied him but so too did a Dominican confessor. When the prince stayed at the abbey of Bury St

Edmund's he requested that he be treated like a fellow monk. Although he was careful to pay off his dicing debts, he made more regular payments towards alms. Above all he wanted to meet the exacting standards of his father, but time and again he fell short. Cast aside in the cold shadow of such an unforgiving taskmaster, the prince turned for solace to the extravagant materialism of his court. It was a court that Gaveston increasingly came to dominate and in which the Gascon provided the humour and warmth that the prince so desperately needed.

Yet the prince persisted in attempting to gain the frustratingly elusive approval of his father. Nothing better illustrates this than an extraordinary incident that occurred in 1305. It was precipitated by a complaint made to Edward I by Walter Langton, bishop of Coventry and Lichfield and the king's treasurer, who claimed that the prince had broken into a wood belonging to him. For such a minor misdemeanour the king's response was entirely out of proportion. The prince and his household were banned from approaching the king closer than a distance of ten to twelve leagues, the Exchequer was ordered to contribute nothing towards the cost of the prince's household, and a number of the prince's favourite companions were removed from his entourage, including Gaveston. The prince did not protest. Rather than complain at his harsh treatment he humbly trailed his father's court as it moved through southern England, never approaching closer than the stipulated limit. The prince borrowed money to finance his truncated household and wrote to his sisters assuring them that his father would eventually forgive him. This pitiful display continued for several weeks until the king finally relented.[16] So desperate was the prince to gain his father's forgiveness that he was reduced to an act of abject subservience. This was no child who had submissively followed after the king but a man of twenty-one who would soon inherit the Crown. The extent to which the young man's will was bent by that of his father was so complete that it prevented him from attempting to assert his own independence. To those who witnessed this humiliating display, it was yet another troubling indictment of the unsuitable character of the future king.

It was these misgivings that led Edward I to engineer the vows sworn at the Feast of the Swans in May 1306. A month after the feast the English host that Edward had summoned mustered at Carlisle. The campaign of 1306 was intended to put an end once and for all to the Scottish wars by destroying Bruce. For Edward the campaign was fuelled by an increasing sense of his own mortality, and by the gnawing fear that, should he die, his heir might not prove capable of bringing the conflict to a successful conclusion. But before he could join the English host, Edward was incapacitated by illness. In his absence the leadership of the campaign passed to the prince. This was another opportunity for him to demonstrate that he was worthy of the Crown. In June the host advanced into Scotland with the prince proudly at its head. As he surveyed the mounted columns of knights and men-at-arms, as he gazed at the trailing line of foot soldiers and listened to the thunderous sounds of the baggage train, a sense of freedom, of finally emerging from the cold shadow of his father, must inwardly have warmed him. He would have been mindful, too, that this would soon be the way of things. The days of his father were numbered. The Crown would soon be his.

But if the prince hoped to win martial glory he was soon disappointed. By the time the English host arrived in Scotland, Bruce had already been defeated. Having been routed by Valence at Methven in June, and having barely escaped with his life from skirmishes at Loch Tay and Dalry, his power had been broken. The prince now had to deal with those who had supported him. Lochmaben Castle, the seat of the Bruces in Annandale, surrendered to the prince's troops without a fight. By July the bulk of the English host was encamped within the walls of Perth. Impatiently awaiting news of the whereabouts of Bruce, the prince and Valence received intelligence that several of his prominent supporters were holed up to the north, in Kildrummy Castle. The English, led by the prince, marched north and arrived before the castle in early August. Some of their quarry had already fled, Bruce's wife and daughter, along with the countess of Buchan, had ridden further north, perhaps heading for Orkney where another of Bruce's sisters was queen. They never made it. Intercepted at the sanctuary of St Duthac in Tain by men of the earl of Ross, a diehard Balliol supporter, they were sent south under armed escort.[17]

Kildrummy Castle, though, remained stubbornly defended. It was occupied by a substantial garrison and commanded by Bruce's brother, Neil. The castle itself was a formidable thirteenth-century sandstone structure, with towers guarding each of its corners and an entrance protected by a strongly fortified gatehouse. A powerful donjon arose from within the castle walls. Built on the solid rock of a ravine, the castle's foundations were impervious to mining. The castle was also well supplied with victuals, the great hall being stacked high with corn. The English had no siege engines, the speed of their advance from Perth precluding the inclusion of a slow-moving siege train. To cut timber and build engines on site was considered inadvisable for an isolated army so far north and with autumn closing in. There was no option for the prince but to order waves of troops to attack the formidable defences of the castle. The garrison met the English at the outworks, fiercely and continually repelling them.

In the end a traitor within the castle brought about its fall. A coulter was placed in a fire. When the metal was aglow with heat it was thrown into the pile of corn that filled the great hall. A huge blaze broke out, flames devouring the interior of the hall and bursting through the roofing boards, clouds of acrid smoke billowing through chambers and up stairways. As the castle burnt the English renewed their attack, but on again being repulsed they decided to let the fire do their work for them. Throughout the hours of darkness they watched the lurid spectacle of the burning castle as it lit the night sky. By morning the gatehouse was a smouldering ruin. Surrender was now inevitable. The laws of war permitted a victorious besieger to do as he wished with an enemy who had held out against him; several of the garrison were hanged from a nearby tree. It is not clear whether the prince ordered this, but as the most senior commander present he evidently did not oppose it. The more prestigious prisoners were temporarily spared, Neil Bruce among them. What was left of Kildrummy Castle was slighted then the English struck camp and headed south.[18]

What followed was horrific even by contemporary standards. During the summer the ailing Edward I had been carried north on a litter and in October he took up residence in the northwest of England, at Lanercost Priory. It was from here that he issued an official ordinance that was barbaric in its brutality: those Scots who had opposed him were to be pursued with hue and cry; those involved in the murder of John Comyn, and all who had advised in and consented to Bruce's actions, were to be drawn and hanged; anyone captured in the act of fighting against the king was to be hanged or decapitated; anyone who surrendered was to be immediately imprisoned and held until the king himself decided their fate; the poor who were captured would be allowed to buy their ransoms at a price they could afford, but which in practice was a price that would financially cripple them.

This ordinance officially sanctioned the excessive depravity of bloodletting into which English recriminations had already descended. In Newcastle, on 4 August, sixteen supporters of Bruce were summarily hanged. Christopher Seton, Bruce's brother-in-law, the man who had killed John Comyn's uncle Robert in the kirk of the Greyfriars in Dumfries six months before, was captured in the castle of Loch Doon. In a symbolic act, Seton was taken back to Dumfries where he was drawn through the streets, hanged and beheaded.

John Stathbogie, earl of Atholl, had been captured as he attempted to facilitate the escape of Bruce's wife and daughter north from Kildrummy Castle. Atholl became the first earl executed in England for more than two hundred years. Edward I's only concession to pleas of mercy was to have the gallows raised higher in regard of the earl's royal blood. Atholl was hanged, decapitated and his remains burnt.

Nor did Edward exhibit any leniency towards those women intimately connected with Robert Bruce. Bruce's wife, Elizabeth, a daughter of the powerful earl of Ulster, was the most fortunate, being held under house arrest in the Lincolnshire manor of Burstwick. Christian, a sister of Bruce and the wife of the executed Christopher Seton, was consigned to a nunnery in Lincolnshire. Mary Bruce, who had openly supported her brother, and the young countess of Buchan, who had deserted her husband to participate in the inauguration of Bruce at Scone, were handed punishments of the most debasing cruelty. Both women were imprisoned in specially constructed cages of timber and iron, the cages having latticed sides so that their occupants were permanently open to view, the only element of privacy being a small, screened-off privy. Mary's cage was attached to the wall of Roxburgh Castle and that of the countess to Berwick Castle. It was a punishment extraordinary for its level of humiliation and public degradation. Bruce's daughter, Marjorie, not yet in her teens, was originally sentenced to occupy a third cage in the Tower of London, but in the event even Edward I could not put a child through such a horrific ordeal; the order was rescinded and Marjorie sent to a Yorkshire nunnery. In 1307 Edward himself appears to have baulked at the extent of the terror he had unleashed, claiming the ordinance he had issued had been interpreted too harshly.

This brutal reign of terror was driven by the rage of the ailing king, yet the prince also had blood on his hands. Those captured at Kildrummy Castle were imprisoned in Berwick. In early October 1306 the prince presided over their trial. Three Scottish knights and a clerk were sentenced to death. Among the knights was Neil Bruce. Along with his comrades, he was drawn, hanged and beheaded. Although acting in accordance with the ordinance issued by his father, the prince was intimately involved in the violent retribution meted out to those who had supported Bruce. Berwick was certainly a grim place to be imprisoned in late 1306, the corpses of the executed being unceremoniously thrown into carts and carried through the streets of the town, above which still hung a butchered and decaying quarter of William Wallace.[19]

The English campaign had proved a dour affair, and the wave of executions that followed provided a gruesome and ignominious epilogue. For the young knights and esquires who had ridden to Scotland beguiled by visions of winning martial glory, it was a disagreeable end to a disappointing campaign. For some the inglorious tedium proved too much to bear. Without obtaining the necessary licence from the king, twenty-two Englishmen left the main host in Scotland and took ship for the continent to participate in a tournament which offered the prospect of renown they so ardently craved. When Edward heard of this he was furious. These men were guilty of deserting the host while Bruce was still on the run. In mid-October the sheriffs of every English county were ordered to arrest these deserters and to seize their lands and goods. Ominously, many of these young men were members of the prince's household, and inevitably Gaveston was among them. At length, in January 1307, sixteen of the deserters were pardoned, and no further action was taken against the others.[20] Yet it was a regrettable episode; whether or not the prince was party to their desertion, the fact that prominent members of his household had left the host and travelled abroad without permission did not reflect well upon him. For King Edward this was another black mark against the character of his son.

In March 1307 the relationship between the king and his heir irrevocably broke down. Gaveston was the rock upon which it ultimately foundered. In an act of appalling misjudgement the prince proposed that Gaveston be granted either the county of Ponthieu or the earldom of Cornwall. Both belonged to the English Crown and were of such prestige and value that they could only be awarded by the king. That the prince should ask his father to consider granting them to a young man who, less than a year ago, had been an impoverished Gascon esquire, was an unprecedented act of folly. That the prince dared not ask this of his father personally but sent Walter Langton, the king's treasurer and bishop of Coventry and Lichfield, to ask him instead suggests he knew what his father's response would be. If so, he underestimated the rage it provoked in Edward. The king gave full vent to his fury. He demanded that his son be brought to him. In a vicious tirade of anger he bellowed at the prince, 'You base-born whoreson. As the Lord lives, if it were not for fear of breaking up the kingdom, you should never enjoy your inheritance.' The king snatched at the prince's hair, grabbing it in both hands and violently tore out a great clump. Spent by this explosion of anger, he ordered that the prince be removed from his presence.[21]

If Edward had sought conclusive proof of his heir's ineptitude, then this was surely it. In proposing these grants for Gaveston, the prince had shown that he had no appreciation of the dignity or authority of the Crown. It was with despair that Edward banished Gaveston into exile. If he could not alter the character of his son, then at least he could remove the chief source of his inappropriate conduct. Gaveston sailed from Dover on 5 May 1307, the hold of the vessel crammed with lavish gifts that the prince had sorrowfully bestowed on his beloved favourite. As the billowing sails disappeared beyond the horizon, so an open breach finally existed between King Edward and the prince.

By the time Gaveston sailed, however, the attention of the king had once again turned to Scotland. In January 1307 intelligence had been received that placed the fugitive figure of Robert Bruce close to the Scottish mainland, near the west coast among the Scottish Isles. During February an English strike force of fifteen knights, thirty men-at-arms and twelve sergeants-at-arms was sent to seek him out. In the same month a fleet of fifteen ships scoured the waters of the Firth of Clyde. In July an English force was ordered to assemble at Carlisle to proceed against Bruce. Edward accompanied it on the journey north. He was again suffering from ill-health. When he led his troops out of Carlisle on 3 July, the indomitable old king was suffering from dysentery. He spent the night of 6 July at the village of Burgh-by-Sands. His condition worsened. It became so bad that the following morning his servants had to lift him from his bed. As they did so Edward I died in their arms.[22] He was sixty-eight.

It was the end of an era. For thirty-four years his will had prevailed over the English realm. Now he was gone. Fearful that his death might encourage the Scots, those closest to him imposed a complete news blackout. More than a week after the king's death the chancellor in London was still sealing writs in the name of Edward I. The prince, now the de facto king, arrived eleven days after the death of his father and with due reverence escorted the embalmed corpse from Carlisle to York. While the archbishop of York accompanied it south to Waltham Abbey, Edward returned to Carlisle and led the waiting troops into Scotland. Less than a month later the army arrived back in Carlisle. It had achieved nothing. The priorities for Edward now lay with the Crown he had inherited and the power that came with it.

The reign of Edward II had begun. With the death of his unforgiving father he had finally emerged from his cold shadow. The immediate future of the English realm, and the course of the war against Bruce, would now be determined in great part by the character and abilities of Edward II. The final bequest of his father, a renowned warrior-king, had predictably been a war. But Edward II himself was no warrior. The solemn vow he had sworn so publicly at the Feast of the Swans on 22 May 1306 was temporarily cast aside. The downtrodden prince was now king. At last he believed he could do what he wanted. This was to be another of his mistakes.

CHAPTER SIX

LORDS OF WAR

For Robert Bruce the death of Edward I was nothing short of a godsend. Before the great warrior-king's death, in the dark days of early 1307, a mysterious rumour had been circulating in Scotland. It was claimed that a prophecy by no less a figure than Merlin had been discovered. The prophecy spoke of the ancient mystic's prediction that when '*le Roi Coueytous*' died the people of Scotland and Wales 'shall league together, and have the sovereign hand and their will, and live together in accord till the end of the world'.[1] The king referred to was interpreted as being Edward I, and like all good prophecies it promised what its audience so desperately wanted to believe. Yet it is a measure of the depths to which the fortunes of Robert Bruce had sunk that this prophecy was almost all that the Scots had to cling to. In early 1307 Scotland remained a beaten kingdom. As for Bruce, his sole objective was to survive. It was no easy task.

The return of Bruce to the Scottish mainland in the first months of 1307 was a fiasco which claimed the lives of two of his brothers and could so easily have cost him his own. Bruce had always intended to come back. His flight and disappearance in late 1306 was not the romantic interlude that it has often been portrayed as. Bruce and his dwindling band of followers spent the last months of 1306 among the Scottish Isles and in the vicinity of the eastern seaboard of Ireland. In view of the composition of the forces with which he returned, it was a time spent in negotiation with the lords of the Isles and with the bellicose Irish chieftains and sub-kings of this largely untamed maritime region. Bruce had been seeking not so much political alliances as access to manpower. Short on numbers, he was also lacking in arms and money; in

February partisans of Bruce secretly slipped into Carrick to collect the rents he was due. By bargaining for support, offering inducements, exploiting his Celtic connections, Bruce began to gather a small but purposeful invasion force.

It was to be deployed in a three-pronged attack. The northernmost landing, to be commanded by James Douglas and Robert Boyd, was on the island of Arran; the largest force, to be led in person by Bruce and his brother, Edward, was to make landfall approximately a dozen miles south of Ayr, at Turnberry; to the south a force commanded by two more of his brothers, Thomas and Alexander, together with an Irish sub-king, Reginald Crawford, and Malcolm MacQuillan, lord of Kintyre, was to land in Galloway. When this simultaneous invasion was launched in early 1307 the latter force immediately met with disaster. It sailed into the waters of Loch Ryan transported in a small but noticeable fleet of eighteen ships and galleys. As soon as the troops waded ashore they were routed by Doungal Macdouall, a local Galloway warlord and a bitter opponent of Bruce. MacQuillan was beheaded on the spot and his decapitated head sent to Edward I. Crawford and the two Bruce brothers, all badly wounded in the engagement, were taken to Carlisle. Thomas Bruce was drawn, hanged and beheaded. Alexander Bruce and Reginald Crawford were both hanged and beheaded. The head of Thomas was displayed atop the keep of Carlisle Castle, and the heads of Alexander, Crawford and MacQuillan were each staked above one of the three town gates.

To the north, Douglas and Boyd enjoyed a measure of success. Landing in secret upon the rugged shores of Arran, they made their way to the castle of Brodick. Having spent time observing the activities of the English garrison, they executed a ruthless ambush when many of the garrison troops were engaged in unloading supply ships. Most of the garrison was killed but enough survived to prevent the castle from being taken. The haul of arms and supplies captured by Douglas and Boyd was invaluable. Unwilling to risk these spoils, they returned to their galleys and slipped quietly away from Arran.

The outcome of the invasion, however, was always going to be determined by Robert Bruce's landing at Turnberry. Carrick may have been Bruce's own earldom but he was certainly taking no chances. A spy named Cuthbert was dispatched to ascertain the situation. Should Cuthbert consider it safe for Bruce and his force to sail, then he would light a fire on the coast at Turnberry Head. Despite the apparent simplicity of this plan, it went dangerously awry. Cuthbert discovered that, in Carrick, no one was prepared to support Bruce openly. Worse, the English occupied Carrick, the garrison based in

Turnberry Castle being so substantial that many of its troops were encamped in the village of Turnberry. As Cuthbert prepared to return to Bruce and impart the terrible news, he saw with horror the bright flames of a fire flickering into the night sky near Turnberry Head. Although the fire was a sheer coincidence, it promised an unmitigated catastrophe.

To Bruce it was the agreed signal. His invasion force of three hundred men and thirty-three small galleys immediately set sail. Concealed by the darkness they made landfall without mishap. As they clambered out of the galleys and splashed ashore, Cuthbert breathlessly hurried to meet them. Urgently he told Bruce of the lack of support and of the presence of the large English garrison. Bruce faltered. To discover that he could not muster ready support in his own earldom was a stunning blow. Undecided, he turned to his closest advisers. There was no one closer to him than his brother, Edward. According to Barbour, it was Edward who stiffened his resolve, pronouncing boldly, 'I'll take my chances here, for good or ill'. The forthrightness of his brother won Bruce over. Silently they led their men forwards, slipping noiselessly into the village of Turnberry where the garrison slept. Then they attacked, breaking down doors and killing men where they lay. The survivors fled to the castle while Bruce and his men ransacked the camp of weapons, armour, silver plate and horses. So great was the fear instilled by this attack that it was necessary for an English relief force to extricate the terrified garrison.[2]

But for Bruce it was hardly a victory. If his position had been weak following the killing of John Comyn and his hasty inauguration at Scone, then it was now horrendously fragile. The terrible rout at Methven and his ignominious flight had stripped Bruce of any semblance of authority or power. Few Scots believed he stood any chance of success. The forces arrayed against him were indeed formidable. It was not only the English who sought his destruction. His actions had created a raft of powerful Scottish enemies, a coalition of influential magnates with links to both Comyn and Balliol. In the north he was opposed by John Comyn, earl of Buchan, a staunch Scottish patriot who had previously fought against the English and who now sought to avenge the murder of his namesake and cousin. David, earl of Brechin, whose lineage could be traced back to David of Huntingdon, had also fought for the Scottish cause until defeat in 1304. John Mowbray, a patriot imprisoned in the Tower of London in 1296, was now guardian of the lands of the murdered John Comyn. William, earl of Ross, was another implacable opponent of Bruce, and the previous year had handed over Bruce's wife, daughter and sister to Edward I. John of Argyll and his father, Alexander, were staunch Balliol and

Comyn supporters. To the south the unruly lands of Galloway, traditional Balliol territory, remained hostile to Bruce, while Galloway, Lothian and the Borders were also studded with castles occupied by English garrisons.

To many Scots it appeared they had no king. Balliol had been discredited and consigned to exile. Bruce was a failed usurper tainted with the terrible crime of murdering a fellow Scottish lord. Nor was Bruce considered a patriot, the treacherous twists and turns of his inglorious career being in stark contrast to the impeccable record of service in the Scottish cause exhibited by many of his influential opponents. The latter would never willingly accept him as king. Bruce was an outcast, a murderer, a traitor and a usurper; the stigma of defeat clung tightly about him. If Bruce was to realise his ambition, if he was to resurrect his claim to be king, then he would first have to defeat his Scottish opponents and win over the Scottish people. Robert Bruce would have to engage in a bitter power struggle; he would have to fight a civil war.

The engagement at Turnberry did not alter anything. Cowed by the excesses of Edward I's barbaric reign of terror, and believing Bruce to be a lost cause, even the Scots of his own earldom of Carrick refused to support him openly, as Cuthbert had discovered. If Bruce was to have any chance of gaining the level of support necessary to win a civil war, then he would have to convince the Scots that he was not a spent force. But in the first months of 1307 it was all he could do to survive. Robert Bruce was a hunted man. Throughout Carrick, Annandale and Galloway armed men scoured the hills and moors for him. Barbour tells of several attempts on Bruce's life, his would-be assassins not Englishmen but Scotsmen. A tracker dog, a sleuthhound, was employed by his enemies, sniffing the rough trackways for the merest hint of his scent. Bruce dared not trust anyone and was constantly on guard, hanging a sword from a strap around his neck so that it was always at hand.[3] It was too dangerous for Bruce to move from one place to another without the most meticulous caution, and when he did move he was forced to keep to inaccessible moors and marshes. To many Scots it was not a question of whether he would be captured or killed, but when.

Nor were his enemies the only ones who believed the days of Bruce to be numbered. Early in the spring of 1307 James Douglas linked up with Bruce in Carrick before departing south to attend to his own pressing business. His ancestral lands of Douglasdale lay here, in the wild surroundings of the ancient expanse of Ettrick forest, and at their heart was the castle of Douglas. In 1298 Edward I had granted the castle and lands to Robert Clifford after they had been confiscated from Douglas's father, William, a notoriously violent and lawless Scottish lord. William had fought alongside Wallace during the revolt of 1297, but had soon been captured. Imprisoned in the Tower of London, he died there on 9 November 1298.[4]

At the time of his father's death James Douglas was probably not yet in his teens. Barbour, as is so often the case, provides our only description of him. The portrait he paints is of a lean, broad-shouldered, thin-faced figure, his inordinately pale skin contrasting starkly with his extraordinarily dark hair. His hair, rather than his ruthless reputation, was to earn him the sobriquet of the Black Douglas. He was not handsome and spoke with a lisp which, according to Barbour, suited him well. Besides recounting conventional attributes such as his fine bearing and generosity, Barbour provides the rather more telling comment that 'When he was cheerful he was engaging, quiet and gentle in company, but if you saw him in battle, he had quite another look'.[5] It was a look many were to witness at the cost of their lives.

James Douglas was an adversary no one wished to face, yet Edward I could have avoided making him an enemy. In his youth Douglas had spent time in Paris and had served the bishop of St Andrews, William Lamberton, occupying the position of the bishop's knife bearer. Following the Scottish defeat in 1304, the bishop had approached Edward I and requested that Douglas's rightful inheritance of Douglasdale be returned to him. Edward dismissed the request. The king was in no mood to return lands to the son of man as unruly as William Douglas, a man who had fought alongside Wallace. Denied his lands, James Douglas waited for his chance. It came with Bruce's usurpation of the Crown in 1306. Douglas had joined Bruce in the spring of 1306 not primarily out of support for his bid to be king, nor purely for the cause of Scottish independence, but to reclaim his lands. Douglas had fought alongside Bruce in the gruelling encounters at Methven, Loch Tay and Dalry. He had fled Scotland with him and led the attack on Arran. Now, it was time for Douglas to turn his attention to the chief reason why he had risked so much for Robert Bruce.

His immediate target was Douglas Castle. However, although Clifford himself was absent, he had installed an English garrison to maintain his hold on the castle. Douglas lured a section of the garrison out of the castle by disguising some of his men as victual carriers. As the English came to seize the goods, they were ambushed and ferociously cut down. So devastating was this ambush, and executed with such speed and precision, that Douglas and his men were also able to force their way into the castle. The fortification was seized and a number of the garrison, including the constable, were taken prisoner. Their fate looked grim. Yet rather than execute his captives, Douglas released them without ransom and even provided them with enough money to cover the expenses of their journey to England. In view of the brutal reputation that Douglas was soon to acquire, such a generous act is entirely at odds with his character. Like his father before him, Douglas was an intensely violent man; he was also immensely practical. There was a simple reason why Douglas released his prisoners: he was in talks with the English and on the point of abandoning Bruce in order to enter into the allegiance of Edward I.[6]

In this he was not alone. David of Atholl, son and heir of the Scottish earl executed by Edward I, was among the most prominent figures in Bruce's meagre band of followers. Early in 1307 he entered into negotiations with the English and subsequently deserted Bruce, pledging his allegiance to the English king. It appears that Douglas and David of Atholl had also come to the conclusion that Bruce was a beaten man. His return to Scotland was an ominous reminder of the dreadfully desperate months of late 1306. Now he was hunted by a legion of enemies, unable to muster support in his own earldom and forced into the wilderness. This sense of hopelessness on the part of Douglas and David of Atholl was compounded by the knowledge that a brutal death awaited them should they be captured, a prospect that seemingly grew more inevitable by the day. In the circumstances it is not surprising they decided to abandon Bruce while they still could. A negotiated surrender would save their necks; it might also save their lands. Before spring was over, David of Atholl had completed his change of allegiance. James Douglas was still in talks with the English when Bruce was finally run to ground.

Aymer de Valence, the victor of Methven, had been charged by Edward I with leading the manhunt for Bruce. A strike force had been placed under his command. In April 1307 an intelligence report placed Bruce at Glen Trool, a deep, steep-sided glen, its interior filled by the implacable waters of Loch Trool. It was typical of the remote and wild areas to which Bruce was increasingly confined. Valence, assailed by Edward I's incessant demands to capture Bruce, was justifiably concerned at the treacherous nature of the terrain. His troops, forced to dismount and go in on foot, would be terribly exposed. Fearful of what might await them, Valence sent a spy into the glen. The ruse backfired. The spy, apparently a woman dressed poorly as if in need of charity, was captured and under interrogation revealed the presence of the English. Hastily the Scots armed themselves. When the spy failed to return, the English cautiously advanced. They emerged from the wood to be confronted by a fully arrayed troop of Scotsmen, with Bruce standing to the fore, his banner raised defiantly above him. As the English faltered, Bruce led his men forwards, plunging into the enemy and driving them back. To find the Scots ready for them was not part of the English plan. With the advantage of surprise lost, they beat a hasty retreat. Yet as the English fled so, it seems, did Bruce. The troops he encountered appear to have been the advance guard of a much larger English force. If so, Bruce fled with good reason; according to an English report, the Scots were hounded relentlessly for twenty-five miles before they finally threw off the English pursuit.[7]

On 10 May Bruce and Valence again clashed. This time it was Bruce who appears actively to have sought an engagement. His target may well have been the English treasurer, Walter Langton, bishop of Coventry and Lichfield, who was travelling between English garrisons in the southwest of Scotland with a substantial amount of money for the payment of their wages. On 8 May the bishop set out from Carlisle, almost certainly escorted by Valence. Perhaps attracted by the money, Bruce planned to ambush the treasurer, choosing as his site Loudoun Hill to the east of Kilmarnock. Here the roadway became narrow due to the encroaching slopes of the hillside. To hinder the English cavalry further, Bruce had three deep ditches dug beside his position, gaps being left in them so that only limited numbers of English horsemen could push through; his intention was to filter them piecemeal towards the waiting Scots.

Valence was aware that Bruce was in the vicinity. The English advanced in two divisions, outnumbering a Scottish force of perhaps no more than several hundred men. When the two sides met a vicious, close-quarter engagement erupted, the Scots fighting on foot so fiercely 'that they impaled both men and horses with spears that sheared sharply, till red blood soon ran from the wounds'. Bruce, his brother Edward, and James Douglas were at the forefront of the action. Valence, now recognising the trap for what it was, and perhaps aware of his responsibility for the bishop and the money, pulled his men out before the main body of his force was committed to the fight. Valence was subsequently reprimanded by Edward I for withdrawing at Loudoun instead of pursuing the engagement against Bruce.[8]

Glen Trool and Loudoun were by no means clear-cut military victories for Bruce. They were little more than intense skirmishes fought between relatively insubstantial forces, neither side ultimately being defeated. Militarily they were far from conclusive. Yet politically for Bruce they were priceless. On both occasions he had met an English force in the field and emerged undefeated. To survive these encounters was in itself a major victory. The stigma of defeat that clung to him was gradually being dispelled. At last the Scots were beginning to have some belief, some hope, in him. Douglas certainly felt hopeful enough to take heart and fight at Loudoun. His faith in Bruce renewed, he broke off talks with the English. Predictably, Barbour portrays Glen Trool and Loudoun as great victories, and in this he was not alone. Bruce was also eager to magnify these engagements. It was five days after Loudoun that news of the 'false preachers' recounting the alleged prophecy of Merlin first reached the English. The preachers were almost certainly acting on the orders of Bruce. If he was going to succeed in the Scottish power struggle, then Bruce realised he needed to win the hearts and minds of the Scots. At Glen Trool and Loudoun he had taken the first step by breaking the cycle of defeat in which he had become entrapped.

Then in July came news of the death of Edward I. If Glen Trool and Loudoun had broken Bruce's run of defeat, the death of Edward I gave him the breathing space he so desperately needed. The half-hearted expedition that Edward II then led into Scotland in August was, to Bruce, a timely reprieve. Edward marched to Dumfries where he received homage from those Scottish lords in allegiance to the English and then headed to Cumnock; by 1 September he had returned to Carlisle. In the same month Valence was replaced by John of Brittany as lieutenant of Scotland. It seemed that the inexorable pressure Edward I had exerted on the Scots was momentarily easing, and Bruce was quick to exploit this. In the autumn he led a punitive raid into Galloway, driving out the local chieftains and forcing the inhabitants to flee into England. Then Bruce turned north. The political power bases of many of his Scottish enemies lay in the lands beyond the Tay. If he was going to reassert his claim to be king, then he would have to defeat these enemies by armed force. Leaving Douglas to operate in the fastness of Ettrick forest, Bruce led his men to Inverlochy and seized the castle there through the 'deceit and treason' of the garrison.[9] The Great Glen now lay open for a rapid advance north.

His support grew. By late October, when Bruce approached the lands of the earl of Ross to the north of Inverness, the force he commanded was so substantial that the earl believed his own force of three thousand men was hopelessly outnumbered, and he entered into a temporary truce with Bruce.[10] His left flank now secured, Bruce moved eastwards along the coast of the Moray Firth systematically destroying the castles of his enemies: Inverness Castle was taken and levelled to the ground; Invernairn Castle was assaulted and burnt by night; Urquhart Castle was seized; the garrison of Elgin Castle, besieged and subjected to heavy attack, was forced to conclude a truce. Moving remorselessly onwards, Bruce laid siege to the castle of Banff. It was here that he was gripped by his first bout of debilitating sickness. Bruce was taken by his troops to Slioch and the siege lifted.

Informed of the whereabouts of Bruce, his enemies took action. The combined forces of John Comyn, earl of Buchan, and David de Brechin, together with the troops of John Mowbray, converged on Slioch in December 1307. In the bitter winter weather they found Bruce's force arrayed defensively among the snow-laden trees. Both sides used their archers, cautiously probing the enemy. For several days the two sides faced one another. Buchan, knowing he had reinforcements on the way, and aware that Bruce's troops were running low on supplies, agreed on Christmas Day to a one-week truce and temporarily withdrew his forces. Conscious that their opponents were increasing in strength, Bruce's men desperately awaited their ailing commander's recovery. In the short days and long nights of Christmas week Bruce did not recover. It was too dangerous to wait any longer. As the end of the week neared, Bruce was placed on a litter and his army quietly slipped away through the trees and snow towards Strathbogie.

Throughout January and February 1308 Bruce's men remained on the move, desperate to avoid their enemies. By March Bruce had at last completed his slow recovery. Mowbray, frustrated by the refusal of the earl of Ross to break his truce with Bruce, had little option but to conclude his own truce. His position secured by these truces, Bruce burnt down the castle of Mortlach (Balvenie) and then marched west to the Black Isle where he took the castle of Tarradale and torched the lands of Alexander Comyn. By 7 April he had again set siege to Elgin Castle, but was forced to withdraw when Mowbray came to the castle's relief on 1 May, the brief truce between them having expired. Bruce again fell ill, the relentless campaigning having taken its toll on his weakened body. Edward Bruce took command, leading the army to Inverurie where supplies could be found.[11]

In an ominous repeat of December the earls again closed in on the bedridden Bruce in late May. The troops of Buchan and Mowbray linked up at Old Meldrum. They were joined by David de Brechin who led his men in an impetuous advance on Inverurie. Bruce's troops were taken by surprise, several being killed while the remainder fled back to the main encampment. In this moment of crisis Bruce struggled from his sickbed and, ignoring the protestations of his closest advisers, demanded that he be helped into his armour and mounted upon his horse. Propped up in his saddle, surrounded by his men, Bruce led a counterattack. Startled by the sight of a fully armoured Bruce, Brechin and his troops fled back towards Old Meldrum where Buchan and Mowbray hurriedly arrayed their forces for battle. Bruce boldly maintained his advance. Indecision gripped his enemies. The cavalry of the earls held off, backtracking towards the foot soldiers. Confronted by the advance of Bruce's men, witnessing the hesitancy of their own cavalry and the indecision of their commanders, the infantry lost their nerve and fled. They were followed by Buchan, Mowbray, Brechin and the rest of the cavalry. Bruce had broken the strength of his chief Scottish enemies without having to engage them in battle. Brechin retreated to his own lands and took refuge in Brechin Castle. Buchan and Mowbray sought refuge in England, the former dying before the year was out. Their lands now lay defenceless.[12]

Victory was the best medicine Bruce could have taken. His army set up camp in a wood within the earldom of Buchan. This was the heartland of his bitter enemies, the Comyns. Determined to eradicate their power base, he presided over a ruthless and systematic devastation of the region. Detachments of troops were sent out, ranging through villages and fields, forests and woods, touching blazing torches to the dry tinderbox of the June countryside, the whole of Buchan disappearing beneath a dense pall of rolling black smoke. So complete was the destruction that the *herschip* of Buchan remained a painful, bitter memory for more than half a century.[13] To the inhabitants of the bustling port of Aberdeen the dark columns of smoke that drifted on the distant horizon were a gloomy portent. By July the town had been besieged by Bruce. It was taken the following month, providing Bruce with an invaluable trading port and also opening lines of international communication. The capture of Aberdeen sealed the success of Bruce's hard-fought campaign in northeast Scotland.

Meanwhile, to the south, in the Scottish Borders, Douglas was emerging as one of Bruce's chief lieutenants. Based in the great forests of the region, Douglas and his armed band struck at their enemies with unrestrained savagery. Back in September 1307 a force led by Valence had tracked Douglas into Paisley forest. Douglas had fought back, his enemies losing a number of horses in a sharp skirmish. Shortly afterwards Douglas ambushed a force led by a Scot, Philip Mowbray, at Edirford eleven miles south of Paisley, and inflicted heavy casualties.[14] However, it was Ettrick forest that Douglas came to dominate. In the spring of 1308, as Bruce campaigned in the north, Douglas executed a second attack on Douglas Castle. It was to result in an infamous act of brutality.

Barbour provides a suitably dramatic account of the assault, which was undertaken on Palm Sunday, 7 April 1308. It was deliberately timed for a moment when most of the garrison were attending a service in the village kirk. The troops in the kirk stood no chance. Most were killed where they stood, their blood spilling over upturned pews and staining the chancel floor. Only a handful of men were taken prisoner. With so many of the garrison slain, the castle was easily taken. It was found that a meal had been prepared, and Douglas had his men sit at the tables in the hall and eat and drink whatever they could. They then ransacked the castle of weapons, armour, valuables and clothes. Victuals that could not be carried, such as wheat and flour, were taken down to the wine cellar and poured out onto the floor. The prisoners were then brought into the cellar. They numbered perhaps a dozen men. On the orders of Douglas they were summarily beheaded. Their heads and truncated torsos fell amongst the wheat and flour. Barrels of wine were broken open and emptied so that the wine congealed with the blood and victuals, defiling the cellar in a scene of horrific carnage. The castle well was then polluted with salt and dead horses. Satisfied with the day's work, Douglas and his men left the castle laden with booty.[15]

The massacre of the Douglas Lardner quickly gained James Douglas a reputation for barbarity among his enemies. Whereas Bruce devastated Buchan for political reasons, Douglas appears to have been motivated purely by his loathing of the English. His generous treatment of the garrison in 1307 had clearly been an aberration; this was the real James Douglas, a man possessed of his father's appetite for violence. It is doubtful whether Bruce would have approved of Douglas's senseless act, but in the bitter civil war in which he was engaged the service of a ruthless and violent man of the calibre of James Douglas was indispensable.

Another man who was to become a chief lieutenant of Bruce was given his first independent command during the summer of 1308. In June, as Bruce presided over the smoking wreckage of Buchan, he dispatched his brother, Edward, to Galloway. It was here, in this wild, predominantly Celtic region of southwest Scotland, that an enclave of former Balliol adherents still aggressively opposed Robert Bruce. The punitive raid in the autumn of 1307 had resulted in some inhabitants of Galloway paying a monetary tribute to Bruce. After his success in the north of Scotland this was now disregarded; subjugation was more important than money. The unenviable task of taming the wilds of Galloway was made yet more difficult by the bellicose local warlords, and the roaming English forces and static garrisons that supported them. Yet if any of Bruce's lieutenants was capable of such a demanding task, then it was Edward Bruce.

Since the murder of John Comyn he had constantly been by his brother's side, offering support and advice and throwing himself into any fight that came his way. It was Edward Bruce who had stiffened his brother's resolve when confronted by the English garrison at Turnberry in early 1307, and it had been Edward who had assumed command of the campaign in northern Scotland during his brother's severe bouts of illness in late 1307 and May 1308. Edward Bruce was a blunt and straightforward man of action. According to Barbour, he was 'extraordinarily bold' and 'had never been defeated by great numbers of men'. Edward was 'renowned above his peers' as he frequently 'defeated many with few'. All he lacked, in the opinion of Barbour, was moderation; if he had possessed this quality, then a worthier man could not have been found except for Robert Bruce himself. Edward was not a thinker but a warrior, a man who lived for the fight. He was an aggressive and capable soldier.

True to character, Edward Bruce did not hold back in Galloway. Two engagements won him an element of dominance though not outright control. Edward first defeated a combined force of Galloway chieftains and English troops in the summer of 1308, shattering their hold on western Galloway, and then in the autumn he destroyed an Anglo-Scottish force which had been sent to regain control of the region. For part of the campaign he had been reinforced by Douglas, though Edward Bruce was still frequently outnumbered – Barbour cited odds of thirty to one against in one engagement. Just as Douglas had gained his notoriety in Ettrick forest, so Edward Bruce built his reputation as a formidable lord of war in the wilds of Galloway.[16]

The third man who was to emerge as a principal lieutenant of Robert Bruce, arguably rising to become the most effective and dependable of them all, featured very differently in the conflicts of 1308. Thomas Randolph was a nephew of Robert Bruce, his mother being the latter's half-sister. Barbour describes Randolph as being 'of moderate stature and well-formed in proportion, with a broad face, pleasant and fair'. The son of a Roxburghshire knight, and with strong family ties to the Bruces, Randolph was a well connected Scottish knight who appears to have embraced wholeheartedly the idealistic values of chivalry. He 'exalted honour' and 'was caring, even loving, in company, and he always loved good knights, for, to tell the truth, he was full of spirit and made of all virtues'. Yet this chivalric spirit did not prevent

Randolph from joining his uncle in 1306 following Bruce's murder of John Comyn. Randolph had fought in the desperate engagement at Methven in June 1306 and had been captured in the rout. Promised his lands by the English if he entered into the allegiance of Edward I, he did so. His change of allegiance most probably saved his life, coming before Edward I had fully instigated the reign of terror which massacred the adherents of Bruce; Randolph did not entirely escape censure, though, for he was imprisoned as a precaution by the English for more than a year. By September 1307 his loyalty to the English was no longer in doubt, and he was among the English force that clashed with Douglas in Paisley forest. Barbour also recounts a story of how Randolph rode against his uncle, pursuing Bruce and seizing the royal banner, a feat that earned Randolph the praise of the English king.[17]

In the summer of 1308 Randolph was again active against Bruce in Scotland. Barbour relates that Randolph was in the company of the Berwickshire knight Adam Gordon, to whose custody he had been committed upon his release from imprisonment. Accompanied by a small troop of men, they entered a house near Peebles where they intended to spend the night. Douglas, lurking in the surrounding environs of Ettrick forest, heard there were enemy troops nearby. Gathering his men, Douglas quietly surrounded the house and attacked those inside. In the confusion several men, including Gordon, escaped. Randolph, however, was captured. Douglas immediately took him to Bruce. Delighted by the reappearance of Randolph, and greeting him warmly, Bruce naturally expected his nephew to return to his allegiance. Randolph, according to Barbour, bluntly refused. He told his uncle that he did not approve of the means by which Bruce was fighting the English. According to Barbour, he boldly said to Bruce 'you should strive to prove your right in open fighting, and not by cowardice nor cunning'. Shocked by this response, Bruce ordered that his nephew be held in close custody.[18]

If Randolph did indeed utter these words then he was evidently speaking from his experience of the war to the south of the Tay. If he had fought in the north of Scotland, however, he would have realised that the strategy adopted by Bruce was much more sophisticated than he believed. The full range of tactics employed by Bruce was in evidence when he undertook his last major campaign of 1308, marching west in the summer to subdue the final enclave of northern opposition, in Argyll. Bruce's growing army, now supplemented by Douglas, advanced into this mountainous region in August. Its passage was facilitated by the existence of a number of separate truces, truces that the English had urged Scots loyal to them to conclude. It was a measure of the paralysis gripping England that Bruce was able to move into Argyll unopposed. John of Argyll and his father Alexander were twice forced to enter into such truces while impatiently waiting for English reinforcements. They never came. Bruce deliberately distorted these truces, claiming falsely that John had come into his peace, an astute piece of propaganda aimed at isolating his enemy and denying him allies. Unable to raise support from the local barons, John of Argyll had no option but to defend himself against Bruce's army with eight hundred of his own men and a fleet of galleys which was based in the region's great lochs. The only advantage he possessed was an intimate knowledge of the treacherous terrain. There was a route along which he knew Bruce would have to advance. It was here that John of Argyll set an ambush.

A narrow track passed beneath one of the sheer escarpments of Ben Cruachan, a rugged mountain rising more than a thousand metres above sea level. John concealed his men above this track and then retreated to the safety of a galley in the loch. Bruce was forewarned of the trap, although the means by which he obtained this vital intelligence remains unclear. Rather than order a withdrawal, Bruce decided to ambush his would-be ambushers. Douglas was instructed to scramble covertly up the escarpment, leading a force of lightly armed men into a position above John's waiting troops. Bruce then led the rest of his force along the narrow track. When a landslide of stones and boulders suddenly cascaded towards them, Bruce instantly withdrew his men from the track and led them in a frantic rush up the escarpment; simultaneously, Douglas led his troops down in a hectic descent. Caught between the two forces, the enemy fled. This fleeting engagement on the slopes of Ben Cruachan subdued yet another region hostile to the claim of Bruce to be king.[19]

John of Argyll had been beaten by a sophisticated combination of truce, propaganda, intelligence-gathering and battle. By employing these tactics, Bruce defeated his enemies in the north of Scotland. He was beginning to show signs of becoming a brilliant military commander, the debacle of Methven now but a distant memory. Yet the astonishing successes of Bruce in the north were also a result of skilful politics. A successful king had to be a consummate politician as well as a capable commander-in-chief. Bruce was adept at both. On 31 October 1308 William, earl of Ross, formally entered into the peace of Robert Bruce. It was Ross who had captured Bruce's wife, daughter and sister in the autumn of 1306, and who had handed them over to Edward I. This act was compounded by the harsh treatment they had subsequently received. Yet Ross was also an influential Scottish magnate, an earl possessed of a vast landed estate and wielding substantial political power. It is a measure of Bruce's political maturity that he placed the need to bolster his kingship above any primitive urge for vengeance. By accepting Ross into his allegiance and returning the earl's lands, Bruce strengthened his claim to be king. He recognised that the support of the great lords of Scotland was essential if his kingship was to attain its full legitimacy. Military success may have won him a measure of dominance, but his position would ultimately have to be consolidated in the realm of politics. After the victory in Argyll, John of Argyll's father, Alexander, also submitted to Bruce, providing further political weight to his kingship. Bruce was also beginning to gain popular support. On Christmas night 1308 the castle of Forfar was seized by a band of Scottish foresters; it is telling that they immediately handed the castle over to Bruce, who subsequently had it destroyed.[20] The success of his campaigns in the north against his Scottish enemies had now won Bruce a measure of political and popular support. Yet his position as king was far from secure. In early 1309 Bruce determined to assert the authority by which he held the Crown. He did so by summoning the first parliament of his tenuous reign.

The parliament that met at St Andrews on 16–17 March 1309 was riven with historical trickery and baseless propaganda. In an attempt to legitimate Bruce as king a document known as the Declaration of the Clergy was produced. It was effectively a manifesto of the Bruce cause, articulating in writing a series of claims supporting the belief that Bruce was the rightful king of Scotland. The Declaration was a poisonous concoction of half-truths and outright lies: it expounded the warped myth that Edward I had selected John Balliol as king although the Scottish people had wanted Robert the Competitor; it advanced the lie that the Competitor had possessed the strongest claim to the Crown; Balliol was erroneously portrayed as a mere puppet of the English king; Bruce was deceptively presented as a disinterested saviour who had come to the rescue of Scotland by means of divine providence; in an absurd inversion of the truth, it was alleged that the Scots had willingly championed Bruce as their leader without any coercion, and that the mercy of Christ had elevated Bruce to such a position. The only claim invested with an element of truth was the statement that Bruce had followed the precedent set by former kings of Scotland in taking and holding the realm by force.

The Declaration was an illusion of smoke and mirrors intended to confuse and persuade. Indeed, as an attempt to assert the legitimacy of Bruce's claim to be king it could be nothing else. Bruce had seized the Crown; he had not acquired it by legitimate means. More presciently, in the Declaration the first attempt was made to fuse the two separate issues of the claim of Bruce to be king and the cause of Scottish independence. Elements of the Declaration were directly borrowed from the diplomatic arguments put forward to the papal curia in 1299 and 1301 for the independence of the Scottish kingdom. Bruce was attempting to hijack the cause of Scottish independence and harness its widespread, if largely latent support, to his own ends. This support for independence, this backing of the 'community of the realm', has been identified as fuelling Scottish resistance to English oppression. But in 1309 Bruce did not enjoy the unequivocal support of this community, nor would he do so for several years to come.

Further efforts were made to legitimate the kingship of Bruce during the parliament. A letter was drafted to Philip IV of France in reply to one sent to Bruce proposing a crusade. Nowhere in Philip's letter did he refer to Bruce as king of Scotland. The carefully drafted reply, however, was effectively an emphatic declaration by the lords of Scotland that Bruce was their rightful king. It had the desired effect, and in the summer of 1309 a messenger from Philip arrived with a letter addressing Bruce as king of Scotland, albeit the letter had been covertly stitched into the messenger's belt to ensure it was not seen by the English. The pope, Clement V, was not so easily moved by the professions of Bruce's legitimacy, and there is no evidence that he ever recognised Bruce as king.

Nor was the Declaration of the Clergy or the letter to Philip IV endorsed by a majority of Scotland's political leaders. The baronial declaration was sealed by three earls in person – Ross, Sutherland and Lennox – while the representatives of five additional earldoms – Fife, Menteith, Mar, Buchan and Caithness – ostensibly set their seals on behalf of earls who were in wardship. Edward Bruce, now styled lord of Galloway, was also present at the parliament, as was Thomas Randolph, lord of Nithsdale, Bruce's nephew and recently reconciled with him. Further notable figures in attendance included the elderly James Stewart, Robert Keith, Alexander of Argyll and James Douglas. Although the seals of several bishops were attached to the Declaration of the Clergy, it is not clear how many bishops were actually present, the two most powerful bishops of Scotland, Wishart and Lamberton, both being unable to attend: Wishart had travelled overseas to the papal curia, and Lamberton, still in English custody, was not allowed to leave the diocese of Durham. The truth was that, despite Bruce's success, many Scottish magnates remained hostile to him, including the earls of Angus, Atholl and Dunbar, and influential lords such as John Mowbray and David de Brechin. The parliament had been aimed both at gaining recognition of Bruce as king abroad, and achieving popular acclamation for him at home. Both aims met with only limited success.[21]

To Bruce it was clear that if he was to consolidate further his authority as king, then he would have to do so by means of armed force. To the south, in the Lowlands and the Borders, he was still confronted by a formidable array of opposition, the most substantial of which was the English garrisons that occupied the chief castles of Scotland. On the Tay the walled town of Perth was also occupied by a large English garrison. If Bruce was to lay claim conclusively to the Crown, if he was to obtain the support of the community of the realm, then he had to rid Scotland of these occupying forces. The expulsion of the English would invest him with the political kudos necessary to establish himself as the legitimate king. It would be a daunting undertaking.

But first he had to survive an English campaign. On 16 September 1310 Edward II led an army across the border at Wark and made for the English-held castle of Roxburgh. After a short period of rest, it advanced tentatively through Selkirk forest before pausing at Biggar. The army followed the Clyde west to Renfrew, to the south of Glasgow, then doubled back, moving eastwards until it reached the relative safety of the fortified English peel at Linlithgow. By November the army had recrossed the border and entered the protective walls of Berwick. As in 1307, the English army had achieved nothing. The campaign lacked the support of most English magnates and was primarily motivated by Edward II's desire to frustrate his domestic opponents.

However, despite the weakness of the English campaign, to Bruce it still posed a considerable danger. In response, Bruce changed his tactics. To the south, rather than openly oppose his enemy, Bruce withdrew his forces before the English army, shadowing it so that his troops 'lurked continually in hiding' and conducting opportunistic hit-and-run raids upon the army. The *Vita* recounts one such attack in which three hundred English and Welsh troops were slaughtered, and relates that the English frequently suffered heavy losses from these ambushes. This was the irregular warfare to which Thomas Randolph had so strenuously objected, condemning it as unworthy of a knight or of a king. The author of the *Vita*, however, recognised the immense practicality of this type of warfare, accurately observing that 'Robert Bruce, knowing himself unequal to the king of England in strength or fortune, decided that it would be better to resist our king by secret warfare rather than to dispute his right in open battle'.[22] Bruce was under no illusion that to take on an English army openly in the field was to invite a catastrophic defeat. If Bruce was to defeat the English, then it was imperative that battle should be avoided and the English embroiled in the unending nightmare of this irregular, 'secret' warfare.

In the summer of 1311, when Edward II finally returned to London, Bruce audaciously took the war over the border. During August, and again in September, he led his forces in devastating raids on northern England, the Scots plundering and burning their way through Northumberland and Cumberland. However, unlike the Scottish raids of the 1290s, the devastation wreaked was not without purpose. In late 1311 Bruce accepted payments of tribute in exchange for local truces, which spared the immediate town or region that had paid. When these truces expired another payment was negotiated. Should a town or county default, or find itself unable to pay, then it was subjected to a devastating raid. This systematic destruction worked due to the level of discipline that Bruce was able to instil in his troops, the people of northern England being of more value to Bruce alive than dead. The tribute payments generated a tremendous amount of money, which Bruce used to finance the prolonged campaign he waged against the English-held castles of southern Scotland.[23]

Despite the failure of an attempt on Berwick in 1312, the town of Perth fell to the Scots on the night of 8 January 1313, Bruce himself leading an assault party as it waded in complete darkness through the moat. The Scots took the castles of Dumfries, Buittle and Dalswinton among several other fortifications, and, as at Perth, subsequently destroyed them. The important town of Dundee had also succumbed to a three-month siege in early 1312. It is clear that from 1311 onwards Bruce waged a costly and determined campaign against the English-held castles and towns of Scotland. The campaign was remarkably successful. In the autumn of 1313 a daring ruse gained the Scots entry into the heavily fortified English peel at Linlithgow; the survivors of the garrison fled and the peel was demolished. Gradually the English foothold in Scotland was being eradicated.[24]

Robert Bruce was becoming increasingly dominant. In November 1313, shortly after the fall of Linlithgow, Bruce delivered a blunt ultimatum. Formally he declared that all Scots had one year to enter into his allegiance. Those who had not done so by the time this deadline expired would suffer the extreme penalty of perpetual disinheritance.[25] To the many Scots who still did not support the claim of Bruce to be king, the choice was stark: either they gave him their backing or they lost their lands. There was to be no compromise.

By delivering this ultimatum, Bruce intended to bring the Scottish civil war to a head. On the back of his incredible run of military success in Scotland he had decided the time had come to consolidate categorically his authority as king. The threat of perpetual disinheritance was shrewdly calculated to make even the most recalcitrant Scot think twice about remaining hostile to Bruce. His ultimatum sought to translate his military success into a definitive political triumph. It was effectively a challenge to any Scotsman who opposed his claim to be king. It was also a challenge that even the embattled Edward II could not afford to ignore. By attempting to bring the bitter Scottish power struggle to a triumphant conclusion, Bruce inadvertently set in motion a large-scale English campaign. It was a campaign that would come to an end south of Stirling, beside an obscure tributary of the Forth known locally as the Bannock Burn.

CHAPTER SEVEN

RAISED FROM THE DUST

By the time Bruce issued his ultimatum, Edward II was emerging from his own bitter power struggle, one that had plunged the English realm into political chaos and brought it perilously close to civil war. Edward had spent Easter 1308 holed up within the formidable defences of Windsor Castle. It was from here that he had issued a flurry of nervous orders. In mid-March he dismissed the constables of twelve major castles in England and Wales, and appointed new and trusted commanders. He ordered that the Tower of London, and towns and castles throughout the kingdom, be munitioned and made ready for war. Troops were to be raised and prepared to join the king. Instructions were given that the bridges across the Thames at Kingston and Staines should be destroyed.[1] Beyond Windsor, in the counties and towns of England, an enemy was gathering. The prospect of war hung heavy in the air. Yet the enemy that Edward prepared to face was not Robert Bruce and the Scots but the magnates of his own realm. Such was the incompetence of Edward II that less than a year after he became king, England was on the brink of civil war.

Fear pervaded the country. The *Vita* vividly captures the mood of foreboding, describing how 'the whole land was much desolated by such a tumult: for every kingdom divided against itself shall be brought to desolation', and observing that if war erupted it would soon escalate, 'for it was held for certain that the quarrel once begun could not be settled without great destruction'. As the king armed so too did the magnates, as they raised troops from their capacious landed estates and readied their castles. It was this 'seditious quarrel between the lord king and the barons'[2] that divided the kingdom. At the heart of the quarrel were two contentious and increasingly inseparable issues: the power invested in the authority of the Crown and, more immediately, the divisive figure of Piers Gaveston.

These were disputes that Edward I had attempted to quell in the last years of his reign. His exile of Piers Gaveston had removed a controversial figure from the realm; the oath extorted at the Feast of the Swans had sought to bind the prince, the magnates and a new generation of knights to the destruction of Bruce and to the vigorous prosecution of the Scottish war. Edward I may also have gone further, for an account relates that as the old king lay upon his deathbed in early July 1307 he had charged Henry de Lacy, earl of Lincoln, Guy de Beauchamp, earl of Warwick, Aymer de Valence and Robert Clifford to watch over the welfare of his heir and ensure Gaveston did not return from exile.[3] All four were leading magnates of the English realm, Valence becoming earl of Pembroke in October 1307, and all had loyally served Edward I. Lincoln, a 56-year-old soldier and politician of tremendous experience, was the most senior. Warwick, Valence and Clifford were all in their mid-thirties, and had first seen combat in the Scottish wars of the 1290s. They had all served alongside the prince, Lincoln directing the operations of the prince's army in 1301 and Valence coordinating with the prince the effort against Bruce in 1306. Lincoln had been one of the two earls who fastened the spurs of the prince when he had been knighted on the day of the Feast of the Swans in May 1306. Yet by Easter 1308 all four magnates were aligned as opponents of Edward II. If civil war began, they would fight against the king.

Even Edward I could hardly have expected such a rapid descent towards civil war. The threat had begun even before the late king was laid to rest. Edward II's first error was prematurely to abandon the Scottish campaign of 1307, easing the pressure on Robert Bruce at a time when the latter was struggling to survive. It was at Dumfries, however, that Edward II made what was to prove his gravest mistake. On 6 August, less than a month after the death of his father, he drafted a hasty charter which recalled Gaveston from exile. The charter also went much further. It granted Gaveston the earldom of Cornwall, immediately placing him among the leading magnates of the realm with a substantial annual income of approximately £4,000.[4] The unprecedented elevation of a household knight, and a Gascon at that, to the rank of earl was compounded by the earldom of Cornwall being inextricably linked to royalty. The two previous earls had been sons of kings and the earldom had been earmarked by Edward I for either Thomas or Edmund, his sons by his second marriage. Edward I had reacted with apoplectic rage to his son's suggestion that Gaveston should be given either the earldom of Cornwall or Ponthieu; now, with his father dead, Edward II was quick to exercise the authority of the Crown and sanction this extraordinary promotion.

Attached to the charter were the seals of seven earls. By witnessing the document, each of these gave their assent to the grant contained within it. Among the seals were those of Lincoln and Valence, men who had purportedly been charged by Edward I with ensuring Gaveston was not recalled from exile. For the magnates who had attended the funeral of Edward I at Westminster Abbey on 22 October 1307, a sense of guilt must have played on their consciences as they reflected on the *volte-face* they had performed. The charter had been sanctioned before the corpse of the old king had even been interred within its tomb. Few could have felt entirely comfortable with the decision of Edward II to recall Gaveston; all must have been perturbed by the unprecedented promotion of the Gascon. Yet Edward went even further, arranging for Gaveston to marry Margaret de Clare, Edward's niece and the sister of the sixteen-year-old Gilbert de Clare, earl of Gloucester. It was a marriage intended firmly to underpin the new found preeminence of Gaveston, with the Gascon becoming a brother-in-law of Gloucester and so directly related to the royal dynasty of the Plantagenet.

None of this, however, provoked any outright opposition. The younger magnates, men who had been attached to the household of Edward when he was prince and who had served in Scotland, knew Gaveston well. They may even have liked his rumbustious character, his martial aptitude originally having even impressed Edward I. Gloucester certainly did not object to the prospect of Gaveston becoming his brother-in-law. Indeed, if some magnates had been unhappy with the charter, they would have been unwilling to say so openly at such an early stage in the reign. It was not in their own interests to antagonise a new king. They would have believed that Edward II must be allowed time in which to establish his rule.

Shortly after Edward I was laid to rest the marriage of Gaveston took place, but it was in December, in the mud of a tournament beside the Thames at the town of Wallingford, where events took a disturbing turn. The tournament was arranged by Edward to celebrate Gaveston's name. Wallingford belonged to the earldom of Cornwall, and as such was a physical symbol of the wealth and status Gaveston had accrued. Two tournament teams were assembled. Humphrey de Bohun, earl of Hereford, John de Warenne, earl of Surrey, and Edmund FitzAlan, earl of Arundel, led a side composed of established lords and knights of the realm. Hereford, a veteran of the Scottish wars, was the most experienced, being a decade older than Warenne and Arundel who were both in their early twenties. The second team was led by Gaveston and comprised young knights of the realm who were eager to prove themselves. Despite the bitter winter weather, crowds would have flocked to Wallingford to watch this colourful chivalric display. They would have cheered as the proud earls and barons were sent tumbling from their expensively caparisoned mounts and fell sprawling into the mud. After several hours the side led by Gaveston emerged triumphant. Edward and Gaveston gloried in his victory. As the *Vita* darkly observed, 'this tournament greatly roused the earls and barons in their hatred of Piers'.[5] Worse was to come.

The first months of 1308 saw both the marriage and coronation of Edward. Prolonged negotiations had resulted in an agreement that Edward would marry Isabella, daughter of Philip IV of France. An excellent political marriage, Isabella, then only twelve, also blossomed to become one of the most noted beauties of the day. The wedding took place in Boulogne on 25 January 1308, the young bride resplendent in a dress fashioned of a mantle of red lined with yellow sindon. On the return of the couple to England, crowds flocked to the shore at Dover, eager to catch a glimpse of their new queen. Edward, however, was more interested in Gaveston. The Gascon had remained in England, Edward having appointed him to the prestigious office of keeper of the realm during his brief absence. As soon as Edward saw Gaveston at Dover, he abandoned Isabella and rushed over to him, throwing his arms around Gaveston and repeatedly kissing him in greeting. The assembled magnates were horrified at such behaviour, as were the French nobles who had made the crossing. It was becoming clear that something would have to be done before events spiralled out of control. Indeed, a number of magnates had already entered into a formal agreement to take action.[6]

In Boulogne, on 31 January 1308, several magnates had attached their seals to a document known as the Boulogne Agreement. Stressing their loyalty and fealty to the king and the Crown, they alluded in the document to 'things that have been done contrary to his [the king's] honour and the rights of the Crown' and the 'oppressions of his people which have taken place and are still taking place daily'. The objective of the agreement, it was stated, was to seek a remedy for these serious maladies, although the issues themselves were not specified. Many were undoubtedly longstanding grievances which went back to the reign of Edward I; the relationship between Edward and Gaveston no doubt served to sharpen others. The four earls who attached their seals were

Lincoln, Hereford, Warenne and Valence, while the most prominent of the five lords was Robert Clifford. At the head of the agreement was the long-serving Antony Bek, bishop of Durham, who was empowered to excommunicate any of the nine magnates who had put their seal to the agreement should they renege upon it.[7]

The Boulogne Agreement was an attempt to identify the areas of government where reform was needed and to encourage Edward to find a remedy for them. The professions of loyalty to the king were not false. But the agreement did contain the first tentative articulation of the concept that the person of the king and the rights of the Crown could be distinguished from one another. The significance of this statement, however, lay in the future. It was in the coronation ceremony of Edward II in February 1308 that a more deliberate attempt was made to affect the constitutional position of the king.

Upon being crowned, kings of England had traditionally sworn a threefold oath; Edward was the first king to swear a fourfold oath. The fourth oath was short and to the point. Edward was asked 'do you agree to maintain and preserve the laws and rightful customs which the community of your realm shall have chosen and will you defend and enforce them to the honour of God to the best of your ability?'; Edward duly replied 'I agree and promise'.[8] Again, this was an attempt to redress old grievances, in particular the promises of reform upon which Edward I had frequently reneged. The 'community of the realm' referred to was slightly different to that of Scotland, the community in England essentially consisting of the politicised community embodied in the knights of the shires who attended parliament as representatives of the commons. In practice, the objectives of the community and of the magnates frequently coincided, and the oath was an attempt to ensure that any promises the king made were kept. It was not an attempt to circumvent the power of the king, but to keep him true to his word. Edward had sworn the fourth oath without a hint of concern.

In the event, it was not the oath for which the coronation was best remembered but the provocative actions of Gaveston. On the day itself, 25 February 1308, the streets of London were so crowded that Edward had to enter Westminster Abbey through a back door. Gaveston was quick to seize the limelight. As the ceremonial procession of magnates and lords wound its way through the heaving streets, Gaveston swaggered haughtily among his peers. According to long-established rites, prominent figures carried the regalia with which the king was to be crowned. Breaking these ancient conventions, Edward decreed that Gaveston should carry the crown of St Edward, the most prestigious item of royal regalia. At the banquet following the coronation, Gaveston acted as if king, making a dramatic entrance bedecked ostentatiously in pearls. Moreover, rather than wearing cloth of gold as did all the other earls, he appeared attired in imperial purple, a colour emblematic of royalty. Gaveston behaved with such arrogance that one unnamed earl allegedly muttered his desire to kill him on the spot. Enraged by Edward's blatant preference for the couch of Gaveston to that of his wife, the uncles of Isabella stormed out of the banquet. A poisoned political atmosphere began to taint the realm.[9]

Shortly after his coronation Edward held a parliament at Westminster. It was to push the country towards civil war. During the interval between his marriage and coronation, it appears Edward had promised the magnates that he would initiate the reforms they believed necessary. At the Westminster parliament he refused to keep this promise. However, rather than bluntly dismissing any reforms, Edward suggested the magnates discuss the business among themselves and present it to him at the Easter parliament. The magnates who desired reform saw this delaying tactic for what it was. Appalled by the backtracking of the king, confronted with a disturbing reminder of the notorious unreliability of his father in such matters and fearing that the Boulogne Agreement and the fourth coronation oath would be rendered meaningless, the magnates seethed with resentment. Yet it was not even these issues that edged them to the brink of war, but the increasingly reviled figure of Piers Gaveston.

At a tournament in Faversham arranged to celebrate the marriage of Edward, Gaveston angered the magnates when he 'contrived to meet them, mocking them on the way'. A subsequent tournament at Stepney intended to celebrate the coronation was cancelled by Edward when Gaveston told him that he believed the earls were plotting his death. It was not the unprecedented promotion of Gaveston that rankled with the magnates so much as his arrogant, condescending attitude, and the fact that 'he was unmindful of his former rank'. Many magnates baulked at the conceit of such a figure as Gaveston, a man who had been 'raised from the dust'.[10] It was in the person of Gaveston that the resentment and disaffection of the magnates crystallised into hardened opposition in the spring of 1308.

This should not be surprising as medieval politics was intensely personal in nature. The magnates were not men who attached themselves to causes for altruistic reasons. Their decisions were ruled by their own best interests. The political world they inhabited was shot through with bitter, frequently venomous personal rivalries featuring rapidly shifting alliances and amoral self-aggrandisement. This was a ruthlessly self-interested, intensely emotive environment, prone to antagonism and feuds, and in which the currency was wealth and status. That several of the magnates were closely related did not necessarily unify them, but rather served to intensify any conflicts that developed. Edward himself had close personal ties to five prominent magnates: Thomas, earl of Lancaster, was his cousin; Gloucester was his nephew; Hereford was his brother-in-law; both Warenne and Gaveston were married to his nieces. Further relationships linked the various magnates, for example Lancaster was married to Alice, the daughter of Lincoln, and Gloucester and Gaveston were brothers-in-law. The magnates operated in an extremely tight-knit, immensely claustrophobic world, in which political disputes were edged with personal rivalries, and where the sole aim of each man was to protect and enhance his own interests.

In 1308 the interests of Hereford, Valence and Warwick were directly threatened. In the preceding years Edward I had granted each man substantial estates in Scotland when it was believed that Scotland was a conquered country. Hereford was granted Annandale, the heartland of the Bruces, along with its caput of Lochmaben Castle; Valence had received lands centred on Selkirk as well as the first-rate castle of Bothwell; Warwick received land worth 1,000 marks per annum following the victory at Falkirk. Robert Clifford had also been granted land in Scotland, receiving the castle of Caerlaverock and the confiscated lands of William Douglas in September 1298.[11] Land was the lifeblood of a magnate and any new acquisition was jealously guarded. The estates these lords had been granted in Scotland promised to yield substantial revenues. But the rebellion of Robert Bruce in 1306, and the lacklustre efforts of Edward II to crush the danger he represented, threatened the loss of their estates. These magnates had a vested interest in the vigorous prosecution of the Scottish war, and the failure of Edward II to make a determined effort against Bruce roused their opposition still further.

Yet Edward I had bequeathed not only a war to his heir but also an enormous debt of approximately £200,000, which he had run up during the incessant warfare of the last decades of his reign. By far the largest creditor was the Italian banking house of the Frescobaldi, from which Edward I had borrowed heavily to finance his wars. Upon the accession of Edward II the customs revenues of England were already mortgaged to the Frescobaldi, and from the outset of his reign Edward found himself in a precariously impecunious position, a situation that seriously curtailed his capacity to prosecute the war against Bruce. The first parliament of his reign, at Northampton in October

1307, had provided Edward with a much needed grant of taxation, while the confiscation of the lands and goods of Edward I's unscrupulous treasurer Walter Langton had also produced a small but valuable windfall early in the reign. Yet Edward had squandered the money he acquired on Gaveston, the Gascon also receiving £500 of the taxation grant to pay a debt Edward owed to him, while Langton's goods also found their way into Gaveston's increasingly bulging coffers. Rumours circulated that the most valuable of Edward's wedding gifts had been given to Gaveston, and that the Gascon had been given the run of the royal treasury, shipping a rich haul of jewels and a golden table to Gascony via the Frescobaldi.[12] That Edward should lavish such wealth on an arrogant foreigner when money was so desperately needed to fight a war further fuelled the magnates' hatred of Gaveston.

Edward found himself trapped in a vicious circle which was largely of his own making. His promotion of Gaveston was an attempt to raise a man he loved above all others to a position worthy of an intimate of a king. But his real mistake had been to continue lavishing gifts and honours upon Gaveston, favouring him above all others, and allowing him to accrue wealth and power at a fantastic rate. When Edward subsequently refused to honour his promises of reform, opposition turned to anger and pushed the realm towards war. Piers Gaveston had come to personify the serious problems of the reign.

The magnates' opposition was not universal but a powerful body of men confronted Edward when parliament met at Westminster on 28 April 1308. Despite the pleas of the king his opponents attended parliament armed. The prospect of civil war still hung over them as Lincoln, the most senior of the earls, stood before the assembled throng and read out a declaration which firmly spelt out the grievances of the magnates. Gaveston was heavily criticised. It was alleged that he had subverted the normal networks of power and had cut the king off from his traditional counsellors; that he had destabilised the natural order of politics and patronage by using his newfound status and wealth to bind men closer to him than to the king and by so doing had engineered a position from which he had the power to depose the king. For this the magnates accused him of treason. He was also charged with disinheriting and impoverishing the Crown during a time of financial hardship, and was consequently accused of being a robber of the people and of the realm. Believing that the relationship between Edward and Gaveston precluded the king from providing impartial judgement, the magnates found Gaveston guilty as charged and declared him traitor and robber in the eyes of the people. They demanded that he should be exiled. Lincoln then invoked the fourth coronation oath, which bound the king to accept the will of the community.[13]

Although Gaveston was the target of these accusations, the declaration was also an attempt to enforce the will of the community upon the king. For Edward to accept the declaration would be to set a dangerous precedent in which the patronage exercised by the king could be held to account by the magnates and subsequently opposed or revoked. The declaration again touched on the concept of separating the person of the king from the authority of the Crown. Edward was not willing to accept a curb on his power or the exile of Gaveston which the magnates demanded. But it was not just the magnates who found the relationship between Edward and Gaveston obnoxious. Philip IV of France, disgusted by Edward's treatment of Philip's daughter Isabella, aligned himself with the opposition magnates, sending letters of support in which he described Gaveston as his enemy and, more pointedly, in which he said that any supporter of Gaveston was his mortal foe. Robert Winchelsey, archbishop of Canterbury, and Margaret, Edward II's stepmother, also lent their support to the magnates. Confronted by this intractable bloc of opposition, Edward eventually relented and on 18 May agreed that his beloved Gaveston should be sent into exile by 25 June 1308.[14]

Curiously, in the midst of this political turmoil, Edward abruptly issued writs for a campaign against Bruce and the Scots. The writs were issued in June and the date of muster set for late August. In the event, the envisaged campaign was soon abandoned. Edward was almost certainly attempting to defuse domestic discord by focusing attention outwards to Scotland, and perhaps thereby seeking a form of reconciliation with the magnates.[15] Whatever his precise intentions, Edward was attempting to use the Scottish war as a means to improve his own position at home. However, the proposed campaign fell short of the serious enterprise required if the inroads Bruce was making in the north of Scotland were to be countered, and it did nothing to assuage the concerns of those magnates whose lands were increasingly threatened by the resurgent Bruce.

This cynical attempt to exploit the Scottish war was at best ill-advised and clumsy. It does, however, illustrate that Edward was well aware that the unequivocal support of the magnates was essential if a serious campaign was to be mounted against the Scots. Although levies of foot soldiers formed the bulk of English armies, the heavy cavalry of knights and men-at-arms would provide an army with its real offensive power. This heavy cavalry was largely supplied by the magnates, each of the great lords of the realm raising substantial numbers of knights and men-at-arms from their vast landed estates. If a magnate was in dispute with the king it was possible, in certain circumstances, for the magnate to refuse to provide a large contingent of heavy cavalry and instead send a minimum quota of mounted troops. The antagonism between Edward and many of his magnates was consequently another serious hindrance affecting the king's capability to prosecute the war. Further complications arose from the fact that military command was firmly founded upon individual status, the high command of an army devolving upon the king and his magnates. The turmoil into which England had descended not only hindered the ability of Edward to raise an effective army, but also carried the danger of the high command of any army being riven with dispute and friction.

But in the summer of 1308 the Scottish war came a poor second to the king's obsession with Gaveston. On 16 June, a mere nine days before the stipulated day of Gaveston's exile, Edward suddenly announced that Gaveston was to become the king's lieutenant in Ireland. Rather than severing Gaveston from sources of wealth and power, his appointment opened up a whole new rich seam for him to plunder. Although physically exiled from England, Gaveston would still be draining money from both the realm and the English Crown. Caught out by this deceitful circumvention of their demand for exile, the magnates could only watch appalled as Gaveston sailed from Bristol for Ireland accompanied by an ostentatious retinue.[16]

Edward was prepared for the furious reaction of his magnates and skilfully employed a charm offensive aimed at placating them and eventually winning them over. The king appealed to their rapacious appetite for wealth and status. Throughout the remainder of the year, Edward 'bent one after another to his will, with gifts, promises, and blandishments, with such success that scarcely a baron remained to defend what had already been decided upon and granted'. Only Warwick stood aloof, his refusal to succumb to the king's overtures being a solitary gesture of defiance. Edward's adept handling of the other magnates suggests that he was not a king entirely without political ability. At a parliament held in August he compliantly accepted a demand that he remove six named knights from his counsel. Tensions still remained, however, the magnates refusing to attend a tournament that Edward had arranged at great expense at Kennington, while a proposed chivalric feast of the Round Table intended to celebrate the marriage of the earl of Gloucester was abandoned by the magnates who feared for their safety.[17]

Edward extended his charm offensive. In January 1309 he sent jewels to the pope, Clement V. For their part the magnates sensed the king was now amenable to change. In early 1309, during a tournament at Dunstable, a new programme of reform was drafted for the forthcoming parliament under the guidance of Gloucester, Hereford, Warwick, Lancaster and Arundel. When it was presented to Edward in the April parliament, however, the king's response was blunt: he would only accept the detailed list of reforms if consent was given for Gaveston to return from exile and be restored to his former titles and lands.[18] It was not a price the magnates were willing to pay. Edward, despite his dire financial position, was not moved by the refusal of parliament to sanction a grant of taxation. The parliament broke up in deadlock. Edward, though, was still outmanoeuvring his remaining opponents. An embassy was dispatched to the papal curia in Avignon, its purpose to have the threat of excommunication that hovered over Gaveston lifted. The presence of Valence among this embassy is a striking example of the success of Edward's charm offensive.[19] In June the embassy returned triumphant and by the end of the month Gaveston, without parliamentary sanction, had returned to England.

When parliament met at Stamford the following month, Gaveston was brazenly present. The deal that Edward had offered the magnates in April still lay on the table: an official recall and restoration of Gaveston in exchange for an agreement to remedy the petition of grievances. But now the odds were stacked in favour of the king. Edward possessed a papal bull lifting the threat of excommunication on Gaveston; there was no cohesive bloc of magnate opposition; Gaveston had already returned. The deal was accepted. Edward promised to remedy the grievances presented, the exile of Gaveston was formally lifted, and his lands and titles fully restored.[20] Of the magnates who had drafted the programme of reform, only Warwick and Lancaster opposed the recall of Gaveston. The victory of the king was complete.

Yet for Edward it was ultimately a hollow victory. Like Robert Bruce between 1297 and 1304, Edward had been fighting the wrong war. The return and restoration of Gaveston was achieved at the apparent cost of the power and authority of the monarchy. For the sake of Gaveston, Edward was prepared to accept a programme of reform which curtailed the power of the Crown, failing to appreciate that the integrity of the Crown was more important than his own short-term personal interests. There is a striking contrast, however, between his disregard for the integrity of the Crown demonstrated in the parliaments of 1309 and Bruce's attitude at the parliament he called the same year at St Andrews. Bruce strove to assert his right to the Crown and to access the authority and power invested in it. He desperately wanted to assert his right to be king, but he also recognised that if he was to win the war in which he was engaged then he needed to appropriate the authority of the Crown. Conversely, Edward endangered the authority of the monarchy, and by antagonising his magnates he also lost the capability to prosecute the Scottish war. Ironically it was Bruce, the usurper, who cherished the authority of the Crown, while Edward, a man destined for kingship since childhood, used it as a currency with which to barter, and in doing so treated it with a callous disregard.

Unable to conduct the Scottish war, Edward sent envoys to negotiate a truce with Bruce in early 1309, which was intended to last for most of the year. Engaged as he was in a bitter civil war, Bruce did not adhere to the truce. Action was now desperately needed. Edward issued writs for a campaign in June, but this was soon abandoned; a new date of muster set for late September was subsequently delayed until October and then cancelled altogether. To support the campaign, Edward had resorted to the hated methods of enforced prise and purveyance, thereby breaking a key promise of reform he had made at Stamford.[21] During these years of political turmoil, 'many colloquies and councils were held for the defence of the land of Scotland and the defeat of Robert Bruce, but the effects of these were not clear nor did they issue in action'.[22] The failure of Edward to prosecute the Scottish war was critically undermining what little credibility he had as king. It is not clear whether the abandoned musters of 1309 were a serious attempt on his part to undertake a Scottish campaign or, as in 1308, whether they were designed to defuse domestic tensions. Whatever Edward's motivations, his attempts proved a dismal failure. Indeed, the delay and eventual abandonment of the September campaign can be traced to a single cause – Piers Gaveston.

Upon his return from Ireland, Gaveston's behaviour became even worse than before. He treated the magnates with blatant contempt, insulting them with derisive nicknames, calling Warwick the 'Black dog of Arden', labelling Lincoln 'Burstbelly', Lancaster 'Churl', and Gloucester, his own brother-in-law, 'Whoreson'.[23] The magnates were understandably enraged. A parliament called for October 1309 was abandoned when five earls refused to attend, bluntly citing the presence of Gaveston as their reason. Summoned to parliament at Westminster in February 1310, the magnates declared they would not attend whilst Gaveston, their chief enemy, a man who had set the baronage and realm in uproar, remained 'lurking in the king's chamber'.[24] Unnerved by this furious backlash, Edward sent Gaveston away from London and requested the earls to attend parliament, ordering them to come unarmed.

His edict fell on deaf ears. Gathering retinues of armed men, in February the magnates descended on London. Their followers encamped threateningly on the outskirts of the city while the earls themselves entered parliament fully armed. They again presented a petition to the king detailing their longstanding grievances. They renewed their attack on Gaveston and the 'evil counsellors' who had so impoverished the Crown that Edward, it was alleged, had sunk to the level of extortion to support himself, the king having squandered the previous taxes he had been granted by parliament. They also levelled a new charge squarely against the king: Edward was accused of dismembering the Crown by losing hold of Scotland.[25] No doubt the magnates who saw their Scottish lands slipping from their grasps were instrumental in advancing this charge. The dismal failure of Edward to prosecute the war against Bruce was coming back to haunt him. It was now the turn of the magnates to deliver a blunt warning: if Edward did not consent to the thorough programme of reform they demanded, then parliament would not grant the king any further taxes. They threatened that if Edward did not grant their demands 'they would not have him for king'. On 16 March 1310, compelled by the dire state of his exhausted finances, Edward agreed to the appointment of a commission of twenty-one prelates, earls and barons, that was to seek out the burdens of the realm and formulate ordinances to remove them.

This commission did not consist of a wholesale bloc of opponents to the king, for moderate earls such as Lincoln and Gloucester were among the Ordainers, Thomas, earl of Lancaster, the king's cousin, being the driving force behind them. Lancaster had played no part in the opposition to Gaveston until 1309, having remained on friendly terms with both Edward and his favourite. But in 1309 Lancaster's position had altered dramatically, most probably due to a perceived personal slight and, crucially, by 1310 he had emerged as the king's most vociferous opponent.[26] For Edward this was an ominous development, not because of any personal ability on the part of Lancaster but due to the wealth and power the earl possessed. Lancaster held the earldoms of Derby and Leicester as well as that of Lancaster. Married to a daughter who was the only surviving child of the earl of Lincoln, he stood to inherit even more political power.

Edward sought to frustrate the efforts of the Ordainers by removing the machinery of government from Westminster. In April 1310 the chancellor and the chancery were ordered to join the king at Windsor; when the chancellor refused he was promptly thrown out of office and a more agreeable successor installed. Then in June, without advice or counsel, Edward abruptly announced his intention to lead an army into Scotland. Writs of military summons were issued and Lincoln was appointed keeper of the realm. The magnates saw this campaign for what it was – a deliberate attempt to derail the Ordainers – and refused to attend the muster. Several earls were Ordainers, while Valence, Lancaster and Hereford were also united in their hatred of Gaveston. Only three earls – Gaveston, Gloucester and Warenne – agreed to join the force which Edward led into Scotland in September 1310. Although the army was back in England by November, Edward was determined not to return to London. The king wintered in Berwick, Warenne at Wark Castle, Gloucester at Norham Castle and Gaveston in Scotland at the English-held castle of Roxburgh. In early 1311 Gaveston ventured to the English-held town of Perth and briefly 'took command' of Scotland beyond the Forth.[27] Edward attempted to raise troops for another campaign, but his finances were exhausted. In July he accepted the inevitable and returned to London. Fearing the conclusions of the Ordainers, he left Gaveston behind within the formidable defences of Bamburgh Castle in Northumberland. Within weeks of the king's departure, Bruce led his first devastating raid into northern England and intensified the pressure on the beleaguered king.

In the summer of 1311, however, Edward was not so much troubled by the charred and blackened landscape of northern England as by the altered political landscape to which he returned. In February, the earl of Lincoln had died and Lancaster had subsequently inherited the earldoms of Lincoln and Salisbury. This marked a seismic shift in political power. Lancaster's possession of five earldoms made him by far the most powerful magnate in England, his annual income reaching the enormous sum of approximately £11,000, almost double that of most other earls. It also gave Lancaster access to an immense source of manpower, providing him with the ability to raise a personal retinue, in size surpassed only by that of the king. When Edward finally returned to London, it was Lancaster who presented him with the conclusions of the Ordainers.

The forty-one Ordinances provided a more far-reaching and detailed version of the grievances previously presented. Edward could perhaps accept criticism of long-running abuses of government such as prise and purveyance.

A demand for the expulsion of the Frescobaldi threatened his tenuous finances. However, Edward objected most vehemently to an attempt by the magnates to take control of the royal household away from him, at last recognising as he did the threat it presented to the authority invested in the Crown. It meant that Edward would be unable to exercise his own patronage, to make war or to leave the realm without the assent of parliament. But in an astonishing display of misjudgement, Edward ultimately offered to accept these reforms if the clauses concerning Gaveston were struck out of the Ordinances, for inevitably the Ordinances called for the renewed exile of Gaveston. Yet again, it seemed Edward was prepared to bargain away the authority of the Crown for the sake of a single, objectionable individual. His attempt to have Gloucester and Warenne intervene on his behalf failed. The Ordainers were not for turning. They declared that if Gaveston was not exiled then 'each man would take steps to defend his own life'.[28] Confronted by this thinly veiled threat of civil war Edward eventually relented, and in October set his seal to the Ordinances. They were proclaimed in every county, and in November 1311 Gaveston again sailed into exile.

By the end of the month he was back. Rumours swept the country, variously claiming that Gaveston was lurking in the company of the king, or was at Wallingford, or at the castle of Tintagel. Infuriated by Gaveston's return, the magnates ordered the counties of southwest England to be scoured for him. The manhunt soon became redundant; by January 1312, Gaveston was at York openly in the company of the king. It was clear that Edward had precipitated his return. Despite the Ordinances, regardless of the sentence of perpetual banishment, ignoring the severe punishments that would befall Gaveston should he return, Edward had recalled him. This was almost certainly the result of a further series of reforms the magnates had produced in November, a raft of supplementary Ordinances which effectively comprised a wholesale cull of the royal household by targeting individuals the magnates wanted removed. To Edward it must have felt like the knife being turned in his back. Furious at what he perceived to be a personal attack, Edward appears to have retaliated by recalling Gaveston. He unilaterally proclaimed the Ordinances illegal and ordered that this be announced throughout the realm. It was a fatal mistake.

The magnates united against Edward and, meeting in London at St Paul's, formulated a plan of action. Gaveston was declared a public enemy and excommunicated. The country was split into regions under tight military control: London and the south were to be held by the earl of Gloucester; the earl of Hereford was responsible for Essex and the eastern counties; the west of England and north Wales were to be controlled by the earl of Lancaster; Valence and Warenne were appointed to head a mounted strike force which was to locate the king and seize Gaveston. In the north, Robert Clifford and Henry Percy were to guard against Gaveston's escape into Scotland, a response to disturbing reports that Edward had offered Bruce the kingdom of Scotland if he would agree to provide Gaveston with safe refuge. A series of tournaments were hurriedly proclaimed throughout the country, tournaments under the cover of which the magnates assembled armed men. In late April the strike force headed north. So too did Lancaster, accompanied by his own mounted force.[29]

Edward, cautiously moving through northern England, was caught out by the speed of the advance. On 4 May the earl of Lancaster suddenly appeared before Newcastle. When his troops entered the town they discovered a rich haul of hastily abandoned jewels and warhorses. But their quarry had fled. Edward and Gaveston had taken ship from Tynemouth, abandoning Queen Isabella on the shore, and sailed south for Scarborough. Leaving Gaveston in Scarborough Castle, Edward continued west to Knaresborough Castle before moving on to York. The earl of Lancaster, having seized the haul found in Newcastle, positioned the bulk of his force between Scarborough and Knaresborough, and sent a contingent of troops to besiege Scarborough Castle. The forces of Valence, Warenne, Clifford and Percy soon surrounded the castle, and the position of Gaveston looked desperate. Surrender negotiations took place and, when the final terms were announced, they were extraordinarily generous. Gaveston agreed to surrender to Valence, Warenne and Percy until 1 August; he would listen to what the magnates decided his fate should be and if he concurred the matter would be settled; if not, then he would be permitted to return to the castle. Meanwhile, as security for his safety, the three magnates agreed to pledge their lands to the king.[30]

On 19 May Gaveston left Scarborough and was escorted south by Valence. On 9 June, upon reaching Oxfordshire, Valence decided to visit his wife in the nearby castle of Bampton. Gaveston was left under guard in the village of Deddington. News of this quickly reached the earl of Warwick. Seizing the opportunity, he gathered his men, burst into the village, seized Gaveston and took him to Warwick Castle, where the Gascon was bound in irons and incarcerated in the dungeon. News of his capture rapidly spread. When the earls of Lancaster, Hereford and Arundel arrived at Warwick Castle, the fate of Gaveston was sealed. The Ordinances provided for the ultimate punishment should Gaveston break the terms of his perpetual exile. On 19 June he was led from the castle to Blacklow, the nearest plot of land owned by Lancaster. Two Welshmen stepped forward. The first ran Gaveston through with a sword; the second severed his head from his body.[31] The hated Gascon was no more.

In the aftermath of this brutal execution the cohesion of the magnates disintegrated. Valence was furious that Gaveston had been seized whilst in his custody, particularly as he had pledged his lands as a guarantee of Gaveston's safety. He adamantly refuted popular allegations that he had been party to his seizure and execution. Indeed, Valence had previously pleaded with Gloucester to intervene and secure the return of Gaveston to his safe custody; Gloucester had dismissed these pleas, stating that it was Valence's fault for agreeing such lenient terms with Gaveston in the first place. A scurrilous rumour circulated claiming that Valence had received a bribe of £1,000 from the king to secure such favourable terms. The more moderate magnates, men such as Gloucester and Warenne, dared not openly support those responsible for the execution. Fully aware of the recriminations they were likely to suffer, the latter had entered into a bond of mutual support.[32] Once again England was plunged into chaos.

When he heard the news of his beloved Gaveston's death, Edward wanted vengeance. Valence, seething at his own dishonourable treatment, firmly allied himself with the king and urged Edward to make war on the offending earls. Parliament was summoned. Lancaster, Warwick and Hereford appeared with substantial armed retinues. Rather than entering London, they sent messengers to the king. Edward considered engaging them in war, but was advised by his anxious counsellors that he might not win. Some cautioned that as 'Robert Bruce had already occupied the whole of Scotland, and forced all Northumberland to pay tribute, it would be better to defend the land rather than destroy its defenders'.[33] The earl of Gloucester now came to the fore. Although only twenty-one he possessed a political sense far beyond his years. According to the *Vita*, Gloucester did not hold back when addressing Edward, cautioning him against attacking his own magnates, and urging him to seek a peaceful resolution to the crisis. With neither side strong enough to dominate the other, protracted negotiations began.

Talks dragged on throughout 1312 and into 1313.[34] Valence was the chief negotiator on behalf of the king, Hereford the spokesman for Lancaster and Warwick. Hereford maintained that the execution of Gaveston was legal as the latter had been declared a public enemy in the Ordinances, a document to which Edward had put his seal; Valence argued that the execution was illegal as Edward had publicly revoked the Ordinances before the execution had taken place. The dispute was exacerbated by the earl of Lancaster holding the jewels and warhorses seized in Newcastle. Lancaster alleged that Gaveston had been in possession of these and claimed this was proof that Gaveston was a thief, a further justification for his execution. Still beset by financial difficulties, Edward impatiently sought the return of the jewels and warhorses. The magnates were determined to be formally absolved from any punishment for the death of Gaveston. Negotiating from two such polarised positions, the two sides did not finally reach a settlement until September 1313. It was entirely favourable to Edward. The earls were absolved of murder, but Gaveston was not declared a traitor nor were the Ordinances provided with any legitimacy. These glaring omissions from the settlement far from guaranteed the safety of the earls. Sinisterly, the preserved corpse of Gaveston, his head sewn back in place, remained deliberately unburied; it was whispered that Edward had sworn to exact his vengeance before his beloved Gaveston was laid to rest.

On 14 October 1313 a feast was held in Westminster Hall. The earls of Lancaster, Warwick and Hereford dined at the same table as the king. The banquet was intended as a symbolic gesture of reconciliation, but it may also have provided a painful reminder of another great symbolic banquet which had taken place beneath the same roof over seven years before. The solemn vows sworn during the Feast of the Swans on 22 May 1306 had become subsumed in the power struggle that had developed from Edward's appallingly mishandled tenure of the Crown. No serious attempt had been made in the intervening years to destroy Robert Bruce. The Scottish war had been unforgivably neglected. In 1306, during the months that followed the Feast of the Swans, Robert Bruce had been a desperate fugitive on the run. By the summer of 1313 the political situation in England had deteriorated to such an extent that, when Edward crossed over to France on a diplomatic mission, it was falsely rumoured that 'Robert Bruce was already in the neighbourhood of York, and proposed to march on London; nor did it seem impossible, since there was none who would resist him'.[35] For several years the Scottish war had been cynically exploited by Edward in an attempt to achieve political gain. It was a tactic of which the magnates were also guilty. During August 1312, in the immediate aftermath of the execution of Gaveston, a proposition had been put to Edward on behalf of Lancaster, Warwick and Hereford: if the king agreed to maintain the Ordinances fully, then not only would the jewels and warhorses seized at Newcastle be returned, but the three magnates would provide Edward with four hundred men for six months to support a Scottish campaign, and they also promised to provide a subsidy to help finance a campaign in the next parliament. Determined to deny the legitimacy of the Ordinances, it was an offer Edward had rejected. Similarly, in December 1312, the king's opponents had promised to consider granting a subsidy for the Scottish war in the next parliament if an acceptable agreement was reached.[36] Despite the increasingly critical situation of the Scottish war, it had consistently been sidelined by the internal disputes that had gripped the English realm. In late 1313 the war could not be ignored any longer.

In October or November a petition was delivered to Edward. Purportedly it came from 'the people of Scotland' – essentially those still loyal to the English – and was headed by the names of Patrick, earl of Dunbar, and the Berwickshire knight Adam Gordon. The petition painted a brutalised picture of southern Scotland. It was claimed that since Edward had departed Scotland in 1311, those loyal to him had suffered losses totalling £20,000. The English garrisons left to fight in isolation had resorted to using force against the local population in order to sustain themselves in terms of victuals and money. The king was left in no doubt as to the gravity of the situation, the petition stating darkly that 'matters are daily getting worse'.[37] At the same time alarming news would have been received in England of the ultimatum of perpetual disinheritance which Robert Bruce had issued. Scotland was on the verge of being lost.

On 28 November 1313 Edward formally replied to the petition. The king announced that he intended to lead an army into Scotland the following midsummer. When parliament met, the king was granted a subsidy to help finance this campaign, with the more contentious domestic issues to be discussed in a parliament set for April 1314. On 23 December writs of military summons were issued to the magnates, prelates and lords of the English realm. The army was to muster at Berwick on 10 June 1314, its objective 'to proceed against the Scottish insurgents, and to repress their rebellion and wickedness'.[38] After seven years of disastrous neglect the full military might of England was to be turned against Robert Bruce and his Scottish adherents.

But underlying tensions in England remained. Several years of bitter political disputes had set the magnates against the king and, ultimately, magnate against magnate. The blood of the leading men of the English realm still ran hot with smouldering grievances and intensified rivalries. Vengeance burnt in the heart of the king. Like the corpse of Gaveston, the disputes that had divided the magnates and their monarch had not been laid to rest. The projected campaign against the Scots had the potential to begin to heal these rifts; it could also splinter apart the brittle rapprochement. As the New Year dawned, it remained to be seen how much strain this uneasy alliance could take. In the first months of 1314 Robert Bruce was about to test that alliance to the limit.

III

1314

For his lord a vassal must suffer great hardship and endure great heat and great cold: he must also part with flesh and blood.

The Song of Roland

CHAPTER EIGHT

A TALE OF THREE CASTLES

THE FIRST BLOW OF 1314 WAS STRUCK BY THE SCOTS. DURING FEBRUARY AN extraordinary revolt erupted within Edinburgh Castle. In an act of mutiny unparalleled in the Scottish wars, the English garrison overthrew its constable, Piers Lubaud, and promoted in his place one of their own. Lubaud was bound in irons and incarcerated in the castle dungeon. This potentially disastrous situation threatened the loss of Edinburgh, a major castle vital to the English war effort. Edward II and his counsellors had been aware of the crisis brewing within Edinburgh, and on 22 February had frantically attempted to defuse it by formally appointing a new constable. But by then it was already too late. Lubaud had been overthrown and was a helpless prisoner in the bowels of the castle he had been committed to command.[1] The spark that ignited this extraordinary revolt was created by the enormous pressure under which the garrison laboured. Beyond the castle walls, below the towering castle rock, Scottish siege lines surrounded Edinburgh Castle with a menacing tightness.

In command of the substantial Scottish force encamped beneath the castle was Thomas Randolph. For both the besieged and the besiegers, the prospect was a dismal one. In the bleakness of a Scottish winter, in the cold and the wet and the mud, the formidable castle remained encircled. For Randolph and his deputies the town of Edinburgh offered a place of lodging, its timber buildings huddled in the shadow of the rock. Most of the besiegers would have taken refuge in a motley encampment of huts and tents, clustering around guttering camp fires to infuse their frozen limbs with a modicum of warmth. It was a dour, desultory affair, far removed from the spectacular English siege of Stirling ten years before. In 1314 the Scots did not possess any siege engines of note and could only press the siege by maintaining a complete blockade, thereby attempting to starve the garrison into surrender. It was a miserable, frustratingly protracted operation. The siege had begun in January, but by late February there was still no sign of success. Desperate to break the deadlock, Robert Bruce had appeared in person among the siege lines and entered into talks with Lubaud before he was overthrown. It was this that had pushed the garrison over the edge.

Barbour believed that the garrison, already alarmed by the closeness of the siege, suspected Lubaud of treachery when they saw him speak with Bruce. The *Vita* similarly labelled Lubaud a 'perjurer and traitor'.[2] But this is far from convincing as an explanation for the drastic action of the garrison. For the besieging commander to have talks with his opposite number was a well-established convention of siege warfare, and Lubaud could hardly be held responsible for the closeness of the siege. Rather, it is in the person of Lubaud himself that the real reasons for his overthrow can be found.

Lubaud was a Gascon knight; more pointedly, he was also a cousin of the despised, and lately executed, Piers Gaveston. Like Gaveston, he too owed his position directly to the notorious favouritism of Edward II. Between 1300 and 1305 Lubaud had been an esquire serving in the garrison of Edinburgh Castle and had subsequently served as a sergeant-at-arms of the king's household in Linlithgow. Lubaud was still in Linlithgow in June 1306; astonishingly he was now a knight and the constable of Linlithgow. His meteoric rise was clearly the product of the king's destabilising favouritism. However, like Gaveston, Lubaud appears to have been a capable soldier, remaining as constable of Linlithgow for seven war-torn years, his tenure only ending with the loss of the fortification to the Scots in 1313. When Linlithgow was lost Lubaud himself was absent, as by then he was also constable of Edinburgh Castle and constable of the logistically important peel at Livingston.[3] This multiple constableship was without precedent. That Lubaud managed to retain these vital fortifications throughout several years of strenuous warfare is testimony to his abilities as a front-line commander.

But Lubaud had been given an impossible task. It was not his abilities that gained him these positions, but the deficiencies of the king. Lubaud was part of the increasingly narrow base of men in whom Edward believed he could fully trust. In these hard-pressed years it was inevitable that at least one of these three fortifications would be lost to the Scots. By the end of 1313 both Linlithgow and Livingston had fallen to them. No blame can be attached to

Lubaud for either loss, nor is there any substance to the suspicion of treachery which gripped the Edinburgh garrison. Their mistrust of Lubaud is, however, understandable. As a Gascon, as a cousin of the hated Gaveston and as a man who owed his position directly to royal favouritism, Lubaud was bound to come under suspicion. The loss of two of his three commands the previous year further undermined his authority. Alarmed at the intensity of the Scottish siege, fearing for their lives, the suspicions of the garrison within Edinburgh Castle hardened. Driven by a sense of panic, they resorted to the drastic measure of overthrowing their constable.

If the Scots knew of the sensational events taking place within the walled confines of the besieged castle, then they must have hoped it was the breakthrough they so desperately needed, for their urgency to take Edinburgh Castle was directly at odds with the painfully slow progress of the siege. Time was against the Scots. Robert Bruce and his lieutenants knew of the writs issued by Edward II on 23 December 1313, which summoned a host to muster at Berwick on 10 June 1314. It was imperative that no siege was still in progress when the English host entered Scotland. The presence of a substantial Scottish besieging force would immediately draw the English and result in a battle, and almost certainly a Scottish defeat. The intransigence of the English garrison in Edinburgh was especially disturbing as the capture of the castle was intended to be the opening move in a major Scottish offensive, the objective of which was the seizure and destruction of the three principal castles of Scotland that remained in English hands. If the Scots could do nothing to prevent the coming of the English host, then they would do all in their power to minimise its impact when it crossed the border. By seizing the great fortresses of Edinburgh, Roxburgh and Stirling, Bruce planned to deliver a devastating preemptive strike against the English campaign.

Robert Bruce was in no doubt as to how vital these occupied castles were to the English war effort. Since the very beginning of the Scottish wars, the English had sought to seize and garrison the major castles of Scotland in an attempt to underpin their position and subdue the Scots. The garrisons of these castles increasingly consisted of mounted troops, the intention being that they should operate beyond the walls and dominate the surrounding region.[4] Through possession of these fortifications, English military power was invasively projected into Scotland. The castles were also crucial in providing essential support to field-armies on campaign, functioning as heavily defended forward bases which could provide an army with victuals, reinforcements, intelligence and refuge. Throughout the wars, English campaigns had revolved around these occupied Scottish strongholds which provided a solid framework on which offensives could be based. By the beginning of 1314 the Scots had seized and destroyed many of these forts. Yet crucially the three great castles of Edinburgh, Roxburgh and Stirling still eluded them. Bruce recognised that if these three could be denied to the English host then the whole English campaign would be irreparably weakened. The objective of the Scottish offensive was brutally simple: to seize and destroy this daunting triumvirate of castles before the English host entered Scotland in five months' time.

It was an enormously ambitious plan. The three strongholds with which the Scots were confronted were like nothing they had encountered before. Their fortifications were formidable, the circuits of vast stone walls and towers placing them amongst the greatest strongholds of Christendom. Perched high upon rocky, isolated volcanic crags, oppressively dominating the skyline, Edinburgh and Stirling in particular possessed a tangible aura of impregnability. Roxburgh Castle was also incredibly well sited, the course of two substantial rivers, the Teviot and the Tweed, passing so close that they effectively formed an impenetrable moat which protected the castle on three sides. The present ruinous site of Roxburgh is completely at odds with the great fortress which once dominated this stretch of the Borders. Nor do the buildings at Edinburgh and Stirling resemble the warlike medieval structures which occupied the crags. As the principal royal castles of the Scottish realm, these were among the most potent physical symbols of the Scottish Crown. Both physically and psychologically these three castles were in a different league altogether from any fortifications the Scots had yet attempted to seize.

However, what stood between the Scots and the taking of these castles was not the bulk of their walls and towers but the English garrisons based within them. The provision of a substantial garrison brought alive the castle as an instrument of war. The size and importance of these castles meant that they contained substantial English garrisons. No figures exist for the precise number of troops they held in 1314, the closest contemporary document being a writ dated January 1313 in which the Roxburgh garrison is recorded as containing 123 men (1 knight, 36 men-at-arms, 15 hobelars, 20 crossbowmen and 51 archers). A detailed payroll account for 1311–12 places the Roxburgh garrison at a total strength of 170 (1 knight, 54 men-at-arms, 21 hobelars, 33 crossbowmen and 61 archers); Edinburgh contained 194 troops (1 knight, 83 men-at-arms, 29 hobelars, 41 crossbowmen and 40 archers). Many of these troops were mounted and as such were well armed and equipped. A significant number were long-serving garrison soldiers who were seasoned veterans of the Scottish wars.[5] The large proportion of men-at-arms in each garrison reveals that these castles were not manned by second-rate troops, but by toughened soldiers who were intended to engage the enemy. On the eve of the Scottish offensive each garrison would easily have comprised more than a hundred combat-hardened troops.

To sustain such large numbers each castle required a substantial support staff. The garrison roll for Edinburgh in February 1300 provides a rare glimpse of these non-military personnel. Serving within the castle was a pantryman, a cook and his boy, a baker and his boy, two brewers, a miller, a cooper, a granary man, a boy keeping the swine, a herdsman, a candle maker, an almoner, two clerks, a water carrier, a sea-coal carrier, and a bowyer and his boy.[6] Every garrison retained a mason, a carpenter, a blacksmith and an *attilator* (an armourer and crossbow maker). The buildings within a castle reflected the skills of this large supporting staff, major castles containing a great kitchen, a bakehouse, a grange, a granary and stables. A fresh-water well within the walls was also a vital requirement. The three principal castles with which the Scots were now confronted were consequently something much more daunting than battlemented walls in which troops were based. A sophisticated, heavily manned castle was not just a fortification but a military institution; it was one of the most formidable obstacles a medieval commander could face. The sheer magnitude of the Scottish objective in early 1314 becomes readily apparent once the nature of the castles and the garrisons installed within them is understood. The Scottish objective was enormously, perhaps impossibly, ambitious.

But despite their immense strength these castles did possess a potentially fatal weakness. To be maintained they needed to be in receipt of victuals, and so were ultimately dependent on external support. The fortress towns of Berwick and Carlisle acted as fortified storehouses, their supplies being transported into Scotland both overland and by ship. Heavily laden vessels destined for Edinburgh docked at the port of Leith, the Forth itself being navigable as far as Stirling. Armed columns of men escorted carts of victuals to landlocked Roxburgh. Dried fish was a major part of a garrison's diet, and meat, both deadstock and livestock, was also plentiful. Salt was essential for its preservative qualities. Drinking needs were met by the brewing of beer, and by the delivery of casks and barrels of wine.[7] All of these victuals were finite. A close siege prevented a garrison from executing a plundering raid. Eventually a garrison would need to be resupplied.

If the castles of Edinburgh, Roxburgh and Stirling were low on victuals in early 1314, then Bruce could reasonably expect their constables to offer terms of surrender in accordance with the established conventions of siege warfare. Should he find them to be well supplied, however, then his offensive ran the risk of ending in abject failure. There was no shortage of troubling precedents, the most remarkable of which was the tenacious resistance in the early years of the Scottish wars of the English garrison besieged in the powerful castle of Bothwell overlooking the River Clyde, the castle holding out for an incredible fourteen months before a Scottish assault finally overwhelmed the starving garrison.[8] Although the conditions endured by the garrison of Bothwell must have been appalling, their intransigence was a striking example of what a determined garrison could accomplish. Encamped below the walls of Edinburgh Castle in February 1314, Randolph would have been reminded that the siege of Bothwell Castle was disconcertingly similar to the siege in which he was presently engaged. On neither occasion did the Scots possess siege engines; both castles were sophisticated, heavily fortified stone fortresses; they were both manned by a substantial number of hardened troops. In fact, Edinburgh possessed a significant advantage for the English in that it enjoyed a real prospect of relief. With the English host due to enter Scotland in June, the garrisons of all three castles knew that if they could hold out until the summer then relief was almost certainly guaranteed.

If the Scots required any further proof of the difficulty of the task in which they were engaged, then the imperviousness of Edinburgh Castle provided it. The castle was well victualled. After two months of siege no headway had been made. Nor did the dramatic overthrow of Lubaud prove to be the breakthrough the Scots so desperately needed. In his place the garrison appointed a constable from amongst themselves, a man of their 'own nationality' who was 'right wary, wise and active' and who used his 'knowledge, strength and cunning to keep his hold of the castle'.[9] There was no thought of surrender. The removal of Lubaud did not originate from the desire of the garrison to secure their leaving the castle on favourable terms, but from a belief that Lubaud was endangering the castle and, consequently, their lives. The garrison remained committed to holding out and evidently believed they possessed sufficient supplies to sustain them until the arrival of the English host. Rather than weakening the garrison of Edinburgh, the overthrow of Lubaud and the appointment of a trusted commander actually strengthened their will to resist.

Despite the increasing urgency Randolph could do nothing but continue to press the siege. The south gate was the only accessible point of the castle and Scottish attacks would have been repelled from the heavily defended gatehouse if they had been attempted. The crossbowmen and archers who manned the castle walls would have unleashed a devastating hail of armour-piercing crossbow bolts and arrows at their attackers. Siege engines kept within the castle would also have been employed against the Scots, springalds would have fired large, oversize arrows, and a *mangonel* or trebuchet hurled great stones at the besiegers. Exposed to the bitter cold of winter, the battlemented walls of Edinburgh Castle towering defiantly above them, the frustrations of the besiegers continued to grow. Edinburgh appeared to be impregnable. The Scottish offensive was in grave danger of falling at the very first hurdle.

Stalled before Edinburgh, Randolph could do nothing but wait. The prospect of a prolonged siege, however, was evidently viewed with disdain by another of Robert Bruce's chief lieutenants. To James Douglas patience was far from a virtue. While the main Scottish effort concentrated on Edinburgh Castle, Douglas headed south to his old hunting ground of Ettrick forest. Here, in this vast ancient tract of rugged woodland, he gathered together a band of men. Lurking in the forest, they attacked those loyal to the English. On the fringes of the forest lay the English-held castles of Roxburgh and Jedburgh. Their garrisons were subjected to a series of hit-and-run raids by day and night. It became unsafe for troops to venture beyond the castle walls. Fuelled by this success, Douglas's ambitions grew in scope. As he watched from the forest he 'turned all his thoughts to work out how Roxburgh might be won by stealth or contrivance'.[10] The answer was not long in coming. There would be no prolonged siege of Roxburgh. Douglas had decided he was going to take the castle by storm.

To undertake an assault on a major castle such as Roxburgh was incredibly dangerous. For Bruce the siege remained his favoured tactic, but a lengthy siege required considerable amounts of manpower and money, resources that remained limited and precluded the simultaneous siege of more than one castle. Only when Edinburgh Castle fell could attention be turned to Roxburgh or Stirling. It is doubtful whether the storming of Roxburgh was a planned component of the Scottish offensive. Although Roxburgh was a key target, it is unlikely that Bruce sent Douglas south with direct orders to make an attempt on the castle. It seems more realistic to suggest that it was only after a period of time spent operating in the forest, during which invaluable intelligence was gathered, that Douglas decided upon an attack. In this sense the assault on Roxburgh may well have been a rogue operation which was not formally sanctioned by Bruce. The audacity of undertaking such an act is certainly in keeping with the impudent character of the Black Douglas.

The assault took place on the night of 19 February 1314. It was the evening of Shrove Tuesday, and the timing of the attack to coincide with the feast day was deliberate. Douglas had used this tactic to devastating effect in his infamous attack on the English garrison of Douglas Castle on Palm Sunday 1308, exploiting the distraction of the feast day to put the garrison at a disadvantage. If he was to storm Roxburgh, it was vital that Douglas exploited every advantage he could get. Surprise was essential. In Ettrick forest a sixty-strong assault party was secretly assembled and carefully briefed. Each man was in possession of a black cloak with which he covered the telltale glint of his chainmail and armour. In the heavy darkness of the winter night, the men dropped to their hands and knees and slowly crawled towards the castle. The immediate danger came from watchmen who patrolled the walkways atop the walls. According to Barbour, a sharp-eyed guard spied movement in the darkness below. Straining to discern the low, shadowy forms, the watchman mistook them for a herd of beasts which had been left out for the night. Dismissively he turned away. The assault party, forced to inch forwards at a painfully slow pace, and pressed close to the walls by the gurgling course of the Tweed and Teviot rivers, risked discovery with every furtive movement. At last they reached the designated section of wall. Rising quietly to their feet, they lifted a specially constructed scaling ladder towards the lip of the wall.[11]

The ladder they raised was of a type that had first been used in the unsuccessful attempt on Berwick Castle two years earlier, ladders considered so ingenious that, when captured by the English, they had been put on public display. An English chronicler marvelled at these 'ladders of wonderful construction' and described them in scrupulous detail. Essentially they were rope ladders, the frame fashioned from hemp, with wooden boards fastened between to form steps. Fenders buttressed the rear of every third step to ensure the ladder did not lay flat against the wall and render it unclimbable. It was raised into position by the tip of a spear or lance being passed through a specially fashioned hole, and then levered upwards until an iron hook attached to the top of the ladder found a grip among the masonry of the battlements.[12] However, the guttural clatter of this iron hook as it caught fast upon the wall gave Douglas and his men away.

In the stillness of the night a watchman heard the distinctive metallic clangour of iron grating on stone. He came across to investigate. As he peered curiously down into the darkness, the first Scotsman had almost ascended the ladder. According to Barbour this was Simon of Ledhouse, the same 'cunning and skilful man' who had constructed the ladder. The watchman tried to knock him down. Ledhouse desperately lunged upwards. He grabbed the watchman by the neck and, grasping him tight, brutally stabbed him with a knife. Ledhouse threw the body down to his companions and urged them to follow him up. Before they could scale the ladder, however, another man rushed Ledhouse. This new assailant was quickly slain; Barbour relates that he was unarmed. The assault party clambered up the ladder and regrouped on the battlements. There was no sign of life, no shouts of alarm. Surprise had been achieved. Swords and knives were swiftly drawn. The great tower of the castle lay ahead of them. Within the tower was the great hall and it was in here that the bulk of the garrison was celebrating the feast day. Swiftly Douglas led his men forwards.

In the great hall the garrison was enjoying much needed respite from the war. The last thing they expected was to find they were under attack in the heart of the castle. In a sudden irruption of violence the black-cloaked assault party burst into the hall, flashing their sword blades viciously in the dancing candlelight. Bellowing the battle cry 'Douglas! Douglas!', the Scots savagely set about the garrison. The English were hopelessly unprepared. Few were armed; hardly any were wearing armour. Entrapped within the confines of the great hall, the garrison were clearly about to be slaughtered.

The constable of Roxburgh, William de Fiennes, was quick to realise this. To resist the Scots in the great hall was suicidal. In the midst of the chaos Fiennes fled from the great hall with a significant number of his garrison and led them into the upper reaches of the great tower. They hastily barricaded the stairs and entranceways to prevent the Scots from breaking in. Throughout the night Douglas's men roamed the castle, taking prisoner or killing anyone they discovered. The only escape from them for fugitive garrison troops was a perilous jump – to almost certain death – from the castle walls. In the great hall guttering candlelight fitfully illuminated the bodies of their less fortunate comrades where they lay sprawled upon the blood-soaked floor.

When dawn broke the following morning, Fiennes and the remnants of his garrison still held out in the tower. In an attempt to dislodge them, Douglas ordered archers to unleash a hail of arrows at the tower, but the defenders remained stoically resolute. Entrapped within their own castle, Fiennes and his men defiantly held the tower for the whole day and throughout the night. A renewed archery assault the following morning finally broke their resolve, an arrow striking Fiennes in the face. Fearing he had suffered a mortal wound, and mindful of his responsibility for the lives of those trapped beside him, Fiennes entered into surrender negotiations with Douglas. Considering the hopeless situation of the garrison, the terms they received were remarkably generous; it is possible the infamously brutal Douglas was moved by the bravery of Fiennes, but it is more likely that Douglas was impatient to gain Roxburgh in its entirety. The defeated survivors of the garrison were taken under escort to the border and released without ransom. By nightfall on 21 February 1314 the first of the three great castles of Scotland had been taken.[13]

In taking Roxburgh Castle by storm, Douglas had achieved a momentous feat of arms. Audacious though the assault had been, it was made possible by meticulous preparation and planning. The capture of Roxburgh was the culmination of seven years of bloody experience for Bruce and his lieutenants in conducting operations against castles, the techniques of assault having gradually been perfected. It is conceivable the garrison were caught off guard, lulled into a false sense of security by the ongoing siege of Edinburgh and the belief that the main Scottish effort was concentrated there, and by the feast day of Shrove Tuesday. But in truth there was little a garrison could do when subjected to such a thoroughly planned and brilliantly executed surprise night assault.

The fighting spirit of the garrison was certainly not in doubt. The arrow wound that Fiennes received did indeed prove fatal and he died shortly after returning to England. No blame can be attached to Fiennes for the loss of Roxburgh Castle, although in mid-century Thomas Gray disparagingly remarked that both Roxburgh and Edinburgh were in the hands of foreigners when they were lost.[14] It is true that Fiennes was a foreigner, a Frenchman, and that, like Lubaud, he too was a favourite of Edward II. Fiennes was only an esquire when appointed constable of Roxburgh, being knighted on 1 August 1311 whilst already in command of the castle. The selection of an esquire to command such a vitally important fortress was an extraordinary state of affairs.[15] Again, as with Lubaud, this was a symptom of the political turmoil of Edward's reign. In 1314 the commanders of the major castles of Edinburgh and Roxburgh were both foreign favourites of the king. Although neither man failed Edward – Fiennes ultimately laying down his life for the office to which he had been appointed – their appointment illustrates the extent to which the domestic conflicts of the reign seriously jeopardised the effective prosecution of the Scottish war.

With the great fortress of Roxburgh in his hands, Douglas immediately sent news of his spectacular success to Bruce. If this was the first Bruce knew of an attempt on the castle, then there is no indication of any surprise on his part, nor did he hesitate in ordering its destruction. Edward Bruce, accompanied by a large company of troops, was promptly dispatched to Roxburgh to effect his orders. Men set to work with a will, digging shafts beneath the fortifications and then firing the timber supports, the tunnels collapsing inwards and bringing the great masonry walls of the magnificent buildings crashing thunderously to the ground in great billowing clouds of dust and splintered stone. It was a sad end for such a striking fortress, an English chronicler being moved to lament that the Scots 'razed to the ground the whole of that beautiful castle'.[16] By March the splendid stronghold of Roxburgh was nothing more than a pitiful ruin.

For Thomas Randolph outside Edinburgh Castle the brilliant success of his rival lieutenant cannot have been entirely welcome news. Douglas had captured Roxburgh in less than forty-eight hours; after two months of siege Randolph was still no nearer to taking Edinburgh. The resolve of the garrison remained strong and their supplies plentiful. Meanwhile, in the siege lines frustration mounted. As the situation dragged on, and with seemingly no end in sight, Randolph desperately sought an alternative means of taking the castle.[17] No doubt prompted by Douglas's sensational storming of Roxburgh, his thoughts turned to devising a new stratagem for success. Inevitably Randolph began to contemplate an assault.

Perched high on its basalt crag, with sheer cliffs dropping away on three sides, Edinburgh Castle was virtually impervious to assault. It could only be approached from the south and the gateway here was consequently well fortified and heavily defended. Nor was this the only problem Randolph faced. A successful assault was dependent on achieving surprise. Roxburgh Castle had been taken on a dark night with the garrison unaware a Scottish force was before the walls. Edinburgh had been subjected to a close siege for more than two months and its garrison was on high alert. Yet it was the very inaccessibility of the castle that provided the besiegers with their only opportunity of achieving surprise. The north face of the castle rock was so steep and treacherous that it was considered unscalable; if an assault party could climb this precipitous rock face, then the garrison would almost certainly be taken by surprise. It was an exceptionally perilous enterprise, but if the Scots were to have any chance of taking Edinburgh by storm then it was from here that they must attack.

Precisely how a way up the north face of the rock was determined remains unclear. Barbour provides a typically romantic account in which a Scotsman, William Francis, revealed the route to Randolph, Francis having once served in the castle and used the route to leave secretly at night to visit a girl in the town below. However, considering the prolonged duration of the siege, there was ample opportunity for the besiegers to reconnoitre the north face and find a way up. The assault party would necessarily be encumbered by ladders for scaling the castle wall once the plateau had been reached. The ascent was to take place at night, in complete darkness, while it was hoped that a diversionary attack on the south gate would draw the majority of the garrison away from the north side of the castle rock.

Thomas Randolph commanded the assault party in person. As Bruce had led the perilous night attack on Perth, and Douglas the assault on Roxburgh, so Randolph was to share with his men the considerable dangers of the night assault on Edinburgh. On 14 March, apparently a particularly dark night, the attack was launched. The assault party of thirty men began the hazardous ascent, groping their way forwards, the sharp edges of rocks cutting into the palms of their hands as they awkwardly clambered upwards through the rugged clefts. The physical exertion of this terrifying climb was immense, a sheer drop and certain death awaiting the slightest slip, and at about halfway the party took a well earned rest upon a ledge. Barbour recounts a tale of how, as they rested, a watchman on the walls high above shouted down in their direction and threw a stone into the darkness towards them; if true, then the nerve of the assault party held and the bluff of the watchman was successfully called. Resuming their precarious ascent, Randolph and his men negotiated the treacherous uppermost reaches of the rock. Heaving themselves onto the plateau, they gazed at the twelve-foot-high section of wall which confronted them.

By now a general Scottish attack upon the south gate was well underway. The sounds of the engagement would have carried clearly through the night to the assault party. At the best of times the north wall appears to have been sparsely defended; with most of its defenders having left to repel the diversionary attack, it now lay invitingly open. Noiselessly the ladders were manhandled forwards and placed against the wall. The assault party scrambled up the rungs and, levering themselves over the wall, dropped down onto the raised walkway. Having climbed the rock and scaled the wall, all that was left for them to do was to cut a path through the garrison to the south gate and let the rest of the besiegers into the castle.

Before the assault party had fully assembled, it was spotted. A cry of treason rang out as watchmen suddenly saw Scots appearing to their rear. Drowned out by the clamour of battle the cry may not have travelled far, but those of the garrison within earshot turned to face their attackers. As the remainder of the assault party frantically clambered up the ladders, Randolph and his men were already engaged in a vicious hand-to-hand fight on the walkway of the north wall. It was an intense skirmish, the Scots exhausted by their climb, the English caught unawares and temporarily outnumbered. The Scots made their numbers pay and 'slew them mercilessly'. The walkway clear, they descended into the castle ward and battled furiously to force a passage through to the main gate.

The fight within the castle was a bitterly hard-fought affair. At the forefront of the embattled garrison was the constable they had selected. Although in name he remains, unfortunately, anonymous, in deed he was everything the garrison had believed him to be. He led the men in a desperate action and fought with such extraordinary strength and determination that, though driven back by the Scots, his tenacity threatened the life of Randolph himself. It was a savage fight, 'swords that had been fair and bright were all bloody to the hilt' and 'cries arose hideously, for those who were struck down or wounded shouted and bellowed with great roaring'. At the height of this frantic struggle the constable was slain, and upon his death the resolve of the garrison broke. The Scots battled through to the south gate. It was thrown open and as the massed ranks of the besiegers poured into the castle, the fate of Edinburgh was irrevocably sealed. Overwhelmed by the Scots, their constable dead, the survivors of the garrison fled for their lives, some sliding down the castle walls in a desperate bid to escape the carnage within.[18]

The storming of Edinburgh Castle was a particularly bloody affair, the garrison being armed and ready for combat. It was a high-risk operation born out of a mounting desperation to seize the castle, and it is a tribute to Randolph and his men that it was brought to such a successful, if sanguinary, conclusion. It was also to have a dark epilogue. In the aftermath of the assault, the Scots discovered Lubaud bound in iron fetters in the castle dungeon. He was granted mercy and entered into the service of Robert Bruce. Such chivalry was to prove short-lived. On 8 March 1316, Lubaud is described in Scottish records as 'deceased, recently convicted in our court of betrayal of us and our kingdom'. Thomas Gray recounted that Bruce, having taken Lubaud into his allegiance, 'afterwards suspected him of treason and had him hanged and drawn' believing that Lubaud 'had always been English at heart, and was waiting for his best chance to harm him'.[19] It is a bitter irony that a man believed by his own garrison to have been guilty of treachery should ultimately be executed for remaining loyal to the English cause. The bleak figure cut by Piers Lubaud is one of the most tragic of the entire Scottish wars.

Edinburgh Castle also met with a sorry but inevitable end. When informed of its capture, Bruce 'hurried there with a company of many men' and supervised its destruction in person. Mine shafts were driven beneath the tower and walls, and the imposing fortifications levelled to the ground.[20] As he watched the castle being reduced to rubble, the optimism that coursed through Bruce must have been immense. At the beginning of the year he had set an enormously ambitious objective by undertaking an offensive aimed at the seizure and destruction of the three great fortresses of Edinburgh, Roxburgh and Stirling. Incredibly, after less than three months, he was already two-thirds of the way towards achieving this objective. There were still more than two months left before the English host was due to arrive in Scotland. The morale of Bruce's troops was incredibly high. Only Stirling Castle remained to be taken.

Although the exact date on which the Scots moved against Stirling is not recorded, it was certainly after the destruction of Edinburgh and Roxburgh, a date in late March or early April 1314 being the most likely. Stirling, situated high on its isolated crag, presented almost identical difficulties to those encountered at Edinburgh. Despite the marked success of assaults against Edinburgh and Roxburgh, the castle of Stirling was besieged. This was with good reason. As the northernmost of the three castles, Stirling was the most vulnerable to the disruption of the supply line on which it depended. Almost certainly, by March the overland supply route had been cut off. The shipment of supplies by sea would have been fitful at best. In late March an order was issued by the English Crown for victuals to be bought and shipped to Stirling Castle, but it is doubtful whether these ever reached the beleaguered garrison. With provisions in the castle running low, and in recognition of the difficulties that an assault presented, Bruce decided to take Stirling Castle by means of an intensive siege.

Whereas Randolph and Douglas had been responsible for the operations against Edinburgh and Roxburgh castles respectively, Robert Bruce himself supervised the initial operation against Stirling Castle before handing command to his brother Edward in late April or early May; on 16 April Edward Bruce had led a raid into Cumberland, his men spending three days laying waste to the district around Carlisle, burning villages and churches, taking men and women prisoner, and driving off cattle. An attack on Carlisle itself was repulsed. After returning from this destructive raid, Edward Bruce took command of the siege of Stirling Castle.[21] The consequences of this change in command were to be immense.

The constable of Stirling was a Scotsman, Philip Mowbray. Mowbray had been a consistent enemy of Bruce, fighting against him at Methven in June 1306 where he had almost captured Bruce when he grasped hold of the reins of the fugitive king's horse. Mowbray himself had lost a horse at Methven, but had again distinguished himself the following year, courageously fighting his way out of an ambush at Edirford, eleven miles south of Paisley, in which James Douglas had attempted to destroy the force he commanded. By 1309–10 Mowbray had been appointed constable of Kirkintilloch Castle, six miles north of Glasgow, and from 1311 he had been in command of Stirling Castle.[22] At the outset of the siege Mowbray would have been offered the option by Robert Bruce to surrender the castle, a request he had evidently declined. Shortly after Edward Bruce took command, he entered into talks with Mowbray and concluded an agreement for the conditional surrender of the castle.

For Mowbray this was a calculated decision. Following the loss of Edinburgh and Roxburgh castles, Stirling Castle was now the focus of the Scottish offensive. In a handful of weeks the English host was due to arrive in Scotland. If Mowbray could negotiate an agreement whereby a deadline for the relief of the castle coincided with the expected arrival of the host, then the relief of the castle could almost be guaranteed. By the nature of such an agreement, hostilities against the castle would be suspended until this deadline expired. Should the host fail to appear, then the castle would be peacefully surrendered. It was an agreement that guaranteed the lives of Mowbray and his garrison, and almost certainly ensured Stirling would not fall. For Mowbray this was the perfect solution, but he could hardly have expected the Scots to contemplate an agreement that was so unfavourable towards them. So Mowbray must have been astonished when Edward Bruce assented to this. The deadline for the relief of Stirling was set as Midsummer's Day, St John the Baptist's Day, 1314; by that day, Monday 24 June, a relieving army had to have come within three leagues of the castle.[23] It was a date that gave the English host ample time to reach Stirling. In one disastrous stroke Edward Bruce had snatched defeat from the jaws of victory.

The Scottish offensive of 1314 lay as assuredly in ruins as the castles of Edinburgh and Roxburgh. By concluding this agreement, Edward Bruce denied the Scots any opportunity of capturing and destroying Stirling before the host arrived. Worse, the primary objective of Robert Bruce, the avoidance of battle, was gravely jeopardised by committing a substantial Scottish force to maintain the siege until the agreed deadline. From the moment the agreement was concluded the English and the Scots were set on a collision course beneath the shadow of Stirling Castle. In a moment of appalling misjudgement Edward Bruce had presented the English with their best opportunity in a generation of bringing the Scots to battle. It was a battle that threatened the destruction of Robert Bruce and the annihilation of the Scottish cause.

But was it an atrocious error on the part of Edward Bruce? Did he really make such a terrible blunder? The true chronology of 1314, as convincingly argued by Professor Archie Duncan, with the siege of Stirling and the agreement for its surrender dated not to the summer of 1313 but to 1314, exacerbates the magnitude of this decision in that Edward Bruce destroyed the momentum of an offensive which was on the brink of success. The consensus is that Edward Bruce did indeed commit such an appalling error. But in truth this does not seem plausible. Whatever his faults, Edward was an experienced soldier and commander who had fought under his brother for eight years. During this time he would inevitably have grasped something of the strategy and tactics at which his brother was so adept. It is inconceivable that Edward did not realise the serious implications inherent in the agreement when he concluded it. He knew when the English host was due to arrive in Scotland and had no reason to suspect that it would fail to appear. It follows that he also recognised the deadline of Midsummer's Day as an invitation to battle. This, it seems, is what Edward Bruce wanted.

If any of Robert Bruce's lieutenants wished for a showdown with the English in 1314, then it would have been Edward Bruce. Such a headstrong desire is entirely in keeping with his bullish character: when Robert Bruce had returned to Carrick in 1307 it was his brother, Edward, who had urged him to attack the garrison of Turnberry; in the winter of 1307–8 it was Edward who had assumed command when Robert was incapacitated by illness and who had defied those enemies seeking their destruction; more pertinently, during the summer of 1308, Edward had made his name in Galloway by taking on and defeating a force that vastly outnumbered his own. As Barbour observed, Edward Bruce was unsurpassed in bravery and daring, but he lacked the moderation of his brother. Physically powerful, ferociously aggressive, Edward Bruce was a hard-headed warrior rather than a calculating commander. Ultimately this was to prove his downfall. In the years following Bannockburn, during the Bruce campaigns in Ireland (1315–18), Edward Bruce was to lead an outnumbered Scottish army into battle at Fochart near Dundalk on 14 October 1318. Hostile accounts claim that he arrogantly refused to wait for reinforcements because he desired all the glory of victory for himself.[24] It was a battle he should not have fought, and in which he was slain.

In the late spring of 1314, with seven years of successful warfare behind the Bruces, Edward Bruce might well have believed that the time had come for them to take on the English in a set-piece battle. Knowing his brother to be adamantly opposed to such a course of action, it is quite possible that Edward's impetuousness led him into engineering just such an occasion. When Robert Bruce heard of the terms of the agreement, he was understandably furious; unlike Edward, he appreciated that a battle with the English host must be avoided at almost any cost.

Yet there was one price that Robert Bruce was not willing to pay. The authority by which Bruce held the Crown ultimately rested upon his military success: should his military reputation be damaged then his authority as king would be undermined. The need to maintain this image of military strength had led Bruce to launch the preemptive strikes against the castles of Edinburgh, Roxburgh and now Stirling. Bruce recognised that the English campaign not only had the potential to destroy him in the field but also to undermine severely his power as king. Should his force merely retreat when confronted by the English host and allow it to roam unopposed through the Borders and the Lowlands, then his authority as king would suffer a tremendous blow. It was essential for Bruce that he should be seen to be willing to oppose the enemy. By destroying Scotland's three principal castles, Bruce not only sought to cripple the English campaign but also to create the ideal conditions by which he could embroil the host in a gruelling nightmare of irregular warfare. Denied the invaluable support of these castles, the English would have had no framework on which to base their campaign. The host would consequently have been vulnerable to ambush and starvation. It was by means of irregular warfare that Bruce had intended to oppose the host.

This plan was irretrievably wrecked by Edward Bruce's agreement for the relief of Stirling Castle. Just as Robert Bruce had recognised that he must oppose the English campaign, so he now realised that his brother's actions had committed him to the siege of Stirling. If he were to lift the siege before the deadline expired, or order an immediate withdrawal when confronted by the English host, then battle could be avoided. The castle would be reinforced and resupplied, but when the host departed from Scotland another siege could be set. Yet Bruce knew such a course of action would harm his authority as king. The deadline for the relief of Stirling was effectively a challenge from which he could not afford to turn away. If Bruce was to underline emphatically the authority by which he held the Crown, then he had to make a show of resistance before Stirling Castle. It was not the cause of Scottish independence that compelled Bruce to undertake this perilous face-off, but his ambition to consolidate his authority as king.

It had been here, on the banks of the Forth within sight of Stirling Castle, that, a decade earlier, Robert Bruce had begun to plot his path to the Crown. Now, by a cruel twist of fate, it seemed that here was where he was destined to be destroyed. If Bruce was to retain his authority as king, he knew he had to make a stand, yet he was painfully aware that should a battle be fought then a catastrophic defeat was almost inevitable. This was the impossible situation in which his brother had placed him. The terrifying prospect of battle loomed as large and as daunting as the towering crag on which Stirling Castle stood defiant. Beneath its oppressive shadow Bruce and his lieutenants began to assemble an army. As he waited for it to gather, a plan began to form in his mind and it was on this that he anxiously dwelt as he prepared to face the formidable might of the English host before Stirling Castle.

CHAPTER NINE

TEARS OF A KING

THROUGHOUT THE FIRST WEEKS OF JUNE 1314, IN THE WAR-RAVAGED COUNTY of Northumberland, the English host began to muster at Wark. For the weary columns of foot soldiers who trudged into its sparse earthen streets there was nothing enticing about their new surroundings. Wark had suffered as much as any other town or village in northern England. Its exposed position on the south bank of the Tweed, on the borderline between England and Scotland, placed it squarely in the path of Scottish raids and English campaigns. Beside the Tweed, fewer than a dozen miles away, the ruins of Roxburgh Castle spoke starkly of the renewed intensity of the war. To most of the foot soldiers who gathered at Wark, the far bank of the Tweed was their first sight of Scotland. They knew of the bitter wars, they had heard of Robert Bruce, they had listened to rumours recounting the savagery of the Scots. It cannot have been with anything other than trepidation that they gazed across the Tweed and wondered what dangers awaited them in Scotland.

The army that gathered at Wark was one which Edward II had frequently despaired of ever raising. If he had dared to believe that the domestic political rapprochement of late 1313 promised a reversal of English fortune in the Scottish wars, then the opening months of 1314 had instantly shattered any such delusion. In December, when Edward had made clear his intention to undertake a campaign, the initiative seemed finally to have passed to the English. No one had countenanced the possibility that Bruce would mount an offensive of his own. News of this unexpected development reached the English in March, messengers arriving with reports 'of the destruction of

Scottish cities, the capture of the castles, and the breaching of the surrounding walls'. The Scottish offensive immediately generated panic in England. News of the fall of Edinburgh and Roxburgh castles, and of their subsequent destruction, was particularly devastating. Edward reeled under the impact of this news, disturbed to such an extent that 'for the capture of his castles [he] could scarcely restrain his tears'.[1] A real fear took hold that the Scots would invade England. It was almost certainly a symptom of this panic that as early as 12 March, even before Edinburgh had fallen, Edward ordered that Bruce's wife, Elizabeth, should be removed from Barking Abbey in Essex where she was being held and taken south of the Thames to Kent and the more secure confines of Rochester Castle, where she was to be kept under close guard.[2] Edward was taking no chances. The pressure of the Scottish offensive was beginning to tell.

Far from regaining the initiative, in the first months of 1314 the war plunged the English into new depths of despair. North of the border Bruce appeared to be all-powerful, ruthlessly directing the relentless onslaught which threatened to destroy the last strongholds of English power in Scotland. It was only too clear to Edward and his commanders that the loss of these principal castles had the potential fatally to undermine their forthcoming campaign. Nor could they do anything to counter this offensive. Formidable though the English war machine was, the raising of an English host required several weeks, even months, for it to be assembled and its infrastructure put in place. The successes of Bruce and the weak English position only added to the sense of panic in English ranks.

Distraught at the unexpected turn of events, Edward felt compelled to respond. At Westminster, on 24 March, a series of writs of military summons was issued which superseded those of December. The wording of the writs leaves no doubt as to the anxiety that gripped England. Edward's clerks wrote of how 'Robert de Bruce and his accomplices have lately attacked, taken, and destroyed various of the king's towns, castles, and fortresses in Scotland and the Marches, and are preparing to invade the English Marches, and to besiege the town of Berwick-upon-Tweed'. The writs clearly reveal that the Scottish offensive was interpreted as a preliminary to a major invasion of northern England, with the vital strategic fortress town of Berwick believed to be the chief objective. The loss of Berwick would be a critical blow and politically it could prove devastating for Edward. If Berwick was endangered then a serious effort must be made to save it. This was the purpose of the new writs. They stated that Edward would be at Newcastle within 'three weeks of Easter, 28 April, with horses and arms, to resist them [the Scots], and to proceed against them powerfully and manfully'. The earls and barons to whom the writs were addressed were also to come to Newcastle on that day with horses and arms so that Edward 'may be then ready to march against the enemy'.[3]

Desperate to be seen to counter the Scottish offensive, Edward had brought the date of muster forward by more than a month. The most immediate impact of these writs, however, was not military in nature, but political. In November 1313 Edward had summoned a parliament to meet at Westminster on 21 April 1314 to discuss 'diverse affairs touching the king and the kingdom'. The new date of muster now forced the cancellation of that parliament, the writs announcing that 'the king cannot hold his parliament at the appointed time, as he could have wished'. This development instantly alarmed the earl of Lancaster and his allies, men who remained extremely sensitive to any perceived threat to their own delicate political position. The patched-up compromise of late 1313 remained fragile and it was certainly not an agreement in which they were prepared to trust their lives. For the earls, parliament was the keystone to their continued pursuit of a programme of royal reforms. The king's abrupt cancellation of the spring parliament went directly against the principles enshrined in the heart of the Ordinances and, more pointedly, threatened the earls' own safety.

Lancaster and his adherents were quick to retaliate. A clause of the defunct Ordinances had stipulated that the king could not undertake a campaign without the consent of parliament. Although the Ordinances did not possess the weight of law, the clause embodied a longstanding convention by which magnates were not compelled to respond personally to a feudal summons which had not received their common assent. They were obliged to provide a minimum quota of knights and men-at-arms, but nothing more. If Lancaster and Warwick should readily respond to this summons, then they would be denying the spirit of the Ordinances and undermining their own position. Despite the potent threat posed by the Scots, they put their own interests first and told Edward that a parliament should be held to discuss the campaign.

Edward bluntly disagreed, citing the urgency of the situation. The recalcitrant earls stated they would not participate in the campaign unless parliament met. At a time of national crisis the domestic battle lines were again being unequivocally drawn. Edward could claim that the implicit assent of the magnates had already been obtained with the subsidy granted in the parliament of late 1313. A number of Edward's hard-line counsellors were more bullish. They urged the king to demand due service from everyone and then set out for Scotland for 'it was certain that so many would come to his aid that neither Robert Bruce nor the Scots would resist'.[4] The counsellors argued that those who refused to come were immaterial, they were not needed, the Scots could be beaten without them. Edward boldly followed their advice.

The English campaign of 1314 would go ahead without the earls of Lancaster, Warwick, Arundel and Warenne.[5] Hereford, however, forewent his former allies and chose to participate in the campaign. The lands he sought to recover in Scotland must have weighed heavily in this decision. In contrast, the intransigence of Lancaster and Warwick, though politically motivated, was also founded upon real fear. An English chronicle recounts that the two earls believed their lives were in immediate danger.[6] Edward had failed to fulfil promises he had made to them, he still sought vengeance for the death of Gaveston, and Lancaster and Warwick feared for their safety should they join the host. In the atmosphere of heightened tensions of early 1314, it was all too easy for rumours to build and fears to grow.

The campaign of 1314 had taken on an importance that transcended the Scottish wars. By refusing to participate, Lancaster and Warwick ran the risk of being dangerously exposed should Edward prove successful. If the king returned from Scotland triumphant, he would gain more than enough political capital to turn against the two earls and exact his vengeance. Yet in pushing ahead with the campaign without allowing parliament to meet, Edward left himself perilously exposed should all end in failure, with the political fallout from such a failure inevitably transferring the political initiative to Lancaster and Warwick. The chronic domestic problems of Edward's reign consequently invested the campaign of 1314 with even greater importance. Disturbingly, the destruction of Bruce and the Scots was becoming a means to an end rather than an end in itself.

The absence of the earls of Lancaster, Warwick, Arundel and Warenne curtailed the manpower which Edward could call upon, but it by no means fatally undermined the prospects of the campaign. As Edward's hard-line counsellors had rightly argued, many of the leading magnates of the realm did respond to the writs of military summons. The earls of Gloucester, Pembroke and Hereford readily agreed to raise troops and participate, as did many barons of the realm, including men such as Robert Clifford, Henry de Beaumont, John de Segrave, Anthony de Lucy and Hugh le Despenser the Younger. All of these earls and barons could call upon their substantial landed estates to raise large numbers of knights and men-at-arms, the mounted core of the English host, while Edward had at his disposal the knights and sergeants-at-arms of the royal household. Despite the absence of several earls there would certainly be no shortage of heavy cavalry.

In terms of foot soldiers, the troops that comprised the bulk of the host, the absence of the earls had no effect whatsoever. The scale of the manpower upon which Edward could call is evident in a further series of writs issued on 24 March attempting to raise a total of more than nine thousand infantry. Over half of these were to come from Wales and the Welsh Marches: Roger Mortimer, the English justiciar of Wales, was instructed to raise two thousand foot soldiers in north Wales and a thousand in south Wales; Mortimer was also to provide three hundred from his own lordships in south Wales and the Marches; Gloucester was to raise two hundred from his lordship of Brecknock; John de Hastings two hundred from Abergavenny; seven hundred were to come from the lordship of Powys. In the west of England the town of Bristol was to provide forty crossbowmen and sixty archers; one hundred foot soldiers were to come from the Forest of Dean; forty foot soldiers from the lordship of Hope; one thousand foot soldiers from the counties of Salop and Stafford. The counties of England north of the Trent, the traditional recruiting ground for campaigns against Scotland, were also to provide substantial numbers of foot soldiers: Chester was to raise five hundred; Yorkshire and Northumberland were each to provide one thousand; another thousand were to come from the combined resources of Nottinghamshire and Derbyshire. All forces were to be sent to the newly arranged muster at Newcastle as, so the writs explicitly state, Edward was 'greatly in need of good foot soldiers'.[7]

In fact, Edward spread his net of recruitment even wider. The same month a writ was issued to the English justiciar of Ireland for the raising of four thousand archers and foot soldiers, who were to be ready by 26 May and shipped to Scotland on board a fleet commanded by Bruce's old Scottish adversary John of Argyll. This force was to be commanded by Richard de Burgh, earl of Ulster, and his troops were also to sail with the fleet. Edward wrote to a number of Anglo-Irish barons requesting them to provide men, and he also took the extraordinary step of sending similar requests to twenty-five native Irish chieftains.[8] If the response of the latter remains doubtful, the fact that Edward sought their help is a measure of the lengths to which he was prepared to go in order to raise a formidable host. By the end of March the writs issued by Edward stipulated that a force of more than thirteen thousand foot soldiers was to muster at Newcastle. Before the month was out, Aymer de Valence had been appointed to the dual office of keeper and king's lieutenant of Scotland. Accompanied by an advance guard of knights and men-at-arms, Valence was ordered to make his way north 'to seek out the ambushes of the Scots, and prepare the king's route into Scotland'.[9] The English campaign of 1314 was beginning to gather a momentum all of its own.

Edward left Westminster and by 1 April the king and his household were at St Albans in Hertfordshire. The long journey north had begun. Twelve days later, having followed the Great North Road, they had arrived sixty miles north in Peterborough. It was from here that, on 13 April, a further series of writs was issued. Their subject was a demand for manpower and money. Addressed to the sheriffs of every English county, the writs ordered that all men of these counties, including the clergy, were either to perform their due military service by mustering for the campaign or pay a fine to the Treasury at Westminster. The inhabitants of the northernmost counties were to pay their fines at York. The ability to commute military service into a cash payment had long since become an accepted feature of medieval society, and Edward was careful to ensure he obtained either the manpower or money which he was due, money that could then be spent on the raising of further troops. A rather belated writ was also issued to the volatile inhabitants of London, informing the citizens that the king was about to depart for Scotland with his army and binding them to keep the peace in his absence.[10]

By far the most intriguing feature of these writs is that the date and place of muster had now reverted to 10 June at Berwick, the original arrangements first announced in December. The attempt to bring the muster forward had been abandoned little more than two weeks after it had been initiated. No reference is made to the envisaged muster at Newcastle. What had happened to make Edward decide that the earlier muster at Newcastle was no longer necessary? Curiously, nothing significant had changed. If Edward and his counsellors had believed Berwick was in immediate danger in late March, then in early April they had no reason to believe that this threat had suddenly disappeared. Indeed, it was on 16 April that Edward Bruce led a raid into Cumberland and oversaw an attempt to take Carlisle. The abrupt abandonment of the Newcastle muster raises serious doubts about the motives that originally lay behind it. There was certainly a real fear in March that a Scottish invasion was imminent, but did Edward exploit this fear to further his own political agenda? By bringing the muster forward, Edward ensured the forthcoming April parliament could not meet. Although Edward professed in the writs of summons that he wished parliament to sit, it was certainly in his interests that it did not to do so. Determined as he was to deny the

Ordinances any semblance of legitimacy, he must have feared that the campaign would be debated in parliament. If parliamentary assent was given to the campaign, as undoubtedly it would have been, then the English host would have been strengthened by the participation of the four intransigent earls. Yet such assent would have lent authority to the Ordinances. Edward was desperate to avoid this difficult situation, and the threat posed by the Scottish offensive provided him with the ideal pretext to cancel the forthcoming parliament. Edward appears to have been willing to sacrifice the significant additional manpower that the earls of Lancaster, Warwick, Arundel and Warenne could have provided in order to buttress his own domestic political position.

A key reason why Edward was able to avoid parliament was that he could finance the campaign from other sources. A subsidy towards the campaign had already been granted in the previous parliament which provided him with a significant sum for the raising and maintenance of a substantial force. The campaign could never have taken place, however, without the financial backing of Antonio Pessagno, a merchant and banker from the city of Genoa. For many years Italian bankers had subsidised English kings, and in particular their wars. Edward I had made extensive use of the banking houses of the Riccardi and the Frescobaldi, and Edward II had retained the services of the latter until their unpopularity marked them out as a target of the Ordinances and they had been expelled from the realm. This financial void was filled in 1312 by the emergence of Pessagno. Within two years he had lent Edward the enormous sum of £111,000, his repayments mainly taking the form of grants of future customs revenue. Part of the total he lent encompassed a loan of £25,000 from the pope, Clement V, which Pessagno proved instrumental in negotiating, the loan being secured against the customs revenue of Gascony. Ironically, this loan had originally been negotiated in 1313 in order to bolster Edward's dwindling finances during his dispute with the magnates. It was not finalised, however, until January 1314, Pessagno receiving the money in March and thereby providing Edward with a timely and substantial amount to support the forthcoming venture. In the months immediately preceding the offensive, Pessagno lent Edward a total of more than £21,000. As well as bankrolling the campaign, Pessagno was also responsible for providing three quarters of the vast amount of wheat and oats that were received at Berwick to sustain the host as it marched north.[11]

An enormous supporting cast worked tirelessly putting the necessary arrangements in place. A tremendous large-scale operation saw victuals gathered from throughout the realm, in particular the eastern counties, and transported north to Berwick and Carlisle. Sheriffs provided set quantities of supplies from their counties, with any shortfall leading to the imposition of the hated system of purveyance and prise by which the necessary victuals were forcibly seized by officials, with recompense given at a later date. It was a system wide open to abuse, and one which had consequently been targeted in the Ordinances.[12] A plentiful supply of victuals certainly arrived in the towns of Berwick and Carlisle in anticipation of the campaign. Pessagno supervised the collection of supplies in the eastern counties and Valence, having arrived in Berwick by 16 April, oversaw their receipt. A large number of English ports were requested to provide ships, the writs envisaging a fleet of over sixty vessels, each vessel to be fully manned by a crew of experienced sailors.[13] Victuals were loaded into their holds and sent north. Many vessels that made the journey along the east coast to Berwick then remained in the fortified port, forming the nucleus of a supply fleet ready to tranship the victuals to the host once it had entered Scotland. The resources necessary to sustain such a substantial army placed an enormous burden on the English state, even though Edward appears to have intended the campaign to last no longer than six weeks.

Exactly what the English intended to do during these six weeks remains obscure. If a plan of campaign was articulated by Edward and his commanders, then no record of it survives. The attempt to summon a substantial Irish contingent and the build-up of supplies in Carlisle suggest a two-pronged invasion of Scotland was planned, with a predominantly Irish force to advance through southwestern Scotland while the main host undertook a simultaneous advance in the southeast. The primary objective of the campaign was, as always, to bring the Scots to battle. It was an objective that had not been achieved since Falkirk sixteen years before. There was certainly no reason for the English to believe that the present campaign would result in this frustratingly elusive battle. If anything, Edward's first-hand experience of the irregular warfare practiced by Bruce's troops during the expedition of 1310–11 should have served as a blunt warning of what the host could expect when it entered Scotland. In all probability the English campaign would prove to be another futile march through the Scottish Lowlands, with the host plagued by sporadic hit-and-run attacks and sudden ambuscades. The raising of a substantial host was far from a guarantee that the campaign would prove successful, and this can only have encouraged Lancaster and Warwick to adopt their intransigent stance.

Yet Edward appears to have viewed the expedition with a surprising degree of optimism. He was certainly determined that the host would display martial prowess. In the late summer and autumn of 1313 he sent no fewer than eleven letters in an attempt to secure the release of the renowned knight, Giles d'Argentan. A veteran of the Scottish wars who had fought against Bruce at Methven and Loch Tay, d'Argentan had incurred the wrath of Edward I when his love of tournaments had enticed him, along with others, to leave the army to participate in a tournament overseas without licence in 1306. It was d'Argentan's martial fervour that led him to undertake a journey to Rhodes in order to join the Knights of St John in the fight against the Saracens, but he had been captured en route and imprisoned in Salonika.[14] Edward's resolve to gain the release of d'Argentan is both a striking demonstration of the king's loyalty and of his need to have knights of this calibre in his company. The flurry of letters was most probably prompted by the prospect of a Scottish campaign, and d'Argentan's release from captivity and presence among the host were undoubtedly a timely boost to the morale of both the king and the army.

The appearance of another singular figure amongst the host also reveals Edward's confidence. Among the king's entourage was Robert Baston, a Carmelite friar and poet. This was most probably not the first military campaign in which Baston had been involved. In 1298 a poem had been composed to celebrate the English victory at Falkirk, its detailed content suggesting that the author had been present at the battle. The successful campaign of 1303–4 was the subject of another detailed poem. Both have been attributed to Baston.[15] In 1314 Edward was evidently keen to employ this noted war poet in his service, clearly intending that Baston compose celebratory verses on the glorious triumph the king sought against Bruce and the Scots. The inclusion of Baston among the English host is striking evidence of the curiously high hopes Edward harboured for the campaign of 1314.

The presence of some individuals was not, however, conducive to establishing cohesion among the host. Henry de Beaumont was a particularly divisive figure. A Frenchman who had become a lord of the English realm, Beaumont had risen to recent prominence due to the favouritism of the king. Although he had participated throughout the Scottish wars and had fought with considerable prowess at Falkirk, his hard-headed acquisitiveness was increasingly resented. Having married a co-heiress of the late John Comyn, earl of Buchan, Beaumont had been granted by Edward the title of earl of

Buchan, which provided Beaumont with a burning desire to defeat the Scots and make good his claim to this valuable Scottish earldom. Beaumont had participated in the campaign of 1310–11 and, while serving in Perth with Gaveston, had asked for, but not received, the constableship of Scotland. Beaumont had become so strongly resented that the Ordinances contained a clause that related specifically to him and demanded his removal from the king's presence. This had been ignored and in 1312 Beaumont had been with Edward and Gaveston when they fled from Newcastle. During the protracted negotiations of 1313, Edward managed to secure the abrogation of the clause demanding Beaumont's expulsion, the king claiming it to be prejudicial to his interests. Yet popular resentment of Beaumont remained unabated. Edmund de Mauley, steward of the king's household, had also been present at Newcastle. Formerly a knight in the retinue of Gaveston, Mauley was among those who had advocated civil war in 1312.[16] Both Mauley and Beaumont featured among the figures that comprised the military high command of the host.

Desperate to ensure his confidence was not misplaced, Edward laboured tirelessly to raise a formidable army. The foot levies were raised by writs of summons and so were essentially a conscript army. In the counties and towns of England, commissioners of array and local officials arbitrarily selected those who would serve. It was an imperfect system open to widespread abuse. Officials were frequently bribed by those with a modicum of money who had no wish to serve, the burden inevitably falling upon the poorest members of society, and consequently the men who were conscripted were frequently of poor calibre. There was no local inspection of the equipment each man possessed, nor were counties and towns obliged to provide the appropriate equipment. The weaponry an arrayed foot soldier possessed could be as basic as a knife and few would have owned any kind of protective padding or armour. Strong regional variations meant that a troop of foot soldiers was a diverse body of men in terms both of ability and equipment. Many would have had no previous experience of serving on campaign or as part of an army. Forcibly snatched from their daily lives, there was little inducement to fight even for those who lived in relative poverty. The pay of 2*d* per day, though undoubtedly a slight improvement for some, was hardly adequate recompense for the dangers and hardships they were certain to endure.

By 20 April the king and his household had reached Lincoln, fifty miles to the north of Peterborough, and it was from here that a further series of writs was issued to satisfy Edward's insatiable appetite for manpower. The counties

1 Remains of Cambuskenneth Abbey, with Stirling Castle in the background. In 1314 the stone buildings of this twelfth-century abbey were impressed by Robert Bruce to act as a supply base for his Scottish army. On the night of 23 June its guards were killed and the stores within it treacherously pillaged by David, earl of Atholl.

2 Edinburgh Castle. Edinburgh was a first-rate fortress that had been in English hands since 1296. In early 1314 the garrison successfully resisted a Scottish siege that lasted several weeks. Thomas Randolph finally took this formidable castle by storm on the night of 14 March 1314.

3 Stirling Castle. Although it was recaptured by the English in 1304, subsequent Scottish successes under Robert Bruce had led to the garrison becoming isolated by 1314. In May of that year the decision of Edward Bruce to conclude a conditional agreement for the surrender of this increasingly vulnerable castle provided the occasion for the confrontation at Bannockburn.

4 Bothwell Castle, South Lanarkshire, interior view. A key English-held castle. In the immediate aftermath of Bannockburn a large company of the defeated English host, including the earl of Hereford, sought temporary refuge within its walls. The Scottish constable, Walter Gilbertson, treacherously surrendered the fugitives to Robert Bruce.

5 Fifteenth-century depiction of Bannockburn, from John of Fordun's *Scotichronicon*. The Scottish army, to the left, is shown as fighting on foot. The town and castle of Stirling appear in the background. The scene in the centre almost certainly represents the famous encounter between Robert Bruce, shown mounted and wielding an axe, and Henry de Bohun.

6 The second Great Seal of Robert I. This contemporary image of a mounted and fully-armoured Robert Bruce vividly depicts a well-equipped knight of the early fourteenth century. The relatively small, flat-topped shield, and the large, heavy-bladed sword that could be held in one hand, are both clearly evident. The armour is a combination of mail and plate, and a great helm protects the head. A rich surcoat and horse trapper complete the stylised image of this warrior-king.

7 Late thirteenth-century aquamanile (water vessel) found in the River Tyne. An exquisitely crafted contemporary representation of a mounted knight. The figure wears a great helm, his arms, hands and legs are protected by mail armour, a decorative surcoat covers his body. The lance and shield which the figure would originally have carried are both missing.

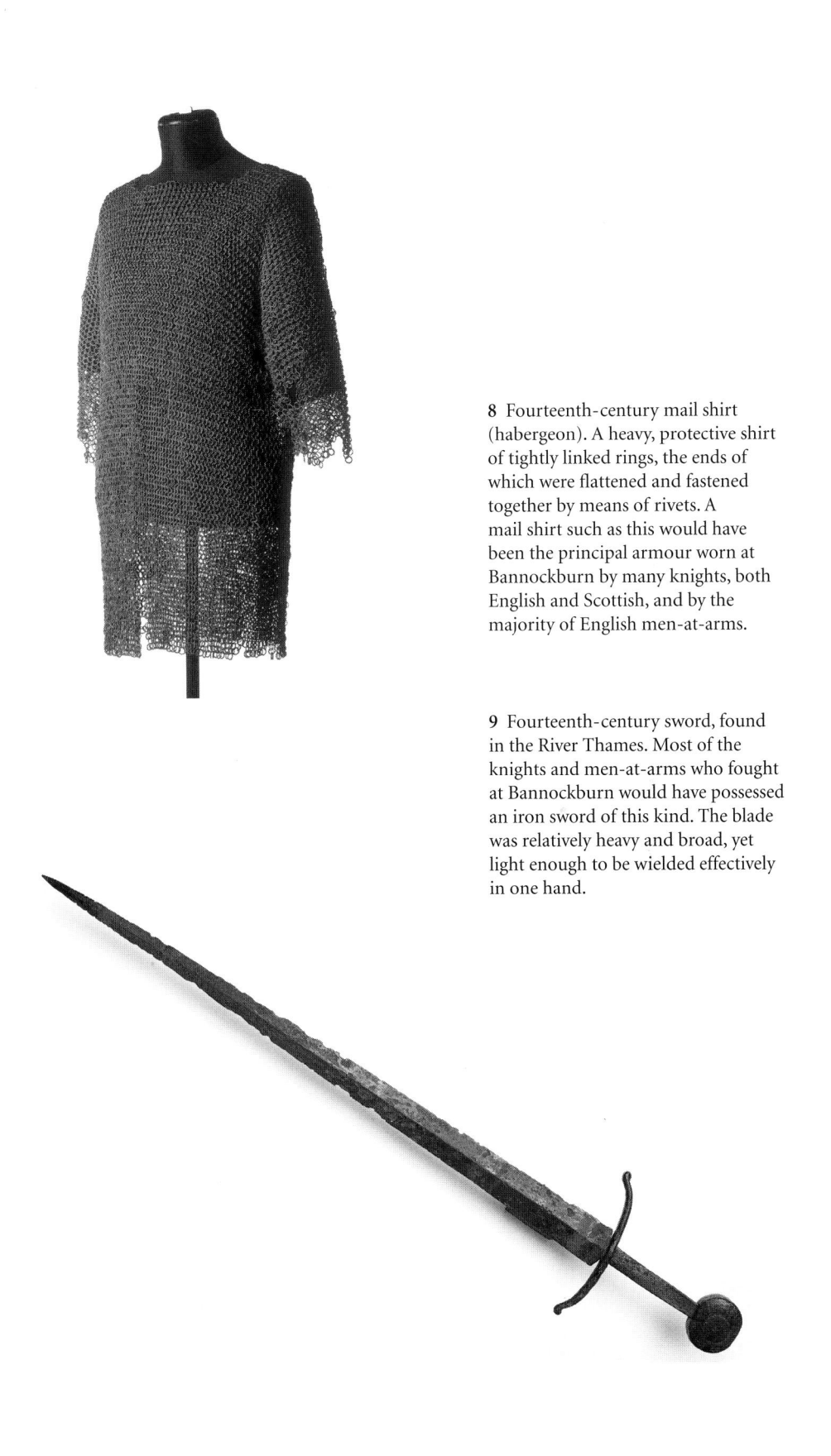

8 Fourteenth-century mail shirt (habergeon). A heavy, protective shirt of tightly linked rings, the ends of which were flattened and fastened together by means of rivets. A mail shirt such as this would have been the principal armour worn at Bannockburn by many knights, both English and Scottish, and by the majority of English men-at-arms.

9 Fourteenth-century sword, found in the River Thames. Most of the knights and men-at-arms who fought at Bannockburn would have possessed an iron sword of this kind. The blade was relatively heavy and broad, yet light enough to be wielded effectively in one hand.

10 Stone carving of two shields from the Cheapside Cross, thirteenth century. The Cheapside Cross was erected in London by Edward I as one of a series of monuments in memory of his wife, Eleanor of Castile, mother of Edward II. The left shield displays the arms of England, and that to the right the arms of Castile. The distinctive flat-topped shield depicted here would have been prevalent among the English cavalry at Bannockburn.

11 Pewter badge of an archer, late fourteenth century. By this time the archer and the longbow had become synonymous with English military triumphs. At the time of Bannockburn, however, the longbow had still to realise its full potential, and archers were not deployed in significant numbers against the Scots. The archer depicted in this badge is a huntsman.

north of the Trent were required to increase the number of foot soldiers dramatically from the quota they had originally been ordered to provide: an additional two thousand foot soldiers were to come from Yorkshire; a further fifteen hundred from Northumberland; Nottinghamshire and Derbyshire were to raise an additional one thousand between them; in the Welsh Marches the counties of Salop and Stafford were together to raise an extra thousand foot soldiers. Edward also plundered for men south of the Trent, summoning five hundred foot soldiers from the combined resources of the counties of Leicester and Warwick. In the north the county of Lancaster was to provide five hundred foot soldiers, and Lincolnshire, the county in which Edward was currently based, was ordered to raise the substantial number of three thousand.[17] These writs more than doubled the total number of soldiers previously requested from England and Wales in late March. A force of almost nineteen thousand foot soldiers had now been summoned, a total that excludes the four thousand Irish foot soldiers who were to sail for Scotland. The host, if only on paper, was beginning to take on intimidating proportions.

From Lincoln the king and his household continued their progress north. A short stay appears to have been made sixty miles from Lincoln in York, and it was not until 10 May that a writ was issued from Easingwold, a small town ten miles to the north of York. From Easingwold the traditional route north was most probably taken, the king passing through the towns of Darlington and Durham, and then on to Newcastle, a journey of approximately sixty miles. By 27 May Edward had arrived in the Northumberland village of Newminster. It was here that the English campaign suddenly burst into life.

Without warning Philip Mowbray rode into the village. Surprise at the unexpected arrival of the constable of Stirling Castle was immediately overshadowed by the startling news he brought. Mowbray approached the king and told Edward of the Scottish siege of Stirling Castle, and of the agreement for its relief that he had concluded. This was the first the English knew of the siege. Despite the long-held belief that the English were given a year to relieve Stirling, in truth they had at most a few short weeks. At Newminster, Edward suddenly learnt that he had less than a month to relieve the castle.

The shock of this revelation was immediately replaced by jubilation. For the first time the English campaign had a definite objective. Yet Edward and his commanders would not have concentrated on the actual siege and relief of Stirling but on the fact that Robert Bruce and a Scottish army lay before the castle. Crucially, the agreement concluded by Mowbray compelled Bruce and his army to remain before Stirling until the deadline of 24 June. It was this army that the English immediately targeted. The Scots had pinned themselves down and in doing so had presented the English with the greatest opportunity in a generation of bringing the Scots to battle. To Edward it was a battle that promised much. Due to the disparity between the forces, an English victory was almost guaranteed; it was not winning that concerned Edward, but gaining the battle. Bruce would almost certainly be destroyed and the Scottish army he commanded annihilated. The war against Bruce would be brought to a glorious conclusion. A victory would provide Edward with a wealth of political capital more than sufficient to exact vengeance against the earls of Lancaster and Warwick. If Edward could engage the Scottish army that lay before Stirling Castle, then the ensuing triumph would provide the catalyst for the resurrection of his faltering reign. Political as well as military pressures required that Edward bring the Scottish army that lay before Stirling to battle. It was an opportunity seemingly handed to Edward by Robert Bruce, and the king seized upon it with alacrity.

But this was not the only intelligence Mowbray brought. As well as imparting news of the siege and of the deadline for the castle's relief, Mowbray also informed Edward of the difficult terrain in which the Scottish army was based. Writs hurriedly issued at Newminster on 27 May announced that 'the king has received intelligence that the Scots intend to assemble in great numbers in certain strong holds and morasses, which are nearly inaccessible to cavalry, and are situate between the king and the castle of Stirling, so as to prevent the castle from being relieved'. The writs were immediately dispatched to those counties and lords that had already been requested to provide foot soldiers, the writs repeating the large totals of foot soldiers they were to raise, and commanding the lords and sheriffs to do their utmost 'to compel the levy to muster at Wark on the 10 June, ready to proceed with the king for the relief of the castle'.[18] It was only now, in late May 1314, that Stirling Castle and the besieging Scottish army became the focus of the English campaign.

Any plan of campaign that had previously existed was instantly discarded. The writs make no mention of the four thousand foot soldiers summoned from Ireland; it was immediately clear this force could not join the host in time for the advance on Stirling. If a simultaneous invasion of southwest Scotland had been planned, it was promptly abandoned. To bolster the size of the host, the bishop of Durham, Richard de Kellawe, was ordered to raise fifteen hundred foot soldiers from his Liberty of Durham. The series of writs issued hastily on 27 May summoned a total force of 21,540 foot soldiers. It was the sudden lack of time that led to the impromptu switching of the place of muster from Berwick to Wark, a change intended to place the host on an almost direct route through Lauderdale to Stirling. The campaign was suddenly invested with a sense of urgency, of real purpose. The entire English effort was now concentrated on Stirling Castle and, more pointedly, the Scottish army that lay before it.

That Edward felt compelled to issue these writs indicates that all was not going well for the English. The need to repeat those that had already been issued in March and April strongly suggests that the foot soldiers the king had summoned were not materialising in sufficient numbers. Indeed, as the writs make clear, the terrain around Stirling made it imperative that large numbers of foot soldiers should march with the host. Edward did not expect all those summoned to appear but, on the basis of previous musters, it was reasonable to expect that approximately half might. The writs and the urging of officials to do their utmost to compel the levy point to an alarmingly lethargic response. With less than a month to relieve Stirling, the assembly of foot soldiers was becoming increasingly critical.

Having delivered his sensational news, Mowbray returned to Stirling. His journey to Northumberland was presumably facilitated by a pass of safe conduct issued by either Robert or Edward Bruce, the Scottish leaders thereby adhering to the conventions of siege warfare. Despite the urgency of the situation, Edward and his household remained in Newminster. It was here that Edward appears to have been joined by Richard de Burgh, earl of Ulster, who would have been accompanied by a significant mounted retinue.[19] Small numbers of foreign troops, mainly cavalry, also joined the host. A contingent of Gascons, subjects of the English king, was almost certainly present, while a number of knights from further afield were drawn by the prospect of winning fame and renown; Baston recounted that 'four Germans joined the ranks as volunteers; I know not what more may be said of their prowess'.[20] Alongside contingents of Welsh and Irish, some Scots were also present, men of rank such as the knight Alexander Seton. Yet despite these various foreign contingents the host remained predominantly English in composition. It was an English army that Edward had summoned, and as the days passed he could do nothing but anxiously wait for an English host to assemble.

At Wark the officials appointed to supervise the muster also awaited with anxiety the arrival of several thousand foot soldiers. In the first weeks of June ragged columns of foot soldiers wearily began to troop into the appointed muster. At best they were reluctant soldiers.[21] Unsurprisingly, such men were notoriously prone to indiscipline and desertion. The Scottish campaigns of

Edward I had constantly been hindered by high rates of desertion among foot soldiers, Edward apparently leaving Stirling in Scottish hands to the rear of his army in 1303 to prevent widescale desertion. A plea roll for the campaign of 1296 reveals a wide range of crimes committed by those serving in the English host, the guilty parties being not just foot soldiers but also men-at-arms and, on occasion, knights. Nearly two hundred offences are recorded, including robbery, assault, trespass, the disobeying of orders and engaging in plunder.[22]

On the march, and theoretically in battle, the infantry was divided into units of a hundred men. Each unit was commanded by a mounted constable, with these hundreds further subdivided into groups of twenty, each of which was commanded by a *vintenar*. The weaponry of foot soldiers varied, some being in possession of spears, knives, or low-quality swords, although many would have been archers, equipped with a bow and arrows. The diversity of foot soldiers is most evident in the troops summoned from Wales, those from the north being noted for their prowess as spearmen, while those from the south were renowned as archers. In the field the crossbow was an unwieldy weapon and, despite its armour-piercing firepower, its short range dictated that the English host would only have contained a relatively small contingent of crossbowmen, such as those raised from Bristol. Among the archers, the longbowmen possessed by far the most potent weapon. In 1314 the potentially devastating firepower of the longbow had yet to gain dominance of the medieval battlefield. A measure of the fear this weapon already instilled is evident in the rumour that James Douglas either gouged out the right eye or cut off the right hand of any English archer he captured. The longbow, fashioned from yew and more than seven foot in length, was a fearsome weapon, but it required the touch of a strong and experienced archer to achieve its full potential. Indeed, it was not the longbow itself that was to prove so devastating in the later years of the century but the deployment of longbowmen in such quantities that they could produce a horrifically destructive arrow storm. A significant number of longbowmen would have been present among the host that mustered at Wark, but the English foot soldiers were far from exclusively composed of such men and it is doubtful that there were enough of them to produce the all-important arrow storm.[23]

Although the quality of foot soldiers was generally poor, they could be raised in substantial numbers. Edward I had frequently summoned large infantry arrays to serve in his Scottish campaigns. In 1298 the incredible total of twenty-six thousand foot soldiers had mustered for the Falkirk campaign, the largest single infantry concentration of his reign. The campaign of 1300 had seen the infantry peak at approximately nine thousand men, and that of 1303 at about seventy-five hundred. Experience had taught the English to expect between perhaps a half and a third of the total number of men summoned actually to appear at muster; local officials were either unable to raise the required numbers or the levies failed to arrive in time for the appointed muster. Occasionally the turn-out could be much worse; the sixteen thousand foot soldiers called out by Edward I for the unpopular winter campaign of 1299 resulted in only twenty-five hundred men arriving at muster.[24] It was in the knowledge of such low turn-out rates that Edward II called upon more than twenty-one thousand foot soldiers in 1314; calculated on the average rate of turn-out, he could reasonably have expected a force of between seven thousand and twelve thousand foot soldiers to be at his disposal at Wark. The difficulty that Edward encountered in raising the required infantry suggests that the total may well have been closer to the lower estimate.

The quality of the English host, its real offensive capability, was provided by the heavy cavalry. At the top of the hierarchy the cavalry consisted of the great magnates and lords of the realm, who were followed by their substantial personal retinues. These comprised knights, esquires and men-at-arms – men who owed a lord military service either through the land they held of him or by means of a formal indenture, whereby knights and men-at-arms received benefits such as annual fees and robes from a lord in return for remaining in his service. Most retinues contained the kinsmen and tenants of a lord, which gave them a strong degree of cohesion. It was upon these retinues that the cavalry force of an army was based.

A retinue could vary in size from a handful of men-at-arms to a troop of more than fifty knights, esquires and men-at-arms. The only retinue for which there is sufficient evidence in 1314 is that of Aymer de Valence, earl of Pembroke. An analysis of the cavalry contingent he contributed to the English host indicates that it consisted of twenty-two knights and fifty-nine men-at-arms.[25] Gilbert de Clare, earl of Gloucester, having access to a larger reservoir of manpower, would have brought a larger retinue than this, while that provided by Humphrey de Bohun, earl of Hereford, would have been on a scale comparable to that of Valence. Individual lords such as Robert Clifford would also have provided significant retinues. By far the largest cavalry contingent was formed by the bannerets, knights and sergeants-at-arms of the royal household. These men received fees and robes from the king, and directly owed him their service. The size of the royal household force fluctuated, but in 1314–15 it contained the substantial total of thirty-two bannerets and eighty-nine knights.[26] In turn, these bannerets and knights could call upon their own personal retinues, and the troops of the royal household consequently provided the nucleus of a substantial mounted force.

In terms of training and equipment, the cavalry possessed quality in abundance. Bannerets, knights and esquires were immersed in the skills of the warrior from an early age, spending long hours in the saddle and being taught the art of combat with both lance and sword, abilities that were further honed in warfare and in the lists of tournaments. On average a quarter of an English cavalry force was composed of bannerets and knights; the real backbone of the cavalry was provided by the men-at-arms. By 1314 many English men-at-arms were effectively professional soldiers. Most were men of little means, the wage they received for military service barely sufficient for their daily subsistence, but the campaigns and garrisons of the Scottish wars had provided them with ample employment. Many were veterans of more than a decade of front-line military service. They were combat-hardened troops who knew how to fight.

The quality of armour that a cavalryman possessed was dependent upon his wealth. The king and his most affluent knights would have owned expensive pieces of heavy plate armour, including a breastplate and backplate, greaves to protect the legs, a gorget to guard the neck, and metal gauntlets. Most would have combined elements of plate armour with the protection afforded by the more widely available armour of chainmail, wearing either a long mail coat, a hauberk, or a shorter mail coat known as a habergeon; the armour of most men-at-arms consisted of either a hauberk or a habergeon. The sleeves of the more expensive chainmail coats might also include mail mittens. A cheaper form of protection was a thick leather coat known as a haketon, the leather in some cases being reinforced with chainmail. Armour could also take the form of the more inexpensive alternative of boiled and hardened leather, known as *cuir bouilli*, which, when dry, became rock hard. To protect the head, the thirteenth-century great-helm remained popular with knights, its all-encompassing metal confines providing complete protection against all but the strongest of blows; the only openings were two slits for the eyes and ventilation slits for the mouth. The bacinet, a much lighter helmet fashioned of chainmail, was worn by the majority of the cavalry, the more sophisticated versions including a movable visor to protect the face. To ward off blows, the cavalry were armed with relatively small, triangular-shaped shields, which had a flat top edge; the shield faces of the more prosperous knights and esquires were decorated to display vividly their familial coat of arms.[27]

Although the range of armour was diverse, the weapons used by cavalry rarely varied from the lance and the sword. The lance shaft was fashioned from ash and was approximately fourteen foot in length, its iron head razor-sharp. Carried into battle held in the vertical position, it was levelled for the moment of charge. It was the cavalry charge, the thunderous impact of several thousand heavily armoured horsemen, which was the most feared phenomenon on the early fourteenth-century battlefield. A successful charge was invested with such raw power that it had the potential to break an enemy and win a battle. To be part of a mass cavalry charge was for many knights their *raison d'être*. During a charge, lances were frequently destroyed upon impact and swords would then immediately be drawn. The most popular swords of the period were large, heavy-bladed weapons, yet light enough to be wielded effectively in one hand. Battleaxes, maces and war-hammers were also carried into battle. However, the most expensive item a cavalryman owned was his horse. Only the richest knights could afford a great warhorse, a destrier, a powerful beast bred purely for combat; the cost of a warhorse was the equivalent of a small fortune.[28] As with armour, the quality of horseflesh was dependent upon the wealth of the knight or man-at-arms and could vary greatly. Many horses were fitted with protective padding, while those of the great magnates and lords were proudly covered with brightly coloured cloth trappers, their coats of arms emblazoned vividly upon them. The brutal business of war was also an opportunity for such men to gain honour and renown.

Similarly, wealth and status dictated those appointed to positions of command. The king was effectively commander-in-chief of the host and the earls his divisional commanders. In preparation for battle, the cavalry was conventionally split into three divisions, or battles, which consisted of a vanguard, a middle-guard and a rearguard. In 1314 Edward commanded the latter, the vastly experienced Valence and Giles d'Argentan by his side. The king appointed Gloucester and Hereford as joint commanders of the vanguard. The middle-guard was commanded by the veteran campaigner Robert Clifford. Chronicle accounts depict the division commanded by Clifford as consisting of three hundred heavy cavalry, while the vanguard and the rearguard both appear to have comprised approximately five hundred men. If these figures are to be accepted then the English cavalry consisted of approximately thirteen hundred men. The *Vita* claims that the host in total contained more than two thousand heavy cavalry, whereas Barbour believed the English had three thousand heavy cavalry at their disposal.[29] The absence of the earls of Lancaster, Warwick, Arundel and Warenne would certainly have had a detrimental impact on the number of cavalry Edward could raise; the retinue that Lancaster brought to the siege of Berwick in 1319 was possibly five hundred strong. In 1314 these four earls together may have contributed no more than sixty cavalrymen. Four years earlier, when Valence had refused to participate in the 1310 campaign, the military service he was obliged to provide consisted of only ten men. In 1298 the great army assembled for the Falkirk campaign had contained a cavalry force of approximately three thousand men; the force assembled in 1314 was certainly smaller than this.[30] A sensible estimate would place the number of heavy cavalry taken by Edward II into Scotland in 1314 at somewhere between thirteen hundred and two thousand.

In the first weeks of June, however, it was the infantry that still troubled Edward. Despite the approaching deadline for the relief of Stirling, he had little option but to wait until more foot soldiers arrived at muster. Edward and his household remained in Newminster as late as 5 June before moving the short distance north to Berwick.[31] The large garrison of the fortress town may well have been plundered for foot soldiers. At Wark the marshal and the constable of the host frenetically set about organising the infantry and cavalry forces which drifted in to the appointed muster. If news of the prospect of a battle fuelled the martial ambitions of knights and men-at-arms, then the common foot soldiers undoubtedly greeted the prospect with horror; they had little to gain from battle and everything to lose.

On 17 June the host finally entered Scotland. That an entire week had passed since the appointed date of muster is indicative of the poor turnout of foot soldiers. But Edward could not postpone the advance indefinitely. The deadline for the relief of Stirling was rapidly approaching. He could not pass up such a glorious chance of battle. At Wark men and horses forded the Tweed. Edward and his household rode out from the safety of the walls of Berwick. Edinburgh lay forty miles away; Stirling Castle was seventy miles off. The two components of the host joined up as they progressed through Lauderdale towards Edinburgh. The host was in Scotland; the advance on Stirling had begun.

The total size of the English host can only be guessed at. If it numbered at the lowest estimate thirteen hundred heavy cavalry and seven thousand foot soldiers, it still remained a formidable force; it may have been appreciably larger, but perhaps not more than two thousand cavalry and twelve thousand foot soldiers. It was certainly the most substantial army Edward II had ever commanded as king. The powerful host that advanced through the Borders was by far the gravest threat to have confronted Robert Bruce since his return to Scotland in 1307. The English host certainly presented a magnificent spectacle. Barbour dramatically recounts that the host was 'so huge it was fearsome' and its troops so numerous 'that it seemed indeed that in a fight they would vanquish the whole world'. The author of the *Vita* was similarly impressed, believing the host to be 'quite sufficient to penetrate the whole of Scotland, and some thought if the whole strength of Scotland had been gathered together, they would not have stayed to face the king's army. Indeed all who were present agreed that never in our time has such an army gone forth from England.' The baggage train in particular was enormously impressive, the *Vita* commenting that 'the multitude of wagons, if they had been placed end on end, would have taken up a space of twenty leagues'. Barbour provides a lavish description of carts loaded with various pieces of equipment including 'tents, plate and furnishing for chamber and hall, wine, wax, shot and provisions, eight score were loaded with poultry'. The host was certainly a 'splendid and numerous army' and was so large that, as it advanced, its sprawling mass 'covered both hills and valleys'. Lit by the sun, 'the whole land was aflame with banners'.[32]

For Edward, though, the voluminous baggage train was a frustrating hindrance, which, together with the infantry, slowed the pace of the advance. Time was increasingly short. If the host was to reach Stirling before 24 June and engage Bruce and his Scottish army before the castle, then speed was of the essence. The weather was unusually hot and the relentless pace that Edward set took its toll. The *Vita*, in an observation heavy with hindsight, recounts critically that Edward 'took confidence from so great and so distinguished a multitude and hastened day by day to the appointed place, not as if he was leading an army into battle but as if he was going to St James's. Brief were the halts for sleep, briefer still for food.'[33] In fact, the pace was dictated by the need to reach Stirling before the expiry of the deadline, the slow accumulation of infantry having delayed the host entering Scotland. Yet in the weeks preceding the campaign, Edward had failed to observe the long-established ritual of visiting the shrines of saints in northern England, and giving prayers and offerings for the success of his enterprise. Nor did Edward ceremoniously take the banners of renowned northern saints St Cuthbert and St John of Beverley from their shrines to accompany his army. The presence of such banners would have had an enormous spiritual effect on troops about to go to war. In failing to acquire them, Edward unaccountably missed an opportunity to boost the morale of his army considerably.[34]

To find himself leading such a formidable army after seven long years of bitter domestic turmoil must have imbued the king with an intoxicating sense of power and purpose. He could have been excused if he believed his time had eventually come. He had raised an army; he had led it into Scotland; the prospect of battle was tantalisingly close. If he could engage the Scots in battle, victory, he believed, was assured. It was a victory that had the potential to cure all the ills of his reign. The defeat of Robert Bruce and the Scots promised the resurrection of his kingship.

On 19 June, two days after entering Scotland, the vanguard of the host reached Edinburgh. Here, beneath the forlorn shadow of the ruined castle, the army rested for two days as it received victuals from the supply fleet that docked at the port of Leith. It was not until 22 June, only two days before the deadline for the relief of Stirling, that the host moved on. By nightfall it had covered the twenty miles to Falkirk. Stirling lay fourteen miles away. Only one full day remained. At daybreak on Sunday 23 June, the host struck camp and began its final advance on Stirling Castle. It was also advancing straight into a trap.

CHAPTER TEN

BAITING THE TRAP

Early on the morning of Sunday 23 June, Robert Bruce ordered James Douglas and Robert Keith to undertake a reconnaissance of the English host. It was known that the English had spent the night at Falkirk. Anxious for accurate information on the English host as it approached, Bruce wanted a detailed report. It was an intelligence-gathering operation of such importance that it was entrusted to two of his most senior commanders. Riding south with a small contingent, Douglas and Keith soon came across their enemy. The English army was indeed a breathtakingly awesome sight; even from a distance its formidable strength was evident. Disturbed by what they had seen, Douglas and Keith immediately returned to Bruce. In secrecy they told him of the size and power of the host. The response of Bruce was simple: he told them to lie. Douglas and Keith were to spread the word among the Scots that the English advanced in poor order.[1] The two commanders did as they were told, but it must have been obvious to them that Bruce was playing an extraordinarily dangerous game.

No one would have understood this better than Robert Bruce. Although he could conceal the harsh truth from others, he could not hide it from himself. The political situation in Scotland dictated that he could not take the most prudent military option of withdrawing from Stirling Castle before the arrival of the English host; such a withdrawal would damage the authority grounded on military success by which he claimed to hold the Crown. An immediate withdrawal would be interpreted as a sign of weakness, yet to remain and engage the English in battle would almost certainly result in defeat. Locked in this dilemma, Bruce recognised that his only option was to chart a course between the harsh political and military realities by which he was confined.

His priority, however, lay in gathering an army. From the moment Bruce learnt of the agreement for the relief of Stirling Castle, the raising of an army had become essential. It was clear that as soon as the English knew of the deadline, the host would be directed to the relief of the castle. Mowbray had been permitted to take news of the agreement to Edward II in late May, and Bruce would have been painfully aware of the subsequent build-up of troops at Wark. If the English king despaired at the lack of foot soldiers, then this fitful turnout was of scant consolation to Bruce. The infantry force that assembled at Wark was of a size Bruce could not hope to match. Indeed, while Edward was encountering difficulties in England, Bruce was beset with his own intractable problems in Scotland.

Dominant though Bruce was, Scotland remained a divided country. The proclamation of perpetual disinheritance that he had issued in late 1313 to those Scots resisting his kingship had been an attempt to consolidate his position by delivering a blunt ultimatum which he hoped would bring the Scottish civil war to a head. Yet the fact that such a measure was necessary is ample proof of the fracture lines that still divided the political landscape of Scotland. Bruce may have beaten and subdued his domestic opponents, but he had not gained their full support. In the former enclaves of his enemies, in regions such as Galloway and Argyll, Bruce could hardly have expected to gain unqualified military backing, while in the north the lordship of Buchan was unlikely to have provided a fertile recruiting ground for the man who had overseen its brutal devastation. To raise an army Bruce was reliant upon the backing of the chief lords of the realm, men who could call upon the military service of the retainers and tenants of their lordships. Yet Bruce still only commanded the allegiance of a handful of the leading men of the Scottish realm.

Of the three earls whose support he did have, two had been raised to their positions by Bruce himself. Edward Bruce, previously the lord of Galloway, had now been granted his brother's former title of earl of Carrick. In northern Scotland the territories of Bruce's defeated opponents had been appropriated and reapportioned to create the earldom of Moray, the title being bestowed upon his nephew, Thomas Randolph.[2] Indeed, of the traditional earls of Scotland, Bruce only enjoyed the support of David of Strathbogie, earl of Atholl, who had returned to Bruce's allegiance following his defection in the desperate days of early 1307. Below those of comital rank,

Bruce could count upon the support of a number of prominent lords. Robert Keith, the marischal of Scotland, was firmly in the allegiance of Bruce, as was the young Walter Stewart, a 'beardless lad' who most probably was still in his teens, while the presence of the bellicose James Douglas was as potent as ever. Although Barbour claims that Bruce had at his disposal the military service of 'many other barons and knights of great repute' their number was in reality limited.[3] In attempting to raise an army, Bruce's problems were further exacerbated by his inability to call upon an all-encompassing Scottish feudal summons, a system that had fallen into disrepair and been further damaged by the bitter civil war. Despite Bruce's best efforts, it would quickly have become apparent to him that his delicate political position precluded him from summoning the full military strength of the Scottish realm.

There was, however, a greater sentiment to which Bruce could appeal. If he could not raise Scots to fight for him as king, then he could exhort them to fight for Scottish independence. It was with this exhortation that Bruce could draw upon a greater reservoir of manpower. Although his authority as king remained tenuous, the underlying strength of Bruce's political position was that, due to his military success in the Scottish civil war, his Scottish enemies had been forced either to join him or fight alongside the English. By 1314 his Scottish enemies relied on the English to continue their war against Bruce. The military successes of Bruce in Scotland had increasingly led him to fight against occupying English forces; the objectives of the civil war in which Bruce was engaged and the national war against the English had begun to merge inextricably. As the weight of the Scottish civil war shifted south of the Tay, the struggle of Bruce forcibly to exert his authority as king increasingly became tied to the fight for Scottish independence. As the objectives of the two conflicts became the same, so Bruce began to acquire the political power inherent in the cause of independence.

Any popular support enjoyed by Bruce originated from the ability to identify him with the cause of Scottish independence.[4] Bruce wanted to consolidate his hold on the Crown, he wanted to be recognised as king, and it was in the figure of such a king that the salvation of an independent Scottish kingdom lay. As these two causes gradually coincided, so the community of the realm gained their desired figurehead of a Scottish king and Bruce gained access to by far the most powerful attribute of the community – manpower.

The size of the Scottish army that mustered to the south of Stirling in the Torwood will never be known. Apart from a force of five hundred light cavalry commanded by Robert Keith, there is a complete absence of information on the numbers and composition of the army. Various attempts have been made to estimate its size, the most notable being a calculation based on the overall Scottish population, while another was founded on the inference of Barbour that the Scottish army was a third of the size of the English host.[5] All that can be said for certain is that the army assembled by Bruce was significantly outnumbered by the English. In all likelihood the Scots would have totalled several thousand men. The only credible contemporary source that provides a general idea of the number of troops under Bruce's command at any one time is the letter written by the earl of Ross in 1308, which alleged that the earl's force of three thousand men was inadequate to oppose Bruce; however, even this figure seems substantially inflated.[6] By 1314 the successes of Bruce would undoubtedly have bolstered recruitment, and a general consensus has been reached that the Scottish army that mustered in the Torwood consisted of a total of approximately forty-five hundred to six thousand men. It would certainly not have been much larger.

In terms of diversity the Scottish army was even more complex than the disparate foot soldiers of the English host. Early fourteenth-century Scotland was a country of cultural contrasts.[7] To the south and east of Scotland, in the Scottish Lowlands, Borders and in the major towns, an implanted Anglo-Norman feudal society was the dominant social force. This feudal society was originally centred on the royal household of the Scottish kings and found its most popular expression in the widely spoken language of French or northern English, the latter being the forerunner of the distinctive language of Scots. In contrast, the western and northern regions of Scotland remained overtly Celtic in character, an ancient society imbued with age-old customs which was heavily dependent on families and clans, and which spoke the Gaelic language. This divide, however, was far from clear-cut. Gaelic was still widely spoken throughout Scotland. In the predominantly Celtic west the Bruce lordship of Annandale was essentially an Anglo-Norman feudal lordship, the Bruces themselves being lords of Anglo-Norman extraction, while the earldom of Carrick, another Bruce possession, was a heavily Celtic region. In the coexistence of this rich blend of cultures, the concept of a homogeneous Scottish kingdom had gradually taken root. Although Bruce and his lieutenants could almost certainly speak Gaelic, the sheer diversity of the regions from which their troops came can only have exacerbated the problem of creating a cohesive and coordinated army.

There is little firm evidence for the regions that contributed the men. Barbour recounts that the division commanded by Robert Bruce included 'all the men of Carrick, of Argyll and Kintyre, and of the Isles . . . he also had a great host of armed men from the Lowlands'.[8] This division in itself was consequently extremely varied, with men from western, predominantly Celtic regions, fighting alongside those from the largely feudalised, Anglo-Norman Lowlands. Thomas Randolph, earl of Moray, presumably commanded those men who came to the army from the northernmost reaches of Scotland, while Edward Bruce would have led those from the southwest, including any troops raised in the Celtic region of Galloway. Individual lords such as James Douglas and Walter Stewart would have brought their own following from the lands of their lordships.

The army that assembled in the Torwood would consequently have had a disorientating amalgam of dialect and language, and a mixture of ancient Celtic and imported Anglo-Norman feudal customs. However, crucially, this disparate body of men was unified against the common enemy of England. Another unifying characteristic was that, apart from the contingent of light cavalry, the Scottish army was composed exclusively of foot soldiers. The rugged landscape of Scotland did not lend itself to the breeding and keeping of large numbers of horses, and this precluded the widespread adoption of the great warhorse, the destrier. This lack of heavy cavalry was also partly the product of the Scottish feudal system which, where it existed, was less developed than its English equivalent. Scottish knights were far fewer in number than their English counterparts and generally were in possession of less wealth and fewer resources.[9] The Scottish army at Bannockburn was overwhelmingly an infantry army and had no option but to fight on foot.

The common foot soldiers of the Scottish army, though varied in culture and appearance, fought with the same weapons. In contrast to the English infantry, only a relatively small proportion would have been archers, the vast majority being armed with long, iron-tipped spears, and with an assortment of knives, axes and swords. Considering the diversity of the force and its hasty summons, it is logical to assume that, like the English foot soldiers, its equipment was at best patchy. Yet, curiously, Barbour recounts that many among the Scottish army were 'well armed and equipped', while the *Vita*, in commenting on the Scottish foot soldiers, claimed that 'each was furnished with light armour, not easily penetrable by sword'.[10] It remains doubtful whether the entire Scottish army was as well equipped as these statements suggest. Bruce had gained substantial sums from the raiding of northern England, money that had been used to trade in arms which were shipped into Scotland mainly through the port of Aberdeen. It is certainly feasible that a proportion of the army was well equipped, presumably receiving the armour, which would most likely have taken the form of a leather haketon, upon their arrival in the Torwood. An English illustration of Scottish troops in 1316 depicts them wearing bacinets and carrying wicker shields, a further indication that an element of the army that fought at Bannockburn might well have possessed some form of armoured protection. If so, most probably the troops wearing armour were those who were to form the foremost ranks of the Scottish force.[11] The ability of the Scottish foot soldiers to withstand the enemy in battle was further strengthened by the presence of chainmail-clad knights and men-at-arms who would stand and fight among their ranks.

The greatest strength of the Scottish army was not to be found in its material possessions, however, but in its morale. Bruce was careful to nurture his troops, making a deliberate point of meeting the various contingents as they arrived in the Torwood where he 'welcomed them with cheerful countenance, saying the right words here and there'.[12] The real source of the army's morale was provided by the core of experienced troops at its heart, veterans of the bitter campaigns waged by Bruce and his commanders against both his Scottish enemies and the English. Among the army that mustered in the Torwood would have been men who had marched north through the Great Glen, who had seized castles along the coastline of the Moray Firth, who had prepared for battle at Inverurie, who had wrought devastation upon Buchan and fought at Ben Cruachan. There were seasoned troops present who had waded into the moat beside Bruce and taken Perth, who had stormed Roxburgh with Douglas and seized Edinburgh with Randolph, men who had fought in Galloway under Edward Bruce and had been present in the siege lines before the castles of Edinburgh and Stirling. There would also have been a handful of survivors from the dark years of 1306 and 1307, veterans of the desperate engagements of Methven and Loch Tay and Dalry, men who had subsequently clashed with English forces at Glen Trool and Loudoun Hill.

In 1314 the morale of these veterans was exceptionally high. For several years they had not suffered a serious reverse. They were on the crest of an incredible wave of success, and had just achieved the amazing feat of capturing and destroying Roxburgh and Edinburgh, two of the most formidable castles in Scotland. It was upon the foundation of this core of experienced and enthusiastic troops that Bruce would have attempted to create a cohesive army from the diverse contingents that arrived at muster. The tight control that Bruce had exercised over Scottish forces during the raiding of northern England demonstrates the discipline he was able to instil into troops who were notoriously unruly. In the Torwood his ability to enforce discipline would have been tested to the limit as he attempted to exert authority over such a diverse body of men. The size of the force Bruce commanded was by far the largest single concentration of troops he had ever had at his disposal. Nor did his commanders possess experience in exercising control over such numbers. The muster, equipping and preparation of such an army undoubtedly proved a great challenge for Bruce and his chief lieutenants.

Never before had they needed to assemble such an army. Following their initial campaigns in the north of Scotland, their successes gained against the English had been achieved by irregular warfare, by engaging in ambuscades, raids and assaults, and by the implementation of a strategy in which battle was deliberately avoided. This 'secret warfare' did not require a large concentration of troops, but rather a number of much smaller, mobile units, able to strike the enemy and quickly withdraw. The raids into England had been conducted by forces limited enough to remain mobile and elusive. The closest Bruce and his lieutenants had come to supervising large numbers of troops was in the preceding months when they had commanded the forces besieging the castles of Edinburgh and Stirling. It would not have been lost on Bruce that the veterans of his army were men experienced in irregular warfare. Few had experience of serving in an army or of engaging in a set-piece battle. This was also true of Bruce and his commanders. The fleeting rout at Methven, the tentative skirmishes at Glen Trool and Loudoun Hill, the frantic engagement at Ben Cruachan and the two vicious encounters that Edward Bruce had fought in Galloway, such was the sum of their experience. These were far from being set-piece battles, and on none of these occasions had those in command led a force large enough to merit the description of an army. Bruce and his lieutenants must have recognised that this gaping void in their experience posed a severe problem.

No time was wasted in attempting to rectify this deficit. The delayed arrival of the English host provided Bruce with an opportunity to instil an element of order and discipline into the diverse Scottish army. A level of rudimentary training was also provided, a course of hasty instruction in which battle tactics would have featured heavily.[13] Although Bruce had no intention of engaging in a set-piece battle, he was cautious enough to prepare his army for such an eventuality. The battle tactics in which the Scottish army was instructed would essentially have encompassed one single theme: the tactical formation known as the schiltrom. Should a set-piece battle take place, then the schiltrom was the only means by which the Scottish infantry could hope to counter the heavy cavalry of the English. The schiltrom itself was a brutally simple formation, consisting of a tightly packed, dense mass of foot soldiers, the front ranks of which presented a vicious forest of spears to an oncoming enemy. Its strength derived from the density of manpower contained within it, a heaving crowd of men pressed so close together that it had the physical potential to absorb the thunderous impact of a full-blooded cavalry charge. Those in the front ranks were horrifically exposed, but the sheer volume of men contained within enabled the schiltrom to suffer significant casualties without the formation being broken.

Yet the strength of a schiltrom was also its greatest weakness. Such a densely packed mass of men was extremely unwieldy and difficult to control. In the field it was a dreadfully cumbersome unit. For this reason it was essentially employed as a static, defensive formation, being firmly rooted to the same piece of ground throughout an engagement. At Falkirk, in 1298, William Wallace had formed the Scottish army he commanded into four separate schiltroms; each took the form of a rough circle, spears projecting outwards to provide all-round protection. Wallace had attempted to anchor these formations down by surrounding each schiltrom with a rope tied to stakes hammered into the ground. These circular masses had withstood incessant English cavalry attacks for a considerable period of time until, at length, they were eventually prised apart, broken by the missile fire of English foot soldiers who unleashed a hail of arrows and stones upon the Scots. The slaughter that followed was a horrific demonstration of the gruesome fate that awaited the troops of a broken schiltrom when assaulted by heavy cavalry. By its very nature the schiltrom was essentially a defensive formation when employed against cavalry, its purpose being to blunt the attacks of the enemy and gradually wear them down in a prolonged battle of attrition, an objective that could be achieved by either physically exhausting the enemy or by inducing them to abandon the engagement out of sheer frustration. If a battle should take place before Stirling, then the ability to form a schiltrom and hold a defensive formation under heavy attack was the only means by which the Scots had the slightest chance of avoiding defeat. Bruce and his lieutenants, therefore, would have trained the army that assembled in the Torwood in the techniques of the schiltrom.

The limitations of such formations make abundantly clear the disparity between foot soldiers and cavalry, between the capabilities of the Scottish army and the English host. Well mounted, well equipped and heavily armoured, the knights and men-at-arms of the English cavalry comprised a powerful mobile offensive force, their primary role being to seek out and attack the enemy. The cavalry could deliver a devastating charge and relentlessly pursue a defeated enemy. As the elite troops of the age, the heavy cavalry of knights and men-at-arms believed themselves to be infinitely superior on the field of battle when confronted by infantry. The Scots, devoid of even the slightest contingent of heavy cavalry, were at an enormous disadvantage. In battle they would have to fight on the defensive; they did not have the means to take the fight to the English. Yet, despite these limitations, a well disciplined infantry force, formed into a tight and dense formation, and tactically fighting on the defensive, could hold its own against heavy cavalry. As the English had found at Falkirk in 1298, heavy cavalry alone could not break a determined schiltrom. At Falkirk it was the missile fire of archers that had ultimately broken the Scottish formations and allowed the English cavalry to wreak carnage.[14] Against a skilful combination of archery fire delivered by English infantry, and the subsequent charge of English heavy cavalry, the Scottish army assembled by Bruce would almost certainly be slaughtered should it engage in battle. Indeed, the Scottish foot soldiers did not even enjoy an advantage over their English counterparts in terms of numbers, the entire Scottish army being comprehensively outnumbered by the English infantry alone. In this respect the significant shortfall in English heavy cavalry caused by the absence of the four English earls was of little comfort to the Scots. Even without the participation of these earls and their retinues, the Scottish army was dwarfed in size by the English host.

Nor would the political conflict that had destabilised England necessarily affect the host. When Edward I had embarked upon the Falkirk campaign he was in the midst of the worst political crisis of his reign, yet victory had still been achieved. Neither could the apparent inadequacies of Edward II as a military commander be relied upon by the Scots to weaken the host. At Edward's side rode Aymer de Valence, veteran of Falkirk, victor of Methven, commander of the English forces that had clashed with Bruce at Glen Trool and Loudoun Hill. The presence of Humphrey de Bohun, earl of Hereford, provided Edward with another high-ranking commander who, in his youth, before he inherited his earldom, had fought at Falkirk. The English high command also comprised another two veterans of Falkirk in the experienced figures of Robert Clifford and Henry de Beaumont. Between them these four lords provided a wealth of knowledge of combat and of command in the field. Crucially, all four had been at Falkirk in 1298, the last major set-piece battle the English had fought. The Scots were outmatched not only in terms of numbers, heavy cavalry and equipment but also in terms of commanders experienced in battle. Should a battle be fought, the English host enjoyed almost every advantage.

Yet recent history did provide one startling event that questioned the assumption of an English victory. In 1302, at Courtrai, urban levies of Flemish foot soldiers had achieved the impossible and routed a substantial force of French knights and men-at-arms, troops rated the best heavy cavalry in Europe. It was a victory of such magnitude that the shock of it reverberated throughout Christendom. The Flemings had arrayed their spearmen in a closely packed formation fronted by an expanse of broken and boggy ground. When an initial attack by French infantry had failed to dislodge the Flemings, the French cavalry had charged, their momentum being disrupted by their own scattered infantry and the treacherous ground. Becoming stranded, they had been slaughtered by the Flemings. The English had revelled in the unexpected defeat of their longstanding enemy, a defeat that had also led to the collapse of the Franco-Scottish alliance; a popular song had been composed in England to honour the victory and, more pointedly, to mock the French.[15] That the English did not read a warning into the battle of Courtrai should not be judged as a failing; it was the unquestioned belief that the French cavalry should easily have beaten the Flemings which led to such popular derision. Courtrai was widely regarded as a singular event which would never be repeated.

Indeed, the assumption that heavy cavalry remained all-powerful was ingrained in the very structure of medieval society, the dominance of the mounted elite being social as well as military in nature, the figure of the landed knight acting as the lynchpin of feudal society. This preeminence was founded on the claim of knights that they were a warrior caste. To believe they were vulnerable to lowly foot soldiers was to question the very foundations of society. Courtrai was consequently dismissed as an unnatural event, a belief reinforced by the much better showing of French heavy cavalry against Flemish foot soldiers two years later at Mons-en-Pévèle.[16] Thomas Gray, in an observation loaded with hindsight, claimed that Bruce took to the field at Bannockburn with Courtrai very much in mind, commenting that the English cavalry 'were not at all used to dismounting to fight on foot, while the Scots had taken the example of the Flemings, who had previously defeated on foot the forces of France, at Courtrai'.[17] This is clearly a corruption of the facts; the Scottish army, consisting of only five hundred light cavalry and lacking any heavy cavalry, had no option but to fight almost exclusively on foot. In the anxious weeks leading up to the deadline for the relief of Stirling, the battle of Courtrai would not have figured prominently in the mind of Robert Bruce. His objective was not to engage in battle, but to do everything he could to avoid it.

The training the Scottish army received was to prepare it for the worst, for the eventuality of a set-piece battle; the strategy Bruce adopted was intended to minimise the chances of such an engagement. Political pressures dictated that he must make a show of opposing the English before Stirling; military realities dictated that he must achieve this without becoming embroiled in full-scale confrontation. This was the awful predicament Bruce faced from the moment the conditional surrender of Stirling had been agreed. The English had less than a month to relieve the castle so Bruce only had a few weeks in which to formulate a strategy that could accomplish the disparate political and military imperatives under which he laboured. It is a measure of his intellect that he could identify these two conflicting imperatives; it is a measure of his abilities as a military tactician that he developed an effective plan.

His greatest ally was the difficult terrain to the south of Stirling through which the English would have to advance.[18] Two roads ran north to Stirling. The easternmost, the high road covering the fourteen miles between Falkirk and Stirling, was encumbered by two major obstacles. To the south it passed through the point of muster for the Scottish army, the Torwood. This was a large tract of ancient woodland, its interior heavily canopied in the height of midsummer and providing a darkened, almost impenetrable entanglement of trees; it was also littered with outcrops of rock. It was through the heart of the Torwood that this road passed before emerging on relatively open ground to the north of the Tor Burn and continuing towards Stirling in a northwesterly direction. After crossing the Bannock Burn it skirted the eastern fringe of the New Park, the second major obstacle on its path. The New Park was a hunting preserve created by Alexander III in the 1260s and took the form of a compact wooded enclosure. Although smaller than the Torwood, the New Park was also heavily wooded and lay just two miles south of Stirling Castle. The second road that led north to Stirling ran to the west of the Torwood, but plunged straight through the eastern side of the New Park. The two roads joined at the northeastern fringe of the New Park, just below the kirk of St Ninians, before covering the last couple of miles to the castle. To the north of the Torwood an old track of Roman origin linked these two routes north.

These roads provided the only means of approach for a large army. Further away to the west, beyond the westernmost road, a slope of rising, broken ground gradually ascended as it progressed further inland; to the east the ground sloped downwards, dropping down a ridge beyond the eastern road and flattening out into a vast expanse of waterlogged carseland. This was a patchwork of bogs interlaced with slow-flowing streams, or *polles* (*pows*), which stretched away eastwards to the tidal course of the Forth. Although in places the ground was dry, the carseland consisted mainly of soft clay and peat. The easternmost road, though on higher ground, passed perilously close to this treacherous carseland; the road to the west was bordered by the rising, broken ground. The line of advance for an army approaching Stirling was consequently restricted to these two roads, one of which ran through the Torwood and the other through the New Park. It was this difficult terrain that Bruce sought to turn to his advantage.

Although the muster of the Scottish army took place in the Torwood, this was not where Bruce intended to make his stand. On Saturday 22 June, having been informed by his scouts that the English host had spent the night at Edinburgh, Bruce ordered his army to decamp from the Torwood and take up a new position further north in the New Park. He instructed a company of men to dig a cavalry trap 'in an open field beside the road, where he thought the Englishmen would have to go if they wanted to move through the Park to the castle'.[19] The precise location of this trap remains unknown. Traditionally, its site has been placed in the immediate vicinity of the New Park, further narrowing the bottleneck through which the English would have to pass. This makes perfect sense and is reminiscent of the trap Bruce employed at Loudoun Hill, his intention then being to break up the cavalry and engage them in smaller, more isolated groups. A more recent analysis proposes that the trap was located further to the south, on the road that ran to the west of the Torwood, the intention being to cut off this route.[20] The trap itself was much more vicious than that constructed at Loudoun, consisting of a honeycomb of holes, each of a foot in diameter and 'as deep as a man's knee', the bottom of each hole being set with a sharpened wooden stake. The Scots worked into the night fashioning this trap, carefully concealing it beneath a layer of sticks and grass. The Carmelite friar and poet Robert Baston was clearly not exaggerating when he described it as 'a contrivance full of evils'.[21]

To further hinder the advance of the English, Bruce also ordered 'the narrow paths through the wood' to be dug up.[22] This ambiguous statement could refer either to the New Park or the Torwood, although the impression of several narrow paths being dug up suggests the larger expanse of the Torwood, an opinion supported by Thomas Gray who referred to it as 'the wood' rather than 'the park'. If the road through the New Park was protected by the cavalry trap, then it was logical for the road that ran through the Torwood also to have been subjected to the attentions of the Scots. By digging up the paths, whether in the Torwood or the New Park, the objective of Bruce was to slow and frustrate the English advance. The means by which Bruce intended to make a show of opposing the English host before Stirling was beginning to take shape.

Shortly after sunrise on Sunday 23 June the Scottish army gathered for the saying of mass. As it was the vigil of the feast of St John the Baptist, they breakfasted on bread and water. It was known that the English had passed the night at Falkirk. Fewer than fourteen miles now separated the two armies. The deadline for the relief of Stirling Castle was due to expire the following day. No one would have felt the mounting tension more keenly than Robert Bruce himself. Having sent Douglas and Keith out to reconnoitre the host, Bruce inspected the cavalry trap that had been completed the previous night.[23] Satisfied with the work, he set about making his final dispositions in preparation for the imminent arrival of the English host.

The 'small folk and carters' were instructed to take the baggage of the Scottish army and move 'a good way away' from the New Park. According to Barbour, this ramshackle body of men positioned themselves in a nearby valley, most probably in the vicinity of Coxet Hill or Gillies Hill, where they would remain hidden from the English. The presence of a Scottish baggage train illustrates the thorough preparations that underpinned the maintenance of the army, as does the existence of a supply base on the north bank of the Forth in the stone buildings of Cambuskenneth Abbey.[24] Evidently a great deal of thought and effort had gone into the raising and maintenance of the Scottish army, and it was with a similar degree of deliberation that Bruce now deployed his fighting forces.

The force was split into three large divisions. Calculated on the basis that the army numbered between forty-five hundred and six thousand troops, each division would have contained approximately fifteen hundred to two thousand men; if a schiltrom was to be formed, then any division larger than this would be almost impossible to command. Alongside the mass of foot soldiers that comprised these divisions there also stood knights and men-at-arms. They too would fight on foot. The divisional commanders would also engage the enemy on foot. Robert Bruce commanded the rearguard, Thomas Randolph the vanguard and Edward Bruce the middle-guard. The presence of a fourth Scottish division, commanded by James Douglas and Walter Stewart, appears to be a creation of Barbour; its existence is not supported by any other source nor does it fit with the conventional system of dividing an army into three divisions. Douglas was almost certainly in charge of a contingent of light cavalry, part of the five-hundred strong force commanded by the marischal, Robert Keith. The rearguard under Robert Bruce remained in the New Park, deployed among the trees at the southern 'entry' where the westernmost road ran into the park. The division commanded by Edward Bruce and the light cavalry under Robert Keith were in close attendance.[25]

The position of the vanguard is more problematic. Bruce instructed Randolph 'to keep the road beside the kirk' and thereby prevent the English from reaching the beleaguered castle should they attempt a flanking manoeuvre across the broken ground to the east bordering the carseland. The kirk has traditionally been recognised as St Ninians, an identification that places the vanguard on the northeastern fringe of the New Park less than two miles from the castle. Yet such a position raises an immediate problem. If the vanguard was deployed here, then it was placed to the rear of the rearguard and, indeed, to the rear of the entire Scottish army. Not only does this awkwardly invert the formation of the whole army, but it also contradicts the tactics Bruce intended to adopt. If all three divisions were concentrated in the New Park, then the English could advance from Falkirk towards the castle with relative ease. An English approach along the easternmost road would avoid the wooded interior of the New Park and force the Scots to confront the host on relatively open ground, the very situation Bruce was determined to avoid. To concentrate the entire Scottish army in the vicinity of the New Park was tantamount to courting battle. A more recent suggestion has placed the vanguard further to the south, in the Torwood, the original place of muster.[26] This makes good sense. A division in the Torwood could hinder any English advance, it could exploit the dug-up paths and it was afforded considerable protection by the large, almost impenetrable expanse of rough woodland. It would slow and frustrate the English advance while providing the Scottish army with a degree of flexibility rather than tying down all three divisions in a single confined location. The deployment of the vanguard in the Torwood and the rearguard in the New Park would, between them, deny the English any opportunity of an uninterrupted advance along either of the two approach roads. The third division, commanded by Edward Bruce, and the light cavalry, could bring help to whichever division was in need from where it was based in the vicinity of the New Park.

The evidence for the deployment of the Scottish vanguard remains inconclusive. A position in the Torwood would run the risk of the vanguard becoming dangerously isolated should the English advance beyond it. Any attempt to bring aid to the vanguard would expose further Scottish forces to the host and might well result in a set-piece battle. Indeed, in the circumstances, it is conceivable that the Scottish army was drawn up in order to be ready to retreat northwards, a scenario that would explain why the vanguard was the northernmost division and the rearguard closest to the advancing English. Whether the vanguard was deployed in the New Park or the Torwood, it is clear that Bruce was determined to avoid a set-piece battle.

Rather than engage the English in battle, the Scottish army was going to oppose the host by means of irregular warfare. This was the plan Bruce had formulated. The broken and wooded terrain to the south of Stirling provided an ideal environment in which to employ these tactics. As the English began their final approach on Stirling they were entering a trap: the Scots had dug up pathways; they had meticulously prepared a concealed ambush of deep holes and sharpened stakes; the Scottish army itself was now hidden from view, its divisions secreted within the impenetrable darkness of the thick woodland.

In the uncomfortable heat of early afternoon, as the midsummer sun blazed high overhead, a faint noise could be heard in the still air. There was a distant clatter of hooves, a muffled stamp of feet. Among the trees of the New Park, and perhaps also within the Torwood, an army of several thousand Scotsmen listened in apprehensive silence to the approach of the English host. From his position on the edge of the New Park, it is possible Robert Bruce could see the gathering dust cloud that arose from beneath the iron-shod hooves and weary feet of the formidable army that sought his destruction. His already anxious mind would further have been troubled by the ominous report he had received earlier that morning of the daunting size of the host and the good order in which it advanced. Bruce had raised an army; he had trained and prepared it; he had formulated a plan. Yet one wrong move, one slight deviation, and his army would be drawn into a catastrophic battle. In attempting to oppose the English host before Stirling Castle, Robert Bruce was playing with fire.

CHAPTER ELEVEN

PLAYING WITH FIRE

THE MIDSUMMER SUN WAS HIGH OVERHEAD AS THE ENGLISH VANGUARD approached the Torwood. Clad in heavy chainmail, uncomfortable beneath the quilted padding of gambesons and the oppressive weight of hauberks and haketons, knights and men-at-arms sweltered in the afternoon heat. Around them the countryside was still and quiet. To the east an expanse of broken, low-lying ground stretched away to the distant banks of the Forth. Here, in the carseland, the soft earth remained perilously marshy even in the height of midsummer. To the north Stirling Castle was now less than ten miles away. Two natural obstacles stood between the vanguard and the castle. The second, the wooded enclosure of the New Park, was still approximately five miles away. The first was immediately before the vanguard. Ahead of them the road to Stirling disappeared into the gloom of the sprawling Torwood. It was with increasing trepidation that Gloucester and Hereford led their men forwards.

Before the vanguard could enter the Torwood it was brought to an abrupt halt by the arrival of Philip Mowbray.[1] Almost a month had passed since Mowbray had appeared in Northumberland with the startling news of the siege of Stirling Castle and the deadline for its relief. In accordance with the well-established conventions of siege warfare Mowbray, as constable of Stirling Castle, had been permitted by the Scots to inform Edward of the deadline and had ridden to England under a pass of safe-conduct. Presumably under protection of a similar pass, Mowbray now approached the host, chivalric convention dictating that the constable should be permitted to converse with the commander of the relieving force when it appeared. It is conceivable Bruce hoped that the news Mowbray was about to impart would cause the English to halt their advance so that an engagement could be avoided. Mowbray was immediately taken to the king. The intelligence he brought was invaluable. Mowbray told Edward that the host need advance no further. He reminded the king that the terms of the agreement specified that if an English army came within three leagues of the castle then it was considered relieved; the vanguard, Mowbray stated, was now the required three leagues from the castle. He then informed Edward that Robert Bruce and the Scots still remained in the vicinity of the castle and had 'dug up the narrow paths through the wood'.[2] Above all Mowbray urged caution. Having witnessed the Scottish preparations, he had grave misgivings about what the host might encounter should it continue its advance.

Edward, however, had none. The revelation that the Scots had not already withdrawn would have immediately been seized upon by the king. The minor details by which Stirling was considered relieved were no longer of any interest to him. He had not come to relieve Stirling but to bring the Scots to battle. The frustrating spectre of a Scottish withdrawal had haunted Edward ever since the host had entered Scotland, and it was this gnawing fear that had led him to drive his army north from Edinburgh with such relentless zeal. The news that the Scots had dug up the paths through the wood, whether the New Park or the Torwood, would only have confirmed his suspicions that the Scots still intended to withdraw behind ruined paths that would seriously hinder any attempt at pursuit by English cavalry. Edward was determined that the Scots should not slip from his grasp. No time could be lost. The host was to continue its advance. Rather than engendering a sense of caution in the king, the intelligence that Mowbray brought only served to intensify the zeal with which Edward drove the host forwards. Mowbray, his prudent counsel ignored, took leave of the king and returned to Stirling Castle. Behind him two English divisions prepared to follow in his wake.

The English plan was simple. Gloucester and Hereford would resume the lead. The vanguard, accompanied by a detachment of Welsh foot soldiers, was to continue onwards through the Torwood and then take the western road which ran to Stirling through the New Park. Simultaneously, to the east, Robert Clifford was to bypass the woodlands and lead his fast-moving mounted division of three hundred knights and men-at-arms across the broken ground that bordered the carseland in a thrust intended to link up with the beleaguered castle garrison. The vanguard was the more powerful force and, as the presence of an infantry detachment indicates, it was expected that Gloucester and Hereford might encounter some resistance. Edward would not have considered this a problem; his primary objective was not to break through to Stirling Castle but to pin down the Scottish army, prevent it from slipping away and destroy it. The presence of Clifford's division to the north of the New Park, in the Scottish rear, would hamper any attempt at a Scottish withdrawal. The third English division, commanded by Edward himself, was to remain in reserve along with the snaking column of weary, dust-covered foot soldiers, that trailed behind the cavalry.

With the departure of Mowbray the vanguard warily resumed its advance. The trees of the Torwood loomed menacingly before them. It was with apprehension that the lead elements of the vanguard entered into the unknown depths of the wood. Daylight disappeared. Momentarily they were blinded by the darkness. An uncomfortable coldness settled on them beneath the shade of the heavy canopy. Vigilantly, knights, men-at-arms and foot soldiers pressed onwards, following the road through the trees, constantly scouring the woodland for the slightest sign of an ambush. It was ideal terrain for such an attack, the enclosed environment perfectly suited for the type of devastating ambuscade in which the Scots had become so chillingly proficient. This unsettling knowledge would not have been lost on those who anxiously advanced through the encroaching woodland. The veterans of the Scottish wars would have been particularly watchful, knowing from hard-earned experience of the lethal ability of the Scots in undertaking irregular warfare.

The vanguard passed through without incident and it was with relief that they emerged unscathed from the darkness of the Torwood to see daylight once again. In the brightness of the afternoon the land beyond the Torwood was seen to be empty of Scots. It was through this area that the English vanguard now advanced. Stirling Castle was less than six miles away. Directly ahead of the vanguard the road entered the wooded enclosure of the New Park. The park was the last obstacle between the vanguard and the castle. From the intelligence Mowbray had imparted, both Gloucester and Hereford knew that the Scottish army had not yet withdrawn; if the Scots were to be found anywhere, it was in the New Park. The two earls decided to proceed with extreme caution. Wary of advancing into an ambush, they ordered forwards the detachment of Welsh foot soldiers, these troops being more suited to the difficult wooded terrain.

This detachment of Welsh foot soldiers was commanded by the English Henry de Bohun, a nephew of Hereford. De Bohun was a young knight, 'valorous and bold' and eager to win renown by virtue of a celebrated feat of arms. The perilous enterprise of leading the Welsh into the confines of the New Park was exactly the kind of opportunity of which such an aspiring knight dreamt. De Bohun was certainly not limited in the scope of his ambitions, believing that 'if he found Robert Bruce there he would either kill him or carry him off captive'.[3] But de Bohun had set his sights on finding Bruce not only out of glory. On 20 October 1306 the ancestral Scottish lands of Bruce, having been stripped from him by Edward I as a result of his treachery, were granted to Hereford, de Bohun's uncle. These confiscated territories included the Bruce heartland of Annandale and the castle of Lochmaben. Scottish success had seen Bruce forcibly reclaim these lands while Hereford, hamstrung by the pitiful exertions of Edward II, had watched helplessly as his new and substantial Scottish estates were lost to him. By defeating the Scots and destroying Bruce, Hereford could retrieve these estates. Therefore, Henry de Bohun's ambition to kill or capture Bruce was inspired not only by glory but also by a practical and very personal motivation. Grasping the reins of his barded destrier in one hand and his iron-headed lance in the other, displaying his shield with its armorial device prominently upon his arm, de Bohun intrepidly plunged into the New Park. The Welsh foot soldiers trailed behind him. The trees closed in around de Bohun. The sunlight was shut off. Undaunted, he pushed on further into the wood.

It is not clear who saw whom first. Concealed near the entry to the New Park was the Scottish rearguard commanded by Robert Bruce. As the English vanguard advanced towards his position, Bruce had begun to prepare his division to face the enemy. Despite his status he did not ride a great destrier, but rather a more humble palfrey, a horse more suited to the woodland in which he was based. The most striking mark of his status was the crown that he wore. This crown sat atop a protective hat of leather, or *cuir bouilli*, which in turn surmounted a bacinet. In his hand Bruce clutched a war-axe, and it was this that he wielded as he set about organising the rearguard.[4] On a palfrey, axe in hand and a crown upon his head, Bruce would have cut a remarkably distinctive figure even amongst the distorting shadows of the thick woodland. It was standard practice that he should do so. The figure of a commander, and in particular of a king, was intended to stand out among an army, his conspicuous presence a powerful means of bolstering the morale of his troops. However, such a presence also served to single out a commander by offering the enemy a target that was frequently too tempting to resist.

Two versions exist as to what happened next. According to Barbour, de Bohun suddenly glimpsed through the trees the particularly eye-catching figure of Bruce. Preoccupied in arranging his division, Bruce was unaware of the English knight's presence. De Bohun immediately seized this opportunity for glory. He spurred his mount and charged at Bruce. The first Bruce knew of de Bohun's approach was the heavy thunder of hooves. Bruce turned his palfrey to meet the threat and, realising that de Bohun was alone, held his ground. When de Bohun saw that Bruce was prepared to face him, he dug in his spurs and increased the thunderous pace of his charge. He lowered his lance into the couched position ready to strike. The trees whipped past. Rapidly he bore down on Bruce. With his full weight behind the lance, he aimed it straight at his unmoving enemy. As the razor-sharp tip rushed towards him, Bruce twisted away and the lance shot past its target. In a single swift and fluid motion Bruce raised himself upwards and, standing in his stirrups, brought his axe round in a powerful, curving blow. The momentum of de Bohun's charge carried him straight into the arcing axe-head. Its sickening impact sliced clean through de Bohun's bacinet and cleaved deep into his skull, killing him instantly. Such was the ferocity of the blow that the axe-head snapped from its haft and remained buried in de Bohun's skull as the lifeless body of the young English knight slipped from the saddle and tumbled heavily to the ground.[5]

The death of de Bohun was spectacularly brutal. With the passage of time it has come to be portrayed as a celebrated heroic encounter between two notable opponents, reminiscent of the chivalric duel of champions which ceremonially preceded several medieval battles. In reality, for both Bruce and de Bohun, it was an appallingly desperate encounter which only one man would survive. The Scottish lords who witnessed it were in no doubt as to its being wildly risky. They were not ignorant of the fact that the one killed could so easily have been Bruce. In fact, the lords were so unnerved that later they openly censured Bruce, for they 'blamed him greatly, for putting himself at risk in meeting so hardy and strong a knight, equipped as he was then seen'. Bruce brushed off their criticisms, downplaying the gravity of what had happened by instead lamenting the loss of his axe.[6] Yet the lords knew that the death of Bruce would also have been the death of their cause.

That Bruce should stand his ground and face de Bohun is entirely in keeping with his character. The Scottish lords, despite their well-founded concerns, could hardly have expected Bruce promptly to flee before the charge of an onrushing English knight, even if the latter was better equipped and astride a powerful warhorse. Rather, their censure implies that the encounter was avoidable, that Bruce deliberately chose to oppose de Bohun. This sentiment lends credence to the only English account of the confrontation. According to this version of the encounter, the *Vita* relates that as the vanguard approached the New Park, 'Scots were seen straggling under the trees as if in flight'. De Bohun, riding ahead of the Welsh foot soldiers, pursued the Scots into the entrance of the wood. As soon as de Bohun entered the New Park 'a multitude of Scots' suddenly broke cover, rapidly emerging from where they had been concealed among the trees. De Bohun found himself surrounded. Desperately, he wheeled his destrier around in a frantic attempt to extricate himself from the New Park. Before de Bohun could escape, Bruce intercepted him and struck him a savage blow with his axe. In a courageous bid to save his lord, de Bohun's squire rode to the rescue, but he was overwhelmed by the advancing Scots and killed.[7]

Whatever the precise circumstances in which de Bohun was so spectacularly slain, the episode had a profound effect. Although Bruce was to be rebuked for risking his life, the immediate result was to enhance immeasurably the morale of his division. Having witnessed Bruce 'right at the first encounter, without hesitation or trepidation, slay a knight thus with one blow, they [the Scottish rearguard] took such encouragement from it that they advanced right boldly'.[8] The dramatic nature of this one-to-one confrontation, of Bruce readily engaging a fully armoured knight whilst he himself was mounted upon a palfrey, of the single axe blow which had slain de Bohun, all served to inspire the Scottish rearguard instantly. The confrontation struck the perfect note of courage and aggression to which the Scots could aspire, and in doing so emphatically set the tone for the fight ahead.

To the English vanguard the death of de Bohun was a stunning setback. For a knight to be killed in combat was an extremely rare event. Afforded a substantial level of protection by the strength of the armour in which they were attired, knights were further safeguarded by the wealth their captors stood to gain from their ransom. The tremendous shock the vanguard felt at the loss of de Bohun would have been magnified by his youth, eagerness and assurance and by the abundance of courage and daring that had coursed through his veins. A nephew of Hereford, a young knight in search of renown, de Bohun was a prominent figure among the vanguard and personified the virtues to which a knight should aspire. The brutal nature of his death would also have startled the vanguard. If they had not witnessed it for themselves, then the Welsh who had accompanied de Bohun would have been quick to inform them of the dreadful axe-blow that had shattered his skull and violently ended his life. It was a blunt reminder to the knights and men-at-arms of the vanguard that the grim fate of de Bohun could so easily be their own; that no one, whatever his rank or status, however fine or costly his armour, was immune from being slain.

Nor was the death of de Bohun the only reason for Gloucester and Hereford to have serious cause for concern. The New Park was teeming with Scots. They now knew that Robert Bruce himself was among them. Indeed, if the account of the *Vita* is to be accepted, then the straggling Scots apparently seen in flight looked suspiciously like a deliberate attempt to lure the English into the wooded enclosure. The New Park bore the unmistakable hallmarks of a trap intended to snare the vanguard and destroy it. Had Gloucester and Hereford known that a carefully disguised cavalry trap of deep holes and sharpened stakes most probably awaited them beside the entrance to the New Park, any suspicions they possessed would have been confirmed. It was almost certainly an attempt to engage the vanguard by means of the 'secret warfare' at which the Scots were so adept. Bruce was playing to his strengths; rather than engage the host in battle, he intended to embroil it in the nightmare of irregular warfare.

The impetuous advance of Henry de Bohun may have prematurely sprung Bruce's carefully laid trap. If de Bohun's death was ultimately the cost of saving the English vanguard, then the young knight had not died in vain. Time for such reflection, however, lay in the future. Before it could recover from the horrific death of de Bohun, the English vanguard was abruptly confronted by a mass of onrushing Scotsmen who poured out from their hiding places within the wood. Emboldened by the inspirational actions of Bruce, they burst forward brandishing spears and axes and bellowing war cries as they streamed towards the vanguard. The English held their ground. Swords rasped from scabbards; lances were levelled. At the entrance to the New Park the two divisions clashed. The Scots of the rearguard lunged at barded destriers with their spears; knights and men-at-arms deftly wheeled their horses round, manoeuvring to avoid the spearheads, thrusting at the Scots with their lances or cutting with the flashing blades of swords.

A vicious skirmish developed, 'a sharp action' in which, the *Vita* claims, Gloucester was unhorsed.[9] Although brief, it was fought with an intense ferocity. Yet it did not escalate into a full-scale engagement between the two opposing divisions. The respective commanders retained a semblance of control. Bruce was painfully aware of the extreme danger to which the Scots would be exposed should they oppose English heavy cavalry in the open. He knew it was imperative that his division should not venture outside the protective cover of the New Park. Conversely, it was clear to Gloucester and Hereford that to engage the Scots within the New Park was to play into the hands of their enemy. A stalemate quickly ensued. The Scots would not advance from out of the New Park and the English would not advance into it. At the entrance to the park the skirmish gradually became a stand-off as each side refused to push forwards. Neither division was willing fully to commit itself to the engagement. Recognising the futility of the action in which they were involved, Gloucester and Hereford ordered the vanguard to disengage and proceeded to conduct a tactical withdrawal. The English vanguard had not been beaten, but its advance had been repulsed. To the Scots this was a victory; to the knights and men-at-arms of the English vanguard, forced to retrace their steps along the road upon which they had so recently advanced, it would have felt very much like a defeat.

The Scottish rearguard remained in the New Park. That there was no reckless pursuit of the retreating English is a measure of the discipline Bruce was able to instil in such a diverse body of men. An impetuous pursuit across open ground would have been sheer folly. As Bruce watched the last of the English disappear back down the road, he could reflect with satisfaction that he had achieved his objective. He had made a stand against the host. Not only had his division survived intact but, by forcing the English to withdraw, he had won a singular success. Crucially, this had been achieved without being drawn into battle. Any contentment he felt, however, would instantly have been dispelled had he known of the savage engagement that raged on the broken ground to the east of the woods. Preoccupied by the action at the New Park, Bruce was unaware that beneath the heat of the afternoon sun the Scottish vanguard was locked in a furious combat with Robert Clifford's cavalry division. Thomas Randolph had broken Bruce's golden rule; he had taken his infantry division into the open field. Now, surrounded by a throng of mounted knights and men-at-arms, he and his men were paying the price in blood.

Bruce had given Randolph strict instructions to guard 'the way beside the kirk'. Although the exact location indicated by Bruce remains uncertain –

whether one accepts the traditional position of the Scottish vanguard in the New Park, or the more recent suggestion that it was located in the Torwood – it is clear that Randolph's brief was to watch the broken ground to the east and ensure that the left flank of the Scottish army was not turned. Bruce had evidently anticipated the very cavalry thrust towards Stirling Castle that Clifford was to undertake. If the Scottish vanguard had indeed been hidden within the Torwood, then it would have endured the agonising experience of remaining still and quiet as the English vanguard advanced through the wood; the Scottish troops would have watched passively from behind cover as columns of English knights and men-at-arms, and Welsh foot soldiers, passed slowly along the road. If Randolph had been in the Torwood, then he would have adhered rigidly to his orders and allowed the English to pass.

Clifford's division appears to have set off slightly after the English vanguard. It was essential that Clifford's force advance at speed and for this reason it consisted exclusively of cavalry. Barbour describes the knights and men-at-arms of whom it was comprised as 'fine young men, anxious for chivalry; they were the best of all the host, in demeanour and equipment'.[10] Its commanders were certainly experienced in combat, being long-serving veterans of the Scottish wars. The most senior figure after Clifford was Henry de Beaumont, a banneret who had fought throughout the wars and who had distinguished himself at Falkirk. Thomas Gray was another notable veteran. A knight of northern England and the father of the author of the *Scalacronica*, Gray had also fought in each phase of the wars and had served as constable of Cupar Castle in Fife. Although the smallest of the three English cavalry divisions, it was certainly not lacking in expertise when it came to the serious business of warfare.

Taking leave of the king, Clifford led the three hundred knights and men-at-arms of his division north in an attempt to break through to Stirling Castle and hinder any attempt at a Scottish retreat. Galloping across the open ground, Clifford's division undertook the flanking movement against which Randolph had been ordered to guard. Curiously, Randolph did not immediately respond. The reason for his uncharacteristic delay in reacting to this advance is obscured by conflicting reports. Barbour recounts that Randolph was simply slow in spotting Clifford's division, relating that when Randolph did finally spy the English he was 'annoyed and angry in his mind that they had passed so far by'. According to *Lanercost* the delay was deliberate, Randolph waiting until the English were 'far distant from their colleagues' before making his move and cutting Clifford's division off from the main body of the host. The *Scalacronica* provides a third alternative, Thomas Gray relating that Randolph, 'having heard that his uncle [Robert Bruce] had thrown back the English vanguard on the other side of the wood, decided that he wanted his share'.[11] That three separate sources all refer to this delay suggests the English had advanced a significant distance towards their objective before any Scottish action was taken. The delay almost certainly arose from a crisis of indecision on the part of Randolph. Although he had been ordered by Bruce to guard the left flank of the Scottish position, he would also have been under strict instructions not to engage the English in the open field. Randolph consequently found himself in an impossible situation. Either he had to let Clifford's division pass through to Stirling Castle or he had to risk taking his division into the field. Caught in this dilemma, Randolph's understanding that the English vanguard had been repulsed by Bruce may well have proved decisive. Rallied by this news, Randolph made his decision. The English cavalry would not be allowed to pass. Rousing the Scottish vanguard, Randolph ordered his men to leave the cover of the wood and form up in the open field.

It was a supremely courageous, if not foolhardy, move. On open ground, foot soldiers were appallingly exposed when pitted against cavalry. To engage in such an encounter willingly was to defy all military convention. The only tactic that infantry could employ to counter this serious disadvantage was for the foot soldiers to form a tightly packed schiltrom, the strength of which was the solid defensive obstacle it presented to cavalry. For a schiltrom to have any chance of success, it was essential that the formation retained its rigidly tight cohesion. The schiltrom Randolph now formed was held together by nothing more than the bravery and discipline of his troops.

Having taken to the open field, the Scottish vanguard drew together in a tight circle, its troops facing outwards and extending their spears beyond the front ranks, the vicious spearheads glinting sharply beneath the glare of the sun. The schiltroms at Falkirk in 1298 had remained immobile; but now Randolph ordered the vanguard to advance towards Clifford's division. Such a compact mass of men was not a formation that lent itself to mobility. The several days that the Scottish army had spent in the Torwood awaiting the arrival of the host had been used profitably by providing the foot soldiers with some rudimentary training in which the tactics of the schiltrom undoubtedly featured prominently. However, theory was one thing; the practice of executing this manoeuvre in the field against a powerful cavalry force was entirely another. Randolph would almost certainly have been positioned towards the middle of the armoured circle, shouting out his orders, directing the unwieldy schiltrom forward, and repeatedly yelling at his men to maintain their formation.

The abrupt appearance of the Scottish vanguard from out of the wood brought the English cavalry to a halt. It was now the turn of Clifford and his commanders to suffer from an anxious bout of indecision. Confronted by the unexpected sight of a schiltrom advancing towards them across open ground, there was disagreement among the commanders of the English division as to the correct tactic to employ against it. Beaumont favoured drawing the Scots further from cover, advising 'Let us pull back a little, let them come, give them the field'. Gray thought such a move would play into the hands of the Scots. He told Beaumont, 'Sir, I doubt that there will be so many of them around in the hour, for they will have the lot all too easily'. Innocuous though this reply was, it riled Beaumont who, perceiving his judgement to be contradicted by a subordinate, retorted petulantly, 'Look here, if you are afraid, flee'. To have his courage openly questioned was an insult no knight could ignore. 'Sir', declared Gray vehemently, 'I shall not flee for fear today.' Before Clifford could intervene, Gray angrily rode out from the division and spurred his destrier towards the advancing schiltrom.

This heated exchange occurred between two senior figures of the host who were well known to each other. Indeed, a decade before, during the English siege of Stirling Castle, Gray had almost been killed when saving Beaumont from capture. Beaumont had been fighting at the barriers of the castle when he had been caught by the hook of a siege engine which the Scots had thrown down from the walls. Gray had come to Beaumont's rescue and dragged him out of danger before the flailing banneret could be lifted into the castle. However, Gray had dangerously exposed himself and was 'struck through the head below the eyes' by the fearsome impact of a bolt fired from a springald. The wound he suffered must have been particularly horrific for he was given up for dead. Only when a party of men was paraded to bury Gray was he seen to move and his eyes flicker open.[12] A full, and no doubt painfully slow recovery followed. Yet this past experience clearly cut no sentiment with Beaumont when Gray now had the temerity to disagree with him. The petulant remark of Beaumont and the hot-headed response of Gray provide a vivid glimpse into the fractious rivalry that existed among the commanders of the host. Although they fought alongside one other, no banneret or knight was ever blind to the need to enhance his personal standing by gaining honour and renown. This desire for individual glory provided the élan on which the fighting spirit of medieval armies was based, but it could also erupt into a personal clash that could seriously undermine an army. As Gray was about to prove, it could also lead even the most experienced of men into an act of recklessness.

Gray was not alone in his rash charge. He was accompanied by William Deyncourt, a fellow English knight, whose motive for undertaking such a reckless act remains unclear. Deyncourt may have become caught up in the drama of the moment or perhaps, like Henry de Bohun, he too was eager for renown. As for Gray, a seasoned campaigner, a man taught in the brutal school of the Scottish wars and who bore the scars to prove it, he should have known better. Whatever the provocation, he should never have undertaken such a desperate charge. It was nothing short of suicidal. Clifford and his men could only watch in horror as the two knights careered across the field and charged straight into the Scottish schiltrom. Spears tore through the flesh of their destriers. Both horses were immediately slain. Deyncourt was killed instantly and Gray thrown violently to the ground. The schiltrom closed in on Gray. Rough hands grabbed the fallen knight and hauled him into the centre of the enclosed formation. Surrounded by a heaving press of Scottish spearmen, Gray became the first notable prisoner of the battle.[13]

The awful fate of the two knights served as a vivid warning to their companions. They had witnessed the dreadful scene unfold; before them lay the corpses of the two destriers and the lifeless body of Deyncourt. The tormenting sight of Gray being manhandled into the midst of the schiltrom would have been profoundly disturbing. It was clear that to act on impulse was disastrous. Although unable to prevent the fatal charge, Clifford quickly recovered control of his division. Clifford and Beaumont had both fought against the Scottish schiltroms at Falkirk in 1298, and the host could not have had two commanders better qualified to deal with the formation with which they were now faced. If experience had taught them anything, it was that there was no short-cut to defeating such a tightly knit and densely packed mass of men. A circular schiltrom had to be prised open; it had to be completely enveloped and subjected to a coordinated and sustained attack. This was not a time for individual glory but for teamwork. Under the expert guidance of Clifford and Beaumont, the knights and men-at-arms 'gathered all in one force, and surrounded them [the Scots] completely, attacking them on every side'.[14]

Encircled by the English cavalry, the Scots staunchly held formation, crowding in against one another as they grimly determined to repel the attack. Fiercely they stabbed outwards with spears, inflicting 'wide wounds' on those horses that came too close. Some foot soldiers daringly darted out from the schiltrom, plunging knife blades into the flanks of horses and unseating their riders. The English, forced to keep their distance, unleashed a barrage of missiles at the schiltrom. Lacking infantry support, they could not call upon the fire of archers and so resorted to throwing whatever they had to hand. They hurled swords and maces at the schiltrom with such ferocity that a 'mountain of weapons' soon built up among the Scots. The schiltrom defiantly resisted the onslaught. The English pressed again and the Scots tenaciously fought back. It was a battle of attrition, the Scots painfully aware that the slightest opening in the schiltrom would result in their massacre; the English knew this too, and frantically Clifford's troops attempted to force that opening and destroy the Scottish vanguard. Both divisions fought with intensity beneath the heat of the blazing midsummer sun, their flesh being 'all wet with sweat' and 'such a cloud rose from them then from breathing, both by horses and by men, and from dust, that such darkness was in the air above them that it was wonderful to see'.[15] Beneath this funereal pall the two divisions remained locked in a desperate struggle.

Any satisfaction that Bruce might have felt at the repulse of the English vanguard was exceptionally short-lived. By the time he became aware of the remorseless battle in which the Scottish vanguard was engaged, the fight was already well advanced. When Bruce eventually came within sight of the terrific struggle, it was with horror that he saw how Randolph 'took the open field recklessly'.[16] Dismay would have been etched on Bruce's face as he stared at the great scrum of well-mounted knights and men-at-arms that surrounded the Scottish vanguard. The appalling clamour of battle – the sharp ring of metal against metal, the screams of the maimed and the dying, hoarse voices frantically bellowing orders – would have carried to him with a terrible clarity on that summer afternoon.

It was evident Randolph was in serious difficulty. According to Barbour the bellicose Douglas, frustrated at not yet having seen action, approached Bruce and requested permission to bring aid to Randolph's division. The reply with which Barbour credits Bruce was at once blunt and startling: 'As Our Lord sees me, you shall not go one foot towards him. If he does well, let him take well. Whatever happens to him, win or lose, I shall not change my plans for him.'[17] To Bruce the grave danger Randolph was courting was only too clear. By taking to the field against English cavalry, Randolph risked the annihilation of the entire Scottish vanguard. Should Bruce allow more of his troops to become involved in this encounter, then he ran the terrible risk of it escalating into a full-scale battle. Bruce's entire plan had been designed to avoid just such an engagement. Now Randolph had placed that carefully planned strategy in dire jeopardy. The encounter between the two opposing armies had reached a critical moment. Bruce, with the insight of an intuitive commander, recognised this. He could not allow his army to be drawn into such a battle. The Scottish vanguard would have to fight on alone.

According to Barbour, Douglas had no such qualms. Whereas Bruce thought in terms of the entire encounter, Douglas could not see beyond this single engagement. Watching the gruelling fight, eager to get into the action, Douglas renewed his appeal to aid Randolph: 'In no way can I see his enemies overcome him when I can give him help. With your leave, assuredly I will help him, or die in the effort'. Despite the hard line that Bruce had resolved to take, it was a plea that would have left him torn between an instinctive desire to send aid to his beleaguered nephew and save the vanguard, and the undeniable need to adhere rigidly to his plans. At length, and no doubt with great reluctance, Bruce gave Douglas permission to help Randolph, although he cautioned him to 'hurry back soon'. Finally able to enter the fray, Douglas assembled his men and set off towards the scene of the bitter fighting.[18]

The force that accompanied Douglas was, however, almost certainly insubstantial. Douglas was not in command of a division. At most he was in charge of a contingent of cavalry and it was probably this that he now led towards Randolph. It is telling that Bruce did not commit either his own division or that of his brother, Edward. Anxious as he was for the survival of the vanguard, his priority was to minimise the risk of a battle. In this moment of crisis Bruce displayed a will of iron in adhering rigidly to his plans. To avoid a full-scale battle he appears to have been prepared to sacrifice the Scottish vanguard.

On the open ground the fight continued to rage. Time and again the knights and men-at-arms rode at the schiltrom, lunging at it with lances, cutting with swords, slinging whatever objects they could find into its unwavering mass. Tirelessly, Clifford and Beaumont exhorted their men to greater efforts, driving them on despite the trenchant resistance they steadfastly endured. From within the heart of the schiltrom Randolph would have yelled out encouragement, urging his men on, bellowing at them to hold formation, to keep steady and remain tightly compressed. The troops of both sides by now were streaming with sweat. They were covered in choking dust. Blood smeared the soil. Assaulted from all sides, still the battered schiltrom held.

Frustration began to mount among the English. They had given their all to break the schiltrom, but with no discernible result. Their exasperation would have been compounded by an earnest belief that, out on open ground, they should have been able to break it. Already fatigued by two long days of continuous advance, they began to falter. Wracked by exhaustion, beset with frustration, their resolve was finally broken by the appearance of the Scottish reinforcements led by Douglas. Gradually the English began to fall back. Ensconced in the heaving heart of the vanguard, Randolph saw his chance. Seizing the moment, he ordered his men to advance. The schiltrom lurched forwards. It passed awkwardly over the corpses of men and horses, and pressed on towards the disorganised crowd of retreating knights and men-at-arms. Douglas, realising that Clifford's division was beaten, brought his troops to a halt. Confronted by this final onslaught, the demoralised English cavalry fled in disarray. Clifford's division ceased to exist as its troops scattered, some riding north to seek refuge in Stirling Castle, their original objective, while others galloped south to rejoin the main body of the host. Behind them the dead and the dying lay sprawled upon the dusty ground.[19]

Exhausted by the gruelling physical punishment of the fight, Randolph pulled off his bacinet and gulped in air. The schiltrom dispersed as men sought a moment of respite from the terrific ordeal they had endured. There was no pursuit of the beaten division, nor did there need to be. In refusing to be broken by the English cavalry, the schiltrom had ultimately broken Clifford's division. The Scottish vanguard had won an unparalleled victory.

Their breath recovered, the battered vanguard wearily trudged to where Bruce and the rest of the Scottish army awaited them in the New Park. Randolph, streaked with blood, sweat and dust, received a hero's welcome.[20] The battle-scarred soldiers of the vanguard were effusively congratulated for their hard-fought triumph. It was a remarkable achievement. Randolph had defied convention by taking an unwieldy schiltrom into the open field against a division of heavy cavalry; in defeating this cavalry division in a prolonged and relentless battle of attrition, he had secured a victory that was without precedent in the Scottish wars. It was a victory no one had believed possible.

As the revelation of this triumph swept through the Scottish army, so the trauma of the defeat rocked the host. Edward II had played no part in the afternoon's fighting. His division, accompanied by the majority of English infantry, had slowly continued its advance northwards. The first ominous sign that all was not going to plan would have been the sight of Gloucester and Hereford retreating towards him, their vanguard division having been repulsed at the New Park. By the time Clifford and Beaumont also forlornly returned with the scattered survivors of their broken division, the main body of the host had already abandoned the road to Stirling and was advancing across the broken ground to the east. Psychologically, the two reverses were immensely damaging, and 'from that moment began a panic among the English and the Scots grew bolder'.[21] It cannot have been with anything other than astonished disbelief that Edward received news of the defeat of an experienced cavalry division of three hundred knights and men-at-arms at the hands of a division of Scottish foot soldiers. In light of Edward's volatile temperament it is unlikely that he held back in expressing the full force of his displeasure.

Yet, as the sun at last set and the first faint shadows of dusk brushed the fields and woods, ostensibly little had changed. In amongst the trees of the New Park the Scottish army regrouped. For Bruce it had been a remarkably successful day, indeed more so than he could possibly have imagined. His plan of engaging the host in 'secret warfare' had led to the repulse of the English vanguard; although Randolph had dangerously disregarded his instructions and taken to the field, the Scottish vanguard had ultimately won a famous victory. Most important of all, Bruce had successfully avoided his army being drawn into a full-scale battle. He had made a stand against the host, he had opposed the might of the English king, and in doing so not only had he emerged undefeated, but he had undoubtedly come off best. Bruce had achieved his objective. There was no longer any need to oppose the host before Stirling Castle. As darkness covered the landscape, his thoughts inevitably turned to ordering a withdrawal.

Nor had the intentions of Edward changed. Despite the reverses the host had suffered, despite his troops being 'cast down and so fearful', he was still determined to bring the Scots to battle.[22] Bloodied the host may have been, but it was by no means irretrievably finished as a fighting force. Many of Clifford's division had returned to the host. The English vanguard had withdrawn from the New Park without suffering significant losses. The main English division, commanded by Edward himself, had not yet seen action, nor had the vast majority of the several thousand foot soldiers who formed the bulk of the host. In the encroaching darkness, as Bruce contemplated withdrawal, Edward relentlessly drove the English host onwards.

The events of that long summer afternoon were, however, to prove decisive. A subtle shift had occurred which was to change the entire nature of the encounter. Only as the night progressed did a handful of men begin to sense this faint but critical swing in the balance of power. Of equal significance were those who remained oblivious to this inexorable shift in power. It was during the hours of darkness on this, one of the shortest of nights, that the outcome of the battle was about to take shape.

CHAPTER TWELVE

THE SHORTEST OF NIGHTS

THERE WAS TO BE NO RESPITE FOR THE ENGLISH HOST. DESPITE THE VEIL OF darkness that masked the landscape, the host maintained its advance. In the previous two days it had covered almost thirty miles. That afternoon it had fought two actions, both of which had resulted in unexpected reverses. Knights and men-at-arms were extremely tired, having ridden in full armour from dawn till dusk on a long and hot midsummer's day. The sore feet of the infantry had pounded incessantly upon the hard earth of dusty roads beneath the glare of the blinding sun. Many men were on the point of exhaustion. Bodies were heavy, minds were tired. The host desperately needed to rest. Yet no relief came. Not once did the pace ease. The host was driven relentlessly onwards by the will of one man and his desire for battle.

Edward was adamant that nothing should stand in his way. He was possessed by the need to bring the Scots to battle. The repulse of the vanguard at the entry to the New Park had compelled him to alter his plans. It was evident from the report Gloucester and Hereford would have brought back that the New Park was heavily defended and, with Bruce himself in command there, could safely be assumed to be the location of the main Scottish army. News of how the Scots had waited in ambush left little doubt in the minds of Edward and his commanders that the New Park was a potential death-trap. Their decision to abandon the road had been taken late in the afternoon, presumably upon the unexpected return of the vanguard. The readiness with which the host left the road and began to negotiate a route across the broken ground to the east may be an indication that a contingency plan was in place; it certainly highlights the eagerness of Edward to get to grips with the Scottish army before it could slip from his grasp. In this the English were aided by possessing a detailed knowledge of Stirling and the surrounding area, having continuously occupied Stirling Castle for the last decade. This was true not only of the men-at-arms of the host who had served in the garrison but also of more influential and high-ranking figures.

Such a man was Ebles de Mountz, a knight of the royal household who was serving in the king's division. The Mountz family was originally from Savoy and had entered royal service in the 1260s, Mountz's father holding the office of steward of Henry III's household and subsequently becoming constable of Windsor Castle. Mountz mirrored this level of royal service when he became steward of Queen Isabella's household in 1311, accompanying Edward and Isabella to France in 1313. He had resigned from this position early in 1314 as, on 22 February 1314, he had been appointed constable of Edinburgh Castle. Edward had hoped that this appointment would defuse the tensions in the mutinous garrison. However, before Mountz could take up office, Piers Lubaud had already been overthrown by the garrison and the following month the castle had fallen. In this moment of crisis Edward turned to Mountz who had a fourteen-year record of illustrious service in the Scottish wars and, more pertinently, unrivalled experience of commanding front-line fortifications, having served as constable of the three strategic castles of Edinburgh, Jedburgh and Stirling. He had been constable of Stirling from 1308 until 1311 and was consequently in possession of a recent and detailed knowledge of the castle and its environs.[1] A veteran of the wars, an intimate of the king and possessing first-hand knowledge of the immediate area, Mountz would have been an indispensable source of information to Edward. Nor would Mountz have been alone in his wealth of local knowledge. The area through which the host advanced may have been hostile but it was far from unknown; the English knew the land to the south of Stirling with a familiarity which might well have equalled that of the Scots.

With the repulse of the English vanguard this knowledge now became invaluable. In order to bring the Scots to battle, Edward knew it was imperative that the host should be brought as close as possible to the Scottish position in the New Park. This was complicated by the need to find terrain firm enough to take the weight of heavy cavalry, yet open enough to provide sufficient room for the full deployment of the host. Ultimately, though, the pressing urgency of finding an alternative route north towards the Scottish position in the New Park overrode all other considerations. The low-lying carseland to the east was threaded with treacherous streams and marshes.

Underfoot it was composed of soft, peaty earth, but the English knew that they would have to advance across this inhospitable landscape if they were to avoid entering the prepared position the Scots occupied in the New Park. If the host could be manoeuvred to the east or north of the New Park before dawn, then, when morning came, it could form up directly adjacent to the Scottish position. Should the Scots still be within the wooded confines of the park, then battle would almost certainly follow. Just one obstacle stood between the host and this objective: the Bannock Burn.[2]

It was a formidable obstruction. The present Bannock Burn is a tame descendant of its medieval ancestor. In 1314 it was a 'foul, deep, marshy stream', its treacherous nature accentuated by it being a tidal tributary of the Forth.[3] Its course was strong and deep, cutting high-banked channels and gorges through the carseland. The ground surrounding much of the Bannock Burn was a perilous morass of soft, swampy earth, which was not guaranteed to take the weight of a man safely, never mind the heavy bulk of a powerful destrier. Any attempt at crossing the stream was bound to be fraught with an unacceptable level of risk and danger. To negotiate such a crossing in the darkness of night with an army of several thousand men and horses was an exceptionally hazardous operation.

No sources record the making of this decision. It is extremely doubtful that it was a preplanned contingency; if so, then it must have been decided beforehand with the agreement of the divisional commanders. If, as is more likely, it was the result of a change of plan, then there is no evidence to suggest that anyone of rank or experience objected to the night crossing of the Bannock Burn. Valence was in close attendance to the king; Gloucester and Hereford had returned to the main body of the host before it abandoned the road; Clifford and Beaumont were present before nightfall. Edward, continually haunted by the spectre of the Scots slipping away, was clearly the driving force behind the night crossing. To Edward the Bannock Burn was an obstacle that stood between the English host and a decisive battle. It is a measure of the undiminished aggressive single-mindedness of the English commanders that they paid no attention to the danger of placing such a difficult natural obstacle to their rear. The prospect of retreat does not appear even to have been considered.

In the darkness of the short midsummer's night the crossing got underway. Foot soldiers were dispatched to a nearby village, probably the small hamlet of Bannock itself, where they ripped out the timber frameworks of buildings, roughly tearing out doors and pulling down roof beams. Grasping hold of the splintered wood, supporting timber planking and beams on their shoulders, they carried the broken remains of the village through the darkness towards the Bannock Burn. Some men were loaded with bundles of thatch, which had been stripped and thrown down from the roofs of the demolished houses. Others no doubt scoured the voluminous English baggage train for timber. (The story of the garrison of Stirling Castle venturing out to provide the English host with doors and windows is almost certainly apocryphal; even Barbour was reluctant to give it credence.) Once collected, the disparate timbers were carefully laid end to end upon the marshy earth and across narrow streams to create crude makeshift walkways to facilitate the passage of men and horses. The Bannock Burn itself was too wide to bridge and it is likely that the English made use of the fordable crossing points with which they were acquainted.[4]

The crossing itself was a very laborious process. Throughout the short night, long lines of troops and horses impatiently occupied the length of the walkways, the slow-moving files close to a standstill as grooms led valuable destriers across the unsteady timbers and broken planking with painstaking deliberation. Queues would have formed at the crossing points as horses reluctantly plunged into the chill waters of the Bannock Burn, iron-shod hooves awkwardly searching for a sure footing as the horses unsteadily splashed their way across before scrambling up the far bank. For men and horses yearning for a rest, the crossing was a hatefully protracted business which took a further toll on already tired and aching bodies. On reaching the far bank there was still no respite for them during this most arduous of nights. In the darkness, encamped in the low-lying Carse of Balquhiderock, the host was uncomfortably close to the Scots. The English who had crossed the Bannock Burn, 'expecting the Scots rather to attack by night than await battle by day', endured an uncomfortable and sleepless night. Knights and men-at-arms remained clad in heavy armour, weapons ready to hand and horses bridled.[5] Tired eyes scanned the darkness. Those men fortunate enough to slumber started at the slightest sound. More than once hands must nervously have reached for knives and swords. Physically the host was exhausted; mentally it was beginning to fracture.

Minds were desperately tired. As men silently queued upon the makeshift walkways or wearily dropped to the ground on the far bank, their thoughts would invariably have returned to the events of the day. It was not an auspicious episode on which to dwell. If the repulse of the vanguard was unnerving, then the defeat of Clifford's division was immensely disturbing. To many it was natural to assume that foot soldiers arrayed in open ground should not stand a chance when pitted against heavy cavalry. The schiltrom should have been broken and the Scottish vanguard slaughtered. That the cavalry had not only failed to achieve this but had actually been beaten by the schiltrom was so startling it bordered on the inconceivable. The *Vita* is adamant that this should never have happened, commenting scathingly that Clifford was 'disgracefully routed' and leaving no doubt that its author held Clifford personally to blame for this miserable defeat.[6] In condemning Clifford in such strident terms, the *Vita* almost certainly reflects how the reverse was perceived by the knights and men-at-arms of the host. So startling was it that they could only explain it by apportioning blame. No credit was given to the Scots; no influential voice of concern was raised at the serious implications of this defeat for the host. It was most probably dismissed as a singular event, something which had never happened before and which was never likely to happen again.

Yet the seeds of doubt had been sown. Knights and men-at-arms were no longer so sure of themselves. The potent threat that a well-organised and solid schiltrom could pose was suddenly uncomfortably real. As a close-knit military community, the knights would have known men who had been killed or injured in the afternoon's fighting. The spectacular deaths of Henry de Bohun and William Deyncourt, both of whom were knights of prominence and renown, would have hit them particularly hard. Knights were rarely killed in battle, yet two had been lost that afternoon. Another well-known knight, Thomas Gray, one of the most seasoned veterans of the Scottish wars, had been unhorsed and dragged as a prisoner into the midst of the heaving schiltrom, an immensely disturbing event which had been witnessed by Clifford's entire division. To those inexperienced in warfare it was a rude awakening to the cruel realities of combat. During the sleepless night they had plenty of time to reflect that victory against the Scots was far from assured, and that a battle might well cost them their lives.

While the knights and men-at-arms dwelt on the troubling events of the afternoon, some personal animosity would have simmered among the English commanders. Clifford was undoubtedly blamed by some for the humiliating defeat of his division, and in light of Edward's capricious nature it is likely that the king vehemently subscribed to this view. Clifford certainly laboured under a cloud of shame, his reputation tarnished and, more importantly, his influence among the English high command consequently diminished. The argument between Beaumont and Gray was itself a disturbing sign of the lack of firm leadership. Clifford was the divisional commander, yet he had allowed Beaumont and Gray to argue as how best to proceed against the Scottish vanguard. In the heat of the moment a petulant quip from Beaumont had led to Gray's impulsive and futile charge. For his own part, Clifford may have had a sense that Beaumont was at fault for this impetuous charge in which Gray was captured and Deyncourt killed. An uneasy tension also prickled between Gloucester and Hereford over the leadership of the vanguard. Rivalry such as this was inherent in a medieval army, its commanders being such proud and powerful figures, and to prevent these rivalries affecting the army a king needed to exercise firm control and to establish a chain of command. In this, as in so many other aspects of his reign, Edward, it seems, was found wanting.

To the rear of the host the conscript levies of foot soldiers could sense that all was not well. Although they were reluctant soldiers, most had scant regard for the Scots and unquestionably believed in the supremacy of the knights and men-at-arms whom they followed. The knights were their social superiors, the lords who owned the land they worked and by whom justice was dispensed. These knights presented an image of themselves as a warrior caste, a military aristocracy, and it was prowess in warfare by which they claimed their elevated position in English society. To the levies of foot soldiers such men were untouchable; to a very real extent they ruled their everyday lives. Yet as the foot soldiers trudged along the walkways, murmurs of discontent would have passed along the trailing columns, troubling whispers drifting through the darkness that something was amiss. Knights had been killed. The vanguard, led in person by no less than two earls, had been repulsed. A cavalry division commanded by experienced bannerets had been beaten in the field by Scottish foot soldiers. The foot soliders' belief in the supremacy of the English cavalry, the invulnerability of knights, was suddenly called into question. For years they had heard of the excommunication imposed on Bruce and, if they despised him, they also knew of his successes. The foot soldiers from northern England had first-hand experience of the devastating impact of Scottish raids. For men who had no wish to be on campaign, the flood of doubts passing through their minds would have bitten with a chill as cold and unsettling as the waters of the Bannock Burn through which they now waded.

Edward appears to have had no such concerns. His fear that the Scots would withdraw and deny him the battle he craved was so all-consuming that he was blind to the deficiencies beginning to afflict the host. In continuing the advance, he appears to have dismissed the events of the afternoon as irrelevant. Tired the host may have been, but Edward was aware that in terms of size and sheer brute force it remained almost completely intact. As the night wore on and the crossing of the Bannock Burn progressed, large numbers of cavalry began to assemble on the far bank. To Edward the potent might of the host was as strong as it had ever been. What he failed to realise was that the scars of his army were etched deeper than mere physical exhaustion. It was only with the coming of daylight that the true depth of these scars would become apparent.

Yet Edward's great fear that the Scots might slip from his grasp was far from a conceit. While to the east the English laboured to accomplish their arduous night crossing of the Bannock Burn, in the darkness of the New Park Robert Bruce was on the brink of ordering a withdrawal. This had always been his intention. The objective had never been to attempt a crushing defeat of the English host but rather to make a show of opposing it, at best of frustrating its progress towards Stirling Castle. In the course of the afternoon this objective had been achieved. Bruce could now order a withdrawal without any loss of authority by which he held the Crown. Indeed, the afternoon had been such an overwhelming success that his position had been immeasurably strengthened. His claim to be king had never been so popularly strong. With his authority substantially bolstered, Bruce would have felt the need to withdraw more pressingly than ever before.

He knew that to stay in the New Park was effectively to commit his army to battle. News that the English were engaged in a night crossing of the Bannock Burn would only have confirmed this; the net around Bruce and his army was gradually beginning to tighten. The pressure to avoid battle, to strike camp and depart, had never been greater. His intention was to withdraw to the region of Lennox, approximately fifteen miles to the south-west of Stirling, its rugged landscape providing 'a more defensible country'.[7] For seven years the entire strategy of Bruce had been built on the guiding principle of avoiding battle with the English. The encounter before Stirling Castle was no different. That afternoon, when he had seen Randolph's division dreadfully exposed in the open field, Bruce had been understandably horrified. His immediate reaction to Douglas's plea to assist Randolph was to hazard sacrificing the division rather than risk a full-scale battle by attempting to save it. He had a plan and he was determined to adhere to it. Yet he could not completely master his instinct to aid the embattled division and, when pressed by Douglas, he had at length relented. There was a conflict within Bruce between his plan and his instinct, between his head and his heart. The support he had allowed Douglas to provide might have been limited, but it was still a deviation from the rigidity of his strict plan. In the darkness of the New Park his instinct again stirred within him. He knew he should give the order to withdraw, yet he found himself increasingly drawn to the prospect of battle.

The successes of the afternoon had surpassed all his expectations. Although the English vanguard had not been mauled in the trap that was the New Park, it had promptly retreated when confronted by the Scottish rearguard. This, together with the adrenalin rush of his single-combat against de Bohun, would personally have emboldened Bruce. The relative swiftness with which the English vanguard had withdrawn was his first inkling of a weakness within the host. Furthermore, the sight of Randolph commanding the Scottish vanguard of foot soldiers to a victory over a powerful heavy cavalry division in the open field caught the attention of Bruce and must have begun to prey on his mind. The schiltrom had shown that, well-handled and strictly disciplined, it could be a formidable weapon. Its success had demonstrated pointedly that it was possible for foot soldiers to prevail against heavy cavalry on open ground. Suddenly an English victory no longer seemed inevitable. But Bruce would also have seized upon the manner of the English defeat. It was clear that the fighting spirit of Clifford's division had been broken by the prolonged engagement. The schiltrom had stood firm despite the terrific onslaught to which it was subjected, and in doing so it had physically and mentally outlasted the English cavalry in a battle of attrition; frustration had eventually broken the spirit of the knights and men-at-arms. Their morale had sunk so low that, at the sight of Douglas and the reinforcements he brought, they had immediately disengaged. When the schiltrom advanced the cavalry had abruptly scattered. Together with the prompt retreat of the English vanguard at the entry to the New Park, this suggested a fragility of spirit among the English so serious that it had the potential to undermine the host completely.

In stark contrast, the mood of the Scottish army was euphoric; its morale could not have been better. If it had previously laboured under the conviction that it stood no chance when pitted against English cavalry, then that belief had been emphatically shattered. A new-found confidence emanated from the army that restlessly awaited its orders in the New Park. However, the Scots did not believe they were invulnerable. They remained beset with nerves and anxiety. The prospect of a brutal death still confronted them. Their high morale was not the result of a belief that they would beat the English but a realisation that the host was no longer assured of beating them. A battle between the two armies was no longer a foregone conclusion. There was a chance the Scots could win. Nor was such a victory without recent precedent. The success of the Flemings at Courtrai suggested the Scots could emerge from battle victorious. The startling success of the Scottish vanguard indicated that they might well have a chance of repeating the outcome of

Courtrai. They were the fresher army, they had the stronger morale, and they had the momentum of the afternoon's successes behind them. In the febrile darkness of night, battle for Robert Bruce became an increasingly tempting prospect.

Yet the risks remained terrible. Defeat would mean the end of Bruce's cause. The army he had assembled, the support he had so painstakingly built up, all of it would be instantly destroyed. Seven years of gruelling warfare would have been for nothing. Everything he had fought so hard to achieve would immediately be rendered worthless. Bruce himself would almost certainly be killed, if not slain in battle then gruesomely executed in its aftermath. His brother Edward would be killed and, with no male heir, the Bruces of Annandale would be no more. In defeat lay the promise of total obliteration. Bruce had achieved so much; was he now to jeopardise everything by fighting a battle he did not have to fight? In the face of such terrible risks he knew he should withdraw, that he should adhere to his plan, but he could not master the temptation to stay and fight. Caught in this appalling dilemma, Bruce delayed his decision. Around him, encamped in the wood, the army he had assembled impatiently awaited an order. While Bruce wrestled with his conflicting emotions, beyond the New Park, out in the darkness of the night, two acts of treachery were about to be committed. One of these was to be of immense significance.

To the east of Stirling Castle, in a bend of the Forth on the north bank of the river, stood Cambuskenneth Abbey. It was here that a decade before Bruce had entered into his secret bond with Bishop Lamberton. On the night of 23 June 1314 it was to be the scene of a less subtle act of treachery. The stone buildings of the abbey had been requisitioned as a storehouse for the provisions of the Scottish army. The man in overall charge of this store was the constable of Scotland, David of Strathbogie, earl of Atholl. Having deserted Bruce in 1307, Atholl had opposed him until as recently as 1312 when, disillusioned by the inactivity of Edward II and the English king's ineffectual prosecution of the Scottish war, he had again switched sides and sworn allegiance to Bruce. Eager as ever to obtain all the influential Scottish support he could muster, Bruce had returned Atholl's earldom and awarded him the prestigious office of constable. This may well have been enough to secure Atholl's loyalty were it not for the careless actions of Edward Bruce. Isabella, Atholl's sister, had once either been betrothed to Edward or been his mistress. An illegitimate son, Alexander, had been born, but the relationship foundered and Edward Bruce turned his amorous attentions to the sister of the earl of Ross. Believing the honour of his family to have been slighted, and no doubt resentful at losing the political influence of his familial alliance with the Bruces, Atholl developed 'a great coolness' towards Edward Bruce. Atholl bided his time and waited for the moment of maximum impact to exact his vengeance. It was on this most dramatic of nights that he finally struck. Without warning Atholl and his men attacked the storehouse at Cambuskenneth, killing the knight in charge, William Airth, and treacherously cutting down many of the Scots who were guarding the abbey. Seizing the provisions, Atholl and his band vanished into the night.[8]

It was an alarming incident. Within the Scottish army there were several prominent Scottish lords who had originally opposed Bruce before coming into his allegiance. In the mounting tensions of the night their loyalty was now stretched to its limit. The prospect of defeat in battle was as awful to them as it was to Bruce; the punishment that the English king would inflict upon them was certain to be dreadful. Through fear these lords might desert the Scottish army or, worse, defect to the host. Bruce could only hope their nerve would hold. The treachery of Atholl, though motivated by a deeply personal grudge, was an unnerving warning to Bruce that these lords might be tempted to look to their own interests. It was a temptation with which he was only too familiar, having himself twice changed sides in the midst of a war. If anyone understood the pressures that could drive a man to defect, it was Bruce. Negligible as the sacking of Cambuskenneth was in military terms, politically it urged a note of caution. It raised questions about the reliability of his army. News of Atholl's treachery would certainly have made Bruce think twice about giving battle.

Yet this was not the only act of desertion that took place that night. Preoccupied by the prolonged exertions of crossing the Bannock Burn, and scouring the darkness in fear of a Scottish night attack, the host failed to notice one of their own quietly slip away. Alexander Seton, a Scottish knight in allegiance to the English, had consistently fought against Bruce for several years. Seton had accompanied the host to Stirling, he had endured the privations which the army had been forced to endure by Edward II, but the humiliating reverses of the afternoon were the final straw. Choosing his moment, Seton deserted the host and surreptitiously made his way to the New Park. He was immediately taken to Bruce. Standing before the man whom he had opposed for so long, Seton spoke bluntly. 'Sir', he urged Bruce, 'now is the time if ever you thought to try your hand at re-conquering Scotland; the English have lost heart and are defeated, they expect nothing but a sudden, open assault'. Seton explained the grave situation of the host in detail, 'saying by his own head and on pain of being hanged and drawn, that if he [Bruce] wished to attack them in the morning, he would defeat them easily without loss.'[9]

Bruce may already have suspected as much, but to hear it confirmed by someone who had been at the very heart of the host was intelligence of the highest order. The very fact that Seton had deserted the host on the eve of battle was in itself resounding proof of the sorry state of that army. Seton emphasised and identified the low morale of the host as the reason why he firmly believed the English could be defeated. He claimed that its morale was so low that if the Scots did the unexpected and were seen to be willing to give battle, then the fragile spirit of the English would be shattered. This was just too tempting for Bruce to resist. His instinct overwhelmed him. The original plan was discarded. He made his decision. The Scots would stay and give battle.

Bruce was taking a gamble of momentous proportions. A Scottish victory was far from assured on the basis of the fragile spirit of the English host alone. Yet Bruce must have realised that this was the best opportunity he would ever have of defeating the English in battle. The morale of the host was abysmally low, its troops were tired, and the elite of the army, the heavy cavalry, was considerably weakened by the absence of the earls of Lancaster, Warwick, Arundel and Warenne, and the mounted retinues that would have accompanied them. Although the English host still outnumbered his own army, Bruce must have been aware that it was considerably weaker than it should have been, both in terms of men and morale. News that the English had precipitously crossed the Bannock Burn and were encamped in the treacherous, low-lying Carse of Balquhiderock, was another enticement for Bruce to give battle; the terrain between the New Park and the Carse was wholly unsuited for heavy cavalry and would severely curtail the full deployment of the enemy. In victory, Bruce could potentially realise his all-consuming ambition of being recognised as the undisputed king of Scotland. Never again would he be presented with the opportunity of achieving so much at a single stroke. If he withdrew now, it would almost certainly take several long years of interminable warfare before he could wrest from the English the recognition he craved. Victory in battle could potentially achieve this in one day. Surrounded by the largest force he had ever commanded, sensing its high morale and aware of the brittle fragility of his enemy, battle was a risk Bruce believed it was worth taking. Although a gamble, it was a supremely calculated gamble. It was a once-in-a-lifetime opportunity and Bruce grasped it with both hands.

This was a chance from which he could not turn away. He realised this could be the defining moment of his life.

The decision made, Bruce summoned a council of war. Picking their way through the darkness of the New Park, the Scottish lords converged on the spot where Bruce was in discussion with his lieutenants. A suspenseful hush descended upon them. They were not clear whether they were to withdraw or give battle. With trepidation they waited for him to speak. Bruce stood before them, their lives in his hands, and in a clear, resounding voice, delivered an impassioned speech.

Bruce urged them to recall those who had suffered in the wars against England, declaring, 'We have lost brothers, friends, relatives; your relatives and friends are prisoners, and now prelates and clergy are shut up in prison'. Of the English he proclaimed 'their glory is in carts and horses, for us hope is in the name of the Lord and victory in war'. Bruce spoke of the low morale of the host, of the hearts of the English being cast down by the reverses they had suffered, 'and if the heart is cast down, the body is not worth a jot'. Boldly he announced his decision to stay and fight. Bruce immediately followed this dramatic announcement by reassuring the assembled lords that they did not have to agree with his decision, that if they believed it right to withdraw then he would do so. Yet Bruce must have known full well that they would readily give their assent. It was nothing more than a skilful oratorical device, and it had its desired effect. The lords cried out their willingness to fight, greeting Bruce's decision with heartfelt acclaim. Emboldened by their response, Bruce confidently pronounced three reasons why the Scots had the edge over their enemy: first, he turned to the traditional claim of a just war, and that the Scottish cause was consequently blessed with divine favour; second, and more prosaically, he appealed to the materialism of the lords and their men, telling them that the English had brought such a wealth of riches with them that 'the poorest of you shall be rich and powerful as well'; third, and most emotively, Bruce declared that they were fighting for their own lives, for the lives of their children and their wives, for their freedom and for their land. The English, by contrast, fought solely for power. Bruce exhorted the Scottish lords not to take prisoners or spoils until the host was in complete disarray. He offered further reassurance by promising that all previous offences would be pardoned, and that the heirs of those who lost their lives in battle would freely receive their inheritance.[10]

It was a perfectly measured pre-battle speech, a rallying cry that appealed to both hearts and minds. To those Scots assembled in the New Park, Bruce was very much their king. Fortified by his passionate words the lords dispersed and, returning to their men, repeated the fervent address which still resounded with clarity in their ears. Throughout the New Park men prepared themselves for battle. Prayers were offered; forgiveness begged for past sins. The Scots were about to engage in a battle they had sought so strenuously to avoid for a generation. There could be no turning back. When daylight came they would fight.

Between three and four o'clock in the morning the first pale shade of dawn tinted the eastern horizon. Slowly the darkness faded. The sky was clear and carried the promise of another warm and sunny day. Beyond the carseland the first rays of sunlight bathed the ground. It was the morning of 24 June 1314. It was the feast day of St John the Baptist. It was dawn on the day stipulated as the deadline for the relief of Stirling Castle.

To the east of the New Park, in the Carse of Balquhiderock, the English host began to stir. Few had snatched more than a couple of hours' rest; almost none had slept. Awkwardly clambering to their feet, knights and men-at-arms stretched aching limbs and flexed tired muscles. The armour they had worn for twenty-four hours felt inordinately heavy, their shoulders and backs straining beneath the oppressive weight. Faces were grimed with dirt and the once colourful trappers of knightly destriers were obscured beneath a thick coating of dust. Squires hurried among the sprawling mass of cavalry, leading horses to be watered, attending to the needs of their lords as best they could. Knights and men-at-arms took stock of their new position, tired eyes taking in the flat terrain which lay before them and which then rose up towards the higher ground where, beyond their sight, stood the wooded enclosure of the New Park.

No one would have stared in the direction of the New Park as intently as Edward himself. If he had passed a slightly more comfortable night than most, it was not by much. Any relief in his mind that a Scottish night assault had not materialised would immediately have been replaced by the fear that the Scots had slipped away during the hours of darkness. It was too dangerous to send scouts into the park and there was little Edward could do but ready the host for the eventuality of battle. In fact, there is an unusual lack of information regarding the preparations of the host on this morning. By convention Edward should have engaged in the creation of new knights on the potential eve of a major battle and delivered a rousing, morale-boosting speech of the kind that Bruce had delivered so skilfully to the assembled Scottish lords. A sliver of evidence suggests that Edward did the former, but there is no indication whatsoever of the latter.[11] A basic breakfast of bread and most probably wine would have been taken. Anxious hands checked weapons and adjusted armour. Few words were spoken.

Beneath the heavy canopy of the New Park the darkness lingered a little longer. The Scots also ate a breakfast of bread and wine or water. Bruce, always careful to observe convention and ever mindful to consolidate his authority as king, ceremoniously knighted those who were due the honour. As was traditional he did so by order of precedence, the 'beardless lad' Walter Stewart receiving this mark of distinction ahead of Bruce's long-serving lieutenant James Douglas. More knighthoods followed, men who were 'of great valour' being similarly bestowed by Bruce in his guise as king.[12] It was the final act in bolstering the morale of his army, compelling those raised to knighthood to prove they were worthy of such a prestigious award and encouraging those with aspirations after knighthood to follow their example. The preparations concluded, there was nothing left for Bruce to do but order his men to take to the field for battle. It was a situation he had never before experienced.

Bruce was far from alone in this inexperience. The nearest he had come to battle was the desperate, disorganised and disastrous skirmish at Methven, and the sharp encounter at Loudoun Hill. These clashes were hardly full-scale engagements. Randolph and Douglas were similarly inexperienced. Edward Bruce had engaged in at least two battles during his time in Galloway, but these were as nothing compared to what he now faced. On the English side Edward II had never fought in battle nor had Gloucester. Valence, Clifford, Beaumont and Hereford had all been present at Falkirk, the only comparable encounter, but there had been no significant battle in the sixteen years that had since passed. Nor did the vast majority of men in each army have experience of battle. The wars had been conflicts of raids, ambushes and expeditions. Even seasoned veterans of more than a decade of warfare were untried when it came to a set-piece battle.

As the rays of the morning sun splintered the horizon, men grimly prepared to enter the unknown. In the preternatural stillness of early morning the silent landscape gave no sign of the appalling clash to come. Before Stirling, within sight of the besieged castle, battle was about to be met.

CHAPTER THIRTEEN

FLESH AND BLOOD

Shortly after daybreak on 24 June the Scots took to the field. It was a simple yet devastating move. Clutching spears in their hands and with battleaxes at their sides, they filed out from the wooded enclosure of the New Park and began to form up beyond its eastern fringe. For several minutes men continued to emerge as the entire Scottish army of upwards of five thousand disgorged from the wood. The rising sun was in their eyes and they gazed with difficulty across the expanse of ground which separated them from the English. In the blinding glare the presence of the host revealed itself in a splintered kaleidoscope of sunlight that reflected off the burnished metal of armour and chainmail. With the sun at their backs the English had no such difficulty in observing their enemy. What they saw, however, touched them with a profound sense of unease.

The sudden appearance of the Scots took the English completely by surprise. The last thing they had expected was for the Scots to take openly to the field. Although plagued by doubts throughout the night, never once did the English countenance the possibility that the Scots would willingly engage them in battle. The night having passed without a Scottish assault, the question that occupied the minds of the English was whether or not the Scots had withdrawn. Many must have expected that the New Park now lay empty. When the first Scottish foot soldiers stepped out from the distant park and advanced towards them, knights and men-at-arms would have ceased their preparations and instead wandered forwards to watch in silence as the Scottish army gradually appeared before them. This was the first sight of their enemy in its entirety. They could see that the army Bruce had assembled was substantial and well armed, but it was not this that troubled them. The wave of disquiet that rippled through the host emanated from the very fact that the Scots should willingly take to the field.

Such an act was unheard of. Throughout the wars the Scots had always sought to avoid battle: the engagement at Stirling Bridge had been an opportunistic attack executed against an isolated section of an English army; at Falkirk, Wallace had been compelled to fight when caught out by the speed of an unexpected English advance. The pattern of the wars had remained unchanged, the English always seeking to gain that elusive battle, and the Scots repeatedly doing all in their power to avoid it. For the English to bring the Scots to battle, it was necessary for them to compel the Scots to stand and fight, and it was the inability of the English to achieve this that was largely responsible for the prolonged nature of the wars. Ever since Edward II and his commanders had been informed of the siege of Stirling and the deadline for its relief, their overriding objective had been to force Bruce and his army into giving battle. It was for this reason that Edward had pushed ahead with the arduous night crossing of the Bannock Burn. The weight of the knowledge that the Scots were liable to slip away had been a terrible burden upon the king. As the sun rose behind him, his great fear was that the Scots had withdrawn during the night. In discovering that they had not done so Edward should have been greatly relieved. Any relief he did feel, however, was tempered by a disconcerting combination of bemusement and disbelief as he watched the Scottish army boldly take to the field before the might of the English host.

The exact location of the field of battle remains an endless source of debate and speculation (see Appendix I). Exiting from their position in the New Park, the Scots would initially have formed up on the broken, hard ground to the east of it. A 'dryfield', believed to be used for the growing of corn, was located on this hard ground. Beyond this, to the east, the land dropped down a relatively steep incline, at the bottom of which was the flat expanse of carseland which stretched away towards the distant Forth. It is not clear whether the Scots advanced down into the carseland to meet the English, or whether they advanced towards the English cavalry after the latter had already ascended the incline and gained the dryfield. Either way, the English cavalry were severely restricted by the unfavourable terrain in which they found themselves, the ground being either soft and boggy or hard and broken. Nor could the full strength of the host be brought to bear against the Scots. Indeed, if the host in its entirety was not still down in the carseland, then the vast majority of

English foot soldiers remained positioned upon this low-lying, treacherous ground. In late May, when Edward had desperately issued writs summoning foot soldiers, he had described this terrain of 'strong holds and morasses' that surrounded Stirling Castle as being 'nearly inaccessible to cavalry'. By crossing the Bannock Burn the king had placed his army on the very land he had identified as being entirely unsuited to cavalry. In his desperation to gain battle, Edward had positioned the host on some of the most disadvantageous ground imaginable. Confronted by the Scots, it was from here that the English would have to fight.

As the initial shock of the Scottish advance passed, a renewed bustle of life possessed the host. Battle was no longer a prospect, but a certainty. Knights and men-at-arms heaved themselves up into the solid bulk of their saddles. They carefully adjusted hauberks and haketons to ensure their heavy coats of chainmail provided all-round protection. They encompassed their hands in gauntlets or mittens of chainmail. The limbs of the wealthier knights were protected by plate armour, those of lesser men guarded by the hard armour of *cuir bouilli*. Squires lifted the colourful trappers that covered destriers to check the fastenings and protective padding beneath. Iron-headed lances of ash were clasped in practised hands. The pommels of swords protruded from scabbards. Some knights carried fearsome, armour-breaking, spiked maces and others falchions, short, broad-bladed swords particularly effective in the confines of close combat.

They manoeuvred their mounts into position, joining the retinues to which they belonged. The colourful panoply of banners that flew brightly overhead of the prominent knights and earls acted as a striking visual guide. Each retinue formed up within its allocated division. At the head of the vanguard the standards of Gloucester and Hereford were raised high and resplendent in the cloudless sky. Above the main English division flew the large royal standard of Edward II; the Plantagenet device of three golden *lions leopardés* on a cloth of deepest crimson was unmistakable in the morning light. Beside the royal standard the glittering jewelled eyes and flickering tongue of the notorious Dragon banner gleamed. Menacing and stark, the banner was a sign that no quarter was to be given. Arrayed beneath the banners of their division, the men commanded by Robert Clifford bore the scars of the previous day's fighting, their armour battered and links of chainmail broken. The three English cavalry divisions formed up with the vanguard slightly in advance. The bulk of the infantry remained to the rear. The Scots were about to receive the shattering impact of a full-blooded cavalry charge.

Edward recognised that this could be the defining moment of his troubled reign. Before the king were arrayed Robert Bruce and his Scottish army, an enemy that had plagued him throughout his rule. Beside Edward the formidable might of the English host awaited his order to attack. He was surrounded by ranks of knights and men-at-arms, the elite of the English war machine, while behind him a mass of foot soldiers stretched back towards the Bannock Burn. Mounted on the best of destriers, attired in the most splendid of armour, tall, muscular and handsome, Edward cut an imposing figure. Yet even he was not immune from the unease that pervaded the host.

It was with 'consternation' that the knights and men-at-arms of the host had hastily mounted, their discomposure caused by the extraordinary sight of the Scots taking to the field, a spectacle that Edward himself found difficult to credit.[1] According to the dramatic account of Barbour, Edward, bewildered by what he saw, turned to the mercurial Scot, Ingram de Umfraville, who was by his side. The king asked incredulously, 'What, do the Scots mean to fight?' 'Yes, indeed,' replied de Umfraville, betraying his own surprise by adding, 'now I see quite the most astonishing sight that I ever saw, when, in order to fight, the Scotsmen have undertaken to give battle against the might of England on open hard ground.' Even de Umfraville, who had once fought against the English, appears to have been astounded by the sight of the Scots taking to the field. Before Edward could comprehend the audacity of the Scots he was confounded by another mystifying spectacle. As he watched, the entire Scottish army, dropped to its knees as one. Astonished, Edward asked if they were pleading for his mercy. 'You are right this time,' responded de Umfraville, 'they ask for mercy, but not from you; for their trespass to God they cry.'[2] Again Edward and the host became curious spectators as another extraordinary event was played out before them.

By the edge of the field the Scots remained on their knees. Their heads bowed, they were led in the saying of mass by the abbot of Inchaffray. The abbot followed this with a brief, rousing speech, calling on the Scots to fight for freedom and the defence of their right. He then proceeded to walk before the massed ranks of the Scottish army, holding a crucifix aloft and urging them to pray.[3] Thousands of foot soldiers, the vast majority of whom were poor and illiterate, fixed their eyes upon the crucifix and prepared their souls for the terror that lay ahead. It was a humbling moment for Bruce; the human cost of his decision to give battle was laid bare as those around him prayed to the Lord for salvation. Having done all he could to fortify the army spiritually, the abbot departed.

Their prayers over, the Scots stood. Clutching spears and axes, they grimly prepared for the fight. Randolph proceeded to the head of the battle-scarred troops of the vanguard. Edward Bruce, perhaps accompanied by James Douglas, took up position with his division. These two formations, each several ranks deep, filled the width of the field of battle. The Scottish rearguard, commanded by Robert Bruce, moved into position behind them.[4] Considering the restricted nature of the ground, the light cavalry under Robert Keith must also have remained to the rear of the army. Belligerently the Scots faced their enemy. In front of them the English cavalry, their armour dazzling in the rising sun, 'shone as brightly as angels'.[5] If Bruce felt a shudder of doubt at what was to come, he did not allow it to show. He gave the order to advance. Foot soldiers trudged forwards. Slowly the Scottish army began to move towards the English position.

Any doubts Bruce may have felt were as nothing, however, compared to the terrible uncertainty that swept through the host. Those who had been most troubled by the astonishing spectacle of the Scots taking to the field were now gripped by an acute sense of foreboding. As the Scottish army advanced towards them, some of these knights and men-at-arms openly voiced the opinion that they should not fight that day. They argued that, as it was the feast day of St John the Baptist, they should show due respect and refrain from battle until the following day. Yet this was little more than an excuse; far more pointedly they stated that the host had already undergone great toil and should be given time to rest before engaging in battle. Critically, it was not those inexperienced in war who urged this delay, but the veterans among the host. As much as they were discomfited by the audacity of the Scots, they were gravely troubled by the state of their own army. Their plea for caution went unheeded. The concerns of these veterans were 'rejected by the younger men as idle and cowardly'; the latter did not listen to this 'practical and honourable advice'.[6]

Yet there was at least one wise head set upon young shoulders. The earl of Gloucester was becoming increasingly perturbed by the situation. As joint commander of the vanguard he was in a position to hear the rumblings of discontent that emanated from amongst the seasoned veterans. Already discomposed by the sight of the Scots taking to the field, he was further disturbed by what he now heard. Since being thrust upon the stage of English politics at the tender age of sixteen, Gloucester had consistently offered the voice of moderation and reason during the vicious factional disputes that had plagued Edward's reign. Gloucester had never shied from providing Edward with his counsel no matter how unpalatable it might prove to be. Grasping the reins of his destrier, he now made straight for the king.

Gloucester reiterated the advice of the veterans. He told Edward the host should not fight that day, citing the need to respect the feast day and the needs of the army to 'recuperate as much as possible'. Edward, bewildered by the unforeseen aggression of the Scots and frustrated by the reverses of the previous afternoon, was in no mood to countenance talk of a delay. He reacted furiously. Bluntly he 'spurned the earl's advice' and, 'growing very heated with him, charged him with treachery and deceit'. Gloucester reeled under this wild outburst of anger. Stung by the savagery of the king's unwarranted rebuke, he hotly declared, 'Today it will be clear that I am neither a traitor nor a liar'. Turning away, Gloucester galloped resentfully back to the vanguard.[7] It was an ugly moment reminiscent of the ill-tempered exchange between Beaumont and Gray the day before. The fault lines among the English command were beginning to crack under pressure. That Edward should accuse Gloucester of treachery appears to indicate that the king had not forgiven the earl for the role he had played in the death of Gaveston, a bitterness that still poisoned the mind of the king. It was an accusation Edward would soon have cause to regret.

For now there was no time for recriminations. As the Scots slowly advanced towards them, so the knights and men-at-arms made the final preparations for their charge: they nervously checked their armour and chainmail; they anxiously flexed their metal-encased fingers around the ashen shafts of lances; they wedged mailed feet firmly into the long stirrups that drooped down below the flanks of warhorses. Squires handed lords their helmets, the very last piece of armour to be put into place. With a sense of bleak finality knights and men-at-arms fastened their bacinets and great-helms. Their job done, the squires hurriedly departed to the rear of the cavalry divisions. The knights and men-at-arms, fully armoured and equipped, made ready for battle.

Few knew what to expect. The cavalry charge was an awesome weapon, but the English had not delivered such a charge for a generation. Indeed, it is unclear whether the engagement at Falkirk actually consisted of a cavalry charge *en masse* rather than a series of separate cavalry actions against individual schiltroms. The vast majority of knights and men-at-arms had never experienced a full-scale cavalry charge, while even the veterans of Falkirk were relative novices. It is unlikely there was a single horseman among the host who had experienced what he was about to undertake. Any sense of familiarity derived from presumption alone. In theory the cavalry charge was exactly what knights and esquires had trained for all their lives, yet the closest many had come to it was in the artificiality of the lists or the mêlée of a tournament. Before them was arrayed a solid mass of several thousand foot soldiers. From their position, the English cavalry could see an impenetrable forest of spears glistening in the sun. For the first time in their lives they were confronted by the brutal reality of delivering a cavalry charge. Nothing could have prepared them for what they now faced.

Edward knew the time had come. He could hear the harsh breath of those who awaited his order; he could sense the bristling energy of the cavalry straining to be unleashed. It is possible the engagement was preceded by a brief exchange of archery fire between a contingent of English and Scottish archers, *Lanercost* recording that 'English archers were thrown forward before the line, and the Scottish archers engaged them, a few being killed and wounded on either side; but the King of England's archers quickly put the others to flight'. If so, it was merely a preliminary to battle which was to be of no significance. Neither Edward II nor Robert Bruce attached any importance to it. Alternatively, Barbour claims that the English attempted to bring archers forward later in the engagement and relates that these were driven off by the light cavalry commanded by Robert Keith. There is no indication in the sources as to where the latter contingent was deployed.[8] Curiously, despite the vitally crucial role they could perform, English archers were to play no significant part in the engagement. The schiltrom was not bombarded by a hail of archery fire. Battle would only be met when the knights and men-at-arms crashed into the heaving ranks of Scottish foot soldiers, an explosive clash between an irresistible force and an immovable object. Both knew one would ultimately have to give way. The moment of truth had arrived. Edward gave the order.

Trumpet calls wailed starkly across the English lines. It was the signal to advance. The silence of the midsummer morning was abruptly shattered. Startled birds took flight from the fields. In the vanguard, knights and men-at-arms dug their spurs into the powerful flanks of their barded destriers and began to move forwards. Those knights and men-at-arms with visors fixed to their bacinets reached up and slammed them shut. They gripped tight their lances, ready to be lowered from the vertical to the horizontal at the moment of charge. Leading the vanguard, the earls of Gloucester and Hereford increased the pace from a trot to a canter. Armour began to clatter; the ground began to rumble. Relentlessly, the charge began to take on a momentum all of its own.

The eerie wail of the trumpet calls carried clearly to the Scots, shrilly piercing the stillness of the morning. The army was ordered to a halt. Ahead of them the lines of the English vanguard had already dissolved into a flurry of confused movement. Thomas Randolph and Edward Bruce immediately organised their two divisions into a single, unbroken schiltrom, which occupied the width of the field. Inexperienced as the English cavalry were in delivering a charge, so the Scots were without experience in receiving one. For those who had fought with such success under Bruce and his lieutenants, their experience of combat had consisted of irregular warfare, of ambushes and raids, sieges and assaults. The prolonged attack the Scottish vanguard had withstood the previous afternoon had not involved a full-scale cavalry charge, and the schiltrom they had formed then had been a compact, circular formation, rather than the solid, front-facing line in which they were now arrayed. The Scots had no experience of withstanding such a charge as they were about to receive.

The two Scottish divisions closed together to form one solid mass of spearmen several ranks deep. The Scots were packed so closely that, according to the *Vita*, they 'advanced like a thick-set hedge, and such a phalanx could not easily be broken'.[9] Having come to a halt the Scottish army now formed a solid, unmoving wall. Planting their feet firmly on the ground, ensuring they gained a firm hold, brandishing spears and holding shields, they turned their bodies to meet the impact of the charge. The foremost ranks raised their spears, a splintered forest of wood and metal protruding outwards to meet the oncoming flesh and blood. The Scottish foot soldiers could hear the first stirrings of the rolling thunder of hooves; beneath them the ground began to tremble. They tensed their bodies and steeled themselves for the shattering impact that was about to tear into them.

Gloucester was at the forefront of the charge. The stinging words of the king would still have rung in his ears as he drove his destrier forwards. Before him he could see the unwavering mass of the schiltrom that stretched across the field. The noise was deafening as the iron-shod hooves of more than a thousand heavy warhorses pounded thunderously upon the hard ground, ripping up earth and grass, and flinging up a trail of mud and dust in their wake. Banners streamed, whipped backwards by the speed of the charge. The massed ranks of the Scottish schiltrom loomed ahead and rapidly took on shape and form. As Gloucester closed on it, he could distinguish grim-set faces and the cruel glint of spearheads. He levelled his lance. The ground raced beneath him. The schiltrom rushed up before him. Then he hit it. In a tremendous collision of appalling violence the vanguard slammed into the schiltrom.

There was a maelstrom of chaos: horses were horrifically impaled upon spears; knights and men-at-arms were thrown to the ground; the schiltrom reeled as foot soldiers were flung backwards by the bone-crunching impact; some were trampled, the razor-sharp heads of lances skewered others. As lances and spears clashed, they snapped with such ferocity 'that men could hear it far away'.[10] Metal sliced through flesh. Bones shattered. Blood sprayed the air. The Scots faltered, but the sheer density of the schiltrom absorbed the devastating blow. The vanguard had driven into the division commanded by Edward Bruce; roared on by their pugnacious commander, the Scots savagely fought back, attacking the English 'with spears that were cutting-sharp, and axes that were well ground, with which many a blow was struck'.[11] Knights and men-at-arms frantically wheeled their destriers around, coming in to attack again, those whose lances remained intact lunging and hurling them at the Scots. Swords were drawn from scabbards and cut at exposed flesh, spiked maces swung at armour and heads, horses were rammed into flailing bodies and shields into faces as battle was met.

Moments after the English vanguard crashed into the schiltrom, the Scots were rocked by a second terrific shock as the bulk of the English cavalry thundered into the Scottish vanguard. There was a 'great crash of the spears that broke', knights and men-at-arms tumbling from their saddles 'for many a horse was impaled there, and many good men felled under their feet had no chance of getting up'. Again the Scots faltered, but Randolph rallied his men and the schiltrom held. The initial impact of the charge had proved indecisive; the full-scale cavalry charge had failed to break the Scottish line. Across the breadth of the field the two armies now became engaged in a desperate battle of attrition: 'there you could see a remorseless battle, some defending, some attacking ... until blood burst through the mail-coat and went streaming down to the earth'. Entrapped in the frenzied mayhem of the mêlée, men frantically fought for their lives. There was a chaos of noise, a blur of sights, senses were disorientated and minds confused. Men fought in the midst of a havoc of murderous violence as they lashed out at their enemies and desperately fended off deadly blows. Physically punishing to even the most powerful of men, the mêlée was psychologically torturous to the strongest of minds: 'there was such a din of blows, as weapons landing on armour, such a great breaking of spears, such pressure and such pushing, such snarling and groaning, so much noise as they struck others, and shouted rallying cries on each side, giving and receiving great wounds, that it was horrible to hear'. As the two armies fought, beneath them 'the grass grew red with blood'.[12]

Neither Robert Bruce nor Edward II had any control over the battle that now raged. The engagement had degenerated into the vicious free-for-all of the hand-to-hand mêlée. Any semblance of influence or command was invested within the retinue leaders and divisional commanders who fought alongside their men. Distinguishable even in the mêlée due to the high class of their armour and equipment, their armorial banners flying above them and emblazoned upon their shields, surcoats and trappers, the commanders provided a critical focal point to inspire and encourage their men, to act as a rallying point.

Gloucester was such a commander. Having led the charge of the vanguard he remained at the forefront of the action, zealously attacking the schiltrom. The venom of his initial charge was most probably motivated by the insulting accusations of the king, which almost certainly fuelled the savagery with which he now attacked the Scots. It may be that the anger that coursed through Glouceter's veins led him to overcommit himself, to take unnecessary risks in an effort to prove himself neither a traitor nor a liar. It could be that he was merely a tragic victim of circumstance. The *Vita* recounts that there was a sudden shift in the battle. Momentarily Gloucester was caught alone. The Scots seized their chance and swept forwards. Gloucester's destrier was slain beneath him. Unhorsed, he tumbled to the ground. The weight of his armour prevented him from scrambling to his feet. As he lay helpless on the blood-soaked grass, the Scottish foot soldiers mercilessly killed the young earl. Later, when his body was retrieved, it was found to be 'pierced by many wounds'.[13]

The devastating effect his death had on the host was immense. Gloucester was the second most powerful English figure present, surpassed only by the king himself; after the king and the earl of Lancaster he was the third most powerful man in the entire English realm. The deaths the previous day of Henry de Bohun and William Deyncourt, both prominent knights, had stunned the host; the impact of the death of Gloucester was staggering in its enormity. He was the first English earl to be killed in the Scottish wars; indeed, no earl had been killed in action for more than sixty years. If the death of a knight in battle was considered a rare event, then that of an earl was almost unheard of. In magnitude the shock felt at the death of Gloucester by those who witnessed or soon heard of it must have been similar to that which had gripped the host when they had seen the Scots take to the field. It was a profoundly traumatic blow.

Such was the enormity of Gloucester's loss, and so great the confusion of the mêlée, that the author of the *Vita* felt compelled to provide two conflicting accounts of Gloucester's death. The version given above is that which the *Vita* gives the most support to. However, in the aftermath of battle, the author was aware of rumours that circulated identifying the rivalry between Gloucester and Hereford, joint commanders of the vanguard, as the cause of the young earl's death. It was said that Hereford believed he should have had the honour of leading the vanguard into battle as he was Constable of England; Gloucester disagreed, stating that his 'forbears had always led the vanguard' and consequently custom dictated that he should have the honour. In an attempt to seize the glory, Gloucester impetuously charged the schiltrom ahead of the vanguard and was unhorsed and killed in the course of this foolhardy attack. It is a measure of the magnitude of his loss that two such conflicting accounts of Gloucester's death continued to have widespread currency after the battle had been fought. It was so unprecedented that such a powerful man should die that there was a need to provide an explanation for the loss. Blame was subsequently heaped upon Bartholomew Badlesmere, a knight of Gloucester's retinue, who was accused of failing to come to the aid of his lord. So severe was the criticism to which Badlesmere was subjected that in England his name became a byword for treachery.[14]

Badlesmere, however, was not alone in his failure to protect the unhorsed Gloucester. Of the entire English vanguard, a force of at least five hundred knights and men-at-arms, apparently not one man came to his aid. It was an apparent dereliction of duty that prompted the *Vita* to remark scathingly, 'Accursed be the chivalry whose courage fails in the hour of greatest need!' and lament, 'Alas! Twenty armed knights could have saved the earl, but among some five hundred not one was found to help'.[15] Yet the failure of the vanguard soldiers to save Gloucester was not the result of their unwillingness to do so; the more disturbing truth is that many were unable to reach him.

The narrowness of the field to which the cavalry was restricted was ominously beginning to tell. As three mounted divisions, perhaps totalling fifteen hundred knights and men-at-arms, attempted to engage the Scots, the whole force began to bunch up dangerously. Those cavalry to the rear pressed forwards determined to reach the fight; beyond them the bulk of the host, a teeming mass of several thousand foot soldiers, closed in behind. Pushed forward by this relentless press of men and horses, the knights and men-at-arms who were engaged in combat were increasingly compressed together and driven towards the spears of the schiltrom. Trapped between the press of their own men and the unmoving wall of the schiltrom, they were denied the space essential to manoeuvre their warhorses and maintain their attack on the Scots. More portentously, they could not manoeuvre to avoid the spears which were viciously thrust towards them, the three cavalry divisions gradually being 'crushed together so that they could not move against them, whilst their horses were being disembowelled by spears'.[16] As the host pressed in on itself, English losses began to mount.

This was the dark heart of the battle. The fight was so intense that at times 'you could hear no noise there; men heard nothing but grunts and blows ... they made neither shout nor yell, but struck each other with all their might'.[17] Swords cut through padded armour; axes cleaved through chainmail and helmets. Shields blocked blows and were thrust into faces. Knives stabbed at exposed flesh. Knees, fists and shoulders were rammed into enemies. Many of those who fell were suffocated and trampled to death beneath a writhing mass of men and horses. Locked in combat, pressed in against one another, the two sides relentlessly fought on.

It was in the midst of this intense mêlée that Robert Clifford was killed. One of the most experienced commanders of the host, Clifford 'was overcome by the Scots and died in the field'.[18] This is the only reference we have to his death. That the demise of a figure as prominent as Clifford should only merit such a vague statement is telling in itself; for the moment and manner of his death to have gone unnoticed suggests he was killed at the height of the fighting as he led the battered survivors of his division who had suffered such an ignominious reverse the previous day. It is fair to assume that Clifford was desperate to atone for the shame of that defeat. Perhaps, like Gloucester, he too believed that he had something to prove, that his reputation was at stake. The stigma of defeat would certainly have led Clifford to refuse taking a backward step as he engaged the schiltrom. Clifford's determination to take the fight to the Scots resulted in his death and with it the loss of a second English divisional commander. It was another devastating blow to the host: Gloucester had been the second most prominent figure among them; Clifford was one of its most experienced commanders. Yet despite these losses the knights and men-at-arms did not falter. Rather it was in the rear of the host that the cracks began to show.

Apart perhaps from a small contingent of archers the English foot soldiers had not yet seen action. Packed between the rear of the cavalry and the Bannock Burn, this force of several thousand men must have begun to suspect that something was amiss. They could hear the sounds of battle, but could not see it. What they did witness, though, was the large number of knights and men-at-arms ahead of them who remained immobile and unable to push through to the scene of the fighting. The foot soldiers were not a disciplined body of men. Desertion and indiscipline were regular features of infantry levies in medieval armies. In the past two days the foot soldiers of the host had been forced to march from Edinburgh to Stirling, a distance of approximately thirty miles, in the long daylight hours and oppressive heat of a warm midsummer. During the night, instead of gaining some much needed rest, they had found themselves wading through the freezing waters of the Bannock Burn.

Physically exhausted, their morale was also precariously low. Unlike the knights and men-at-arms of the host, the foot soldiers had little hope of achieving fame or renown, nor were they likely to enrich themselves against an enemy who was relatively poor. Dispiritedly they had heard of the inauspicious actions fought the previous day and of the casualties suffered. During the night, queuing upon the makeshift walkways beside the Bannock Burn, their concerns had grown. Now, as the cavalry stalled before them and the clamour of battle rang ominously in their ears, their last reserves of morale began to fall away. News of the death of Gloucester may have filtered through to them. At this point the 'small folk' appointed by Bruce to watch over the Scottish baggage, 'yeomen and boys and carters', may have appeared in significant numbers on a distant rise in the vicinity of Coxet Hill or Gillies Hill to the west in the hope of gaining plunder.[19] The fragile morale of the foot soldiers finally collapsed. To the rear of the host demoralised foot soldiers started to drift away from the army and make their way back towards the Bannock Burn. Others began to follow. The drift of men became a trickle and the trickle a flow, and with a startling rapidity the foot soldiers of the English host began to retreat *en masse*. Panic set in and 'the men in the English rear fell back on the Bannock Burn ditch, falling one over another'. The contagion of retreat spread rabidly through the host. For those unable to push through to the fighting, whether infantry or cavalry, 'there remained nothing but to take flight'.[20]

As the rear disintegrated, so the host gradually began to break apart. A vacuum developed behind the front ranks. The cavalry engaged in the thick of the fighting 'disarrayed by the blows of spear points to their horses, began to flee'.[21] Suddenly Edward II himself was dangerously exposed. The two renowned warriors entrusted with his safekeeping and his destrier's reins, Aymer de Valence and Giles d'Argentan, saw the crisis that was developing and were quick to realise the battle was all but lost. Although a significant number of knights and men-at-arms were still engaged in the fight, Valence and d'Argentan knew their priority was to ensure the safety of the king. The consequences of Edward being captured or killed were too appalling to contemplate. It was essential for the king to be extricated from the field of battle before the host completely broke apart.

Obstinately, Edward refused to leave: 'The king, taking the ruin and flight of his men with a bitter spirit, and despising the fear of death from a strength of rage ... rushed fiercely against the enemy like a lion which had lost its whelps'. In desperation Valence and d'Argentan were forced to lead him physically from the field, pulling his destrier away by its reins, doing so against Edward's will 'for it pained him to leave'. The Scots were frighteningly close and a contingent of Scottish knights, fighting on foot, 'grabbed the caparison of the king's warhorse with their hands to bring him to a halt'. Beset by bitterness and anger, and beside himself at the prospect of defeat, Edward 'struck behind him with a mace, so forcefully that there were none that he hit, whom he did not beat to the ground'. It was with tremendous difficulty that the king was escorted from the field, his destrier being seriously wounded in the fierce exchanges and unable to go on. A riding horse was quickly brought up, a courser, and the king hastily remounted. Having left the field, the knights and men-at-arms of the royal household closed in protectively around him.[22]

According to one account, d'Argentan, his duty to the king fulfilled, turned and addressed him. For a knight renowned as the third best in Christendom after the Holy Roman Emperor Henry VII and Robert Bruce, the humiliating defeat in which d'Argentan found himself was too much for his honour to bear. 'I am not accustomed to fleeing,' he announced to Edward, 'and I do not wish to go any further. I commend you to God.' Without another word d'Argentan turned his destrier and charged alone at the Scottish schiltrom. Bellowing the battle cry 'Argentan!' he rode headlong into Edward Bruce's division. He was met by a vicious wall of spears. His horse was slain. D'Argentan, set upon by an onslaught of knives, axes and spears, was overwhelmed and immediately killed.[23] D'Argentan's charge was to win him great fame; the charge was also a measure of the depth of despair that he felt at the unfolding defeat.

With the departure of the king from the field, the English host finally collapsed. When those knights and men-at-arms who were still tenaciously engaging the Scots saw the royal standard leave the field, they recognised that all was lost. Because of the withdrawal of the king, they were no longer obliged to stay and fight. Desperate to save their own lives they turned their mounts and fled. Only around Edward was any semblance of order maintained. The contingent of cavalry that surrounded him was substantial, numbering around five hundred men. They rode north, intending to take refuge within the walls of Stirling Castle. It was with shock, however, that they found the 'drawbridge was raised and the gate closed', the king 'repulsed as if he were an enemy'. There were murmurs of treachery. Philip Mowbray and his garrison had remained inside throughout the battle, though it was rumoured that Mowbray had been seen in armour as if to fight.[24] Rather than acting treacherously, Mowbray appears to have realised that if Edward entered the castle then he would effectively become a prisoner, for he would almost certainly be captured when the castle was subsequently surrendered. For Edward and his large escort, caught out by this unexpected development, there was a moment of dreadful indecision. Only one chance of escape remained – for Edward to flee south to the border accompanied by his cavalry escort. If necessary they would have to fight their way out of Scotland. Grasping the reins of their horses they turned away from the castle and, riding 'all the way round the Torwood' to the west to ensure they gave the victorious Scots a wide berth, they galloped southwards.[25]

Those still on the field of battle were not so fortunate. Many knights, men-at-arms and foot soldiers also attempted to flee south towards the border. Blocking their way was the Bannock Burn. When it had been crossed in the night, it was viewed as a barrier separating the host from gaining battle and a glorious victory. No thought had been given to the lethal obstacle it would prove to be in the event of a retreat. Thousands of men and hundreds of horses now descended upon it as they desperately fled for their lives.

Frantically they scrambled down its banks, tripping and falling into the freezing water, pushing and pulling others out of their way. Those who fell were crushed and trampled. Warhorses lost their footing and tumbled in. Weighted down by armour and chainmail, knights and men-at-arms were dragged beneath the surface and drowned. More fugitives followed as the defeat became a rout, men wildly plunging in where there was no hope of crossing, pressing down on those already struggling to keep their heads above water. Those trapped below the water, unable to free themselves from the clinging morass of mud that lined the bottom, flailed helplessly in the Bannock Burn's murky depths. It took a terrible toll as 'many nobles and others fell into it with their horses in the crush, while others escaped with much difficulty, and many were never able to extricate themselves from the ditch'. So many died within the Bannock Burn it was claimed that 'men and horses could then pass dry-foot over it on drowned horses and men'. The *Vita*, more simply but with no less horror, recounts that 'a great part of our army perished in it'.[26] The number of lives lost, and the horrendous manner in which those entrapped within the Bannock Burn died, leave no doubt as to the magnitude and terror of the disaster that befell them.

That so many men undertook this desperate crossing was due to their anxiety to escape the brutal slaughter that was the fate of their companions caught on the field of battle. Not only the triumphant Scottish foot soldiers savagely killed any Englishmen they found alive. The rabble of 'small folk', who had been ordered to watch over the Scottish baggage, had now appeared among the carnage of the battlefield. As soon as they saw the host had been defeated, they swarmed over the field and 'ran among them [the English] and killed them like men who could put up no defence – it was dreadful to see'.[27] They enthusiastically indulged not only in an orgy of killing but also of pillaging. The corpses of men-at-arms and, in particular, knights, were rich pickings for men who lived in relative poverty. They vied with the Scottish foot soldiers as they ruthlessly stripped bodies of 'silver, gold, clothes and armour'. Soon an even greater haul of riches presented itself as the rampant Scots overran and sacked the vast English baggage train, despoiling it of such a wealth of armour, gold and silver plate, jewels and costly garments that the *Vita* claimed goods to the amount of £200,000 were seized.[28] Whatever the precise amount, it was a spectacularly rich haul which must have made some individuals extremely wealthy.

In his pre-battle speech Robert Bruce had offered the wealth that the English brought with them as one of the incentives for his troops to fight. It was an enticement he now had cause to regret, as his victorious army chose plunder over pursuit of the fleeing remnants of the defeated enemy. In defeat the English host irretrievably broke apart; in the exultation of victory and with the prospect of booty, the Scottish army lost all semblance of discipline and chaotically dispersed. Bruce ceased to have a cohesive army at his disposal at the very moment when he needed to consolidate his victory by pursuing the host. As the *Vita* recognised, it was extremely fortunate that 'a great part of the Scottish army was occupied in plunder' as 'if all the Scots alike had been attending to the pursuit of our men, few would have escaped'.[29] For those who managed to flee the field of battle and scramble across the Bannock Burn, the danger was far from over. In their haste to escape, knights shed their armour; the more fortunate fled on horseback, but many knights and men-at-arms were forced to take flight on foot. To their rear they were constantly harried by disorganised bands of Scotsmen, while the inhabitants of the countryside, realising with surprise that the English had been defeated, rose up against them and indiscriminately slaughtered any they caught.[30]

Another group of English fugitives had followed the initial route of Edward II north and sought refuge in Stirling Castle. They too had been refused entry by Mowbray and, in desperation, had recourse to climbing onto the escarpments of the crag on which the castle was perched. So substantial were their numbers, 'the rocks about the castle' being 'all covered here and there by those who fled', that Bruce found it necessary to gather together a large company of men for fear that if those on the crag regrouped they could pose a significant danger. To eradicate this threat Bruce ordered an attack. The English, however, no longer had the stomach for the fight. Recognising the futility of their situation, they surrendered without a struggle and were taken prisoner.[31] It was the last significant act on the field of battle.

To the south Edward II made good his escape. After Mowbray had refused him entry to Stirling Castle, the king with his substantial escort of five hundred knights and men-at-arms had ridden non-stop through the Lowlands as the sun beat down upon their backs. They were pursued by Douglas, who had gathered together a band of sixty Scottish light cavalry, together with another Scottish knight, Laurence Abernethy, and his mounted contingent. Abernethy was in allegiance to the English and had been bringing aid to the host; on hearing of the Scottish victory he promptly joined Douglas. Unperturbed by the odds stacked against him, Douglas persisted in following the king and caught up with the English at Linlithgow. However, even Douglas knew that an attack would be suicidal. Instead, he continued to track Edward to Winchburgh – a small village to the west of Edinburgh – where both groups watered their horses, then trailed the king to Dunbar. Here Edward was received by Earl Patrick of Dunbar, a Scot in allegiance to the English. Adhering to strict feudal custom, the earl delivered his castle of Dunbar to the king and moved out his own household. A ship was immediately made ready and Edward, accompanied by a select escort of close companions, set sail for England. The cavalry that had escorted the king to Dunbar were left behind. Drawing together in a close company, they set out again riding south for the border and the fortress town of Berwick.[32]

Meanwhile, Robert Bruce had remained on the field. Throughout the mêlée, Bruce and his lieutenants had commanded their respective divisions as they battled fiercely against the English cavalry. Now, strewn around him were the dead and the dying, both Scots and English. In the Bannock Burn the deep waters were stilled as those trapped within succumbed to its icy embrace. Among the carnage of the battlefield those attempting to identify the corpses of notable men were hindered in their task by coats of arms being covered in blood, and by the hordes of victorious Scots who were frantically stripping the dead in their hunt for wealth. The enormity of what Bruce and his Scottish army had achieved could be seen in the devastation around them. It was a battle that Bruce, his lieutenants and his army had not merely survived but had resoundingly won. They had not only defeated the formidable might of the English host but had emphatically routed it. Robert Bruce stood at the epicentre of a victory of seismic proportions, the shockwaves of which were only just beginning to be felt.

IV

THE SHOCKWAVE

*O day of vengeance and disaster, day of utter loss and shame,
evil and accursed day, not to be reckoned in our calendar . . . .
So many fine noblemen and valiant youth, so many noble horses, so
much military equipment, costly garments and gold plate – all lost
in one unfortunate day, one fleeting hour.*

Vita Edwardi Secundi

CHAPTER FOURTEEN

ONE FLEETING HOUR

EDWARD II MAY HAVE BEEN FORTUNATE TO ESCAPE THE FIELD OF BATTLE, BUT THE political fallout of the catastrophic defeat threatened to engulf him. Having taken ship from Dunbar, he disembarked at Berwick and made for York.[1] Here, in the principal town of northern England, Edward tried to come to terms with the calamitous rout that had shattered the English host. The king was joined in his troubled deliberations by Valence and Beaumont, both commanders most probably having sailed from Dunbar with Edward. News of the shocking defeat spread quickly throughout the kingdom. In few places was alarm voiced as openly as in the narrow, claustrophobic streets of York, where the king and his close companions now resided in a state of numb bewilderment. Beyond the town walls chaos reigned.

The collapse of the host led to an alarming outbreak of rumour and confusion. It was not known who was alive and who dead. News, most of it unsubstantiated, constantly filtered through to Edward. It was not until 22 July, nearly a full month after the battle had been fought, that Edward learnt for certain that Ingram de Umfraville had been taken alive by the Scots.[2] That the fate of such a prominent figure should remain unknown for so long indicates the enormous scale of the confusion which the defeat generated. The host, broken apart and dispersed, had fled in panic towards the border; troops scattered throughout the Scottish Lowlands and northern England. It would take months before the fate of many of these survivors became clear.

The fate of Hereford, however, soon became known. If Edward had believed the situation could not get any worse, then the news of what had befallen his brother-in-law was to prove him wrong. Hereford and a number of prominent lords, accompanied by a large force of knights, men-at-arms and foot soldiers, had managed to extricate themselves from the battlefield. As Edward fled east to Dunbar, they had taken a more direct route to the border and headed south. At Bothwell, seven miles to the south of Glasgow, they had broken their journey, and the more prominent of the fugitives, Hereford among them, had taken temporary refuge in Bothwell Castle. The great stone fortress of Bothwell had been in English hands for more than a decade. In 1314 its keeper was Walter Gilbertson, a Scottish knight in allegiance to the English. From the moment Hereford and his men arrived, Gilbertson appears to have begun to reconsider where his best interests lay. This crisis of loyalty did not prevent him from admitting the fugitives into the castle, though ominously he deliberately placed them in separate timber houses within the castle ward, careful to split them up. It is not clear at what point Hereford realised that his intended place of refuge had become a prison. Entrapped within the formidable curtain walls of Bothwell Castle there could be no escape. Gilbertson immediately entered into negotiations with Edward Bruce and, upon securing favourable terms, he transferred the bewildered earl and his comrades as prisoners to Robert Bruce.[3]

The capture of Hereford was a devastating blow for Edward. He had no choice but to negotiate for the earl's release; however, it was painfully clear that Bruce would demand a high price for such a prestigious captive. Moreover, that price would not be financial, but political. On 18 July Edward ordered the prior of Sixhills in Lincolnshire to deliver Christian Bruce, Robert's sister, to the sheriff of Lincoln, who was to bring her to Edward at York. Similar orders stipulated that Bruce's wife, Elizabeth, should also be brought to York, along with Robert Wishart, bishop of Glasgow, and Donald, earl of Mar, together with a number of prominent Scots who were also in English custody. Elizabeth Bruce was still in London a week later, on 26 July the constable of Rochester Castle being ordered to transfer her to the Tower of London. The intimates of Robert Bruce remained in York throughout the late summer while protracted negotiations for the release of Hereford were conducted. It was not until 2 October that orders were issued for Wishart, Donald, earl of Mar, Elizabeth, Christian and Marjorie, Bruce's daughter, to be escorted to Carlisle Castle, and then on to a location arranged by Hereford where the exchange of prisoners was to take place.[4] In obtaining the release of family and allies who had been lost to him as prisoners for eight years, Bruce had achieved a great personal and political coup. The cost to Edward of securing the release of

Hereford was immensely damaging both for the Scottish war, in terms of popular propaganda, and for his own fragile political authority.

The exchange may well have been delayed due to the English parliament, which met at York in September. It was a parliament that Edward did not want to summon but that the defeat at Bannockburn had made inevitable. The parliament he dreaded opened on 7 September. The earl of Lancaster was now preeminent. During the campaign he had remained in Yorkshire, residing in his favourite castle of Pontefract and anxiously awaiting news of the host. At best he must have expected to hear that the campaign had proved futile and that the Scots had predictably withdrawn before the host and refused to give battle. Such an ineffective campaign would have provided Lancaster with the political ammunition to mount another attack on the king and push for the implementation of the Ordinances which had first been drawn up in 1311. When Lancaster was informed that the host had been defeated in battle, he would have been as startled as anyone. Yet he must also have experienced a grim sense of elation. On the back of such a disastrous defeat the resurgent authority of Edward was broken. At the York parliament Lancaster found himself to be virtually unopposed. Edward feebly agreed to observe the Ordinances and made no attempt to protest against a subsequent purge of the royal household. Lancaster, however, was also acutely aware of the Scottish threat, and a series of measures were taken for the defence of northern England. What is immediately striking is that there was no attempt to enter into peace negotiations with Robert Bruce.[5]

Nor did Bruce believe that Bannockburn had won him the war. He was quick to follow up his astonishing victory. In August he led a raid with Douglas that reached as far south as Richmond in Yorkshire, only forty miles from York itself, and subsequently the raiding force wreaked devastation on Cumberland as it made its way back to Scotland.[6] This raid deep into northern England was clearly intended as a ruthless follow-up to the victory won at Bannockburn, providing the English with a frightening demonstration of the extensive reach of Bruce and the Scots – a raid that Bruce must have hoped might convince Edward, or indeed Lancaster, to consider a settlement. Such an agreement would also seem to be behind the magnanimous gestures Bruce made towards his defeated enemy in the aftermath of Bannockburn. The bodies of Gloucester and Clifford were respectfully removed from the battlefield and freely transported to England. Marmaduke Tweng was freed without ransom and allowed to depart with his costly armour. Edward's privy seal and his shield, both lost in the rout, were found upon the field of battle and diplomatically returned to the king.[7] Bruce, ever the skilful politician, recognised that he needed to convince the English to reach a settlement; he did not want to alienate Edward by heaping further humiliation upon him. The truth was that, despite the shattering defeat of the English host, Bruce was not in a position to dictate terms.

In November 1314 Bruce held the second parliament of his reign.[8] It took place at Cambuskenneth Abbey just east of the once mighty Stirling Castle – which Bruce had destroyed in the immediate aftermath of the battle – and only a few miles from the battlefield of Bannockburn itself. As Bruce presided over the parliament it cannot have been lost on him that a decade before, in this same abbey, he had first begun to plot his way to the Crown. His domestic position was now immeasurably strengthened. The political kudos of his victory at Bannockburn was immense, while materially the spoils of battle – consisting of copious amounts of armour, weapons, silver, plate and, later, ransom payments – were so substantial that Scotland now 'overflowed with boundless wealth'.[9] With victory at Bannockburn, the tide of the Scottish power struggle in which he was engaged had irrevocably turned. Walter Gilbertson was only one of a number of Scots who now entered into Bruce's allegiance. Philip Mowbray, the constable of Stirling Castle, having duly handed over the castle, had come into Bruce's peace. Patrick, earl of Dunbar, having seen Edward II to safety, also felt the irresistible shift of the political tide and submitted to Bruce. At Cambuskenneth Abbey, adhering to the blunt ultimatum he had delivered the previous year, Bruce disinherited those who had not come into his allegiance, along with those Scots who had died fighting against him on the field of battle. By formally carrying out this act, Bruce effectively consolidated his authority in Scotland as king.

But an impasse remained. Bruce could still not gain the crucial English recognition of his status which he required to secure his hold on the Crown. If Edward had been captured, then Bruce could almost certainly have extorted this formal recognition as the price of the king's ransom, a recognition that would also have implicitly established the independence of the Scottish kingdom. The failure to capture the English king was critical in denying Bruce the opportunity fully to exploit the victory won at Bannockburn. Yet this may not be the only reason the battle did not ultimately prove decisive. By the autumn of 1314, as both the English and the Scots took stock of the implications of Bannockburn in their respective parliaments, the disorientating fog of war that obscured the last day of the battle was gradually being dispersed. Only as the weeks passed did the character of the English defeat slowly become apparent. Indeed, it was the manner of this defeat that also precluded Bannockburn from being a decisive Scottish victory.

With the passing of time the events of 24 June 1314 have once again disappeared into an obscuring mist. Nearly seven centuries after the battle was fought, it is only to be expected that our knowledge of what actually happened on that extraordinary day is imprecise and fragmentary. Exactly how the mêlée unfolded will never be known. The horror of the battle is evident, as is the terror of the desperate hand-to-hand combat, the panicked flight of the English and the appalling death of those who drowned in the mud-churned waters of the Bannock Burn. There can be no doubt that it was an unexpected and spectacular Scottish victory. For the English the humiliation of such a comprehensive defeat at the hands of the Scots was devastating. This much is clear. Yet many questions about the crucial engagement on 24 June remain unanswered; indeed, several fundamental questions have rarely, if ever, been asked. If the extraordinary outcome of the battle of Bannockburn is to be truly understood, then it is by means of a thorough re-examination and re-evaluation of the surviving sources which recount that fateful day.

In the late summer of 1314, as Edward anxiously awaited the September opening of parliament in York, the number of casualties suffered by the host would gradually have become apparent. It would have been impossible then, as it is now, to establish anything approaching an approximate estimate of the number of those of the English host killed in the battle. Nor would any attempt have been made to ascertain these figures. The only men whose fate would eventually have become known were those of rank, the lords and knights of the host. Although no official casualty list exists, contemporary chronicles record the death of forty-nine such men. Besides Gloucester, Clifford and d'Argentan, the *Vita* records the deaths of Payn Tibetot and William Marshal, while the deaths of Edmund de Mauley, steward of the king's household, and John Comyn, lord of Badenoch (son of the John Comyn killed by Bruce in 1306), are referred to in *Lanercost*. Edmund Comyn also died fighting on the English side. Several knights of Valence's retinue were slain, including John de Riveres and William de Vescy. A contemporary English chronicle, the continuation of Nicholas Trivet's chronicle, provides by far the most detailed list of English casualties. This source names twenty-seven high-ranking fatalities and claims that an additional, unnamed, thirty-three knights also perished, making a total of sixty. The *Annales Londonienses* provide the names of nineteen men of rank slain, which are not identified by the continuation of Trivet (see Appendix II).[10] On the first day of battle alone, 23 June, the killing of just two knights, Henry de Bohun and William Deyncourt, had been sufficient momentarily to stun the host. The psychological impact of the brutal death of so many men of rank and status on the English must have been immense.

That such an unprecedented number of knights were killed has led to the assumption that the host suffered horrendous battlefield losses. If casualty figures were so high among knights, then it follows that this should also be true of the host at large. It was also a contemporary belief, the late fourteenth-century Scottish chronicler John of Fordun recording that 'the earl of Gloucester and a great many other nobles were killed; a great many were drowned in the waters, and slaughtered in pitfalls; a great many, of diverse ranks, were cut off by diverse kinds of death'.[11] So grievous were English losses presumed to have been that Bannockburn has frequently been portrayed as a battle in which the flower of English chivalry was slaughtered, and the host so decimated that the English realm was temporarily destroyed as a fighting force.[12] This is the traditional view of Bannockburn, the mêlée fought on the second day being seen as a prolonged battle of attrition in which the host was gradually annihilated in a horrific massacre.

The sources suggest this was not the case. On 17 August 1314 a substantial force of approximately 120 troops was dispatched from York to reinforce the English garrison of Berwick. This force was composed entirely of troops of the royal household. It was headed by William Montagu and twenty household knights, these knights being accompanied by forty-three of their esquires and forty of the king's sergeants-at-arms, along with a number of additional troops.[13] It was a powerful force, well armed, well equipped and mounted. The crucial factor, however, is that it was composed exclusively of royal household troops. There is every reason to believe that most, if not all, of this household force had been present with the king at Bannockburn. Indeed, one knight among this force, Ebles de Mountz, the former constable of Stirling Castle, was definitely present at the battle. A writ dating from 1316 states that he was still owed money for horses he had lost in the king's service at Stirling in 1314.[14]

The assembly of this substantial household cavalry force less than two months after Bannockburn strongly suggests that the defeat did not even temporarily destroy the English as a fighting force. It questions the assumption that the elite of the English host, the cavalry, was massacred by the Scots. Indeed, the existence of this force may be explained by the very fact that they were troops of the king's household and had been serving in the king's division. Barbour is quite specific that, when the host began to break apart,

Edward fled from the field with his mounted escort of five hundred knights and men-at-arms, a figure he consistently repeats throughout his narrative of Edward's flight to Dunbar. Similarly, *Lanercost* recounts that Edward made for Dunbar 'with many others mounted and on foot'. Thomas Gray writes that 'those who came away with him [Edward] were saved, all the others came to grief'.[15] The sources agree that a large number of the troops of the king's division, the main cavalry element of the host, emerged from Bannockburn relatively unscathed. If the figure Barbour provides is roughly accurate, then the vast majority of the main English cavalry division not only survived the battle but returned safely to England.

This is not to claim that the division did not suffer significant casualties. The retinue of Aymer de Valence, who throughout the campaign had been in the company of the king and who helped him flee the battlefield, appears to have suffered particularly: four of his twenty-two knights were slain and a further ten taken prisoner. It has been suggested that these casualties were the result of a prolonged rearguard action fought by Valence to cover Edward's escape and to hinder his pursuit by James Douglas. As we have seen, an alternative and perhaps more likely scenario places Valence himself as departing with the king and taking ship with Edward from Dunbar.[16] As earl of Pembroke, Valence's foot soldiers largely consisted of Welshmen; Barbour recorded that Maurice de Berkeley, another of Valence's knights, 'departed from the army with a big force of Welshmen' and that 'they held their way at a pretty pace, but before they came to England many of their company were taken, and many of them too were slain'. This is the only specific reference to a large number of Welsh foot soldiers escaping from the field of battle, but again it adds to the impression that the host did not suffer a horrendous massacre at Bannockburn. Many knights and men-at-arms must also have fled on foot. In August 1314 Hugh de Audley the elder, a prominent English lord, was due compensation from the Crown totalling £410 6s 8d for horses he had lost in the king's service at Stirling in June 1314; with the mean value of a warhorse at the time being nearly £12, this almost certainly represents a loss of more than twenty horses, perhaps even thirty.[17]

Although the earl of Hereford was ultimately captured, he too survived the battle. Moreover, he fled to Bothwell, approximately twenty miles south-west of Stirling, accompanied not only by a number of lords but also, according to *Lanercost*, 'with a great crowd of knights' and 'six hundred other mounted men and one thousand foot', the majority of whom made for the safety of Carlisle.[18] Whatever the precise numbers, clearly a significant proportion of the host fled towards Carlisle. Presumably many of the cavalry had formed the vanguard of the host, the division of which Hereford had been joint commander. That so many of the vanguard should have survived is extremely surprising considering it was the first division to engage the dense ranks of the Scottish schiltrom. Yet the *Vita* also implies this when, in condemning Gloucester's men for not coming to his aid when he was unhorsed, it asserts that 'of the five hundred cavalry whom he had led to battle at his own expense, he almost alone was killed'.[19] Here the *Vita* is almost certainly alluding to the vanguard as a whole rather than to Gloucester's personal retinue; either way, it is quite specific that of these five hundred knights and men-at-arms very few indeed were killed. Clearly the vanguard did suffer significant casualties, *Lanercost* recounting that three prominent lords were killed along with Gloucester, but it appears that it was far from destroyed.

From the accounts of these contemporary chronicles, both Scottish and English, it is evident that two substantial bodies of troops that formed part of the English host extricated themselves from the battle and made their way south, one heading to Berwick via Dunbar, and the other to Carlisle via Bothwell. If the figures that the chronicles provide are to be believed (and those given are by no means outlandish), then these two forces together contained more than a thousand cavalry and approximately a thousand foot soldiers. The cavalry figure is most striking. If the host had consisted of the lowest estimate of approximately thirteen hundred cavalry, then this figure effectively represents at least two entire divisions. Should the cavalry have numbered upwards of two thousand men, then this does not alter the startling fact that so many retreated from the battle as part of one of these two groups. Many others would have fled individually or in small groups. The *Vita* conveys a sense of the confusion engendered in the aftermath of defeat with the arresting statement that, of the English host, 'five hundred and more were thought to be dead who had been taken captive and were later ransomed'. In this the *Vita* is almost certainly referring to knights and men-at-arms, and if this five hundred includes some of the above two groups who had later been captured, then it must also encompass a significant number of individuals who fled from the field of battle but were apprehended before they could reach the border. This statement of the *Vita* is also supported by an official document. On 13 July, nineteen days after the battle, Edward II issued an order to the English escheators who had responsibility for the counties north of the River Trent. As was their duty, in the weeks immediately following the battle they had taken into the hands of the Crown the 'lands of divers bannerets, knights, and other tenants in chief believed to have been slain at Stirling'. Edward now instructed the escheators to ensure these lands were kept safely, 'as the king is informed that many of them are still alive in his enemy's power'.[20]

Indeed, the vast majority of casualties suffered by the cavalry of the host appear to have been knights and men-at-arms taken prisoner. Even Fordun, despite his reference to the great number of English killed, lays particular emphasis on the vast haul of prisoners, recounting that 'many – a great many – nobles were taken, for whose ransom not only were the queen [Elizabeth Bruce] and other Scottish prisoners released from their dungeons, but even the Scots themselves were, all and sundry, enriched very much'. An English chronicle relates that those captured included 'magnates and knights some six score in number, besides clerks and men-at-arms, who were later ransomed for various prices'.[21] Again, as with those killed, the chronicles record only the capture of the most prestigious figures of the host. Robert de Umfraville, earl of Angus, was taken prisoner, as were a number of distinguished English lords including John de Segrave, Anthony de Lucy and John Giffard. Roger Northburgh, keeper of the king's shield, was also captured, together with a knight of his retinue and one of his clerks. The constable of Bamburgh Castle, John de Eslington, was taken prisoner, his presence at Bannockburn raising the possibility that troops from the garrison of this Northumberland castle were present at the battle. Robert Baston, the Carmelite friar and poet, was also captured. Ironically, Baston was compelled by Bruce to compose verses to glorify the Scottish victory in order to gain his release.[22]

The continuation of Trivet is again singularly notable for naming a significant number of those men of rank who were captured. Fifty-one individuals are identified as being taken prisoner during the battle and subsequent pursuit, and the chronicle states that another, unnamed, thirty-four were also captured. This total of eighty-five is slightly contradicted by the chronicle itself which subsequently claims that ninety men of rank were taken prisoner, of which twenty-two were earls, barons and bannerets, and sixty-eight were knights (see Appendix II).[23] A few more precious slivers of evidence hint at the large numbers of Englishmen captured. In 1315, following an unsuccessful Scottish assault on Carlisle, a prominent Scottish lord, John de Moray, was captured by the English. At Bannockburn, according to *Lanercost*, Moray had enriched himself by taking prisoner twenty-three knights and esquires, along with a number of other men of various ranks.[24] In the immediate aftermath of the battle, the large numbers of Englishmen who fled to the rock of Stirling

Castle and were subsequently taken prisoner were so substantial that Bruce felt threatened by their presence. Many of those who survived the desperate crossing of the Bannock Burn were either killed or captured, the *Vita* recounting that 'many of our men perished and many, too, were taken prisoner'. The indiscriminate slaughter of these fugitives by the local inhabitants was quickly halted on the direct orders of Bruce, a proclamation being issued that the English should be taken prisoner and held to ransom. *Lanercost* suggests a similar story when it reveals that 'certain knights were captured by women'.[25] It is also evident that these prisoners were almost exclusively taken during the pursuit which followed the rout. Few appear to have been captured on the field of battle itself. It seems that the edict Bruce pronounced before the battle, in which he forbade the Scots to take prisoners until the host had been comprehensively defeated, had been followed to the letter. This edict might well account for the brutal deaths of Gloucester, Clifford and d'Argentan, lords who, if captured, would have fetched enormous ransoms.

Many of those killed at Bannockburn also appear to have met their deaths during the pursuit. *Lanercost* recounts that 'some who were not so speedy in flight were killed by the Scots', and adds that of those who fled towards Carlisle 'many, also, were taken wandering around the castle [of Bothwell] and hither and thither in the country, and many were killed'. The statement of Thomas Gray, though an inaccurate generalisation, that those who escaped with the king were saved while 'all the others came to grief', again conveys the impression that many of the English casualties occurred during the pursuit.[26] That this was the case should not come as a surprise, for in medieval warfare the most horrendous casualties were inflicted during the pursuit of a defeated army. Bannockburn was no different. For those who fled the field of battle on foot the danger of death or capture was as great, if not greater, than it had been during the battle. Once broken, the host could have been annihilated. That it was not was due to two simple reasons: the lack of Scottish cavalry, and the bulk of the Scottish army becoming distracted by the pillaging of the English baggage train. These were the factors that prevented a defeat from becoming a massacre and ultimately saved the majority of the English host from death, and many others from capture.

It is impossible to attempt an accurate estimate of English casualties, both in terms of those killed and those captured. Barbour makes the absurd claim that at least thirty thousand English were killed, though his rather more circumspect assertion that 'two hundred pairs of red spurs were taken from dead knights' may contain a grain of truth.[27] The continuation of Trivet proclaims that the total number of English casualties, both those killed and those captured, suffered by individuals of the rank of knight and above was 154 men. The separate totals the continuation also provides of 60 killed and 90 captured work out at 150 casualties.[28] A casualty figure of between 150 and 200 men of rank killed and captured is entirely feasible, and it may be this to which Barbour alludes. There is no reference whatsoever to the total number of casualties suffered by the esquires, men-at-arms and foot soldiers of the English host. The Bannock Burn certainly claimed the lives of many of those who were killed; the sources are unanimous in their agreement that a significant number drowned within its murky depths. It is a measure of the paucity of evidence that only one man, Edmund de Mauley, steward of the king's household, is specifically identified in one source as having drowned in the Bannock Burn.[29]

Of those captured there is the most fleeting of glimpses in the later petitions submitted by men-at-arms who had been impoverished by the payment of their ransoms. John Hesilrigg, a man-at-arms of Northumberland, informed the king that he had been made a prisoner during the 'discomfiture' at Stirling, where he had lost horses and armour worth 200 marks. Hesilrigg's ransom had also been set at 200 marks and he evidently encountered problems in raising the necessary funds, remaining imprisoned by the Scots for two years and losing all the profits of his land in Northumberland for five years; he reckoned the total financial cost of his capture at a substantial 600 marks. Lucas de Barry, an esquire of the king's household, had served in several front-line garrisons since the outbreak of the wars. At Bannockburn he was captured and so heavily ransomed that he had been forced to sell and lease all his lands. Another long-serving veteran of the Scottish wars was Robert de Blakebourne. At Bannockburn his brother had been killed and the warfare of the following years had left de Blakebourne completely destitute. Robert de Clifford, namesake of the great lord killed in the battle on 24 June, had also been deprived of everything of value after being taken prisoner, losing horses and harness worth 100 marks and his ransom being set at £100. The registers of the archbishop of York, William Greenfield, record four payments in 1314 towards the costs of ransoms for individuals captured in Scotland: 20 marks was paid to aid Edmund de Rypariis; the knight Simon Warde was granted £20 in the form of a loan; and his fellow knights John Giffard and Baldwin de Fryvill received 200 marks and 100 marks respectively. Clearly the ransoms set by the Scots were extraordinarily high. In November 1314 the Exchequer was instructed to aid Alan de Walingford, a sergeant-at-arms of the king, in the ransom of his son Robert, a prisoner of the Scots, Alan being unable to raise the necessary sums himself. Being taken prisoner may have spared the lives of many men, but financially it ruined them. The defeat at Bannockburn altered their lives forever.

These petitions provide a vital glimpse of the very real human cost of the battle. For those who had a father, brother, husband or son killed or captured, the impact was often devastating. Walter de Fauconberg, a man of some social standing, survived the battle, but his eldest son was killed and his youngest son captured – the latter being released upon the payment of a ransom of 500 marks – while several of the retinue Fauconberg had led into battle had also been slain. Times could be hard even for the families of knights who had been killed. In December 1314 the widow of James Torthorald was granted eight quarters of wheat and ten quarters of beans and pease from the king's stores at Carlisle for the sustenance of herself and her children throughout the harshness of winter.[30] Profound as the impact of defeat at Bannockburn was on Edward II and the English realm, it was individually devastating to those who suffered the cruel blow of a personal loss.

To Edward, ensconced in sorrow within the walls of York, the survival of the majority of the host would gradually have become apparent. Men assumed dead were found to be held prisoner; some drifted into England in 'abject confusion';[31] others safely reached the border and made their way home. This is not to say that such unprecedented losses were not startling, but that they were far from shattering. The English realm was not temporarily destroyed as a fighting force. If the number of knights lost led to the belief that the flower of English chivalry had been killed, the backbone of English military might was still intact. Yet any solace this brought Edward must have been tempered by increasing confusion as to what exactly had happened to the English host on that fateful Midsummer's Day. The casualties suffered were not nearly as severe as was at first feared, and the majority had occurred not during the hand-to-hand combat of the mêlée but in the ensuing pursuit. If the host had not been decimated in the mêlée then how had it been so comprehensively defeated? What had taken place during that savage engagement that caused such a formidable army to collapse? How had Bruce led the Scots to such an extraordinary victory?

The most obvious factor contributing to the outcome of the engagement was the field of battle itself. Confined to the limits of the 'dryfield' or to the Carse of Balquhiderock, the English cavalry became dangerously bunched up and began to press in upon one another. Unable to manoeuvre their horses, knights and men-at-arms became ineffective and vulnerable to the vicious forest of spears brandished by the Scots. As we have seen, to the rear of the host the great mass of English foot soldiers was prevented from advancing by the crush of cavalry before them and it was here, to the rear, that the host had begun to fall apart. There can be little doubt that the bulk of the English host, the levies of infantry, did not participate in the mêlée, apart perhaps from a small contingent of archers. The failure of Edward and his commanders to deploy the missile fire of archers against the dense mass of the schiltrom was a fatal error. Although the longbow had yet to dominate the battlefields of Europe, it was archery fire that had proved decisive in breaking apart the schiltroms at Falkirk. Astonishingly, despite this precedent, archers were not central to the English battle plan at Bannockburn; instead, a heavy cavalry charge had been used in an attempt to break the schiltrom. English foot soldiers played almost no part in the hand-to-hand combat of the mêlée, and the majority of those foot soldiers who were killed would have lost their lives as they fled.

The failure of experienced commanders such as Valence, Hereford, Clifford and Beaumont to ensure the large-scale employment of archers reveals the extent to which the host was poorly led. This breakdown in command stemmed from the ineffective leadership of King Edward himself and the resentments that simmered among the earls and lords. Edward's appointment of Gloucester and Hereford as joint commanders of the vanguard was almost certainly an attempt to placate both earls, men who had recently figured among his domestic opponents, yet this dual appointment bred instability and rivalry. Edward's unwarranted berating of Gloucester when the latter urged a postponement of the battle was most likely a hangover from the political conflict within England; and the dispute between Beaumont and Gray, unchecked by Clifford, the result of weak leadership failing to control notoriously headstrong men. Within the high command there would have been lingering enmity. In 1312 it was Valence who had urged war against the earls responsible for the death of Gaveston, one of whom was Hereford. In the same year Gloucester had bluntly refused to intervene on behalf of Valence. Beaumont himself was a divisive figure who had been directly targeted in the Ordinances and his expulsion demanded. Tensions, therefore, pervaded the high command of the host. Under the weak leadership of Edward, and exposed to the pressure of battle, the fracture lines had begun to rupture.

The failure of the English to deploy large numbers of archers meant that the mêlée was a straight fight between English heavy cavalry and Scottish foot soldiers. The cavalry, fighting in difficult terrain and opposed by a strong defensive formation, found themselves in a distinctly unfavourable position. Indeed, the restrictions of the field appear to have prevented the full strength of the English cavalry engaging the dense mass of the Scottish schiltrom. *Lanercost* reports the words of an eyewitness who recounted that 'the English in the rear could not reach the Scots because the leading division was in the way, nor could they do anything to help themselves'. This reference to the 'leading division' suggests it was not just the English infantry that could not get through to the Scots but also a substantial contingent of cavalry. The *Vita* is in no doubt that this was the case, recounting that 'two hundred knights and more, who had neither drawn their swords nor even struck a blow, were reduced to flight'.[32] As this statement immediately follows the *Vita*'s account of the withdrawal of the royal standard from the field of battle, it suggests that these two hundred knights were part of the king's division.

Indeed, the absence of any reference to Edward II or Aymer de Valence taking part in the fierce fighting of the mêlée is particularly noticeable; it is highly unlikely that the contributions of two such prominent figures would have been overlooked by the chroniclers. The first mention of Edward and Valence is in their withdrawal from the field, and this immediately raises questions about their role in the mêlée. Of the three cavalry divisions, the vanguard was the first to charge the schiltrom. A second charge followed, although there is no mention of this comprising one division or two. There was certainly a lack of organisation, Barbour commenting that, apart from the vanguard, all the English cavalry were bunched together, almost certainly due to 'the extreme narrowness of the place that they were in to await the fight'. An English chronicle recounts that 'the English did not join battle all together, but separately, because they did not want to help each other'.[33] The restrictions of the terrain clearly led to disorder and confusion among the English cavalry at the moment they delivered their charge. In the circumstances, upon being confronted by the unexpected appearance and advance of the Scots, it is quite possible that the cavalry charge was an instinctive response rather than a calculated action; two contemporary sources claim that the English advanced impetuously.[34] If the cavalry charge was an instinctive reaction to the unexpected advance of the Scots, then this would help explain the failure of the English to deploy significant numbers of archers.

Presumably the previous day's chain of command remained in place. Clifford would consequently have led the charge of the second division, his death providing clear evidence that it was fully committed to battle. Considering the restrictions of the field and the silence of the chroniclers, the suspicion must be that the third English division, commanded by Edward himself, was prevented from fully engaging the schiltrom. That Valence and d'Argentan, despite the confusion of battle, were clearly able to see that the host was falling apart lends further weight to the idea that they were not heavily engaged in the fighting. The failure of the king's division fully to engage the Scots would also go some way to explain the suicidal charge of d'Argentan despite the battle having already been lost; it may not have been the shame of defeat that troubled d'Argentan so much as the humiliation he felt at not even having come to blows with the enemy. The failure of the king's division fully to engage would also explain the survival of the substantial force of cavalry, almost divisional in strength, which accompanied Edward to Dunbar.

Nor is it clear that the division commanded by Robert Bruce was fully committed to the mêlée. The formation of the Scottish forces at the outset of the engagement suggests that Bruce's division, the Scottish rearguard, also remained on the periphery of the fighting. It is clear that the divisions commanded by Thomas Randolph and Edward Bruce formed the front ranks of the schiltrom, and it was behind these that the rearguard was deployed. The dense mass of the schiltrom occupied the breadth of the field and, as no flanking manoeuvre was attempted by the Scots, the only means by which the rearguard could have engaged the English was if the schiltrom had parted, faltered or broken. It did none of these. Although Barbour vividly describes Bruce leading his division into battle at some length, the English chroniclers completely omit Bruce from the fighting.[35] As with Edward II, it is inconceivable that they should fail to mention the entrance of the Scottish commander, and with hindsight the Scottish king, into the chaos of the mêlée. Barbour could not deny his hero a role in such a key moment; the English chroniclers laboured under no such obligation. Bruce may have been the architect of the victory won at Bannockburn, but the extent of his involvement in the mêlée remains questionable.

If neither the divisions of Edward II nor Robert Bruce were fully engaged in the fight, then a serious question arises with regard to the duration of the mêlée. Unusually, no chronicle provides a clear indication of its length of time. Only an English chronicler, John Trokelowe, claims it was a long engagement. *Lanercost* provides the ambiguous statement that, when the two armies met, 'they remained without movement for a while'.[36] The sense that it was a prolonged engagement originates from the belief that the host was slowly slaughtered in a battle of attrition, but the evidence suggests that such a slaughter did not take place. The failure of a significant proportion of both armies to engage the enemy implies that the battle was not a prolonged affair in which more and more troops were drawn into the carnage. Evidently the engagement began early in the morning, the English having passed a troubled and sleepless night, and the Scots and the English, after a short breakfast, taking to the field. On Midsummer's Day, dawn would have broken between three and four in the morning; if allowance is made for the abbot of Inchaffray saying mass with the Scots and for the arraying of each army, then the first clash would almost certainly have occurred before the hours of eight or nine at the very latest. Trokelowe recounts that the fight began at about the third hour of the day.[37] Barbour's description of the English knights shining as brightly as angels may well be more than a mere literary device; with the still-rising sun behind them, their armour would indeed have blazed gloriously in the bright morning light.

A sense of time can also be gained from the flight of Edward II. Upon leaving the battlefield he initially rode to Stirling Castle. Refused entry, he turned south, rode around the western edge of the Torwood and then made for Dunbar. Although none of the sources state when Edward reached Dunbar, it is clear that by nightfall on 24 June he had completed the greater part of his journey; Barbour recounted that the flight was broken just once, at Winchburgh, to the west of Edinburgh.[38] The distance from Stirling to Dunbar is approximately sixty miles. Riding on fairly good roads, and without a change of horses, it would have taken Edward much the greater part of a day to have covered such a significant distance by nightfall. Even allowing for the exceptionally long hours of daylight, Edward must have begun his flight well before noon. Therefore, it is extremely unlikely that the engagement lasted throughout the morning.

Internal contradictions within the sources also indicate that the mêlée was not a prolonged affair. The two different accounts of the death of Gloucester provided by the *Vita* emphasise the confusion of battle. The sense of timing they infer is also intriguing. The version favoured by the *Vita* is that which places Gloucester's death as occurring during a shift in the fighting, with battle having already been engaged; the second version cites Gloucester as being killed before the fighting began in earnest, rashly charging ahead of the vanguard. Clearly, the death of Gloucester was an incident witnessed by many of the English vanguard. That these two accounts had widespread currency suggests that Gloucester was killed shortly after battle had been met. There can be little doubt that he was killed early in the mêlée. In relation to

Gloucester's death, the *Vita* contains a curious account of the death of Giles d'Argentan. Although other chronicles are quite clear that d'Argentan was killed whilst delivering a futile solo charge against the Scots after Edward had been led from the field, the *Vita* alone claims that d'Argentan met his death when he witnessed the unhorsing of Gloucester and courageously went to aid the earl 'thinking it more honourable to perish with so great a man than to escape death by flight'.[39] This account of the death of d'Argentan is almost certainly wrong; with the battle already lost, his suicidal charge was a striking episode recorded by more than one chronicler. Yet it is intriguing that the author of the *Vita*, a man with access to eyewitness accounts, could link the deaths of Gloucester and d'Argentan to a single episode. Gloucester was killed early in the engagement; d'Argentan was killed towards its end. The ability of the *Vita* to connect these two events suggests that they were not separated by a significant length of time. It appears that the start of the mêlée and its end were not widely separated events. The confusion surrounding the engagement, and the contradictions inherent within the sources, may not be due to the prolonged nature of the mêlée but rather to its brevity.

In fact there is no significant evidence to suggest that the engagement fought on Midsummer's Day was a prolonged encounter. If the precedent set by many other medieval battles is to be considered, then it would by no means be unusual for the mêlée that decided Bannockburn to have been of relatively short duration. The decisive battle of Tinchebray, fought in 1106, appears to have lasted little more than an hour. When the English and French clashed at Crécy in 1346, the battle began late in the afternoon and was over by nightfall. At Agincourt, in 1415, the main engagement lasted for two or three hours. Considering the brutal physical punishment of the mêlée, a particularly lengthy engagement was often not necessary for an army to be broken or, as both Crécy and Agincourt demonstrate, for horrific casualties to be inflicted. Indeed, the survival of so many of the English host at Bannockburn was almost certainly due to the shortness of the battle. In terms of duration, it is clear that the engagement fought on 24 June was nothing remotely approaching the extraordinarily long battle of Neville's Cross, an encounter fought between the English and the Scots near Durham in 1346, which lasted from nine in the morning until the service of vespers in the evening. In many cases the pursuit following a battle was longer than the battle itself.[40]

A picture of the grim mêlée fought at Bannockburn on the morning of Midsummer's Day 1314 emerges gradually. The engagement began early in the morning and was over by noon at the very latest, almost certainly much sooner. Restricted by the confines of the field of battle, a substantial proportion of each army was unable to engage the enemy before the mêlée was over. Most of the English casualties occurred in the aftermath of the rout as the infantry and cavalry attempted to flee, rather than during the engagement itself. Two substantial elements of the defeated host, both of which included large numbers of knights and men-at-arms, not only survived the battle but headed south in close company. The majority of casualties suffered by the English were not in terms of men killed but those taken prisoner. However, an unprecedented number of English bannerets and knights were slain in the engagement along with two high-ranking English commanders, Gloucester and Clifford. These men, driven by notions of martial prowess and chivalry, would have been at the forefront of the heavy cavalry charges. Forced to fight on a narrow front, advancing on entirely unsuitable ground and prevented from manoeuvring their destriers, the bannerets and knights suffered disproportionately heavy casualties. It was the startling death of such a high number of men of rank that sent shockwaves rumbling throughout the English realm. A significant number of men-at-arms must also have met their death on the field of battle. Yet although unprecedented numbers were killed, the elite of the host, the bannerets and knights, together with the esquires and men-at-arms, survived in substantial numbers. It is also telling that, according to Barbour, only two Scottish knights, William Vipont (Vieuxpont) and Walter Ross, were killed.[41] The number of casualties among the massed ranks of Scottish foot soldiers is impossible to estimate. A significant number must have lost their lives. None of the Scottish high command, however, was killed. At no point was the schiltrom in danger of being broken. The English host was defeated without even coming close to breaching the Scottish lines. In a battle that the English host should have expected to win, why did it perform so dreadfully? If it was not destroyed in the mêlée, then how was it so comprehensively defeated?

The simple answer is that it broke apart. All the sources are quite clear that the initial retreat began to the rear of the host with levies of disgruntled foot soldiers drifting back towards the Bannock Burn. As more followed so the cohesion of the host disappeared. Alarmed by this spectacle the king was reluctantly led from the field, and with the departure of his standard the host fell apart. The knights and men-at-arms engaged in the mêlée did not precipitate this disastrous retreat, but rather the large mass of infantry which had not yet been committed to battle. Unable to advance, panic spread through the ranks of these reluctant foot soldiers. Their morale was already incredibly low, their minds and bodies fatigued by days of relentless marching and the night crossing of the Bannock Burn, their spirits disturbed by the unexpected reverses of the previous day. Although the knights and men-at-arms applied themselves to the fight, their morale was also precariously fragile. Many had not wanted to engage in battle that day. They, too, were tired and troubled by the reverses they had suffered. Few would have been unaware of the dissensions among their commanders. The death of Gloucester at the outset of the mêlée would further have undermined their resolve.[42]

Robert Bruce had crucially identified this appallingly brittle English morale on the night of 23/24 June. That same night Alexander Seton had sought out Bruce with first-hand intelligence that 'the English have lost heart and are defeated'. It was intelligence that Bruce himself then echoed in addressing the assembly of Scottish lords, when he declared of the English that 'if the heart is cast down, the body is not worth a jot'.[43] The momentous decision of Bruce to stay and give battle was largely based on his belief that psychologically the English were there to be beaten. It was for this reason that Bruce had his army boldly take to the field and advance towards the English, a show of aggression intended further to undermine their opponents' faltering resolve. In contrast the Scots, buoyed by their unexpected successes of the previous day, were ready for the fight. When the English were held by the schiltrom, the shock of their cavalry charge absorbed, it did not take long for the pressure of battle to splinter and crack the morale of the host, and for the host disastrously to break apart.

In many ways Bannockburn was a victory of spirit over might. The English host was not physically annihilated in battle, but its morale was catastrophically broken. This was the character of the English defeat.[44] Indeed, on closer inspection, it was not so much defeat at the hands of the Scots for which the English chroniclers reserved their invective, but the humiliation of the rapid flight of the host. Trokelowe recounts that the English 'gripped with fear, fled', while a contemporary poem comments that 'when the two sides engaged, that one [the Scots] remained firm, but that which had shown so much pride fled'. In describing Edward and his escort departing the field of battle, *Lanercost* does not hold back in its condemnation, declaring that 'to their perpetual shame [they] fled like miserable wretches to Dunbar Castle'. Similarly, the *Vita* indulges in a dramatic lament, declaring, 'O famous race unconquered through the ages, why do you, who used to conquer knights, flee from mere footmen?', before voicing the opinion that it was almost unheard of in living memory 'for such an army to be scattered so suddenly by infantry'.[45] This last statement is particularly revealing. In recounting that the English were scattered 'so suddenly', the *Vita* reinforces the impression that the hand-to-hand combat of the mêlée was of relatively short duration. In fact the evidence suggests that, although the English lost so much on 'one unfortunate day', the crucial mêlée itself, as the *Vita* alludes, might well have lasted little more than 'one fleeting hour'.[46]

CHAPTER FIFTEEN

THE LEGACY

Almost twenty years after Bannockburn, on 11 August 1332, a heavily outnumbered English force was confronted by a Scottish army deep inside Scotland at Dupplin Moor to the south of Perth. The political figurehead of this modest invasion force was Edward Balliol, son and heir of the late John Balliol, the former king of Scotland. Real military command resided in the controversial figure of Henry de Beaumont, erstwhile target of the Ordinances and a veteran of Bannockburn. The force commanded by Beaumont was chiefly the product of a handful of English lords who had lost lands which English kings had formerly granted them in Scotland. These men, the Disinherited, had come to reclaim these lands by armed force. Their chances of success did not look good. They did not enjoy the official support of the English king, Edward III. Their force hardly merited the description of an army, comprising at most five hundred knights and men-at-arms, and perhaps little more than a thousand foot soldiers. They were opposed by a multitudinous Scottish army which, though hastily raised, was commanded by no fewer than five earls. It appeared that the Disinherited were about to pay the ultimate price.

As the Scots advanced the English cavalry dismounted. Knights and men-at-arms sent their horses to the rear and formed a line at the end of a narrow glen through which the Scots would have to approach. The English foot soldiers, many of whom were archers, formed up beside the knights and men-at-arms. The Scots came towards them on foot. When the advancing Scots came within range of the longbows of the English archers, they were met by a relentless hail of arrows. The Scots grimly pressed onwards, the front ranks engaging the English knights and men-at-arms in vicious hand-to-hand combat. Savaged by the ceaseless rain of arrows, the troops on the Scottish flanks pushed in towards the centre. The attack lost its momentum as men pressed in upon one another. To the rear the largest Scottish division advanced straight into this sprawling mass of disorganised men. Entrapped between their own rear division and the English, the Scots fell in their hundreds, some crushed underfoot, others suffocated beneath the weight of those who fell upon them. Many who attempted to flee were cut down by the English cavalry which had remounted to conduct the pursuit.

Of the five Scottish earls present at Dupplin Moor, three were killed. At least two thousand Scotsmen lay dead upon the field of battle. English casualties were extremely slight. Despite their apparently hopeless situation the Disinherited had won a resounding victory. Beaumont was quick to follow it up. On 24 September 1332 Edward Balliol was inaugurated as king of Scotland at Scone. It was an act intended to overthrow the incumbent king of Scotland, David II, son and heir of the late Robert I of Scotland, better known as Robert Bruce. However, though David II was only eight and his authority was exercised by a Guardian, he enjoyed substantial Scottish support. Scotland was once again plunged into civil war. The following year Edward III, like his father and grandfather before him, entered the fray. An English army besieged Berwick, and on 19 July 1333, at Halidon Hill, to the north of the town, the English destroyed a Scottish army. The war between England and Scotland was reignited. In the following years Edward III led a series of campaigns into Scotland. He had the ruined castles of Edinburgh, Stirling and Roxburgh rebuilt and installed large garrisons within them. The Scots sought to attack these castles, they adopted the tactics of irregular warfare, and above all they determined to avoid being brought to battle by the English.[1] Those Scots with long memories could be forgiven for thinking that Bannockburn had never been fought. Two decades after the most spectacular of Scottish victories, the Lowlands were once again occupied by English forces. The independence of the Scottish kingdom was once again gravely threatened. Bannockburn, it seems, had changed little.

In the immediate aftermath of his great victory in 1314, Robert Bruce had quickly recognised that Bannockburn was not a decisive battle in the conflict with England. The rout of the English host had not won him the war. Indeed, only the capture of Edward II could potentially have achieved such a decisive victory. Moreover, in terms of those killed, the English military machine was far from wrecked; in the months following the defeat, Edward II could still call upon a much greater reservoir of manpower than Bruce could in terms of knights, men-at-arms and foot soldiers. The character of the English defeat, the fateful breaking apart of the host, was as much a psychological collapse as a physical disintegration. Although this did nothing to diminish the spectacular nature of the Scottish victory, it exacerbated the difficulties encountered by Bruce in attempting to exploit Bannockburn fully to gain a decisive political advantage over the English. The recognition that Bannockburn alone was not sufficient to win the war resulted in the Scottish raid deep into northern England immediately afterwards. Similarly, as we have seen, Bruce demonstrated that he desired peace by means of individual acts of magnanimity, such as releasing Marmaduke Tweng without ransom, returning the corpses of Gloucester and Clifford, and sending Edward his lost shield and privy seal. Bruce also appears to have sent a peace envoy to the parliament held by the English at York in September; if so, it was more in hope than expectation.

The English were deaf to such entreaties. Indeed, the domestic conflict that had torn England apart now, for the first time, worked against Bruce. A central accusation levelled against Edward had been the loss of Scotland. It was a charge Lancaster had vehemently supported. In late 1314, having gained political dominance on the back of the catastrophic defeat inflicted by Bruce and the Scots, Lancaster could hardly now support a peace settlement which would inevitably entail formal recognition of an independent kingdom of Scotland. Nor could he risk antagonising those magnates who still had hopes of ultimately reclaiming their Scottish estates. Indeed, by being seen vigorously to counter the Scottish threat, Lancaster could most readily consolidate his authority, and from September a series of military appointments were made in an attempt to safeguard northern England.[2] In the aftermath of the humiliating rout at Bannockburn, it is almost certain that Edward himself would not have countenanced the possibility of a peace settlement, an act that, in the circumstances, would have been tantamount to admitting defeat. It was not a confession that any English king would openly make. The Scottish war would continue to be waged.

This was the intractable difficulty for Robert Bruce: the need to translate the great battlefield victory of Bannockburn into a tangible political triumph in the war against England. In popular terms, the impact of Bannockburn was dramatic. The shock of the English defeat at the hands of the Scots resounded throughout Christendom. More pertinently, as the English author of *Lanercost* relates, 'After the aforesaid victory Robert de Bruce was commonly called King of Scotland by all men, because he had acquired Scotland by force of arms'.[3] In the aftermath of Bannockburn, with the surrender and destruction of Stirling Castle, Scotland had been all but cleared of English garrisons, and the following year it was finally freed from almost all occupying forces.

Although it was not a decisive battle, Bannockburn irrevocably changed the character of the war. No longer did the English possess strongholds in Scotland. Their ability to project power north of the border so severely curtailed, the mounting of a successful campaign became that much harder. Bannockburn consequently marked a significant turning point in the conflict with England. The primary objective of Bruce was no longer to establish his authority as king in Scotland, but to wrest formal political recognition of his position as king from his English counterpart. In defeating his Scottish opponents and pushing the English out of Scotland, Bruce had effectively made good his claim to be king through military conquest; this position could only be secured, however, by formal English acknowledgement of Bruce as king of Scotland. It was an acknowledgement that Edward and his magnates would never voluntarily make. To them, Bruce himself remained a faithless murderer and a traitor who had instigated rebellion, crimes for which he still remained under excommunication. More pointedly, any recognition of Bruce as king was also an implicit acknowledgement of an independent kingdom of Scotland. The struggle of Bruce to assert his authority as king and the fight for Scottish independence had become one and the same. Although Bruce was popularly viewed in Scotland and England as king of Scotland, he now devoted all his efforts to make his kingship a political reality.

In the years following Bannockburn he took the war to the English. He exerted incredible pressure upon the exposed northern counties. Scottish raids plunged deep into England, fast-moving forces commanded by Randolph and Douglas cutting a path of devastation as far south as Yorkshire. In 1315 the fortress town of Carlisle was besieged by the Scots, although determined attempts to take the town by means of siege engines and then by assault were repulsed. The following year an audacious operation to storm the town of Berwick under cover of night also met with failure. A new horror descended upon the war-torn counties of northern England in 1315 and 1316, with two years of abnormally heavy rainfall causing a severe European-wide famine which claimed thousands of lives. In the already devastated county of Northumberland, and in the isolated garrison town of Berwick, the twin disasters of warfare and famine took a horrendous toll. Within Berwick, troops starved to death at their posts, horses were boiled and eaten when they died, and essential military equipment was pledged for meagre rations of food. As a petition from the town plaintively recounted, it was a 'pity to see Christians leading such a life'. A desperate foray to seize victuals ended in slaughter when, on St Valentine's Day, 14 February 1316, eighty of the garrison were killed in a ferocious ambush led by Douglas.[4] In the dark years of famine which followed Bannockburn, the war became increasingly futile and remorseless.

The human cost of the conflict was exacerbated by the opening of a new front in 1315. The landing of a Scottish invasion force in Ireland in May signalled the beginning of a desultory and wasteful three-year campaign which diverted precious Scottish money and resources from the main theatre of war in northern England. Speculation still surrounds the precise motivation for Bruce's invasion of Ireland. It is unclear whether Bruce intended to free Ireland from the presence of the English and create a Celtic alliance against England, or whether his objective was to deny the resources of Ireland to the English in any future Scottish campaigns. The motives ascribed to Bruce have been many and varied. Barbour, however, believed the impetus did not come from Bruce himself, recounting that it was Edward Bruce who 'felt that Scotland was too small for both him and his brother; therefore he formed a purpose that he would become king of Ireland'.[5] Edward Bruce was certainly the driving force behind the invasion and either in the summer of 1315 or in May 1316 he was crowned king of Ireland. His reign, if it can be called that, was to be short-lived. Edward was killed in battle at Fochart near Dundalk, approximately fifty miles north of Dublin, on 14 October 1318; his severed head was placed in a salted box and sent to Edward II. Ironically, Philip Mowbray also met his death at Fochart. Having entered into the allegiance of Robert Bruce after surrendering Stirling Castle, Mowbray sailed to Ireland as a member of the Scottish invasion force and fought alongside his former enemy, Edward Bruce, at Fochart. Seriously injured in the rout, Mowbray later died of his wounds.[6] Four years after Bannockburn, the two men who had been responsible for concluding the agreement at Stirling Castle which effectively led to the great battle were both dead, killed in the same engagement, two former Scottish adversaries meeting their deaths not as enemies, but as comrades.

Ireland, however, was a wasteful distraction for Robert Bruce, who knew that the real issue of the war could only be settled by inflicting further damage upon English soil. He achieved a tremendous coup in early 1318 when the vital strategic town of Berwick was taken by assault, initial entrance having been gained via a traitor in the garrison, and Berwick Castle fell to the Scots after a prolonged eleven-week siege. Berwick was immediately occupied by the Scots and its defences strengthened. The calamitous loss of the town at last provoked an English reaction. In 1319 Edward II led an English army north and besieged Berwick. There was a bitter struggle with both sides employing great timber siege engines. Internal political struggles within the English camp, however, prevented the town from again changing hands. The tensions between Edward II and Lancaster ruptured into an outright dispute when the besiegers received news that a force led by Randolph and Douglas had raided deep into Yorkshire and defeated a hastily assembled band of Englishmen, mainly clergymen, at Myton. Edward wanted to maintain the siege of Berwick; Lancaster supported the northern lords who wanted to abandon the siege in order to protect their lands.[7] The army dissolved and the English campaign fell apart. Berwick remained in Scottish hands.

Bruce further ratcheted up the pressure on the English by targeting the castles of Northumberland. Following the capture of Berwick, the Scots seized the castles of Wark, Harbottle and Mitford; all three were subsequently destroyed. The first-rate castles of Bamburgh and Warkworth were so hard-pressed by the Scots that their constables entered into negotiations with their enemy for a temporary respite.[8] In December 1319 a two-year truce was agreed between Bruce and Edward II. If Bruce was tempted to believe that the English were finally weakening, then any such illusion was immediately shattered upon the expiry of the truce. Early in 1322 Edward II summoned the largest host of his reign. In anticipation of this English campaign, Scottish forces raided northern England, but they could do nothing to prevent the host from entering Scotland. In August Edward led an army of more than twenty thousand men north. Bruce withdrew his forces before it and emptied the Lowlands of victuals. The English host, suffering from starvation, prematurely headed for the border and, due to the lack of victuals, immediately dispersed. Edward, accompanied by a small force, remained in northern England. Suddenly, Bruce was presented with a glorious opportunity to capture the English king. Gathering his men, Bruce, along with Randolph and Douglas, rapidly crossed the border. Edward was in Yorkshire, residing first at Byland Abbey, then at Rievaulx Abbey. An English force desperately attempted to prevent the Scots from reaching the king and made a stand at Byland. The English were defeated by Randolph and Douglas, but enough time had been bought for Edward to make good his escape.[9] As at Bannockburn, the English king had narrowly slipped from Bruce's grasp.

The enormous pressure exerted by the Scots on northern England was, however, at last beginning to tell. In this sense 1322 was a crucial year. The abysmal failure of the English campaign, further Scottish raids conducted with impunity, a close Scottish siege of Norham Castle and the near capture of Edward II – leading to the humiliating spectacle of the English king fleeing from the Scots within his own kingdom – all lent indisputable weight to the truth that Bruce could not be dislodged from his position of power in Scotland. The war had ground to a bleak stalemate. In 1323 Andrew Harclay, a lord of northern England who had fought strenuously against the Scots and who the previous year had been awarded the earldom of Carlisle, took it upon himself to negotiate a peace treaty with Bruce. Edward could hardly tolerate such unilateral action and Harclay was arrested and brutally executed.[10] But a dialogue between Bruce and Edward had been opened, and negotiations led to the Thirteen-Year Truce at Bishopthorpe, near York, on 30 May 1323, the truce being formally confirmed by Bruce at Berwick on 7 June.[11] The truce did nothing to resolve the most contentious issues of the war – the independence of Scotland and the claim of Bruce to be king remaining unconfirmed by the English – but it did herald a period of much needed peace and potentially provided the basis for the conclusion of a definitive settlement in the near future. Despite the spectacular victory won at Bannockburn in 1314, it had taken Bruce and the Scots a further nine years of gruelling warfare to force the English into accepting the inevitability of a lengthy truce.

Yet only four years after the truce was concluded it was on the point of collapse. It was undermined not by a resurgence of the conflict between England and Scotland but by the domestic political turmoil in which England remained embroiled. Although the political fallout from the shocking defeat at Bannockburn had threatened to engulf Edward, the king had managed to survive that crisis. In the months following the battle, Edward had concurred with the penalties of defeat, accepting the dominance of the earl of Lancaster and agreeing to adhere to the Ordinances. The body of Piers Gaveston had been laid to rest in December 1314, Edward having failed to gain vengeance for the death of his beloved favourite. Lancaster, however, had also suffered a series of misfortunes. The most grievous had been the sudden death of Warwick, his greatest ally, on 12 August 1315, a loss that caused Lancaster to become increasingly isolated; his other former ally, Hereford, remained close to the king after he was ransomed from captivity in late 1314. The great famine of 1315–16 further undermined Lancaster's period of authority. The dearth of food was exacerbated by the substantial sums of money Edward had spent in undertaking the Bannockburn campaign, along with the material losses suffered in the defeat.[12] Attempts by Lancaster to raise an army to fight the Scots could not overcome these deep-rooted problems.

The death of Gloucester at Bannockburn had been another enormous setback to Edward as it removed one of the few moderating voices of his reign. Gloucester had also been the last male heir of the great Clare family, and when the body of the young earl was laid to rest in Tewkesbury Abbey it marked the break-up of this powerful earldom. Its estates were eventually split among Gloucester's three sisters and their husbands, so further destabilising the volatile political climate. Indeed, the political vicissitudes of Edward's reign took another, intensely personal, twist in 1317, when Lancaster's wife, Alice, was abducted by the earl of Warenne, a crime in which the earl of Hereford may also have had a hand. Lancaster became increasingly hostile, engaging in a private war with Warenne and accusing Edward of failing to adhere to the Ordinances as he had promised. Edward retaliated, declaring Lancaster an enemy of the king and the kingdom for failing to attend a council.[13] It was as these bitter disputes escalated that the startling news arrived of the loss of Berwick in early 1318. For once personal arguments were put aside to deal with the Scottish war. In August 1318 a formal compromise between Edward and Lancaster was agreed in the Treaty of Leake, and the following year the two men led the English army that besieged Berwick, the tensions generated by the siege causing their fragile understanding to break down. In the poisoned atmosphere of the failed campaign, rumours were rife that Lancaster was in league with Bruce and had been paid to ensure that the siege failed.[14]

As open hostility resumed between Edward and Lancaster, the king committed what ultimately was to prove a fatal mistake. Having previously split the realm apart over his unrestrained favouritism of Gaveston, he now promoted a new favourite, Hugh le Despenser the younger. Despenser had been close to the king for several years. He had fought at Bannockburn and was almost certainly one of the select few who took ship with Edward from Dunbar following the battle. Despenser had accrued a significant inheritance following the death of Gloucester, being married to the late earl's eldest sister. The location of this landed inheritance, which was centred on the lordship of Glamorgan, caused Despenser and his father, Hugh le Despenser the elder, to turn their acquisitive gaze upon south Wales. Enjoying the full backing of

Edward, they set about extending their estates.[15] In doing so, they ran foul of the Marcher lords, a powerful group of English barons whose lands were based in Wales and the Welsh borders, and who jealously guarded their power and privileges. The most prominent of the Marcher lords was Hereford.

Lancaster at last found the semblance of allies in the disgruntled Marcher lords. Furious at the favouritism lavished on the Despensers, father and son, the lords seized their lands and castles in Wales and the Marches, and demanded the expulsion of the two favourites. Fearing war, Edward accepted these blunt demands and exiled the Despensers. But, even as he did so, he was engineering a counterattack. In early 1322 Edward raised troops and moved against the Marchers. Some submitted; others, including Hereford, fled north to link up with Lancaster. There is good reason to believe that Lancaster was in contact with Bruce; as the fugitives headed north through Yorkshire their ultimate destination was popularly believed to be Scotland.[16] At Boroughbridge their route was blocked by Andrew Harclay, who had arrayed his troops on the far bank of the River Ure. Experienced in fighting the Scots, Harclay had his men dismount and form up to fight on foot. A ford and a narrow bridge afforded the two crossing points. Both were guarded. On 16 March, with the king and his troops closing in from the south, Hereford and Lancaster made the decision to attempt a crossing. Hereford, accompanied by a contingent of knights and men-at-arms, led a charge across the bridge. Due to its narrowness they were forced to attack on foot. Harclay's men were ready and waiting. Spears were thrust at the onrushing earl. Hereford fell, mortally wounded. His standard bearer was struck down and killed beside him. An English chronicle claims that Hereford was killed by 'a thief, a ribald' who 'skulked under the bridge, and fiercely with a sword smote the noble knight in the bottom, so that his bowels came out there'.[17] So died the earl of Hereford, veteran of Falkirk, joint commander of the English vanguard at Bannockburn, killed in England by a fellow Englishman, having taken up arms against his brother-in-law, the king.

The earl of Lancaster was captured the following day. After a brief trial he was beheaded at his castle of Pontefract on 22 March 1322, his body having been turned to the north in accordance with the belief that he had colluded with Bruce.[18] At long last Edward had exacted vengeance for the death of Gaveston. An orgy of officially sanctioned bloodletting followed, Edward II instigating a series of arrests, trials and executions of those he believed had taken up arms against him. The king indulged in an excess of barbaric violence reminiscent of the brutal reign of terror that his father Edward I had unleashed upon the supporters of Robert Bruce in 1306. Flushed with success, it was in the triumphant wake of Boroughbridge that Edward undertook his last campaign into Scotland. Bruce, however, proved an infinitely more capable opponent than Lancaster ever had. The abysmal failure of this campaign, together with Edward's humiliating flight and the defeat at Byland inflicted by Randolph and Douglas, finally convinced the English king to conclude a truce. What is interesting is that Edward should choose to do so at a time when his domestic position was approaching its zenith. The victory at Boroughbridge, the execution of Lancaster, the trial and execution of those adjudged rebels and the ensuing formal annulment of the Ordinances in parliament, all these combined to ensure that for the first time Edward ruled without restraint. The years of impecuniousness which had continually afflicted his reign were also a thing of the past, the confiscated lands of those who had taken up arms against him, the Contrariants, alone providing the king with an enormous financial windfall. Indeed, though the campaign of 1322 proved an abysmal failure, it is clear that Edward had the resources to muster a substantial and well-equipped host.

The truth, it seems, is that Edward's heart was never in the Scottish war. Like the financial debt he had inherited from his father, the war was a bequest which he could have done without, and in which he had little interest. Throughout his reign the Scottish war had always come a poor second, his priority being the domestic struggle with his own magnates. Even in 1314 the prospect of a successful Scottish campaign was increasingly viewed as a means to an end with regard to the domestic conflict rather than as an end in itself. Writing in mid-century, Thomas Gray commented that, in the years following Bannockburn, Edward 'hardly troubled himself at all about Scotland, since through apathy, he had lost as much as his father had gained', and Gray further observed that after the loss of Berwick the English 'did not bother themselves with the war, but allowed it to die out'.[19] Reluctant though Edward was to acknowledge the loss of Scotland, there is an unmistakable sense that he allowed the English war effort gradually to wind down, the campaign of 1322 being a final, ultimately futile flourish, prompted by the heady success of victory at Boroughbridge. With the failure of the campaign Edward sought a period of peace, although he still refused formally to recognise Bruce as king. In his new-found position of predominance in his own realm, Edward knew there would be no wholesale domestic political opposition to the conclusion of a truce with Bruce and the Scots. By the end of 1323 England was ostensibly a country at peace.

THE LEGACY 247

This illusion was soon shattered. The downfall of Edward II, when it came, originated from an entirely unexpected source. Having returned from exile in early 1322, and devoid of opponents following the purge of the Contrariants, the Despensers had run riot, gorging themselves on land and money, resorting to blackmail if necessary to increase their already exorbitant wealth. Edward, blindly indulging his new favourites, failed to recognise the growing resentment they provoked in his queen, Isabella. When the prospect of a conflict with France threatened in the mid-1320s, it was Isabella, herself a French princess, who was sent to smooth negotiations. Valence, having been involved in negotiating the truce of 1323 with the Scots, was also dispatched as an envoy to France. He was never to return. Aymer de Valence, earl of Pembroke, died on 23 June 1324, exactly ten years to the day since the English and Scots had clashed at Bannockburn. He died of natural causes, collapsing in a doorway shortly after having eaten, and apoplexy has been advanced as the most likely cause of his death, although a malicious English chronicler, sympathetic to the executed earl of Lancaster and so hostile to Valence, derisively claimed that Valence 'was murdered suddenly on a lavatory seat'. The body of the late earl was returned to England and interred in Westminster Abbey.[20] The loss of Valence, a respected man of authority on whom Edward had increasingly come to rely, was a serious blow for a king who was already too close to his detested favourites.

Determined to avoid having to travel to France himself and do homage to the French king for Gascony, one of the contentious issues for which Isabella and Valence were to have negotiated, it was decided by Edward and the Despensers that the king's twelve-year-old son and heir, Edward, should accompany his mother Isabella and do homage in place of the king. In the autumn of 1325, with both the queen and the young prince in France, Isabella refused to return until the Despensers were removed. With the heir to the English Crown at her side, Isabella was in a powerful position. She was further strengthened by the support she received from several influential English exiles, men who had fled the tyranny of Edward and the Despensers. Isabella found common cause with Roger Mortimer, a powerful Marcher lord, who scandalously became her lover.[21] Securing military backing, Isabella and Mortimer sailed for England and on 24 September 1326 made landfall on the east coast at Harwich, at the mouth of the River Orwell. So widespread was the unpopularity of Edward and the Despensers that the invasion force encountered no serious opposition. Edward and his favourites were captured, the king being taken in Wales near Neath. The Despensers were executed and Edward was incarcerated in Kenilworth Castle in Warwickshire.

The murderous endgame was now played out. Edward was forced to resign the Crown in favour of his young son, and the coronation of Edward III took place on 1 February 1327. But until the young Edward came of age real power in England was exercised by Mortimer. The former king Edward II was moved to Berkeley Castle in Gloucestershire, and it was here that he died between 20 and 22 September 1327. The exact circumstances of his death remain unresolved. If he was murdered, the most likely scenario, then it would have been at the behest of Mortimer, and perhaps with the connivance of Isabella. His funeral took place in Gloucester on 20 December 1327 when the tragic king was laid to rest in St Peter's Abbey, his tomb surmounted by a wooden effigy. The lack of knowledge regarding Edward II's death led to persistent rumours that he had escaped and fled abroad, a seemingly fanciful tale; but one curiously supported by the existence of a credible contemporary letter which recounts how Edward secretly travelled on the continent and ended his life as a hermit.[22] Even in death this most bemusing of English kings left a legacy of ambiguity and uncertainty.

For Bruce the emergence of the Mortimer regime threatened the truce he had concluded with Edward II. The earl of Mar, brought up in the household of Edward II and having refused to leave the English king when terms for the earl's return to Scotland had been secured by Bruce after Bannockburn, had vainly plotted for the restoration of the deposed Edward. Although Bruce, as the price for such a restoration, could feasibly have demanded from the deposed Edward II a formal recognition of himself as king of Scotland, it was not a possibility he pursued. Instead, on the night of Edward III's coronation, 1 February 1327, Bruce delivered a pointed reminder to Mortimer by ordering an assault on Norham Castle. Mortimer responded to this failed assault by raising an army which the teenage Edward III dutifully led north in the summer of 1327. A Scottish force had also entered northern England, and the English campaign became a desultory and frustrating pursuit of their elusive enemy across the exposed northeastern landscape of Weardale. When the English army disbanded, Bruce led an invasion of Northumberland in which the castles of Alnwick, Warkworth and Norham were besieged. It was at the siege lines around Norham Castle that the first English envoys approached Bruce in order to seek peace.[23] The Scots withdrew and the series of negotiations that followed ultimately resulted in the Treaty of Edinburgh. This was the definitive peace that Bruce had fought so hard to gain. By the terms of the treaty, the English abandoned all their claims to the Scottish kingdom and recognised Bruce as king of Scotland. For his part Bruce agreed to pay the English a total sum of £20,000 in annual instalments, a payment that ostensibly was 'for the sake of peace'. The treaty was concluded on 17 March 1328 and formally ratified by the English on 4 May in a parliament at Northampton.[24] To reinforce the treaty it was agreed that Bruce's son and heir, David, should marry Joan, daughter of Edward II and sister of Edward III. Special arrangements were required as both David and Joan were still only children. The wedding of the two minors duly took place at Berwick on 12 July 1328. A final settlement, it appeared, had at last been reached between Scotland and England.

Despite the great Scottish victory won on the field of battle at Bannockburn, it had taken another fourteen years before Robert Bruce finally achieved the formal English recognition of his kingship that he had sought for so long. It was not Bannockburn, therefore, that ultimately brought the English to the negotiating table but the long years of attritional warfare that followed. Indeed, thirteen years after Bannockburn it had been necessary for Bruce to undertake one final campaign to pressurise the English into reaching a definitive peace settlement. Although Bannockburn was by far the single most spectacular episode of the war Bruce fought against England, it was not the decisive factor that ultimately gained Bruce and the Scots their objectives. Nor, after Bannockburn, did Bruce ever fight another set-piece battle against the English: in 1319 no attempt had been made to confront the English army besieging Berwick; in 1322 the Scots had withdrawn before the English host, reverting to their former tactics of irregular warfare; during the Weardale campaign of 1327 the Scots had deliberately ensured they were not brought to battle. Despite the remarkable success won at Bannockburn it is clear that Bruce was determined never again to take on the English in battle. An extremely capable military commander, Bruce knew that he had taken a supremely calculated risk on the night of 23 June 1314, his decision to stay and fight being based on a set of very particular circumstances. He was acutely aware that Bannockburn had been a singular victory which could almost certainly never be repeated. Crucially, Bannockburn had not seduced Bruce into believing a battle-seeking strategy could win the war against England; on the contrary, he had known that the next battle would most likely have resulted in a Scottish defeat. Bruce clearly understood the unique nature of the circumstances that had made a Scottish victory at Bannockburn possible.

This recognition, however, was only part of the reason why Bruce never again engaged the English in a set-piece battle. After Bannockburn the political imperatives under which Bruce laboured had also irrevocably changed; no longer was he weighed down by the need to establish himself as king in Scotland. Victory at Bannockburn had effectively sanctioned his authority as king within Scotland, and it was this need to establish his authority in Scotland that had led to the battle. The perilous face-off before Stirling Castle had not been brought about by the cause of Scottish independence but had originated in Bruce's desire to consolidate his claim to be king. Having risen to dominance by force of arms, it was essential that his military reputation remain untarnished; the extraordinary victory that followed at Bannockburn had sealed his reputation and effectively concluded an armed conquest of Scotland. Although few of his enemies at Bannockburn were Scots, the battle had still been of critical importance in dictating the outcome of the bitter power struggle in Scotland. In this sense Bannockburn was the last battle of the Scottish civil war, and domestically it proved to be a decisive victory for Bruce. Within a year of Bannockburn, on 27 April 1315, Bruce made his first formal provision for the succession of the Scottish Crown, stipulating that if he should die without a male heir then his brother, Edward, was to become king. The death of his brother in October 1318 led to a new provision, and the birth of his son and heir, David, had necessitated a further change in 1326.[25] The enactment of such provisions illustrates that, with his victory at Bannockburn, Bruce believed he had firmly acquired the Crown.

The only potentially serious challenge to the supremacy of Robert Bruce in Scotland came in 1320. In that year, as part of ongoing attempts to gain formal international recognition for Bruce as king of Scotland, a letter had been sent to the pope, John XXII, unequivocally asserting both the rightful independence of Scotland and the legitimacy with which Bruce reigned as King Robert. This letter, better known as the Declaration of Arbroath, is chiefly remembered for its eloquent declaration of Scottish independence, but it was the presentation of Bruce as the legitimate king, as a selfless saviour of the Scots, that stuck in some influential Scottish throats. A plot was hatched, its objective presumably being a Balliol restoration. Bruce, however, was tipped off, probably by Patrick, earl of Dunbar. The alleged conspirators were immediately arrested and tried in the Black Parliament of August 1320. Several were executed; others were sentenced to perpetual imprisonment. Among those implicated in the plot was Ingram de Umfraville, the mercurial Scottish lord who had fought against Bruce at Bannockburn and who had subsequently been captured. Having since served Bruce, in 1320 he now returned to English allegiance. His ultimate fate remains unknown.[26]

This half-hearted conspiracy was the only significant domestic threat to Bruce's reign after Bannockburn, and it was strangled at birth. No further attempt was made to depose Bruce. So strong was his hold on the Crown that there was no opposition when, upon his death in 1329, his son was inaugurated as David II of Scotland. The authority of Bruce as king within Scotland had been secured not by the peace settlement of 1328 but by the great victory he had won at Bannockburn fourteen years before. The settlement of 1328 had gained him the formal English recognition that legitimised his position; however, it was as the victor of Bannockburn that Bruce had gained the acclamation of the Scots as their king. In this respect Bannockburn had been a profoundly decisive battle.

On 7 June 1329, the year after the peace settlement had finally been concluded, Robert Bruce died in his home at Cardross, near Dumbarton, aged fifty-five. Since 1307 he had suffered bouts of incapacitating illness. Barbour believed the cause of his ill-health to have been the 'days of great tribulations' when Bruce had been a hunted man on the run. In 1328 Bruce had again been gravely afflicted by sickness and was unable to attend the wedding of his heir at Berwick. The exact nature of the illness that took his life remains unknown although a contemporary chronicle recounts that he died of leprosy, a theory that is still debated and includes modern analysis of the cast of his skull. The achievements of Bruce are all the more remarkable in light of the serious ill-health he suffered. Before his death Bruce had declared that he wished his heart to be taken into battle against the Saracens, and then finally interred at Melrose Abbey. His heart was duly removed and embalmed. The body of Robert I of Scotland was laid to rest in Dunfermline Abbey and surmounted by a fine tomb of Parisian marble.[27] Perhaps it was an act of mercy that Robert Bruce did not live to hear the peace settlement he had fought so strenuously to obtain talked of in derogatory terms by the English. Within little more than three years of his death the war would be renewed.

In February 1330 James Douglas set out for the Holy Land. Although accompanied by a contingent of Scots, his most precious possession was a silver casket in which was contained the embalmed heart of Robert Bruce. The route Douglas had chosen went via Spain. Here a conflict raged between the Christians, led by Alfonso XI of Castile, and the Saracens. The reputation of the Black Douglas went before him and he was appointed to the command of a division of the Christian army. On 25 August 1330 an engagement was fought near Turon. Although it resulted in a Christian victory, Douglas was slain on the field of battle. Contemporary accounts suggest that Douglas, eager to be the first into the fray and inexperienced in fighting the Saracens, advanced prematurely. His division was temporarily cut off and Douglas killed. After the battle his body and the casket containing Bruce's heart were recovered by the Christians from the battlefield. His body was subsequently boiled until the flesh was separated from the bones. The flesh was buried in consecrated ground in Spain, and his bones and the casket were reverentially brought back to Scotland. The bones of James Douglas were interred in his ancestral kirk of Douglas; according to the dying wishes of Robert Bruce, the casket containing the late king's heart was ceremonially buried at Melrose Abbey.[28]

In accordance with the provisions made by Bruce for the succession, his nephew Thomas Randolph was appointed Guardian of his five-year-old son, now king, David II, and of the Scottish realm. Randolph, however, did not long outlive his former comrades. He died at Musselburgh, near Edinburgh, on 20 July 1332. It appears Randolph may have died of cancer of the liver, an account of his last days revealing him to have been swollen and flushed. Yet the timing of his death coincided with the sailing of the invasion force of English lords, the Disinherited, and it was consequently alleged by a Scottish chronicler that Randolph had been poisoned by an English friar.[29] Within weeks the Disinherited had landed in Scotland and, under the command of Henry de Beaumont, defeated the Scots at Dupplin Moor on 10–11 August 1332. Notably, of the commanders of both sides who had fought at Bannockburn, it was Beaumont, the longest-surviving, who proved to be the driving force behind the reopening of the war. Beaumont died in France on 10 March 1340. Despite the English victories of Dupplin Moor in 1332 and Halidon Hill in 1333, his ambitions in Scotland were never realised.

Yet the repercussions of Bannockburn were to endure well beyond the deaths of those who had fought in this most famous of battles. As we have seen, in terms of the wars between England and Scotland the battle of Bannockburn did not prove conclusive, nor did it resolve the political conflicts within England. Only in terms of the Scottish civil war did Bannockburn prove pivotal; in establishing Bruce as king in Scotland, it consequently marked a significant shift in the war with England. The truth is that, in this period, no battle proved decisive in terms of the ongoing war. At Falkirk in 1298 the annihilation of a Scottish army had no significant impact in bringing the Anglo-Scottish wars to an end. The destruction of another Scottish force, at Neville's Cross in 1346, a defeat that resulted in the Scottish king, David II, being captured and many Scottish earls and lords being killed or taken prisoner, only served to halt the wars temporarily. By the last decades of the fourteenth century England and Scotland were again fighting in earnest. The ultimate importance of Bannockburn, however, is not to be found in assessing the merits or failures of its short-term decisiveness but in recognising its long-term legacy.

The English certainly did not forget this most humiliating of defeats. Bannockburn was a stain on their character, a defeat they took very much to heart. The *Vita* lamented that it 'blemished the reputation of the English', and as far afield as Italy it was derogatorily observed that the English were 'inferior to the wretched Scot'.[30] In the decades following Bannockburn a serious overhaul of the English military machine was fitfully implemented by means of trial and error in an attempt to understand how such a catastrophe could have occurred, and to learn how it could be prevented from ever happening again. On the field of battle at Dupplin Moor in 1332, and again at Halidon Hill in 1333, the results of this overhaul began to emerge. Knights and men-at-arms dismounted and fought on foot, taking up a tactically defensive position alongside the infantry. The latter consisted almost exclusively of archers armed with the devastating firepower of the longbow, and the entire army operated as a single cohesive and coordinated force. By the late 1330s this overhaul was completed by the introduction of the mounted archer – remaining mounted for the march and then fighting on foot – and recruitment by means of contracts with individual lords and captains, each of whom agreed to provide a set number of cavalry and mounted infantry. This latter development led to the raising of mixed retinues of cavalry and infantry. In 1346, within a matter of seven weeks, two separate English armies achieved stunning battlefield victories: at Crécy on 26 August an army led by Edward III spectacularly routed the French; in northern England on 17 October, outside the walls of Durham, an invading Scottish army led by David II was destroyed at Neville's Cross.[31] The English had learnt the hard lesson they had been taught at Bannockburn. Their development of a new military system and tactics saw them dominate the battlefields of France in the mid-fourteenth century. This was the enduring legacy of Bannockburn for the English.

For the Scots the immediate benefits of Bannockburn may have seemed rather disappointing considering the spectacular nature of their unexpected victory. The battle did not gain the Scottish kingdom its independence, nor did it bring an end to the wars. In contrast, for Bruce personally, the immediate rewards of Bannockburn were of immense importance. In leading a Scottish army into battle against the might of the English host, a host led in person by the English king, and in inflicting such a comprehensive and unprecedented defeat upon it, Bruce had popularly established himself as king of Scotland. On the field of battle before Stirling Castle he had emerged victorious from the bitter Scottish power struggle which he himself had triggered. It was not the independence of the Scottish kingdom that was won amidst the devastation of Bannockburn, but the right of Bruce to call himself king. In this sense it was not Scotland that emerged from Bannockburn as the real winner, but Robert Bruce himself.

Yet for Scotland the battle had another, more ethereal and infinitely more enduring legacy. By making his fateful decision not to withdraw but to stay and commit his army to the fight, Bruce inextricably bound his cause to that of an independent Scottish kingdom. It was a union forged in blood in the horrific terror of the mêlée. After the furnace of battle, the two causes had become inseparably fused. Bruce came to personify Scottish independence, and it was from the Scottish kingdom that Bruce drew his strength. It was a fusion that with the passage of time came to transcend warfare and politics, and developed into the spiritual core of the emerging Scottish nation. Robert Bruce and Bannockburn became synonymous with independence, and as such they became the touchstone of a shared sense of a Scottish national identity. In this way the decision of Bruce to stay and fight did indeed do much to dictate the fate of the Scottish nation. As the defeat of the English host at Bannockburn had been possible due partly to their hopelessly low morale, so the enduring legacy of the battle for Scotland was also psychological in nature. It is as a potent symbol of Scottish independence and nationhood that the legacy of Bannockburn survives to this day.

APPENDIX I

24 JUNE 1314:
THE FIELD OF BATTLE

THE SITE WHERE THE MÊLÉE WAS FOUGHT ON THE MORNING OF 24 JUNE 1314 was critical in determining the outcome of the engagement; unfortunately, the exact location of this field of battle has proved impossible to identify with any degree of certainty. During the twentieth century it was the subject of substantial debate and speculation, and it remains so to this day. In 2001 the conclusions of a thorough historical investigation led by Fiona Watson were published by Stirling Council. A site was suggested, but still the field of battle could not be identified for certain. The likelihood is that it never will be. The documentary evidence remains inconclusive, and no compelling archaeological finds have ever been made. This should not be considered unusual as medieval battlefields are notoriously difficult to pinpoint; the site of the great battle fought between the English and Scots at Neville's Cross in 1346 also remains largely unknown. In both cases an approximate area for the engagement can be identified, but little more.

In fact, even the approximate location of the mêlée of Bannockburn was originally wrong. Traditionally, the site was thought to be on the eastern edge of the New Park in the locality of the Borestone. This is where the present heritage and visitor centre stands, but it has long since been dismissed as a viable site. In the early twentieth century a radical reinterpretation by Mackay Mackenzie placed the field of battle well to the east, right out in the treacherous expanse of the Carse of Stirling. This extreme proposition was tempered in the 1930s by the separately published studies of Thomas Miller and R.A. Carruthers, both of which suggested that the engagement occurred on the 'Dryfield' of Balquhiderock, on firm ground bordering the ridge which dropped down into the carseland. In the 1950s Philip Christison argued for a site in the Carse of Balquhiderock, placing the engagement in the triangle formed by the Bannock Burn, the Pelstream Burn and the ridge which marked the beginnings of the carseland. Geoffrey Barrow favoured the 'Dryfield' of Balquhiderock, though he would not completely rule out the Carse of Balquhiderock. A report, written by Fiona Watson and Maggie Anderson in 2001, identified the site of battle as being either in the Carse near Millhall or upon the 'Dryfield' of Balquhiderock, part of which now forms the playing fields of Bannockburn High School. The report favours the 'Dryfield' and suggests that the English were subsequently driven back into the treacherous carseland. In contrast, the most recent of these many studies, undertaken by William Scott, argues strongly for a field of battle down in the Carse of Balquhiderock.[i]

Both the Borestone and Mackenzie's site, the latter located well out in the great Carse of Stirling, can be discarded. Neither fits either the evidence or the course of events. The approximate location in which the battle was fought can be narrowed down to an area extending east from the New Park to the boundary formed by the converging courses of the Bannock and the Pelstream burns. This area consisted of two contrasting terrains, the 'Dryfield', which may have been a restricted field of cornland perhaps half a mile wide, and the soft, treacherous terrain, of the Carse of Balquhiderock, laced with slow-flowing polles. Separating these two terrains was a ridge, or rather an abrupt incline, which rose steeply for approximately fifty to sixty foot from the low-lying carseland. The engagement was fought somewhere within this area.

Precisely where this was remains unclear. We know that, in their desperation to bring the Scots to battle, the English had crossed the Bannock Burn during the night of 23 June. The chronicles indicate that most, if not all, of the English host spent what remained of the night encamped in the Carse of Balquhiderock. Their intention in the morning cannot have been anything other than to advance towards the New Park in the hope that the Scots were still present, and in doing so they would have ascended the incline and

---

[i] W.M. Mackenzie, *The Battle of Bannockburn* (Glasgow, 1913); T. Miller, *The Site of the Battle of Bannockburn* (Historical Association, 1931); A. Carruthers, 'The Site of the Battle of Bannockburn', *Chambers Journal* (February, 1933); P. Christison, 'Bannockburn, 23 and 24 June 1314', *Proceedings of the Society of Antiquaries in Scotland*, xc (1959); *Robert Bruce*, 301–10; F. Watson and M. Anderson, *The Battle of Bannockburn: A Study for Stirling Council* (Stirling, 2001); W. Scott, *Bannockburn Revealed* (Rothesay, 2000).

reached the 'Dryfield'. The Scots spent the night encamped in the New Park. During the short hours of darkness, Bruce would have received intelligence that the English were attempting a crossing of the Bannock Burn, and he would have known that, when dawn came, they would be somewhere to the east of the New Park, in the vicinity of the Carse of Balquhiderock. The English had placed themselves in an extremely unfavourable position, and knowledge of this must surely have been a key factor in Bruce's decision to stay and give battle. The vital question is how Bruce thought he could best exploit the unfavourable position of the host.

Having resolved to give battle, he essentially had two options. He could preempt an English advance by leading his army down into the carseland and attempting to entrap the English in the Carse of Balquhiderock, penning them in between the Bannock and Pelstream burns, both of which were much more formidable natural obstacles in the fourteenth century than they are today.[ii] This would force the English heavy cavalry to fight upon appallingly soft terrain and so considerably diminish their effectiveness. Alternatively, Bruce could allow the English to ascend the incline and gain the restricted confines of the 'Dryfield'. If he should then advance against the host, the English would be compelled to fight on an extremely narrow front and the host would most probably have become awkwardly disjointed, many of the foot soldiers being unable to ascend the incline and reach the battlefield. Bruce required a field of battle that was both restricted in size and unsuitable for heavy cavalry. Both sites appear to have had the potential to meet these requirements.

A third factor must surely have been the fifty-foot (approximately fifteen-metre) ridge or slope, which separated the hard ground from the low-lying carseland. Bruce was an experienced military commander and it is difficult to believe that he would readily have surrendered the advantage of height. As the English were to learn, the ideal position for an army arrayed on foot was to fight from a tactically defensive position on higher ground. If Bruce had deployed his army at the summit of this ridge, then the range and firepower of the English archers in the Carse below would have been curtailed. Forced

---

[ii] Barrow is at pains to stress that it was most unusual for a battle to be named for any location other than a village or town, and believes that it was named after the small settlement of Bannock(burn) rather than the burn itself, an argument that, if correct, would tend to lend credence to the battle being fought upon the 'Dryfield' which was relatively near to the settlement: see *Robert Bruce*, 280–2. Although contemporary references to the battle frequently referred to it as 'Stirling', the name 'Bannockburn' was also used by contemporaries, mainly in reference to the actual burn in which many English were killed. For examples, see *Scalacronica*, 75–7; *Lanercost*, 208.

to advance uphill, the momentum of the English cavalry charge would have been substantially reduced. It is hard to imagine Bruce leading his army down into the treacherous carseland to confront the English; it is equally difficult to envisage him allowing the English cavalry to mount the ridge unopposed. No contemporary source explicitly refers to this ridge or invests it with any importance in the engagement. Indeed, a position on the ridge may not have restricted the field of battle to the extent that Bruce required. All that can be said is that the ridge was another factor which Bruce would have had to take into consideration when deciding upon the best site from which to confront the English.

Geoffrey le Baker, however, recounts that the English cavalry foundered at a ditch or ditches (*fossas*) into which their horses tumbled, the Scots killing many of those who were dismounted and taking others prisoner. In an attempt to save the cavalry, English archers tried to lay a field of protective arrow fire between the cavalry and the Scots, but in doing so shot their own cavalry in the back. Baker mistakenly identifies this ditch as the cavalry trap dug by the Scots on 22 June, and compounds this error by claiming that it stretched across the entire front of the Scottish army. Although the account of the battle provided by Geoffrey le Baker is characteristically melodramatic and riddled with inaccuracies, it is worth considering whether there may not be an element of truth hidden within the confusion; perhaps, as they attempted to advance against the Scots on 24 June, the cavalry foundered not in a ditch but as they advanced out of the Carse and up the steep incline.[iii]

There can be little doubt that it was Bruce himself who dictated where the mêlée would be fought that morning. It was the Scottish army that initially advanced in full array towards the English and precipitated the engagement. The *Vita*, however, claims that this was a Scottish response to the fact that 'the English line had occupied the field', a view echoed by Barbour.[iv] Interestingly, when the Scots emerged from the New Park and dropped to their knees to say mass, the chroniclers are in agreement that this was witnessed by the English. At this point the two armies must have been within sight of one another, but exactly where the Scots said mass is not clear. If it was beside the New Park, then the English must have ascended the ridge; if it was after an initial Scottish advance, then the English might still have been down in the Carse.

[iii] See *Chronicon le Baker*, 7–8.
[iv] *Vita*, 52; *Bruce*, 468–9.

Contemporary chroniclers are of little help. Thomas Gray recounts that 'in the morning at sunrise, they [the Scots] came out of the woods on foot in three divisions, and steadily held their course towards the English army, which had been armed for all the night, their horses bridled'. This appears to suggest that the Scots advanced upon the location where the English had spent the night. Barbour writes of the 'plane' upon which the Scots were deployed, but claims that the English cavalry had already occupied the 'hard feld'. Robert Baston, an eyewitness to the engagement, writes that 'the dry ground [*arida terra*] of Stirling sustains the first conflicts', but this is in reference to the engagements fought on Sunday, 23 June. Of the encounter fought on 24 June, Baston provides two intriguing comments. First, he writes that 'The English fighters look expectantly for Scots whom they may do to death – Scots no longer remote but close at hand'. Secondly, Baston dramatically recounts, 'Many a sob escapes from the rampart of the countenance; rushing down, the raging Scottish fighters advance on foot . . .'. Both comments give the impression that the Scots advanced towards the English, the latter comment being especially interesting for its description of the Scots 'rushing down' to engage the host; could this be a reference to the Scots advancing down the incline to meet the English in the Carse of Balquhiderock? Another poem, possibly also written by Baston, recounts of Edward II that he 'attacks while there is no retreat . . .', and subsequently states that 'Between the stony stream and the obstruction of their camp the treacherous English people come to grief'.[v] Again, the impression here is that the host was pinned down in the Carse, with the Bannock and Pelstream burns preventing any ordered retreat. The fact that Baston specifically refers to the encounters of 23 June being fought on the 'dry ground' also suggests that the mêlée of 24 June was fought on appreciably different terrain. Clearly, the Scots halted to receive the charge of the English cavalry, but an unexpected Scottish advance towards the host at the outset, perhaps even an advance down into the carseland, may well have provoked a hasty and disorganised English cavalry charge. Scottish foot soldiers would also have found the soft ground of the carseland difficult, but if Bruce believed it presented insurmountable problems to the English cavalry then he may well have decided to fight the engagement there.

The inescapable truth is that the exact site of the engagement is impossible to pinpoint with any degree of accuracy. However, whatever its precise location, it is abundantly clear that the English host had entrapped itself on

[v] *Scalacronica*, 75; *Bruce*, 468–9; *Bower*, 359–61, 372–3.

appallingly unfavourable ground. This terrain, whether it consisted of soft carseland or of hard, broken ground, was entirely unsuitable for heavy cavalry. Restricted to a narrow 'Dryfield', or hemmed in on a narrow front by the Bannock and Pelstream burns, the full might of the host could not be deployed. In his desperation to bring the Scots to battle, Edward II had imperilled his army by placing it in the most treacherous and hostile of terrains. The only way out was to break the Scottish schiltrom; if the Scots stood firm, then the host would be pushed further back into the carseland, its line of retreat fatally obstructed by the Bannock and Pelstream burns. Although the field of battle cannot be identified for certain, its critical contribution to the outcome of the battle is clear. If the host had not been placed in such a terribly unfavourable position during the night, then it must be doubted whether Bruce would have decided to stay and give battle. Ironically, it was the all-consuming desire of Edward to bring the Scots to battle that placed the host in such a hazardous position, and it was by placing the host in such appallingly unfavourable terrain that Edward inadvertently provided Robert Bruce and his Scottish army with a rare opportunity to defeat it. As the agreement for the relief of Stirling had given the English a tremendous opportunity to bring the Scots to battle, so Edward's desperation to achieve that battle gave the Scots a chance of emerging from it victorious.

APPENDIX II

ENGLISH CASUALTIES

The following individuals are identified in contemporary sources as being casualties of the engagements fought on 23 and 24 June 1314 and of the subsequent Scottish pursuit. All are men of the rank of knight and above.

The following are recorded as killed in the rout:[i]

Gilbert de Clare, earl of Gloucester
Robert Clifford

Payn Tibetoft
William Marshal
John Comyn, lord of Badenoch
William de Vescy
John de Montfort
Nicholas de Hastelegh (Hastele)
William Deyncourt[iii]
Giles d'Argentan

Ralph de Beauchamp
John de Penebrigge (Henebrigge)
Anselm Marshal
John de Riveres (Ryvere)
Robert de Hastele[ii]
Robert Botevilyn
Oliver de Picton
Gerald del Idle
John de Gosorald
Robert de Pulford

[i] Nineteen of these individuals are named as being killed in two or more sources. *Trivet* is the sole authority for eight of them, the *Annales Londonienses* for a further eighteen and the *Gesta* for one. The death of James Torthorald is recorded in the grant made to his widow and children. See ch. 14.
[ii] It is possible that Robert was related to Nicholas Hastelegh (Hastele), another knight among the list of those killed.
[iii] William and Reginald Deyncourt, both killed in the rout, were brothers. See *Gesta*, 46.

Edmund Comyn
John Lovel (le Riche)
Edmund de Hasting
Miles de Stapelton
Simon Ward[iv]
Robert de Felton
Michael de Poinynge
Edmund Mauley

Henry de Bohun
Thomas Ufford
John de Elsingfelde (Elsefeld)
John de Harecourt
Walter de Hakelut
Philip de Courtenay

Thomas de Bosford
Reginald Deyncourt
Robert de Applyndene
Thomas de Conradi
Thomas de St Leger
Reginald de Lem
William de Gosyngtone
Nicholas de Vieuxpont (Vespont)
Thomas le Ercedekene[v]
John Cabery
Robert Bertram
Hugo de Scales
James de Torthorald
John de Grey

The following are recorded as captured:[vi]

Humphrey de Bohun, earl of Hereford
Robert de Umfraville, earl of Angus
John Giffard
William le Latimer
Maurice de Berkeley
Ingram de Umfraville
Marmaduke Tweng

Giles de Beauchamp
John Cysrewast
John Bluwet
Roger Corbet
Gilbert de Bohun[vii]
Bartholomew de Enefeld
Thomas de Ferrers

[iv] The registers of Archbishop William Greenfield of York record that a payment was made for the ransom of the knight Simon Warde. See ch. 14. *Trivet* is the sole authority for a knight called Simon Ward being killed and, though he may have been mistaken, it is also conceivable that there were two separate knights, perhaps related, who shared the same name.

[v] The *Annales Londonienses* record that Thomas was killed, while *Trivet* recounts that Thomas and Odo le Ercedekene were taken prisoner. Again, this may be the result of confusion in the sources, or a reference to two separate individuals. A third possibility is that Thomas may have died of wounds whilst in captivity.

[vi] Eleven of these individuals are listed as captured in two or more sources; *Trivet* is the sole authority for the rest. In addition the knight Roger Mortimer also appears to have been taken prisoner.

[vii] Gilbert de Bohun (spelt Boun in *Trivet*) would have been a relation of Humphrey de Bohun, earl of Hereford, and presumably was captured alongside the latter whilst taking refuge in Bothwell Castle. Their capture and the cost of their subsequent ransoms, together with the brutal death of Henry de Bohun, Hereford's nephew, would have cast Bannockburn as a particularly dark episode in the annals of the Bohun family.

ENGLISH CASUALTIES 263

John de Wyletone
Robert de Mauley
Henry filius (son of) Hugo
Thomas de Gray
Walter de Beauchamp
Richard de Charonis
John de Wevelmtoun
Robert de Neville
John de Segrave
Gilbert Pecche
John de Clavering
Anthony de Lucy
Ralph de Camys
John de Euere
Andreas de Arembyn
Thomas de Berkeley
filius (son of) Roger Tyrel
Anselm de Marshal

Ralph Botetourt (Butetort)[viii]
Thomas Botetourt (Butetort)
John de Kingestone[ix]
Nicholas de Kingestone
William Lovel
Henry de Wiletoun
Baldwin de Frevile (Fryvill)
John de Clivedone (Clindon)
Adomar la Souche (Zouche)
John de Merewode
John Manse
Thomas le Ercedekene[x]
Ode le Ercedekene
Robert Beaupel filius (son)
John Mautravers filius (son)
William Giffard[xi]
William Giffard
Roger Northburgh
Roger de Wikenfelde[xii]

[viii] Ralph and Thomas are listed together in *Trivet*'s list of casualties, and it follows that they were either father and son or, most probably, brothers. They were presumably related to the household banneret John Botetourt, who himself had been a strong adherent of Edward II, but who had also served as an Ordainer.

[ix] *Trivet* relates that John and Nicholas were brothers.

[x] Thomas and Odo are listed together by *Trivet*. See also n. v above.

[xi] Both Williams are listed together by *Trivet*. They were almost certainly related to the banneret John Giffard, who was also taken prisoner. The *Vita* relates the capture of the latter immediately after recounting the capture of Hereford, and in doing so raises the possibility that John was also captured in Bothwell. That two of his relatives were also taken prisoner lends further support to this.

[xii] According to *Trivet*, Wikenfelde was serving in the retinue of Roger Northburgh, perhaps as one of his two clerks, both of whom were captured.

ABBREVIATIONS

Ann. Lond.	'Annales Londonienses', *Chronicles of the Reign of Edward I and Edward II*, vol. i, ed. W. Stubbs (Rolls Series, 1882–3).
Annales Paulini	'Annales Paulini', *Chronicles of the Reign of Edward I and Edward II*, vol. i, ed. W. Stubbs (Rolls Series, 1882–3).
Bower	*Scotichronicon by Walter Bower*, vols vi and vii, ed. D.E.R. Watt et al. (Edinburgh, 1991, 1996).
Bruce	*The Bruce by John Barbour*, ed. and trans. A.A.M. Duncan (Edinburgh, 1999).
Brut	*The Brut*, vol. i, ed. F.W.D. Brie (Early English Text Society, original series, cxxxi, 1906).
CDS	*Calendar of Documents Relating to Scotland*, 4 vols, ed. J. Bain (London, 1881–8); vol. v, ed. G.G. Simpson and J.D. Galbraith (Edinburgh, 1986).
DNB	*Dictionary of National Biography* (Oxford, 2004).
EHR	*English Historical Review*.
Foedera	*Foedera, Conventiones, Litterae, et Acta Publica*, I, ii, ed. T. Rymer (Record Commission, 1816).
Fordun	*John of Fordun's Chronicle of the Scottish Nation*, 2 vols, ed. W.F. Skene (1993 reprint of 1872 original).
Gesta	'Gesta Edwardi de Carnarvan', *Chronicles of the Reign of Edward I and Edward II*, vol. II, ed. W. Stubbs (Rolls Series, 1882–3).
Guisborough	*The Chronicle of Walter of Guisborough*, ed. H. Rothwell (Camden Society, lxxxix, 1957).

Lanercost	*The Chronicle of Lanercost, 1272–1346*, ed. and trans. H. Maxwell (Glasgow, 1913).
Parl. Writs.	*Parliamentary Writs and Writs of Military Summons*, 2 vols in 4, ed. F. Palgrave (London, 1827–34).
Robert Bruce	*Robert Bruce and the Community of the Realm of Scotland*, G.W.S. Barrow (Edinburgh, 4th edition, 2005).
Rot. Scot.	*Rotuli Scotiae*, 2 vols, ed. D. Macpherson et al. (Record Commission, 1814).
Scalacronica	*Scalacronica by Sir Thomas Gray, 1272–1363*, ed. and trans. A King (Surtees Society, ccix, 2005).
Stevenson	*Documents Illustrative of the History of Scotland*, 2 vols, ii, ed. J. Stevenson (Edinburgh, 1870).
Trivet	*Nicolai Triveti Annalium Continuatio*, ed. A. Hall (Oxford, 1722).
Trokelowe	*Johannis de Trokelowe et Henrici de Blaneforde Chronica et Annales*, ed. H.T. Riley (Rolls Series, 1866).
Vita	*Vita Edwardi Secundi*, ed. and trans. N. Denholm-Young (London, 1957).

NOTES

1. A BATTLE WON

1. *Bruce*, 506–8.
2. *Guisborough*, 298–303. For a comprehensive account of Stirling Bridge, see A. Fisher, *William Wallace* (Edinburgh, 1986), 49–56.
3. *Stevenson*, 232–3.
4. *DNB*, xii, 107–8.
5. *CDS*, ii, no. 887; Fisher, *Wallace*, 41, 44–5.
6. *CDS*, ii, no. 1432; Fisher, *Wallace*, 117.
7. *Bruce*, 496; *Bower*, vii, 52–7.
8. *DNB*, xxii, 750–1.

2. THE WOLF IN THE FOLD

1. Details of the siege are to be found in *CDS*, ii, nos 1491, 1498–1500, 1504, 1519, 1536, 1539, 1556; M. Prestwich, *Edward I* (London, 1988), 501–2.
2. Richardson and Sayles, *The English Parliament in the Middle Ages*, xiii (London, 1981), 311.
3. *Stevenson*, 481–5; *CDS*, ii, 1510.
4. Comprehensive accounts of the political and legal intricacies that led to the outbreak of war can be found in *Robert Bruce*, chs 1–4; Prestwich, *Edward I*, 356–75. For contemporary documents central to the crisis, see E.L.G. Stones, ed., *Anglo-Scottish Relations, 1174–1328* (London, 1965); E.L.G. Stones and G.G. Simpson, eds, *Edward I and the Throne of Scotland 1290–96: An Edition of the Record Sources for the Great Cause* (Oxford, 1978).
5. *Robert Bruce*, 78.

3. A POISONED CHALICE

1. Prestwich, *Edward I*, 78, 215–26, 330–1. See also J.E. Morris, *The Welsh Wars of Edward I* (Oxford, 1901).
2. T.H. Riley, ed., *Chronica Willemi Rishanger* (Rolls Series, 1865), 373–4; *Guisborough*, 271–3; Prestwich, *Edward I*, 470–1.

3. *Robert Bruce*, 96–7.
4. *Scalacronica*, 39.
5. Fisher, *William Wallace*, 49–56.
6. Prestwich, *Edward I*, 479–81.
7. Ibid., 496.
8. For Courtrai, see J.F. Verbruggen, *The Battle of the Golden Spurs: Courtrai, 11 July 1302* (Woodbridge, 2001 edition).

4. THE DARK STAIN OF TREACHERY

1. *Bruce*, 66–81; *Fordun*, ii, 330–3; *Guisborough*, 366–7. Due to the sensational nature of this event, the chronicles provide various accounts of the circumstances surrounding the murder. They largely agree that Bruce arranged the meeting because he suspected John Comyn of betraying him to Edward I, or of attempting to blacken his reputation with the English king. The claim by Fordun that Bruce fled from London having been warned that he was about to be arrested is almost certainly untrue. Although the chroniclers imply that Bruce intended to kill Comyn for this perceived betrayal, it would seem Bruce merely intended to confront Comyn, not murder him. But see also n. 13 below.
2. *Vita*, 12.
3. *Robert Bruce*, 31–4.
4. Ibid., 119; *Guisborough*, 295.
5. *Guisborough*, 295–8. Although Bruce may have been a patriot, 'neither he nor we may entirely distinguish this sentiment from his interest in the throne'. See A.A.M. Duncan, 'The War of the Scots, 1306–23', *Transactions of the Royal Historical Society*, 6th Series, ii (1992), 136.
6. *Robert Bruce*, 34–5.
7. Ibid., 103; *Bower*, vi, 75.
8. *Robert Bruce*,110–12; Fisher, *William Wallace*, 41, 44–5.
9. See A. Young, *Robert Bruce's Rivals: The Comyns, 1212–1314* (Edinburgh, 1997). For Comyn's claim to the Crown, see A. Grant, 'The Death of John Comyn: What Was Going On?', *Scottish Historical Review*, lxxxvi (October, 2007), 176–224.
10. *CDS*, ii, no. 1290. Wallace appears to have travelled to the continent on a diplomatic mission. See Fisher, *Wallace*, 96–8.
11. *Robert Bruce*, 155–6; *Stevenson*, nos 579–80, 586, 603.
12. The full text of this ambiguous agreement, and a discussion of its meaning, is provided in *Robert Bruce*, 160–1. See also Prestwich, *Edward I*, 496–7.
13. It is difficult to believe that Bruce arranged to meet Comyn with the intention of killing him, although a strong argument has recently been advanced that the killing was indeed premeditated. Comyn – as a nephew of John Balliol, and grandson of Dervorguilla, a granddaughter of David, earl of Huntingdon – was arguably next in line to the Crown after the Balliols. It has been suggested that Bruce reacted to this threat by deliberately setting out to kill Comyn. See Grant, 'The Death of John Comyn', *passim*.
14. F. Palgrave, ed., *Documents and Records Illustrating the History of Scotland*, i (London, 1837), 323–4; *Robert Bruce*, 170–1.
15. The contents of Wallace's letters can hardly have been incriminating for Edward I took no immediate action against Bruce. As Barrow suggests, they probably dated to the period before 1302 when Bruce had been fighting against the English. See *Robert Bruce*, 181.
16. Although there is no firm evidence that Bruce was waiting in expectation of the death of Edward I, in the circumstances it is extremely likely.

17. E.L.G. Stones, ed., *Anglo-Scottish Relations, 1174–1328* (London, 1965), 34. It has even been suggested that Wishart may have persuaded Bruce to take the throne rather than seek a deal with Edward I. See *Bruce*, 88 n., 175–7; Duncan, 'War of the Scots', 136. Barrow curiously terms Bruce's usurpation of the Crown a 'revolution', partly due to the later emergence of the community of the realm in support of Bruce, but Barrow qualifies this by also admitting that it was the 'private revolution of an ambitious man'. See *Robert Bruce*, 187.
18. *Robert Bruce*, 194–7.
19. *Bruce*, 92–104; *Guisborough*, 368. Barbour recounts that it was Ingram de Umfraville, a Scottish lord in allegiance to the English, who advised Valence on this course of action. Barbour reprises Umfraville's position as a shrewd adviser to the English at Bannockburn.

5. BEQUEST OF A WARRIOR-KING

1. Edward initially refused to accept that Bruce was guilty of Comyn's murder, believing that reports of his involvement were merely rumours intended to destabilise Scotland. See Prestwich, *Edward I*, 505.
2. H. Johnstone, *Edward of Carnarvon, 1284–1307* (Manchester, 1946), 105, 108–9.
3. The definitive biography of Edward I is Prestwich, *Edward I*.
4. *Ibid.*, 42–58, 412–35. The intricacies of the Barons wars are covered in J.R. Maddicott, *Simon de Montfort* (Cambridge, 1994).
5. *Bruce*, 154; *Scalacronica*, 65; *Vita*, 40.
6. Prestwich, *Edward I*, 126–7; Johnstone, *Edward of Carnarvon*, 11, 15.
7. Johnstone, *Edward of Carnarvon*, 25, 28.
8. *Vita*, 40.
9. Prestwich, *Edward I*, 484–90; N.H. Nicolas, *The Siege of Carlaverock* (London, 1828).
10. Prestwich, *Edward I*, 493–4; Johnstone, *Edward of Carnarvon*, 73.
11. Prestwich, *Edward I*, 498–500; Johnstone, *Edward of Carnarvon*, 83, 90.
12. Johnstone, *Edward of Carnarvon*, 90.
13. *Ibid.*, 51. Prestwich, *Edward I*, 226–7, 553. During the political crisis of 1297, Edward I had cynically exploited the position of the prince for political gain, but this was out of necessity rather than choice. See Johnstone, *Edward of Carnarvon*, 34; Prestwich, *Edward I*, 425.
14. For Gaveston, see J.S. Hamilton, *Piers Gaveston, Earl of Cornwall, 1307–12: Politics and Patronage in the Reign of Edward II* (Detroit, 1988); P. Chaplais, *Piers Gaveston, Edward II's Adoptive Brother* (Oxford, 1994).
15. Johnstone, *Edward of Carnarvon*, 83.
16. *Ibid.*, 305.
17. *Bruce*, 152–4.
18. *Ibid.*, 154–8; Johnstone, *Edward of Carnarvon*, 112. Some of the garrison may have been hanged. See *Lanercost*, 170.
19. *Bruce*, 150; *Guisborough*, 369; Prestwich, *Edward I*, 508–9; Barrow, *Robert Bruce*, 228–31.
20. Prestwich, *Edward I*, 509–10; Johnstone, *Edward of Carnarvon*, 112. The countess of Buchan was released from her cage in 1310, and Mary Bruce, presumably also released from her cage by 1310, returned to Scotland after Bannockburn. See *Robert Bruce*, 210.
21. Johnstone, *Edward of Carnarvon*, 122.
22. Prestwich, *Edward I*, 510, 556–7.

6. LORDS OF WAR

1. *CDS*, ii, no. 1926.
2. *Bruce*, 166–96.
3. *Ibid.*, 212–22, 224–32.
4. *Ibid.*, 60–6.
5. *Ibid.*, 62–4.
6. *Ibid.*, 242–6; Duncan, 'War of the Scots', 140. Barbour almost certainly errs by placing the 'Douglas Lardner' (see below) before this attack on Douglas Castle. See *Bruce*, 202 nn. 225–462. Barbour appears to have mistakenly reversed the chronology.
7. *Bruce*, 282–8. Duncan believes that the encounter at Glen Trool took place in June 1307 and so followed the engagement at Loudoun Hill, a reversal of the traditional chronology. See *Bruce*, 282 nn. 509, 296 nn. 131–3.
8. *Ibid.*, 296–308.
9. *Ibid.*, 319 n. 34.
10. These details are contained in a letter sent in April 1308 by Duncan de Frendraught, sheriff of Banff for the English, to Edward II. The letter is given in full in *ibid.*, 318 n. 5.
11. *Ibid.*, 318–26, 318–20 n. 34.
12. *Ibid.*, 326–8, 326 n. 189.
13. *Ibid.*, 332–4.
14. *Ibid.*, 290–4.
15. *Ibid.*, 202–10.
16. *Ibid.*, 344–52, 354.
17. *Ibid.*, 374.
18. *Ibid.*, 354–8.
19. *Ibid.*, 360–6.
20. *Ibid.*, 334 and 334 nn. 311–24.
21. *Robert Bruce*, 237–41; Duncan, 'War of the Scots', 131–5.
22. *Vita*, 12.
23. The raiding of northern England is thoroughly analysed in J. Scammell, 'Robert I and the North of England', *EHR*, 73 (1958), 385–403; C. McNamee, *The Wars of the Bruces: Scotland, England and Ireland, 1306–28* (Edinburgh, 2006), ch. 3. See also Duncan, 'War of the Scots', 148.
24. *Bruce*, 334–42, 366–72; *Lanercost*, 202.
25. Duncan, 'War of the Scots', 149. See D. Cornell, 'A Kingdom Cleared of Castles: The Role of the Castle in the Campaigns of Robert Bruce', *Scottish Historical Review*, lxxxvii (October, 2008), 241–4.

7. RAISED FROM THE DUST

1. J.R. Maddicott, *Thomas of Lancaster* (Oxford, 1970), 77–8.
2. *Vita*, 4–5.
3. *Brut*, 202, 206; J.R.S. Phillips, *Aymer de Valence, Earl of Pembroke* (Oxford, 1972), 24.
4. Chaplais, *Piers Gaveston*, 24–32; Hamilton, *Piers Gaveston, Earl of Cornwall*, 37.
5. *Vita*, 2.
6. Hamilton, *Piers Gaveston, Earl of Cornwall*, 47.
7. Phillips, *Valence*, 26–8, in which the agreement is given in full.
8. *Foedera*, i, 36.
9. *Annales Paulini*, 261–2.
10. *Ibid.*, 259; *Vita*, 3.

11. *DNB*, iv, 587; *ibid.*, vi, 445; *ibid.*, xii, 107; Maddicott, *Lancaster*, 69–70; Phillips, *Valence*, 24.
12. *Brut*, 206.
13. *Gesta*, 33–4; Maddicott, *Lancaster*, 81–2; Phillips, *Valence*, 27–8.
14. Maddicott, *Lancaster*, 83–4; Phillips, *Valence*, 28.
15. *Parl. Writs*, ii, 373–4; Maddicott, *Lancaster*, 106.
16. *Annales Paulini*, 263–4; *Brut*, 206; *Gesta*, 35; *Vita*, 5–6.
17. *Annales Paulini*, 264; *Vita*, 6.
18. Maddicott, *Lancaster*, 97–103.
19. Phillips, *Valence*, 29.
20. Maddicott, *Lancaster*, 103–5.
21. *Parl. Writs*, ii, 381–3; Maddicott, *Lancaster*, 109.
22. *Vita*, 7.
23. *Brut*, 206–7; *Vita*, 7.
24. *Vita*, 8.
25. *Ibid.*, 8; Maddicott, *Lancaster*, 110–11.
26. Maddicott, *Lancaster*, 91–4.
27. Bower, vi, 347; *Lanercost*, 190; *Vita*, 11–12. The author of the *Vita* believed that the campaign was primarily a shrewd attempt by Edward to avoid the summons of Philip IV of France to do homage for the lands he held of the French king.
28. *Vita*, 17–18. The contents of the Ordinances are discussed in Phillips, *Valence*, 31–2; Maddicott, *Lancaster*, 118–20.
29. Maddicott, *Lancaster*, 124–5; Phillips, *Valence*, 32; *Vita*, 21–2. The *Vita* claims that Bruce refused to countenance such an eventuality because if Edward broke the promises he made to his magnates, how could Bruce possibly trust his word.
30. Maddicott, *Lancaster*, 127; Phillips, *Valence*, 33–4; *Vita*, 24.
31. Maddicott, *Lancaster*, 127; *Vita*, 26–7.
32. Maddicott, *Lancaster*, 127–9; Phillips, *Valence*, 33–6.
33. *Vita*, 31.
34. Maddicott, *Lancaster*, 130–54; Phillips, *Valence*, 39–67.
35. *Vita*, 39.
36. Maddicott, *Lancaster*, 135–6; Phillips, *Valence*, 49.
37. *CDS*, iii, no. 337. A similar plea was made by the devastated county of Cumberland earlier in the year. In response Edward had sought a truce with the Scots and unhelpfully instructed the inhabitants of the county to look after themselves until his return from France. See Maddicott, *Lancaster*, 149.
38. *Parl. Writs*, ii, 110.

8. A TALE OF THREE CASTLES

1. *Bruce*, 376–8; *Calendar of Fine Rolls, 1307–19*, 189.
2. *Ibid.*, 376–8; *Vita*, 48.
3. *Vita*, 48. For Lubaud, see D. Cornell, 'English Castle Garrisons in the Anglo-Scottish Wars of the Fourteenth Century', unpublished Ph.D. thesis (University of Durham, 2006), 100–2.
4. *CDS*, iii, app. vii, 393–412.
5. *Ibid.*, app. vii, 393–412; *Parl. Writs*, ii, 95. For length of service, see Cornell, 'Castle Garrisons', 145–80. A hobelar was a lightly armed cavalryman mounted on an unarmoured horse.
6. *CDS*, ii, no. 1132.
7. Cornell, 'Castle Garrisons', 61–78.

NOTES to pp. 116–32 271

8. The resolve of the constable, Stephen de Bramptone, led to his harsh imprisonment in Scotland for three years. See *CDS*, ii, no. 1867. The siege took place in either 1298–9 or 1300–01.
9. *Bruce*, 378.
10. *Ibid.*
11. *Ibid.*, 378–86; *Vita*, 48; *Scalacronica*, 71–3; *Lanercost*, 204.
12. *Lanercost*, 201–2.
13. *Bruce*, 378–86.
14. *Scalacronica*, 71.
15. *CDS*, iii, app. vii, 406.
16. *Bruce*, 386; *Lanercost*, 204.
17. Randolph sought to win the castle 'by cunning mixed with good chivalry', *Bruce*, 386.
18. *Ibid.*, 388–96; *Lanercost*, 204; *Scalacronica*, 71; *Vita*, 48.
19. *Bruce*, 398; *Scalacronica*, 73; A.A.M. Duncan, ed., *The Acts of Robert I, King of Scots, 1306–29*, Regesta Regum Scottorum, v (1988), 84.
20. *Bruce*, 400; *Lanercost*, 204.
21. *Lanercost*, 205. See also *Bruce*, 406 n. 31.
22. *CDS*, v, no. 472; *Bruce*, 90–2, 98, 100–2, 290–5.
23. Thomas Gray believed the agreement stipulated that an English army had to approach at least three leagues from Stirling Castle within eight days of 24 June 1314. See *Scalacronica*, 73. However, as Professor Archie Duncan has demonstrated, both Gray and Barbour are almost certainly wrong in claiming that the Scots granted the English a year in which to relieve the castle. See *Bruce*, 402 n. 810–30; Duncan, 'War of the Scots', 149–50; D. Cornell, 'A Kingdom Cleared of Castles: The Role of the Castle in the Campaigns of Robert Bruce', 244–8. The *Vita* (48) and *Lanercost* (205) both relate that the siege of Stirling followed the taking of Roxburgh and Edinburgh, and the series of writs issued for the English campaign make no mention of Stirling until as late as May 1314. See *Parl. Writs*, ii, 117. A recent attempt to argue that the agreement was indeed of a year's duration has centred on the fact that, in November 1313, Edward II declared his intention to bring an army to Berwick before the feast of St John the Baptist, 1314. It has been argued that the reference to this date is irrefutable proof that the agreement for the surrender of Stirling was already in place in late 1313. See W. Scott, *Bannockburn Revealed* (Rothesay, 2000), 115–19. In fact, the feast of St John the Baptist was an important date in the medieval calendar and was frequently cited in official documents, for example in 1313 a temporary truce that had been in place in Scotland between the English and the Scots expired on the feast of St John the Baptist. See *CDS*, iii, no. 337. It is far more likely that, following Edward's declaration in November, the knowledge that an English army would have entered Scotland by St John the Baptist's day 1314 prompted Philip Mowbray to agree to it as the stipulated deadline in spring 1314. The truth is that, rather than a year, the English only had a matter of weeks in which to relieve Stirling.
24. *Bruce*, 670–4.

9. TEARS OF A KING

1. *Vita*, 49.
2. *CDS*, iii, 354. Elizabeth was to be allowed expenses of 20*s* a week, and was permitted to take exercise within the castle and the neighbouring priory of St Andrew's at suitable times.
3. *Parl. Writs*, ii, 112.
4. *Vita*, 49–50.

5. Warenne was in dispute with Lancaster and was also attempting to have his marriage to Edward II's niece, Joan of Bar, annulled. Arundel may have followed the lead of Warenne, his brother-in-law, or perhaps believed the faction led by Lancaster to be the most powerful. See Phillips, *Aymer de Valence*, 73–4. The earl of Oxford, a rather anonymous figure in this volatile period, did not participate in the campaign. The earl of Norfolk was too young to attend.
6. J.R. Lumby, ed., *The Chronicle of Henry Knighton* (1889–95) i, 410.
7. *Parl. Writs*, ii, 112–13.
8. *Ibid.*, 113; *Rot. Scot.* 118–24.
9. *Parl. Writs*, ii, 112; *Vita*, 50.
10. *Parl. Writs*, ii, 114–15.
11. McNamee, *Wars of the Bruces*, 61, 126 charts 3 and 4; M. Prestwich, *The Three Edwards: War and State in England 1272–1377* (London, 1996 edition), 106; N. Fryde, 'Antonio Pessagno of Genoa, King's Merchant of Edward II of England', *Studi in Memoria di Federigo Melis*, ii (Rome, 1978), 159–78; Phillips, *Valence*, 71–2.
12. For a detailed survey of military logistics in the fourteenth century, see H.J. Hewitt, *The Organisation of War under Edward III* (Manchester, 1966).
13. *Rot. Scot.*, 118–24.
14. *Calendar of Close Rolls*, 1313–18, 76; *Bower*, vii, 52–7; *Robert Bruce*, 271.
15. A.G. Rigg, 'Antiquaries and Authors: The Supposed Works of Robert Baston', in M.B. Parkes and A.G. Watson, eds, *Medieval Scribes, Manuscripts and Libraries: Essays Presented to N.R. Ker* (London, 1978), 317–31. The poem is given in full in *Bower*, vi, 366–75.
16. *DNB*, iv, 659; *Gesta*, 41–2; Phillips, *Valence*, 66; *Vita*, 30.
17. *Parl. Writs*, ii, 115.
18. *Ibid.*, 117.
19. *Bruce*, 408 nn. 101–3. A protection exists, dated 30 May 1314, which states that the earl of Ulster is ready to come from Ireland to Scotland. See *CDS*, v, no. 2974.
20. *Bower*, vi, 369. Barbour undoubtedly exaggerates the number of foreign troops among the English host, and wrongly claims that the count of Hainault was present. See *Bruce*, 408 nn. 91–4.
21. The best general survey of English foot soldiers is to be found in M. Prestwich, *Armies and Warfare in the Middle Ages: The English Experience* (Yale, 1999 edition), ch. 5. See also J. Bradbury, *The Medieval Archer* (Woodbridge, 1985).
22. C.J. Neville, ed., 'A Plea Roll of Edward I's Army in Scotland, 1296', *Miscellany XI*, Scottish History Society, 5th Series, iii (1990). The existence of this plea roll does, however, demonstrate that an attempt was made to instil discipline within the army.
23. Prestwich, *Armies and Warfare*, 131–3; *idem*, *Three Edwards*, 70; A. Ayton, 'Arms, Armour and Horses', in M. Keen, ed., *Medieval Warfare: A History* (Oxford, 1999), 203. See also Bradbury, *Medieval Archer*; R. Hardy and M. Strickland, *The Great Warbow* (Stroud, 2005).
24. Prestwich, *Edward I*, 479, 481, 483, 485–6, 493, 498; *idem*, *Armies and Warfare*, 116–17.
25. Phillips, *Aymer de Valence*, 75. Substantial numbers of knights, esquires and men-at-arms were granted protections for service in the 1314 campaign. There are approximately 830–890 protections. See *Robert Bruce*, 269, 474 n. 20. Protections, however, are not proof of service, but of an intention to serve. Those named within them cannot be known to have fought at Bannockburn for certain, but the likelihood must be that the majority were indeed present. See *CDS*, v, nos 1705–30, 2961–74.
26. Prestwich, *Armies and Warfare*, 40.
27. *Ibid.*, 18–30. For a more detailed study of armour and weaponry, see F. Lachaud, 'Armour and Military Dress in Thirteenth- and Early-Fourteenth-Century England', in M. Strickland, ed., *Armies, Chivalry and Warfare in Medieval Britain and France* (Stamford, 1998), 344–69. See also P.R. Coss, *The Knight in Medieval England 1000–1400* (Stroud, 1993).

28. Prestwich, *Armies and Warfare*, 30–7.
29. *Bruce*, 410; *Vita*, 52–3; *Scalacronica*, 73.
30. Phillips, *Valence*, 3; Prestwich, *Edward I*, 479, 484–5, 493.
31. *Parl. Writs*, ii, 118.
32. *Bruce*, 408; *Vita*, 50; *Lanercost*, 206. Barbour's reference to 'shot' is clearly an anachronism which alludes to the appearance of gunpowder weapons at the time he was writing in the 1370s. The chronicles provide notoriously fabulous figures for the total size of each army, Barbour believing that the English host numbered one hundred thousand (410) and the *Vita* placing the Scottish army at a strength of forty thousand men (52).
33. *Vita*, 50–1.
34. *Lanercost*, 206. During the Falkirk campaign of 1298, Edward I had visited the shrine of St John of Beverley in Yorkshire and had taken with him into Scotland a banner of the saint, together with the banner of another prominent northern saint, St Cuthbert; see Fisher, *Wallace*, 71–2.

10. BAITING THE TRAP

1. *Bruce*, 428.
2. Edward Bruce was made earl of Carrick in 1312, and the newly reconciled Randolph attended the parliament of 1309 as the lord of Nithsdale. See *Ibid.*, 372 n. 262, 400 n. 796. Randolph was made earl of Moray in 1312. See *DNB*, xlvi, 13.
3. *Bruce*, 416.
4. Barrow believed the community of the realm to be so crucial that it provided the subtitle of his seminal work on Bruce.
5. *Robert Bruce*, 272–3; *Bruce*, 416 n. 244.
6. *Bruce*, 318 n. 5.
7. For a study of Scotland in this period, see A. Grant, *Independence and Nationhood: Scotland 1306–1469* (London, 1984).
8. *Bruce*, 420–2.
9. Duncan, 'War of the Scots', 144–5.
10. *Bruce*, 416; *Vita*, 52.
11. Legislation enacted in 1318 has been seen as attempting further to improve the armour of Scottish troops. See Duncan, 'War of the Scots', 145.
12. *Bruce*, 418.
13. Although the fact that Scots received rudimentary training prior to the battle is generally accepted, there is actually no definitive documentary evidence to support this. In such a situation it must be assumed that some training was provided.
14. For the ability of infantry forces to withstand heavy cavalry in this period, see K. De Vries, *Infantry Warfare in the Early Fourteenth Century: Discipline, Tactics and Technology* (Woodbridge, 1996); M. Bennett, 'The Myth of the Military Supremacy of Knightly Cavalry', in M. Strickland, ed., *Armies, Chivalry and Warfare in Medieval Britain and France* (Stamford, 1998), 304–16.
15. T. Wright, ed., *The Political Songs of England* (Camden Society, 1839), 187–95.
16. See De Vries, *Infantry Warfare*, ch. 3.
17. *Scalacronica*, 75.
18. The most comprehensive discussions of the terrain to the south of Stirling are to be found in *Bruce*, 440–7; *Robert Bruce*, 276–83.
19. *Bruce*, 422.
20. *Robert Bruce*, 283; *Bruce*, 442.
21. *Bruce*, 422; *Bower*, vi, 373.

22. *Scalacronica*, 73. Curiously, neither the cavalry trap nor the dug up paths feature again in contemporary accounts of the battle.
23. *Bruce*, 424.
24. *Ibid.*, 426, 504–6, 506 n. 496–500. Duncan suggests that the provisions stored in Cambuskenneth Abbey consisted of feed for horses. However, since the abbey was located on the banks of the Forth between Stirling Castle and the sea, it is conceivable that its stone buildings were impressed by Bruce as an *ad hoc* siege-castle or supply base for the troops who had been besieging the castle for several weeks. Bruce's possession of the abbey would have made English attempts to ship victuals to the castle along the Forth extremely difficult.
25. *Ibid.*, 443–5.
26. *Ibid.*, 426, 440–7; *Robert Bruce*, 283.

11. PLAYING WITH FIRE

1. Although some historical accounts claim that the English vanguard had already advanced before the arrival of Mowbray, this is not borne out by the chronicles. In fact, Thomas Gray, in recounting that the 'the young men would not stop, but held their way', suggests that the English vanguard had heard and subsequently ignored Mowbray's warning before advancing. See *Scalacronica*, 74.
2. *Ibid.*, 73.
3. *Vita*, 51.
4. *Bruce*, 448.
5. *Ibid.*, 448–52; *Scalacronica*, 73, in which Gray inexplicably errs by recounting that the knight killed by Bruce was a certain Peter de Montfort.
6. *Bruce*, 452.
7. *Vita*, 51.
8. *Bruce*, 450.
9. *Ibid.*, 450–2; *Vita*, 51. It is not clear whether Gloucester was actually unhorsed in this engagement or whether this episode is the result of confusion with his death the following day.
10. *Bruce*, 430–2; *Scalacronica*, 73–5.
11. According to Barbour, Bruce chided Randolph that 'a rose had fallen from his chaplet'. See *Bruce*, 432; *Lanercost*, 207; *Scalacronica*, 73–5.
12. After 1308 Gray had frequently served in Scotland alongside Beaumont. See *Scalacronica*, xxvii, 47, 75.
13. *Bruce*, 434; *Scalacronica*, 75. Thomas Gray later resumed his career of military service, presumably having been ransomed.
14. *Bruce*, 434.
15. *Ibid.*, 434–8.
16. *Ibid.*, 436.
17. *Ibid.*, 436–8.
18. *Ibid.*
19. *Ibid.*, 452–6; *Lanercost*, 207; *Scalacronica*, 75.
20. *Bruce*, 456.
21. *Lanercost*, 207.
22. *Bruce*, 466.

12. THE SHORTEST OF NIGHTS

1. In 1314 Edinburgh had fallen to Randolph before Mountz could take up his new command. The career of Mountz is detailed in Cornell, 'Castle Garrisons', 96–9.
2. The actual site of the engagement fought on 24 June remains a source of debate and speculation. All that can be said for certain is that the field of battle was extremely restricted and favoured infantry rather than cavalry. The terrain between the New Park and the Carse of Balquhiderock was certainly not suited for the deployment of heavy cavalry. See Appendix I.
3. *Scalacronica*, 75.
4. *Bruce*, 466–8; *Scalacronica*, 75; *Robert Bruce*, 289–92.
5. *Scalacronica*, 75; *Vita*, 51.
6. *Vita*, 51.
7. *Scalacronica*, 75.
8. *Bruce*, 506. See also *Ibid.*, 506 nn. 496–500; *Robert Bruce*, 355. See ch. 10, n. 24.
9. *Scalacronica*, 75. It was not unknown for an apparent defector to be primed with disinformation, and some of Bruce's commanders may have suspected that the news Seton brought was an attempt to lure them into battle. However, as Seton risked losing his life in undertaking such an action, and as the intelligence he brought only confirmed what Bruce already suspected, Seton was evidently trusted.
10. *Bruce*, 456–65. For two further versions of this speech see *ibid.*, 458–9 nn. 210–327.
11. Apparently Reginald Deyncourt, brother of the slain William Deyncourt, had been made a knight before the battle. See *Gesta*, 46.
12. *Bruce*, 468; *Vita*, 52.

13. FLESH AND BLOOD

1. *Scalacronica*, 75.
2. *Bruce*, 470–2. Barbour has de Umfraville reprise the role of adviser he apparently played at Methven, counselling Edward to feign a retreat, allow the Scottish army to plunder the baggage and then attack the disorganised Scots. If de Umfraville did indeed advise such a tactic, which in itself is most doubtful, then Edward would never have countenanced a retreat in the face of the Scots, even if feigned.
3. *Ibid.*, 472; *Bower*, vi, 362–6; *Lanercost*, 207; *Robert Bruce*, 294.
4. 'They had so arranged their army that two columns went abreast in advance of the third, so that neither should be in advance of the other; and the third followed, in which was Robert', *Lanercost*, 207–8.
5. *Bruce*, 468–70. The chronicles are quite clear that the Scots initially advanced towards the English position, ready to give battle; see *ibid.*, 468–70; *Scalacronica*, 75; *Vita*, 51–2. The *Vita* claims that the English already occupied the field, perhaps confusing the location of the field of battle with the area in which the English had encamped overnight.
6. *Vita*, 52.
7. *Ibid.*, 51–2.
8. *Lanercost*, 206; *Bruce*, 481–2. Trokelowe claims that the English placed archers in the front line before battle was met. See *Trokelowe*, 84. The problematic nature of archers being brought forward and a cavalry action occurring once the two armies were already locked in battle suggests the former scenario to be the most likely. See *Bruce*, 482 nn. 41–9. That neither the *Vita* nor the *Scalacronica* refers to a skirmish between archers illustrates the inconsequential and ineffective nature of any such action. The unsubstantiated claim that English archers ended up firing arrows into the backs of their own cavalry appears to be an elaboration by a later chronicler, Geoffrey le Baker.

See E.M. Thompson, ed., *Chronicon Galfridi le Baker de Swynebroke* (Oxford, 1881), 8–9. However, see also Appendix II. Presumably the Scottish light cavalry under Robert Keith remained to the rear of the Scottish army, ready to repel any flanking manoeuvre attempted by English foot soldiers.
9. *Vita*, 52.
10. *Bruce*, 473–4.
11. *Ibid.*, 474.
12. *Ibid.*, 476–8, 486–8.
13. *Vita*, 52–3. Trokelowe also states that Gloucester was killed during a shift in the fighting, although he places his death later in the engagement. See *Trokelowe*, 85. The claim that Gloucester was slain because he had attacked impetuously and in his haste had failed to put on his distinctive surcoat, the Scots consequently failing to recognise his identity and value as a prisoner, is almost certainly a later fabrication. See *Chronicon le Baker*, 8. Many English lords and knights were killed in the battle; clearly the Scots were not taking prisoners.
14. *Vita*, 53. A contemporary poem on the battle of Bannockburn alludes to one 'Bartholomew' who treacherously failed to come to the aid of Gloucester, his lord. See 'The Battle of Bannockburn', in *Political Songs*, 263.
15. *Vita*, 53. According to the poem, a number of knights and esquires were also killed alongside Gloucester. See 'The Battle of Bannockburn', *ibid.*, 265.
16. *Scalacronica*, 75.
17. *Bruce*, 480–2.
18. *Vita*, 54.
19. *Bruce*, 490.
20. *Lanercost*, 208; *Scalacronica*, 75.
21. *Scalacronica*, 75–7.
22. *Ibid.*, 77; *Vita*, 54; *Bruce*, 494; *Trokelowe*, 86.
23. *Bruce*, 494–6; *Scalacronica*, 77. An alternative account, which is discussed in the following chapter, is contained within the *Vita*, 53.
24. *Bruce*, 498; *Vita*, 54.
25. *Scalacronica*, 77. Barbour recounts that the king and his escort went 'beneath the castle ... and then they went round the Park'. See *Bruce*, 498. Barrow believes that Edward would not have had time to engage in such a lengthy detour to the west of the Torwood. See *Robert Bruce*, 478–9, n. 149.
26. *Bruce*, 496; *Lanercost*, 208; *Vita*, 54.
27. *Bruce*, 496.
28. *Ibid.*, 502; *Vita*, 55–6.
29. *Vita*, 55.
30. *Ibid.*
31. *Bruce*, 502.
32. *Ibid.*, 498–500, 508–12; *Lanercost*, 208–9; *Scalacronica*, 77; *Vita*, 55–6.

14. ONE FLEETING HOUR

1. Barbour alone states that Edward sailed to Bamburgh in Northumberland. See *Bruce*, 512.
2. *CDS*, iii, no. 373. De Umfraville, however, remained in Scotland in the service of Bruce until 1320. See Duncan, 'War of the Scots', 127.
3. *Bruce*, 500; *Lanercost*, 209–10; *Scalacronica*, 73.
4. *CDS*, iii, nos 371, 372, 393. Having spent his childhood in the household of Edward II, the young Donald, earl of Mar, refused to return to Scotland and stayed with Edward, a striking indication of the more agreeable aspects of Edward's personality. The

ransom for the banneret John de Segrave was also costly in political terms, Edward ordering that four prominent Scottish prisoners held in England should be handed over to Segrave's son, Stephen, in order to help secure his father's release. See *CDS*, iii, no. 402.
5. Maddicott, *Thomas of Lancaster*, 160–6; Phillips, *Valence*, 76.
6. *Lanercost*, 210.
7. *Bruce*, 506–8; *Trivet*, 15–16; Thomas Walsingham, *Historia Anglicana*, ed. H.T. Riley (1863–4), 141–2. According to *Trivet*, the privy seal was sent to England in the company of the English knight Roger Mortimer, who was released without ransom by Bruce. See A. Gransden, *Historical Writing in England*, ii (1982), 9; I. Mortimer, *The Greatest Traitor: The Life of Sir Roger Mortimer* (London, 2003), 276 n. 15.
8. Duncan, 'War of the Scots', 149.
9. *Fordun*, ii, 340.
10. *Ann. Lond.*, 231; *Brut*, 207; *Gesta*, 46; *Lanercost*, 208; *Scalacronica*, 73–7; *Trivet*, 14–16; *Vita*, 56. For those English casualties who are named, see Appendix II.
11. *Fordun*, ii, 339.
12. A sentiment indirectly expressed by a comparison with Courtrai where 'the flower of France fell before the Flemings'. See *Vita*, 56; M. McKisack, *The Fourteenth Century* (Oxford, 1991 edition), 40.
13. *National Archives*, London: E159/101, m. 156.
14. *CDS*, iii, no. 495.
15. *Bruce*, 508; *Lanercost*, 208–9; *Scalacronica*, 77.
16. Phillips, *Valence*, 75.
17. *Bruce*, 500–2; *Calendar of Close Rolls*, 1313–18, 111; A. Ayton, *Knights and Warhorses: Military Service and the English Aristocracy under Edward III* (Woodbridge, 1999), 195. Not all of these would have been warhorses. The number of English horses killed at Bannockburn must have totalled in the hundreds. In 1298 at Falkirk, 110 horses are recorded as slain and that is only among the cavalry which was directly in the pay of the English king. See Prestwich, *Edward I*, 481.
18. *Lanercost*, 209–10.
19. *Vita*, 53.
20. *Ibid.*, 55; *Calendar of Close Rolls*, 1313–18, 109.
21. *Fordun*, ii, 339; *Gesta*, 46.
22. *Gesta*, 46; *Lanercost*, 210; *Scalacronica*, 73–5; *Trivet*, 15–16; *Vita*, 55; *Ancient Petitions Relating to Northumberland*, ed. C.M. Fraser, Surtees Society, clxxvi (London, 1966), 61–2.
23. *Trivet*, 15–16.
24. *Lanercost*, 215–16.
25. *Ibid.*, 210; *Vita*, 55.
26. *Lanercost*, 209–10; *Scalacronica*, 77.
27. *Bruce*, 504. *Bower* followed Barbour in claiming that two hundred English knights were killed; vi, 365.
28. *Trivet*, 15–16. The 'six score' – 120 – prisoners of rank to whom the *Gesta* refers would also fit with a total casualty figure of between 150 and 200 men of rank. Although there is no accurate figure for the overall number of men ranked knight or higher in England at this time, a sense of proportion can be gained from the fact that more than 260 esquires were knighted at the Feast of the Swans in 1306, and that in 1314 the royal household contained 121 bannerets and knights.
29. However, although Mauley was certainly killed, only one chronicle directly attributes his death to drowning in 'a fresh river that is called Bannock Burn'. See *Brut*, 207. Robert Baston gives the impression that Mauley was killed by the Scots, recounting that he was 'overcome by a hostile people abounding in ferocity'. See *Bower*, vi, 375.

30. *CDS*, iii, nos 399, 413, 624, 627, 676, 714; *Archbishop Greenfield's Register*, v, cliii (Surtees Society, 1938), nos 2455, 2457.
31. *Lanercost*, 210.
32. *Ibid.*, 208; *Scalacronica*, 75–7; *Vita*, 54.
33. *Bruce*, 470; *Gesta*, 46.
34. 'The Battle of Bannockburn', in *Political Songs*, 262–7; *Trokelowe*, 263.
35. Professor Archie Duncan first suggested that Bruce may not have been engaged in the mêlée. See *Bruce*, 486 nn. 112–61. Barrow, however, follows Barbour, and states that the entrance of Bruce's division into the engagement proved decisive. See *Robert Bruce*, 297–8.
36. *Trokelowe*, 84–5; *Lanercost*, 208.
37. *Trokelowe*, 84.
38. *Bruce*, 508–12.
39. *Vita*, 53. Trokelowe similarly places the death of Gloucester during a shift in the fighting when battle had already been joined, and cites his death as the catalyst that prompted the flight of the English. This placing the death of Gloucester at either the start or end of the battle again suggests the engagement was of short duration. See *Trokelowe*, 85.
40. Contemporary letters record that at Crécy approximately fifteen hundred French knights and esquires were killed in battle, a total that includes ten counts, eight barons and eighty bannerets. Contemporary estimates of French losses at Agincourt vary considerably, but it would seem that at least fifteen hundred knights, and almost a hundred men of a rank higher than that of banneret, were killed. An English chronicler places the number of French knights and esquires killed there at approximately three thousand. Scottish losses at Neville's Cross were also particularly high and took a significant toll on those of high rank, with two earls being killed, together with the constable, marshal, chamberlain and chancellor of Scotland.
41. *Bruce*, 504.
42. It has been argued that the low morale of the English host was overplayed by English chroniclers in light of the humiliating defeat. See J.E. Morris, *Bannockburn* (1914), 71; Scott, *Bannockburn Revealed*, 440. Such an argument is far from convincing. Only Edward II and the younger knights and esquires of the host appear to have been eager for battle. The host was clearly tired, and the unexpected reverses and losses suffered on 23 June could not but have served seriously to undermine English morale. More pointedly, it was the morale of the English foot soldiers that ultimately proved to be crucial, and there can be little doubt that on the night of 23–24 June these conscripted soldiers would have viewed the prospect of battle with a dreadful sense of foreboding.
43. *Bruce*, 456; *Scalacronica*, 75.
44. As a great military historian once observed, 'the balance between victory and defeat turns on mental impressions and only indirectly on physical blows'. See B. Liddell Hart, *History of the First World War* (London, 1976 edition), 463.
45. 'Battle of Bannockburn', 263; *Lanercost*, 208–9; *Trokelowe*, 85; *Vita*, 54, 56.
46. *Vita*, 56.

15. THE LEGACY

1. The renewal of the war, together with the battles of Dupplin Moor and Halidon Hill, are described in detail in R. Nicholson, *Edward III and the Scots: The Formative Years of a Military Career* (Oxford, 1965).
2. Maddicott, *Lancaster*, 165–6.
3. *Lanercost*, 210.
4. *CDS*, iii, nos 470, 477, 486; *Bruce*, 566–70.

5. *Bruce*, 520. For the campaigns of the Bruces in Ireland see McNamee, *Wars of the Bruces*, ch. 5; S. Duffy, ed., *Robert the Bruce's Irish Wars* (Stroud, 2002). The latter argues that Edward Bruce was made king of Ireland in the summer of 1315 rather than in May 1316; see ch. 1.
6. *Bruce*, 672–6. According to Barbour, prior to the battle of Fochart, a certain Gib Harper had attired himself in a surcoat that belonged to Edward Bruce, Harper presumably being Bruce's herald. Barbour recounts that in the aftermath of the defeat the corpse of Harper was mistaken for that of Edward Bruce and it was Harper's head, not that of Edward, which was erroneously sent to Edward II. There is no evidence to support this claim; see *ibid.*, 670 n. 94–7. Although Mowbray appears to have died of wounds sustained at Fochart, an English source raises the possibility that he was still active in Scotland in 1319; see *ibid.*, 674 n. 159.
7. *Ibid.*, 616–64; *Lanercost*, 219, 226–7; Maddicott, *Lancaster*, 244–53; Phillips, *Valence*, 184–5.
8. *Lanercost*, 220; *Scalacronica*, 81.
9. *Bruce*, 676–90; *Lanercost*, 237–40; N. Fryde, *The Tyranny and Fall of Edward II* (Cambridge, 1979), ch. 9.
10. Harclay was made earl of Carlisle for his success at Boroughbridge. For details of the agreement see Barrow, *Robert Bruce*, 322–4. See also *Lanercost*, 235, 241–5; McNamee, *Wars of the Bruces*, 154–5.
11. For the treaty, see Barrow, *Robert Bruce*, 324.
12. According to the English chronicler Thomas Walsingham, there were rumours that Warwick had been poisoned by members of the king's inner circle. See *DNB*, iv, 588. For the period of Lancaster's dominance, see Maddicott, *Lancaster*, ch. 5.
13. *Vita*, 87; Maddicott, *Lancaster*, 190–1, 197. Lancaster's wife, Alice, remained estranged from him.
14. It was alleged that Lancaster had been paid the fantastically large sum of £40,000 by Bruce. See *Vita*, 97.
15. This period is the subject matter of Fryde, *Tyranny and Fall*.
16. *Vita*, 123.
17. *Brut*, 219.
18. *Ibid.*, 220–3; *Gesta*, 76–7; *Lanercost*, 234; *Vita*, 124–6.
19. *Scalacronica*, 79, 81. Interestingly, the *Vita* expresses the opinion that Edward's failure to counter Bruce was due to the king pursuing the two diverse objectives of attempting to retain Gaveston whilst also seeking to wage the Scottish war, commenting that 'He who hunts two hares together, will lose now one, or else the other', *Vita*, 13. An incongruous allusion by a later Scottish chronicler, namely, that the English defeat at Bannockburn was divine retribution for the brutal mutilation of Simon de Montfort in the previous century (1265), is a consequence of the Ordinances being identified with the cause Montfort had represented, which by implication identifies the domestic disputes of Edward's reign as instrumental in the English defeat. See Bower, vi, 355.
20. *Brut*, 232; Phillips, *Valence*, 233–4. His widow, Mary de St Pol, commissioned Valence's tomb which can still be seen in Westminster Abbey, and founded Pembroke College, Cambridge, in honour of his memory. See *DNB*, lvi, 44.
21. See Mortimer, *Greatest Traitor*.
22. T.F. Tout, 'The Conspiracy and Death of Edward of Caernarvon', in *idem, Collected Papers*, ii (London, 1934). For a recent analysis of his mysterious death, and for an argument that Edward actually survived, see Mortimer, *Greatest Traitor*, 185–99.
23. *Bruce*, 710–40, 742–4; Nicholson, *Edward III*, 14, 26–47, 63.
24. For details of the treaty see *Robert Bruce*, 331–5; Nicholson, *Edward III*, 47–52.
25. *Robert Bruce*, 381–2.

26. *Ibid.*, 394–403; *Bruce*, 698–704, in which Barbour claims that de Umfraville asked Bruce for permission to leave Scotland, as he was appalled by the execution of David de Brechin. See also M. Penman, 'A fell conuiracioun agayn Robert ye douchty king: the Soules Conspiracy of 1318–20', *Innes Review*, 50 (1999), 25–57. The text of the Declaration of Arbroath is given in *Bruce*, 779–82.
27. *Robert Bruce*, 418–19; *Bruce*, 748–52, 754–6; M. Kaufman, 'Analysis of the Skull of Robert the Bruce', *History Scotland*, 8, no. 1 (2008), 22–30.
28. Barbour claims that Douglas was killed in an attempt to rescue William Sinclair, a fellow Scottish knight. See *Bruce*, 752–4, 758–66, 762 nn. 407–500; *Robert Bruce*, 419–20.
29. *Bower*, vii, 63; *Bruce*, 772, 772 nn. 619–20.
30. *Vita*, 56. The Italian comment is from Petrarch, quoted in C.J. Rogers, *War Cruel and Sharp: English Strategy under Edward III, 1327–60* (Woodbridge, 2000), 39.
31. For a recent analysis of Crécy, see A. Ayton and P. Preston, eds, *The Battle of Crécy* (Woodbridge, 2005). For Neville's Cross, see M. Prestwich and D.W. Rollason, eds, *The Battle of Neville's Cross 1346* (Stamford, 1998).

BIBLIOGRAPHY

I. Primary Sources

The Acts of Robert I, King of Scots, 1306–29, Regesta Regum Scottorum, vol. v, ed. A.A.M. Duncan (Edinburgh, 1988).
Anglo-Scottish Relations, 1174–1328, ed. E.L.G. Stones (London, Nelson, 1965).
'Annales Londonienses', *Chronicles of the Reign of Edward I and Edward II*, i, ed. W. Stubbs (Rolls Series, 1882–3).
'Annales Paulini', *Chronicles of the Reigns of Edward I and Edward II*, i, ed. W. Stubbs (Rolls Series, 1882–3).
The Anonimalle Chronicle, 1307–34, ed. W.R. Childs and J. Taylor (Yorkshire Archaeological Society, Record Series, cxlvii, 1991).
Archbishop Greenfield's Register, 1306–15, 5 vols (Surtees Society, 1873–1952).
The Bruce by John Barbour, ed. and trans. A.A.M. Duncan (Edinburgh, 1999).
The Brut, vol. i, ed. F.W.D. Brie (Early English Text Society, original series, cxxxi, 1906).
Calendar of Documents Relating to Scotland, 4 vols, ed. J. Bain (London, 1881–8).
Calendar of Documents Relating to Scotland, vol. v, ed. G.G. Simpson and J.D. Galbraith (Edinburgh, 1986).
Calendar of Close Rolls.
Calendar of Fine Rolls.
Calendar of Patent Rolls.
Chronica Willemi Rishanger (Rolls Series, 1865).
Chronicon Galfridi le Baker de Swynebroke, ed. E.M. Thompson (Oxford, 1881).
The Chronicle of Henry Knighton, vol. i, ed. J.R. Lumby (1889–95).
The Chronicle of Lanercost, 1272–1346, ed. and trans. H. Maxwell (Glasgow, 1913).
The Chronicle of Pierre de Langtoft, vol. ii, ed. T. Wright (Rolls Series, 1890).
The Chronicle of Walter of Guisborough, ed. H. Rothwell (Camden Society, lxxxix, 1957).
Documents Illustrative of the History of Scotland, 2 vols, vol. ii, ed. J. Stevenson, (1870).
Documents and Records Illustrating the History of Scotland, ed. F. Palgrave (1837).
Edward I and the Throne of Scotland, 1290–96: An Edition of the Record Sources for the Great Cause, 2 vols, eds E.L.G. Stones, G.G. Simpson (Oxford, 1978).
English Historical Documents, vol. iii, ed. H. Rothwell, 1189–1327 (London, 1975).
Flores Historiarum, 3 vols, ed. H.R. Luard (Rolls Series, 1890).

Foedera, Conventiones, Litterae, et Acta Publica, I, ii, ed. T. Rymer (Record Commission, 1816).
'Gesta Edwardi de Carnarvan', *Chronicles of the Reigns of Edward I and Edward II*, vol. ii, ed. W. Stubbs (Rolls Series, 1882–3).
Historia Anglicana, Thomas Walsingham, ed. H.T. Riley (1863–4).
The Household Book of Queen Isabella of England, ed. F.D. Blackley, G. Hermansen (Edmonton, Alberta, 1971).
Johannis de Trokelowe et Henrici de Blaneforde Chronica et Annales, ed. H.T. Riley (Rolls Series, 1866).
John of Fordun's Chronicle of the Scottish Nation, 2 vols, ed. W.F. Skene (1993, reprint of 1872 original).
Nicolai Triveti Annalium Continuatio, ed. A. Hall (Oxford, 1722).
The Original Chronicle of Andrew of Wyntoun, 6 vols, ed. F.J. Amours (Scottish Text Society, 1903–14).
Parliamentary Writs and Writs of Military Summons, 2 vols in 4, ed. F. Palgrave (London, 1827–34).
'A Plea Roll of Edward I's Army in Scotland, 1296', *Miscellany XI*, ed. C.J. Neville (Scottish History Society, 5th Series, iii 1990).
The Political Songs of England, ed. T. Wright (Camden Society, 1839).
Rotuli Scotiae, 2 vols, ed. D. Macpherson et al. (Record Commission, 1814).
Scalacronica by Sir Thomas Gray, 1272–1363, ed. and trans. A King (Surtees Society, ccix, 2005).
Scalacronica: The Reigns of Edward I, Edward II and Edward III as recorded by Sir Thomas Gray, ed. and trans. H. Maxwell (Glasgow, 1907).
Scotichronicon by Walter Bower, vols vi and vii, ed. D.E.R. Watt et al. (Aberdeen, 1991, 1996).
Scotland in 1298: Documents Relating to the Campaign of Edward I in that Year, ed. H. Gough (London, 1888).
The Siege of Carlaverok, ed. N.H. Nicolas (London, 1828).
Vita Edwardi Secundi, ed. and trans. N. Denholm-Young (London, 1957).
Vita Edwardi Secundi, ed. W. Childs (Oxford, 2005).

II. Secondary Sources

Ayton, A., 'English Armies in the Fourteenth Century', in *Arms, Armies and Fortifications in the Hundred Years' War*, ed. A. Curry, M. Hughes (Woodbridge, Boydell, 1994).
——, 'Arms, Armour and Horses', in *Medieval Warfare: A History*, ed. M. Keen (Oxford University Press, 1999).
——, *Knights and Warhorses: Military Service and the English Aristocracy under Edward III* (Woodbridge, Boydell, 1999 edition).
Ayton, A., and P. Preston, eds, *The Battle of Crécy* (Woodbridge, Boydell, 2005).
Barker, J., *Agincourt* (London, Abacus, 2006 edition).
Barron, E.M., *The Scottish War of Independence*, 2nd edn (Inverness, 1934).
Barrow, G.W.S., *Robert Bruce and the Community of the Realm of Scotland*, 4th edn (Edinburgh University Press, 2005).
Bennett, M., 'The Myth of the Military Supremacy of Knightly Cavalry', in *Armies, Chivalry and Warfare in Medieval Britain and France*, ed. M. Strickland (Stamford, Paul Watkins, 1998).
Bradbury, J., *The Medieval Archer* (Woodbridge, Boydell, 1985).
Carruthers, A., 'The Site of the Battle of Bannockburn', *Chambers Journal* (February, 1933).
Chaplais, P., *Piers Gaveston, Edward II's Adoptive Brother* (Oxford, Clarendon Press, 1994).
Christison, P., 'Bannockburn – 23rd and 24th June, 1314: A Study in Military History', *Proceedings of the Society of Antiquaries in Scotland*, xc (1959).

Contamine, P., *War in the Middle Ages*, trans. M. Jones (Oxford, Blackwell, 1986 edition).
Cornell, D., 'English Castle Garrisons in the Anglo-Scottish Wars of the Fourteenth Century', unpublished Ph.D. thesis (University of Durham, 2006).
——, 'A Kingdom Cleared of Castles: The Role of the Castle in the Campaigns of Robert Bruce', *Scottish Historical Review* lxxxvii (October, 2008).
Coss, P.R., *The Knight in Medieval England, 1000–1400* (Stroud, Alan Sutton, 1993).
Davies, I.M., *The Black Douglas* (Oxford, 1974).
De Vries, K., *Infantry Warfare in the Early Fourteenth Century: Discipline, Tactics and Technology* (Woodbridge, Boydell, 1996).
Dictionary of National Biography (Oxford University Press, 2004).
Duffy, S., ed., *Robert the Bruce's Irish Wars* (Stroud, Sutton, 2002).
Duncan, A.A.M., 'The Community of the Realm of Scotland and Robert Bruce: A Review', *Scottish Historical Review*, xlv (1966).
——, *Scotland: The Making of the Kingdom* (Edinburgh, Mercat Press, 1975).
——, 'The War of the Scots, 1306–23', *Transactions of the Royal Historical Society*, 6th Series, ii (1992).
——, 'The Battles of Ben Cruachan, 1308', *West Highland Notes and Queries*, 2nd Series, no. 20 (August, 1999).
Fisher, A., *William Wallace* (Edinburgh, John Donald, 1986).
France, J., *Western Warfare in the Age of the Crusades, 1000–1300* (London, Routledge, 1999).
Fryde, N., 'Antonio Pessagno of Genoa, King's Merchant of Edward II of England', *Studi in Memoria di Federigo Meltis*, ii (Naples, 1978).
——, *The Tyranny and Fall of Edward II, 1321–26* (Cambridge University Press, 1979).
Gillingham, R., 'Richard I and the Science of War in the Middle Ages', in *Anglo-Norman Warfare*, ed. M. Strickland (Woodbridge, Boydell, 1992).
Gransden, A., *Historical Writing in England*, 2 vols (1974, 1982).
Grant, A., *Independence and Nationhood: Scotland 1306–1469* (London, Edward Arnold, 1984).
——, 'The Death of John Comyn: What Was Going On?', *Scottish Historical Review*, lxxxvi (October, 2007).
Hamilton, J.S., *Piers Gaveston, Earl of Cornwall, 1307–12: Politics and Patronage in the Reign of Edward II* (Detroit, Wayne State University Press/London, Harvester, 1988).
Hardy, R., and M. Strickland, *The Great Warbow* (Stroud, Sutton, 2005).
Hewitt, H.J., *The Organisation of War under Edward III* (Manchester, 1966).
Housley, N., 'European Warfare, c.1200–1320', *Medieval Warfare: A History*, ed. M. Keen (Oxford, Oxford University Press, 1999).
Johnstone, H., *Edward of Carnarvon, 1284–1307* (Manchester University Press, 1946).
Kaufman, M., 'Analysis of the Skull of Robert the Bruce', *History Scotland*, 8, no. 1 (2008).
Keen, M., ed., *Medieval Warfare: A History* (Oxford University Press, 1999).
Lachaud, F., 'Armour and Military Dress in Thirteenth- and Early Fourteenth-Century England', *Armies, Chivalry and Warfare in Medieval Britain and France*, ed. M. Strickland (Stamford, Paul Watkins, 1998).
Liddell Hart, B., *History of the First World War* (London, Pan, 1972).
Lynch, M., *Scotland: A New History* (London, Pimlico, 1991).
Mackenzie, W.M., *The Battle of Bannockburn: A Study in Mediaeval Warfare* (Glasgow, 1913).
——, *The Bannockburn Myth* (Edinburgh, 1932).
McKisack, M., *The Fourteenth Century* (Oxford, Oxford University Press, 1991).
McNamee, C., 'William Wallace's Invasion of England in 1297', *Northern History*, xxvi (1990).
——, *The Wars of the Bruces: Scotland, England and Ireland, 1306–28* (Edinburgh, John Donald, 2006).

Maddicott, J.R., *Thomas of Lancaster* (Oxford, Oxford University Pres, 1970).
—, *Simon de Montfort* (Cambridge, Cambridge University Press, 1994).
Miller, T., *The Site of the Battle of Bannockburn* (Historical Association, 1931).
Morris, J.E., *The Welsh Wars of Edward I* (Oxford, 1901).
—, *Bannockburn* (Cambridge, 1914).
—, 'Mounted Infantry in Medieval Warfare', *Transactions of the Royal Historical Society*, 3rd Series, viii (1914).
Mortimer, I., *The Greatest Traitor: The Life of Sir Roger Mortimer, Ruler of England, 1327–30* (London, Pimlico, 2004).
Nicholson, R., 'The Last Campaign of Robert Bruce', *English Historical Review*, 77 (1962).
—, *Edward III and the Scots: The Formative Years of a Military Career, 1327–35* (Oxford, Oxford University Press, 1965).
—, *Scotland: The Later Middle Ages* (Edinburgh, 1974).
Penman, M., 'A fell conuiracioun agayn Robert ye douchty king: The Soules Conspiracy of 1318–20', *Innes Review*, 50 (1999).
Phillips, J.R.S., *Aymer de Valence, Earl of Pembroke* (Oxford University Press, 1972).
Prestwich, M., *Edward I* (London, Guild Publishing, 1988).
—, *The Three Edwards: War and State in England, 1272–1377* (London, Routledge, 1996).
—, *Armies and Warfare in the Middle Ages: The English Experience* (New Haven and London, Yale University Press, 1999).
Prestwich, M., and D. Rollason, eds, *The Battle of Neville's Cross 1346* (Stamford, Paul Watkins, 1998).
Richardson, H.G., and G.O. Sayles, *The English Parliament in the Middle Ages* (London, 1981).
Rigg, A.G., 'Antiquaries and Authors: The Supposed Works of Robert Baston', in *Medieval Scribes, Manuscripts and Libraries: Essays Presented to N.R. Ker*, ed. M.B. Parkes, A.G. Watson (London, 1978).
Rogers, C.J., 'The Age of the Hundred Years' War', in *Medieval Warfare: A History*, ed. M. Keen (Oxford, Oxford University Press, 1999).
—, *War Cruel and Sharp: English Strategy under Edward III, 1327–60* (Woodbridge, Boydell, 2000).
Scammell, J., 'Robert I and the North of England', *English Historical Review*, 73 (1958).
Scott, W., *Bannockburn Revealed* (Rothesay, 2000).
Stones, E.L.G., 'The Submission of Robert Bruce to Edward I c. 1301–2', *Scottish Historical Review*, xxxiv (1955).
Strickland, M., ed., *Armies, Chivalry and Warfare in Medieval Britain and France* (Stamford, Paul Watkins, 1998).
Tout, T.F., 'The Conspiracy and Death of Edward of Caernarvon', *Collected Papers*, ii (1934).
—, 'The Tactics of the Battles of Boroughbridge and Morlaix', *Collected Papers*, ii (1934).
Verbruggen, J.F., *The Battle of the Golden Spurs: Courtrai, 11 July 1302* (Woodbridge, Boydell, 2001).
Watson, F., *Under the Hammer: Edward I and Scotland, 1286–1307* (East Linton, Tuckwell Press, 1998).
—— *The Battle of Bannockburn: A Study for Stirling Council* (Stirling, 2001).
Young, A., *Robert Bruce's Rivals: The Comyns, 1212–1314* (Edinburgh, Tuckwell Press, 1997).

INDEX

Abbey Craig, 6, 27–8
Aberdeen, 14, 31, 59, 78, 153
Abergavenny, 133
Abernethy, Laurence, 212
Agincourt, battle of (1415), 233
Airth, William, 191
Alexander II, king of Scots, 20
Alexander III, king of Scots, 16–17, 20–1, 159
Alfonso XI, king of Castile and Leon, 251
Alice, wife of Thomas of Lancaster, 94, 244
Alnwick Castle, 248
Alphonso, son of Edward I, 57
Annandale, 8–9, 40–8, 94, 152, 168, 190; lords of, *see* Bruce Robert, lord of Annandale, the Competitor; Bruce, Robert, lord of Annandale, earl of Carrick
Aquitaine, 23
Arbroath, Declaration of (1320), 250
archers: English, 142–3, 202, 229; Scottish, 202
Argentan, Giles d', 9–10, 137, 145, 209, 221, 226, 231, 233, 261
Argyll, 81–2, 150, 153
Argyll, Alexander of, 71, 82–4
Argyll, John of, 71, 82–3, 133
army: English: at Stirling Bridge (1297), 27–8, at Falkirk (1298), 29, raising of (1314), 132–4, financial and logistical support, 135–6, plan of campaign, 136, 139–40, high command, 145, 229, baggage train, 147, advances on Stirling Castle (1314), 146–8, casualties, 221–7, 261–3; Scottish: at Stirling Bridge (1297) 27–8, at Falkirk (1298), 29, raising of (1314), 151–3, divisional commanders, 152–3, 161–2, council of war, 193, and schiltrom, 29; *see also* cavalry; infantry
Arran, 70, 73
Arundel, earl of, *see* FitzAlan
Atholl, earls of, *see* Strathbogie, David of; Strathbogie, John of
Audley, Hugh de, 223
Avignon, 98
Ayr, 46, 59, 70

Badenoch, lords of, *see* Comyn, John, lord of Badenoch, the Red Comyn; Comyn, John, lord of Badenoch
Badlesmere, Batholomew, 206
Balliol, Edward, son and heir of John Balliol, 237–8
Balliol, John, king of Scots, 20–3, 26, 30, 32, 40–5, 50, 63, 71–2, 83, 237, 250
Balquhiderock, Carse of, 185, 192, 194, 228, 256–9
Bamburgh Castle, 101, 225, 242
Bampton Castle, 103
Banff Castle, 77
Bannock, 184
Bannock Burn, stream, xiv, 87, 159, 184; English night crossing, 184–5, 187–8, 191, 192, 197–9, 235; and English retreat, 208, 210–13; English casualties, 221, 226–7; and field of battle, 256–7, 259–60

286 INDEX

Bannockburn, battle of: location, 183–4, 194, 197–8, 228–9, 255–60; duration of mêlée, 231–3; English casualties, 221–7, 261–3; Scottish casualties, 234; significance of, 239–40, 249–51; legacy, 253–4
Barbour, John, 5, 39, 42, 57, 73, 76, 80, 118–19, 122, 126, 145, 147, 151–3, 162, 169, 173, 177–8, 185, 202, 223, 226, 230, 231, 232, 258
Barking Abbey, 130
Barons' Wars, 24, 40, 56
Barry, Lucas de, 227
Baston, Robert, 137, 141, 160, 225, 259
Beauchamp, Guy de, earl of Warwick (c. 1272–1315), 60; and promise to Edward I (1307), 89; granted lands in Scotland (1298), 94; opposes Edward II and Gaveston (1308–10), 97–9; and capture and death of Gaveston (1312), 103–4; in negotiations with Edward II (1312–13), 104–5; refusal to participate in Scottish campaign (1314), 131–2, 135–6, 139, 146, 192; death (1315), 243
Beaumont, Henry de (c. 1280–1340), 132; background, 137–8; military experience, 157, 195; and problems among high command (1314), 229; at Bannockburn, 173; dispute with Thomas Gray, 175, 186–7, 201; engagement with Scottish vanguard, 176, 178, 180, 184; in York with Edward II (1314), 217; at Dupplin Moor (1332), 237–8, 252; death (1340), 252
Becket, Thomas, archbishop of Canterbury, 43
Bek, Anthony, bishop of Durham, 92
Ben Cruachan, battle of (1308), 82, 154–5
Berkeley Castle, 248
Berkeley, Maurice de, 223
Berwick, 7, 14, 22, 65, 85–6, 101, 106, 113, 115, 130, 222, 238, 240, 249; sack and capture of (1296), 24–6; and Scottish campaign (1314), 134–6, 140, 146; escape of Edward II to (1314), 213, 217, 224; captured by the Scots (1318), 241–2, 246; English siege of (1319), 244
Berwick Castle, 65, 118, 242
Biggar, 85
Birgham, Treaty of (1290), 18
Bishopthorpe, Thirteen-Year Truce concluded at (1323), 243
Black Isle, 77
Blacklow, 104

Blakebourne, Robert de, 227
Bohun, Henry de, 168–72, 176, 184, 186, 189, 205, 222, 262
Bohun, Humphrey de, earl of Hereford (c. 1276–1322), brother-in-law of Edward II, 94; military experience, 195; at Feast of the Swans (1306), 53; at Wallingford tournament (1307), 90; Boulogne Agreement (1308), 91–2; granted lands in Scotland, 94, 168; at Dunstable tournament (1309), 98; and Scottish campaign (1310–11), 101; capture and death of Gaveston (1312), 103–4; negotiations with Edward II (1312–13), 104–5; participates in Scottish campaign (1314), 132; retinue, 143; appointed joint commander of English vanguard, 145, 157; advance on Stirling and engagement at New Park, 165–8, 171–2, 180, 182, 184; alleged rivalry with Gloucester, 187, 206, 229; and engagement on 24 June, 198, 202, 206; flees from battlefield, 223–4; capture and ransom of, 217–19, 262; becomes an ally of Edward II, 243; dispute with Lancaster (1317), 244; death at Boroughbridge (1322), 245
Boroughbridge, battle of (1322), 245–6
Bothwell Castle, 94, 116, 218, 223–4, 226, 263
Boulogne, 91
Boulogne Agreement (1308), 91–3
Boyd, Robert, 70
Brechin, 14
Brecknock, 133
Bristol, 97, 133, 142
Brodick Castle, 70
Brougham Castle, 8
Bruce, Alexander, 46, 70
Bruce, Christian, 65, 218
Bruce, David II, king of Scots, 238, 249, 250–3
Bruce, Edward, earl of Carrick (c. 1280–1318), xv, 46; character, 80; returns to Scotland (1307), 70–1; at Loudoun Hill (1307), 75; campaigns in northern Scotland (1307–8), 77; campaigns in Galloway (1308), 79–80; at St Andrews parliament (1309), 84; destroys Roxburgh Castle (1314), 121; raids Cumberland (1314), 124–5, 141; assumes command of siege of Stirling Castle (1314), 124; concludes agreement for conditional surrender of Stirling

(1314), 125–7, 141; at Scottish muster in Torwood, 150, 153; appointed commander of Scottish middle-guard, 162, 178; and hostility with earl of Atholl, 190; limited experience of battle, 195; and engagement on 24 June, 200, 203–4, 209, 231; invasion of Ireland and death (1315–18), 127, 241, 250
Bruce, Elizabeth, queen of Scots, 46, 63, 65, 130, 218, 225
Bruce, Marjorie, mother of Robert Bruce, 40
Bruce, Marjorie, daughter of Robert Bruce, 42, 63, 65, 218
Bruce, Mary, 65
Bruce, Neil, 63–5
Bruce, Robert, lord of Annandale, the Competitor (d. 1295), 20–1, 39–40, 43, 45, 83
Bruce, Robert, lord of Annandale, earl of Carrick (d. 1304), 41–2, 46
Bruce, Robert I, king of Scots (1274–1329), xiv–xvii, 3–11, 20, 31, 32–3; enters into secret bond with Bishop Lamberton (1304), 15–16, 46–8, 190; influence of his grandfather, 39–40; birth (1274), 40; breaks allegiance to Edward I (1297), 41–2; as Guardian, 43–4; submits at Irvine (1297), 45; resigns Guardianship (1299), 45; returns to allegiance of Edward I (1302), 45–6; second marriage (1302) and inheritance (1304), 46; creates network of alliances, and his relationship with John Comyn (1304–6), 48; kills John Comyn (1306), 37–9, 47, 49; inaugurated as king of Scots (1306), 50; routed at Methven (1306), 51–2, 63; flees from the Scottish mainland (1306), 52, 69; Edward I vows destruction of (1306), 53–5; punishment of family and adherents (1306), 64–5; returns to mainland (1307), 67, 69; and death of Edward I (1307), 69, 76; assaults garrison of Turnberry (1307), 70–1; Scottish enemies of, 71–2; and James Douglas, 73–4, 79; at Glen Trool and Loudoun Hill (1307), 74–6; campaigns in northern Scotland (1307–8), 76–8, 79; bouts of illness, 77, 85–6, 251; and Thomas Randolph, 80–1; strategy and tactics of, 81–2, 159–61, 166; subdues Argyll (1308), 81–2; accepts allegiance of William, earl of Ross (1308), 82–3; holds first parliament at St Andrews (1309), 83–5; and English campaign (1310), 85; initiates raiding of northern England (1311), 86; seizes English-held fortifications in Scotland (1311–13), 86; issues ultimatum of perpetual disinheritance (1313), 86–7; at siege of Edinburgh Castle (1314), 112–13; instigates offensive against castles of Edinburgh, Roxburgh and Stirling (1314), 114, 116, 130; and Douglas's assault on Roxburgh Castle, 117–18; orders destruction of Roxburgh Castle, 121; and Piers Lubaud, 123–4; supervises destruction of Edinburgh Castle, 124; at siege of Stirling Castle, 124–5; and agreement for the relief of Stirling, 126–8, 139–40, 141, 149–50; raises a Scottish army, 150–5; supervises training of army, 155–6; prepares to oppose English host before Stirling, 159–61, 166; deploys army, 161–4; encounter with Henry de Bohun, 168–70; engagement with English vanguard, 171–2, 174; issues instructions to Randolph, 172; reluctance to aid Scottish vanguard, 177–8; and successes of 23 June, 179–81; contemplates withdrawal, 189; tempted to stay and fight, 190; and treachery of Atholl, 191; receives intelligence from Alexander Seton, 191–2, 235; decides to stay and fight, 192; holds council of war, 193; dubs knights, 195; final preparations for battle, 199–200; and mêlée, 205, 211–12, 213, 226, 231; exchanges earl of Hereford for relatives and adherents, 218; attempts to follow up Bannockburn, 219; holds parliament at Cambuskenneth (1314), 220; popularly acknowledged as king, 239–40; and invasion of Ireland (1315), 241; captures Berwick (1318), 241–2; undertakes further campaigns in northern England, (1315–16) 240–1, (1318 and 1322) 242–3, (1327) 248; foils Soules Conspiracy (1320), 250; concludes Thirteen-Year Truce (1323), 243; concludes Treaty of Edinburgh (1328), 248–9; death (1329), 251; heart of, 251–2; importance of Bannockburn to, 249–50, 251, 254

Bruce, Thomas, 70
Buchan, earldom of, 78, 150, 154
Buchan, earls of, *see* Comyn, John, earl of Buchan
Buittle Castle, 86
Burgh, Elizabeth de, *see* Bruce, Elizabeth
Burgh, Richard de, earl of Ulster, 11, 46, 60, 65, 133, 141
Burstwick, 65
Byland, engagement at (1322), 242, 246
Byland Abbey, 242

Caerlaverock Castle, 58–60, 94
Caernarfon Castle, 57
Cambridge University, 46
Cambuskenneth Abbey, 16, 47, 161, 190–1, 220
Cardross, 251
Carlisle, 25, 42, 62, 70, 75–6, 115, 125, 134, 136, 225, 228, 240; flight of English army to (1314), 223–4, 226
Carlisle Castle, 41, 70, 218
Carrick, 42–3, 70, 126, 152–3
Carrick, earls of, *see* Bruce, Edward, earl of Carrick; Bruce, Robert, lord of Annandale
castles: siege engines, 12, 14–15, 175; siege warfare, 63–4, 76, 111–12, 116–17, 125, 175; assaults on, 71, 73–4, 76, 79, 117–20, 121–3; role of, 113–14, 124; garrisons of, 114–15
cavalry: English: heavy cavalry, raising of 96–7, 132–3, weaponry, 135, retinues, 143–4, men-at-arms, 143–4, armour, 144, warhorses, 145, cavalry charge, 145, numbers at Bannockburn, 146–7, offensive power of, 157; Scottish: light cavalry, 151, lack of heavy cavalry, 153
Chester, 133
Clare, Gilbert de, earl of Gloucester (1291–1314), 10–11; nephew of Edward II, 94; becomes brother-in-law of Gaveston (1307), 90; marriage of (1308), 97; opposes Edward and Gaveston (1309), 98–9; appointed Ordainer (1310), 100; participates in Scottish campaign (1310), 101; and capture and death of Gaveston (1312), 102–4; acts as mediator (1312–13), 104; and Scottish campaign (1314), 132; retinue of, 143–4; appointed joint commander of English vanguard, 145; advance on Stirling and engagement at New Park on 23 June, 165–7, 172, 180, 182, 184; alleged rivalry with Hereford, 187, 206, 229; military experience, 195; role in mêlée of 24 June, 198, 200–5; death, 205–6, 207, 221–2, 224, 226, 232–5, 261; corpse of, 219, 239; division of the Clare inheritance, 244
Clare, Isabel de, wife of the Competitor, 39
Clare, Margaret de, 90
Clement V, pope, 84, 98, 135
Clifford, Robert (1274–1314), 8–9, 31, 43, 46; granted lands in Scotland (1298), 72–3, 94; and promise to Edward I (1307), 89; and pursuit and capture of Gaveston (1312), 103; participates in Scottish campaign (1314), 132; retinue of, 144; appointed commander of English middle-guard, 145, 157; and problems among high command, 229; leads advance towards Stirling Castle, 166–7; engages Scottish vanguard on 23 June, 172–80, 184, 185–7, 189; experience of battle, 195; engages the Scots on 24 June, 198, 230; death, 207, 221, 226, 230, 234, 261; corpse of, 219, 239
Clifford, Robert de, 227
'community of the realm': Scottish, 84, 151; English, 92
Comyn, Alexander, 77
Comyn, Edmund, 221, 262
Comyn, John, earl of Buchan (1289–1308), 44, 71, 77–8, 137
Comyn, John, lord of Badenoch, the Red Comyn (d. 1306), 60, 64; negotiates Scottish surrender (1304), 31; murder of (1306), 37–9, 50, 51, 52, 53–4, 71, 80–1; background, 44; as Guardian, 44; political importance of, 48
Comyn, John, lord of Badenoch (d. 1314), 221, 262
Comyn, Robert, 38, 64
Contrariants, 246, 247
Cornwall, earldom of, 66, 89
Courtrai, battle of (1302), 30–1, 158–9, 189–90
Coxet Hill, 161, 208
Crawford, Reginald, 70
Crécy, battle of (1346), 233, 253
Cressingham, Hugh, treasurer of Scotland, 27–8
Cumberland, 25, 86, 124, 134, 219
Cumnock, 76

Cupar Castle, 173
Cuthbert, 70–1

Dalry, 52, 63, 73, 154
Dalswinton Castle, 86
Darlington, 139
David I, king of Scots, 20
David, earl of Brechin, 71, 77–8, 85
David, earl of Huntingdon, 21, 71
Declaration of the Clergy (1309), 83–4
Deddington, 103
Derby, earldom of, 100
Derbyshire, 133, 139
Despenser, Hugh le, the elder, 244–5, 247
Despenser, Hugh le, the younger, 132, 244–5, 247
Deyncourt, William, 176, 186–7, 205, 222, 261
Disinherited, the, 237–8, 252
Donald, earl of Mar, 218, 248
Douglas, James, lord of Douglas (d. 1330), 142; lands on Arran and attacks Brodick Castle (1307), 70; character and appearance 72–3; first capture of Douglas Castle (1307), 73–4; in talks with the English (1307), 74; at Loudoun Hill (1307), 75–6; executes ambush in Paisley forest (1308), 78; and Douglas Lardner (1308), 78–9; aids Edward Bruce in Galloway (1308–9), 80; captures Thomas Randolph (1308), 81; campaigns with Robert Bruce in Argyll (1308), 81–2; at St Andrews parliament (1309), 84; takes Roxburgh Castle by assault (1314), 117–22, 124–5, 154; undertakes reconnaissance of English host (1314), 149, 161; at Scottish muster in Torwood (1314), 151, 153; pleads with Bruce for permission to aid Randolph, 177–9, 188; knighted by Bruce, 195; and engagement of 24 June, 200; pursues Edward II to Dunbar, 212, 223; conducts raids into England (1315, 1319), 240, 242; ambushes Berwick garrison (1316), 241; at Byland (1322), 242; crusade and death (1330), 251–2
Douglas Castle, 72–4, 78–9, 118
Douglas, kirk of, 252
Douglas, William, 8, 72–3, 94
Douglasdale, 72
Dover, 67
Dreux, Yolande de, queen of Scots, 16–17
Dublin, 241
Dumbarton, 251

Dumfries, 37, 47, 64, 76, 89
Dumfries Castle, 8, 38, 86
Dunbar, battle of (1296), 25–6, 29, 42
Dunbar Castle, 212–13, 217–18, 223–4, 231–2, 235, 244
Dunblane, 14, 60
Duncan, Professor Archie, 126
Dundalk, 127, 241
Dundee, 86
Dunfermline Abbey, 31, 251
Dunstable, tournament at (1309), 98
Dupplin Moor, battle of (1332), 237–8, 252, 253
Durham, 139–40, 233, 253
Durham, diocese of, 84

Easingwold, 139
Edinburgh, 22, 111, 146–8, 208, 212, 232
Edinburgh Castle, 13, 16, 26, 115, 183; siege of (1314), 111–14, 116–17, 155; taken by assault (1314), 120–3, 154; destruction of (1314), 124–7, 130, 148; rebuilding of, 238
Edinburgh, Treaty of (1328), 248–9
Edirford, 78, 125
Edmund Plantagenet, son of Edward I, 89
Edward I, king of England (1239–1307), 9; at siege of Stirling (1304), 13–16, 32; approached by Guardians (1286), 17–18; claims suzerainty over Scottish kingdom (1291), 19–20; and Great Cause (1291–2), 20, 83; attempts to enforce Scottish oaths of fealty (1293), 21–2; summons Scottish lords to serve overseas (1294), 22–3; background, 24, 56, 91–2; and sacking of Berwick (1296), 24–5; and battle of Dunbar (1296), 25; strips John Balliol of kingship (1296), 26–7; reaction to battle of Stirling Bridge (1297), 28; at battle of Falkirk (1298), 29; beset by financial and diplomatic pressure (1299–1302), 30; and Scottish campaign (1303–4), 31–2, 59; and the Bruces (1296–7), 41–3; accepts Bruce back into his allegiance (1302), 45–6; treachery of Bruce against (1304–6) 47–9; reaction to killing of Comyn (1306), 50, 53, 74; and Feast of the Swans (1306), 53–5; character and appearance, 55–7; and Edward II, 58–61, 66–7, 89; incapacitated by illness (1306), 63; orders brutal punishment of Bruce's adherents (1306), 64–5, 72, 246;

Edward I (*cont.*)
  initiates campaign against Bruce (1307), 67; death (1307), 67, 69, 89; funeral (1307), 90; makes grants of Scottish estates, 94; financial debt on death, 94
Edward II, king of England (1284–1327), xvii, 46; knighted (1306), 53; at Feast of the Swans (1306), 54–5; participates in Scottish campaigns (1300–4), 58–60; birth and childhood, 57–8; appearance and character, 57–8, 61–2, 186; lands and titles granted to, 60; relationship with Gaveston, 60–2, 91; banished from Edward I's presence (1305), 62; leads campaign against Bruce (1306), 63–4; punishes adherents of Bruce (1306), 65; quarrels with Edward I (1307), 66–7; succeeds to the Crown (1307), 67–8; undertakes Scottish campaign (1310), 85, 101; incurs hostility of magnates (1308), 88–9, 95–6; recalls and promotes Gaveston (1307), 89–90; at Wallingford tournament (1307), 90–1; marriage of (1308), 91; coronation of (1308), 92–3; inherits financial debts of Edward I, 94; personal ties with magnates, 94; squanders money (1307–8), 95; issues writs for a Scottish campaign (1308), 96; appoints Gaveston lieutenant of Ireland (1308), 97; wins over magnates (1308–9), 97–8; recalls Gaveston and negotiates with magnates (1309), 98; apparent disregard for the rights of the Crown, 99; issues writs for a Scottish campaign (1309), 99; accepts appointment of Ordainers (1310), 100; and Ordinances (1311), 101–2; recalls Gaveston (1311), 102; pursued by magnates (1312), 103, 138; response to death of Gaveston, 104–5; failure to prosecute the Scottish war, 105; apparent reconciliation with magnates (1313), 105; issues writs for the 1314 campaign (1313), 106, 113, 129; and Piers Lubaud, 112, 120; and William de Fiennes, 120; distress at Scottish offensive (1314), 130; brings date of muster forwards (1314), 130–1; cancels parliament, and renewal of dispute with Lancaster and his allies, 131–2, 134–5; issues writs for the raising of foot soldiers, 133–4, 139, 140–1, 143; and preparations for the campaign, 135–7; and Henry de Beaumont, 137–8; receives news of the deadline for the relief of Stirling, 139, 150; commands rearguard division, 145; leads advance on Stirling, 146–7; fails to take the banners of saints, 147; receives news of Scottish preparations, 166–7; intentions on the evening of 23 June, 180–2, 187–8; orders night crossing of the Bannock Burn, 183–4, 198; and problems among high command, 187, 229; prepares for battle on the morning of 24 June, 194–5; disquieted by Scots taking to the field, 197–9; rebukes Gloucester, 200–1; orders English advance, 202; and mêlée, 205, 230–1; led from field of battle, 209; flees to England, 210, 212–13, 217, 223, 232, 233; and capture of Hereford, 217–18; in York, and parliament (1314), 217, 219, 221, 228; issues order to escheators, 224–5; refuses to recognise Bruce as king, 239; at siege of Berwick (1319), 242; concludes truce with Bruce (1319), 242; concludes Thirteen-Year Truce (1323), 243; renews quarrel with Lancaster, 243–4; and Despensers, 244–5; sanctions execution of Lancaster (1322), 245; attitude to the Scottish war, 246; overthrow, deposition and death of (1326–7), 247–8
Edward III, king of England, 237–8, 247, 248
Eleanor of Castile, queen of England, 57
Elgin Castle, 76–7
Eslington, John de, 225
Essex, 103
Ettrick forest, 9, 72, 76, 78, 80–1, 117–18
Evesham, battle of (1265), 56

Falkirk, 29, 148–9, 159, 161, 162
Falkirk, battle of (1298), xiii, 9, 29, 44, 56, 60, 94, 136–7, 142, 146, 156–7, 173–4, 176, 195, 197, 201, 229, 245, 252
famine of 1315–16, 240, 244
Fauconberg, Walter de, 228
Faversham, tournament at (1308), 93
Ferre, Guy de, 57
Fiennes, William de, 119–20
FitzAlan, Edmund, earl of Arundel: at Wallingford tournament (1307), 90; at Dunstable tournament (1309), 98; and capture and death of Gaveston (1312),

103–5; refuses to participate in Scottish campaign (1314), 135, 146, 192
Flemings, 30–1, 158, 189
Fochart, battle of (1318), 127, 241
foot soldiers, *see* infantry
Fordun, John of, 44, 222, 225
Forest of Dean, 133
Forfar Castle, 83
France, 30, 56, 158
Francis, William, 122
Franco-Scottish alliance, 23, 31
Fraser, Simon, 13, 31–2
Frescobaldi, 94–5, 102, 135
Fryvill, Baldwin de, 227

Galloway, 27, 41, 70, 72, 76, 79–80, 126, 150, 153–5
Gascony, 60, 95, 135, 247
Gaveston, Arnaud, 60
Gaveston, Piers, earl of Cornwall (d. 1312), 112–13, 244, 245; first introduced to Prince Edward (1300), 60–1; banished from Edward's household (1305), 62; deserts Scottish campaign (1306), 66; first sentence of exile (1307) 66–7; recall and promotion (1307), 89–90; incurs wrath of the magnates (1307–8), 90–6; second exile, and appointment as lieutenant of Ireland (1308), 97; returns to England (1309), 98; personally insults magnates (1309), 99–100; participates in Scottish campaign (1310), 101; targeted in Ordinances (1311), 102; third exile and return (1311–12), 102; capture and death (1312), 103–5; corpse of, 106, 243; repercussions of death, 132, 138, 201, 229
Genoa, 135
Giffard, John, 225, 227, 262, 263
Gilbertson, Walter, 218, 220
Gillies Hill, 161, 208
Glamorgan, lordship of, 244
Glasgow, 14, 50, 85, 125, 218
Glen Trool, 74–6, 154–5, 157
Gloucester, 248
Gordon, Adam, 81, 106
Gray, Thomas, 173, 175–6, 186–7, 201, 229
Gray, Thomas, chronicler, 57, 61, 120, 123, 158, 161, 174–6, 226, 259
Great Cause, 20–1, 23, 40, 42–3
Great Glen, 76, 154
Greenfield, William, archbishop of York, 227, 262

Guisborough, Walter, 42

Halghton, John de, bishop of Carlisle, 41
Halidon Hill, battle of (1333), 238, 252, 253
Happrew, 9, 31
Harbottle Castle, 242
Harclay, Andrew, earl of Carlisle, 243, 245
Harwich, 247
Hastings, John de, 21, 133
Henry II, king of England, 43
Henry III, king of England, 17, 40, 56–7, 183
Henry VII, Holy Roman Emperor, 9, 209
Hereford, earl of, *see* Bohun, Humphrey de
Hesilrigg, John, 227
Hope, 133

Inchaffray, abbot of, 199, 232
infantry: English, 138–9, at Wark muster, 129, 141, 142, 146, raising of, 133–4, 139, 140–1, armour and weaponry, 138, 142, indiscipline, 141–2, numbers, 142–3, 147, Scottish: numbers, 151–2, 161, Torwood muster, 151–3, armour and weaponry, 153–4, training and tactics, 155–6, morale and experience, 154–5; *see also* army
Inverlochy Castle, 76
Invernairn Castle, 76
Inverness, 76
Inverness Castle, 76
Inverurie, 77, 154
Ireland, 97, 127; troops summoned from (1314), 133; Bruce invasion of (1315–18), 241
Irvine, 8, 43
Isabel of Fife, countess of Buchan, 50, 63, 65
Isabella, sister of earl of Atholl, 190
Isabella of France, queen of England, 60, 91, 93, 96, 103, 183, 247–8

Jedburgh Castle, 117, 183
Joan of the Tower, queen of Scots, 249
John, king of England, 56
John XXII, pope, 250
John of Brittany, earl of Richmond, 60, 76

Keith, Robert, marischal of Scotland, 84, 149, 151, 161–2, 200, 202
Kellawe, Richard de, bishop of Durham, 140

Kenilworth Castle, 248
Kennington, tournament at (1308), 97
Kildrummy Castle, 63–5
Kilmarnock, 75
Kinghorn, 16, 18
Kingston, 88
Kintyre, 153
Kirkintilloch Castle, 125
Knaresborough Castle, 103

Lacy, Henry de, earl of Lincoln (1249–1311), 59; at Feast of the Swans (1306), 53; promise to Edward I (1307), 89; and recall of Gaveston (1307), 90; Boulogne Agreement (1308), 91–2; father-in-law of Thomas of Lancaster, 94; and dispute with Edward II and Gaveston (1308–10), 95–6, 99–100; as an Ordainer (1310), 100; appointed keeper of the realm (1310), 101; death (1311), 101
Lamberton, William, bishop of St Andrews, 16, 19; appointed Guardian (1299), 44; enters into secret bond with Bruce (1304), 46–9, 190; and inauguration of Bruce at Scone (1306), 50; surrenders to English (1306), 51; and James Douglas, 73; in English custody (1309), 84
Lamouilly, Jean de, 14
Lanark, 27, 41, 46
Lancaster, 139
Lancaster, Thomas earl of (c. 1278–1322), 60; cousin of Edward II, 94; becomes an opponent of Edward II and Gaveston (1308–9), 98–100; driving force behind Ordinances (1310–11), 100; refuses to participate in Scottish campaign (1310), 101; inheritance and wealth (1311), 101, 205; capture and death of Gaveston (1312), 103–4; negotiates with Edward II (1312–13), 104–5; refuses to participate in Scottish campaign (1314), 131–2, 135–6, 139, 146, 192; at York parliament (1314), 219; enacts measures for the defence of the north (1314), 239; at siege of Berwick (1319), 242, 244; quarrels with Edward II (1317) 243–4; at Boroughbridge, and execution of (1322), 245, 247
Lanercost, chronicle of, 173, 202, 223–4, 225, 226, 230, 231, 235, 239
Lanercost Priory, 64

Langley, manor of, 58
Langton, Walter, bishop of Coventry and Lichfield, English treasurer, 66, 75, 95
Lauderdale, 141, 146
Leake, Treaty of (1318), 244
Ledhouse, Simon of, 119
Leicester, 139
Leicester, earldom of, 100
Leith, 115, 148
Lennox, 188
Lennox, Malcolm II, earl of, 50, 84
Lewes, battle of (1264), 40, 56
Lincoln, 138–9
Lincoln, earldom of, 101
Lincoln, earl of, *see* Lacy
Linlithgow, 59, 85–6, 112, 212
Livingston, 112
Lochmaben Castle, 8, 40, 45, 63, 94, 168
Loch Doon Castle, 64
Loch Ryan, 70
Loch Tay, 10, 52, 63, 73, 137, 154
Loch Trool, 74
London Bridge, 49
London, 26, 46, 50, 53–4, 67, 100–2, 104, 134
Loudoun Hill (1307), 75–6, 154–5, 157, 160, 195
Lubaud, Piers, 111–13, 116, 120, 123–4
Lucy, Anthony de, 132, 225, 263
Lundie, Richard, 27

Macdouall, Dougal, 70
MacQuillan, Malcolm, lord of Kintyre, 70
Magna Carta (1215), 56
Malcolm IV, king of Scots, 20
Margaret of England, sister of Edward I, wife of Alexander III, 17
Margaret of France, queen of England, 12, 15, 96
Margaret, Maid of Norway, 17, 18, 21
Marshal, William, 221, 261
Mauley, Edmund de, 138, 221, 227, 262
Melrose Abbey, 251–2
Merlin, prophecy of, 69, 76
Methven (1306), 9–10, 51–2, 63, 71, 73, 81–2, 125, 137, 154–5, 195
Mitford Castle, 242
Mongols, 24
Mons-en-Pévèle, battle of (1304), 158
Montagu, William, 222
Montfort, Simon de, 56
Moray, earl of, *see* Randolph
Moray, John de, 225

INDEX 293

Mortimer, Roger, earl of March, 133, 247–8, 262
Mortlach Castle, 77
Mountz, Ebles de, 183, 222
Mowbray, John, 71, 77–8, 85
Mowbray, Philip, xv; ambushed in Paisley forest (1307), 78; concludes agreement for surrender of Stirling Castle (1314), 125; arrives at Newminster, 139–41, 150; imparts news of Scottish army on 23 June, 165–7; refuses to admit Edward II and English fugitives into Stirling, 210, 212; transfers allegiance to Bruce (1314), 220; participates in Bruce invasion of Ireland, and death (1318), 241
Murray, Andrew, 6, 8, 27, 32, 43
Musselburgh, 252

Neath, 248
Neville's Cross, battle of (1346), 233, 253, 255
Newcastle, 14, 64, 103, 105; and Scottish campaign (1314), 130–1, 133–4, 138–9
Newminster, 139, 141, 146
New Park, xiii–xiv; prepared for conflict by Bruce, 159–63; on 23 June, 165–7, 173–4, 182–3; regrouping of Scottish army in, 188–9; council of war held in, 193–4; and relationship to field of battle, 255–8
Norham Castle, 19, 101, 243, 248
Northburgh, Roger, 225, 263
Northumberland, 25; raided by Scots (1311), 86; troops summoned from (1314), 133, 139
Northumberland, Earl Henry of, 20
Nottinghamshire, 133, 139

Old Meldrum, 77–8
Oliphant, William, 13, 15
Ordainers, 100–6
Ordinances (1311), 101–2, 131, 135–6, 138, 219, 229, 237, 244, 246
Orkney, 63

Paisley, 78, 125
Paisley forest, 78, 81
papacy, 30, 45, 84
Paris, 73
parliament: English, (1307), 94–5, (1308), 93, 95–6, (1309), 97, (1310), 98, (1312), 104, (1314), 219, cancelled (1314), 131, 134–5; Scottish, (Norham, 1291), 19, (Rutherglen, 1300), 45, (St Andrews, 1304), 13, (St Andrews, 1309), 83–8, (Cambuskenneth, 1314), 220, (Black Parliament, 1320), 250
Patrick, earl of Dunbar, 106, 212–13, 220, 250
Peebles, 9, 31, 44, 81
Pelstream Burn, 256–7, 259–60
Pembroke, earl of, see Valence
Percy, Henry, 43, 103
Perth, 10, 14, 18, 51–2, 60, 63, 85, 86, 101, 122, 138, 154, 237
Pessagno, Antonio, 135–6
Peterborough, 134, 138
Philip IV, king of France, 22–3, 30–1, 84, 91, 96
Picardy, 30
Pontefract Castle, 219, 245
Ponthieu, county of, 66, 90
Powys, 133

Ragman Roll, 26
Randolph, Thomas, earl of Moray: character and appearance, 80–1; in English custody (1306–8), 81; captured by Douglas (1308), 81; at St Andrews parliament (1309), 84; besieges Edinburgh Castle (1314), 111, 116–17; takes Edinburgh by assault (1314), 121–4, 154; at Scottish muster in Torwood, 150, 153; appointed commander of vanguard, 162; and engagement with Clifford's division, 172–9, 180, 188–9; lacking experience of battle, 195; and engagement on 24 June, 200, 203–4, 231; conducts raids into England (1315, 1319), 240, 242; at Byland (1322), 242; death (1332), 252
Remonstrances, 56
Renfrew, 85
Rhodes, 137
Riccardi, 135
Richmond, 219
Rievaulx Abbey, 242
Riveres, John de, 221, 261
Robert I, see Bruce, Robert I, king of Scots
Rochester Castle, 130, 218
Roslin, 31
Ross, Walter, 234
Round Table, 97
Roxburgh, 22

Roxburgh Castle, 29, 65, 85, 101, 113–14; seized by Douglas (1314), 117–22, 154; destruction of (1314), 121, 124–7, 129–30; rebuilding of, 238
Rutherglen, 50; Scottish parliament at (1299), 45
Rypariis, Edmund de, 227

St Albans, 134
St Andrews, 31; Scottish parliament at (1309), 83–5, 99
St Cuthbert, 148
St Edward, crown of, 93
St James's (London), 147
St John, John de, 45, 58
St John, Knights of, 137
St John of Beverley, 148
St Ninians, kirk of, 159, 162
St Paul's (London), 102
St Peter's Abbey, 248
Salisbury, earldom of, 101
Salonika, 137
Salop, 133, 139
Savoy, 183
Scalacronica, 174
Scarborough Castle, 103
Scone, 21, 27, 50, 65, 71
Segrave, John de, 132, 225, 263
Selkirk, 94
Selkirk forest, 85
Seton, Alexander, 141, 191–2, 235
Seton, Christopher, 38, 64–5
Sixhills, prior of, 218
Slioch, 77
Soules Conspiracy (1320), 250–1
Soules, John de, 13
Spain, 251
Stafford, 133, 139
Staines, 88
Stamford, English parliament at (1309), 98–9
Stepney, tournament at (1308), 93
Stewart, James the, 43–4, 84
Stewart, Walter the, 151, 153, 162, 195
Stirling, 208, 223
Stirling Bridge, battle of (1297), 6–9, 11, 27–9, 44, 51, 197
Stirling Castle, xv, 7, 26–7, 44–7, 113–14, 117, 151, 164, 183, 188, 190, 250, 254; English siege of (1304), 12–15, 32, 60, 112, 175; Scottish siege of (1314), 124–6, 154–5, 162, 195, 222; agreement for surrender of (1314), 125–6, 139–41, 146–8, 149–50, 161, 194; difficult terrain surrounding, 159–60, 163, 183; on 23 June, 165–7, 173–4, 179–80; garrison of, 185; English refused refuge in, 210, 212, 225–6, 232; surrender and destruction of (1314), 220, 240, 241; rebuilding of, 238
Stone of Destiny, 26, 50
Strathbogie, 77
Strathbogie, David of, earl of Atholl, 74, 85, 150, 190–1
Strathbogie, John of, earl of Atholl, 50, 60, 65
Strathearn, 59
Strathearn, Malise III, earl of, 60
Strathord, 31
Surrey, earl of, see Warenne, John de, earl of Surrey (d. 1304); Warenne, John de earl of Surrey (1286–1347)
Swans, Feast of the (1306), 53–5, 62, 68, 89, 105

Tarradale Castle, 77
Temple Church (London), 53
Tewkesbury Abbey, 244
Thomas Plantagenet, son of Edward I, 89
Tibetot, Payn, 221, 261
Tinchebray, battle of (1106), 233
Tintagel, 102
Torthorald, James, 228, 261
Torwood, 7, 44; muster of Scottish army in, 151, 153–6; terrain of, 159; prepared for conflict by Bruce, 160–3; on 23 June, 165–7, 173–4; and flight of Edward II, 210, 232
Tottenham, 46
Tower of London, 7, 26, 65, 71, 73, 88, 218
Trokelowe, John, 231
Turnberry, 70, 126; Head, 70–1
Turnberry Castle, 59, 71, 80
Tweng, Marmaduke, 5–7, 11, 28, 32–3, 44, 219, 239
Tynemouth, 103

Umfraville, Ingram de, 45, 199, 217, 250–1
Umfraville, Robert de, earl of Angus, 225, 262
Urquhart Castle, 76

Valence, Aymer de, earl of Pembroke (d. 1324), commands English forces against Bruce (1306–7), 51–2, 63; at Glen Trool and Loudoun Hill (1307), 74–5; departs office of lieutenant of Scotland (1307), 76; encounters Douglas in Paisley forest (1307), 78; and promise to Edward I (1307), 89; and recall of Gaveston (1307), 90; Boulogne Agreement (1308), 91–2; granted lands in Scotland by Edward I, 94; travels to papal curia at Avignon for Edward II (1309), 98; refuses to participate in Scottish campaign (1310), 101; capture and death of Gaveston (1312), 103–4; participates in Scottish campaign (1314), 132; appointed keeper and lieutenant of Scotland (1314), 133–4; receives victuals at Berwick, 136; retinue of, 143, 146; as keeper of the king's reins, 145, 157, 184; previous experience of battle, 195; and engagement of 24 June, 209; takes refuge in York with Edward II (1314), 217; retinue of, and casualties, 221, 223; and problems among high command, 229; role in mêlée on 24 June, 230–1; death (1324), 247

Vescy, William de, 221, 261
Vipont (Vieuxpont), William, 234
Vita Edwardi Secundi, 57, 85, 88, 91, 145, 147, 153, 170–3, 186, 203, 205–6, 211, 212, 224, 226, 230, 231, 235, 239

Waldegrave, Richard de, 7
Wales, 18, 23, 24, 56, 103; troops summoned from (1314), 133, 138, 142
Walingford, Alan de, 227–8
Walingford, Robert de, 228
Wallace, William, 6–9, 13, 27–9, 31, 32, 43–6, 48–9, 51, 65, 73, 156, 174, 197
Wallingford, tournament at (1307), 90–1, 102
Waltham Abbey, 67

Warde, Simon, 227, 262
Warenne, John de, earl of Surrey (d. 1304), 6, 25–6
Warenne, John de, earl of Surrey (1286–1347): at Wallingford tournament (1307), 90; Boulogne Agreement (1308), 91–2; related to Edward II, 94; participates in Scottish campaign (1310), 101; pursuit and capture of Gaveston (1312), 103; refuses to participate in Scottish campaign (1314), 132, 135, 146, 192; engages in private war with Lancaster (1317), 244
Wark, 85; muster of English army at (1314), 129, 140–2, 146, 150
Wark Castle, 101, 242
Warkworth Castle, 242, 248
Warwick, 138
Warwick Castle, 103
Warwick, earl of, *see* Beauchamp
Weardale, 248–9
Westminster, 93, 95, 130, 134
Westminster Abbey, 53–4, 90, 92, 247
Westminster Hall, 54–5, 105
Westminster Palace, 53
Westmorland, 8
William, earl of Ross, 63, 71, 76–7, 82–4, 152, 190
William the Lion, king of Scots, 20–1
Winchburgh, 212, 232
Winchelsey, Robert, archbishop of Canterbury, 96
Windsor Castle, 88, 101, 183
Wishart, Robert, bishop of Glasgow, 43–4, 48–51, 84, 218

York, 67, 102–3, 134, 139, 243; in aftermath of Bannockburn (1314), 217–18, 219, 221–2
Yorkshire, 133, 139

CW01209474

Taliman Sluga
Christmas in Europe
Recipes · Customs · Specialities

> Rodeln hoch 2
> twice the tobogganing experience

Eure Winterhighlights
Your winter highlights

> **Skifahren & Snowboarden** im > *Skiing & snowboarding in the* Snow Space Salzburg & Shuttleberg Flachauwinkl-Kleinarl
> **Langlaufen, Winterwandern & Schneeschuhwandern**
> *Cross country skiing, winter hiking & snow shoe hiking*
> **Stille Nacht - Adventveranstaltungen** > *Silent Night - Events*
> Events: **Winterfeste, Heimat- & Brauchtumsabende, Snow Volleyball Tour, Ski amadé Ladies Week**
> *Events: Winter festivals, Folk Heritage Evenings, Snow Volleyball Tour, Ski amadé Ladies Week*
> **Täglich freier Eintritt** in die Wasserwelt Wagrain (3 Stunden)
> *Daily free entrance to the Wasserwelt Wagrain (3 hours)*
> **Wagrainis Winterwelt** im Snow Space Salzburg
> *Wagrainis Winterwelt in Snow Space Salzburg*
> **Absolut Park** am Shuttleberg Flachauwinkl-Kleinarl
> *Absolut Park at the Shuttleberg Flachauwinkl-Kleinarl*
> **Salzburger Sportwelt Card** mit Ermäßigungen in der Region
> *Salzburger Sportwelt Card with discounts in the region*

wagrain-kleinarl.at

WAGRAIN® KLEINARL

> Skifahren hoch 2 in zwei Skigebieten
> *Twice the skiing experience at two skiing areas*

> Stille Nacht - Veranstaltungen für die ganze Fami
> *Silent Night - events for the whole fam*

Taliman Sluga

Christmas in Europe

Recipes · Customs · Specialities

VERLAG ANTON PUSTET

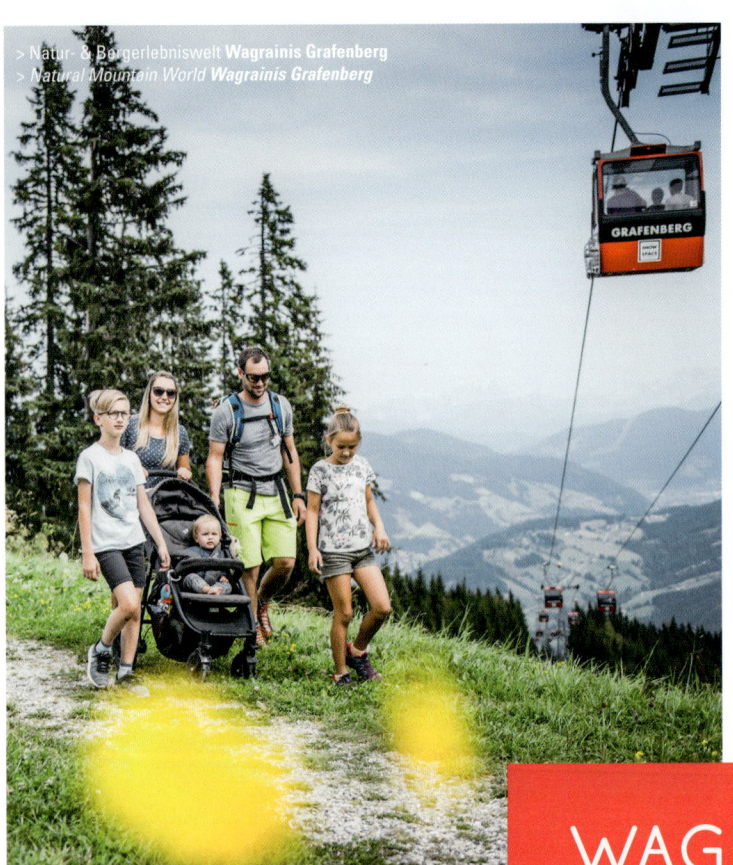

> Natur- & Bergerlebniswelt **Wagrainis Grafenberg**
> *Natural Mountain World **Wagrainis Grafenberg***

> Täglich gratis Eintritt in das **Erlebnisbad Wasserwelt Wagrain**
> *Daily free entrance to the **Wasserwelt Wagrain***

WAGRAIN® KLEINARL

Eure Sommerhighlights
Your summer highlights

> **Wanderregion** mit 140 km markierten Wanderwegen
> ***Hikingregion** with 140 km of marked hiking trails*
> **KLETTER-WELT Wagrain-Kleinarl** mit Hochseilgarten & Flying Fox
> ***KLETTER-WELT Wagrain-Kleinarl** with high rope course & flying fox*
> **BIKE-WELT & Bikepark Wagrain**
> ***BIKE-WELT & Bikepark Wagrain***
> Events: „Musik auf den Almen", „Musik & Theater", Red Bull X-Alps, NIVEA Familienfest, **Bauernherbst-Festwoche** mit Kürbisfest & Almabtrieb
> *Events: „Music at the huts", „Music & Theatre", Red Bull X-Alps, NIVEA Familienfest, Bauernherbst festive week with pumpkin festival & Almabtrieb*
> **Soccerpark Wagrain-Kleinarl** - Der Freizeitspaß
> ***Soccerpark Wagrain-Kleinarl***
> **Salzburger Sportwelt Card** mit Ermäßigungen in der Region
> ***Salzburger Sportwelt Card** with discounts in the region*

wagrain-kleinarl.at

> Mountainbiken & E-Biken für die ganze Familie
> *Mountainbiking & e-biking for the whole family*

Contents

Foreword	7
Authors's foreword	8
Introductory notes	9
Albania	12
Belgium	17
Bulgaria	22
Denmark	27
Germany	34
Estonia	42
European microstates	50
Finland	51
France	56
Greece	64
Great Britain	70
Ireland	80
Iceland	85
Italy	89
Former Yugoslav States	
Croatia	96
Serbia	104
Slovenia	110
Bosnia, Macedonia, Kosovo, Montenegro	116
Latvia	118
Lithuania	122
Luxembourg	128
Malta	134
Netherlands	139
Norway	144
Austria	148
Poland	156
Portugal	164
Romania	168
Russia, Ukraine, Belarus, Moldova	174
Sweden	177
Switzerland	182
Slovakia	188
Spain	194
Czech Republic	202
Hungary	208
Cyprus	214
Acknowledgements	218
Bibliography	221
Recipe index	222
Picture credits, Copyright	224

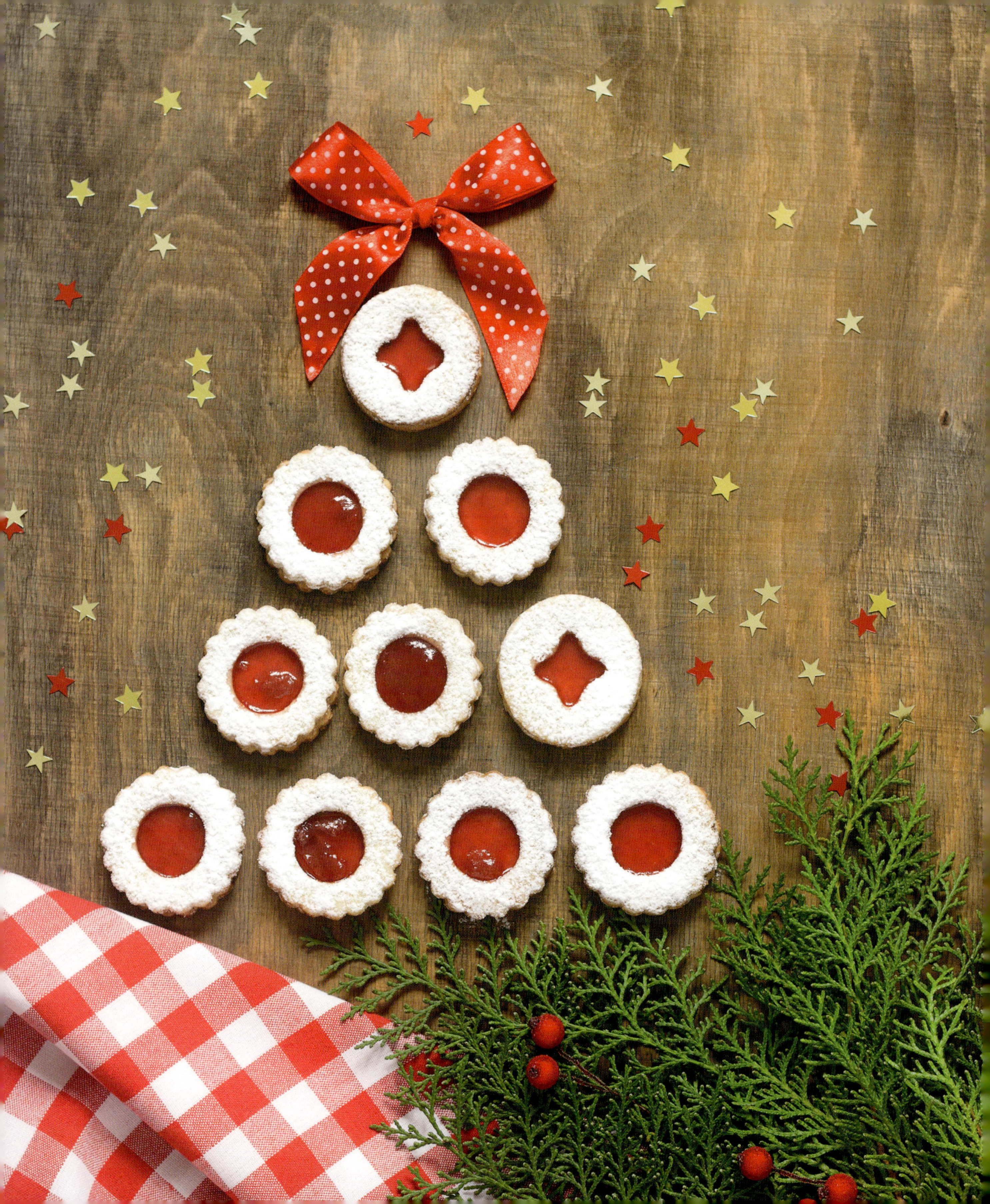

Foreword

"Jesus, all nations on earth": this line from the song Silent Night was the inspiration for Wagrain's Advent of Cultures. At its heart, this involved inviting people from many different countries to display their Christmas decorations and serve up their Christmas treats at the local Christmas market, as well as including music groups and choirs from various regions into the local Advent concert.

Schools were also involved in this project. Every year for more than ten years, schoolchildren have prepared three different Christmas meals from various countries and regions in their home economics classes. Under the guidance of recipe book author and cultural mediator, Taliman Sluga, the students first of all learnt about the run up to Christmas, how people in other countries celebrate the birth of Christ and about their traditions and specialities. As part of this, the author was supported by teachers Margarethe El Makarim, Anita Moser and Monika Huber.

Students were able to discover that Christmas celebrations are highly varied, yet in all countries, the most important part is eating and sharing traditional regional dishes.

Eugen Grader,
Mayor of Wagrain

Dear Readers,

For many years, Joseph Mohr, the author of the lyrics to the famous song, lived and worked in the holiday destination Wagrain-Kleinarl. As a result, the local villages and associated tourism are closely linked to the theme of "Silent Night", even today, making Advent in the region all the more unique and authentic! Guests from many different countries enjoy spending their holidays in Wagrain-Kleinarl, which means that people from many nations encounter one another in the communities during the Advent season. As a result, there is much joy in sharing customs, dishes and chatter at Advent markets, for example during the "Advent of Cultures". As a successful tourist destination, we regularly come across people from all over the worlds and different cultures, under the slogan "Zest for life, squared!" This is why it was of the very important for us at for Wagrain-Kleinarl Tourism to give this project our full and enthusiastic support.

Come and experience the magic of "Silent Night" for yourself at the very place it started in Salzburger Land and celebrate 200 years of "Silent night, holy night" with us!

I wish you all the happiness when cooking and tasting the delicious dishes!

Stefan Passrugger
Manager
Wagrain-Kleinarl Tourism

Author's Foreword

Christmas is a celebration that takes place in almost every country in the world. Over the course of time, regional quirks, sagas and ancient rituals have been combined with Christian beliefs, resulting in individual customs and traditions in every country.

"Jesus, all nations on earth!" are the words to the fourth verse of "Silent night, holy night". And the Salzburg region of Austria, including Wagrain-Kleinarl, invites all these nations to visit them and not only celebrate Christmas together, but also get to know the country and its people.

And what could be more obvious for Wagrain, as a tourist destination and the "Silent night" parish, to make both of these things, the world-famous song and the Christmas celebration, the focus of a somewhat special project. A project that connects the people – at least those in Europe – to the festive period. Cooking, eating, drinking and celebrating know no borders – and this is especially true of the Christmas period.

Right from the start, this initiative to bring different people together has been championed along with students from Wagrain and Kleinarl.

To fill in the backstory, in 2009 I was able to work alongside cultural events pro, Heinz Leitner, on the concept of a contemporary implementation of Christmas activities in Wagrain in the run up to Christmas. This was when the "Advent of Cultures", featuring a peaceful Advent market in Kirchboden in Wagrain, was brought to life. Since then, there has been a new guest country every year that is able to display their Christmas cuisine and arts and crafts and thus enrich the local Advent concerts that are typical in this region.

As part of this project, cooking groups of children from Wagrain and Kleinarl in all six school years spent more than ten years focusing on the specific Christmas traditions of European countries and created menus featuring the most popular Christmas meals. They cooked the dishes in class and then enjoyed these together, adding to the festive spirit.

The clear objective was to find out more about the similarities and peculiarities of the customs and culinary dishes in European countries during the Christmas period: for example it stood out that in the Czech Republic they have numerous traditions that are said to predict the future, or in Italy that there are so many occasions when the children receive presents. Then there's also Eastern Europe, where it is very common to burn a "Yule log", or Northern Europe, where goblins, gnomes, spirits, imps and trolls all get up to mischief, sometimes meant friendlily, but often with more malicious intentions.

This recipe book is the result of this intensive interest, to encourage you to read, cook and taste.

Hopefully this task will be a nudge for other schools to also use food and cooking as way of understanding different cultures.

The recipes generally serve four. In terms of ingredients and cooking techniques, they are easy to follow. That being said, the dishes will allow you to get a sense, or a "taste," of the regional spirit of each country.

At Christmas, everyone sings "Silent night", each in their own language and as part of specific customs and dishes. Let's hope this culinary message of peace will delight the hearts and stomachs for the 200th-anniversary celebrations of the song "Silent night".

Taliman Sluga
Author and project leader

Introductory notes

Before we really get all Christmassy and culinary, I just want to add a couple of tips to make it easier to understand the book and give the recipes a go, each of which is intended to feed four people.

As an introduction to each country, you will be wished "Merry Christmas and Happy New Year!" in each respective language, or languages, and you will also see the first line of the song Silent Night.

The collection of the Christmas customs and traditions itself is then selected as a snapshot. For every country you could, of course, fill an entire book with customs and ceremonies since, in some cases, even small individual regions celebrate Christmas very differently.

Nevertheless, I have hopefully managed to successfully reflect the similarities and the differences between the Christmas traditions and cultural atmosphere in European countries.

With regards to the culinary pages, we also wanted to give an interesting overview which should inspire you to try out the respective country's cuisine.

The meals described according to the recipes form a selection of typical Christmas dishes from one country for the entire holiday, compiled in the classic menu sequence of starter/soup, main course and sweet pudding.

The recipes can also be easily followed with average cooking knowledge and without vast amounts of technical kitchen equipment. The ingredients are also all readily available.

As the slow food slogan says, "Enjoyment requires education" – the more I know about specific dishes, their preparation and background, the greater the spiritual and culinary enjoyment as well.

I wish you an enjoyable pre-Christmas read, every success when cooking and all the delights of eating.

Taliman Sluga

Following double page: Students from Wagrain and Kleinarl cooking Christmas menus.

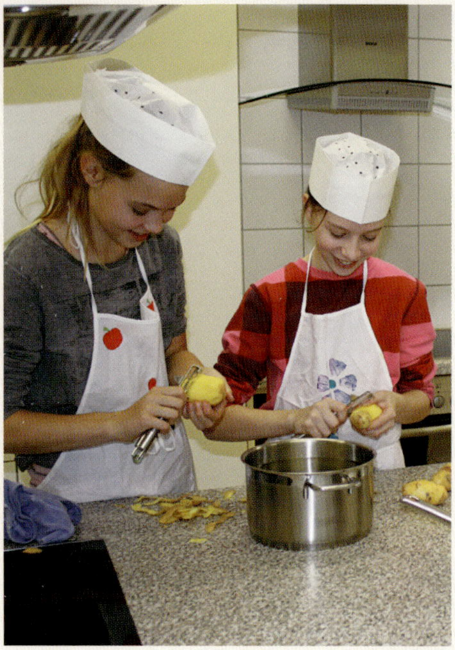

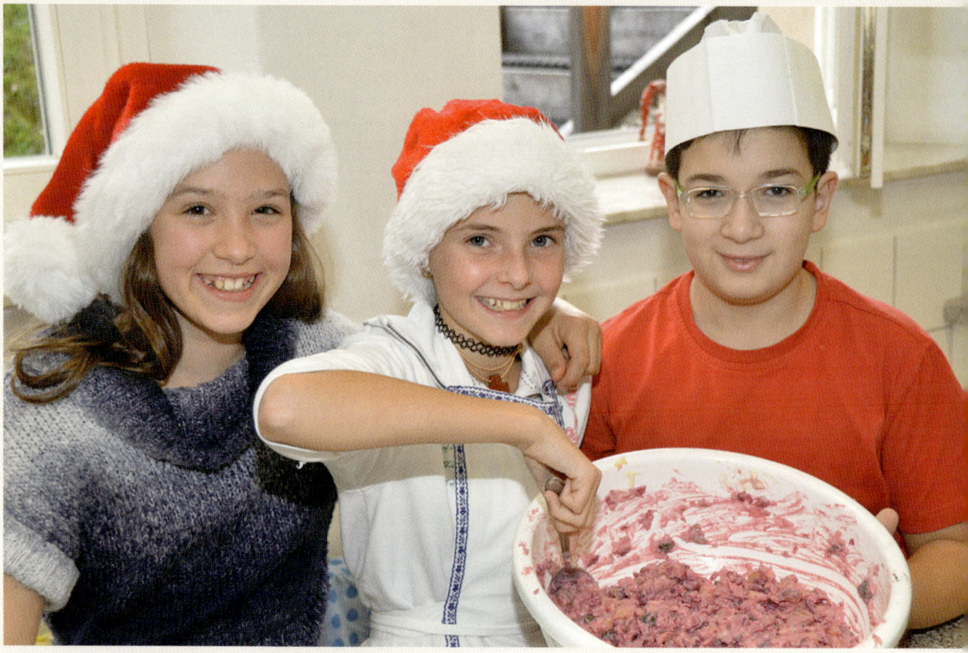

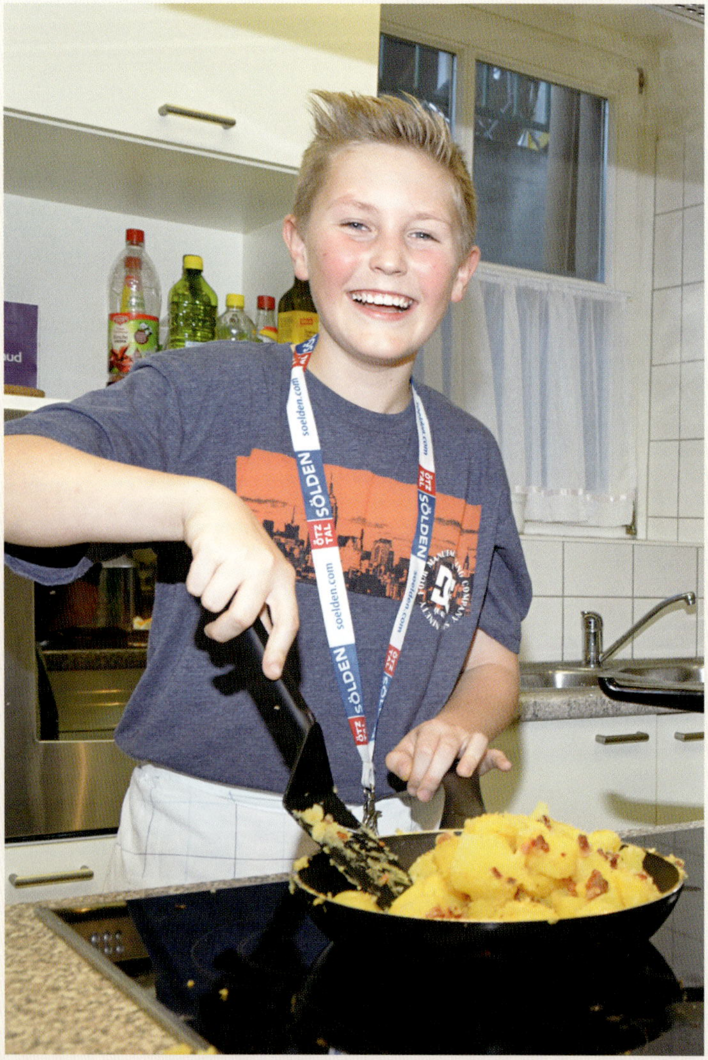
SÖLDEN
soelden.com

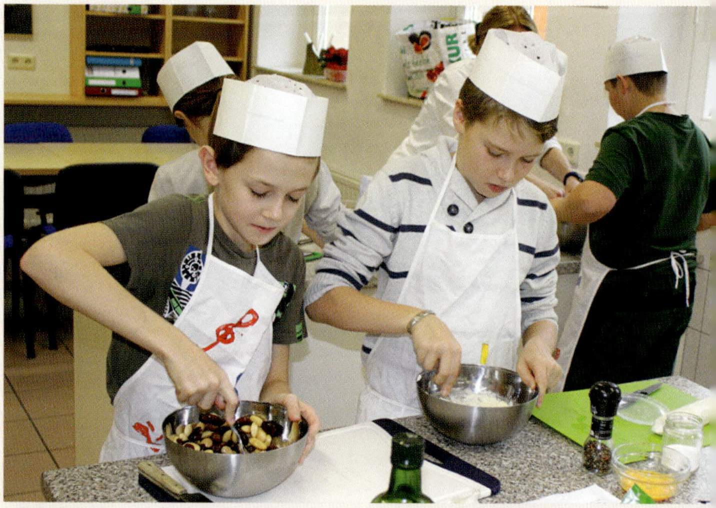

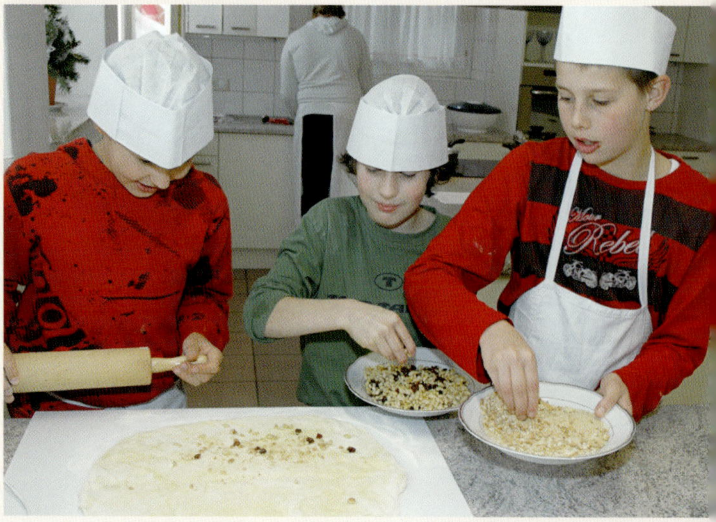

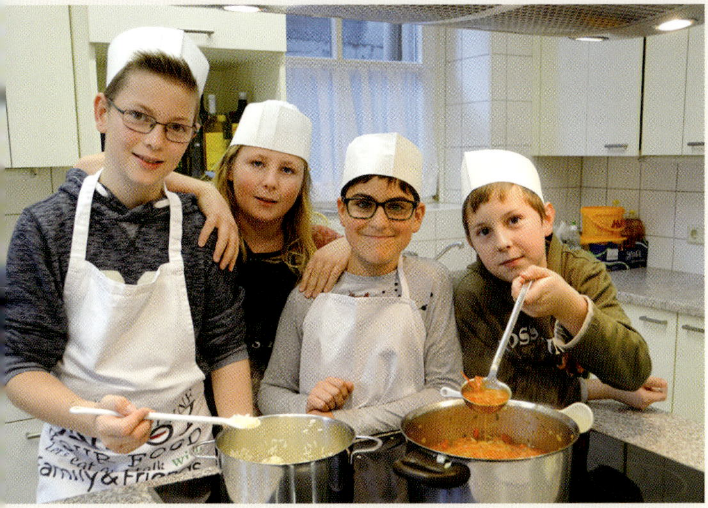

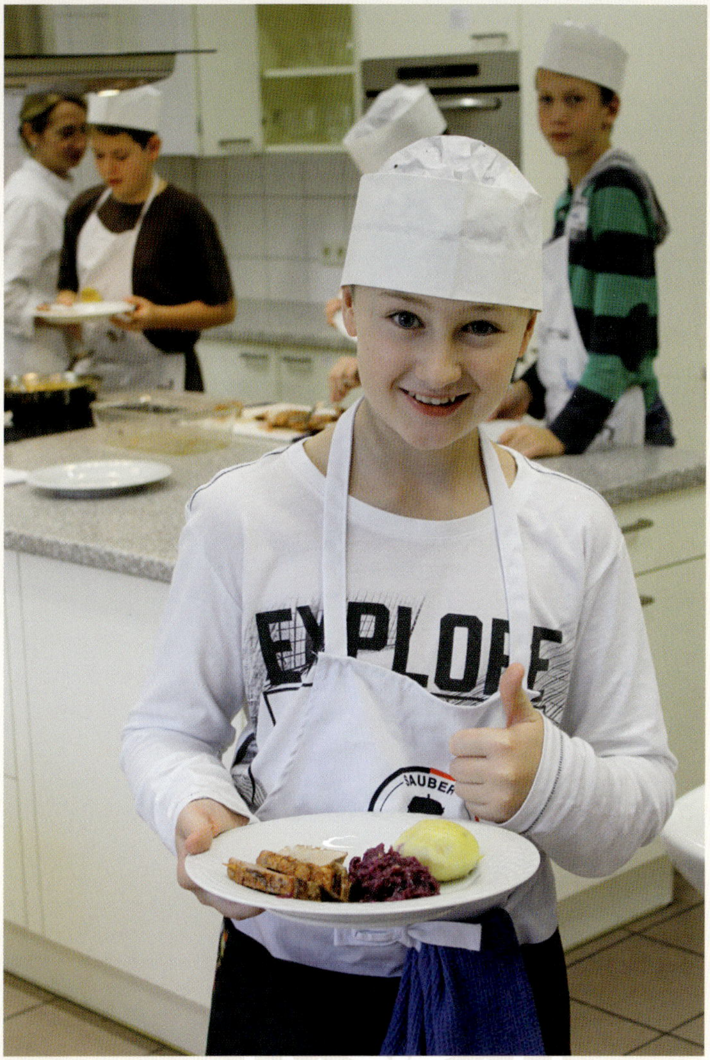

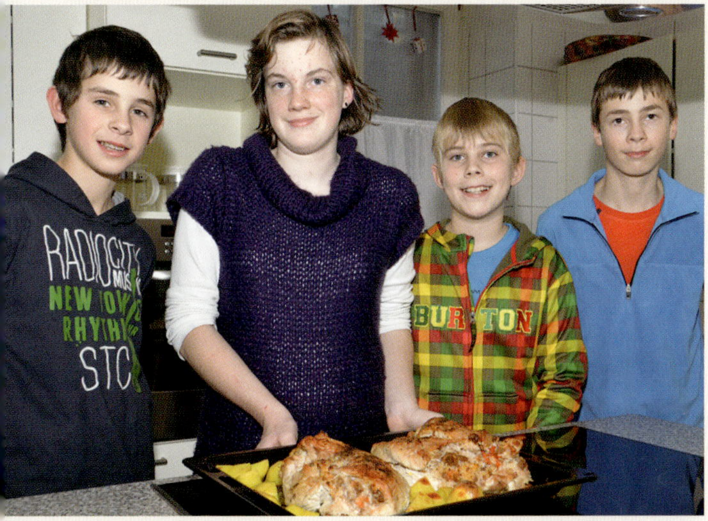
BURTON

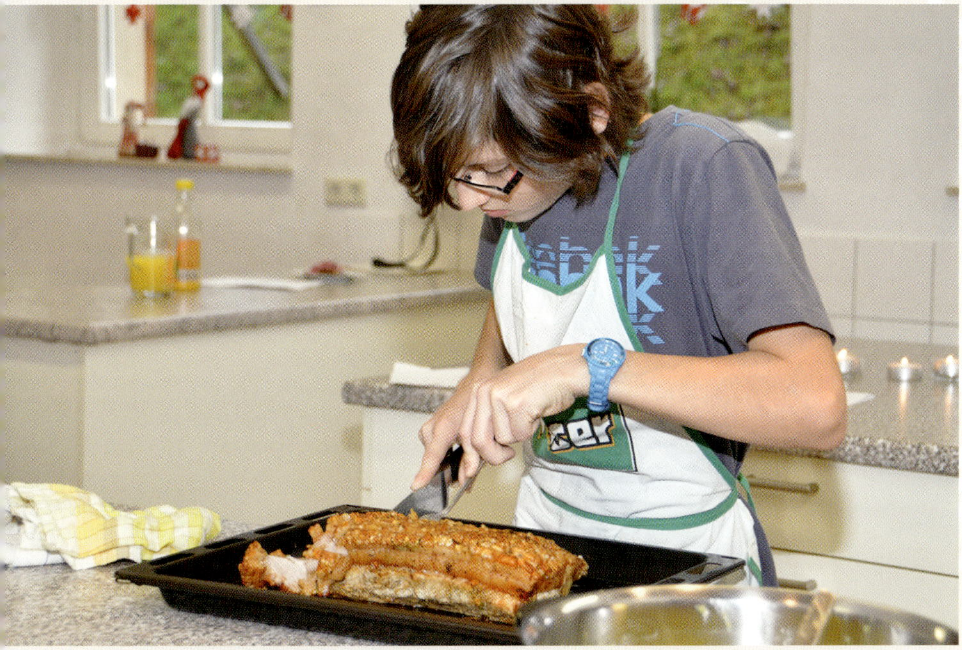

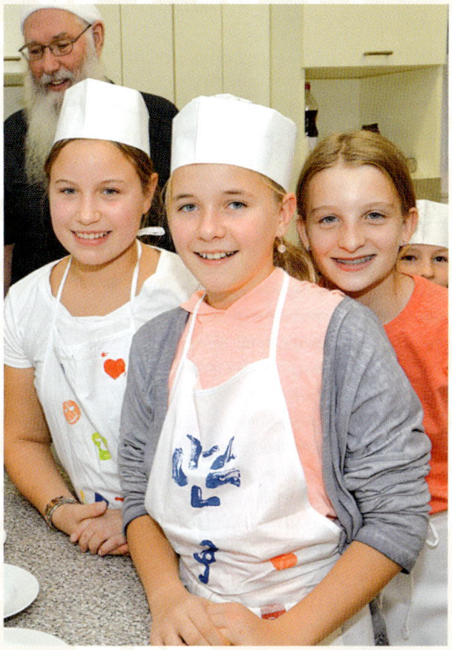

ALBANIA

Gëzuar Krishtlindjet dhe Vitin e Ri

Natë e shenjtë! Natë e qetë!

From a religious point of view, Albania is a very remarkable country. This is particularly noticeable during Advent and Christmas. Dignitaries of different religions invite one another to celebrate sacral feasts together. Some of the customs are similar to those in neighbouring countries, such as donating food, letting off loud volleys of gunfire or burning yule logs. Traditionally there are strict instructions, such as lopping down tree trunks, transporting them and setting them alight. And it is said that the ashes of the yule log have an interesting effect.

Christians make up only a sixth of the population of Albania. Nevertheless, they also celebrate Christmas here on 25 December – a public holiday. Christian and non-Christian Albanians alike celebrate again on 6 January, the Orthodox Christmas day of celebration. Religious leaders attend large celebrations together and wish each other a merry Christmas. Here, there is clearly a long tradition of different religions coming together peacefully.

In the past, there was a religious custom of slaughtering a ram at Christmas and leaving part of the meat for the poor as alms.

Something similar was also common in the north of Albania. In the Kelmendi region on the border with Montenegro, cheese, bread, cream and yoghurt would be placed on the graves of dead relatives and then given to the poor.

Light has also always played an important role. On Christmas Eve, the people are always careful to ensure the candles at home do not go out –a symbol for the warmth of the stable in Bethlehem.

Many of these old customs are upheld today, which is why church bells still chime at midnight to this day and many people attend Holy Mass.

Gunfire, previously common at midnight, has been replaced in the meantime with fireworks. Nevertheless, in some regions, loud gunfire at this time of year is still common, such as in the Mirdita region, where shots are fired on Christmas Eve at sunset. And shots also resound from kneeling worshippers after mass and the abbot's blessing.

As in many European countries, there are also customs in Albania which are said to ensure a good harvest. For example, at Christmas, a bundle of straw is touched with an axe under the kitchen table, and they say "Bind or I'll hack you apart!" This straw is then bound around the fruit trees with the hope that this will prevent the fruit from falling prematurely from the branches in the coming summer.

In Albania, much like the rest of the Balkans, for centuries it has been tradition to set fire to a piece of a tree trunk, the yule log, on Christmas Eve. The burning wood giving off warmth and light has a similar meaning to the fir tree further north in Europe. In many places, this custom, which often has rigorous instructions, is upheld to this day.

Exactly according to tradition, before sunset on 24 December, a tree is felled with only three blows of the axe. It is important that the trunk tilts to the east. The tree is caught by helpers so that it does not touch the ground. This would, of course, bring bad luck.

Byrek.

The night before Christmas, *Nata e Krishtit* (Night of Christ), worshippers attend church services. Christmas Day is then a true family celebration. Family members gather for good food, good wine and a certain type of biscuit. In the past, these baked goods were given to the children as they went from house to house for Christmas.

Traditional Christmas meals are bean soup, fish and puff pastry filled with walnuts and pumpkin. On Christmas Eve, the table is not cleared after the meal and the light is not turned off – out of gratitude for prosperity and in the hope of also having sufficient food in the coming year.

Since the Communist era, presents are not shared for Christmas but only on New Year's Eve. There is also a very typical New Year's Eve treat known as *baklava*, from the Balkans to the Middle East.

Wine is poured onto the cut in order to reconcile the tree's soul. The yule log is then brought into the inner yard and is initially leant against the wall of the house.

The wood is only carried into the house in the evening. When doing so, the log is treated with the utmost care and is gracefully called the "noble yule log" as though it were an important guest they are all pleased to see. As a sign of hospitality, food and drink is placed on the trunk before it is thrown onto the open fire after sunset and set alight. The piece of wood then burns for the whole night.

In some regions in Albania, the yule log is set alight on Christmas Eve but only extinguished after the festivities, and then again on New Year's Eve and finally on Epiphany, 6 January, for the third and final time.

It is said that the ashes of the trunk have a healing effect that will also ward off illness. They are scattered over the fields and gardens for a healthy harvest and thrown into the air to expel the "hail demon".

The custom of the burning log is practised not only by Catholics, but also by Muslims, and in all likelihood originates from a pre-Christian festival connected to the winter solstice.

Although most Albanian regions are predominantly Muslim, the towns and squares are decorated for Christmas during the Advent season, and there are even Christmas markets in the larger towns. This fact alone shows the open Albanian attitude towards different religions. Furthermore, it is quite common to fly the Albanian national flag in churches and mosques.

Baklava.

Albania

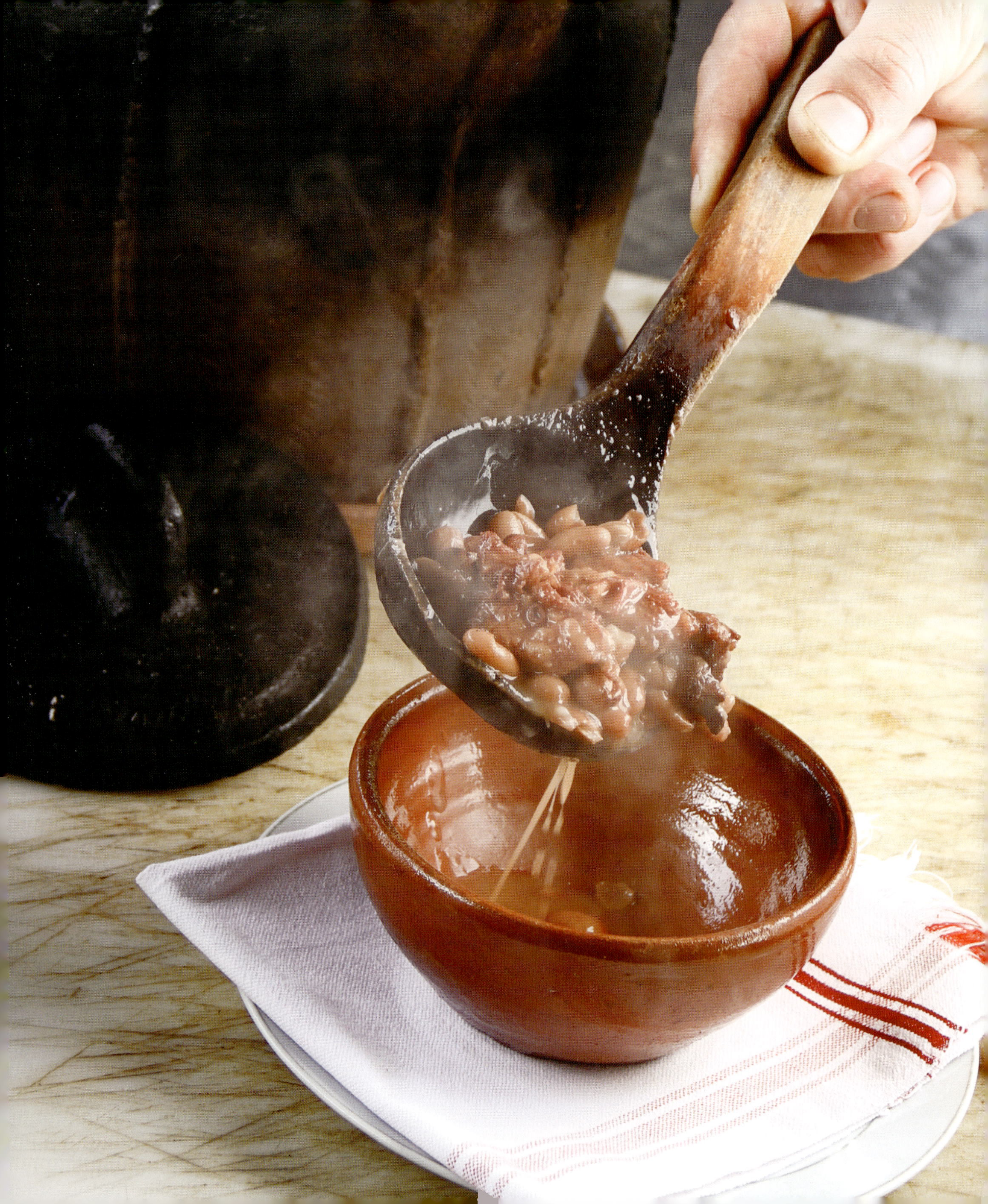

Pasul

(Albanian bean soup)

350 g	dried white beans, soaked overnight
1 tbsp	butter
1	onion
2 tsp	ground sweet paprika
1 tsp	flour (if necessary or desired; thickens soup)
	Hot red peppers, dried, to taste
	Double cream, to taste
250 g	beef or lamb, possibly cooked as a whole
	Salt, pepper

Cook the beans in the butter until they are soft, then take the pan off the heat.

Meanwhile, peel and finely chop the onions, then lightly fry them until they turn translucent.

Stir in the ground paprika, adding in a little flour. Deglaze with the cooking water from the beans and stir well with a whisk to avoid lumps.
Return everything to the beans in the pan and season with salt, pepper and double cream. Let simmer on a low heat for about a further 30 minutes.

Meat can also be cooked too. Goes very well with warm, fresh bread.

Shkodra Carp

1 kg	carp, ready to cook in portion-sized pieces
1	bread roll, stale, cut into thin slices
350 g	onion, finely chopped
50 g	almonds, finely chopped
50 g	raisins
	Lemon slices
	Allspice kernels, whole
	Peppercorns, whole
1 tbsp	butter
1	bay leaf
5 tbsp	oil
	Salt

Preheat the oven to between 220°C and 250°C.

Heat the oil in a heatproof dish and lightly sauté the onions in the oil. Add the almonds and raisins. Brown the sliced roll as well.

Add the lemon slices, bay leaf, allspice and pepper and stir, before browning for a few minutes. Rub salt into the pieces of carp. Place the carp in the mixture in the pan and spread flakes of butter over the top.

Put a dish in the preheated oven and bake the carp for 30 to 45 minutes (depending on the oven) until it reaches the desired brownness.

Serve with vegetables, potatoes, rice, for example.

Albania

Petulla

(Albanian doughnuts – sweet or savoury)

500 g	flour
2	medium eggs
1 tsp	salt
½ cube	yeast
	Pinch of sugar
½ tsp	bicarbonate of soda
	Water with milk, lukewarm, mixed as needed
	Oil for frying

Dissolve the yeast and sugar in a glass with some of the milk-water mixture. Put the flour, eggs, salt and yeast in a bowl. Then add enough of the mixture and stir with a wooden spoon to produce a stringy, elastic dough, which falls heavily from the spoon. Let the dough stand and only then work in the bicarbonate of soda well with the wooden spoon.

With wet fingers, pull the dough apart to form thin flat cakes and fry in the hot fat on both sides.

The petullas are eaten sweet with jam or honey or savoury with feta cheese, olives, tomatoes, ajvar or torshi (pickled vegetables).

BELGIUM

Vrolijk kerstfeest en een gelukkig nieuwjaar
Joyeux Noël et bonne année
Fröhliche Weihnachten und ein gutes neues Jahr

Stille nacht, heilige nacht
Nuit de Paix, Sainte Nuit
Stille Nacht, heilige Nacht

In Belgium, the appearance of *Sinterklaas* and *Zwarte Piet* marks St Nicholas' Day, and brings with it a great exchange of presents. The Christmas period doesn't only include "living" nativity scenes but also culinary treats, such as speculoos, marzipan hearts, the Belgian version of mulled wine and, of course, beer brewed especially for this time. Along the Meuse, games are played for sweet stollen. Incidentally, Father Christmas does not play a fundamental role. For this, as with their northern and eastern neighbours, the "bean king" has more significance on the name day of the Magi. If, on 2 February, the *crêpes* are successfully flipped in the pan, it promises to be a good year.

In Belgium, as in the Netherlands, 6 December is the actual day for presents. Indeed, here Christmas is also a family celebration, but for the expectant little ones, Nikolaus is the much greater event.

The Belgian *Sinterklaas* travels from Spain on a steamboat and lands in Antwerp in the middle of November. His arrival is broadcast on TV across the whole country and flocks of children greet *Sinterklaas* with a song.

St Nikolaus is accompanied by his helper, *Zwarte Piet* (Black Peter). The two of them ride from house to house, filling the prepared boots with sweets and presents. In return, the children leave out hay, carrots and sugar for *Sinterklaas*' horse.

In Belgium, the Advent period also features special shows. Across the whole country, "living" nativity scenes, Christmas plays or famous paintings of the birth of Jesus are put on or displayed, and the churches organise colourful processions.

Christmas Eve in Belgium is a normal working day which is celebrated with a festive meal with the family and, not uncommonly, by attending midnight mass. Eventually, the Belgians see out the evening over mulled wine.

25 December is an official bank holiday, predominantly a religious event, and is celebrated by families with good food. Belgian Christmas food is heavily influenced by French cuisine. This includes stuffed turkey and a chocolate Christmas cake. Of course beer brewed especially for the Christmas celebration, speculoos, marzipan hearts and pralines are must-haves.

A lovely tradition has developed along the River Meuse. Here, they bet money for Christmas stollen. Everyone who puts in a small contribution receives a playing card. Finally, the dealer turns over the top card of the stack and whoever has the highest number of the same colour as the uncovered card receives the Christmas stollen.

26 December is another normal working day and the Belgians mostly celebrate New Year's Eve in restaurants

with good food and dancing. On the second Christmas day, the whole family attends one of the many classical concerts.

On New Year's Day, light cakes in the shape of hearts or people are served. Once again, they enjoy good food, often accompanied by sauerkraut. A coin is hidden under one of the plates. Whoever finds this becomes the first lucky one of the new year.

On Epiphany, a cake is baked with a bean inside. The lucky one who manages to get hold of this particular slice of cake is then the "Bean King".

2 February is the day of *Chandeleur* (Candlemas). Traditionally, Belgian (French) families cook *crêpes* on this day – or the weekend after. *Crêpes* are similar to Austrian pancakes made of eggs, (buckwheat) flour and milk or water. Normally very thin, on this occasion they are thick.

To prepare them, you must hold a piece of gold in your left hand and, with your right hand, throw the first *crêpe* out of the pan into the air. It should turn over once and land flat back in the pan. This promises a good harvest and thus prosperity for the coming year. Even without the piece of gold, a successfully flipped *crêpe* still promises luck for the whole year.

Christmassy atmosphere in Brussels

Waterzooi

(Flemish poultry stew)

1	chicken
A little	butter
2	leeks
250 g	carrots
250 g	celery
200 g	mushrooms
500 g	potatoes
1 l	chicken soup, seasoned with garlic and bay leaf
100 ml	double cream
	Bay leaf, thyme, parsley, finely chopped
	Salt, pepper
	Olive oil, for roasting

Cut the chicken into four parts and fry in butter until crispy. Then place in the oven at 160 °C for 20 minutes.

Peel the potatoes, cut into medium-sized chunks, then boil in salted water.

For the sauce, fry half of the leeks, mushrooms, celery and carrots, the bay leaf and thyme with the olive oil in the pan until brown. Then fill it up with chicken stock, reduce, add the cream and leave to simmer. Finally, strain through a sieve. Fry the second half of the leeks, celery, carrots and mushrooms in olive oil.

Then, place on top of the chicken cut into small pieces, generously pour the sauce over, distribute the potatoes around and serve scattered with some parsley.

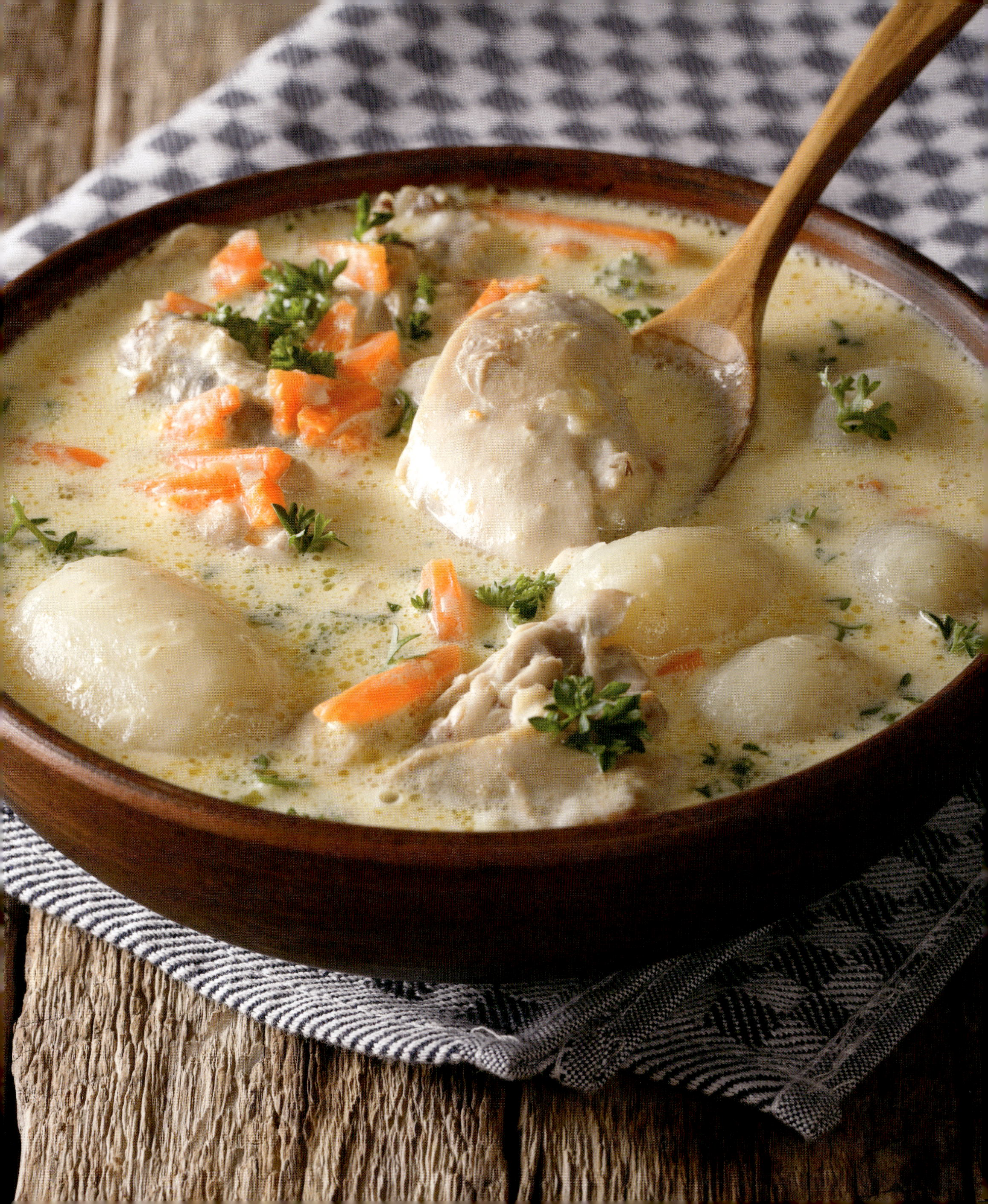

Stoofvlees with chicory

(Belgian beef dish)

800 g	beef (goulash meat), cut into rough chunks
50 g	butter
2	onions
2	bay leaves
¼	baguette
300 ml	dark beer (Belgian)
100 ml	red wine or thinned balsamic vinegar
	Thyme
	Sugar
	4 cloves
	Mustard (Dijon mustard)
	Salt, pepper

Chicory au gratin

4	medium chicories
75 g	butter
75 g	flour
1 l	milk
1 tbsp	crème fraiche
2 tbsp	double cream
6	slices of ham
	A little grated nutmeg
140 g	Gruyere cheese
	Salt, pepper

Sear the meat in a pan. Chop the onions and quickly sear them in the same pan. Then, add the bay leaf, cloves, thyme and salt and pepper, cover the pan and leave to simmer (Flemish: stoven) over a low heat for about an hour at 180 °C in the oven. Taste from time to time and flavour to taste.

Meanwhile cut the baguette into slices 1cm thick and spread with mustard.

Then add the beer, a little wine and as well as the baguette and a spoonful of sugar to the meat and leave to cook until the meat is tender.

Finally mix in the sauce.

Wash the chicories, boil for c. 15 minutes, dry on kitchen roll and cut off the stems.

For the bechamel sauce, melt the butter, add the flour and leave to brown, remove from the heat and add the milk, stirring continuously with a wooden spoon. Then return to the heat, stir and add in the double cream and crème fraiche. Flavour with salt, pepper and nutmeg.

Roll each chicory in one slice of ham and place in a gratin dish. Add the sauce, generously scatter grated cheese on top and gratinate in a preheated oven for c. 20 minutes at 200 °C.

Serve the meat in the sauce with the chicory.

Nic Nac Guimauve

(Belgian Christmas biscuits with meringue)

140 g	butter
140 g	icing sugar
1	sachet vanilla sugar
2	eggs
2 tbsp	rum or rum flavouring
	Juice of half a lemon
270 g	flour (soft)
	Pinch of Salt

Meringue

3	egg whites
200 g	icing sugar
	Pinch of salt
	Hundreds and thousands (for decorating)

For the crumbly piped biscuit, preheat a fan oven to 180 °C.

Beat the butter, sugar and vanilla sugar until light and fluffy. Stir in the two eggs. Add the rum and lemon juice. Finally, fold in the flour.

Transfer the biscuit dough to a piping bag and pipe kisses onto a baking tray lined with greaseproof paper.

Bake for c. 15 minutes and leave to cool.

For the meringue, beat half of the icing sugar with the egg white until it forms stiff peaks. The mix is stiff enough when you can turn the bowl upside down without the mixture sliding out. Then gently stir in the rest of the sugar.

Transfer the meringue to another piping bag, using a star nozzle, pipe onto a baking tray lined with greaseproof paper and bake in the oven until the shapes are solid. Immediately place the fresh meringue onto the freshly baked biscuits, which are a little damp.

You can also pipe the meringue roses directly onto the biscuits and bake them together, but this does not always work as well. The meringue can be coloured using different food colouring.

Belgium

Bulgaria

Vesela koleda i shtastliva nova godina **Tíxa nóšt, svjáta nóšt**

In Bulgaria, many customs that were suppressed during the Communist period have now been brought back to life. *Pitka*, a fortune bread, is baked once more, the yule log *Budnik* is set alight and *snejanka*, the snowflake, helps Father Christmas to hand out presents. The Christmas celebration takes three whole days. According to Bulgarian tradition, the number of celebration days must be an odd number. It's not just nuts and certain spices on the table that will decide whether or not the coming year will be a success, but also whether the men are successful when diving into the ice-cold river for the cross.

The upheaval at the end of 1989 also had an effect on celebration days and customs in Bulgaria. The socialist holidays were abolished, while Christian traditions were once again revived. Among other things, *pitka* is baked, the traditional fortune bread in the shape of flowers, crosses or other Christian motifs. Whoever finds the coin hidden in the dough in their piece will have a happy and successful year ahead.

On 6 December, *Vater Roger* fills St Nicholas sacks for the children, and fish is eaten to commemorate St Nicolas.

In Bulgaria, as in many other countries in Europe, an important element of Christmas preparations is the yule log, *Budnik*, often the trunk of an oak tree, elm or pear tree. This is fetched from the forest by a young man of the family, who wears his best suit to do so. On the way back to the house, the trunk is not allowed to touch the floor. Once home, the wood is placed in a small fireplace which is filled with wine, oil and incense. The whole family gathers round and recites prayers as the log burns.

The Christmas celebration, called *Koleda*, begins on 25 December and lasts for three days. This also signifies the end of the fasting period that begins in the middle of November for the Orthodox Church. The celebrations are already underway one day before.

However, on Christmas Eve, only vegetarian food is served, such as bean soup, *sarma* (sour cabbage leaves stuffed with rice), dried chillies with beans, stuffed peppers, *Baniza* (puff pastry with various fillings), pickled vegetables and honey with garlic and nuts.

All these dishes and ingredients have symbolic meanings. The onions ensure prosperity and the garlic protects from evil spirits. The legumes stand for health and the honey for the sweetness of life.

An uneven number of dishes is important, which is why families conscious of this tradition prepare seven, nine or even thirteen courses. This final number is evocative of the twelve apostles with Jesus during the Last Supper.

To drink there is beer, wine and schnapps, often a home-brewed fruit schnapps.

As a gift for the future, each guest receives a nut placed on their plate, which must be cracked immediately. It is said that the coming year will be as good as what's inside. If the nut is somewhat shrivelled, this indicates rather bad times ahead.

After this glimpse into the future, the oldest person at the table gives out a piece of bread to everyone.

In Bulgaria, there will always be a small bunch of basil on the table as part of the decorations, which is bound

Baniza.

together with a red thread. Red symbolises the colour of life and the basil is said to bring good health.

In the past, a silver coin hung on the red thread and a small candle was attached in the middle of the bunch, which had to burn on Christmas Eve, Christmas day and New Year's Day. You could call this Bulgaria's answer to the Advent wreath.

After the meal, the table is actually not cleared away since, in the old days, the people in Bulgaria believed that their dead relatives would come for dinner during the night.

One custom that is slowly fading from memory is the young, unmarried men singing, the *Koledari*. As part of this, the group go from house to house bearing *Survatschki*, which are cherry branches decorated with many colours. The men lightly pat the residents on the back and wish them wealth and good health in a traditional manner. For their efforts, the singers are rewarded with money, food and other gifts. Moreover, they carry long wooden rods with which they skewer *kravai* prepared by the residents –round bread with a hole in the middle.

In the night on 24 December into 25 December, *Djado koleda* (Father Christmas) brings presents for all the children who have been good throughout the year. *Snejanka*, the "snowflake" helps him to hand out the presents.

During the communist period in Bulgaria, there were only Christmas trees for New Year. Nowadays, they are often put up two days before *Koleda* and decorated with colourful lights or candles, ornaments and small cotton balls, which are supposed to look like snow.

In Bulgaria, 25 and 26 December are national holidays. On these days, rich dishes with pork and chicken or puff pastry filled with cheese are served up, with cake for pudding.

In some villages and small towns, they also celebrate *Jordanov* den, 6 January, according to the old calendar. There is one very special custom for this. The village priest throws a cross into the nearest river and the young men jump into the ice-cold water, diving after the cross. Whoever successfully emerges with the treasure will go into the new year with happiness, prosperity and wealth. After his freezing dive, the grateful victor visits all his neighbours to wish them all the best for the coming year. In some regions, the men sing, dance and play music, sometimes even with drums and bagpipes, during the ritual in the wintry cold depths.

Shiroka Laka, a village in South Bulgaria.

Bulgaria

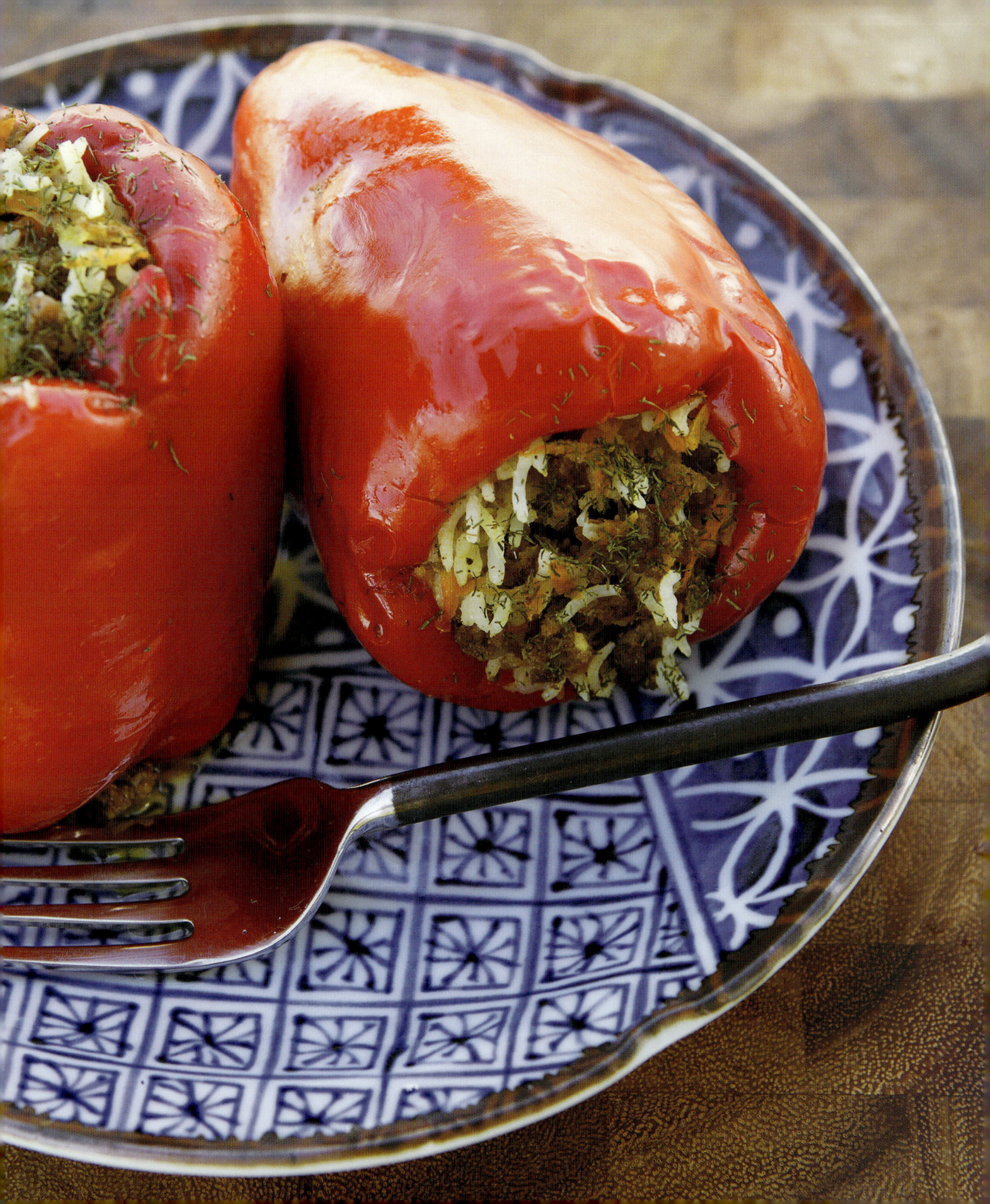

Bob chorba
(Bean soup)

250 g	beans, white, brown or black
2	carrots
2	onions
1-2	bell peppers
2	tomatoes
	Salt
	Oil
	Parsley, chopped
	Mint, chopped

Wash the carrots, onions and bell peppers and cut them into small pieces.

Having soaked the beans the previous day, boil them in a pan with salted water and a little oil. After boiling for 20 minutes, add the chopped vegetables. When the beans are done, mix in the chopped tomatoes. After boiling for a further 10 minutes, add the parsley and mint to the pan. Add salt to taste.

Spicy pepper emphasises the character of the soup.

Palneni chushki s oriz
(Stuffed peppers)

10–12	large peppers (c. 500g)
250 g	minced meat
125 g	rice
125 g	fresh mushrooms, or a few dried mushrooms
1–2	onions
1–2	carrots
1–2	tomatoes, diced
	Salt
	Oil
	Picantina (typical Bulgarian taste-enhancing spice mix)
	Parsley, dill
	Yoghurt

Fry the onions, mushrooms and carrots in 100-150 g oil. Add the minced meat and stir it all together. Meanwhile, put the rice in a bowl with hot water. Then rinse with cold water, add to the pan and mix everything thoroughly. Season with half a teaspoon of salt and some *Picantina*. Finely chop the parsley and dill and add to the pan.

Stuff the peppers with the mixture and seal with diced tomato. Pour some oil over the stuffed peppers. Then put them on a baking tray in the oven.

Sprinkle ½ cup of water onto the baking tray. Bake the peppers in the oven at 250–300 °C for about an hour. They can be served with yoghurt.

Pitka

(Christmas bread)

500 g	plain flour
	Pinch of baking powder
15 g	yeast
½ l	yoghurt, lukewarm
	Pinch of sugar
2	eggs
100 g	butter, melted
1 tsp	salt

For brushing

1	egg yolk, mixed with
1 tbsp	water

Mix the flour and baking powder in a bowl. In a well in the middle, add the yeast to 1/8 l yoghurt, with the sugar dissolved in this. Then stir everything together with the flour to make a dough. Leave the mixture to rise for 15 minutes.

Thoroughly mix the rest of the yoghurt along with the eggs, melted butter and some salt into the dough and knead until smooth. Cover the mixture and leave to rise in a warm place for another c. 45 minutes.

Turn the dough onto a worktop dusted with flour and knead again, incorporating a coin, and shape into 4 small loaves. Place on a greased baking tray, cover with a tea towel and leave to rise for another c. 15 minutes. Then brush the loaves with the egg yolk and bake in the pre-heated oven for c. 25 minutes.

DENMARK

Glædelig jul og godt nytår

Glade jul, dejlige jul

In Denmark, the Advent period starts as early as November when the Danes enjoy drinking *Julebryg* and *Glögg*. In the weeks running up to Christmas Eve, advent calendars, wreaths and candles are common sights. St Lucy's Day is also celebrated during this light-deprived wintery waiting period. Gift-bearing Nicholas is not known: they have *Nisse* for that, legendary imps whose image is used everywhere for Christmas decorations and decorates the Christmas tree. The Danes celebrate Christmas itself with a feast, all very *hyggeligt* (cosy)!

Pubs across the whole country start serving *Julebryg*, a Christmas beer, very early, from the so-called j-day, the first Friday in November. Similarly, *Juleforkost* takes place during the Advent period. For the most part, these are work parties where they enjoy various fish and meat dishes.

This popular Christmas beer is not the only thing available from November. This is when the Danes can also buy Christmas stamps, freshly printed every year, the *julemærke*. They were brought to Advent life in 1904 by post office clerk *Einar Holbøll*. Profit from their sales is donated to charity.

In addition, the weeks before Christmas in Denmark are marked with an Advent wreath in the classical manner. There is also a widely popular alternative to this – large Advent candles with 24 tick marks.

As well as conventional Advent calendars, the *Julekalendar* is also very popular on TV, a 24-part Christmas series. Both children and adults settle down in front of their TV screens to watch Christmas tales featuring nisser, Danish dwarves.

Imagine a *nissen* as an old man with a white beard and a red hat, roughly as tall as a ten year-old child. According to old legends, he traditionally lives in houses and stables.

From here, the comical creature can look after the property and the animals. However if the attentive imp is not treated well then he will play tricks on the occupants or might even leave the house completely. The name *Nisse* is a derivative of Niels, which is the Danish form of Nicholas.

While in Denmark it might be unheard of for St Nicholas to deliver presents, the *Julenisse* (Christmas nisse) is a fixed part of Danish Christmas tradition. He helps Father Christmas to prepare all the presents.

On farms, it was, and still is, customary to place a large bowlful of semolina pudding or *Risengrød* (rice pudding) on the roof. This dish is the Christmas meal for the *Nisser* who live there, to put them in a good mood.

On 13 December, *Lucia* is celebrated in Denmark as this date marked winter solstice in the Middle Ages. Light returns and the days get increasingly longer. In schools, nurseries and some care homes it is traditional for the "Lucia bride", dressed in white from head to toe, to light up the wintery darkness with candles in a wreath on her head. A small group of children dressed in white robes follow her holding candles and singing the Lucia song. This custom originates from Sweden.

Hygge (cosiness) is an important attitude towards life in Denmark.

23 December is "little Christmas Eve". The Christmas tree is often decorated on this day. Any other preparations for the cosy Christmas celebration get underway the following day, and the Danes enjoy lots of *Glögg* – the Danish version of mulled wine.

Julehjerte is THE Danish Christmas decoration, a red and white woven Christmas heart made of glossy paper. These hearts are not only hung on the Christmas tree, but are used as decorations everywhere. Small pictures of the Danish Christmas dwarf can also be found all over the place.

On 24 December, many Danes go to church during the day. In the evening, a traditional Christmas dinner is on the menu, with goose, duck, turkey or roast pork served. Red cabbage and boiled potatoes, caramelised in the pan, are served alongside this.

For pudding, the Danes enjoy the popular *Ris á l'amande*, with a whole almond inside, and cherry sauce. Whoever is lucky enough to find the almond receives a present.

After dinner, the candles are lit on the Christmas tree and there is singing and maybe even dancing around the tree. The presents come after this.

The family meet again on 25 December for a cold buffet with some additional small, warm dishes. Of course, there will always be herring – it is said to "swim" the best in beer and schnapps.

For many Danes, 26 December is celebrated in much the same way as the previous day, only not at home but at someone else's house.

Christmas time in Denmark is a celebration of family, and *Hygge* (cosiness) plays a very important part. Everyone sitting peacefully together, warmed by the *Glögg*, the scent of Christmas baking, and candles burning – a particularly *hyggeligt* (cosy) scene in Denmark.

Sildesalat

(Danish herring salad)

2	herring, marinated
1	apple
2	small boiled potatoes
2	small red turnips, pickled
1	small pickled gherkin

Dressing

75 g	mayonnaise or crème fraiche
4 tbsp	yoghurt
1	onion, finely diced
3 tbsp	vinegar
½ tsp	mustard powder
	Salt, pepper

Mix all the ingredients for the dressing together thoroughly. Cut the other ingredients into small cubes and stir together with the dressing. Serve with bread (dark rye bread).

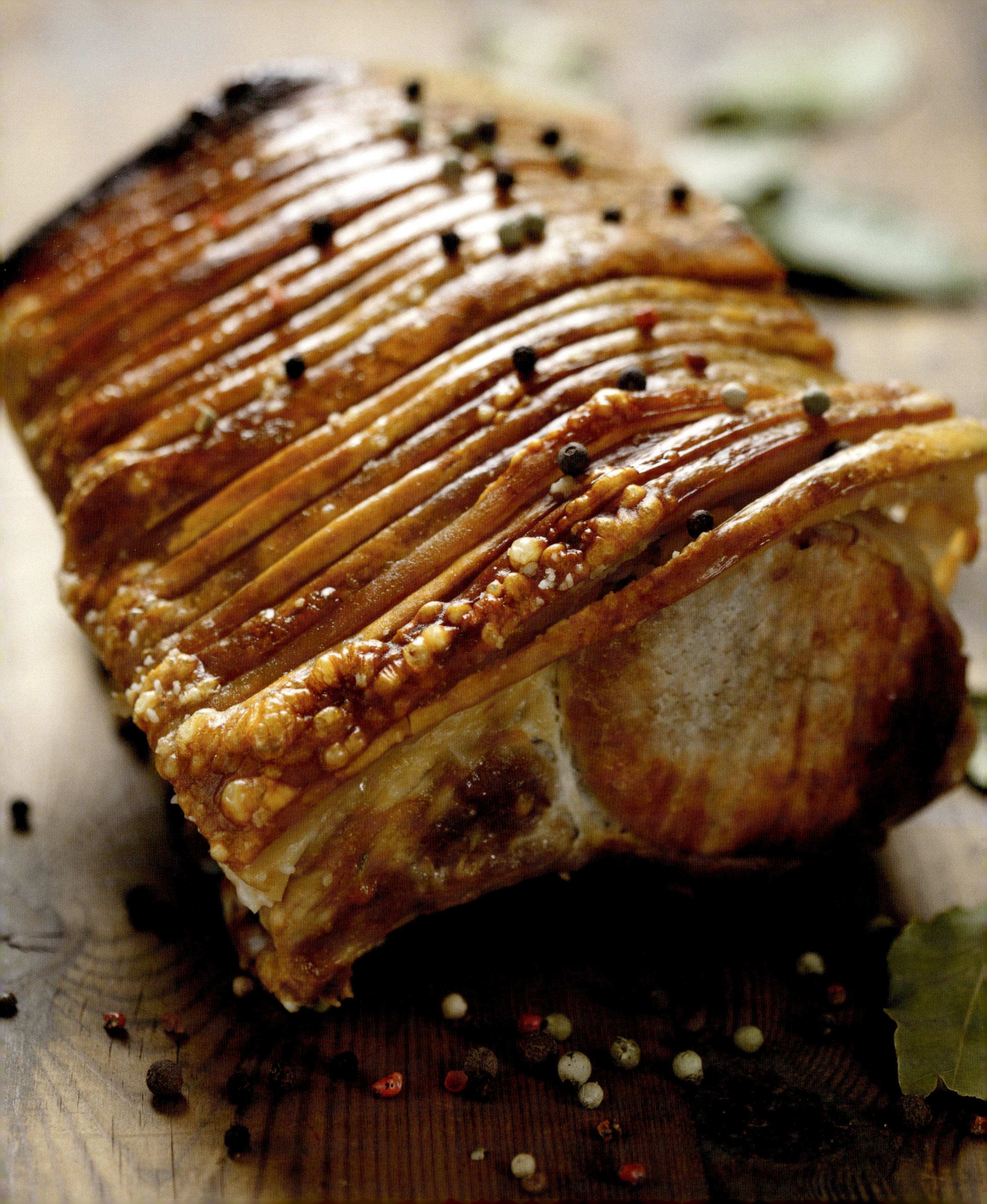

Flæskesteg

(Roast pork with crackling,
with potatoes and Danish red cabbage)

1 kg   roast pork, with rind
Salt, pepper
Garlic powder
Orange salt
Thyme pepper
Bay leaves
Caraway seeds, ground

For the sauce
Savoury sauce lebkuchen (Reibelebkuchen,
a plain, slightly spiced Lebkuchen)
Mustard
Curry powder
Ketchup
Vegetable stock

Place the roast pork rind side down in boiling water or in stock about 3cm deep and boil for c. 20 minutes. The now soft rind can then easily be cut into pieces.

Then rub the salt, pepper and other herbs into the rind. Place in a roasting tin or casserole dish and generously sprinkle the garlic powder onto the rind. Roast in the pre-heated oven at 220 °C for 25 minutes. If necessary, add a little oil. The core temperature should be at least 75 °C. Now switch on the grill in the roasting oven and grill for a further 20 minutes. If the core temperature reaches 85–90 °C, switch off the oven and leave the roast meat in the oven to keep warm.

Bring the roasting broth to the boil on the hob. The flavoursome juices from cooking the meat can also be dissolved with a little water. Thicken with the sauce lebkuchen and flavour with mustard, ketchup, curry powder and vegetable stock.

Brown glazed potatoes
1 kg potatoes, small, boiled and peeled
85 g sugar
75 g butter

Dry the boiled, peeled potatoes with a piece of kitchen roll. Brown the sugar in a pan. Add the butter and the potatoes. When the butter has melted, quickly heat the potatoes over a high heat and brown them by stirring.

Danish red cabbage
1 head of red cabbage (c. 1 kg)
100 g lard
1 glass red wine
½ cup vinegar (wine vinegar), diluted
1 onion, finely diced
5 tbsp jelly (currant jelly)
Salt, pepper
Sugar
Pinch of ground cloves

Shred the red cabbage and heat up the lard. Add the diced onion and leave until they start to go translucent. Add in the shredded cabbage and the remaining ingredients, mix well and stew for about an hour. Add salt and pepper to taste and serve.

Denmark

Ris à l'amande

(Danish Christmas almond rice pudding)

250 g	pudding rice
1 l	milk
250 ml	water
	Pinch of salt
250 ml	double cream, lightly beaten
100 g	almonds, chopped
	Sugar, vanilla sugar
	Cinnamon
1 tsp	butter

Put the pudding rice into the boiling water and boil for two minutes. Add the milk, cover and leave to simmer over a very low heat for about 35 minutes, stirring frequently. Serve the rice pudding with butter, sugar and cinnamon. In Denmark, they like to drink malt beer with this.

For the Danish *ris à l'amande*, fold the almonds and lightly beaten cream into the cooled rice pudding and add sugar to taste.

Æblekage

(Danish apple cake)

1 kg	apples, tart, peeled and cut into slices
5 tbsp	sugar
1 tsp	cinnamon
75 g	butter
100 g	sugar
200 g	cream cheese
3	eggs
100 g	bread for toasting, chopped into small cubes
100 g	almonds, chopped

Scatter the cinnamon and sugar over the apples and place in a greased baking dish. Separate the eggs and beat the egg whites until they form stiff peaks. Stir together the butter, sugar, cream cheese, egg yolks, almonds and cubes of bread to form a mixture.

Fold in the egg whites and spoon the mixture over the apples. Bake at 200 °C for c. 30 minutes.

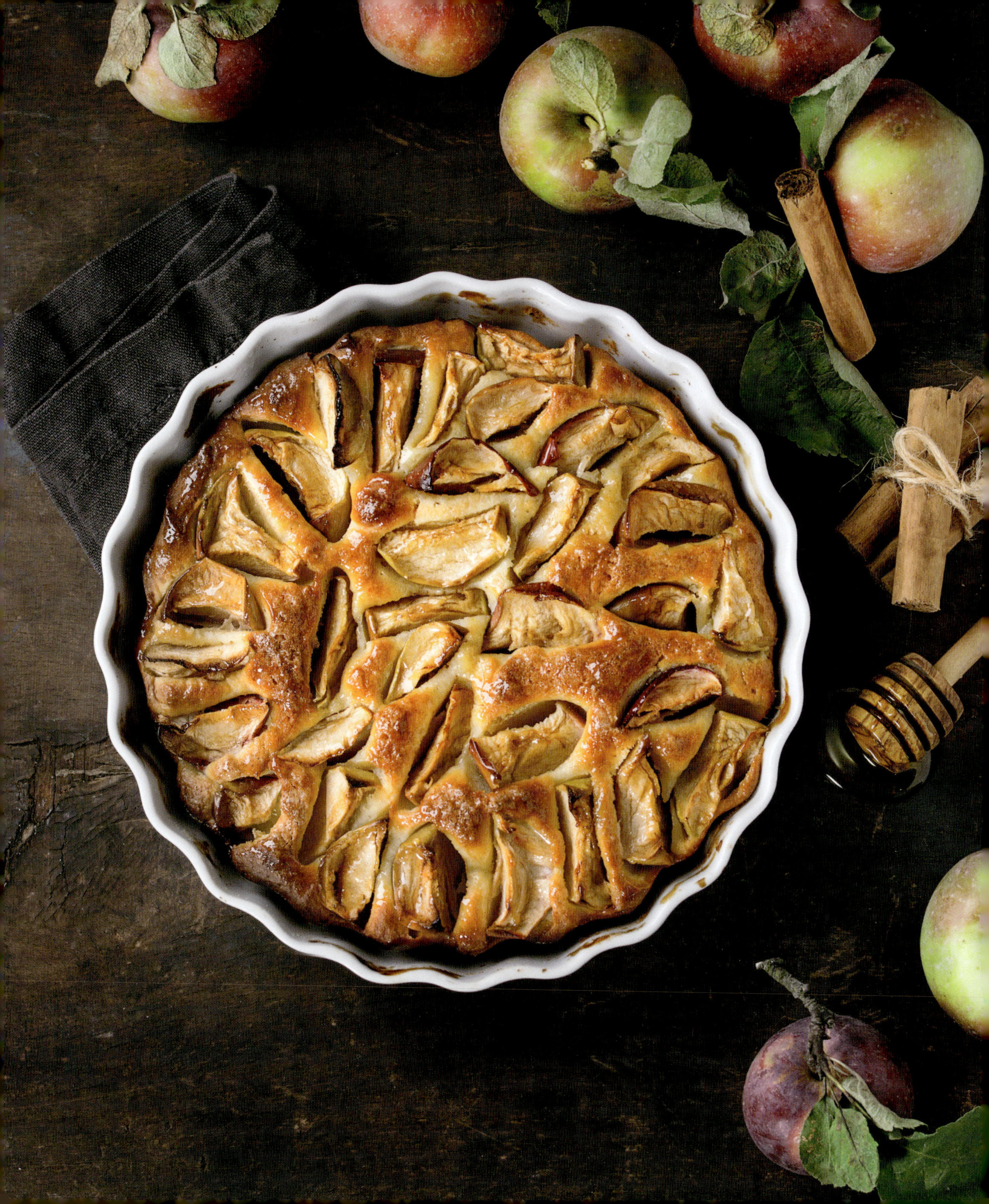

Germany

Fröhliche Weihnachten und ein glückliches neues Jahr　　　　　　　**Stille Nacht, heilige Nacht**

Wooden arches adorned with candles, colourful nutcrackers, Räuchermännchen (incense-smoking figurines) and wooden toys – all of these things are inextricably linked to the Ore Mountains in Germany. Here, the mining culture is reflected in their Christmas customs which in turn represent the diverse nature of Christmas traditions across Germany. Here, Advent begins with the *Männelwecken.* This involves fetching the wooden Christmas figures from the loft and setting them up. *Glückauf- und Lichtlabende* are typical events during this time. The *Neunerlei* feast is served up on Christmas Eve with every course having its own symbolic meaning.

In the Ore Mountain region, the cosy and bright Advent period starts with the *Männelwecken*. The famous wooden Christmas figures, including Räuchermänner, angels and miners, nutcrackers, candles arches, pyramids, mangers and all the rest of the *Mannelzeig* (display) are dusted off and used to decorate rooms and windows from the Saturday before the first day of Advent.

Family and friends gather in front of the large wooden pyramids, often four storeys high, light the candles and, with a gentle nudge, they set the large fan wheel spinning. The rising heat propels the pyramids that have been lovingly hand-crafted, and these table carousels keep on spinning until the candles have burned all the way down. This happy scene is rounded off with a glass of herbal schnapps.

There is a long tradition of Christmas markets in the Ore Mountains. Cosy log cabins entice passers-by with local wooden crafts, creative wooden toys, candles and tasty Christmas delights. The oldest of these markets is thought to be the Striezelmarkt in Dresden.

During Advent, *Glückauf- und Lichtlabende* take place across the whole mining region of the Ore Mountains, which explains why the roots many of their customs can be found in mining culture. Nowadays, there is singing and chattering in the traditional *Hutznstube* where, in the past, the miners would whittle away while the women sat at the spinning wheel. The old mining days and their traditions live on. The largest mountain parade in Germany takes place every year in Annaberg-Buchholz in front of myriad guests, marking the start of the Advent period – with thousands of miners dressed in Renaissance clothing.

Every family will have their own Christmas Eve traditions. One example might be lighting a Christmas Eve candle, in a candlestick passed down from one generation to

A Christmas Market in the Black Forest.

Christmas stollen.

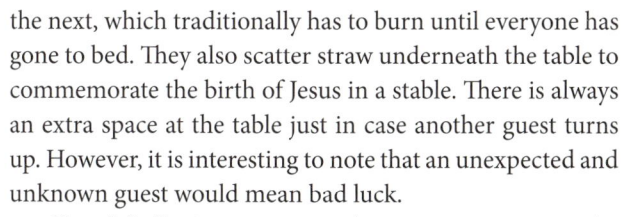

Night watchman at Christmas.

the next, which traditionally has to burn until everyone has gone to bed. They also scatter straw underneath the table to commemorate the birth of Jesus in a stable. There is always an extra space at the table just in case another guest turns up. However, it is interesting to note that an unexpected and unknown guest would mean bad luck.

Church bells ring out across the country at 6pm on the dot, which means it is time for the "Neunerlei", traditional Christmas food in the Ore Mountains. Every family member must have a bite of each dish, since every course has its own symbolic meaning.

Bratwurst is supposed to bring geniality, sauerkraut should stop life taking a sour turn, lentils are said to ensure you are never short of cash and *Klöße* (dumplings), carp and herring should guarantee that any "riches" never get lost. Christmas goose, roast pork and rabbit (*Kuhhase*) should bring happiness and faithfulness, and kompot symbolises a certain joie de vivre. Rolls or buttermilk are thought to prevent illness and headaches, nuts and almonds should ensure peaceful everyday life in the coming year, and finally mushrooms or beetroot are supposed to bring joy, happiness and a good harvest. Before or after eating, and in any case before the presents are handed out by *Rupperich*, a kind of St Nicholas figure, they sing a specific Christmas Eve song, which includes stanzas dating from 1862, as well as additional individual verses. They tuck into the Christmas stollen, everyone's favourite, between *Neunerlei* and *Mettenschicht* (midnight mass).

The customs in this *Losnächten* are based on the pre-Christian celebration, Winter Solstice, which also included processions of the dead and spirits. One relic of this is the tradition of pouring lead on New Year's Eve. This traditionally involves molten metal being poured through an old bowl that has been handed down through the generations.

Epiphany, also known as *Hochneujahr*, is followed by the *Mariä Lichtmess* on 2 February, marking the end of the Christmas period. This is interesting because it is an example of a Catholic celebration that is upheld in a Protestant region. Later on, the Christmas tree is taken down and put away, the *Mannelzeig* packed into boxes and put away for safekeeping until the next *Männelwecken*.

Germany

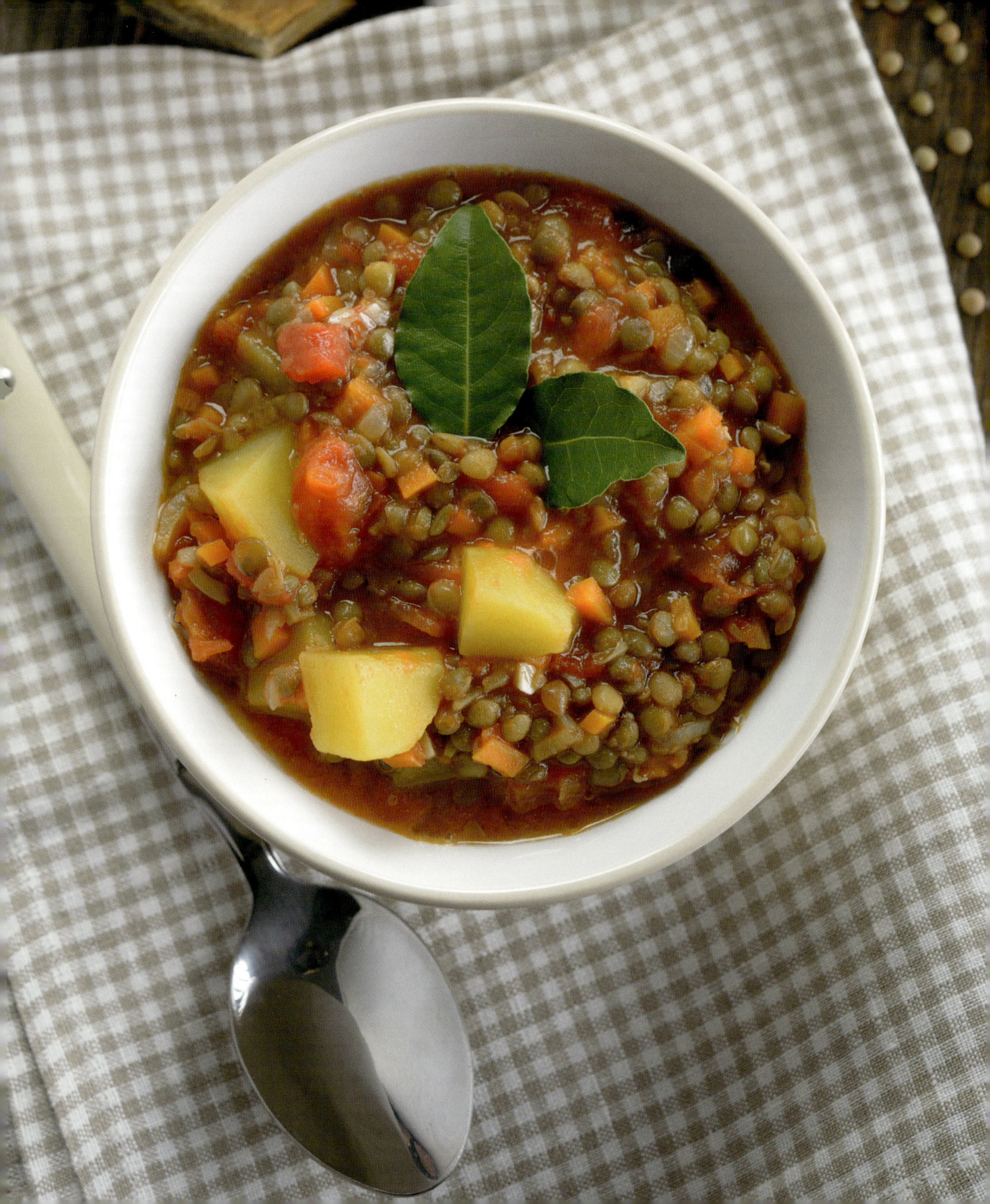

Lentil soup

	Leftover vegetables or 1 bunch of soup greens
500 g	lentils
400 g	potatoes, peeled and cubed
400 g	onions, cut into rings
½ packet	(Chemnitz) savoury lebkuchen, finely diced
2	knockwurst
1½ l	water or vegetable stock
2 tbsp	sugar
2 tbsp	vinegar
	Salt
	Freshly ground pepper

Boil the lentils together with the soup vegetables and a pinch of salt until soft. Boil the potatoes separately with a little water and salt until soft.

Cut the knockwurst into slices and fry. Then, add in the onions and fry further until they are transparent and soft. Now add the sugar and savoury lebkuchen and continue to stir.

Remove the soup greens from the soft-boiled lentils, chop them into small pieces and add the potatoes and the knockwurst-onion mixture. Pour over a little water or stock. Stir well and add 1–2 tbsp vinegar. A pinch of freshly ground pepper finishes the soup off wonderfully!

Tip: Left to stand and then reheated, the soup tastes even better!

Baked carp

600 g	carp fillets, bled and ready to cook
2	eggs
	Flour and breadcrumbs for coating
200 g	butter
	Oil
2	lemons
½ bunch	parsley, finely chopped
	Salt, pepper

Cut the carp into strips 1–2 cm thick. Season the eggs well with salt and pepper in a deep dish and beat well.

Put the breadcrumbs in another deep dish. First coat the strips of carp with flour, then cover in the egg mixture and coat with the breadcrumbs on all sides.

Melt the butter with a little oil over a medium heat in a large, heavy pan and then fry the carp pieces in there until golden brown.

Finally, remove, leave to dry on kitchen roll and serve with finely chopped parsley.

Tip: When coating, always mix salt and pepper into the eggs. This does not dry out the fish and it remains succulent.

Always leave the coated fillets for 30–60 minutes before frying. The breading will stick better.

Germany

Potato salad

3	medium-sized potatoes
100 g	boil beef or sausages, cut into strips (for example Extrawurst, Polish sausage, etc.)
1 tub	natural yoghurt
1	small jar of sour pickles
3 tbsp	oil
2	apples, peeled and cored
1	onion, finely chopped
	Pepper, salt
	Fresh parsley, 1 tomato and 1 pepper
2 tbsp	Bautzner mustard, average strength

Wash the potatoes, boil with their skins on, then peel and cut into slices about 0.5 cm thick. Flavour the meat or sausage with yoghurt, pepper, salt, oil and a little of the liquid from the pickles.

Cut the sour pickles, apples, tomatoes and pepper, if necessary, into cubes and fold into the warm potatoes with the mustard, onions and the meat salad yoghurt mixture.

Leave the potato salad to stand and infuse – preferably leave overnight in the fridge. If it becomes too solid, add in a little more of the liquid from the pickles. Finally season to taste. To serve, scatter with finely chopped parsley.

Potato cake

500 g	potatoes from the previous day, boiled and peeled
250 g	flour
250 g	butter
3	eggs
2 tbsp	sugar
1 cup	raisins (soaked overnight in apple juice, amaretto liqueur or rum)
1 sachet	baking powder
	Cinnamon sugar mixture

Knead the mashed potatoes, flour, baking powder, 150 g of the butter, the eggs, sugar and raisins together to form a smooth dough. Roll out thinly onto a greased baking tray and spread 50 g of the remaining butter over the top.

Bake in a preheated oven at 225 °C for c. 25 minutes. Take out of the oven and spread another 50 g of butter over it and scatter with the cinnamon sugar. Best eaten warm.

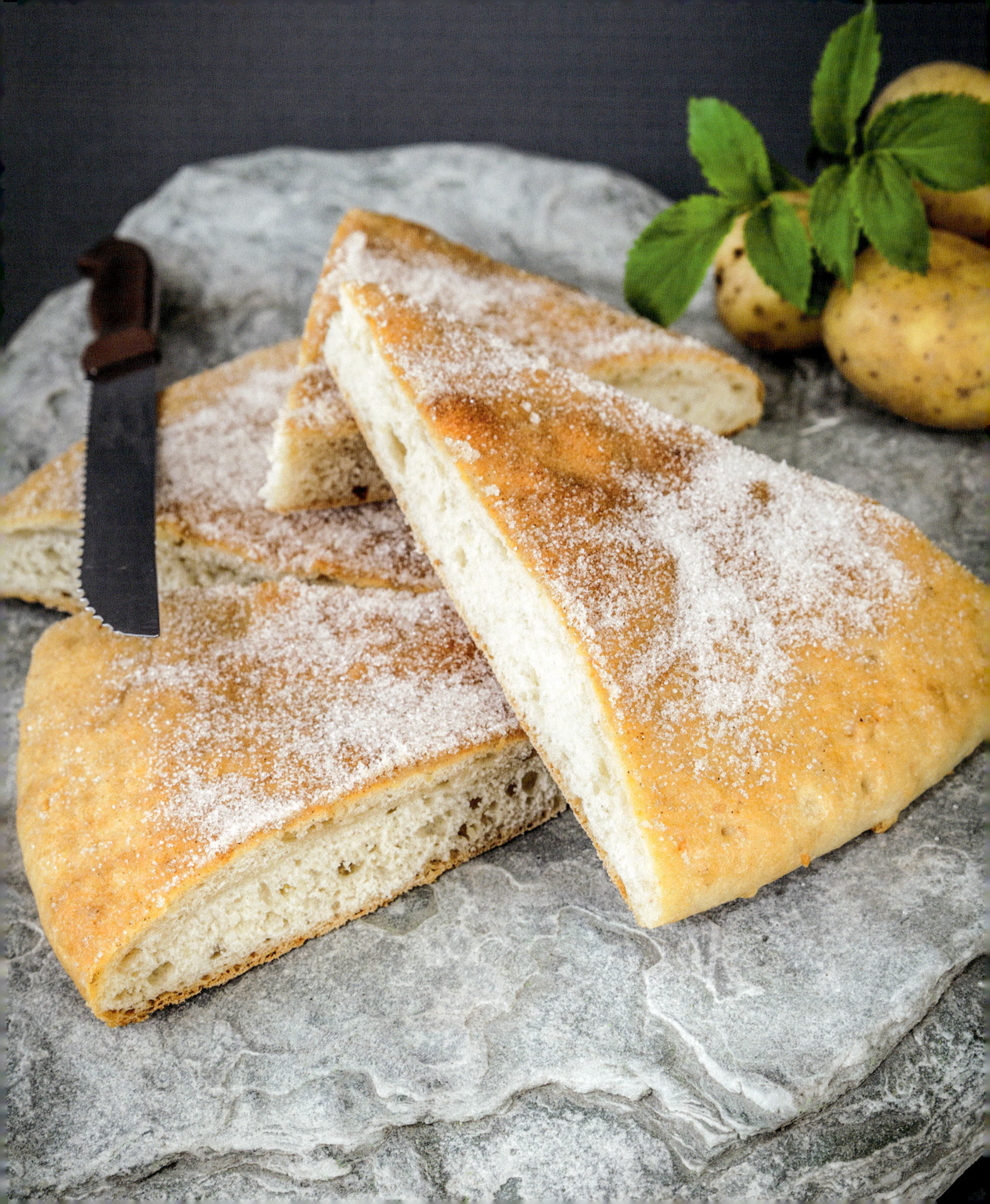

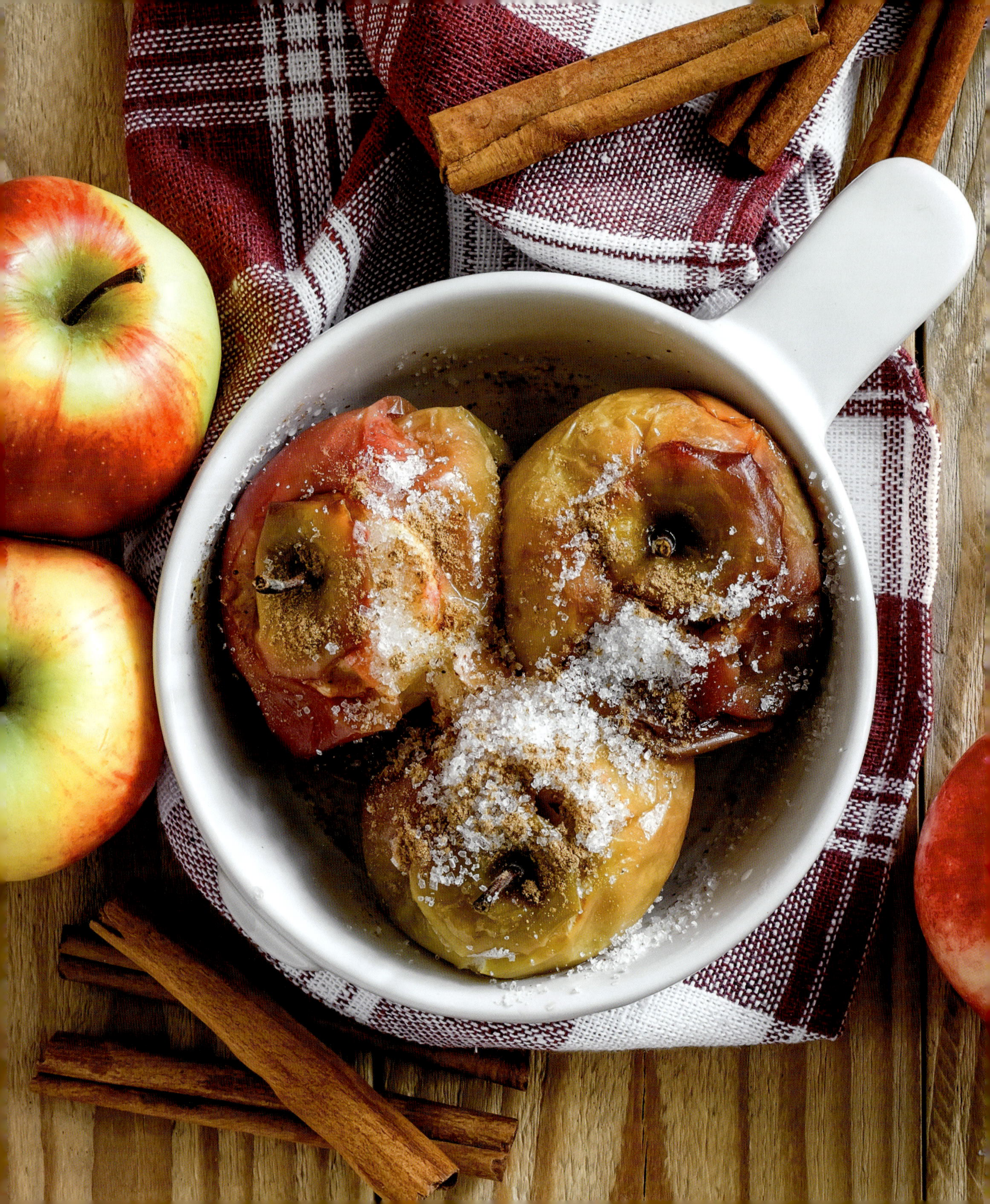

Baked apples

4	large crunchy apples
	Butter
	Oil
	Aluminium foil
	Custard, for serving
3 tbsp	marzipan
2–3	hazelnuts, grated
	A little lemon juice
	Hot water

Wash and dry the apples. With an apple corer, cut out the core, stem and any flowers. Stir the marzipan with a little hot water, mix in the grated nuts and add lemon juice to taste. Fill each cored apple with the mix and top with a small knob of butter. Make small packets out of the aluminium foil, grease them and place the apples inside.

Then, put the apples in a preheated oven and roast at 175 °C for half an hour.

When the apples are done, open the foil slightly and scatter sugar over the apples.

The apples can be served with custard.

ESTONIA

Häid jõule ja head uut aastat **Püha öö, õnnistud öö**

How long does the Christmas period last in Estonia? What do gnomes and pixies have to do with Christmas in this country and when should you expect their evil tricks? How long have Christmas trees been around in Estonia? Who brings the presents and when are they given out? Who declares Christmas peace? For how long do you wish each other a happy new year and what do you use to help to hold back the tears? The answers to these questions are just as interesting as the pursuit of the culinary specialities *Verivorst, Sült, Jõululeib* and *Pipparkogid* that are typical of this country.

The advent period begins on the first of four Sundays before Christmas. In Estonia, the Christmas holiday itself lasts for several days and mixes old pagan customs with new religious ones. In the past, Christmas was traditionally celebrated from *Thomasdat*, that is from 21 December, until Epiphany, 6 January, today "only" for four days, from 24 to 27 December.

Unlike in many other European countries, St Nicholas is not particularly well known. This is why it is gnomes and witches who get up to their (evil) tricks during the Estonian winter.

Just before Christmas Eve, the brooms from the house and garden are thoroughly cleaned. However, should the goblins deem the brooms to be too dirty, then they are supposedly allowed to get up to their nasty tricks.

While gnomes reward children with sweets during the Advent period, witches have never had anything good in mind. They set out to cause misery and perform all manner of ill deeds on the locals. What is the logical answer to this? Clean your brushes! Witches can't possibly fly with a clean broom, meaning they'll have no way to get up to no good.

There is an all-round decorative festive spirit in the cities. The streets are decorated with baubles and chains of lights, and the shops are full of Christmas goods. In the period leading up to Christmas, the Estonians love to celebrate and party with good food, punch and vodka.

On the evening before 24 December, the Estonians prefer a quiet night. Families come together and go to the sauna to relax.

Every year on 24 December, the President of Estonia officially declares Christmas peace and takes part in a church service in Tallinn.

Since Estonian independence, Christmas has become a contemplative and religious festival – of course with a Christmas tree too, which has supposedly been tradition since the 15th Century. It is decorated with some sweets, a small toy, baubles and strings of light. Candles were only added more recently.

On Christmas Eve, on 24 December, there are presents under the pine tree and a large Christmas meal with *Vervivorst* (black pudding), *Sült* (head cheese), roast beef or goose, potatoes and rye bread. To wash it down, the Estonians like to drink beer or homebrewed schnapps. As well as marzipan, popular sweets are the Christmas bread *Jõululeib*, a type of fruit cake, and *Pipparkogid*, biscuits with pepper, cocoa and cinnamon.

In fact, many Estonian meals are of Russian, German or Scandinavian origin.

Jouluvana, Father Christmas, comes all the way from Finland to bring presents to the children on Christmas Eve. The Finnish gnomes are also in on the plan, specifically as Father Christmas's helpers. The small imps hand out the presents along with *Jouluvana* to anyone who is singing a song, reciting a poem or dancing.

During Christmas night, the leftovers of the Christmas meal are left out on the table for ancestors and dead relatives, according to old traditional beliefs. The lights are also left on. In Estonia, another Christmas tradition is visiting the graveyard. Once there, a candle is lit and they commemorate their ancestors.

25 December lies right at the heart of the excitement and is called *Jõulupüha*. On this day, the people in Estonia like to visit their families. Many also like to go to a restaurant or go dancing.

The festivities of the Estonian-Russian Orthodox Church do not fall on 25 December, but on 6 January. On this holiday, Epiphany is celebrated as part of midnight mass. "Jack Frost" brings small presents for the children. Many Estonians with Russian roots begin the festivities early, on New Year's Day, and these last up until 7 January – or even longer.

But let's go a few days back before the turn of the year. On New Year's Eve, the old year is bidden farewell to with a large party. Many culinary delights are prepared and it's always "dress to impress". Until midnight, they eat, drink and dance. At midnight the people gather in the streets, glass of fizz in hand, the fireworks start, and the corks are popped.

A typically Estonian custom is also pouring molten lead into the snow or in cold water. When you later examine the hardened lead by candlelight, you can harness the power of your imagination to read your fate for the coming year.

When the children are still small, they stay at home on New Year's Eve, but as soon as the kids are old enough, they all go out with their friends. In recent years, the New Year's Eve parties have been getting bigger and more glamorous.

In Estonia, people want to start the year with as few tears as possible. Therefore, they drink a glass of water on the streets at midnight so that, symbolically, they no longer have to cry that number of tears in the coming year.

They wish each other "Happy New Year" until 6 January, Epiphany. This is also a public holiday in Estonia.

The Nordic winter in Estonia is bitterly cold.

And then there is yet another celebration day that we should point out during the long, but no longer as tough, winter. Estonians celebrate *Vastlapäev* on the second Tuesday in February. In Estonia, it is said that on this day, the "backbone of winter has now been broken".

If there is still enough snow on the ground, the Estonians traditionally go ice-skating and then eat pea soup, pork knuckle and *Vastlakuklid* (sweet biscuits). For a long while, ice skating has been common on *Vastlapäev*. In the past they believed that it would result in a better harvest of grains, linseed and hemp.

Estonia 43

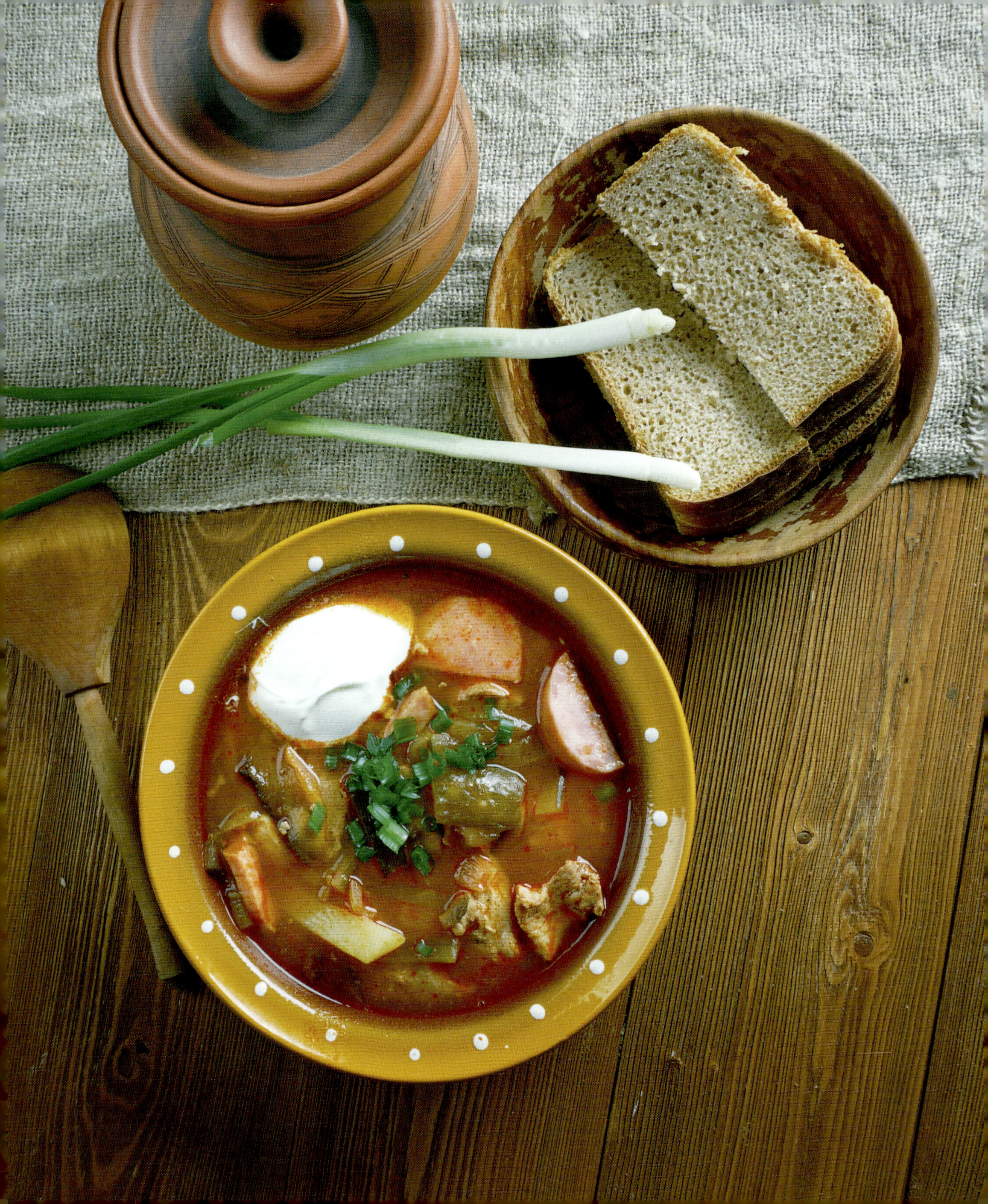

Seljanka

(Russian-style sausage stew)

200 g	salami
200 g	sausage (jagdwurst)
200 g	sausage (poultry sausage)
200 g	lardons
5	medium onions
4	red peppers
150 g	tomato puree
5	pickled gherkins and water from the jar
1 tbsp	Sambal Oelek (spiced chilli sauce or 1 chilli pepper, dried)
1	bay leaf
	Stock (stock cube)
1 tsp	mustard
3	cloves of garlic
	Dill
	Lemon
	Sour cream

Fry the lardons, then add the diced sausage, except the salami. Leave everything to sizzle away nicely for a bit. Then, mix in the salami, leave to brown for a little longer, then add the onions until they are transparent. If necessary, add a little water.

Now, mix in the diced pepper, the tomato puree and the crushed garlic and leave to simmer. Then, add the gherkins with a little of the water from the jar and all the herbs.

Pour over up to 1 ½ litres of water, then add the stock and leave to simmer gently for 20 minutes.

Important: Leave the Seljanka to stand for a few hours before eating. Just eat with crusty bread and sour cream.

Verivorst

(Black pudding)

1 ¼ kg	pearl barley, part cooked in salted water
¾ kg	pork belly, cut into small pieces
4	medium onions, cut into slices
½ l	pig blood
	Enough pork intestines, cleaned
	Marjoram, oregano
	Powdered kummel
	Oil or lard
	Salt, pepper

Fry the onion and meat until slightly brown, add to the pearl parley and cook everything together until the mixture is cooked. Then leave to cool.

Now add the blood to the meat-barley mixture and season with salt and the herbs. Loosely fill the pig intestines with the sausage mixture and securely tie off at 15 cm intervals.

Place the sausages in lukewarm water, then bring the water to simmering point – not boiling point – and cook for about 30 minutes. After this, quickly refresh in cold water.

The black puddings are generally often baked or fried and served with sauerkraut, fried bacon, cranberry jelly or pumpkin salad.

Estonia

Mulgikapsad

(Meat dish with sauerkraut from the Mulgi region)

1 kg	sauerkraut
500 g	pork meat, thoroughly washed, or salted meat
50 g	bacon
150 g	pearl barley (pot barley), washed
1	onion, finely chopped
	Stock or water
	Salt, sugar

Fry the onion and bacon, then place the meat and the sauerkraut in alternating layers on top, placing the fattier meat below the cabbage.

Scatter the pearl barley over this and pour water over the top until the barley is covered.

Stew over a low heat until the dish is cooked. Then mix and by all means flavour with sugar.
Cut the meat before serving. Salted potatoes go well with this.

Kodused kohukesed

(Curd cheese sweets)

250 g	curd cheese
50 g	soft butter
50 g	nuts, chopped
40 g	sugar
1 tsp	vanilla sugar
200 g	chocolate icing, bittersweet

If necessary, leave the curd cheese to dry or wring out with a tea towel.

Then stir together with butter, nuts, sugar and vanilla sugar until everything is really well mixed together. Then shape the mixture into a log 2 cm thick or little balls 2 cm big and wrap in cling film and place in the freezer for half an hour.

Just before taking them out the freezer, melt the chocolate over a water bath, stirring occasionally. Then, take the curd cheese mix out, cut into pieces, place the pieces or balls into paper cases and carefully pour a teaspoon of icing over the top. Then, leave everything to cool again in the fridge, and the curd cheese sweets are ready to eat.

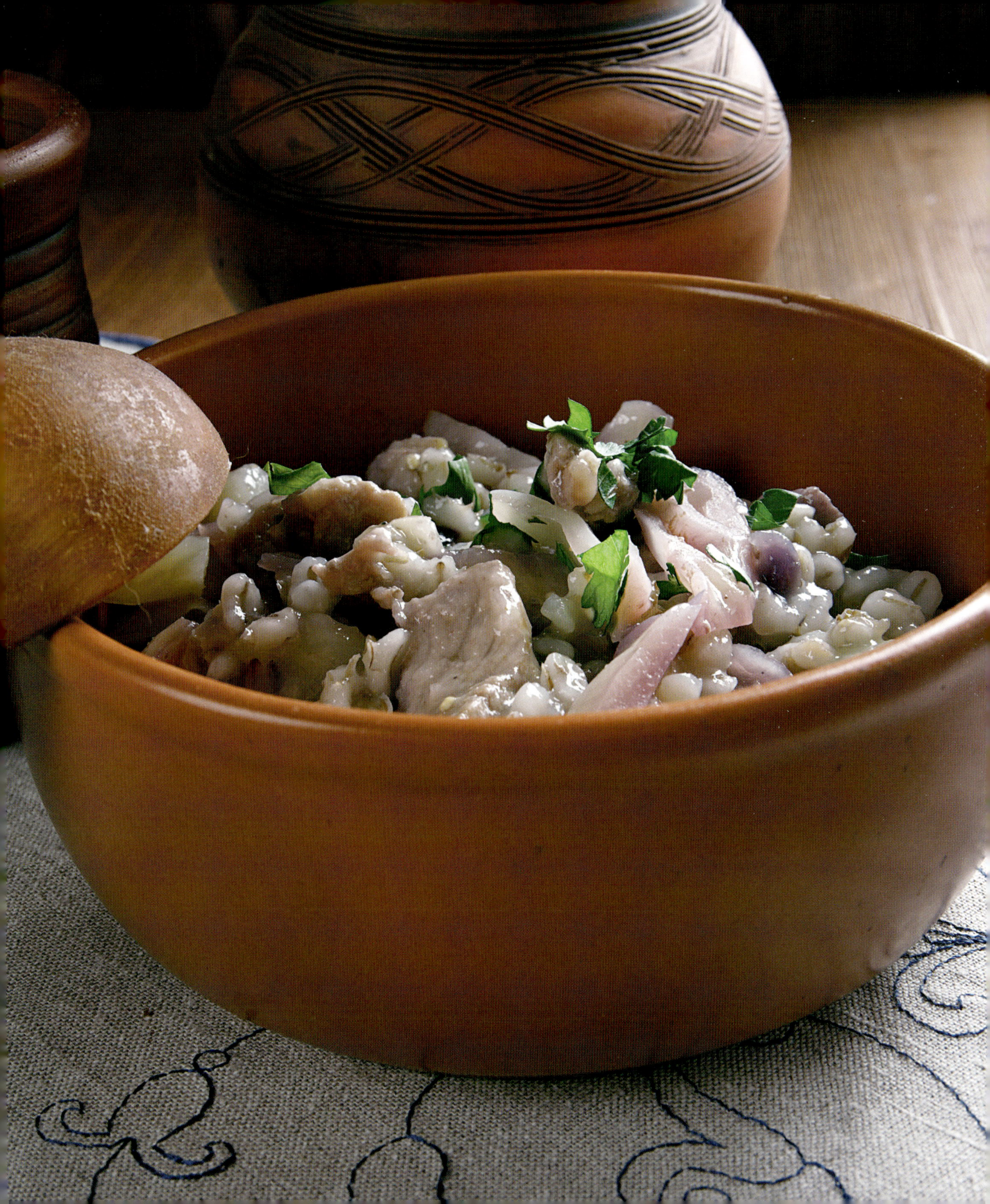

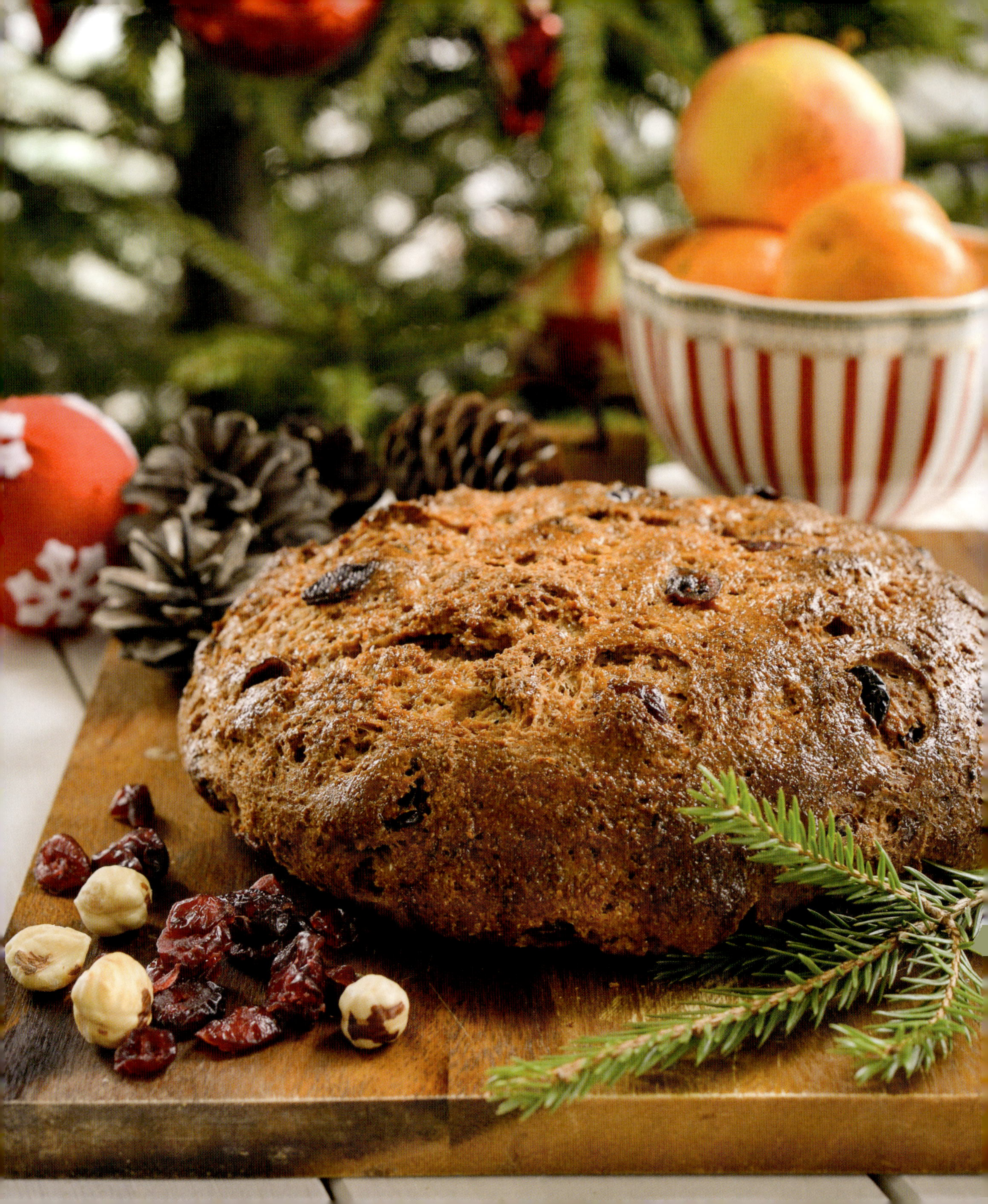

Jõululaib

(Christmas bread)

300 g	flour
1	egg
1/8 l	milk
1	cube of yeast
1 sachet	vanilla sugar
80 g	butter
	Sugar
	Salt

Nut filling

250 g	chopped nuts
150 g	breadcrumbs
2 tbsp	butter
60–80 g	granulated sugar
1 sachet	vanilla sugar
3 tbsp	honey
150 ml	milk
2–3 tbsp	raisins (optionally soaked in rum)
	Zest of one lemon
	Cinnamon

Prepare a smooth yeast dough from the ingredients for the dough. Wrap in cling film and leave to rise in a cool place.

For the filling, fry the breadcrumbs in a frying pan with the butter until golden brown.

In another pan, leave the milk to heat slowly and then dissolve the sugar, vanilla sugar and honey in the milk. Then stir in the nuts and remove from the heat.

Now add the raisins, breadcrumbs, cinnamon and lemon zest and mix well. In required, add a little extra milk.

Roll the dough out on a lightly. Floured worktop, work in the nut filling and then join together to form a loaf, wreath or nest and bake at 170–180 °C for about 30 minutes until golden brown.

Estonia

Christmas in European Microstates

Andorra · Liechtenstein · Monaco · Athos · San Marino · Vatican City

With an extensively Catholic population, Christmas in Andorra is celebrated similarly to Catalonia or neighbouring France. It's much the same in Liechtenstein: Christmas is celebrated much like in its neighbouring countries. The various stamps with Christmas motifs delight many philatelists. French and Italian influences are also reflected in Monaco's Christmas festivities. The customs in San Marino for Christmas and New Year do not differ from those in Italy.

In the monastic republic of Athos, Christmas is celebrated according to orthodox rituals, and the Christmas festivities in the Vatican (abb.) are conducted according to Roman Catholic ceremonies. The papal Christmas address *Urbi et Orbi* (Lat. "the city [Rome] and the world") is broadcast across the world on TV and radio.

Finland

Hauskaa joulua ja onnellista uutta vuotta **Jouluyö, juhlayö**

In Finland, the Christmas period starts well before the actual celebrations. During this time, you'll see lots of people wearing pointy red hats and there are parties aplenty. On 6 December, the focus isn't on St Nicholas, instead they commemorate Finnish Independence. There is no shortage of *Glöggi* in the run up to Christmas, as well as there being an abundance of Lucy girls wearing crowns of candles. Along with his wife and helpers, *Joulupukki*, the only real Father Christmas, is quite at home in Finland. In fact, every child in Finland knows his exact address. Once the Christmas tree has been decorated with *Himmeli* and Finnish flags, there is nothing left to prepare before the celebrations can get started.

Strictly speaking, Christmas in Finland starts early with the *pikkujoulu*, the name for office Christmas parties in Finland. And these might even be as early as the end of October.

A few weeks before Christmas, the streets will be teeming with people wearing pointy red hats. Children in particular like to slip into the role of Father Christmas's helpers, or *Joulupukki* as they know him.

As in many other countries, mulled wine and lebkuchen are also a big part of the Advent period in Finland. There is also a non-alcoholic version of Finnish *Glöggi*, with raisins and blanched almonds, made using a healthy dose of currant juice. Gingerbread and *Joulutortut* (Christmas stars) with a blob of jam on top can always be found at Christmas parties.

The first Sunday of Advent kicks off the actual festive season, and Georg Joseph Vogler's "Hosianna" is played in churches across the country.

6 December is not only St Nicholas's Day, but also *Itsenäisyyspäivä*, Finnish Independence Day. They remember all the casualties of the War of Independence in 1917.

St Lucy's Day is one of the high points of the Advent season – in particular in the Swedish-speaking regions of Finland. An impersonator of St Lucy, crowned with candles and accompanied by ten other girls, spreads festive cheer in hospitals and schools.

A particularly important figure is *Joulupukki*, the Finnish Father Christmas, and supposedly the only real Father Christmas in the world. *Joulupukki* lives on the mountain of Korvatunturi in Lapland, along with his wife *Joulumuori* and his reindeer *Petteri punakuono*. Many *tonttus*, small Christmas elves, spend the whole year making Christmas

Festive Christmas meal in Finland

Joulupukki on his way with *Petteri punakuono*

presents. If you have written a Christmas list, it is best to send this straight to Father Christmas himself. *Joulupukki's* exact postal address is Maakunta Katu 10, ss-96100 Rowaniemi. It is always Christmas in Santa's village and visitors travel from within Finland and from other counties all year round.

A special Christmas stamp is released every year in Finland. In 2007, it even smelt of lebkuchen. Fathers are usually responsible for sourcing the Christmas tree, which the children then decorate festively with candles, baubles and tinsel, as well as little paper flags, not just Finnish ones, but other countries too. *Himmeli* is also popular, an intricate hand-made straw decoration.

The real Christmas celebrations start in the evening on 23 December. Once the children have gone to bed, the adults decorate the house and prepare for the coming Christmas days.

For many Finnish families, a Christmas church service is part of Christmas Eve along with lighting candles in the graveyard. Christmas songs are also an important part of Christmas celebrations in Finland – not only in churches but also together with family after a traditional Christmas dinner.

Along with a wide selection of different kinds of pickled fish, such as *lasimestarin silliä*, or pickled herring, or herring in a mustard or garlic sauce, salt cod is also often served as a starter as part of their large Christmas dinner.

A central culinary element is *Joulukinkku*, Christmas ham, also known as "baked Swede". Carrot and turnip casserole is also a traditional dish, as well as rosolli salad made with beetroot, carrots, apples, gherkins and cream coloured with beetroot juice. An almond is hidden in the Christmas porridge: an oaten porridge made with cinnamon, sugar and cold milk. Finns with a Swedish background also enjoy eating *Pulla*, a yeasted pastry made using cardamom.

And before Father Christmas hands out any presents, most Finnish people go to the sauna together. In the past, they took care to remember to look after the spirit of the house before they went, leaving it a bowl of porridge in the corner of their shed and even dedicating the last pour of the water over the rocks in the sauna to it. After all this, they enjoy a hearty meal, usually celebratory roast pork.

Finnish pets are even lucky enough to receive their own Christmas presents. For example, birds are given suet balls stuffed with sunflower seeds.

Another traditional part of Christmas in Finland is the Christmas Peace, which is proclaimed in Turku on 24 December every year at midday.

25 December is first and foremost for relaxing. The second Christmas day, *Tapani* day, is dedicated to St Stephen. Finnish people go to "Tapani dances" where they enjoy a good tango or waltz, but some of them would rather just meet up with friends.

On New Year's Eve, the Finns often invite friends round or they meet up in restaurants, attend organised dances and enjoy lively concerts. Of course, there are also huge firework displays and some people try their hand at lead blowing.

The Christmas period lasts until Epiphany on 6 January, which is when the Christmas tree is also tidied away.

Finnish-style Christmas ham

Sillisalaatti

(Finnish herring salad)

1	medium-sized salted herring or soused herring fillets
150 g	waxy potatoes
2	carrots, finely diced
100 g	beetroot, boiled, finely diced
100 g	sausage, finely chopped
1	pickled gherkin, finely chopped
1	large apple, peeled and cored
1	small onion, cut into rings
4 tbsp	white wine vinegar
150 ml	double cream
1	boiled egg, cut into eighths
	Freshly chopped parsley
	Freshly chopped chive
	Salt, pepper

Gut, skin and bone the salted herring. Then soak for one hour – or just use soused herring fillets.

Boil the potatoes and carrots until al dente.

Stir the double cream and vinegar together and season with salt and pepper. Then mix all the ingredients and leave to stand for at least 30 minutes, before garnishing with egg and herbs.

Joulukinkku

(Christmas ham with turnip and carrot casserole)

  1 large ham,
placed in pickle brine for 4–5 days

Coating
- 1 egg yolk
- 1 tbsp brown sugar
- 2 tbsp breadcrumbs
- 2 tbsp mustard
- Cloves

Turnip and carrot casserole
- 2 medium turnips, finely diced
- 4 carrots, finely diced
- 3 eggs
- 100 ml cream
- 3 tbsp breadcrumbs
- 3 tbsp ground hazelnuts
- Salt
- Coarsely ground pepper

Score the skin of the ham with rectangles and season with the cloves. Put in the oven with the skin facing upwards and cook at 125 °C for about 1 hour per kilo. Then, you can cut off the skin and coat the surface with breadcrumbs. Put back in the oven until the coating is golden brown.

Peel the turnips and carrots and boil in salted water until al dente. Drain away the water, leave the vegetables to dry and blend them or mash them using a potato mash.

Mix together the cream and the breadcrumbs and leave to swell up. Beat the eggs and season with salt and pepper. Add the hazelnuts and beat again.

Mix the creamy breadcrumb mixture and the blended turnips and carrots together and fold in the beaten eggs. Turn everything out into a greased tin, smooth the top and bake in the oven at 175 °C for about 1 hour.

Ginger biscuits

(makes 200)

300 g	margarine
300 g	sugar
3	eggs, separated, egg whites beaten to form stiff peaks
250 g	birch or maple syrup
2 tsp	cinnamon
2 tsp	powdered ginger
2 tsp	ground cloves
1 tsbp	chopped Seville orange zest
1 kg	flour
3 tsp	bicarbonate of soda

Boil the syrup with the spices, add the margarine and stir until everything has cooled. Then beat the egg yolks and sugar until light and fluffy.

With the spiced syrup mixture, first stir in some of the flour and bicarbonate of soda, then the beaten egg whites and then stir in the remaining flour. Do not knead the dough any further but cover with foil and leave to chill until the following day. Cut out biscuit shapes and bake until brown.

Finland

France

Joyeux Noël et bonne année **Nuit de Paix, Sainte Nuit**

What don't the French do to celebrate Christmas! Christmas markets, Advent wreaths, *Saint Nicolas*, Father Christmas, Christmas trees, midnight mass and, in particular, lots of artistic nativity scenes with fabulous figures that are supposed to mirror society and tell all kinds of tales. One of the largest nativity scenes is in Paris. And what would Christmas Eve in France be without an extravagant delicious meal with seven courses and 13 puddings! They have even more special sweet cakes to celebrate Epiphany, and whoever finds the bean hidden inside their slice of cake becomes king for the day.

The celebrations in France begin on the first week of Advent and last until Epiphany. Towns and villages are lit up all across France. Both young and old enjoy beautiful nativity scenes, steeped in tradition, and *Marchés de Noël* (Christmas markets). Houses and flats are also decorated with branches of mistletoe, nativity scenes and festive decorations.

In Alsace, they are careful to maintain numerous traditions which are part of the festive period. For example, some of the most beautiful Christmas markets can be found in this region. Similarly, Paris has one of the largest nativity scenes in the world.

Provence is known for its *Santons* markets featuring traditional nativity figures made of porcelain. Every profession imaginable from the last few centuries is represented here. In total, there are about 50 typical figures with very characteristic names, such as *Roustido*, a pleasant lady sheltering from the rain under the umbrella her husband is holding. In contrast, *Bartomiou* is an incorrigible drunkard with a long hat who is bringing a piece of salt cod for Jesus. *Pistachié*, a "beanpole" who is goading on a packhorse carrying sacks of grains, is also featured, as well as *Lou Ravi*, a man throwing his arms above his head in wonder. Among the other figures there is also a garlic merchant, a fishmonger, farm hands carrying lanterns, a fisherman with his net thrown over his shoulder and lots of people kneeling, praying to baby Jesus.

Other than in the Alsace and in some parts of Lorraine, *Couronne de l'avent*, the Advent wreath, is not often lit in French households. However, colourful Advent calendars of all shapes and sizes have started popping up in French playrooms in a big way in the last few years.

According to old Provençal tradition, wheat is sown on 4 December, or rather planted in cotton wool which has been moistened with water. Then, if the wheat seeds have germinated nicely by 25 December, then tradition has it that there will be a good harvest in the following year. Naturally rotten seeds are a bad omen. Similarly, if fruit branches that were cut down on 4 December and placed in a vase to bloom by Christmas, this is also a good sign.

In France, 24 December is a perfectly normal working day. But by the evening it becomes peaceful, tranquil and cosy. In some regions they sprinkle holy water over the wood in the fireplace in that hope that, according to old

Galette des Rois, the traditional French puff pastry cake eaten on Epiphany

beliefs, the ashes will protect the house from being struck by lightning in the following year.

Everyone who has gathered together goes to a restaurant or stays at home, and *Réveillon de Noël*, the traditional Christmas meal with its seven courses and 13 puddings, can begin. They start off with an aperitif. This is followed by oysters and salad, with smoked salmon and a dry white wine. After this comes *foie gras*, with savoury onion chutney, crispy toast and a sweet white wine.

The main course is either turkey stuffed with chestnuts or roast lamb or beef, a stuffed capon, a fish dish or even *ente à l'orange* or a goose with chestnuts, liver and cabbage, accompanied by various vegetables and red wine.

The famous 13 puddings

The *Bûche de Noël*, a cake in the shape of a tree trunk, is an absolutely essential pudding. The other sweet dishes are symbolically dedicated to the Last Supper and include *Fougasse* (pancakes), white hazelnut nougat and pistachios as well as dark nougat with honey. Similarly, in Alsace, *Bredle*, small dried pastries with aniseed, almonds or cinnamon, *Kouglof*, the Gugelhupf as well as *Beerawecka*, a Christmas bread with dried fruit and lebkuchen are also popular. There are also dried figs, raisins, almonds, nuts, dates, various different fruits and pumpkin cake on offer.

After this extravagant meal, many religious people conclude Christmas Eve by attending mi dnight mass. Presents are already exchanged on 24 December, but the main event takes place on 25 December.

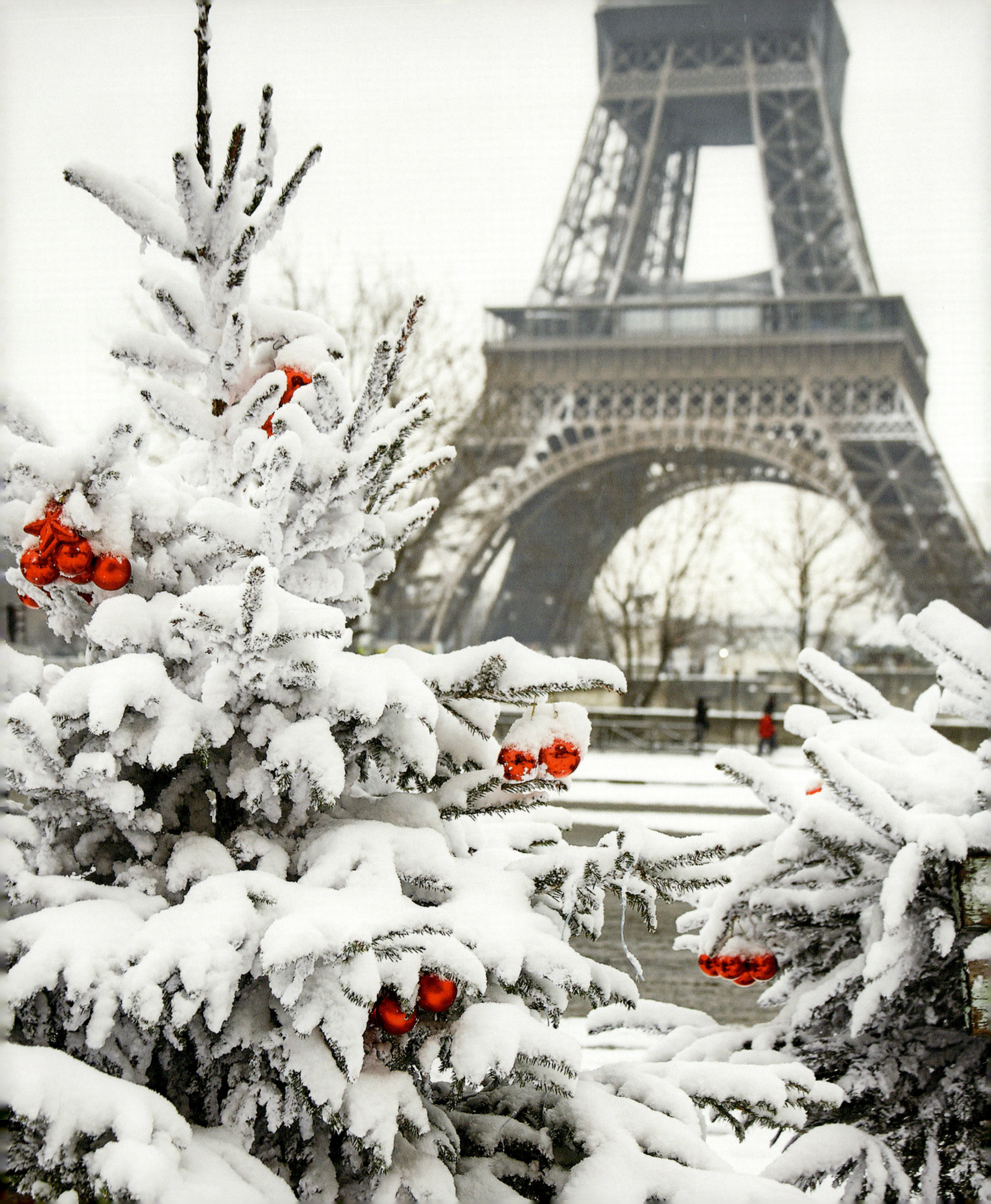

Père Noël (Father Christmas), dressed in a long red gown and pointy hat, leaves presents for the children under the Christmas tree. This is particularly common in Alsace.

In the past, *Saint Nicolas*, accompanied by his helper dressed in black, *Père Fouettard*, a figure similar to Knecht Ruprecht or Krampus, also left presents for the children on 6 December.

Réveillon de la Saint-Sylvestre, which is how 31 December is known in France, is celebrated in the company of family, friends and acquaintances, either at home or a restaurant.

At midnight on the dot, they kiss each other on the cheek two, three or four times, depending on the region and wish each other a happy new year.

In France, it is not uncommon to continue to wish people a happy new year well into January.

One French peculiarity for New Year and the following days is *les étrennes*, little New Year gifts.

During this time, the French like to give "everyday helpers", such as postal workers, caretakers or refuse collectors, presents in the form of money.

The celebrations in France do not finish on New Year's Day. Epiphany is still very popular, which always takes place on the first Sunday in January. *Galette des Rois*, the Epiphany puff pastry cake made of marzipan, is THE traditional speciality on this day. The family gather together and the youngest is allowed to hand out the slices of cake. Whoever then finds *la fève* (the bean) hidden in the pastry, but it might also be a porcelain figure, can crown themselves king for the day or choose someone else to be regent.

The king can then enjoy royal freedoms for that one day. But they then have to supply a new Epiphany cake the following day. It is obvious why this tradition can sometimes last the whole week; the ritual is always the same.

Smoked salmon salad

300 g	frozen peas
½	cucumber
1	head of lettuce
3	tomatoes
150 g	smoked salmon (slices)
2	hard-boiled eggs, each cut into eight
1	pinch of sugar
1 tbsp	salt
1	unwaxed lemon

Marinade

1 tbsp	dill vinegar
3 tbsp	olive oil
	Sprigs of dill for garnishing
	Salt, pepper

For the smoked salmon salad, boil the peas with a pinch of salt and sugar for 3 minutes, drain and leave to cool.

Remove the green base of the stem from the washed tomatoes. Cut the tomatoes and cucumber into slices and add the peas.

Hard boil the eggs, rinse in cold water, peel and cut into eight pieces.

Make the marinade by stirring together the salt, olive oil, dill vinegar and pepper, mix with the vegetables and leave to infuse in the fridge for 30 minutes.

Wash the head of lettuce and place on a plate. Serve the salmon, vegetables and eggs on top and decorate with dill before serving.

Duck breast à l'orange with potato dumplings stuffed with red cabbage

2	large duck breasts with the skin on
3	unwaxed oranges
	Oil for frying
50 ml	Grand Marnier/orange syrup
200 ml	double cream
1 tsp	chicken stock
1 tbsp	balsamic vinegar
	Salt, pepper

Potato dumplings with red cabbage stuffing

1 kg	floury potatoes
3	eggs
5 tbsp	flour
	Salt
1 pinch of sugar	
1 pinch of ground nutmeg	
5 tbsp	chunks of bread
1 tbsp	butter
400 g	red cabbage with grated apples

Wash the duck breasts, pat dry and carefully score rectangles into the skin using a sharp knife. Take care not to cut into the meat!

Rinse one of the oranges under hot water, finely peel and cut the zest into strips (producing about 1 to 2 tbsp). Filet the fruit flesh. Juice the other two oranges.

Heat a little oil in a pan until very hot and place the duck breasts in the pan with the fatty layer down. Fry for about 8 minutes.

Turn the duck, pour over Grand Marnier/orange syrup and fry for a further 5 minutes. Remove the duck breasts from the pan, season with salt and pepper and keep warm in the oven.

Deglaze the pan with the orange juice, with the juices from frying still in there, and stir in the double cream. Add the chicken stock and balsamic vinegar and simmer for 5 minutes. Add the orange segments and strips of zest to the sauce and season to taste with salt and pepper.

For the potato dumplings, boil floury potatoes, leave to cool, peel and mash with a potato mash or puree with a flour mill.

For the red cabbage filling, firstly fry the red cabbage with the grated apple until cooked, leave to cool and squeeze out well. Stir the eggs into the potato mixture, add the flour and knead thoroughly with salt, sugar and nutmeg to form a dough. The dough is ready when it no longer sticks to the bowl.

Fry the chunks of bread (or a stale roll cut into cubes) in a little oil in a pan. After this, mix into the potato dough.

Split the potato mixture into large pieces and shape each of these into a dumpling. Press 1 to 1 ½ tbsp of red cabbage into the middle of the dumplings and seal the dumplings again with the dough.

Bring a pan of salted water to the boil, place the potato dumplings in the pan, bring to the boil and leave to cook over a lower heat for about 10 minutes. The dumplings are ready when they float to the surface.

Cut the duck breast into slices 1cm thick and dish up on 4 plates with the dumplings and the sauce.

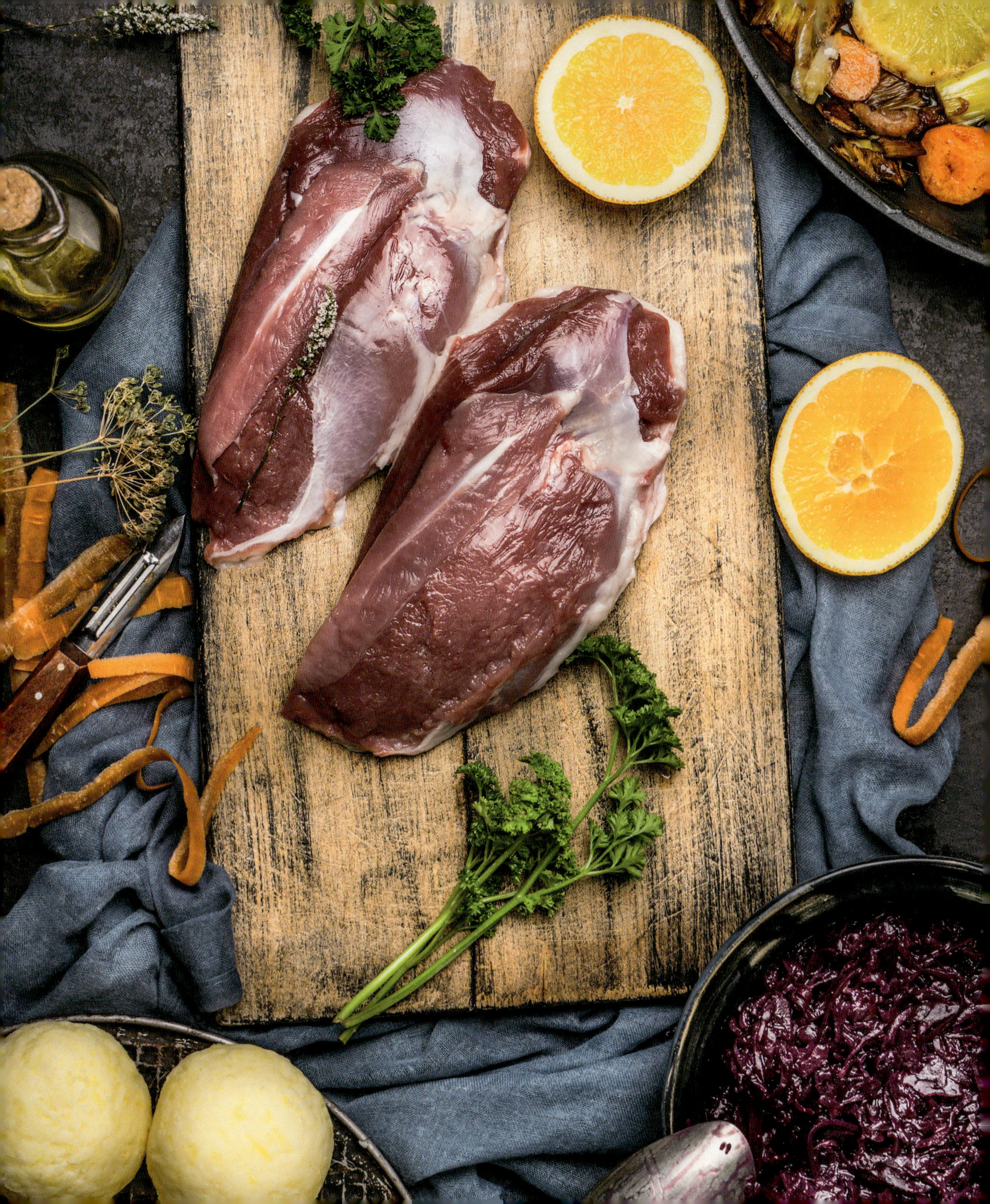

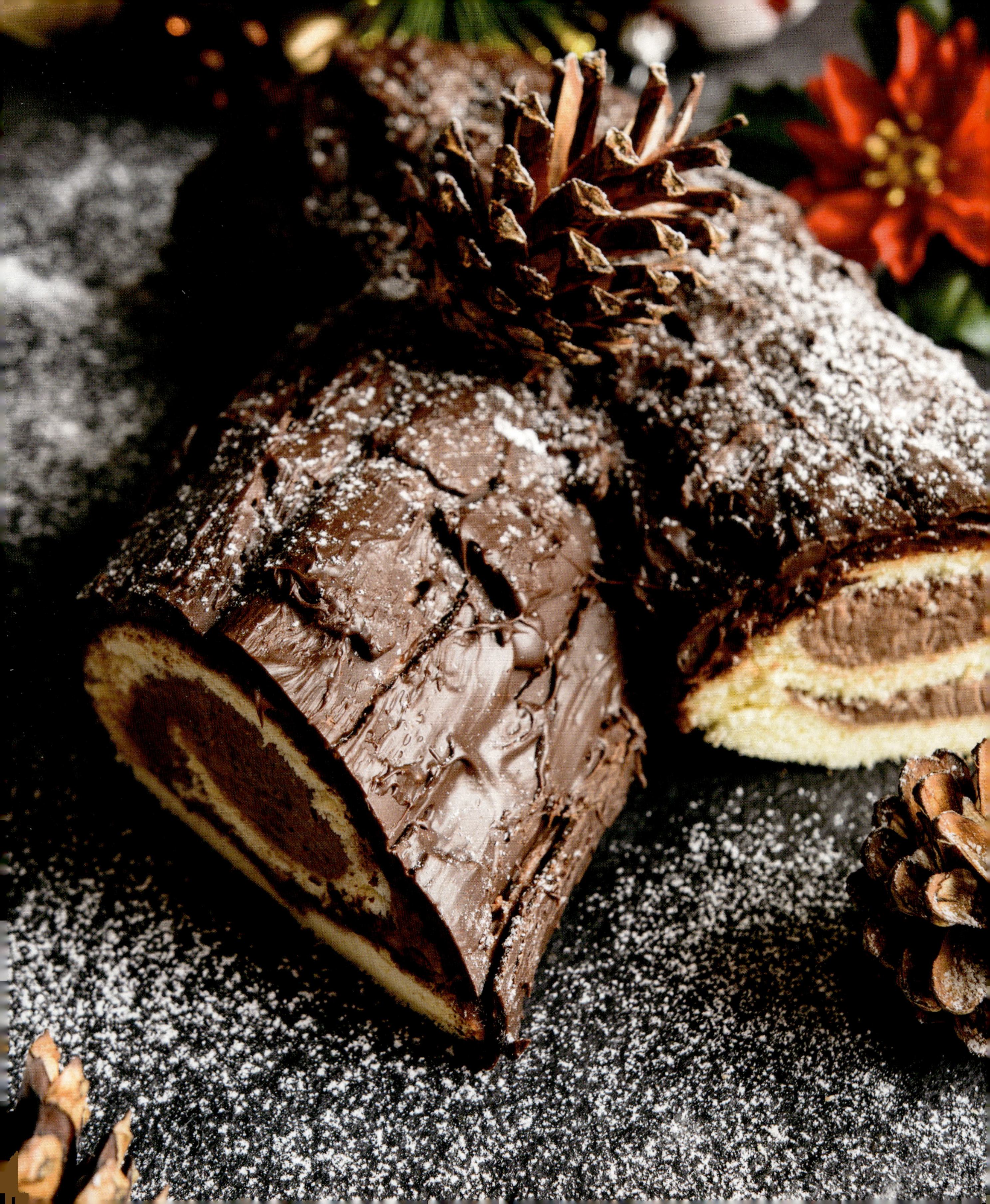

Bûche de Noël
(Yule Log)

Sponge base
4	eggs, separated
200 g	flour
160 g	sugar
1 tbsp	baking powder
	Sugar for turning out

Filling
100 g	dark chocolate
150 g	butter
100 g	sugar
1 tsp	instant coffee powder
50 g	milk chocolate
	Icing sugar for dusting

For the sponge base, beat the egg yolks with the sugar until very light and fluffy. Sieve the flour and baking powder then add spoonful by spoonful to the egg-sugar mix and stir well.

Beat the egg whites until they form stiff peaks and carefully fold into the egg yolk mixture. Spread the mixture out evenly on a baking tray lined with greaseproof paper.

Bake in a preheated oven at 200 °C for about 12 to 15 minutes. Immediately after baking, turn the sponge out onto a sugared tea towel. Remove the greaseproof paper and roll the sponge up.

For the filling, melt the different kinds of chocolate in a bain-marie. Beat the butter and sugar together until light and fluffy. Add the chocolate and coffee powder and stir well. Place the creamy mixture in the fridge until it is spreadable.

Remove the sponge from the towel and spread from the middle using half the creamy mixture, then roll back up. Cut both ends of the roll diagonally in the same direction and stick these pieces onto the roll as branches using some more of the creamy mixture. Spread the rest of the creamy mixture over the top of the roll.

Using a fork, introduce grooves into the icing (like the pattern of a tree trunk). Keep cold until eating. If you want, dust later with icing sugar to look like "snow" and decorate with pine branches.

France

Greece

Kalá Christoúgenna kai eftychisméno to néo étos

Ágia Nýchta, se prosménoun

Christmas in Greece is celebrated according to the Julian calendar, that is a few days later than in Central Europe. This period is marked by Christmas songs to bring happiness and Christmas fires to offer protection. According to old legends, *Kalikanzari* (goblins) play an important role right up until 6 January. Above all, it is important to keep them away from your house and garden. The Christmas tree has ancient symbolism and is therefore of particular significance. During the night of 1 January, St Basil brings gifts to well-behaved children. Christmas food is varied and, ending with *kourabiédes* and *melomakarona*, very sweet.

In Greece, celebrations get off to a very noisy start with the children taking to the streets, causing an uproar with bells and drums and, at the same time, striking up songs to bring happiness. These hymns are called *kalanda*, which differ depending on the region. As a reward, the little ones receive presents. In the past, these were nuts, dried figs and Christmas baked goods; nowadays it is mostly money.

Furthermore, from 24 December, the Greeks light Christmas fires that burn for twelve nights as well as leaving the fireplaces aglow in their houses. For Christmas Eve, the largest and best piece of wood is placed in the fire to symbolically warm up Baby Jesus.

Furthermore, according to old beliefs, the Christmas fire keeps the pesky goblins away. They are called *Kalikanzari* in Greece and have nothing but mischief in store.

There is a myth about these little villains. Nowadays, the Greek Christmas tree is inspired by West Europe and decorated splendidly; however it does have another archaic meaning which is linked to the Greek goblins. That is, from time immemorial it has symbolised the "Tree of Life", and the *kalikanzari* spend the entire year trying to saw it down. However, before the evil spirits can succeed, Jesus is born. According to old Greek beliefs, the goblins leave their underground world for twelve days at Christmas in order to bring trouble to mortals, and the Christmas fire offers protection from them.

Especially up until the 1950s, many Greeks decorated their homes with a small, illuminated ship meaning the start of a new journey in life, corresponding to the birth of Jesus. Even today, there are often large illuminated replicas of ships erected in squares in Greek towns and villages.

Traditionally, a festive Christmas meal is also part of the celebrations in Greece. Nowadays, stuffed turkey is very popular and widespread. A typical Christmas meal in Greece further includes the following dishes: fish soup with saltwater fish and then cold fish, on a plate decorated with mayonnaise and vegetables, goat or lamb fricassees and goat with potatoes from the oven. *Kourabiédes* (Christmas biscuits), *Christospomo*, a sweet bread, and *Melomakarona* (honey macarons) are served as sweet dishes.

On 1 January, St Basil's Day, the children once again sing songs of praise and go from door to door, as on 24 December. When doing so, the young singers carry paper

Christmas lights in the port of Kalamata.

stars and sometimes a paper ship with them as decoration. They tap the man of the house and his wife on the back with a twig. Since this is also said to bring good luck, the children are rewarded with nuts, cakes or money.

Usually, handing out the children's presents takes place on the night of 1 January. St Basil is the gift bearer, who places the presents in front of the children's beds. Then, on New Year's Day, there is traditionally *vasilopita* in honour of the saint. This is a cake with a gold coin inside in. Whoever finds the gold coin is said to have good luck for the rest of the year.

St Basil lived and worked in the 4th Century and, even then, was known as an important ascetic, bishop and Doctor of the Church. In Greece, he was already worshipped as a saint soon after his death. Basil is the patron saint of the poor and the sick and of peace.

On 6 January, the Greeks celebrate the divine revelation of theophany and the baptism of Christ. On this date, it is also high time to banish the mischievous *kalikanzari* to the underworld once again. This happens symbolically by ceremonious, priestly blessings of all houses and waters.

Kakavia
(Greek fish soup)

1 ½ kg	various Mediterranean fish, decaled, washed, filleted and boned (or a good half a kilo of fish fillets)
1 ½ l	fish stock
4	shallots, cut into rings
3	tomatoes, blanched, peeled, cored, cut into cubes
2	carrots, peeled, cut into cubes
3	small potatoes, peeled, cut into cubes
2	garlic cloves, finely chopped
1	bay leaf
1 branch	parsley, finely chopped
1 branch	dill, finely chopped
	Celery leaves
3 tbsp	lemon juice
4 tbsp	olive oil
	Salt

Lightly sauté the shallots in olive oil until transparent. Add the potatoes, carrot, garlic and bay leaf to the pan and pour in the fish stock or water. Leave to simmer for about fifteen minutes.

Meanwhile, cut the fish or the filets into bite-sized pieces, salt them and also place them in the soup. Leave over a low heat for 5 to 10 minutes.

Then put the tomatoes in the soup. Season with lemon juice and sea salt. Serve the finished soup with parsley and dill and the finely chopped celery leaves.

Greek Christmas Turkey

1	small turkey or 4 turkey fillets with an incision, washed and well dried
400 g	tomatoes, diced
250 g	mincemeat
250 g	rice
½ cup	butter, melted
100 ml	white wine
	Cinnamon, cloves
	Potatoes
	Mint
	Lemon juice
	Olive oil
	Paprika powder
	Salt, pepper

For the filling, fry the butter with the mincemeat and rice, season with mint, salt and pepper. Then add the tomato pieces and leave to simmer. The rice may still not yet be soft.

Stuff the resulting filling into the turkey or turkey fillet pockets. Seal or sew up the turkey or the fillet pockets with skewers so that nothing spills out. Rub salt and pepper into the outside and sprinkle over the paprika. Spread some butter over the top so that the skin becomes wonderfully crispy and juicy.

Put the turkey meat into a roasting tin and add some peeled, quartered potatoes around it. Full the dish half full of water, lemon juice and oil and roast in a preheated oven 250 °C for 2 to 2.5 hours, adjust accordingly for the smaller fillet pieces.

Tip: various salads, sheep's cheese and olives work well as accompaniments.

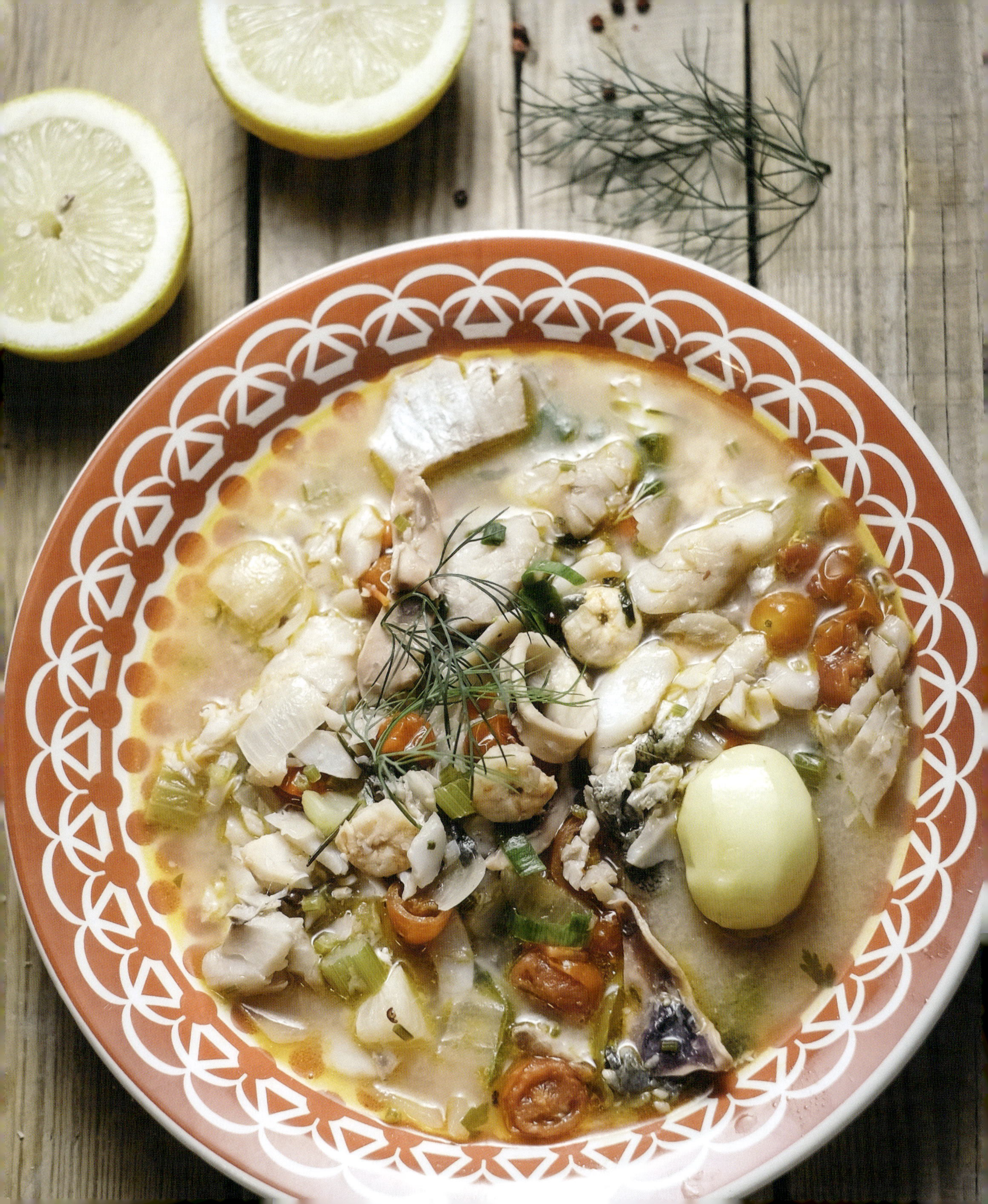

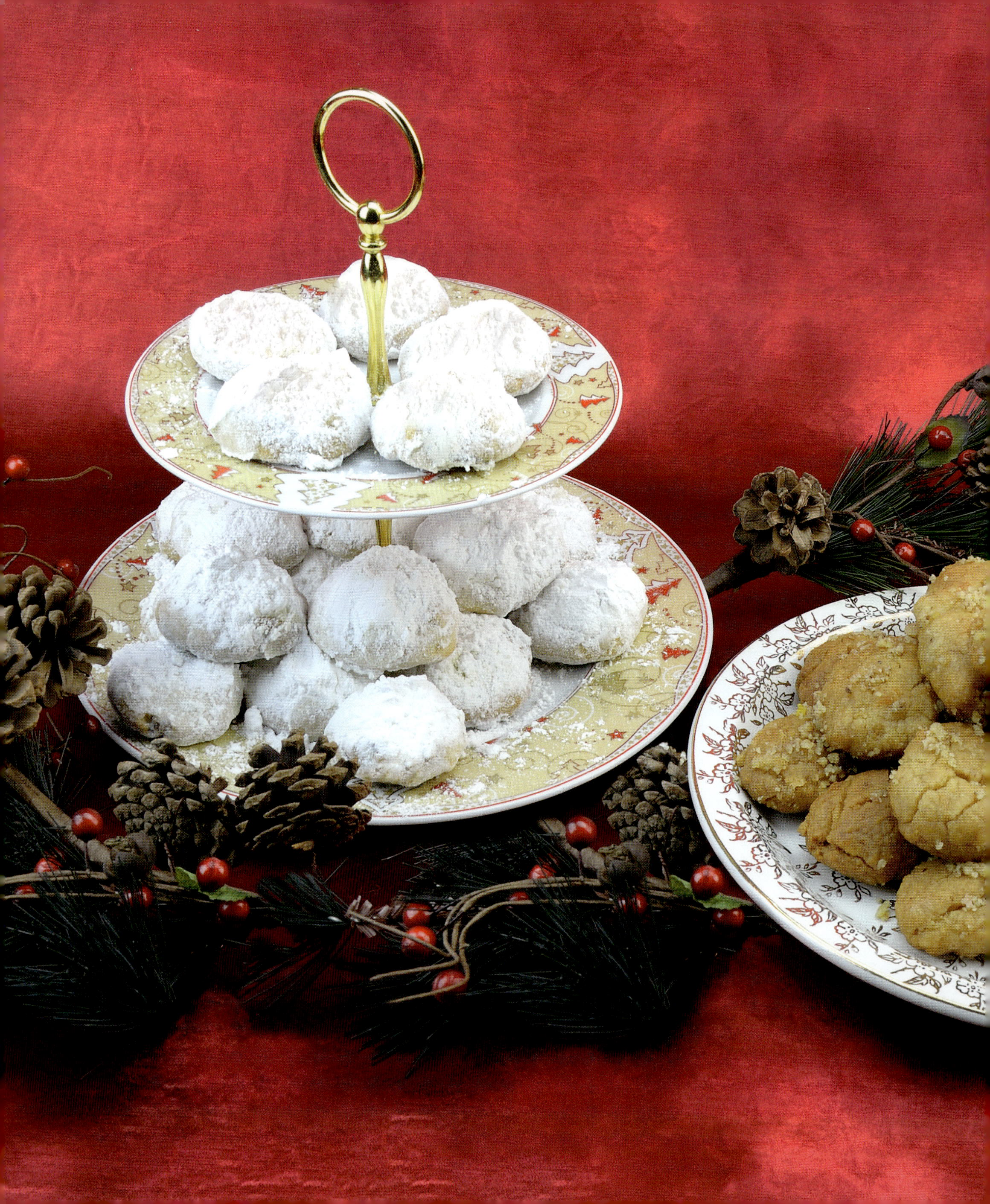

Arnaki frikassee

(Lamb fricassee with chicory salad and lemon sauce,
as an alternative main course)

750 g	lamb, cut into portion sizes
4	spring onions, washed, finely chopped
250 g	lettuce (chicory or Greek Marouli lettuce), washed, roughly chopped
80 g	dill, finely chopped
80 g	parsley, finely chopped
⅛ l	olive oil
2	eggs, whisked
80 ml	lemon juice
	Salt, pepper

Heat the olive oil in a pan over a high heat and fry the pieces of meat in the pan. Season with salt and pepper and deglaze with a little water. Seal the pan with a lid and leave to simmer lightly until the meat is about half done.

Add the spring onions and lettuce leaves, together with the dill and parsley, to the meat and leave to simmer further. Do not stir any more, otherwise the green leaves will crumple.

Slowly mix the eggs and the lemon juice with a little liquid from the pan. Add this lukewarm mixture to the meat that has finished cooking in the meantime and mix well.

Serve as soon as possible.

Melomakarona

(Honey macarons)

125 ml	olive oil
3 tbsp	sugar
40 ml	water
40 ml	orange juice, freshly pressed
10 ml	cognac
1 sachet	baking powder
500 g	flour
1 tsp	cinnamon
¼ tsp	ground cloves

Syrup

300 g	sugar
5 tbsp	honey
180 ml	water
1	cinnamon stick
4	cloves
150 g	walnuts, roughly chopped

Put all the ingredients for the dough into a bowl and knead it well, preferably by hand. The dough should be very soft and oily.

Shape the dough into small loaves, press a small dent into the top with a spoon and into the bottom with the tip of a finger so that the syrup is absorbed from below and the walnuts remain stuck to the top. Place on a baking tray and bake at 200 °C for about 20 minutes, until dark brown, and leave to cool completely. You can dunk them into the syrup straight after this on the same day, but preferably even later.

For the syrup, bring all ingredients to the boil, constantly skimming the bubbles from the mixture. Reduce to a low heat, but make sure it remains quite fluid. Using the skimming spoon, dunk some of the pieces of melomakrona into the simmering syrup for 3 to 5 minutes each. Then remove them, place on a plate and scatter over the chopped walnuts.

Greece

Great Britain

Merry Christmas and a Happy New Year   **Silent Night, Holy Night**

In Great Britain, Christmas is a merry, rather than contemplative, affair. The *yule log* found across Eastern Europe is also popular here. Mistletoe and garlands of evergreen leaves hang above doorways. Christmas cards were invented in London and are still a big hit today. *Father Christmas* leaves presents in large red stockings. You are sure to find turkey, *Christmas pudding* and Christmas crackers at every Christmas dinner. 26 December is called *Boxing Day* and is marked in quite a specific manner. According to tradition, servants received a small gift on this day.

Christmas is the most popular holiday in Great Britain. The traditions and ceremonies are rooted in ancient pagan customs. Remnants of these can still found in today's Christmas celebrations – such as hanging mistletoe to the doorframe. Anyone standing underneath may be kissed.

The *yule log* dates back to Viking times, which was once burnt in honour of the god Thor. The English have assumed this custom for the celebration of the birth of Christ.

Advent begins four Sundays before Christmas. For children, an Advent calendar makes the time until the holidays pass more quickly.

Handmade wreaths and garlands made of branches (pine, holly and ivy) can be found all over the place – on the door, on the window, above the fireplace or on the table. The green of the leaves symbolises eternal life.

The Advent period is peak season for charity events, which always involve plenty of *mulled wine* and *mince pies*.

In local theatres, young and old alike put on pantomimes, a kind of fairy-tale musical with a crude sense of humour. In schools and churches, children rehearse nativities and Christmas plays and sing *Christmas carols*.

Christmas Eve is considered to be preparation time for the actual celebration the following day, Christmas Day. Many people attend midnight mass. On 24 December, children hand up large red stockings in the hope that *Father Christmas* will fill them with presents. Most children also leave something by the front door for Father Christmas and his reindeer to eat and drink, such as *mince pies*, a carrot or even a glass of whisky. In general, Christmas in Britain is colourful and high-spirited. In some cases, they hang up colourful garlands and don little paper hats.

Presents are opened on the morning of the first Christmas bank holiday. Later, the family gather together for a traditional Christmas dinner, which often consists of *roast chicken* or *roast turkey* with *roast potatoes* and lots of vegetables, such as peas, carrots, broccoli, Brussel sprouts, cabbage and swede. Small sausages wrapped in bacon and boiled ham are also very popular. For pudding, there are sweet *mince pies* or *Christmas pudding*. *Christmas cake* is a rich fruit cake with marzipan and royal icing.

Christmas crackers are also very popular. Something resembling a large, brightly coloured bonbon with twisted ends is laid on the table with the cutlery, which goes bang when pulled apart and is filled with a small crown, a rhyme or a toy. Of course the paper crown is worn for the whole duration of the meal.

London ablaze with light at Christmas

The custom of sending Christmas cards to friends and family also originates from Great Britain. In 1843, the artist John Calcott Horsley designed the first greeting card. Christmas feasts, church bells and other religious images were the motifs on it.

Even today, about a billion Christmas cards are sent in Great Britain – despite digital media.

In 1840, Prince Albert brought the tradition of putting up a decorated, illuminated Christmas tree with him from Germany. Every year, a giant Christmas tree is lit up in Trafalgar Square.

On Christmas Eve, choirs go from house to house and perform *Christmas carols*. This tradition dates back to the Middle Ages when beggars took to the streets singing and begged for gold, food or drink.

On 26 December, Britons celebrate *Boxing Day*. The name refers to the colourful boxes in which, in the past, apprentices received their Christmas pay. Today, they traditionally spend the day visiting friends and family and any free time is used for shopping, since many shops lure customers with very special cheap offers on *Boxing Day*.

Christmas Crackers.

On this day, people also give thanks to others who make everyday life as smooth as possible, such as postmen, milkmen or bus drivers. They receive small gifts. On *Boxing Day*, there are many charity events, such as hikes or even diving into the sea.

On 27 December, some normality returns and they then celebrate New Year's Eve, even if the turn of the year is not celebrated in a big way in England.

The Christmas period ends on 5 January with so-called *Twelfth Night*. Up until 1752, Christmas in Great Britain was still celebrated on 6 January, according to the Julian calendar. A quite specific tradition takes place in Wales. On this day, *Mari Lywd*, a person dressed as a horse and clothed in white goes from door to door. They present the inhabitants with a riddle. Anyone who does not know the answer has to not only be "bitten" by *Mari Lwyd*, but also has to ask them into the house and feed them.

Great Britain

Vol-au-Vent

(Puff pastry tarts with a chicken and ham filling)

250 g	puff pastry
125 g	chicken, cooked and cut into small pieces
125 g	ham, cooked and diced
50 g	mushrooms, sliced
1 tbsp	lemon juice
2	egg yolks
	Some parsley and chive, finely chopped
	Salt, pepper

Bechamel sauce

270 ml	milk
1 tbsp	butter
2 tbsp	sour cream
1 tbsp	flour
	Salt

Roll out the puff pastry. Now, cut out 6 cm discs using a round cookie cutter. Leave 8 pieces as they are and cut out a hole about 3 cm wide from the middle of the others. Bake eight of these small pastry discs from the middle as well. They will later serve as a lid for the vol-au-vents. Knead the rest of the dough together again, roll out and cut out more discs.

Cover the eight whole pastry discs with two dough rings each, one on top of the other, brushing with egg yolk in between. Then place these on baking trays and bake for just about half an hour until golden brown.

In the meantime, prepare the filling. To do so, lightly brown the mushrooms in butter for 5 minutes, combine with chicken and ham and season with lemon juice, pepper, salt, parsley and chive.

For the bechamel sauce, melt the butter, brown a little flour in it and pour over the milk, stirring constantly so that there are no lumps. Then, fold in the sour cream and season with salt. Fill the baked vol-au-vents with the cooked mixture and place the little lids on top. The vol-au-vents can be served warm or cold as a starter.

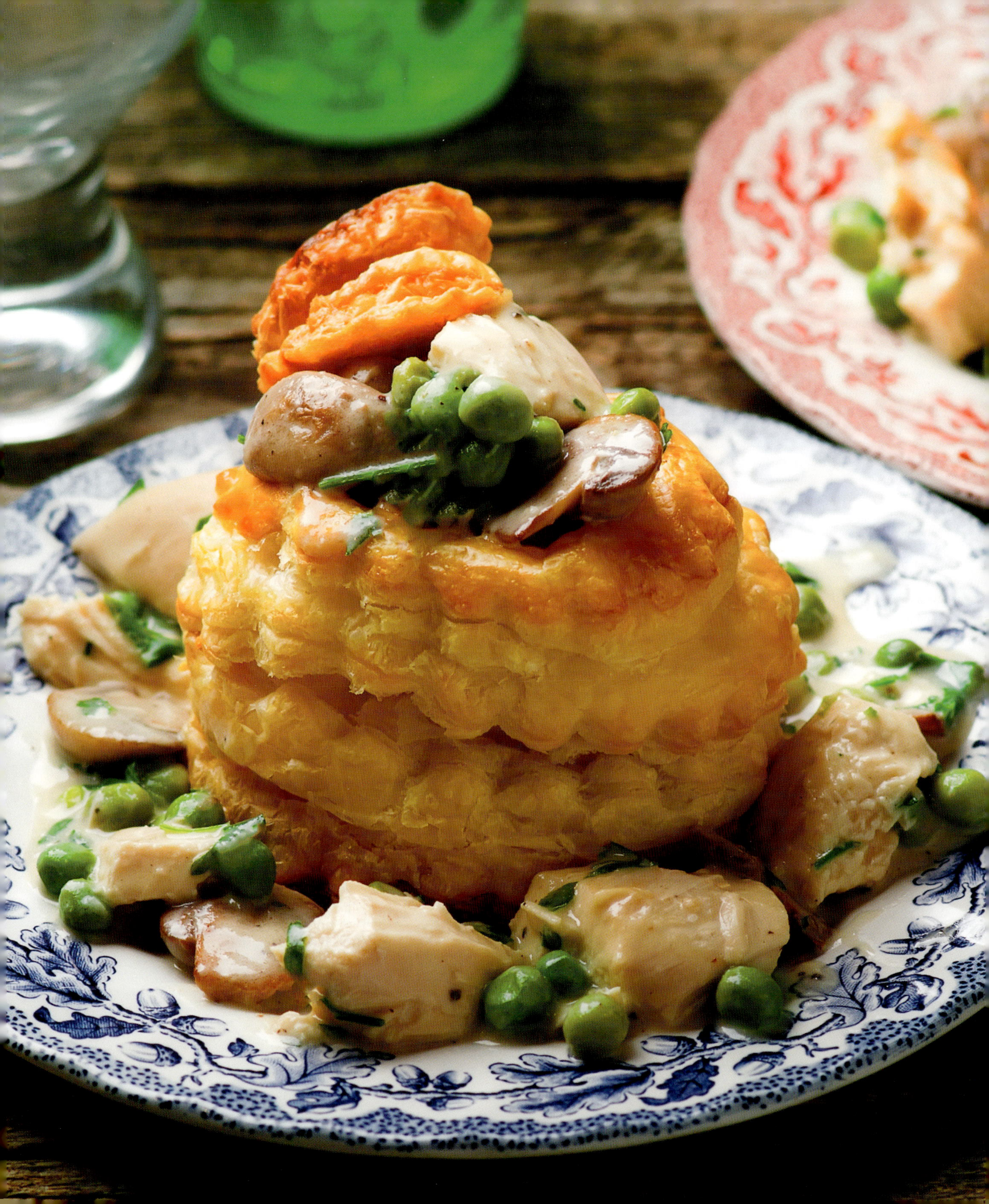

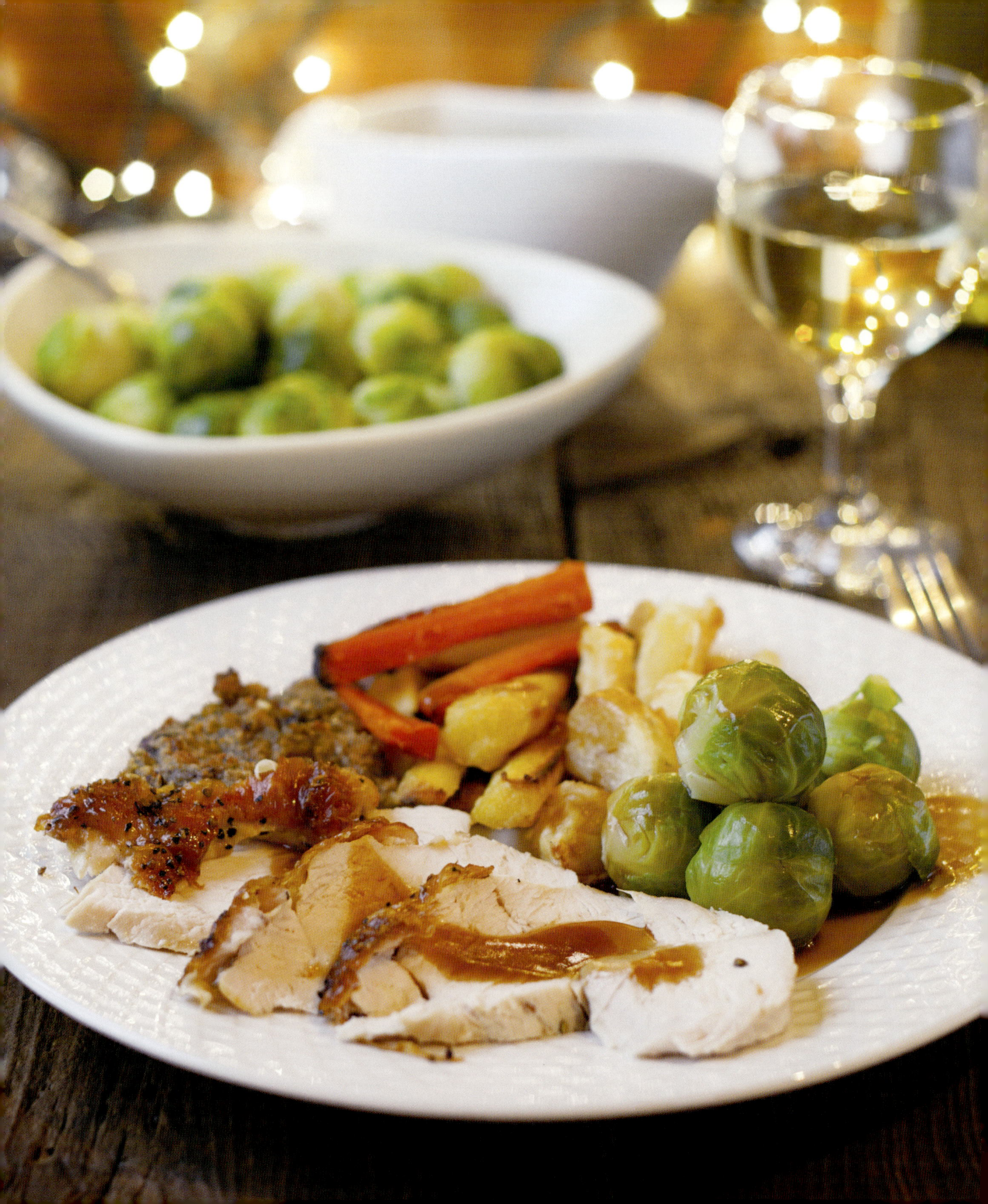

Roast beef with Brussel sprouts, roast potatoes and remoulade sauce

400 g	joint of beef
	Pepper, course and varied
4	cherry tomatoes
800 g	waxy potatoes
100 g	onions, cut into thin rings
4 tbsp	olive oil
	Salt, pepper
½ tsp	caraway seeds
1 tbsp	parsley

Remoulade sauce

70 g	mayonnaise
70 g	yoghurt
50 g	onion, finely chopped
1	gherkin
1	egg, hard boiled and diced
	Salt, pepper
	Pinch of cayenne pepper
½ tsp	Worcestershire sauce
½ tbsp	parsley
½ tbsp	chives, finely chopped
1 tbsp	cress

Brussel sprouts

500 g	Brussel sprouts
	Salt, pepper
	A little butter

Thoroughly wash the potatoes, place in cold, lightly salted water and boil until soft. Pour the water away, leave to cool, peel and cut into slices. Heat the oil and brown the onion rings in the oil. Add the potatoes and fry until crispy, season with salt, pepper, caraway seeds and parsley.

Clean the Brussel sprouts, score a cross on the stalk end and cook in plenty of water until firm. Then toss in butter and season with salt and pepper.

For the remoulade, stir the mayonnaise and yoghurt together in a bowl until smooth. Add the onions, gherkin and diced egg to the bowl. Add the spices and finely chopped herbs and carefully mix everything together. Garnish with cress when dishing up.

Take the meat out of the fridge about 1 hour before roasting, pat dry and score a grid into the fat with a sharp knife. Then, season with salt and pepper and fry in hot oil in a large pan over a high heat, until all the sides are brown. Then place onto a baking tray. Stick a roasting thermometer into the thickest point into joint of beef to reach the middle of the beef. Roast in the lower third of a hot over at 140 °C with static upper and lower heat. The thermometer should display a core temperature of 60 °C.

Then wrap the joint of beef tightly in aluminium foil and leave to rest for 15 minutes. Cut into thin slices and dish up, season with pepper to taste. Quarter the cherry tomatoes, remove the stems and season, garnishing the roast beef with them. Add the roast potatoes, Brussel sprouts and remoulade sauce.

Great Britain

Mince Pies

(sweet English Christmas tarts, makes 12)

Pastry

400 g	flour
80 g	sugar
30 g	icing sugar
	Pinch of salt
2	egg yolks
280 g	cold butter
	Butter for the tin
	Flour for the tin

Filling (mincemeat)

100 g	apple
2 tsp	lemon juice
30 g	candied lemon peel
30 g	candied orange peel
250 g	blanched almonds
50 g	blanched hazelnuts
2 cl	brandy
50 g	currants
100 g	soft butter
80 g	sugar
20 g	honey
1 tsp	cinnamon
½ tsp	ground cloves
	Pinch of ground cardamom
2	egg whites
	Pinch of salt

For the pastry, mix the flour with the sugar, icing sugar and salt, turn onto the worktop and make a well in the centre. Add the egg yolks and place the pieces of butter around the outside. With a large knife, chop the butter into the flour, until it is crumbly. Then quickly knead together with both hands to form a smooth dough. Shape into a ball, wrap in cling film and chill.

Peel and core the apples and finely grate. Mix together with the lemon juice.

Chop up the lemon peel, orange peel and nuts very finely in a cutter.

Stir together the brandy (leave out for children!), the currants and the squeezed out apple. Beat the butter and sugar until light and fluffy, add the honey, cinnamon, cloves and cardamom. Stir the mixture from the cutter into the butter mixture. Pre-heat the oven to 170 °C with convection. Grease and flour a muffin tin or muffin moulds.

Roll the pastry out on a lightly floured surface to 3 mm thick and cut out circles about 10 cm in diameter, as well as lots of stars. Place the circles into the dents in the tray or place in the moulds, press well into the edges. Leave in a cool place for a short while longer.

Meanwhile, beat the egg whites with the salt until they form stiff peaks and carefully fold in the mincemeat mixture. Divide the mixture between the mice pies, cover with the stars and bake on the middle shelf in the preheated oven for about 20 to 25 minutes.

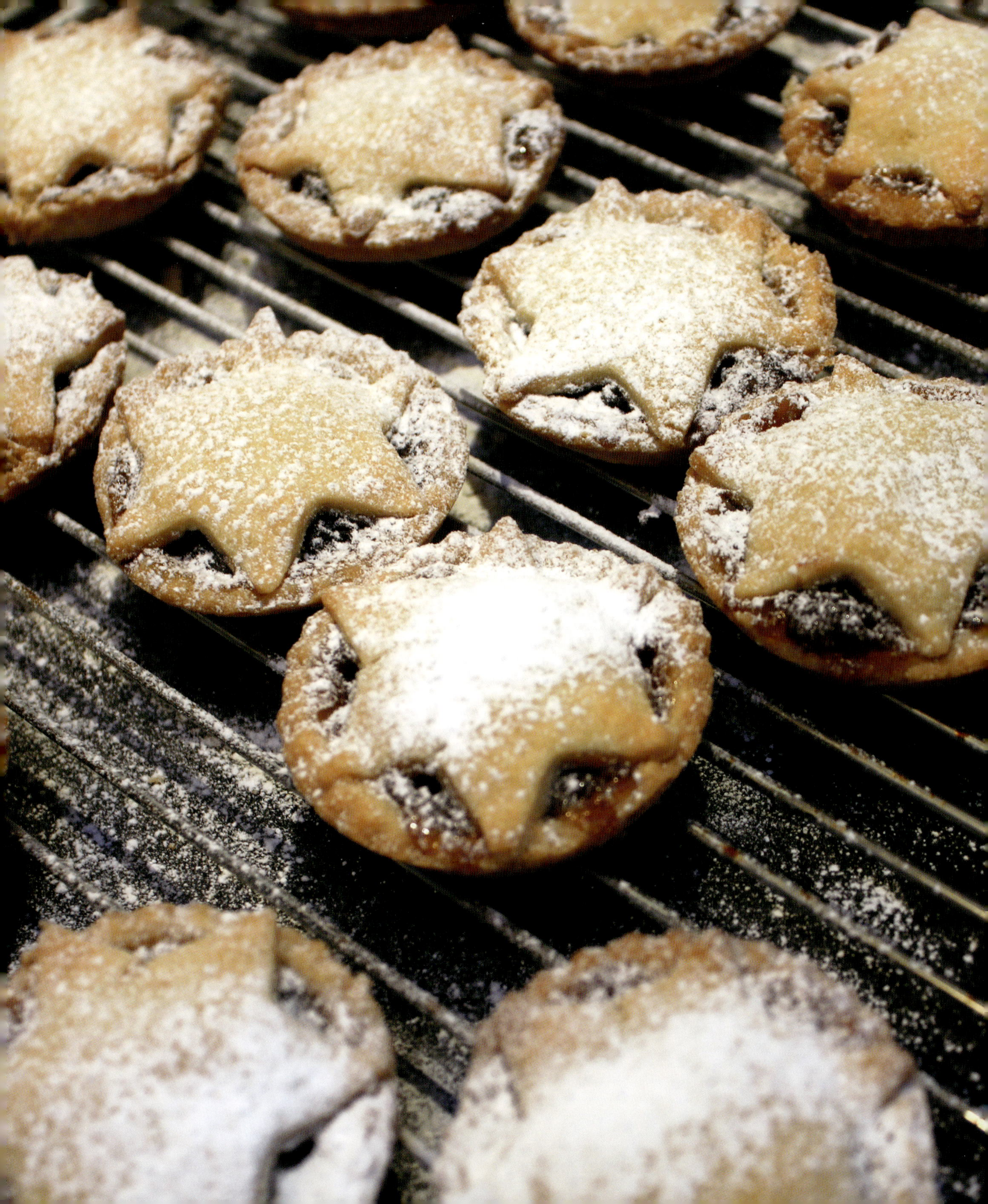

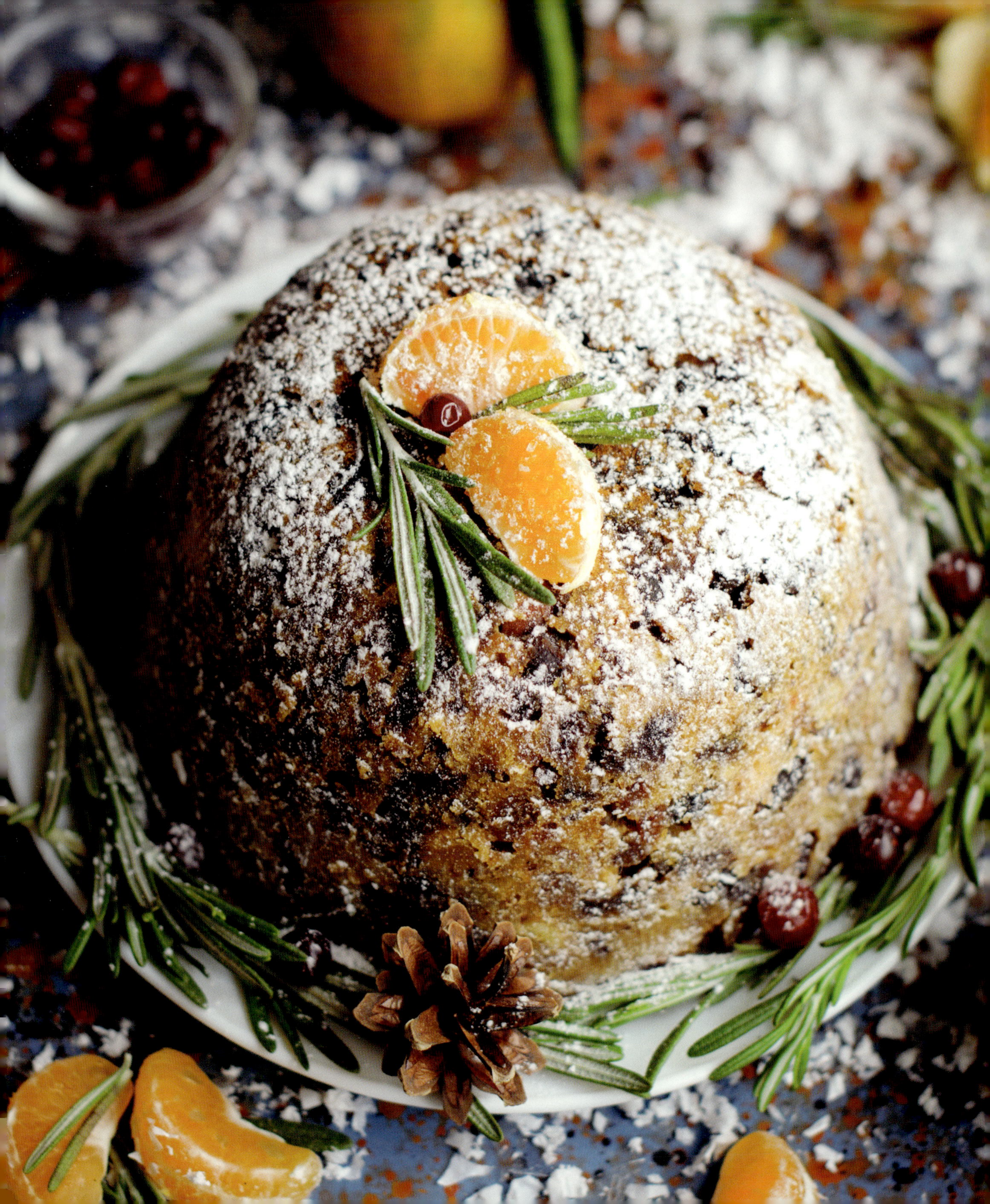

Christmas Cake

300 g	raisins, soaked in rum
200 g	candied lemon peel
200 g	candied orange peel
150 g	hazelnuts, chopped
150 g	almonds, chopped
300 g	flour
250 g	butter
200 g	sugar
150 g	butter
4	eggs
1 sachet	baking powder
100 ml	whisky
	Cinnamon, cardamom
	Salt
	White royal icing
	Candied fruit, to taste

Combine all the nuts and fruit with a cup of flour. Beat the butter, sugar and eggs until creamy, then add the rest of the sieved flour with the baking powder, spices and salt and stir to form a smooth dough. Then, stir in the nuts and fruit and add the whisky. Mix well and place in a spring-form cake tin lined with baking paper.

Bake for about 2 hours at 180 °C on the lowest shelf.

Leave to cool, take out of the tin and wrap in aluminium foil. After about 3 days, coat with white fondant icing and decorate with chopped candied fruit. Then, wrap again for at least another three weeks and then the cake will taste delicious.

Christmas pudding

100 g	sultanas
50 g	each of currants, candied orange peel, candied lemon peel and breadcrumbs
80 g	dried plums
2 tbsp	butter
75 g	ground hazelnuts
1	apple, peeled, finely grated
40 g	(brown) sugar
4 cl	rum
2	eggs
	Crushed cloves
	Cinnamon

Blanch the sultanas and raisins and leave to dry, add the plums and pour the rum over the fruit. Then, mix in the grated apple, candied lemon peel and candied orange peel. Now gradually combine all the remaining ingredients and stir until the mixture forms a homogeneous dough.

Then, pour the dough into a greased pudding bowl with a lid and seal (with aluminium foil).

Preheat the oven to 150 °C and place the pudding in a hot water bath on a grate and leave to simmer for about three hours. Then turn the pudding onto a plate and preferably leave to stand for a few days (or weeks) before serving.

Great Britain

IRELAND

Nollaig Shona agus Bliain Úr faoi mhaise
Merry Christmas and a Happy New Year

Oíche chiúin, oíche Mhic Dé
Silent Night, Holy Night

Mistletoe, garlands and windows decorated with candles are all part of the Christmas period in Ireland, which officially begins on 8 December, as well as *Christmas pudding*, *mince pies* and hot egg liqueur punch, *eggnog*. *Santy* brings the presents and the time-honoured *Wexford Carols* are sung. Swimming at Christmas is just as typically Irish as "Little Christmas" or "Women's Christmas", when the women all head to the pub leaving the men home alone to look after the household.

Christmas in Ireland starts as early as October, with cards and decorations popping up in shops.

Plum pudding is also prepared at this time so that it has enough time to mature before Christmas day.

The Irish often spend the Advent period cleaning their houses or flats. After they have finished cleaning, they traditionally hang up red Christmas lanterns.

Officially, the actual Christmas period in Ireland begins on 8 December with festive lights and Christmas markets. During this time, the Irish return home from all across the world to celebrate with friends and relatives. Houses are then decorated with garlands and candles, and wreaths and mistletoe branches with berries to bring as much luck as possible are hung on front doors.

As in England, in the past, mistletoe was used to "steal" kisses. Today, the Irish decorate their houses with mistletoe branches as a symbol of peace – although kissing is of course not completely out of the question as it is often a lovely token of peace. According to old beliefs, mistletoe branches are said to predominantly protect against evil spirits and thoughts.

Another specific tradition in Ireland is placing Christmas candles in windows. When doing so, every little flame represents one inhabitant. It's also possible that the lights are supposed to be reminiscent of Mary and Joseph looking for lodgings.

You also have to have Advent wreaths. In Ireland, they have five candles, three purple ones, a pink one and a white one in the middle. The latter is only lit on Christmas Eve.

The smell of *mince pies*, small pastries stuffed with fruit, ultimately provides a tranquil atmosphere and anticipation for the Christmas celebrations.

Dublin at Christmas

In Ireland, evergreen pine trees have only been used at Christmas for a relatively short amount of time. Holly and ivy were traditionally used instead of pine trees.

On Christmas Eve, children hang their Christmas stockings up to be filled during the night by *Father Christmas*. As a thank you, they also leave a glass of beer or whiskey and a pie ready so that *Santy* has enough provisions for his strenuous working day.

Then midnight mass in Ireland ushers in Christmas itself.

In terms of culinary traditions, *Christmas pudding* – with brandy or rum sauce, brandy butter and cream, turkey, *trifle* (a sweet dish made of several layers with custard, cream, fruit or jam, sponge fingers soaked in alcohol and whipped cream) and ham are all part of Christmas dinner.

Other popular dishes include smoked salmon, seasoned roast beef, prawn cocktail, ham, cranberry sauce and bread sauce, cocktail sausages, potatoes and vegetables. The *Christmas cake* is fluffy, moist and rich and is made of dried fruit, lots of whiskey and spices.

An alternative to this is *Christmas pudding*. The preparation takes a lot of time. Among other things, the dough consists of currants, almonds, cherries, breadcrumbs, flour and spices. Before serving, whiskey or brandy is poured over the pudding and set alight.

Gifts are handed out in the morning on 25 December: they often enjoy singing Christmas songs when doing this; one of the oldest, the *Wexford Carol*, allegedly originates from the 12th Century and tells the story of the birth of Jesus.

26 December is an official public holiday in both Northern Ireland and the Republic of Ireland. In Northern Ireland it is known as *Boxing Day*, in the Republic of Ireland as *St Stephen's Day*. In Dingle in County Kerry (Republic of Ireland), the *Wrenboys* ("wren hunters") make their way through the streets singing and dancing in costumes made of straw to collect money for charity.

The traditional Christmas swim takes place in many coastal regions in Ireland. Thousands of bathing beauties and mermen plunge into the waves of sea. When doing so, many participants conquer their "weaker selves" for a good cause. After swimming, everyone is very happy and proud of having managed to survive jumping into the cold depths. And spectators shout and cheer enthusiastically for

Hot Toddy, a popular winter drink in Ireland

the toughened participants. Eggnog is commonly served, a kind of egg liqueur with whiskey and spices or Hot Toddy made of whiskey, hot water, sugar, lemon zest and cloves.

The Christmas period ends on 6 January. Epiphany is called "little Christmas" or "women's Christmas". On this day, the female population make their way to the pub and the men have to "tend to the fire" at home. An important task for the men on 6 January is taking down the Christmas decorations, since superstition has it that it's bad luck not to do so. On "Women's Christmas", the men obviously also prepare all the meals.

Ireland

Butternut Squash Soup

1	small butternut squash, washed and cut into small cubes
1	leek, finely chopped
1	onion, finely chopped
1	piece of root ginger, peeled, finely chopped
1	clove of garlic
700 ml	vegetable stock
1 tbsp	crème fraiche or mascarpone with double cream
	Olive oil
	Butter
	Chilli oil
	White bread
	Salt, pepper

Brown the onion in butter and olive oil, add the butternut squash, garlic, leek and ginger and fry for a little while longer. Pour over the stock and leave to simmer on a medium heat for about 20 minutes until the vegetables are soft. Then press through a strainer or blend and season with salt, pepper and crème fraiche. Finally drizzle over some chilli oil and serve with toasted white bread.

Irish Tournedos
with dry-cured ham in a port and orange sauce

4	fillet steaks about 125g each
150 ml	port, red
3	oranges, zest
2 tbsp	orange juice
1	cinnamon stick
2 tbsp	raspberry vinegar
2 sprigs	thyme
4 tbsp	hazelnut or walnut oil
4	slices of dry-cured ham
½ head	red cabbage, finely grated
40 g	butter
400 ml	fish stock
300 g	potatoes
	Salt, pepper

Finely grate the orange rind and squeeze out the juice. Stir the orange juice with the vinegar, oil, salt and pepper in a large bowl to make the dressing. Fold in 1 tbsp of orange rind. Mix the red cabbage with the dressing and leave to stand for at least one hour.

Put the meat stock into another pan with the port, the rest of the orange juice, the cinnamon stick and the sprigs of thyme, bring it all to the boil and reduce by about half.

Rub salt and pepper into the fillet steaks and wrap the slices of ham around the fillet steaks. Fry them in hot butter for about 5 minutes until nice and golden. However they should still be pink on the inside. Remove from the pan and wrap them in aluminium foil to keep warm. Strain the boiled, reserved stock and boil down with the meat juices to make a sauce.

Cover the finished tournedos with some sauce and serve with the red cabbage. In Ireland, a fitting accompaniment would be (roast) potatoes.

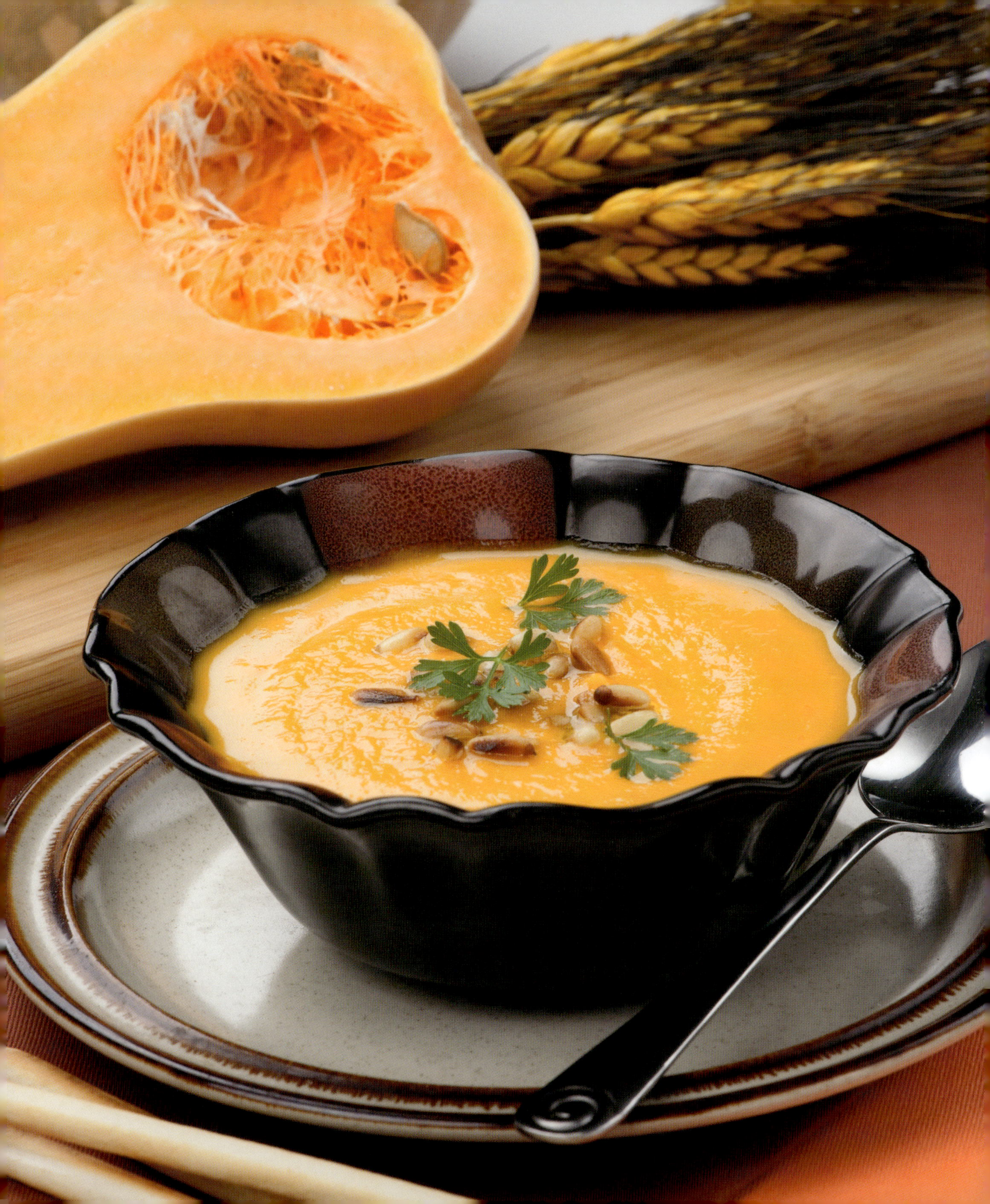

Mince Pies

(Nutty fruit tartlets, makes 12)

180 g	cold butter, cubed
2 tbsp	orange liqueur or orange extract
200 g	flour
80 g	chopped mixed nuts
80 g	dates, dried and finely chopped
1	egg yolk
100 g	dried apricots, finely chopped
	Ground allspice
	Butter
	Flour
	Sugar
	Salt

For the pastry, rub the cubes of butter into the flour to form fine breadcrumbs. Add the salt, sugar, egg yolk and some cold water and knead to form a smooth dough. Shape the dough into a rectangle, wrap in cling film and put in the fridge for about an hour.

For the filling, boil about 250 ml water, stir the dried fruit and nuts into it and remove from the hob. Then mix in the allspice and liqueur and leave to cool further, drain away the excess water. Roll the dough out on a lightly floured work surface to about 3 mm thick and cut out circles about 7 cm in diameter. Grease and flour a muffin tin and press the circles of dough into it. Put 1 tbsp of filling into each mould. Cut out circles about 5 cm in diameter from the remaining dough. Then – because it's Christmas – cut out a small star for each one and place on top of the filling as a cover, lightly pressing around the edges.

Bake in a preheated oven at 180 °C for a good half an hour. Then turn the cooled pies out of the mould.

Tip: As long as there's no one around with a sweet tooth, the mince pies will keep in a cake tin for 1 to 2 weeks.

Ireland

Iceland

Gleðileg jól og farsælt komandi ár

hljóður nótt, heilagur nótt

Some Christmas traditions are similar to those in other countries; others are very typical of Iceland and only customary there, such as "rotten stingray" and the not altogether harmless "Yule Cat". Decorative Christmas lights brighten up this dark time of the year and a varied selection of dishes is served up for Christmas. The "13 sons of the giantess" bring the presents. Their peculiar names are indicative of their respective nature and the roles they play, many of which are antagonistic. Surely you weren't expecting something good from *Skyrgámur*, the "skyr gobbler?"

In Iceland, Christmas is first and foremost a celebration of family and of light. Because the sun has been setting at midday since November, festive lighting plays a special role here. Houses, gardens and shops are decorated with colourful lamps. The Christmas season begins four days before Christmas Eve when Advent wreaths are put up.

Þorláksmessa, or "Little Christmas", is generally celebrated on the day before Christmas in Iceland. The day commemorates Iceland's patron saint, Bishop Thorlak, who lived in the 12th Century and died on 23 December 1193. One old custom is thoroughly cleaning the house on *Þorláksmessa*. According to pagan beliefs, this will banish evil spirits.

Something very special is cooked up on the celebration day before Christmas, namely *Kæst Skata*, "rotten stingray". This unique Icelandic delicacy does exactly what it says on the tin: (half) decayed, pungent stingray which is made palatable by the fermenting process. This fish is in fact highly poisonous since it does not discharge uric acid but instead concentrates it in its blood or in its tissue. Yet if the fish is left to rot for four to five weeks at a constant temperature, the poison escapes and the stingray is "ripe". The fermented flesh is then boiled in salted water, stirred to form a pulp and prepared with melted sheep fat to form a paste. Seasoning is not really necessary - *Kæst Skata* has an intense strong aroma anyway, for both the nose and the pallet, as I'm sure you can imagine. They usually raise a glass of milk, not schnapps, with this dish at Christmas.

On the morning of *Aðfangadagur* (24 December, Christmas Eve), the Icelanders remember the dead and light up their graves with candles. Of course they also decorate the Christmas trees with candles, even if trees are rather difficult to find on the volcanic island.

In Iceland, the *Jólasveinar* are responsible for the Christmas presents, the "13 sons of a giantess". They all arrive on their own day between 12 and 24 December and their names are: *Stekkjastaur* (Sheep-Cote Clod – is skinny and stiff, steals milk from ewes in the stables), *Giljagaur* (Gully Gawk – sneaks milk from cowsheds), *Stúfur* (Stubby – steals pots and pans to eat the burnt leftovers), *Þvörusleikir* (Spoon Licker), *Pottaskefill* (Pot Scraper), *Askasleikir* (Bowl Licker), *Hurðaskellir* (Door Slammer), *Skyrgámur* (Skyr Gobbler), *Bjúgnakrækir* (Sausage Swiper), *Gluggagægir* (Window Peeper – peers wide-eyed into the warm, cosy rooms from outside the window), *Gáttaþefur* (Doorway Sniffer), *Ketkrókur* (Meat Hook – loves to munch on the Christmas roast) and *Kertasníkir* (Candle Stealer).

The Hallgrimskirkja in Reykjavik

In the past, the "sons of the giantess" were known for playing tricks on people from 12 December. However in the meantime, they have taken over the responsibility of distributing Christmas presents. On 6 January they return to their caves. Of course Father Christmas, dressed all in red, has also found his way into Iceland in more recent times.

It is said that the "Yule Cat" will gobble up anyone who has been too lazy to bother spinning any wool in the Autumn. However those who have made the effort will receive *Jólaföt* (clothes) for Christmas. There is a very popular Icelandic Christmas song about this tale.

Christmas Eve is officially ushered in at 6pm with church bells and they exchange Christmas wishes.

Christmas food in Iceland is very traditional, with dishes typical of the country. In December, *Laufabrauð* (Christmas biscuits) baked in oil and other smoked dishes are prepared, such as *Hangikjöt*, a lamb dish, or pork loin, but also fish such as salmon or trout.

Furthermore, even hunted rock ptarmigan is on the menu, as well as "snowflake bread", *Laufabrauð*, with colourful patterns, similar to the Indian lentil bake *Papadam*.

There is also a white potato sauce called Uppstúfur, served with peas and red cabbage.

The sweet and salted *Hamborgarhryggur* is a particularly popular dish – essentially salty roast pork coated with a sweet glaze and served with a Coca-Cola sauce. Caramelised potatoes, pickled red onions, vegetables and often a Waldorf salad are served with this.

These are the most common dishes, but there are also others that are becoming more and more popular. These include turkey, expensive cuts of beef, goose and luxurious seafood (Icelandic lobster) or salmon. Seafood soup and lobster soup are also popular as starters or main courses.

For a true Icelandic Christmas, boiled sweet rice pudding also has to be included in which an almond is hidden. The child who finds it receives an extra present.

Icelanders also love to bake Lebkuchen, chocolate biscuits, liquorice tops, and many other sweets.

Christmas beer and *Malt og appelsin*, a kind of malted drink made of apple juice, make up the traditional drinks.

Presents come after diner and some Icelanders then go to midnight mass where they meet neighbours and friends. However others stay at home and turn their attention to their gifts. They enthusiastically read books or play cards and enjoy their sweets.

Jóladagur, the first day of Christmas, is spent within the family circle; they relax, eat good food and watch films.

On the second day of Christmas, *Annar í jólum*, it is similar, but many people also celebrate in bars in the evening which are open until late at night. They start to let off fireworks even a couple of days before New Year's Eve. The greatest spectacle is obviously at midnight on New Year's Eve.

These explosions go on until 6 January, albeit slightly quieter, when Epiphany is celebrated in Iceland.

Hangikjöt (smoked lamb) is a raw Icelandic ham speciality of smoked lamb or mutton, often the legs on the bone and a fatty layer. Firstly, the meat is rubbed with coarse sea salt and then cured for two to four days. Then, depending on the thickness, it is cold-smoked for two to four weeks at about 22 °C with birch. Then the *Hangikjöt* is matured in fresh air. *Hangikjöt* is offered throughout the entire year. It can be cut into thin slices and eaten with bread or boiled with potatoes, peas and a white bechamel sauce as a main course. Generally, every Icelander will eat *Hangikjöt* at least once during the Christmas period.

Lebkuchen – a popular sweet

Hangikjöt, smoked lamb

Poached salmon fillet with hazelnut

1 kg	salmon fillet, no skin, cut into portion-sized chunks
2 l	water
½ tbsp	salt
1 tbsp	white peppercorns
1	bay leaf
2	unwaxed lemons
50 g	chopped hazelnuts, for scattering
	Lettuce

Boil the water with the herbs in a large pan, add the juice of half a lemon, slice the other half of the lemon and add this to the water. Remove from the heat, add the pieces of fish and leave to cook for about 10 minutes (no longer boiling).

Lift the pieces of fish out of the stock, dish up on a plate garnished with lettuce and scatter over the chopped nuts. Garnish with lemon slices. You could also serve with a remoulade sauce. Delicious warm or cold.

Laufabrauð
("Snowflake bread", Christmas baking)

700 g	flour
1 tsp	baking powder
½ tbsp	sugar
50 g	butter or margarine
½ l	milk
	Coconut oil, for frying
	Salt

Make a smooth dough from the flour (wholemeal flour or rye bread flour would also work), a little warm milk, salt and baking powder, and finally a little sugar. Divide the mix into small pieces and then roll each one out as thinly as possible to that you get circles with a diameter of 15 to 20 cm. After rolling the dough out, cut small patterns into the dough or roll over them with relief rollers. Finally, the "snowflake bread" is fried in hot fat until golden brown. Laufabrauð is crispy and traditionally eaten during the Christmas period and on New Year's Eve with smoked lamb or ham.

ITALY

Buon Natale e felice Anno nuovo

Astro del ciel, pargol divin

Christmas time in Italy is a carousel of presents for the children. Celebrating *San Nicola*, St Lucia, Father Christmas *Babbo Natale*, the Baby Jesus *Gesù Bambino* and the witch *Befana*, each one an occasion for children to receive presents. *Santa Lucia* plays a significant role during the Advent period. According to old traditions, the poor are provided with food on this occasion. Mangers are customary across the whole of Italy and often form the focal point at family gatherings and in churches. New figures are added again and again to these. And of course, there is an abundance of food – from roast meats and various fish to the popular sweet dishes *Panettone* and *Torrone*.

Italians also celebrate Christmas very extensively. The vast number of customs is astounding, which almost always include gifts for the children.

On the island of Sicily, the people are invited to a game of Christmas poker. The winnings help to fund all the presents.

In Italy on 6 December, *San Nicola* is not allowed to be glimpsed by the children; he sneaks unseen into houses during the night of 5 to 6 December and places presents for the kids in front of their bedroom doors.

13 December is *Santa Lucia's* day, the "messenger of light". She comes in the night of 13 December and places *Dolci* (sweet delicacies) or even small presents on the windowsill or in shoes for the children. The saint once bequeathed her entire fortune to the poor. Today, *Torrone dei poveri*, a meal for the poor, is still prepared on this day. According to old tradition, it includes chickpeas, which are cooked with sugar, until they become solid.

Mangers have been customary all across Italy from the early 14th Century. *Il presepe* (the Christmas manger) is the most important attribute before and during the Christmas celebrations in Italy. The wonderfully designed Christmas mangers are put up in living rooms and churches about two weeks before Christmas. They are then the focal point in the family circle and during church services.

New figures from the Christmas story, family history, village events or from friendship circles are added throughout the years, since everyone wants to have their own individual manger. However, the figure of the Baby Jesus is only allowed to be placed into manger during the night from 24 to 25 December – and that is at midnight on the dot.

Francis of Assisi is seen as the "inventor" of the Christmas manger. After a visit to Bethlehem in the year 1223, he thought about how he could present the Christmas message to the ordinary people of his hometown as emphatically and vividly as possible. The oldest written document in which the construction of a manger is mentioned comes from the year 1384.

In the meantime, beautifully decorated Christmas trees have become more and more common on the celebration days but are not traditionally part of Christmas celebrations in Italy. On 23 December, children in some regions dress up as shepherds and go singing from house to house accompanied by flutes – in the manner of poor herdsmen

Italian nativity figures.

of previous times. During the Advent period, they used to play old folk tunes on bagpipes and pan pipes, for which they were given, and still are given, some money or sweets.

In Rome, canons are fired from the Castel Sant'Angelo on Christmas Eve to mark the start of the Christmas celebrations and at the end of the strict 24-hour fasting period.

Presents are brought by either *Babbo Natale*, the Italian Father Christmas, or by the witch *Befana* only on 6 January – or even by both.

In the region surrounding Trieste, on Christmas Eve every family member pulls a slip of paper with the number of their present out of a little bag. Then there is a large celebratory meal. This includes fish, fried vegetables (*Fritti*) or turkey. *Panettone* is most commonly served as a Christmas cake for pudding. Yet many inhabitants of Trieste also eat salad with herbs and tropical fruits, *Prosciutto*, *Salami*, *Pasta scampi* or truffle pasta, pumpkin with mushrooms, winter squid, salmon, cooked suckling pig, turkey, lemon sorbet and *Gubana* (a kind of nut strudel) at Christmas.

A typical Christmas menu in neighbouring Muggia is *Baccala alla triestina in bianco*, *Mussoli alla scottadeo*, *Frutti di mare*, *Polipi insalata*. (Trieste stockfish in white wine, boiled mussels, seafood, stockfish salad).

A specific sweet festive speciality is *Torrone* – nougat made of honey and egg white with nuts or almonds.

Traditionally for *Torrone*, a copper kettle is heated from below with an agitator early in the morning, for example at about 7am. The light honey is prepared with the egg whites, beaten until they form soft peaks. Until the 1960s, it was customary to stir the ingredients at home by hand, a long and strenuous task. To do so, two to three women always took it in turns to thoroughly mix the honey mixture, which could weight up to 15 kg to then later fold in the same amount of nuts or almonds.

Midnight mass, celebrated by the Pope in St Peter's Basilica, is watched on TV, before *Gesù Bambino* (Baby Jesus) arrives early in the morning on 25 December. He places presents in front of the children's bedroom doors or under the pine tree. Then, the family all meet up for the great Christmas meal. The table is covered in all the delicacies that Italian cuisine has to offer. Then they play games together, often there is also a small tombola.

Various forms of feasts and celebrations have become established in different regions of Italy. In some areas, an olive tree is felled and prepared for the fire in the fireplace. In Rome and Naples, the children go from house to house carrying a large paper star above a small, illuminated manger.

On New Year's Eve, it has always been customary to wear red underwear, much like in China. This is said to bring happiness, love and health into the new year.

6 January is the high point of a happy Christmas period in Italy, since the children receive presents with the arrival of the Three Kings at the stable. On the evening of 5 January, the children place their shoes in front of the door or hang their stockings on the fireplace.

The witch *Befana* brings the presents. She is depicted as an ugly but very kind-hearted old woman. La *Befana* flies from roof to roof and down the chimney into the houses. She leaves sweets and presents for good children, but she has black lumps of coal ready for the bad children.

Pasta con scampi

(Pasta with prawns)

500 g	pasta (spaghetti, tagliolini)
3 tbsp	olive oil
4	cloves of garlic, finely chopped
500 g	prawns
	Pinch of chilli powder
1 bunch	chives, finely chopped
	Salt, pepper

Cook the pasta in salted water until al dente. Then drain and mix with the olive oil to prevent it sticking together.

Fry the garlic until translucent, then add the prawns, season and cook until done. Add the cooked pasta and heat again, stirring constantly. To serve, scatter over the chopped chive.

Salmon with crab in a mascarpone sauce

600 g	salmon fillet, cut into 4 portions
2	fennel bulbs, finely chopped
3	carrots, finely chopped
1	onion, finely diced
⅛ l	dry white wine, or diluted white wine vinegar (optionally balsamic vinegar)
2	bunches parsley
4 tbsp	vinegar
1	lemon, cut into slices
90 g	mascarpone
2 tbsp	lemon juice
3 cl	grappa (only for adults!)
200 g	prepared prawns
50 g	butter
2 tbsp	olive oil
	Salt, pepper

Boil the parsley, salt, sugar, vinegar and lemon juice in about 1 l water. Then, add the pieces of fish and simmer over a low heat for 3 to 4 minutes.

Remove the pieces of fish and keep warm on an oiled baking tray. Save some of the cooking liquid. Cook the fennel and carrots in salted boiling water until al dente. Drain, drizzle with olive oil and keep warm.

Boil the onion with the white wine or diluted white wine vinegar, add about ¼ l of the fish stock or vegetable stock and allow to thicken slightly. Then stir in the mascarpone and season with lemon juice, grappa (only for adults!), salt and pepper. Cook the prawns in the sauce. Serve the salmon and vegetables on plates and pour the sauce with the prawns over the top. White bread, potatoes or rice go well with this.

Panettone
(see also Switzerland)

1	cube yeast
250 ml	milk
150 g	sugar
650 g	flour
200 g	butter
1	egg
4	egg yolks
1 tsp	salt
1	unwaxed lemon, zest
50 g	chopped almonds
100 g	candied lemon peel, finely diced
100 g	candied orange peel, finely diced
150 g	raisins, soaked in rum
	Butter for the tin
	Baking paper

Crumble the yeast into the lukewarm milk, add a pinch of sugar and leave for 10 minutes for the bread starter or pre-ferment. Put the flour, sugar, melted and cooled butter, egg, egg yolks (leaving a little for brushing later), salt, lemon zest and starter in a bowl and knead well together.

Mix in the almonds, candied lemon peel, candied orange peel and raisins and quickly knead together. Cover the dough and leave to rise until doubled in size.

In the meantime, grease a cooking pot that is 12 cm tall (c. 15 cm diameter, oven safe) and line with baking paper. Knock the dough back, place in the pot and leave to rise again (c. 15 minutes). Brush the mixture with egg yolk and cut a cross into the top. Bake in a preheated oven at 175 °C for about 90 minutes.

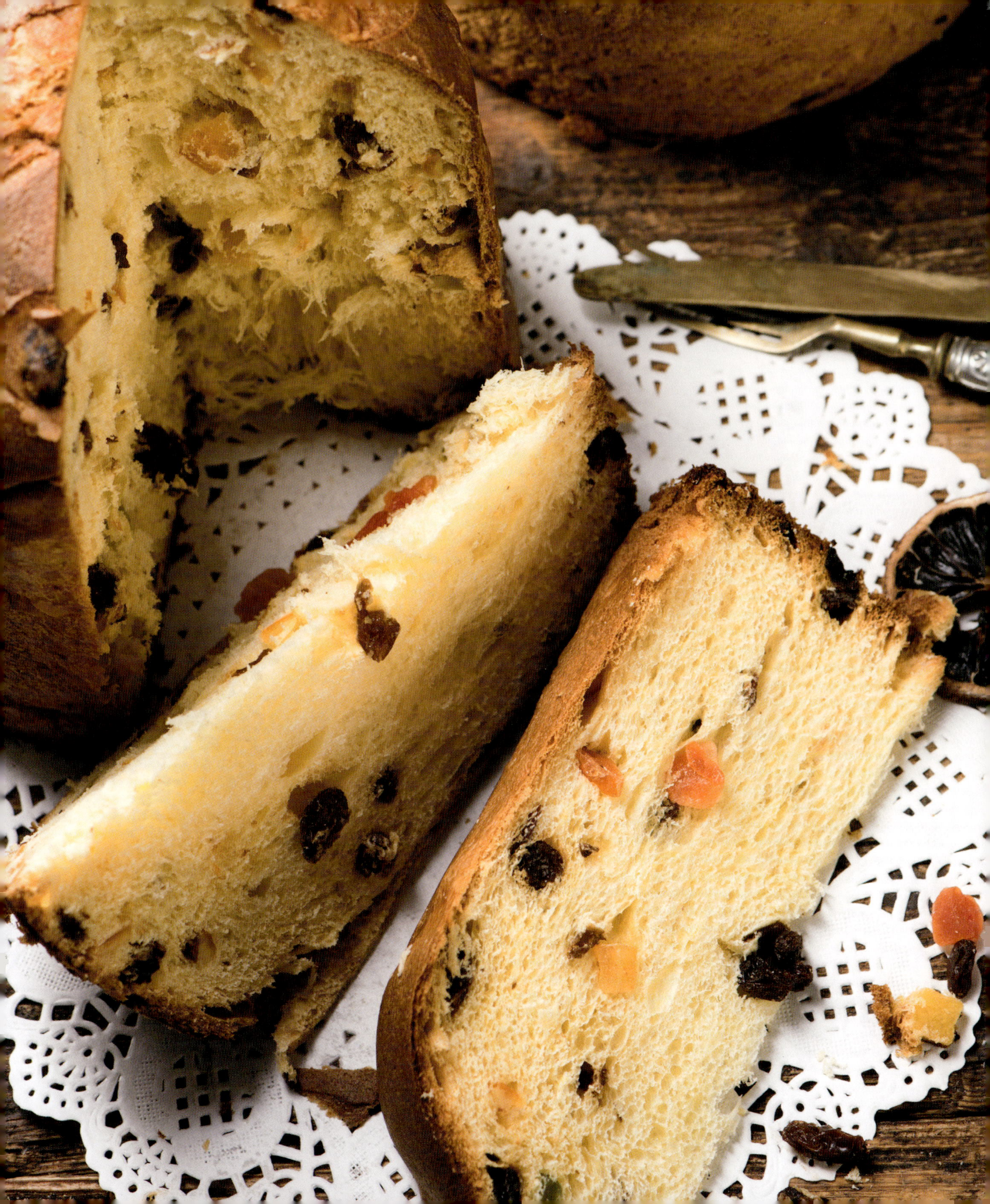

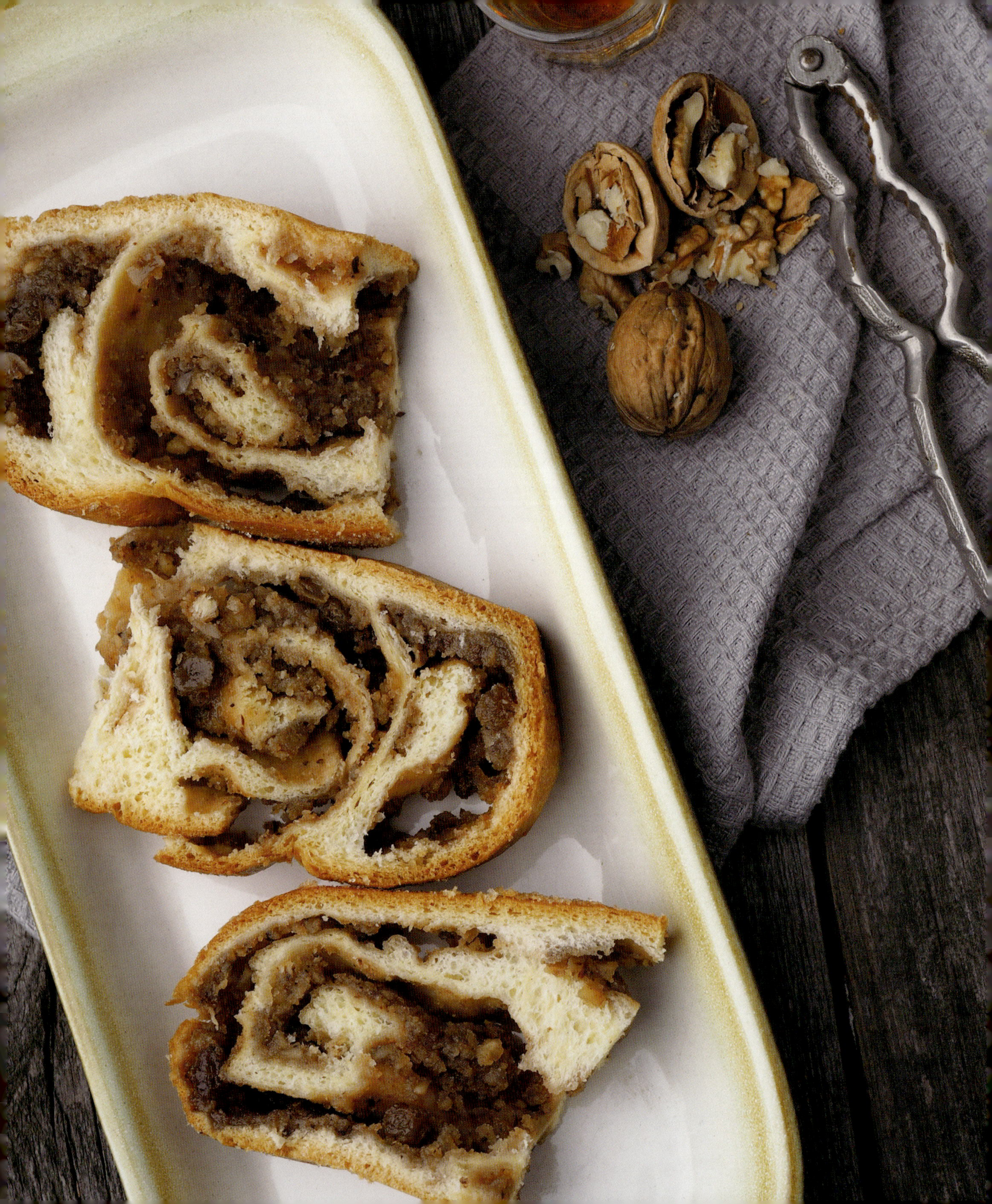

Gubana

(Friulian Reindling, Preßnitz)

Dough

125 g	butter
	Pinch of sugar
2 tbsp	icing sugar
1 cube	yeast
4	egg yolks
¼ l	milk, warmed
450 g	flour, soft
1 sachet	vanilla sugar
1	unwaxed lemon, zest
	Salt
	Cinnamon
	Butter and flour for the worktop or the backing tin

Filling

¼ kg	chopped hazelnuts
100 g	pine nuts, soaked
100 g	raisins, soaked
50 g	sugar
50 g	biscuit crumbs (or cake crumbs)
50 g	chocolate, grated
50 g	candied orange peel, finely chopped
50 g	candied lemon peel, finely chopped
70 ml	rum or 1 vial of rum flavouring
80 g	butter shavings

Stir the crumbled yeast together with a pinch of sugar, the milk and some flour, cover, and leave to rise in a warm place with no draughts to form a bread starter, a pre-ferment.

Beat together the butter, icing sugar, vanilla sugar and a little salt until soft and then gradually beat in the yolks. As soon as the starter is well risen, add the butter mixture and flour and beat everything together to form a smooth dough. Cover and leave to rise again in a warm place.

Roll the dough out on a floured surface into a rough rectangle. Scatter nuts, sugar, pine nuts, raisins, cake crumbs, chocolate, candied orange peel, candied lemon peel and cinnamon over the top. Drizzle with the rum (flavouring) and distribute the butter shavings over the top.

Now roll the dough up and place the roll in a round baking tin, greased well with butter. Leave covered in a warm place until the Gubana has once again doubled in size. Then brush with butter and bake in a preheated oven at 170 °C for about an hour.

Italy

Croatia

Čestit Božić i sretna nova godina **Tiha noć, sveta noć**

"Kathrein stops the dance", they also say in colloquial Croatian. The quiet weeks before Christmas provide plenty of opportunities for exchanging gifts. Similarly to in Italy, in Croatia it is above all the children who receive presents. *Sveti Nikola* brings the first presents on 6 December. Advent is also an important time to sow Christmas wheat. On 24 December, the Christmas log common in the Balkans, *Badnjak*, is set alight and straw is scattered. There are delicious feast day dishes that vary between regions, and then it's off to mass at midnight. New Year's Eve is celebrated exuberantly and on 6 January the mood is once again very tranquil.

As in all Christian countries, Christmas customs are an important part of the tradition and culture of Croatia. This Balkan country has a surprisingly high number of associated customs, which differ from region to region.

In some parts of Croatia, preparations for the Christmas period start as early as 25 November with the saying "*Sveta Kata zatvara vrata*". In English: "St Catherine closes the door." This means the start of the fasting Advent. Weddings and other great celebrations are then no longer held.

Large towns such as Zagreb and Dubrovnik are decorated for the feast days, for example with giant pine trees in town squares, decorated with splendid red and gold baubles. Thousands of lights shine brightly and people love to visit one of the many Christmas markets.

The first Sunday of Advent kicks off the reflective pre-Christmas period, which, up until the 16th Century, used to last for six weeks. Nowadays, the first candle on the Advent wreath is also lit in Croatia.

On 6 December, *Sveti Nikola* introduces the days for gift giving. On the previous evening, children in north Croatia polish their boots, place them on the windowsill and hope for presents from Nicholas. He is accompanied by Krampus, a furry figure who the children are supposed to be afraid of. Often there are sweets or toffee apples.

With the celebration of St Lucy on 13 December or the 3rd Sunday of Advent – the "Father-proceeds day" – the rounds of gifts get underway. Fathers surprise their children with a little something. The "Mother-proceeds day" is on the 4th Sunday of Advent. On this day, mothers give their children apples, nuts, dried figs and plums.

On St Lucy's Day, sometimes also on St Barbara's Day on 4 December, mothers or daughters sow the *Božićna pšenica* (Christmas wheat). The taller the crop grows in the flowerpots until Christmas, the more successful the coming year is said to be.

On Christmas Eve, the wheat – hopefully tall, green and sumptuous by then – is bound together with a ribbon in the colours of the Croatian flag.

Christmas Eve in Croatia is called *Badnja večer*. On this day, the yule log is set alight (normally by the father of the family). The log is then supposed to burn for the whole of the first Christmas holiday, which today is only the case in rural regions.

Yet on Christmas Eve, in some places three yule logs are burnt as a symbol of the Holy Trinity. The embers are used to light all the candles in the house, which should bring riches to the inhabitants.

When the head of the family brings straw into the house as a reminder of the birth of Jesus in the stable, this symbolises the start of the Christmas holidays. *Medenjak* (Lebkuchen) are baked and enjoyed far and wide.

Christmas trees were not common in Croatia until the middle of the 19th Century. Before then, broad leaf trees were used, then later evergreen pine trees. The wooden manger, usually handmade, is placed under the Christmas tree.

On Christmas Eve, children have the creative task of decorating the house with home-made paper decorations, flowers, gilded nuts and fruits.

Whoever can, then goes to Midnight mass on Christmas Eve. And at 5 o'clock in the morning on Christmas Day, they then visit the pastorate.

After the church service, there is hot slivovitz, Christmas biscuits and pastries are exchanged and wishes for a "blessed Christmas" as well, with the traditional response being, "Together with you – thanks be to God." When doing so, the people kiss one another as a symbol of peace.

Of course the Croatians also sing the song "Silent night". Furthermore, a typical Croatian Christmas song is "*Narodi nam se*" (Unto us is born).

Djed Mraz (Jack Frost), who came back to life during the period of socialism in the 1960s, disappeared again in the 1990s and made way for a new gift bearer, *Djed Bozicnjak* (Father Christmas).

Cod (*Bakalar*) is one of the traditional foods eaten on Christmas Eve, which is prepared in one of two possible ways: as *Brudet* (stew or soup) or *Bianco* (boiled). *Sarma* (cabbage roulade, filled with meat and rice) are also typical, suckling pig. Homemade sausages, *Pašticada* (pot roast beef in Dalmatia) and Kulen (a kind of aromatic pork sausage, particularly common in Slavonia).

Slanina (bacon) and *Panceta* (pork belly) are also very popular. Moreover, cheese and *Pršut* (ham, typical in Dalmatia) are served. On Christmas Eve, there are also many kinds of sweet dishes, such as *Fritule* (mini doughnuts) or *Uštipci*, similar to a doughnut, often with raisins.

However the Croatians normally don't enjoy these specialities before the evening. Christmas presents are first opened on Christmas morning. In Croatia, Christmas lasts for three days. 26 December, St Stephen's Day, is viewed as the second Christmas Day, and that of St John as the third.

New Year's Eve is the biggest party of the year. In the evening, they eat heartily and leisurely, with suckling pig and all kinds of side dishes and a huge number of cakes on the menu. At midnight, the new year is greeted with fireworks on the streets, followed by extensive celebrations in bars and restaurants.

Sveta tri kralja oder *Bogojavljenje* (Epiphany) marks the end of the Christmas period. On this day, the Christmas decorations are usually tidied away and the tree is disposed of.

Around 6 January, groups go on a pilgrimage with papal stars to their families and sing sacral songs. In northern and north-eastern Croatia, in each case three young men go on a pilgrimage from house to house and receive small gifts. The star bearers are sometimes also accompanied by other young people who sing fitting songs.

Christmas wheat

Buzara

(Seafood)

800 g	prepared shellfish (loosened mussels, prawns, calamari, precooked)
150 ml	olive oil
4	tomatoes, peeled, finely chopped
4	cloves of garlic
2 tbsp	breadcrumbs
4 tbsp	chopped parsley
200 ml	white wine
1 tsp	vegeta (Croatian spice powder, you could use a stock cube instead)
	Pepper

Quickly fry the garlic, tomatoes, breadcrumbs, parsley, wine, vegeta and pepper in a pan in hot olive oil. Add the shellfish and leave to simmer with the lid on until everything is cooked. This will only take a few minutes. Serve with white bread.

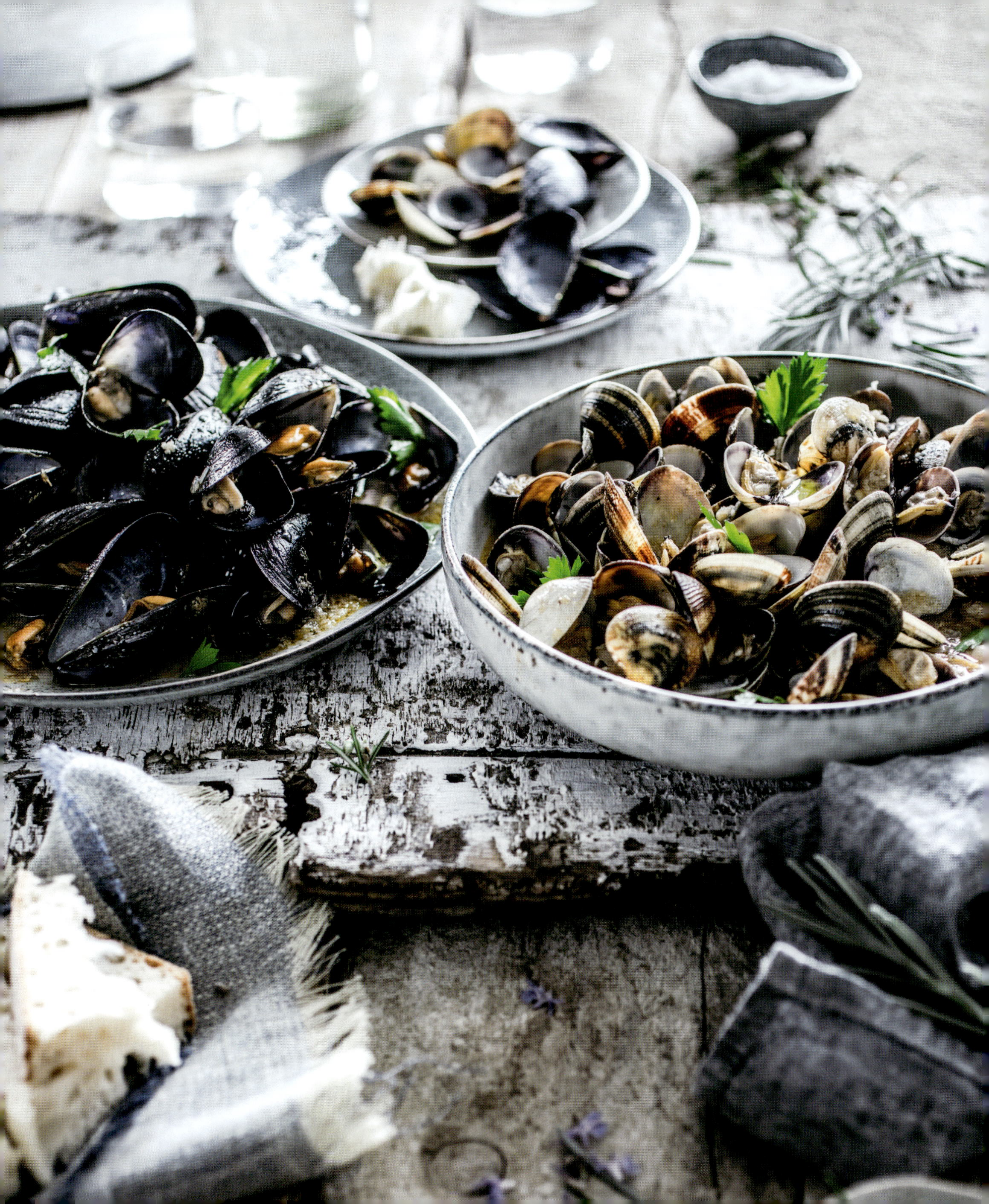

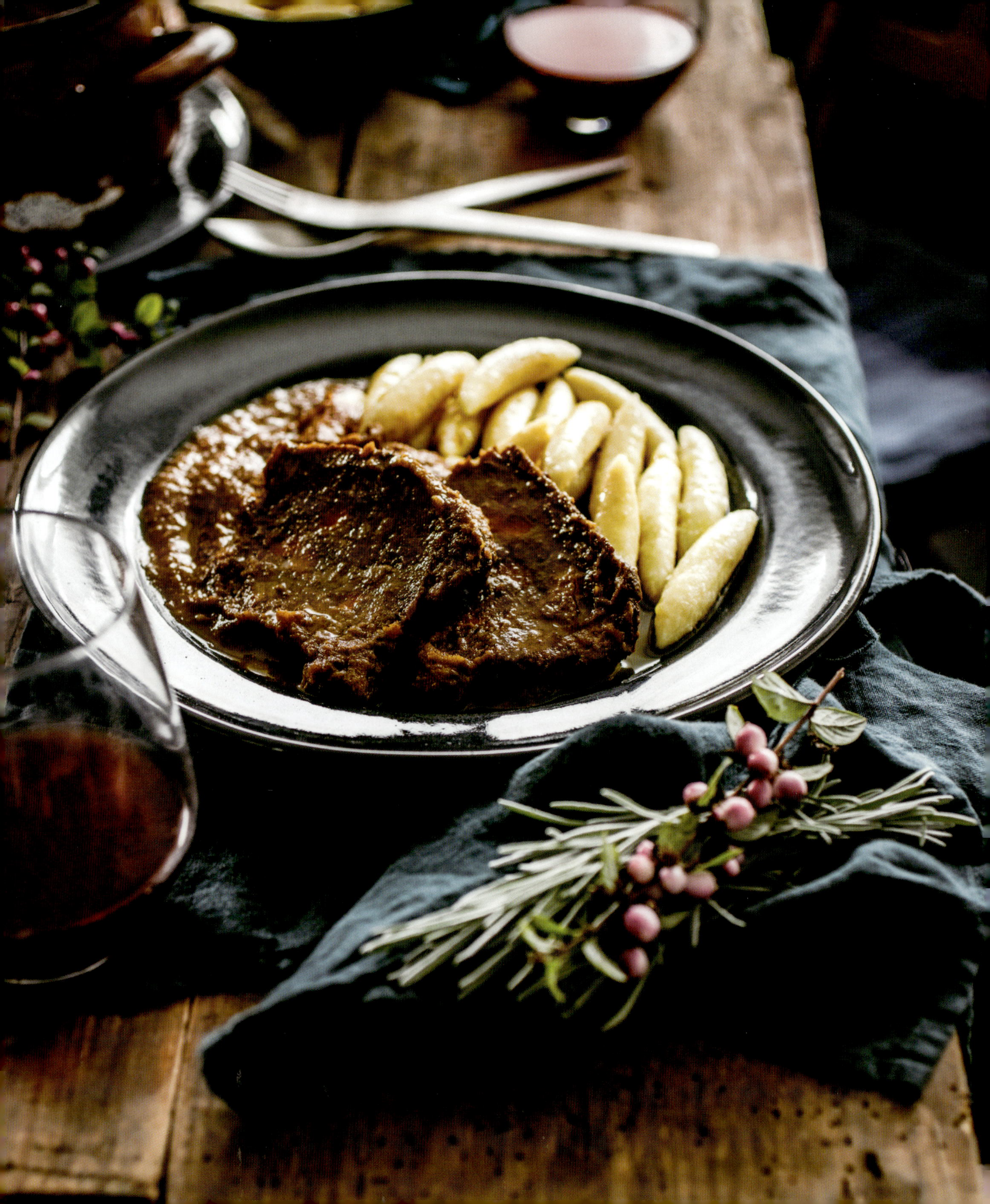

Pašticada
(Pot roast beef)

1 kg	beef (leg)
100 g	smoky bacon, cut into strips
2	onions, finely chopped
1	small celery stick, finely diced
3	carrots, cut into sticks
250 ml	red wine
3	beef tomatoes, skinned, de-cored, finely chopped
250 ml	beef or vegetable stock
1 tbsp	tomato puree
5	cloves of garlic, roughly chopped
	Cloves
1–2	bay leaves
	Olive oil
	Sugar
	White wine vinegar
	Nutmeg
	Salt, pepper

Stud the meat with 3 to 4 cloves, the carrots, garlic and the smoky bacon.

Marinate overnight in the white wine vinegar, then pat dry and brown around the edges in hot oil in a deep pan. Add the onions and celery, then stir the tomato puree as well as a little sugar into the oil. Brown everything together quickly.

Add the tomatoes to the meat, deglaze with red wine and stock, add salt and pepper and place the bay leaves inside. Leave the roast to stew over a low heat for about 3 hours. Regularly douse with hot water or stock.

When the meat is soft, cut into thick slices and leave to simmer in the sauce for a further 10 minutes. Finally bind the sauce with flour, breadcrumbs or butter to make it thick and creamy. Dish up the slices of meat on a plate and serve with the sauce.

Potatoes or Njoki (Gnocchi) go very well with this, as well as spinach or Blitva (Croatian chard with potatoes and garlic).

Dalmatinska Rožata

(Dalmatian crème caramel)

4	eggs, well beaten
12 tbsp	sugar
800 ml	milk
1 sachet	vanilla sugar
1	lemon, zest
	Rosewater
	Syrup or runny honey
	Ovenproof small tins

Caramelise two thirds of the sugar in the pan and share between four small ovenproof tins. Heat the milk together with the rest of the sugar and removed from the heat before it boils.

Then mix with the eggs and also stir in the vanilla sugar, lemon zest and 3 to 4 drops of rosewater. Share the mixture between the tins and leave in a bain-marie until solid and they have come away from the edge of the tins.

After cooling, turn out onto dessert plates, drizzle with syrup or honey and serve.

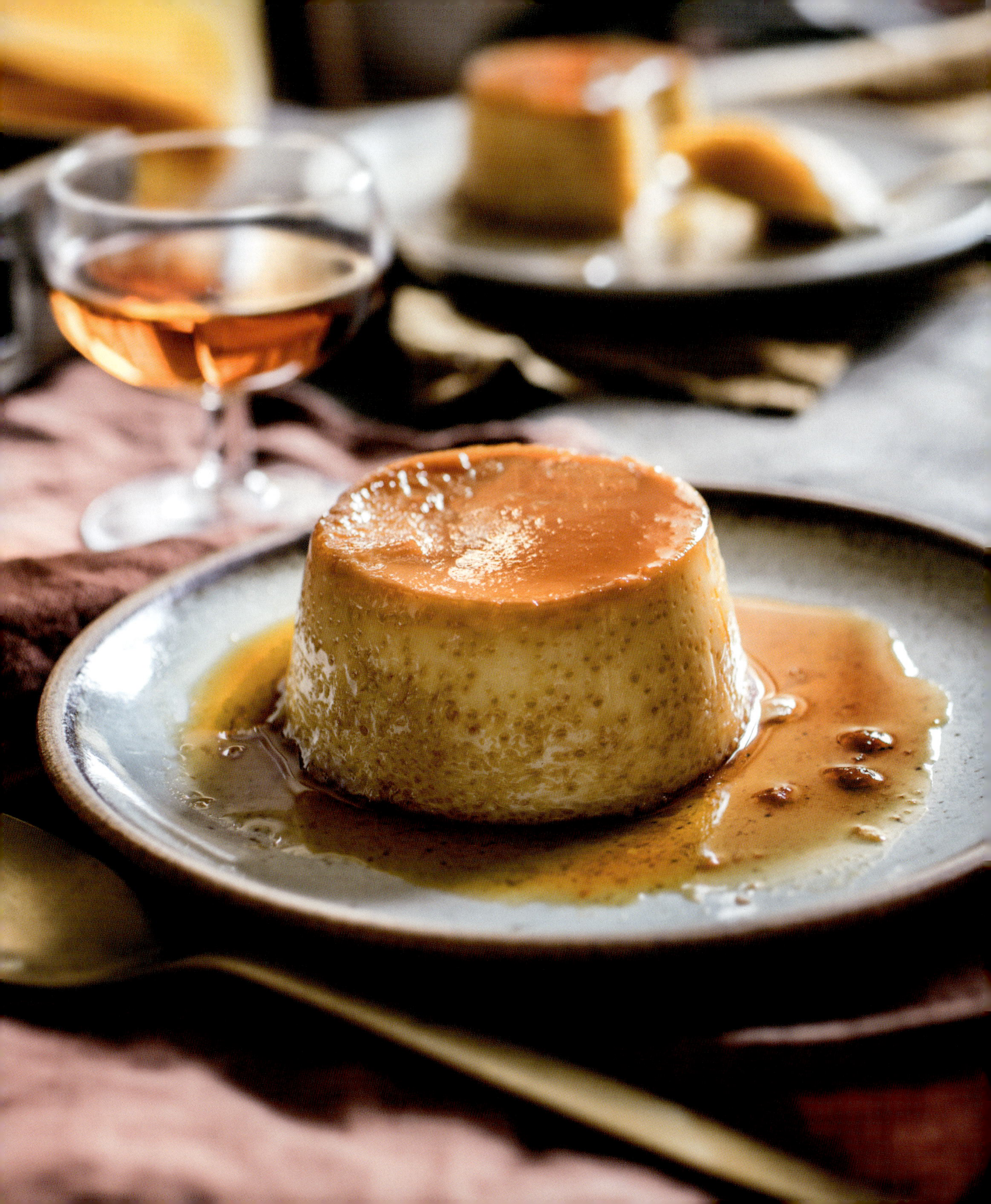

Serbia

Hristos se rodi – vaistinu se rodi!
(Christ is born – he is truly born!)

Tiha noć, sveta noć

In Serbia, the pre-Christmas fasting period is upheld before and on Orthodox Christmas Eve. There are family feasts to honour the patron saints of the house. For Christmas, Traditional Serbian families burn a yule log or branch of oak. Straw with sweets is scattered under the table. But the sweet offerings are only eaten on 7 January when the fasting period comes to an end. Then, bean soup, suckling pig, roast lamb, *Cesnica*, or Christmas bread, are also on the table. *Sliwowitz* and wine complement the feast. New Year's Eve is also celebrated, but the Orthodox turn of the year only takes place on 13th to 14th January.

Christmas markets with mulled wine and mulled cider, mangers and Christmas trees are not especially popular in Serbia.

Instead, there are specific Orthodox festivities to honour the family's patron saints. These traditional celebrations are called Slava – in Serbian *slaviti* means "to celebrate"). "Slava of St Nicholas" is on 19 December.

Badnji dan means "holy day" and falls on 6 January in Serbia. A gun is fired into the air very early in the morning and this announces that everyone should go into the forest to beat trees. This symbolically stands for the wood which the shepherds brought to warm the stable where Jesus was born. Nowadays, a simple bundle of oak branches with dried leaves is also used instead.

Badnje vece is Christmas Eve on 6 January. It is not only mass which is celebrated in churches, but also *Badnjak*, that is the tree that was felled on that day, and the straw, which is reminiscent of Baby Jesus's manger, is consecrated.

When the people return home from mass, the consecrated tree trunk and the straw are brought into the house with them.

Since Christmas Eve, like the previous six weeks, is still a time for fasting, believers eat specific meals. There is no meat, but often fish, salad and beans.

After eating, straw is spread out under the table with sweets and coins hidden in it. In this traditional *Pijukanje*, the children can then look for the sweets in the straw – by

Cesnica, Serbian Christmas bread

The *Badnjak*, a tree trunk or bunch of twigs, is part of the Orthodox Serbian Christmas celebration

shouting *Piju-piju*, like small chicks. Yet the sweets have to wait to be eaten until the following day since the fast is still going on.

On Christmas, that is on 7 January, the fasting period is over, and then they eat well and heartily. This great holiday is called *Božić* in Serbia.

All the church bells peel early in the morning on the Christmas holiday. The people attend morning mass in their Sunday best.

After the church service, *Nafora* (bread) is served. The people traditionally greet each other with the festive words "Christ is born!" and they answer, "That is true, he is born!". At home, they then light a candle, the head of the household takes incense and consecrates every inhabitant, the house and the icons.

After morning mass, there is usually *Cicvara* for breakfast, a dish made of flour, eggs, butter and cheese. There are also small dried cakes on the table, dried figs and homemade *Sljivovica*.

On Christmas Day, the very rich lunch starts earlier than usual and lasts for longer.

A traditionally essential component of the Christmas meal is *Cesnica*, a flat, round Christmas bread. A branch from the *Badnjak* is placed on top and a coin is hidden in the bread. Whoever finds it will supposedly have a particularly happy life for the whole year.

The traditional Christmas roast – the suckling pig – is only common in the villages; families in cities almost always buy roast pork from the butcher.

Pasulj prebana (baked beans), *Sarma* (stuffed herb leaves), *Corba* (bean soup), almond cakes and barrel cakes.

The Orthodox New Year celebration is celebrated extensively with folk singers, firecrackers and fireworks at midnight on 13 January – but in Belgrade, for example, they also take place on 31 December. For children, 31 December is usually a kind of "Nicholas Eve". The following morning, shoes and stockings are filled with nuts, chocolate or other gifts. In Serbia, 14 January finally heralds the new year for everyone.

Corba od pasulja

(Serbian bean soup)

2	potatoes, peeled, cut into cubes
300 g	pork or pork ribs, smoked
1	onion, peeled and halved
250 g	white beans, dried
1 tbsp	sweet paprika
1	parsley root, peeled, cut into slices
3	carrots, peeled, cut into slices
4 tbsp	olive oil
2	cloves of garlic, finely chopped
100 g	sausage, spicy, e.g. Debreziner, cut into slices
½ bunch	parsley, finely chopped
	Salt, pepper

Rinse the beans on the previous day, pour off the washing water and soak the beans overnight in fresh cold water. The following day, heat the beans with the soaking water, add half an onion and the garlic, cover and bring to the boil, cook until al dente and then drain.

Boil the meat separately in water until soft, then pull off the bone and chop up into small pieces.

Finely dice the second half of the onion and fry it with the carrots, the parsley root and the peeled potatoes in hot olive oil. Then dust with the sweet paprika, stir and pour over a little of the cooking water from the meat. Leave to cook further until done.

Now, add the beans and the meat with the remaining meat boiling water to the vegetables and add the sausage.

Boil through everything thoroughly, add more salt to taste or season.

Serve with chopped parsley scattered on top.

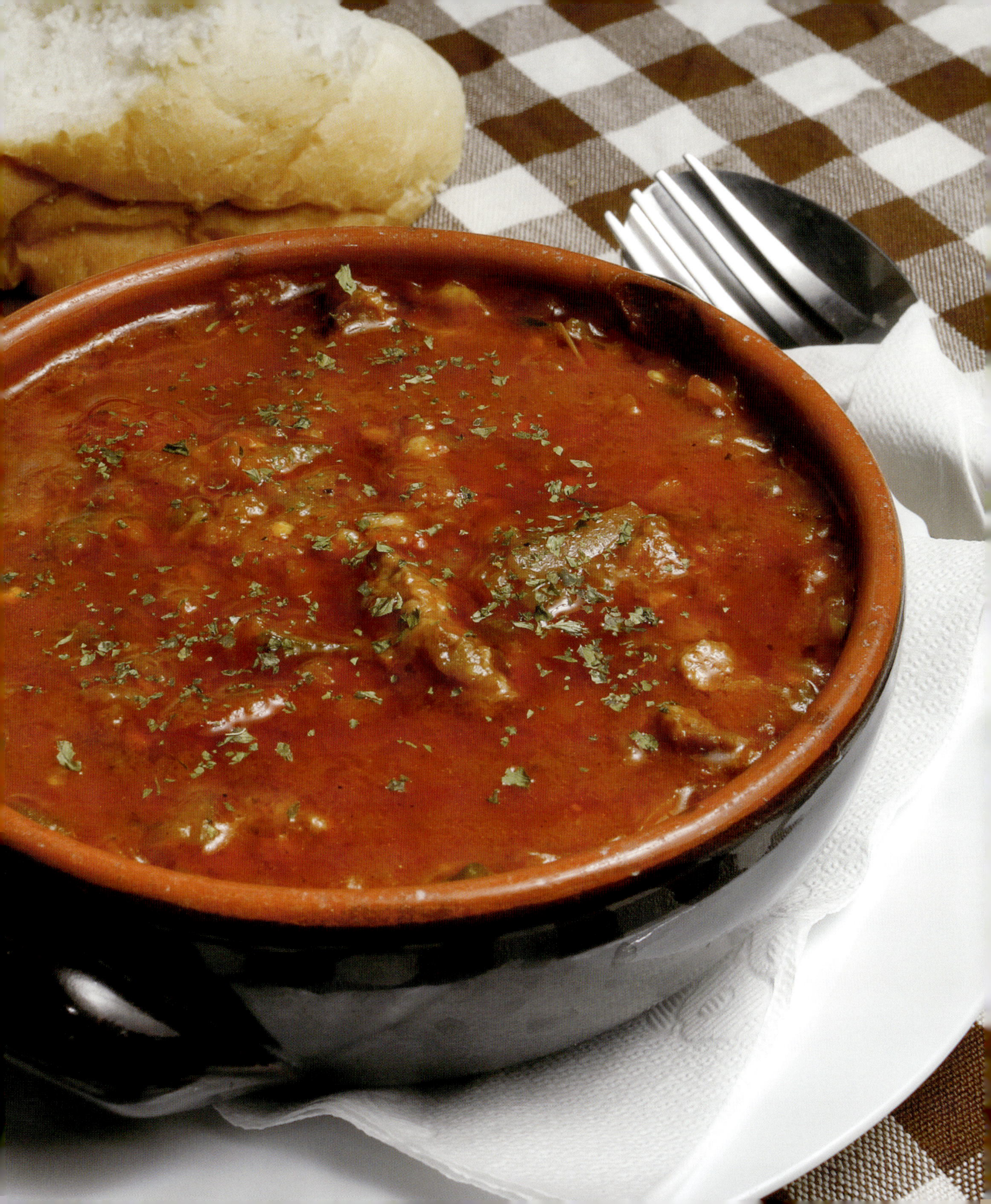

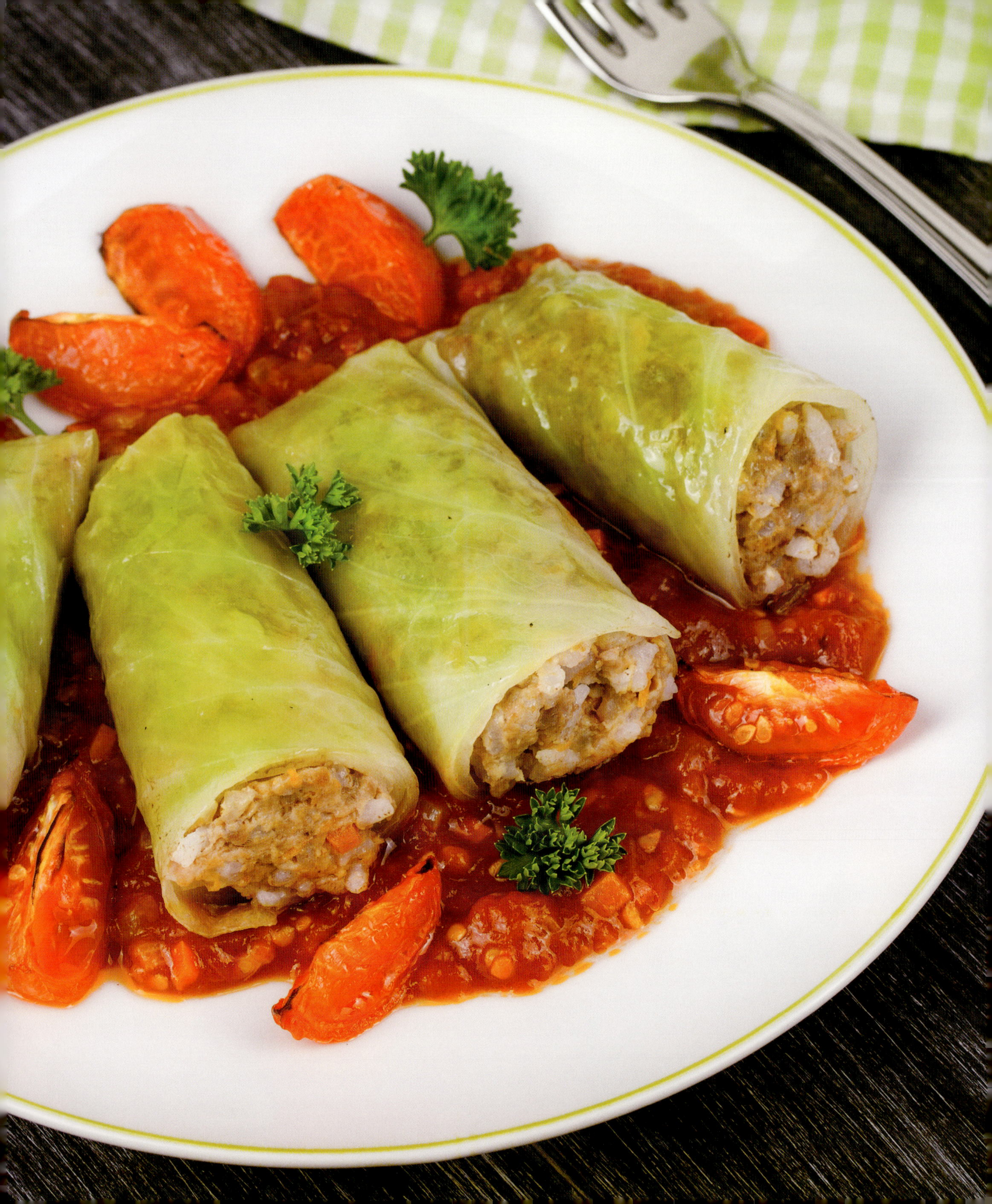

Sarma
(Stuffed cabbage rolls)

1	head of cabbage, large
2	onions, cut into small cubes
500 g	mincemeat
250 g	rice
2	eggs
1 tbsp	herb or spice mix, dried
1 tbsp	powdered sweet paprika
1	clove of garlic, finely chopped
500 g	tomatoes, passata or from a can
	Vinegar, oil
	Salt, pepper

Cook the rice in well salted water until not quite cooked, drain and leave to dry.

Fry the onions in hot oil, add the mincemeat, fry and deglaze with some diluted vinegar.

Then add the rice, season with the herb mixture and powdered paprika, and cook for a further 10 minutes, stirring continuously. Add the clove of garlic and season with salt and pepper. Leave to cool and stir in the eggs. For the cabbage head, remove the stalk and blanche in simmering water until the leaves are flexible. Then remove the large leaves, fill each with some of the meat-rice mixture, roll up and place into an oiled pot.

Pour over a little water, add the passata, and cook the whole thing over a low heat for about 30 minutes. Finally, dish up the cabbage wraps with the tomato sauce. Salted potatoes are a suitable accompaniment.

Cesnica
(Serbian Christmas cake)

½ l	milk
1 sachet	yeast
2	eggs
1 kg	flour
	Sugar
1	coin
	Salt
	Butter for greasing the cake tin
1	egg yolk for brushing the dough

Put the flour into a bowl, make a well in the centre of the flour. Crumble the yeast into it, cover and leave to rise with a pinch of sugar and some lukewarm milk for about 10 minutes.

Beat the eggs and place in the yeast, add a little salt and then the rest of the milk. Beat the mixture well with a wooden spoon so that you get a smooth dough. Cover the kneaded mixture with a clean tea towel or leave to stand in a yeast dough bowl with a cover. As soon as the dough starts to grow, carefully knead it again. It should rise only by a half. Now press the coin into the dough and place it all in a buttered tin. Using a fork, a pair of scissors or wooden pick, score various motifs (doves, flowers etc.). Brush the surface of the dough with egg yolk.

Bake in a preheated oven at 170 °C until the cesnica has turned golden brown.

Cesnica is usually not cut with a knife but broken by hand. Tradition has it that whoever finds the coin will be blessed for the current year and can expect a lot of happiness, success and money.

SLOVENIA

Vesele božične praznike in srečno novo leto　　　　　　　　　　**Sveta noč, blažena noč**

In Slovenia, the Christmas period covers a very long period of time, that is from 13 November to 2 February the following year. In Slovenia, old folk customs are mixed with religious and modern traditions. One example of this are the magical powers that the Christmas bread is said to possess. The homemade Christmas manger, St Nicholas with angels and devils and the Holy Spirit are also part of Slovenian Advent and Christmas culture, as well as colourful Christmas trees, blessings with holy water and incense to ward off evil spirits. *PolnoĐnica*, the midnight mass, and *Dedk Mraz*, "Jack Frost" who brings the gifts, combine obviously Christian ceremonies with socialist customs.

In Slovenia, the Christmas period begins as early as 13 November with a festive meal which heralds the start of the pre-Christmas fasting period.

Miklavž (Nicholas) comes on 6 December, accompanied by angels and devils. The small villains leap around wildly, rattle their chains and threaten any naughty children. In the meantime, *Miklavž* shares out presents. In Slovenia, Nicholas usually lives together with *Lady Winter* in ice hole no. 9 on Slovenia's highest mountain, Triglav.

During the Advent period, the Slovenes collect green moss and twigs, as well as beautiful stones for *Jaslice*, the Christmas manger, which is only put up on Christmas Eve.

In rural areas, religious Slovenes set up a "little corner of God". This consists of a small fir tree that is not decorated and a hand-carved dove, which symbolises the Holy Spirit.

Bôžič means Christmas in Slovenian, which means something along the lines of "little God". According to Indo-European myth, this title can be seen in close conjunction with the rebirth of the son of God.

Christmas bread made of rye, wheat or buckwheat also has pagan roots. In fact, it is said to possess magical powers which give both humans and animals health and strength for the new year. Moreover, the classical Slovenian nut roulade *Potica* has culinary significance. It can be sweet or savoury.

It is somewhat uncommon to invite friends and acquaintances over on Christmas Eve. Families tend to keep themselves to themselves. In some regions, visits from non-family members are even seen as a bad omen.

Bled Castle – festively illuminated

You can't get through Christmas in Slovenia without a warming fire

The great Christmas celebration begins as the sun sets on 24 December. The house is sprinkled with holy water and tradition has it that incense will protect against evil daemons.

Nowadays, most families have a colourfully decorated Christmas tree, similar to the central European model.

Simple dishes are eaten, and afterwards they head to midnight mass.

In some places, after the Christmas church service, a few small fireworks are let off in front of the church. Back at home, they tuck into a late Christmas meal of black pudding or pork. Yet Slovenian children still have to wait until the following morning for their presents.

On New Year's Eve, the Slovenes celebrate the next "Christmas". Blessings with holy water are repeated, this time for the house and grounds, to smoke out the last of the evil spirits.

On New Year's Day, there are more gifts for the children, this time from *Dedek Mraz*. "Jack Frost" is a relic of the socialist era. He appears clad in a white sheepskin and with a dormouse fur cap on his head.

As in most countries, New Year's Day in Slovenia also ends with exuberant celebrations and splendid fireworks.

The final time you will say and hear any Christmas greeting is on Epiphany – referring back to the Orthodox Church.

Yet up until 2 February, the celebration of the "Presentation of the Lord", the *Jaslice* (Christmas manger) remains in its place and other festive songs are also sung.

Vegetable soup with homemade pasta

400 g	root vegetables (carrots, celery, parsley root), finely chopped
1	leek
3	potatoes, peeled, finely diced
80 g	peas, fresh or deep-frozen
80 g	porcini mushrooms, soaked
1	small onion, diced
1	clove of garlic, chopped
	Peppercorns
1	bay leaf
1	sprig of thyme
1 tsp	marjoram
50 g	flour, soft
1 tsp	(white wine) vinegar
1 ½ l	water
2 tbsp	fresh parsley, finely chopped
	Salt, pepper
	A little oil

Pasta dough (Štrukli dough)

500 g	flour, soft
1	egg
2 tbsp	oil
	Salt
1 tbsp	mild vinegar
	Water, lukewarm

Soak the dried porcini mushrooms in water for about 20–30 minutes. Wash the root vegetables and potatoes, peel them and cut into small cubes. Halve the leek lengthways, wash thoroughly and roughly chop.

Heat the oil in a large pan, sauté the flour in the pan until golden brown, add the onions and fry further, add the root vegetables and fry them altogether for a little longer. Pour over water and simmer over a low heat for about 20 minutes.

Now, add the leek and leave to simmer further for a few more minutes.

Finally, mix in the finely chopped, soaked porcini mushrooms, leave to boil and season with salt and pepper.

For the pasta, mix the ingredients together well and knead to form a smooth dough. Leave to rest for a little while. Then roll the dough out flatly (with a pasta maker) and cut into noodles or stamp out Christmas stars.

Cook in salted water or directly in the soup until al dente. Scatter finely chopped parsley over the finished soup and serve. You could also add pork rind or streaky bacon. Then also use the pasta dough for *Štrukli*.

Christmas roast with Štrukli

(Braised turkey with boiled soft quark strudel)

1 kg	roast turkey (rolled roast), alternatively 1kg turkey breast
1 bunch	parsley, finely chopped
3	leeks, cut into rings
1 tbsp	root vegetables, dried
1 tsp	mustard
200 g	whipped cream
100 ml	chicken stock
3	oranges
	Salt, pepper
	Butter for the tin and cold butter for the sauce

Štrukli dough, see p. 112

Filling

100 g	butter
2	eggs, beaten
400 g	curd cheese, strained
100 ml	sour cream
3 tbsp	fresh tarragon, finely chopped (or 1.5 tbsp dried)
	Butter
	Breadcrumbs
	Salt

Grease a spring release tin with butter. Wash the turkey, pat dry, season with salt and pepper and place in the tin. Preheat the oven to 200 °C.

Using a knife remove the peel from two of the oranges and cut out the individual segments. Juice the third orange. Place the orange segments, parsley and leek on top of the meat. Stir together the orange juice, mustard, cream and stock. Season with salt and pepper. Pour over the turkey and roast in the oven at 200 °C for about 45–50 minutes. Then, drain off the sauce and season it, beating it together with cold butter.

Prepare a *Štrukli* dough as described on page 112. Split the mixture into three, brush with oil, cover and leave to rise in a warm bowl for about half an hour.

For the filling, beat the butter with the curd cheese, the eggs and a little salt until creamy. Finally, add the sour cream and tarragon and a little salt and mix well. Dust a tea towel with flour.

Roll out one of the three pieces of dough very thinly or pull apart with the backs of your hand, as if making normal filo pastry, and leave to dry for a little while. Cut away the pastry ridge remaining around the edges. Spread a third of the filling over one half of the pastry, put some flaked butter over the top and roll to make a thin strudel. Using a wooden spoon, press in Štrukli about 10 cm in length and then separate these with a pastry cutting wheel. The cut surfaces should seal easily.

Repeat the above with the remaining two pieces of dough. Leave the *Štrukli* in small portions in boiling water for about a quarter of an hour, take out, coat quickly in breadcrumbs and put on a plate to keep warm. To serve, cut the roast into pieces and dish up with the *Štrukli* and the sauce.

Potica

(Nut roulade)

Dough
500 g	flour, sieved
80 g	sugar
80 g	butter
1 cube	yeast
250 ml	milk, lukewarm
3	egg yolks
1	unwaxed lemon, zested
	Lard, butter or oil and breadcrumbs for the tin
	Salt

Filling
500 g	nuts, chopped (such as walnuts)
100 g	sugar
50 g	butter
300 ml	milk
150 g	breadcrumbs (Crisp bread or milk bread breadcrumbs)
	Ground cinnamon
2 tbsp	rum or 1 vial rum flavouring
1 sachet	vanilla sugar
1	egg, beaten, for brushing
	Icing sugar for dusting, optional

Carefully stir together the flour, yeast, 2 tsp sugar and 5–6 tbsp of lukewarm milk to form a starter. Dust with a little flour, cover and leave to rise in a warm place for a good quarter of an hour.

For the filling, boil the milk with the sugar, the butter and the vanilla sugar. Add the nuts, breadcrumbs, cinnamon and rum, stir well and then leave to cool.

Melt the butter in milk that is not too hot and add to the starter. Then also add the egg yolk, sugar, a pinch of salt and lemon zest and knead everything together to form a smooth dough. Cover and leave to rise again in a warm place for about an hour. If it has clearly increased in volume, knock back and roll out to be as rectangular as possible.

Brush the filling evenly over the dough.

Now, roll the dough out either from both sides to the middle or, very traditionally, roll it out from just one side. Grease a suitable baking tin, scatter with breadcrumbs and place the roulade in the tin. Cover and leave again for a good quarter of an hour. Then brush with the beaten egg and then bake on the middle shelf in the preheated oven at 180 °C for about 45 minutes. Once cool, dust the Potica with icing sugar.

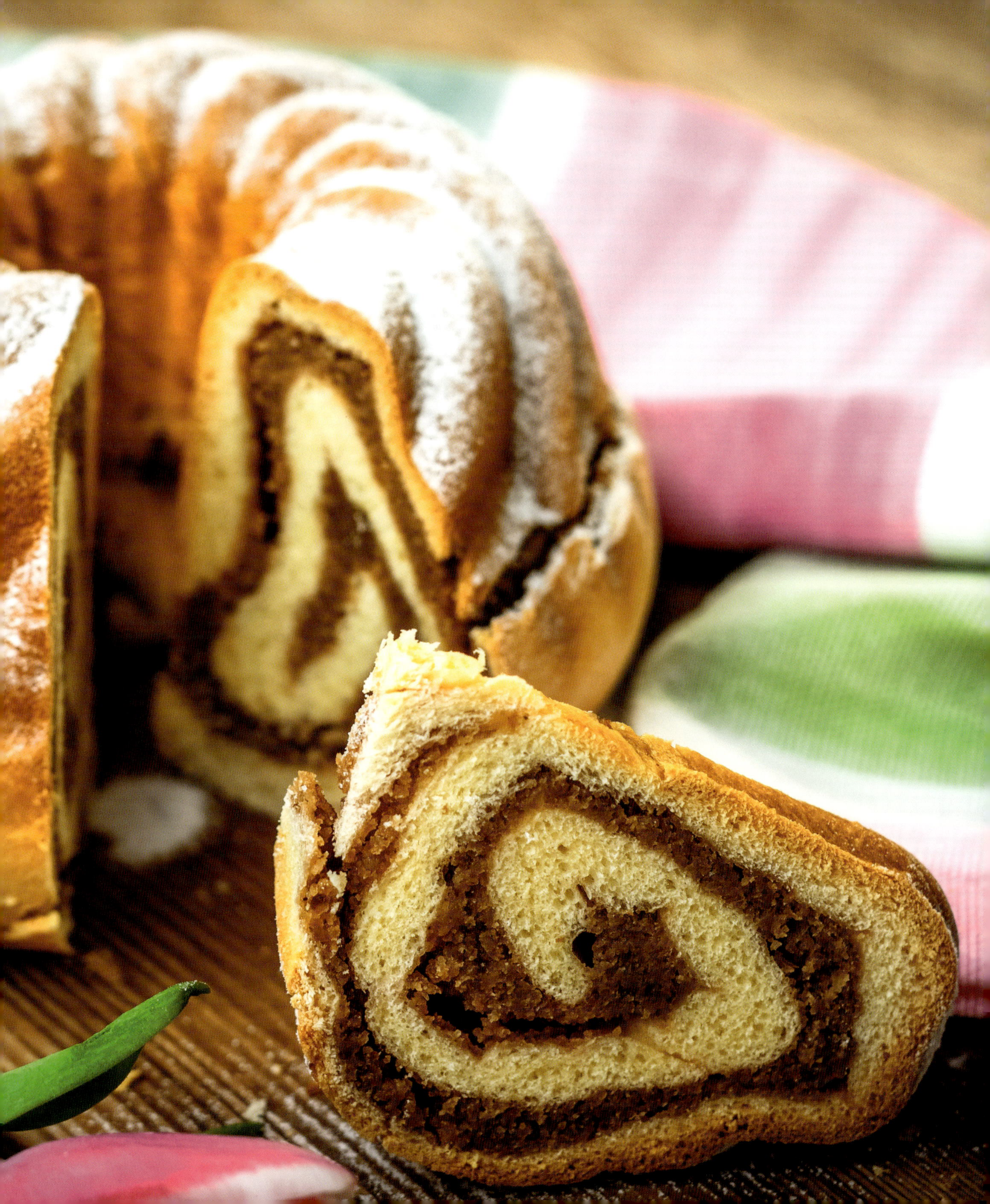

Bosnia · North Macedonia · Kosovo · Montenegro

Bosnia

Sretan božić i srećna nova godina

Tiha noć, sveta noć

In Bosnia-Herzegovina – as in Serbia or Russia – presents are handed out over New Year, and this makes New Year's Eve the most important celebration of the year. In any case, Christmas is celebrated on two dates.

A peculiarity not only in Bosnia but also in many Balkan countries and across Eastern Europe is that followers of different religions take part in each other's celebrations.

Nowadays, in Sarajevo, for example, Christmas Eve is celebrated on 24 December within the family circle. Then, Christians, Muslims, Orthodox Christians and Jews gather together for midnight mass in the Sacred Heart Cathedral. In socialist former Yugoslavia, religious celebrations were only private affairs, but New Year's Eve was celebrated by all religions alike.

The oak tree, *Badnjak*, is traditionally burnt on 6 January, the day before the Orthodox Christmas Day. On Christmas Day, they feast on specialities such as Christmas bread, *Česnica*, before it really gets going a week later for the second New Year festivities.

North Macedonia

Sreḱen božiḱi sreḱna nova godina

Tiha noḱ, sveta noḱ

In North Macedonia, it is also common for people of different religions to come together peacefully over Christmas. Christians and Muslims even share the same pilgrimage sites: the limewood Madonna of Letnica in Kosovo, the Nicholas Church in Albanian Laç and the Tomorr mountain in central Albania. In certain regions, even today some families give their children a Christian and a Muslim name.

In Makedonski Brod, in western North Macedonia, there is one building that is both a church and a mosque. Icons and images of Bektaschi saints hang next to each other, prayer mats lie on the floor – a characterisation of religious life in Macedonia. Christmas decorations consist of dried oak leaves, among other things.

On the evening of 5 January, before the start of the actual holidays, the people come together for *Koleda*, a neighbourhood feast. Special sweetmeats are baked for this and are given as gifts along with other small presents. Music plays around an open fire into the early hours of the morning and they warm themselves with hot *Rakija* (fruit brandy).

On Christmas Eve, called *Badnik*, the actual Christmas celebrations begin with a communal meal in the family. A *Zelnik* (a kind of Macedonian lasagne with various fillings) is served in decorated dining rooms as the traditional dish. For *Badnik*, a special round bread is prepared by a baking a coin into it. Whoever finds it gets a small present and many good wishes for happiness in the coming year. The festive table is traditionally only cleared away early the following day.

In the morning of 6 January, the children finally get their money's worth. They head out in groups, knock on doors, sing and ask for sweets and other little presents.

The three Christmas holidays on 7, 8 and 9 January are traditionally observed with family feasts, visits to relatives and church services.

Kosovo

Gëzuar Krishlindjet vitin e ri (Albanian)
Hristos se rodi – vaistinu se rodi! (Serbian: Christ is born – he is truly born!)

Natë e shenjtë, natë e qetë (Albanian)
Tiha noć, sveta noć (Serbian)

Even if Kosovo is more Muslim on the whole, Christmas is still celebrated by the Christian minority.

In Kosovo, fir trees have a special significance. Because of the atheist communist period in the past, they stand not only for Christmas itself, but for the New Year. Then there was also the "winter man" as the atheist counterpart to Father Christmas.

At 4pm on Christmas Eve, a family member chops four small branches off a walnut tree. Beans, cream, cheese, schnapps and wine are then rubbed into the place where it was cut. Then the branches are bound together to form a cross. When it is dark enough, everyone – apart from the oldest male family member – goes outside the front door and asks the man inside, "Grandfather, would you like us to come over with the cross and the food that God has made?" The traditional answer is "You are all very welcome, come inside!"

Then there is usually beans, *Pite* (yeasted bread) with pumpkin, lettuce, fish and wine.

On the first Christmas day, everyone gets up early and goes into the garden with freshly baked bread and with wine. Here, the oldest in the family will have set up a large circle made of straw with a cross in the middle. Everyone positions themselves around the circle and prays. After the reflective part of the ceremony, fireworks are let off.

Montenegro

Montenegrin is the official language of Montenegro, along with Bosnian, Albanian and Croatian. Christmas greetings are thus just as varied. Christian Orthodox is the predominant religion here, meaning they celebrate the Christmas holidays in the same way as in neighbouring countries, so according to Orthodox rituals. The traditional Christmas meal in Montenegro also corresponds to its surrounding neighbours. *Bakalar* (cod or stockfish), for example, is a typical Christmas dish in Montenegro, but a kind of salad is also prepared. Accompanying this is a famous Montenegrin wine, which is also exported to other countries.

A popular Montenegrin Christmas pastry is the cake *Pogaca* with a coin baked into it.

LATVIA

Priecīgus Ziemassvētkus un laimīgu Jauno gadu   **Klusa nakts, svēta nakts**

The Christmas period in Latvia reflects many pagan and Soviet customs and rituals. Loud music, clothing, dancing and singing shape the Advent period. There have been Christmas trees in Riga for more than 500 years. Typical Christmas food includes a whopping thirteen tasty dishes, often very hearty, which are enjoyed throughout the course of the day. *Pírági* is one of these festive dishes, as well as roast pork with sauerkraut and *Sklandu rausi*. New Year's Eve in the capital city is accompanied by all manner of things, from fireworks to artistic performances. In addition, Latvians enjoy a glass of their "Riga Black Balsam".

It is also the case in Latvia that Christian traditions have mixed with those that are seemingly archaic. For example, for both Winter Solstice and Christmas Eve, they go from house to house with an oak beam, causing an uproar with loud music. The log is burnt in the final garden to ward off evil and to give new strength to the sun. When doing so, participants sing and dance. As well as just dancing, symbolic plays are also on the programme. One of them is called "The wolf eats the goat". In it, the wolf symbolises darkness and the little kid the light.

Another Latvian Christmas tradition is called *Budéli*. To celebrate this, the children dress up as animals, as well as the sun or death, and go from door to door to chase away evil spirits, according to ancient beliefs. As a small reward they receive sweets. The adults accompanying them sometimes also get a shot of schnapps.

The country's first Christmas tree was erected about 500 years ago in Latvia's capital city, Riga, and they celebrated this anniversary in 2011. Today, Christmas trees are very colourful and are decorated with lots of cotton and real candles, as well as dried flowers. The tree is also adorned with straw stars. They symbolise the beaming sun.

At Christmas the Latvians also have a total of thirteen dishes spread throughout the day, often hearty ones, such as black pudding with peas, sauerkraut, pearl barley, *Pírági* (pierogi), *Sklandu rausi* (tartlets filled with mashed potato and carrots), pig snout, roast pork or fish – lamprey, for example, with cucumber sauce. Often, the Latvians stash away any large fish scales in their wallets, which is said to bring heaps of riches in the new year.

Whoever eats these dishes nine times is also is said to also be prosperous and happy in the new year. In addition, the Latvians traditionally drink *Ruguspiens*, which is soured milk or kefir.

Russian Orthodox Latvians celebrate Christmas on 6 January. However, during the Soviet period, it was entirely forbidden to celebrate the birth of Christ. New Year celebrations took place during the Advent period, but any Christian Christmas songs were forbidden.

In schools and factories they were allowed to celebrate with a New Year's Tree, as well as the figures "Jack Frost" and Snow White.

On New Year's Eve, the people in Latvia can enjoy an interesting entertainment programme of Latvian artists on the quay in Daugava followed by an impressive firework display at midnight. To mark the occasion, the revellers drink "Riga Black Balsam". This is a national drink in Latvia made of peppermint, St John's wort, vermouth, birch buds, ginger, calamus and melissa.

Pīrági
(Pierogi)

Dough
500 g	flour, sifted
¼ l	milk, mixed with water
1 cube	yeast
75 g	butter
1 tbsp	sugar
1	egg
	Salt

Filling
350 g	bacon, smoked, finely chopped
1	medium onion, finely chopped
	Pepper

For the filling, mix the bacon and onions together well and fry briefly in a pan, pepper, and then leave to cool.

Make a starter out of the crumbled yeast with a little warm water and flour and leave to rise in a warm place for 15 minutes. Dissolve the salt and sugar in milk or water that is about body temperature. Add the beaten egg and add everything together with the melted butter and the rest of the flour to the starter and knead well until the dough comes away from the spoon or your hands. Then leave again in a warm place until doubled in size. Then, knock back the dough briefly, shape into a roll about 5 cm in diameter and cut it into pieces about 3 cm long.

Mould each piece into a ball and leave these to rise again for about 15 minutes. Then flatten the balls, put some of the filling on top, fold the dough in half to make a crescent shape and seal well. Place on a baking tray, brush with egg yolk and bake in the oven until light brown. Finally, brush the Latvian pierogi with melted butter.

Latvia

Roast pork with sauerkraut and potatoes

Roast
- 600 g roasting pork with rind
- 400 g pig bone
- 2 carrots
- 1 parsley root, roughly cubed
- 200 g celery, roughly cubed
- 2 onions, roughly chopped
- 2 garlic cloves, roughly chopped
- 500 ml beer, dark

Stock
- 1 tbsp oil
- 1 tsp caraway
- 1 bay leaf
- Peppercorns, juniper berries, salt, freshly ground pepper

Sauerkraut
- 800 g sauerkraut
- 1 onion, finely cubed
- 100 ml dry white wine
- 400 ml stock
- 1 slice smoked streaky bacon, finely cubed
- 1 bay leaf
- Apple sauce
- Peppercorns, juniper berries
- Oil
- Sugar

Parsley potatoes
- 500 g waxy potatoes
- 2 tbsp butter
- ½ bunch parsley, freshly chopped

Preheat the oven to c. 220 °C using a fan oven. Rinse the pork bones with cold water and leave to dry and, with the root vegetables but not the garlic, distribute in a roasting dish coated with oil.

Wash the pork rind, pat dry and score crosses into it. Rub the salt, pepper and caraway well around over the meat. Now boil the joint skin down in boiling water or stock two fingers deep for about 15 minutes. Then place on top of the vegetables with the fat layer face up and slide into the oven. When the vegetables have browned, pour over a little beer and turn the temperature down to 180 °C. Add the garlic, bay leaf, some peppercorns and juniper berries and leave to roast in the oven for another 1 ½ hours. Keep pouring in a little beer, stock or water at regular intervals during this time.

Turn the vegetables and the bones from time to time. Take care not to pour any liquid over the rind (otherwise it will not go crispy)! At the end of the roasting time, turn the temperature back up to 220 °C so that a crunchy crust forms.

For the sauerkraut, fry the onions in hot oil until transparent. Dust with a little flour and then stir in the cabbage. Then, pour in the wine and leave to simmer and reduce almost completely. Simmer over a low heat for about 45 minutes. After about half an hour, add some peppercorns, juniper berries and a bay leaf as well as some apple sauce and simmer these too.

Boil the potatoes in salted water until soft, drain and leave to steam off. Then fry the potatoes in a pan with hot butter until golden brown. Scatter parsley over the top and keep warm.

Finally, take the roast out, simmer off the sauce a little, degrease if necessary and season with salt and pepper. Cut the meat into slices, drizzle with sauce, dish up with the sauerkraut and the potatoes on preheated plates and serve.

Piparkuka

(Christmas biscuits, Lebkuchen)

1	egg
125 g	runny honey
125 g	butter
125 g	sugar
½ kg	flour
½ sachet	baking powder
½ tsp	ground black pepper
½ tsp	ground ginger
½ tsp	ground cinnamon
½ tsp	ground cloves
½ tsp	ground nutmeg

Heat the honey, sugar and butter in a bowl set over a pan of boiling water. Remove from the heat just before it boils and add the spices. Add half the flour to the mix, stir well and leave to cool.

Then add the rest of the flour, egg and baking powder and knead to form a smooth dough. Wrap in cling film and leave to rest in the fridge (for two days if possible).

Knead the dough again, then roll out thinly and cut out different shapes.

Back the biscuits in a preheated oven at 200 °C for c. 10 to 12 minutes.

Latvia

LITHUANIA

Linksmų Kalėdų ir laimingų Naujųjų metų　　　　　　　　　　　　　　　　　　　　　　　**Tyli naktis, šventa naktis**

What would Christmas in Lithuania be without Christmas markets and without the legendary Christmas procession and carousel in Vilnius? The pre-Christmas period starts very early – as early as November. Even though St Nicholas and the Advent wreath are relatively unknown in Lithuania, Christmas is nevertheless celebrated lavishly, but thoughtfully at the same time. Here fish, mushrooms, poppyseeds, beetroot, various baked goods and *Kisielius* are preferred, Kisielius being a syrup-like cranberry drink. Father Christmas brings presents and then the rest of the holidays are observed with a hint of superstition and magic.

In Lithuania, the Advent and Christmas period gets going as early as the end of November. This is when the formal ceremony to open the Christmas market in Cathedral Square in Vilnius takes place. A tall, illuminated Christmas tree is erected, a merry Christmas procession takes place and, in Bernardinai Garden, there is an enchanting fountain with dancing jets of water and a carousel for grown-ups and kids alike.

There are Christmas markets in almost every town and city for the entire Advent period, offering various types of mulled wine, culinary specialities and handmade Christmas souvenirs. However, in Lithuania there is no sign of St Nicholas on 6 December and you'd also probably have to look very hard to find an Advent wreath anywhere in the weeks leading up to Christmas.

The actual Christmas celebration on *Kūčios*, 24 December, is a rather quiet family affair. On this important holiday, they go swimming or cleanse themselves in a steam room since there is an old Lithuanian belief that Christmas Eve will be representative of the whole year to come.

Since the start of the 20th century, the children spend the morning decorating the Christmas tree with straw stars, handmade crafts, toys, apples, nuts and biscuits. They start with *Kūčia*, the first part of the Christmas meal as soon as it gets dark and the first star rises in the sky. This traditional dish is made up of porridge and Christmas Eve biscuits, both of which are prepared with poppyseed milk.

As in many other countries, the Lithuanians also usually enjoy twelve dishes in total, a reference to the twelve apostles. Before eating, they pray together, and there are wafers ("God biscuits") in the middle of the table. Together with bread, these are handed around the table with good wishes.

Seven, nine or twelve other meat-free dishes are laid out on the table. Often, various variations of fish, poppyseed milk soup, mushrooms, bread, *Kūčiukai* (small baked goods made of a sweet dough with poppyseeds) and wine are served. On Christmas Eve, traditional Lithuanians will eat neither meat nor dairy products.

The meal ends with everyone drawing straws. At every place at the table there is a piece of straw under the tablecloth. If it is long and thick it promises to be a good year ahead. In contrast, thin pieces of straw or straw that might even be even broken is seen as a bad omen. The straw is a reminder of the birth of Jesus in the stable.

Traditional drinks are *Kisielius*, a syrup-like cranberry drink, and Kompot made of dried fruit. Once all the dishes are on the table, candles are lit and the family take their seats. There is always a spare space for any member of the family who has died in the previous year. Some Lithuanians even invite homeless people or those less fortunate than themselves to join them or give them food. This is thought to guarantee the family's happiness in the coming year.

At the start of the meal on Christmas Eve, a communion wafer is handed around the table, together with good wishes. After this, everyone is supposed to take at least one bite from every dish to guard against any bad luck in the future.

After eating, the family exchange and unwrap gifts which were brought by Father Christmas, *Kalėdų senis*. In the meantime, the leftovers from the meal are left on the table for the souls of any dead relatives or they are placed on the windowsill after the meal for their ancestors.

Christmas Eve dinner is finally cleared away on Christmas morning and they are then able to enjoy meat again – for example boiled pig's head, suckling pig or ham. Sweet breads and other sweets are also popular. On the following Christmas holiday, 26 December, many Lithuanians visit their friends.

All across the country, New Year's Eve is celebrated with large firework displays and then New Year's Day is the time to enjoy and savour some fish soup.

The festivities for Christmas and the new year end on 6 January with the celebration of Epiphany.

Festive spirit in the main square in Vilnius

Šaltibarščiai

(Christmas borscht, beetroot soup with dried mushrooms)

2	beetroot, boiled, peeled, finely sliced
2	cucumbers, diced
2	hard-boiled eggs, egg yolk and egg white diced
100 g	mushrooms, dried
100 g	sour cream
1 l	curdled milk
10	sprigs of dill
100 g	spring onions, finely chopped
	Salt

Put the dried mushrooms in a little hot water. Mix together the egg yolks, chives and a little salt with a spoon and put into a soup pan together with the cucumbers and the egg white. Add the mushrooms together with the soaking water, sour cream, curdled milk and beetroots, stir well and leave to simmer for a little while.

Scatter finely chopped dill over the soup. Hot potatoes are often served with this.

Kepenimis įdaryta veršiena riešutų padaže

(Veal roulade stuffed with liver in a nut sauce)

600 g	veal tenderloin, cut into thin slices
1	egg, beaten
1	lemon
	Fat
	Breadcrumbs
	Flour
	Lemons
	Allspice
	Salt, pepper

Filling

200 g	veal liver, boiled
40 g	butter
1	egg, hart boiled, thinly sliced
½ cup	peas
	Salt

Sauce

20 g	butter
1 tbsp	flour
1 tbsp	chopped hazelnuts
1 ½ cups	meat or fish stock
	Salt

Lightly pound the slices of meat and rub in a mixture of salt and the herbs.

For the filling, mince the liver. Add the egg, peas, seasoning, salt and butter and mix well. Brush the filling over the slices of meat and roll these up tightly, fastening with a toothpick. Then coat in flour, egg and breadcrumbs and roast in a well-greased roasting tin at 180 °C for about an hour.

For the sauce, prepare a roux with butter and flour, deglaze with the stock, season with salt, add the nuts and leave to simmer until the sauce has thickened.

Cut the finished roulades, place on a plate and garnish with slices of lemon. Serve with the nut sauce.

Traditionally, roast potatoes and raw or preserved vegetables are served with it.

Kuciukai
(Christmas biscuits)

500 g	flour
200 ml	milk
50 g	oil
½ cube	yeast
2 tbsp	poppyseeds, blanched
100 g	sugar
	Salt

Make a starter from the yeast, sugar, some warm milk and half of the flour. Leave to stand in a warm place for about an hour. Then knock back the dough and add the rest of the flour, oil and the poppyseeds. Mix well and knead until the dough no longer sticks to your hands or to the dough hook or the wooden spoon. Leave to rise again for a while.

Then shape the dough into logs 1cm in diameter and cut these into lengths about 2 cm long.

Bake in the oven at 160 °C until golden brown.
Serve with poppyseed milk.

Aguony pienas
(Poppyseed milk)

1 cup	poppyseeds
1 l	water, boiled and cooled
½ cup	sugar

Finely powder the poppyseeds and grind them until a thick mixture emerges. Add the water and sugar and stir well.

Serve with Lithuanian *kuciukai* (Christmas biscuits).

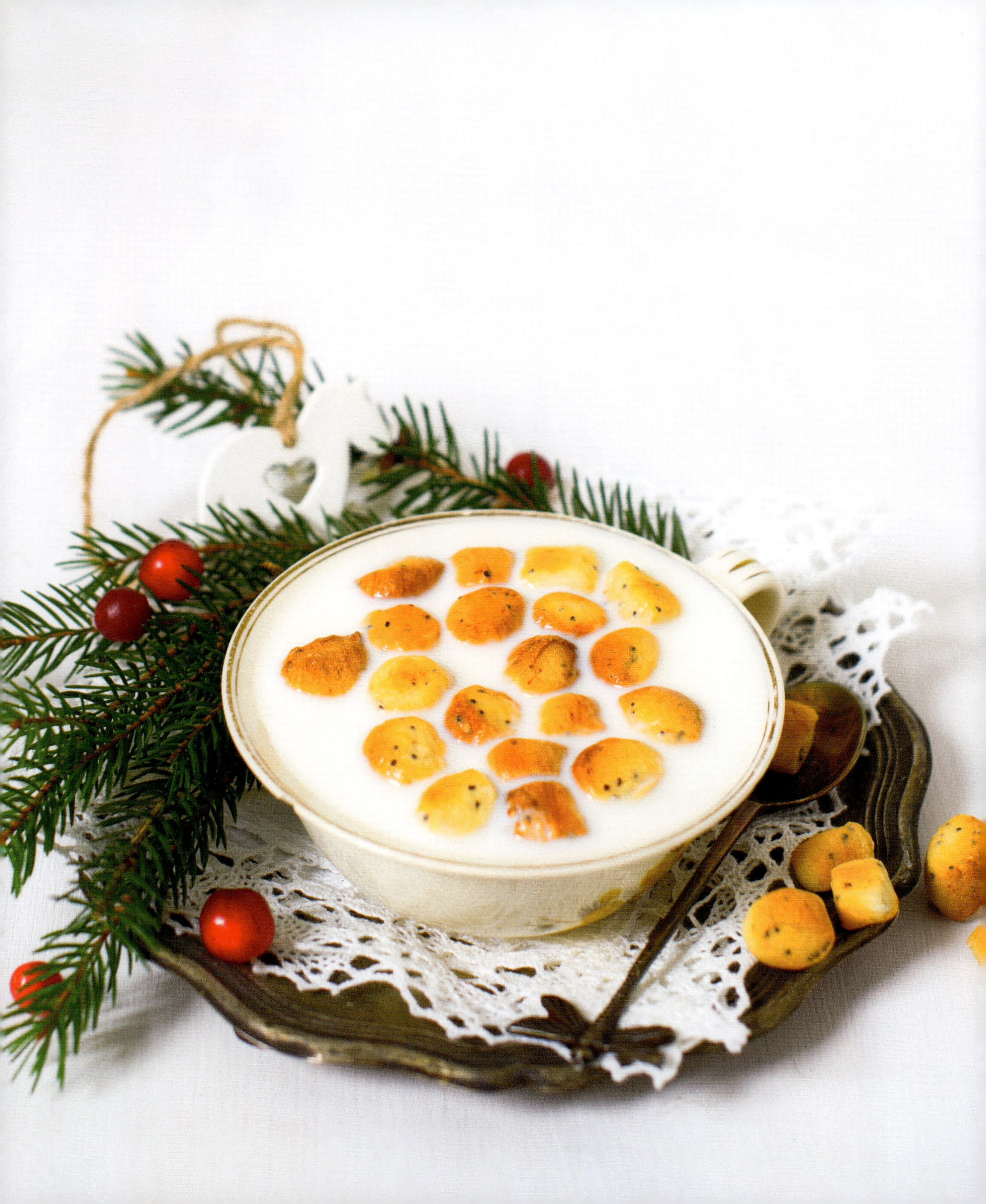

LUXEMBOURG

Schéi Chrëschtdeeg an e gudde Rutsch an d'neit Joer
Schöne Weihnachten und ein gutes neues Jahr
Joyeux Noël et Bonne Année

Se'leg Nuecht! Hélleg Nuecht
Stille Nacht, heilige Nacht
Nuit de Paix, Sainte Nuit

Christmas decorations, markets and the "Winter Lights" festival delight the Luxembourgers during Advent. *Kleeschen* and his helper, *Houseker*, bring gifts on 6 December. Then, the *Chrëschtkëndchen* hands out all kinds of surprises to children at Christmas. Presents are often only exchanged after attending midnight mass or even on 25 December. In Luxembourg, the Christmas holidays are a family affair and a time to enjoy hearty cuisine. Typical delicacies are, for example, *Träipen*, *Gromperekichelcher* and the *Lëtzebuerger Grillwurscht*. There are also special puddings, much to the delight of the local people.

For many Luxembourgers, Christmas is the most important celebration of the year. 25 December (*Chrëschtdag*) and 26 December (Stiefesdag) are public holidays.

In Luxembourg, Christmas is above all a celebration when the whole family gathers together for a hearty feast.

Winter magic at *"Chrëschtmaart"*.

The majority of the population in Luxembourg is Catholic. To celebrate Christmas, practising Catholics either attend midnight mass – such as the particularly festive service in the Cathedral of Notre-Dame, Luxembourg, for example – or there are also Christmas services in churches on 25 December.

In the past it was tradition to all eat *Träipen* (black pudding) with mashed potato and apple sauce after midnight mass. Nowadays, festive food in Luxembourg has been influenced by many other European countries. Turkey, fondue, seafood, *Weihnachtsbûche* (cake in the shape of a log) and stollen are all very popular.

Nevertheless, there are still some typically Luxembourgish dishes that play an important role during the Christmas period such as *Gromperekichelcher* (mashed potato), *Lëtzebuerger Grillwurscht*, *Boxemännercher* (gingerbread men-shaped biscuits), *Glühwäin* (mulled wine) or *Egg Nogg* (a sweet drink with egg, double cream, vanilla and rum).

Little Luxembourgers do not receive their Christmas presents from Father Christmas but from the *Chrëschtkënd-*

Atmospheric blaze of lights at the Christmas market in Luxembourg City.

chen (Christ Child). Some families wait until after midnight mass to unwrap any presents under the tree, while others only exchange their presents on 25 December.

However, the customs during the Christmas period start much earlier. On each of the four Sundays before Christmas Eve, the corresponding candles of the Advent wreath are lit, the wreath being made up of fir, pine or mistletoe branches.

In these weeks, Christmas parties also take place in nurseries, schools, care homes, sports clubs and other social groups. The Luxembourgers enjoy attending celebratory concerts in churches, schools and at Christmas markets during the Advent period.

Every year Luxembourg City conjures up the holiday spirit with "Winter Lights", a series of events during the Advent period on the subject of light: Christmas parades, Christmas markets, public concerts, exhibitions and other events.

The evening before 6 December is also very important during Advent. This is because the children place a shoe outside the front door which *Kleeschen* (Nicholas) and his helper (*Houseker*) fill with sweets and fruit.

The Christmas decorations are already up from the 1st Sunday of Advent. They include magnificent Christmas lights, pyramid-shaped Christmas decorations, as well as giant mangers and impressive Christmas trees.

Many families also set up a manger at home. Furthermore, in many villages, the children stage a wonderful nativity play.

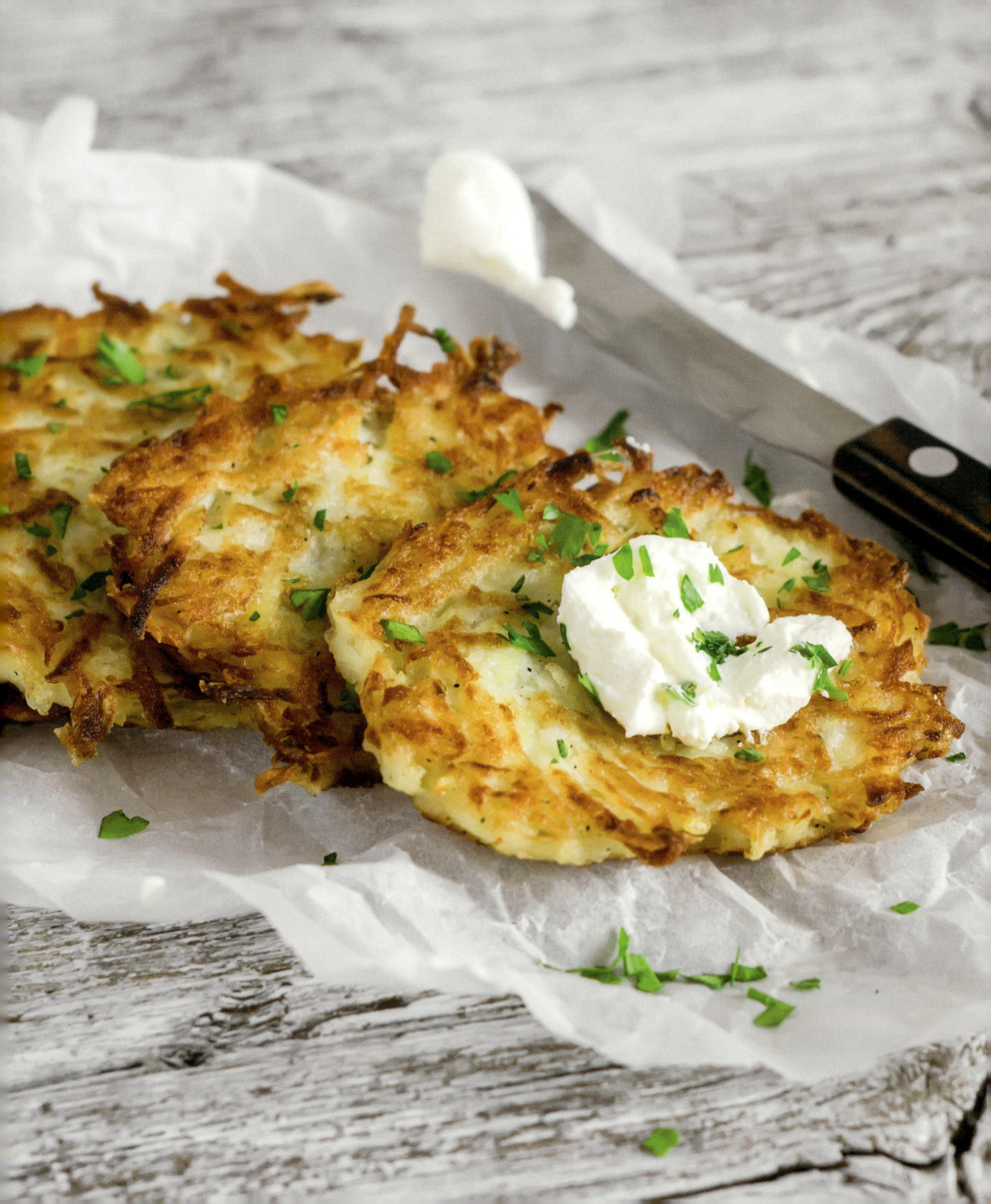

Gromperekichelcher mat Ierbsebulli

(Mashed potato with pea soup)

Soup

750 g	peas (frozen also works)
1 bunch	soup greens, finely sliced
2	small onions, finely sliced
1 l	stock
500 g	smoked pork, pre-boiled if preferred
	Whole nutmeg
	Salt, pepper

Gromperekichelcher

12	medium potatoes
2	onions, finely sliced
2	eggs
	Chives, finely chopped
	Ground nutmeg
	Salt, pepper

Boil the smoked pork for about 1 ½ hours until soft or use a pre-boiled joint.

Peel the vegetables and, together with the peas, put them into a saucepan with the stock and also boil them until everything is soft. Then season with salt, pepper and nutmeg and blend until smooth.

If the soup seems too thin, you can improve this somewhat with a roux. If it is too thick, thin with some of the water from boiling the meat or with stock. Cut the meat into small pieces and then add to the soup.

For the Gromperekichelcher, roughly grate the potatoes and wring out with a tea towel so that the mixture is as dry as possible.

Mix the chives and onions with the seasoning. Beat the eggs, add the potato mixture and mix everything together in a bowl.

In each case press one heaped tablespoon of the potato mixture in a pan until flat and fry in hot oil on both sides until golden brown. Leave to dry on a piece of kitchen roll and serve separately to the soup.

Luxembourg

Träipen

(Black pudding with creamed potato and apple sauce)

300 g	black pudding
2	onions, cut into rings
1 tbsp	finely chopped chive
	Flour
	Oil

Creamed potato

1 kg	floury potatoes
100 ml	milk
60 g	butter
	Grated nutmeg
	Salt

Apple sauce

½ kg	apples, peeled and cored, cut into chunks
2–3 tbsp	sugar
1 tbsp	lemon juice
300 ml	water

For the apple sauce, put the apples, water, lemon juice and sugar in a large pan and boil until soft. Pour over the water and puree the apple mixture, season or sweeten to taste.

For the creamed potatoes, finely mash the boiled potatoes and mix with the warm milk, butter, salt and nutmeg.

Peel the onions, cut into rings and put in a bowl. Dust with flour and fry in hot oil until golden brown.
Peel the skin off the black pudding, cut into medium chunks and fry well in a second pan.
Put the creamed potato in the middle of the plate as a base. Put the fried black pudding on top of the creamed potato, share the onion rings over the top, scatter with the chive and serve. Dish up with the apple sauce.

Snowflakes

(Simple biscuits in the shape of snowflakes, makes about 100)

250 g	butter
125 g	flour
200 g	potato flour of cornflour
100 g	icing sugar
1 sachet	vanilla sugar
	Salt

Mix all ingredients together well in a bowl and knead to form a smooth dough. Then leave to rest in a cool place for about an hour.

Then, shape the mixture into a log about 3 to 4 cm in diameter and cut into small equal slices (about 1 cm thick) and shape into small balls. Press them flat using a floured spoon and bake at about 175 °C for 10 to 12 minutes.

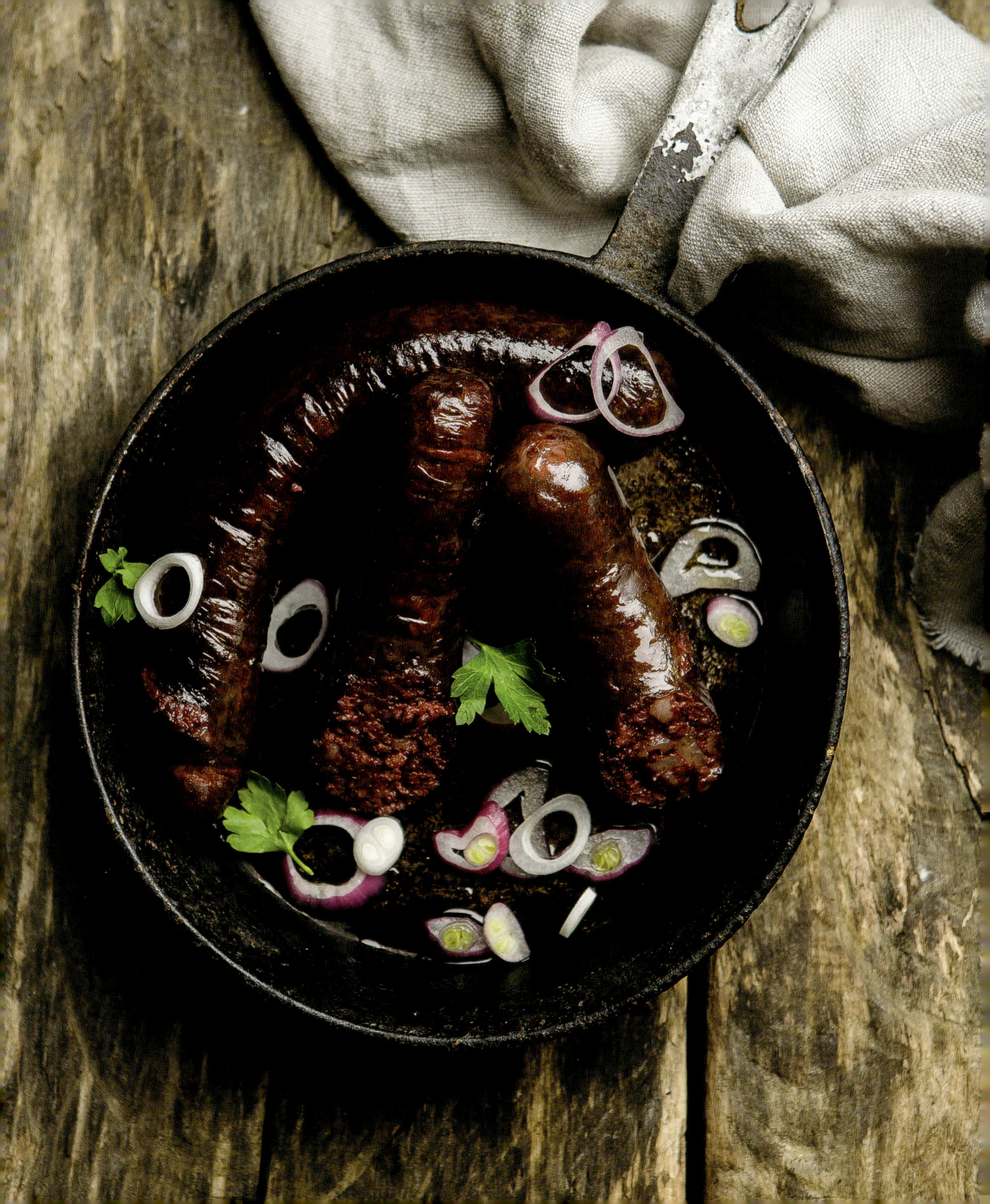

MALTA

Milied it-tajjeb u sena ġdida kuntenta
Merry Christmas and a Happy New Year

O lejl ta' skiet, lejl tal-Milied
Silent Night, Holy Night

Malta and its neighbouring islands are all very Catholic. As a result, Christmas is also marked in a very religious manner. This includes numerous church services during the Advent period, as well as processions featuring the figure of Baby Jesus, accompanied by a lot of singing. Visiting nativity scenes is also very popular, which is why Christmas nativity scenes can be found practically all over Malta. Specific features of a Maltese Christmas include "Nicholas's beard" and one unique feature of Maltese Christmas is for a child to speak at the midnight sermon on Christmas Eve. The famous pantomime is staged in Valletta. The sumptuous food on Christmas Eve is influenced by British traditions, but also by North Africa and Italy.

Maltese people love celebrating Christmas. This is easy to see during Advent with the festive sea of lights. Christmas symbols blaze virtually everywhere along the streets and inside passageways in towns. Especially in Valletta, the capital city, Christmas music blares out from speakers, even outside, and there is a Christmas tree on every corner imaginable. Food shops even have a Christmas tree on top of the deep freezers and shelves.

That being said, religion plays an important role in the Advent period in Malta. Evening mass with sacral music takes place more often during this time, especially during the last few days before Christmas Eve

The capital city is also famous for the annual *Christmas pantomime* in the beautiful Teatru Manoel. The pantomime is an entertaining mix of satire and slapstick humour and is enjoyed by children and adults alike.

A typically Maltese tradition is *Ġulbiena*. As part of this, grains of wheat, corn and grass are sown in flat trays on a bed of cotton wool and placed in a dark place. This is how the seeds produce long white shoots, similar to grass. They call this "Nicholas's beard". Come Christmas, this is then used to decorate mangers and statues of Baby Jesus.

In fact, Christmas mangers, often lovingly hand-crafted, can be found absolutely everywhere on the island – whether in private living rooms, churches or in small chapels. During the Advent and Christmas period, the Maltese enjoy strolling around all the public *Presepij* (mangers) in their neighbourhoods.

Christmas Eve in Malta begins with a festive procession through the streets and lanes in almost every town. People sing well-known Christmas songs and carry a figure of Baby Jesus around with them.

Of course, being a deeply Catholic island, the people of Malta and the neighbouring island, Gozo, also go to church on Christmas Eve. The places of worship are decorated wonderfully festively. Since the 17th Century, the figures from the magnificent nativity scenes, such as shepherds or angels, who nowadays move around mechanically among themselves, have been known as *pasturi*. During Christmas mass, the Baby Jesus is placed on the high altar. The Three Kings are only placed in the *Presepij* on Epiphany.

An unusual Maltese Christmas tradition is *Priedka tat-Tiefel*, the "child's speech". A child, usually seven to ten years old, leads the sermon during Christmas mass, instead of the priest. The child's address always includes the Christmas story with the birth of Jesus in Bethlehem.

Most Maltese celebrate Christmas at home with a Christmas tree, which, if at all possible, should be a pine tree – something quite exotic for the islanders. The Christmas tree is traditionally decorated with lights, tinsel and glittering trinkets.

While they head to work as usual on 26 December, in Malta, 25 December is the festive Christmas day. Usually, the family celebrates with an extensive lunch. They then exchange presents after this. Here, *Santa Claus* brings the gifts for the children. Santa blows the presents in through the closed windows as there are no chimneys in Malta.

For the Christmas meal, the fattest Hasi, a hen, is roasted in a large casserole dish, together with potatoes and vegetables. This is served with *Timpana* (baked pasta) as an accompaniment. For pudding, *Qaghaq tal-ghasel* (honey pastry ring) is traditionally served, stuffed with dried citrus fruits, cocoa, spices, orange blossom water, syrup and honey. To end the meal, the Maltese are rather partial to another glass of *Imbuljuta tal-qastan*. This is a hot drink made of chestnuts and cocoa powder which is often drunk instead tea or coffee during the Christmas period.

There is one more speciality that should be mentioned: *Bigilla*. The Maltese bean paste is a delicious vegetarian dish for snacking. The bean paste is a kind of dip and can be enjoyed warm or cold. It is usually eaten with fresh bread.

As a legacy of the British sovereignty in Malta from 1800 to 1964, turkey is often served at Christmas instead of Maltese chicken. And instead of the typical honey pastry ring, Christmas cake, *Christmas pudding* and *mince pies* are also enjoyed. The Italian Christmas cake *Panettone* is also very popular.

The Maltese people bid farewell to the old year with exuberant New Year's Eve parties and greet the new year with magnificent firework displays.

Bigilla

(Bean paste)

400 g   beans
4   cloves of garlic, crushed
    Olive oil
    Parsley, chopped
    Salt, pepper
    Baking powder

Leave the beans to soak for 1–2 days in salted water along with the baking powder. Change the water occasionally. Then, dry the beans and boil in unsalted water over a low heat until they are al dente. Then drain the beans and mash to a pulp.

Stir the bean mash well and season with salt, pepper, garlic, olive oil and parsley. Bigillia is often eaten warm, but it can also be enjoyed cold with white bread.

Pastizzi

(Stuffed puff pastry pockets, makes 6)

3 packets	puff pastry
500 g	ricotta cheese
2	eggs
	Milk
	Salt, pepper

Mix the ricotta cheese in a bowl with the eggs and seasoning.

Cut the puff pastry into squares about 10 cm x 10 cm and put a teaspoon of the cheese mixture in the middle of each square. Now, fold over to form pockets, leaving a little bit of the filling showing at the top.

Brush the pastizzi with milk and bake in the oven at 200 °C for about 30 minutes.

You can stuff the puff pastry pockets with all kinds of ingredients: in Malta, examples include bean paste or mushrooms with ham or chicken stuffing.

Orange and rosemary chicken

1	prepared chicken, split into four parts
4	unwaxed oranges
3	sprigs of rosemary, picked
2	cloves of garlic, peeled, roughly chopped
2	sprigs of basil, picked
400 ml	chicken stock
50 g	cold butter, cubed
	Ground sweet paprika
	Salt, pepper
	Tabasco
	Tagliatelle
	Bread
	Wine

Peel one of the oranges and split it into segments. Juice the remaining oranges.

Now spread the orange segments, the pieces of garlic, basil leaves and rosemary out evenly under the skin of the chicken.

Season the chicken portions with salt, pepper and paprika, place in a roasting dish and pour over the chicken stock and orange juice and roast for 45 minutes at 140 °C with circulating heat.

Then take the chicken portions out the oven and keep warm. Strain the stock and leave to reduce slightly, then gradually cream in the butter and season with tabasco and salt. Tagliatelle, salad, bread and a good wine go very well with this.

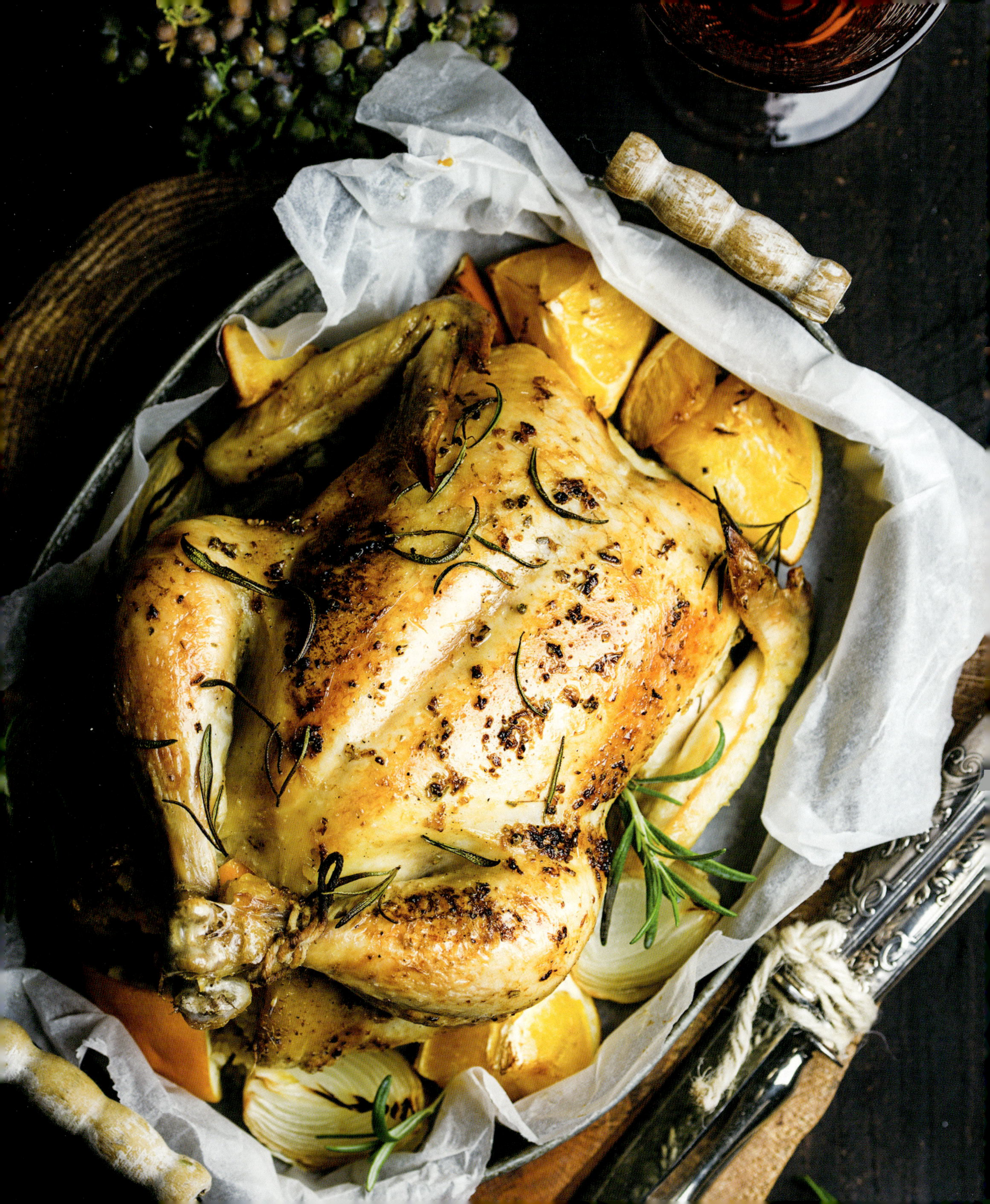

Qaghaq tal-ghasel

(Maltese pastry ring)

200 g	flour
4 tbsp	semolina
2 tbsp	sugar
75 g	cold butter, diced
75 ml	water
100 ml	orange juice
200 g	black treacle
200 g	sugar
1 tbsp	cocoa powder
1 tbsp	aniseed
	Pinch of ground cloves
1	unwaxed lemon, zested

Mix the flour, 2 tbsp semolina and sugar together in a bowl, then add the butter cubes and water. Knead well until it forms a smooth dough.

For the filling, put the treacle, sugar, cocoa, aniseed, cloves and lemon zest in a pot and slowly bring to the boil. Then add the remaining semolina and boil until a firmer mixture emerges.
Roll the dough out and cut into strips about 8 x 30 cm.

Share the filling in the middle of each of the strips, roll up and join the ends together. Now place the pastry rings on a baking tray lined with greaseproof paper and score several times with a knife. Bake in a preheated oven at 180 °C for 25–30 minutes.

Netherlands

Vrolijk Kerstfeest en een gelukkig nieuwjaar

Stille nacht, heilige nacht

Sinterklaas comes over from Spain to Holland by boat, along with *Zwarte Piet*, and the children are always more than happy to entertain him – although they may well be hoping for something in return! After this, the Christmas tree is put up and half of Holland makes their way to markets selling mulled wine, lebkuchen and Christmas stars. Accompanied by delicious food, the large celebration is rather familial and tranquil; until New Year's Eve, it seems as if the clocks just tick that little bit slower. But then the whole country parties hard! On Epiphany, the Christmas tree has to vanish away and the lucky fellow, the "bean king," moves in.

In the Netherlands, *Sinterklaas* takes the place of St Nicholas. He carries a crosier and wears a red coat and mitre. He is accompanied by *Zwarte Piet* (Black Peter). He is a similar figure to "Knecht Ruprecht" in Germany and the "Krampus" in Austria.

Since he was introduced into the Netherlands in the 19th century, he was portrayed as a dark-skinned servant in oriental clothes, with a black face, big red lips and gold earrings. But in 2013, this image was criticised for being racist. Since then there have been emotional debates in the Netherlands between advocates and opponents of this figure. Meanwhile, there are alternative Zwarte Piet costumes, where the black on the face is just supposed to be soot, or the actors' faces are made up using other colours.

Legend has it that *Sinterklaas* and his companion spend the year in Spain and come over by steamboat in the middle of November. This tradition originates from the time of Philip II of Spain who was also King of the Netherlands in the 16th Century.

As a result, the main event is the arrival of *Sinterklaas* in the Dutch city of Amsterdam. He lands on the day of *Sinterklaasavond* (Sinterklaas evening on 5 December) and the children gather in the harbour, eagerly awaiting his arrival. From here, he continues his journey on a white horse. The little ones write their wish lists and the horses are provided with hay, bread, carrots and water.

On this day, lots of children also leave their clean shoes in front of the door hoping to find surprises inside them the following day. However anyone who finds coal in their boots was clearly not good enough.

Popular sweets for *Sinterklaas* are chocolate coins, gingerbread biscuits and marzipan. In Holland, there is also a long tradition of chocolate letters. During the Christmas period, the Dutch eat about 20 million sweet letters. In the past, Nicholas' gifts were covered with a sheet and the letter-shaped biscuit placed on top revealed the name of the person to whom the gifts belonged.

On *Sinterklaasavond*, the Dutch also get together with family for a meal. Then they hand out presents which include a funny, original poem about each recipient. The presents are often beautifully wrapped and there are often so-called *surprises* included as part of the wrapping. This means that a smaller box might be hidden inside a bigger box and there might even be another box even smaller still inside the second one until a matchbox containing a lovely little trinket is revealed.

In the Netherlands, the Christmas tree is already up and decorated when *Sinterklaas* leaves the country again on 6

Sinterklaas fills shoes with sweet delicacies.

December. Thousands of Dutch people make their way to German Christmas markets during the run up to Christmas for mulled wine, lebkuchen and Christmas stars.

Kerstmis (Christmas itself) in the Netherlands is a rather religious celebration for which the whole family comes together without a great exchange of gifts or presents. To mark the occasion, a sumptuous feast is served up in some families. The selection of dishes varies depending on individual taste. In some families, they eat roast beef or venison, as well as festive biscuits. Nowadays, popular dishes also include fondues such as raclette with meat and vegetables.

Many people go to church on Christmas Eve and on the first Christmas Day.

On 25 or 26 December, quite a few people travel to see their parents, where they happily shoot the breeze during the sumptuous feast and over a slice of Christmas stollen. Dishes steeped in tradition are served up.

In the Netherlands, the time between Christmas and New Year is called *Tussen kerst en oud en nieuw*. This one week is an allegory for the clock ticking more slowly, and the hecticness of everyday life is supposed to fade to a distant memory. The Dutch are famous, or infamous, for their fireworks, and New Year's Eve is no exception.

Something quite special on 1 January is *Nieuwjaarsduik*, the "New Year's Dive". The biggest event of this kind takes place on the beach in Scheveningen. Anyone can take part, regardless of age, as long as the water isn't too cold for you. After the start, the order of events is "run, scream, dive.". Afterwards there is hot pea soup for all the brave swimmers.

The Christmas Tree stays up in Dutch living rooms until *Dreikoningen*, or Epiphany, on 6 January. For Epiphany, a cake is baked with a bean inside. The lucky one who manages to find the slice of cake with the bean becomes the "Bean King".

There are also men dressed as kings, who go from house to house singing songs and are rewarded for this by the families.

Traditionelle *Oliebollen* for New Year

140 Netherlands

Bacon pancakes

330 g	flour
27 g	yeast
½ tbsp	sugar
½ l	lukewarm milk
2	eggs
4 tsp	oil
200 g	bacon, cut into strips
27 g	beet sugar syrup
2 tbsp	sunflower oil
	Freshly ground pepper
1 tbsp	wholegrain mustard
	Pinch of salt

Put some flour in a bowl, make a well in the centre and add the crumbled yeast together with 1 tbsp sugar. Then, add 1tbsp of the lukewarm milk and stir to form a starter dough.

Cover and leave in a warm place for about 15 minutes. Then add the salt, both eggs and the rest of the flour and the lukewarm milk to make a liquid yeasted dough. Cover again and leave in a warm place for a further 20 minutes or so.

Now cook the dough in a lightly greased pan: when doing so, fry the strips of bacon in the pan in portions until crispy, allow a good 50 g per person.

Then, for each bacon pancake, pour two ladlefuls of the yeasted dough over the strips of bacon and cook until golden brown on both sides. Keep the cooked pancakes warm in a preheated oven at 150 °C.

Preistamppot met paddestoelen
(Roast beef with leek mash pot and mushrooms)

750 g	potatoes
500 g	leeks
250 g	mixed mushrooms
50 g	hazelnuts or almonds
20 g	butter
2 tbsp	sunflower oil
	Freshly ground pepper
1 tbsp	wholegrain mustard
	Salt

Peel the potatoes and cut into pieces. Wash the leeks, cut in half lengthways and cut into strips. Wash the mushrooms and cut into slices. Roughly chop the nuts or the almonds.

Boil the potatoes in salted water for about 20 minutes until cooked. Halfway through the cooking time, add the leeks and boil them too.

Heat the butter and oil together in a pan and fry the mushrooms over a high heat until dark brown. Sprinkle over salt and pepper.

Drain the potatoes and leeks, reserving some of the cooking water. Mash the potatoes, leeks and mustard together. If necessary, add a little of the cooking water. Spread the mushrooms over the Stamppot.

Serve with roast beef, scatted with the nuts or almonds.

Netherlands

Marinated pot roast à la Marianne

1 kg   beef
       Vinegar water (²/₃ cider vinegar, ¹/₃ water)
       Salt, pepper
1   bay leaf
1   onion

Cut the beef into bite-sized chunks, put in a bowl and cover with the vinegar water. Add the peeled raw onions. Leave to stand overnight. Drain off the vinegar water the following day and reserve (we will use it later!).

Season the meat with salt and pepper and roast gently (it will be quite watery).

Add the bay leaf and the onion that has been cut into pieces and cook slowly for about 5 minutes. Add all the vinegar water and cook until the meat is done and the sauce is a creamy consistency. Serve with mashed potato. Don't forget to remove the bay leaf!

Baked alphabet letters for names

400 g   puff pastry
200 g   marzipan
        Poppyseeds
1   egg
       Greaseproof paper

Roll the puff pastry out to a strip 4 cm wide and 2 cm thick. Roll the marzipan into a thick sausage and place on the strip of dough.

Now, wrap the dough around the marzipan, brush the edges with water and press them firmly together.

Cut the resulting puff pastry sausage into pieces. Then, roll these into thin sausages and shape into the corresponding letter. If a letter is made up of several parts, press the ends together firmly.

Brush the finished letters with egg yolk, scatter with poppyseeds and place on a baking tray lined with greaseproof paper. Bake at 200 °C for about 25 to 30 minutes.

Simple Spekulatius

½ sachet	baking powder
250 g	butter
1	egg, egg white
50 g	flaked almonds
60 g	ground almonds
500 g	flour
6 tbsp	milk
1 tsp	cinnamon
250 g	sugar

Pile the flour, baking powder, sugar, cinnamon, ground almonds and the cold butter cut up finely onto the worktop. Make a well in the middle and pour in the milk.

Slice at everything with a large knife and quickly knead together to form a shortcrust pastry dough. Cover and chill for about 1 hour. Then, preheat the oven to 180 °C.

Roll the dough out thinly on a lightly floured surface (about 3–4 mm thick) and cut out shapes. Place the shapes on a tray lined with greaseproof paper, brush with beaten egg white and scatter the flaked almonds over them.

Bake on the central shelf in the oven for 12 to 15 minutes.

Netherlands

Norway

God jul og godt nytt år

Glade jul, hellige jul

A good *Julbord*, often enjoyed as part of the office Christmas party, kicks off the pre-Christmas period in Norway. Advent calendars and Christingle oranges are a daily reminder for the Norwegians that Christmas is coming. St Lucy's Day on 13 December brightens the dark winter period. Christmas Eve is reserved for family. After mass on 24 December, the buffet *Julbord*, in the past consisting of up to 60 different dishes, is served. Christmas songs by the famous *Sølvguttene* are played on the radio. The presents fly through the window at the call of *Julklapp*, but house imps and pets also receive a little something. As in Sweden, the Christmas trees are taken down by 13 January at the latest.

During the pre-Christmas period many employers in Norway host the traditional *Julbord*, a kind of buffet, as part of their work Christmas celebrations. At this time of year, Christmas church services and markets, as well as Advent concerts, take place in most Norwegian towns.

So what do the Norwegians do to entertain themselves in the time leading up to Christmas Eve? Lots of children have an Advent calendar. In some families, it is also common to decorate an orange with 24 cloves. The cloves are pulled out one by one every day until 24 December. It is also traditional to bake seven kinds of Christmas biscuits during the Advent period and to make decorations for the tree.

St Lucy's Day, which is also popular in Sweden, is celebrated in schools and nurseries on 13 December. As part of the celebrations, a choir goes through the rooms in the morning holding candles, handing out *Lussekatter* (Lucy bakes) and singing Lucy songs.

On 23 December, the Norwegians celebrate *Lille julaften*. On this "little Christmas Eve", many families spend the evening at home watching the short film "Dinner for one".

For many Norwegians, the most important Christmas celebration day is *Julaften*, Christmas Eve. Individual family traditions often determine exactly how they spend the day. Today's Christmas celebrations in Norway stem from ancient midwinter and harvest traditions. Back then, winter solstice was celebrated, and the ancient symbol for the sun was a wheel.

Nowadays, many families eat rice pudding at lunchtime on 24 December.

Along with handmade decorations, Christmas baubles, tinsel and candles, it is also common to hang Norwegian bunting on the tree.

At 5pm, the bells ring in Christmas Eve, which is when many Norwegians attend Christmas church services. The famous boys' choir *Sølvguttene* (The Silver Boys) sings on the TV. In Norway, the choir's songs are without a doubt an important part of Christmas. It's finally the evening and high time for *Julbord*, the festive feast. Similar to a buffet, it is quite spectacularly varied and extensive. In the past, friends and family members would have been served up to 60 different dishes. There aren't quite as many dishes today, but there are still certain delicacies that are traditionally enjoyed.

Christmas dishes in Norway are influenced by the individual regions. There is either *Svineribbe* (ribs), *Pinnekjøtt* (cured lamb ribs) or cod. *Mølje* ("mishmash") is also very popular, a speciality made of meat, fish and crispbread. They drink special Christmas beer and aquavit with this.

Cured lamb ribs (*Pinnekjott*).

The children enjoy sweet reed Judelbrus, a Christmas lemonade.

There is often *Riskrem* for pudding, which is creamy rice pudding with an almond hidden inside. Whoever finds it gets a small present, a marzipan pig, for example.

It's also important not to forget the *Nisse* (goblin). This Christmas imp lives in the stable and plays tricks on people if he isn't treated well. Therefore, before the meal, he is offered a large bowl of rice pudding made with butter, sugar and cinnamon, which is placed outside the front of the door. You mustn't forget the animals in the surrounding area either. A bundle of corn is strapped to the fence for the birds, and the cows in farmyard receive special Christmas food.

After the meal, the Norwegians dance around the Christmas tree and exchange presents. It is also customary for one member of the family to anonymously throw the presents into the room while shouting "J*ulklapp, Julklapp*". With a little imagination, this is supposed to represent the imps hard at work.

In Norway, *Julemann*, Father Christmas, is nowhere near as significant as in other countries. That being said, in some families, he still brings the children their presents.

In Norway, 25 December is a quiet and peaceful day when they attend Christmas church services. There is *Lutefisk* (leached salted cod), different kinds of pickled herring, smoked meat and *Julepølse* (a kind of white sausage) to eat.

The children go as *Julebukk* (Christmas ram). Or they dress up as *Nisser* (goblins) and go from house to house, singing Christmas songs, and they receive sweets in return.

The time between Christmas and New Year's Eve is called *Romjul*. In this week, the Norwegians visit their relatives for more Christmas meals and cosy evenings with the family.

31 December is called *Nyttårsaften*. New Year's Eve is celebrated in Norway much like in other countries in Central Europe. They either celebrate at home with friends and family or go to restaurants and take part in the celebrations there.

Then, during the night, the bells ring in the new year, followed by firework displays. They wish each other "*Godt nytt år!*" Often, people go for a walk in the forest while it is still night-time. 1 January is called *Nyttårsdag* and is the official flag day in Norway.

The Christmas period in Norway doesn't come to an end on 6 January, but only on *St. Knuts dag* or rather *Tyvendedags jul* on 13 January. On this day, the Norwegians traditionally take the candles and decorations down from the Christmas tree, as is also customary in other countries in northern Europe.

Traditional Christmas bread.

Norway

Lamb's lettuce with nutty vinaigrette and Gjetost-Knusti

(cheesy crust)

250 g	prepared lamb's lettuce
50 g	cheese, Gjetost (Norwegian goat's whey cheese)
3 tbsp	raspberry vinegar
1 tbsp	orange juice
4 tbsp	hazelnut oil
2 tbsp	vegetable stock
4	slices of toast, crusts removed
1 tsp	butter
50 g	pine nuts, toasted
80 g	almonds, browned
	Sugar
	Salt, pepper

Mix together the raspberry vinegar, orange juice, hazelnut oil and stock and season with salt, pepper and a little sugar.

Cut out small circles or stars from the toast with a cookie cutter. Heat the pieces of bread in hot butter in a pan and fry on both sides until golden brown, then lightly salt.

Place small slices of Gjetost on the bread and put under a preheated grill for about 4 minutes. Drizzle the vinaigrette over the lamb's lettuce and serve with bread, nuts and almonds.

Torsk (cod) in mustard sauce

400 g	cod fillets
2	medium shallots, finely diced
40 g	butter
50 g	mustard, medium strength
100 ml	white wine (or diluted white wine vinegar)
100 ml	double cream
	Sugar
	Salt, white pepper

Fry the shallot cubes in a pan with melted butter. Place the cod fillet on top and pour over the white wine. Simmer for a further 10 minutes with the lid on.

Then remove the fish and keep warm. Add the mustard and double cream to the fish stock and reduce everything by a third.

Season with salt, pepper and some sugar to taste. Plate up the fish and pour the reduced sauce over the fish.

Serve with salted potatoes or root vegetables.

Kransekake

(wreath cake)

500 g	ground almonds
500 g	icing sugar
3–4	egg whites

Icing

1	egg white, stiffly beaten
	Lemon juice
	Icing sugar

Blitz the almonds together with the icing sugar until very fine. Beat the egg whites until they form soft peaks and stir the mixture together to form a dough. Leave to chill overnight. If possible, grease circular Bundt cake rings well with fat and lightly flour. Press the dough out with a dough syringe into an even, finger-thick sausage about 1–2cm in diameter or roll the dough out into a correspondingly thick log. Add a little flour if necessary.

Place the dough pieces into the rings and join the ends together firmly. If you do not have a suitable tin, then place the rings on a piece of greaseproof paper. Bake on the middle shelf in the oven at 200 °C for about 20 minutes. Then, leave the rings to cool.

For the icing, mix all the ingredients together and fill into a piping bag with a very thin nozzle. Decorate the largest ring with a zigzag pattern, then place the rings one on top of the other in size order and also decorate each ring with the icing. In doing so, the icing acts as a glue for the Kransekake tower.

You can decorate the wreath cakes however you would like – such as with colourful marzipan. The Norwegians like to use bright crackers and little Norwegian flags. The tip of the cakes is decorated depending on the occasion: christenings, confirmations, weddings, Christmas, New Year…

Norway

Austria

Fröhliche Weihnachten und ein glückliches neues Jahr

Stille Nacht, heilige Nacht

It's almost impossible to find a house in Austria where they haven't played the song "Silent night" at some point over the Christmas period. Barbara branches, Krampus processions, visits from St Nicholas, Advent wreaths and Christmas markets are all typical features of the pre-Christmas period in Austria. There is also certainly no shortage of Christmas biscuits, fruit bread and lebkuchen. Austrians spend their cosy Christmas holidays surrounded by family, observing regional traditions, going to church parties and enjoying special Christmas food. The Pummerin, the big bell in Vienna's Stephansdom ring out on New Year's Eve, and actors dressed up as the Three Wise Men make their way through the country on 6 January. The Christmas season ends on *Maria Lichtmess*.

Since 1818, Christmas in Austria has been closely related to the world-famous Christmas song "Silent night, holy night". This moving song was first heard 200 years ago in the parish church of St Nikola in Oberndorf in the Salzburg region.

Curate Joseph Mohr was responsible for the lyrics, while Franz Xaver Gruber, a teacher from Arnsdorf near Oberndorf, came up with the melody.

Unfortunately, due to flooding at the end of the 18th Century, St Nikola church, which was constructed in around 1100, fell into such a ruinous state that it had to be demolished.

As a result of this incessant flooding and the risk of it in the future, Oberndorf's village centre was completely reconstructed further upstream, including the Salzachbrücke and the church. Since 1937, the Silent Night chapel has stood on the site of the original church, in memory of it. Every year on 24 December they hold a festive party there to commemorate the first time this world-famous song was heard.

In the "Silent night" parish of Wagrain in the Salzburg region, they go about singing this world-famous song in a very reserved and traditional manner. Officially, it is only sung on St Barbara's Day, the anniversary of the death of the song's lyricist Joseph Mohr, by his grave, and also on Christmas Eve.

Advent in Austria is "a b'sondere Zeit" (a special time). Despite stressing about presents and manically fitting in their Christmas shopping, the Austrian people always manage to find some quiet time to reflect with family and friends.

From a religious perspective, Advent is indeed a fasting period. This is why, for many years, they say "Kathrein stellt das Tanzen ein" (Kathrein stops the dance) or "Kathrein schließt Bass und Geigen ein" (Kathrein puts away the bass and violins).

This ban, originating from folklore, dictates that there should be no exuberant parties such as weddings or dances from Kathreintag on 25 November onwards.

Originally supposed to last for 40 days, the fasting period has now shrunk down to just four weeks. These four weeks are symbolised by the four candles on the Advent wreath. In the past, it was traditional for the four candles to each match the liturgical colour of the four Sundays before

Husarenkrapferl.

Vanillekipferl.

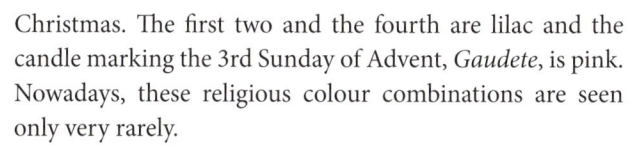

Christmas. The first two and the fourth are lilac and the candle marking the 3rd Sunday of Advent, *Gaudete*, is pink. Nowadays, these religious colour combinations are seen only very rarely.

From the end of November, Advent or Christmas markets take place in many towns across Austria. You can smell the punch and the mulled wine from miles off. Visitors can be tempted by a marvellous array of Christmas biscuits, regional crafts and Christmas decorations. The most popular Christmas biscuits in Austria include Vanillekipferl (vanilla crescents), lebkuchen, Linzer Augen, Kokosbusserl (coconut macaroons), cinnamon stars, Nussecke (nutty wedges), Anisbögen (aniseed snaps), Husarenkrapferl (jam thumbprint biscuits), rum truffles, meringue, Hausfreunde cookies, nut strudel, Nusspotize (swirled nut bread) and Christmas stollen, of course, which, dusted with icing sugar, is supposed to be reminiscent of the shape and colour of swaddled Baby Jesus.

Kletzenbrot made of rye flour, salt and a yeast or sourdough mixture, and bread seasoning as well as *Kletzen* (dried pears), prunes, nuts, raisins, figs, candied orange peel, sugar, run and schnapps are also very common.

From 1 December, the children have Advent calendars, hoping to make the time pass more quickly, and more sweetly, before Christmas. They open a little door or box every day to reveal a sweet little surprise. The first Advent calendar made of paper was printed in 1904 featuring pious images behind every closed door.

Wichteln (Secret Santa) is quite common in many offices, schools and clubs during the Advent period. In Austria, this playful gift exchange is also known as *Engerl und Bengerl*,

The popular group game originally comes from Scandinavia and the concept is based on a benevolent spirit from Norse mythology. The often do Secret Santa at Christmas parties. For this, everyone finds out whom they will be buying a little gift for a few weeks before the party. Whom everyone has picked should remain a secret. This makes the whole thing more exciting. Then the presents are anonymously exchanged at the Christmas party.

Another very popular tradition during Advent is the game *Herbergssuche*. Two children dressed as Mary and Joseph go around singing from house to house asking for somewhere to stay ("Herberge"). The whole exchange is sung and usually starts with the man of the house asking "Who's that knocking at our door?" In some regions, a statue of the Virgin Mary is left with the host family for a day.

As part of this custom of *Anglöckeln* (knocking), which has taken place for more than 500 years, a group of children, young people or even adults sings songs suitable for the Advent period, recite poems and play festive music on the flute.

Religious people in Austria brave the cold early on weekday mornings to go to church for *Roratemessen* (Advent Eucharist celebrations). The word rorate is a shortened form of the text in the Old Testament from the Book of Isiah called *Rorate caeli desuper* (Drop down ye heavens from above).

On St Barbara's Day, 4 December, there is a custom that is supposed to allow young women, above all those hoping to marry, a glimpse into their future. Before sunrise, apple, forsythia and cherry tree branches are chopped down and placed in a vase. If they have blossomed come Christmas Eve, this means there will have their wedding the coming year, or maybe just luck, joy and good health.

In many regions in Austria, St Nicholas and *Krampus* come the evening before 6 December. In the past, the presents included apples, nuts, lebkuchen and simple toys. Anyone who could afford it would have also received oranges, mandarins and peanuts or *Bockshörndln*, dried sweet fruit from the carob tree, but these are very difficult to find now.

St Nicholas takes *Krampus* along with him to terrify any "naughty" children. He can really scare the little ones with rods made from willow branches, and by rattling chains loudly and carrying a basket around with him to take them away.

Most bakeries sell *Krampusses* made of yeasted dough in various sizes. Lebkuchen in the shape of St Nicholas, with coloured icing on top, are also very popular during this time to buy as presents or to simply enjoy. In many places, there are *Krampus* and *Perchten* associations whose members not only accompany St Nicholas wearing spectacularly ugly masks and clothes but also feature in exuberant Krampus processions.

8 December, the *Immaculate Conception*, is a national holiday in Austria, but one that hasn't really worked its way into the festivities. Because shops are still open on this day, as has been the case for the last few years, it has a lot of economic importance for businesses during Advent. The *Lucia-Tag* on 13 December is basically not celebrated at all in Austria, unlike in Sweden or Italy.

The twelve nights from 20/21 December up to *Dreikönigstag* (Epiphany) on 6 January are known as *Raunächte* in Austria. This is the time for "purifying" the house and garden with a smouldering mixture of embers, incense, palm branches and herbs. According to ancient beliefs, during these special nights, evil spirits can be easily "smoked out" of the house and disaster can be averted.

During these Raunächte, there are processions in many alpine villages, wherein the "good" *Schönperchten* and the "evil" *Schiachperchten* (*schiach* = ugly) are said to drive out winter itself with their bells, while others believe they drive out the evil spirits of winter by creating a racket. The most important *Raunächte* are the Thomasnacht, Christnacht, New Year's Eve and Epiphany.

Thomasnacht from 20 to 21 December is not only the first *Raunacht*, it is also a time where young women, in particular, can have a look at the future of their relationships. The related customs are called *Lasseln* (raising hats) and *Baumschütteln* (tree shaking). Depending on what the women find under the hat, this will give them an indication of their future partner. With *Baumschütteln*, the young ladies try to express their desire for a partner.

In many regions in Austria, homemade nativity scenes are put up in churches and homes. In some places, it is even possible to admire "living" nativity scenes in large squares. Around Christmas, numerous museums and relevant exhibitions display the true variety of Austrian nativity scenes and the amazingly detail handicraft involved.

24 December is Christmas Eve, which is when *Christkindl* brings the presents in Austria. Imagine him as a child with curly hair, wings and a halo. Just before giving out the presents, a window in the house is opened so that he can fly in.

When all the presents are ready under the Christmas tree, which has been lit up with candles and stars, a little bell is secretly rung.

Present opening can now begin in front of the decorated Christmas tree and the song "Silent night" can be heard. In many families, they sing and play this themselves.

Some families have their Christmas meal before their presents, others afterwards. The meal on Christmas Eve is often quite simple, such as a plate of cold meats, sausages, sauerkraut and a potato or mayonnaise salad.

In Wagrain, lots of families have a simple sausage soup. This is also common in some regions in the Tyrol. In Salzburger Pinzgau, *Bachlkoch* is traditionally prepared

Christmas market on Rathausplatz in Vienna

at Christmas, a milk pudding made with honey and poppyseed.

However, raclette and fondue have become more and more popular; and some families already have a splendid Christmas meal on Christmas Eve with Christmas carp, roast beef, Christmas goose or silverside of beef with horseradish.

For religious Austrians, attending midnight mass is the high point of 24 December. Christmas day on 25 December and 26 December are cosy holidays celebrated all across Austria when they invite their relatives round or visit them. Either way there are distinct festive meals.

In Upper Austria, *Stefanitag* (26 December) is known for being the only date when *Störibrot* spiced with aniseed can be baked. In the past, it was traditionally brought to your parents-in-law for *Störibrotanschneiden* and *Störibrotkosten* (cutting and tasting the Störibrot).

In other states, the so-called *Stefaniritt* (Stefani ride) takes place for consecrating horses, since St Stephen is in fact the patron saint of horses and grooms, as well as of masons, tailors and carpenters.

On 28 December, the "day of the innocent children", the people in some regions remember the slaughter of infants ordered by the biblical King Herod. On this day, children go from house to house in order to *schappen* or *pissnen*, which means that they lightly beat the people with brushwood. Along with this, the children say rhyming blessings for which they are, of course, rewarded, especially with money.

Celebrating New Year's Eve has old Germanic roots. Since time immemorial, "evil spirits" were banished with fire and noise. Nowadays, fireworks and firecrackers are used instead. This is how they bid farewell to the old year and welcome in the new, as well as church bells peeling, the most famous being the Pummerin, the bell of Stephansdom in Vienna. Its chiming, broadcast on TV and the radio, traditionally ushers in the new year in Austria. Dancing the well-known Blue Danube Waltz by Austrian composer and "Waltz King", Johann Strauss II, is an absolute must for many revellers in the first few minutes of the new year.

Raising a glass of champagne, the Austrian people wish one another "Prosit Neujahr!", and they also exchange lucky charms like lucky pigs, shamrocks, figures of chimney sweeps, fish scales, horseshoes, ladybirds and lucky coins.

One custom on New Year's Eve, which has only become a tradition in the past few years, is everyone watching the comedy sketch "Dinner for One" together on the TV. On the first day of the new year, the Vienna Philharmonic Orchestra's New Year's concert, is broadcast across the world on TV and radio from the Golden Hall of the Wiener Musikverein.

Sternsinger, people dressed up as the Three Kings, go from house to house right up until 6 January. They deliver blessings for the inhabitants for the new year and collect money for their charitable actions. When leaving the house, they write the number of the year and the letters C+M+B over the front door. This stands for *Christus mansionem benedicat* (May Christ bless this house). Others interpret the letters as simply being the first letter of the names of each of the Three Wise Men, *Caspar, Melchior* and *Balthasar*.

The majority of Christmas trees are cleared away on 6 January. But in some living rooms, they leave them up until Candlemas, 2 February. This is when Christmas really is over. Until 1912, Candlemas was also an official bank holiday when servants could change their posting.

Wagrain sausage soup

300 g	braised beef leg
3–4	marrowbones
½	onion, finely chopped
	Celery, finely chopped
	Carrots, finely chopped
	Oil
	Soup pasta
	Sausages (Frankfurters or a different kind of boiled sausage), sliced
2	bay leaves
	Salt
	Whole peppercorns

Quickly fry the onions, then the braised beef, marrowbones, bay leaves, peppercorns, celery and carrots in a pan, fill with water, bring to the boil and leave to simmer gently for a little while longer.

After about 1 ½ hours, the soup should be ready. Remove the braised beef and the bones and save for using in something else. Then boil the sausages and the pasta in the soup for about 10 minutes. Serve garnished with chive and parsley.

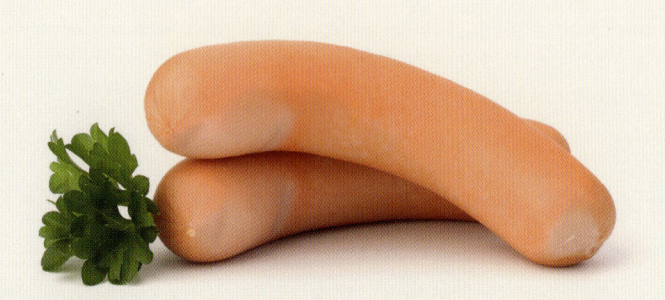

Christmas carp

1	whole carp, about 1.5 kg
	Juice of 2 lemons
	Dash of vinegar
	Butter for the tin
200 g	potatoes
500 g	root vegetables
500 ml	fish stock
	Horseradish

Gut and bone the carp. Drizzle the lemon juice over the fish and leave to marinate. Then season the carp and blanche quickly in vinegar water.

Grease an ovenproof dish with butter and place the carp with the stomach opening upright onto a second flipped ovenproof bowl or larger cup. By doing so, the fish cooks evenly but remains juicy.

Peel the potatoes and cut into slices. Peel the root vegetables as well and cut into thin strips. Place both of these in the dish around the fish, pour over a little fish stock and cook in the oven at 200 °C for 30–45 minutes.

Before serving, scatter some freshly grated horseradish over the fish and serve with root vegetables and potatoes.

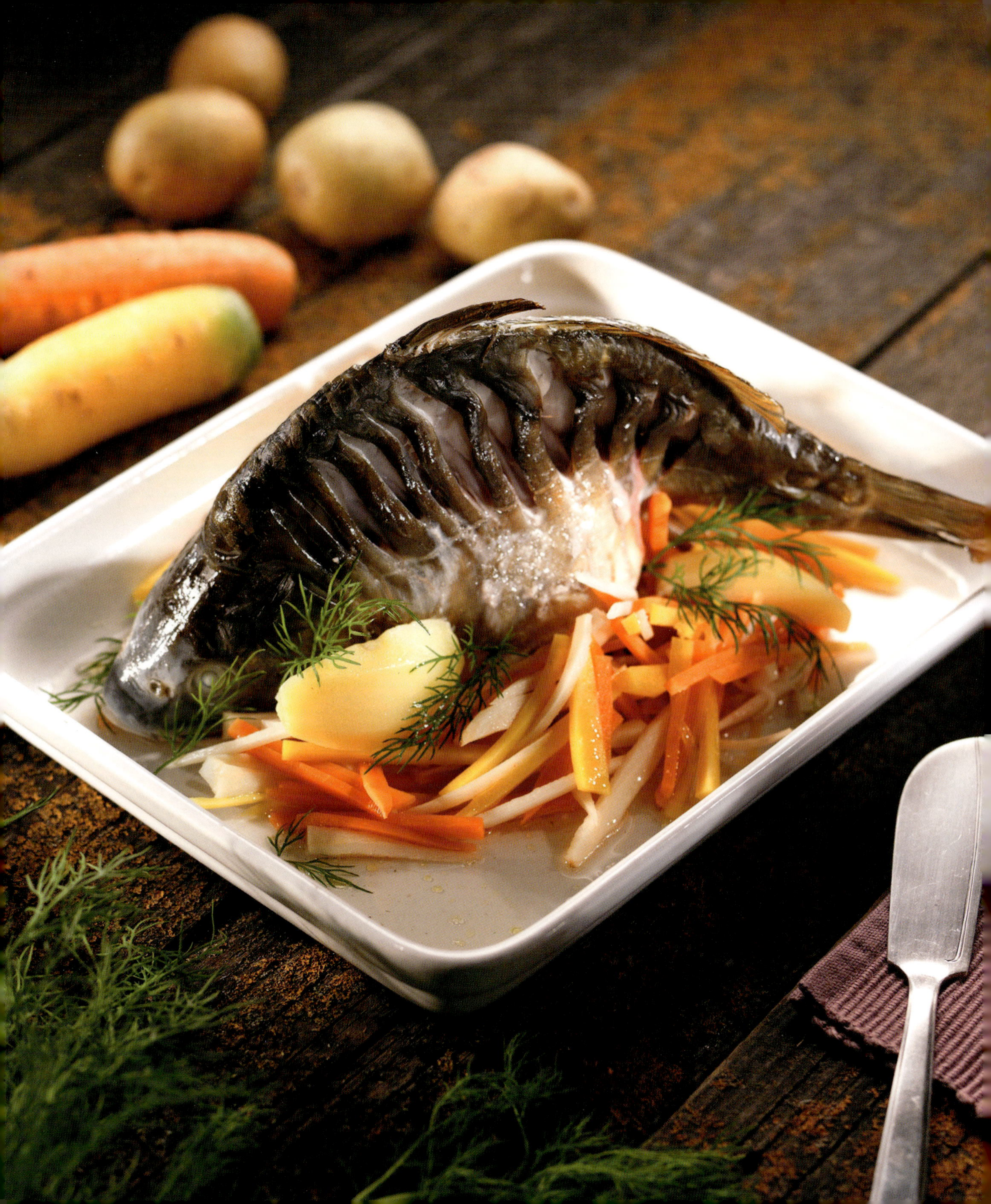

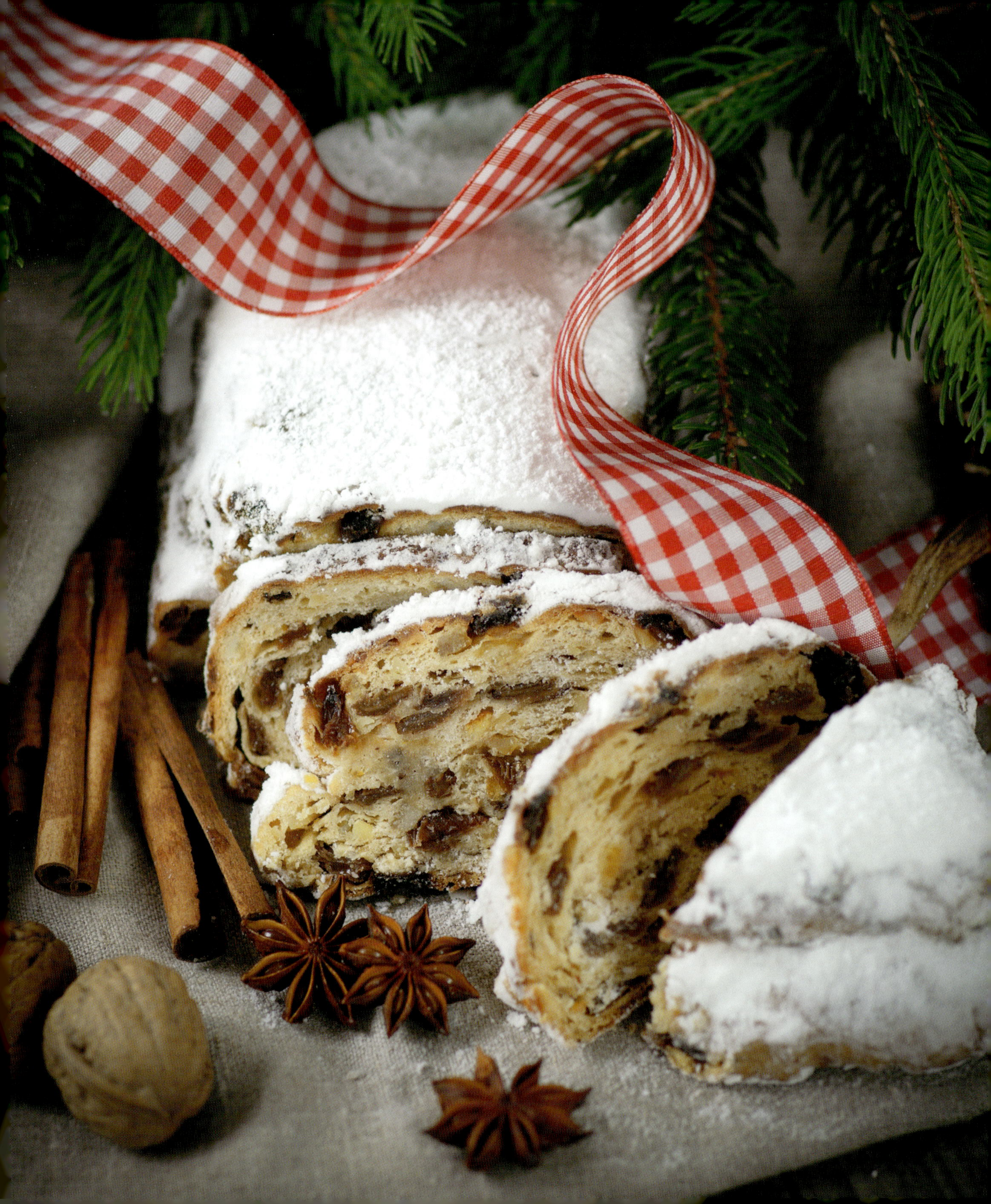

Christmas stollen

1 ½ kg	flour
3	cubes of yeast
	Lukewarm milk
4	eggs
300 g	sugar
100 g	strips of candied lemon peel
100 g	sweet blanched almonds, finely chopped
10 g	bitter almonds
1	lemon, zest
	Ground cinnamon
	Grated ginger
	Grated nutmeg
	Grated cardamom
600 g	butter
500 g	raisins
200 g	currants, soaked in rum overnight
5 tbsp	rum
	Butter
	Icing sugar
	Salt

Make a starter from the yeast, a little lukewarm milk and sugar. Dust over some of the flour, cover and leave for about half an hour. Then, mix in the rest of the flour, add the eggs, sugar, a little salt and the necessary amount of lukewarm milk and knead to form a relatively firm dough.

Add the candied lemon peel, almonds, lemon zest and spices to taste, soft butter and raisins and currants. Knead the dough until it bubbles. Split into pieces, throw these at one another with force and then knead them all together again until the dough is very smooth. Then, cover again and leave for about two hours.

On a floured pastry board, shape into a long plaited bun. Then, something quite specific happens: roll out half the dough from the middle to one edge, using a rolling pin, moisten this section of the dough with water and fold it back over the other half of the dough. This is how the stollen gets its typical shape.

Line a baking tray with greaseproof paper, grease with butter, place the stollen on this and also brush with butter. Leave to rise a third time and then bake for about 60 minutes at 170 °C. After baking, brush the hot stollen with butter again and dust generously with icing sugar.

POLAND

Wesołych Świąt Bożego Narodzenia i szczęśliwego Nowego Roku **Cicha noc, święta noc**

There is a long tradition of splendid Christmas markets in many cities across Poland, which epitomise the "most peaceful time" of the year for many people in Poland. St Nicholas rides through the streets on white horses. On Christmas Eve, straw is scattered on the ground to be reminiscent of the stable in Bethlehem, and the Gospel is read out as soon as the first star can be seen in the sky. After this, many Poles serve a traditionally home-cooked meal, often made up of twelve components. There are soup, fish and cabbage dishes, as well as various sweet baked goods. At midnight, believers go to *pasterka*, midnight mass. They celebrate exuberantly on New Year's Eve, and New Year's Day is greeted with sweet *Pierogi*. The Christmas period comes to an end on Epiphany.

Advent and Christmas are particularly significant for the predominantly Catholic population of Poland. The Christmas period begins on the first Sunday of Advent and, according to old customs, the fasting period also commences. Despite fasting, the Poles still enjoy visiting Christmas markets. In my opinion, the most beautiful ones can be found in Warsaw, Wrocław, Poznan, Gdansk and Szczecin. The oldest Christmas market can be admired in the cultural city of Krakow.

During Advent, pre-Christmas gatherings and meals, similar to those enjoyed on Christmas Eve, are organised in companies, schools and other institutions. The meals are either homemade or brought in from home or catered for. This is the Polish equivalent of our Christmas parties or Austrian people meeting at Christmas markets.

In Poland, *Święty Mikołaj*, St Nicholas, comes down from the sky on a sleigh pulled by white horses. Children recite prayers and religious texts and receive images of the saints, red apples and holy biscuits – either handed to them in person or placed under their pillows or in polished shoes. In Poland, Christmas Eve is called *Wigilia* (from the Latin *viglare*, meaning to wake). According to traditional customs, the course of events for the celebration is very important and determines whether the coming year will be a happy one. If *Wigilia* is celebrated peacefully together with family then, according to old beliefs, this will have a positive effect on events in the future.

Any housework should have been finished before nightfall. Therefore, they start preparing the evening meal together and decorating the Christmas tree from the early hours of the morning.

Traditionally, bundles of grains, hay and straw are also part of the festive decorations as they are supposed to ensure a good harvest and symbolise Jesus' manger in the stable.

There is also a small bundle of hay that is placed under the dining table to remind them of the birthplace of Jesus. In most Polish families, a coin is placed under everyone's plate in the hope of preventing them from falling into poverty.

The celebratory meal, which friends and relatives are invited to, does not start until the first star appears in the sky. And they always set one place too many just in case there should be an unexpected visitor. This is also in memory of their ancestors.

Before the meal, the story of the Nativity is read out. Only then can they tuck in. But before they start eating, they share a sacred white wafer among themselves. This symbolises peaceful cooperation, love and kindness. And everyone wishes each other all the best for the following year. In families with animals, a colourful wafer is also shared with the animals. According to one Polish legend, animals are able to talk for the night.

In Poland, the Christmas feast is made up of twelve components. Each dish stands for one of the twelve apostles. A chunky clear soup, cabbage dishes and a fish dish (unlike in many other countries, there are no meat dishes), are all part of the traditional *Wigilia* meal: carp, pickled herring, salted herring or other cooked fish are popular.

Since the 1940s, carp has become a popular fish for *Wigilia*. It was often brought while still alive so that they could be sure that the fish really was fresh. Then it is kept in a tank until Christmas to be served up as fillets or in jelly etc.

There is of course no shortage of sweet dishes: *Kutia*, a mixture of flour, poppyseeds, raisins, honey and nuts, *Makówki*, a layered dish made of poppyseeds, raisins, milk and slices of white bread or *Moczka*, a kind of lebkuchen sauce, *Strucla z makiem* (poppyseed stollen), *Ciasteczka* (Christmas biscuits) and *Pierniki* (lebkuchen) are also popular. After eating, they tuck a fish scale or a fish bone into their wallets which is thought to provide prosperity and happiness in the coming year.

As a game, the children pull some of the hay out from under the table. Green means a year full of prosperity or possibly a marriage, while black hay supposedly promises bad misfortune. A nut is also often hidden in a cake. Whoever finds it in their slice is said to have a successful year, according to old tradition.

At midnight, they attend *Pasterka* (shepherd's mass) in church.

In the countryside, it is customary to this day for fancy-dress Christmas carollers to go from house to house with a star or with one of the typical Polish nativity scenes – the very colourful ones from Krakow are particularly famous – and they expect a small reward for this.

The first Christmas Day is traditionally reserved for family. The Poles prefer to stay at home, eat together, relax and watch television. What to watch, or what programme, is always a hotly debated topic. "Home Alone" obtained cult status quite a while ago. Nowadays, Christmas isn't Christmas in Poland without it.

New Year's Eve is shaped by fireworks, lashings of bubbly and a roaring fire. Usually, they don't do any cleaning on this day since otherwise, legend has it, this would drive happiness from the house. The fridge must always be well stocked – as a symbol of full coffers in the new year.

At midnight on the dot every clock is wound up to welcome in the coming year on time.

"Good spirits" are invited into the house by leaving the door wide open. Women looking for a partner fill their shoes with some poppyseeds. This can allegedly considerably increase the number of admirers.

On New Year's Day, they eat sweet *Pierogi* filled with nuts hoping to spend the whole year in good health and good spirits.

6 January has been a bank holiday since 2011. A procession with Caspar, Melchior and Balthazar riding on camels and horses passes through the streets, surrounded by many other people dressed in colourful clothes. The route is lined by many spectators, with the children wearing bright, cheery cardboard crowns.

Kutia, a sweet Christmas dish.

Zurek

(Sourdough or roux soup with sausage and egg)

500 ml	sourdough soup
20 g	dried mushrooms
	Soup vegetable mix (3 carrots, 2 parsley roots, ½ celery stick), peeled, roughly chopped
1	onion
300 g	sausage, Polish, white or smoked
50 g	streaky bacon
6	hard-boiled eggs, peeled
2	cloves of garlic
1	beaker sour cream
½ tsp	horseradish, freshly grated
150 g	streaky bacon
1 kg	potatoes
	Soup powder
	Allspice
	Bay leaf
	Dried marjoram
	Salt, pepper

Sourdough or roux soup

1 tbsp	oil
1 tbsp	flour, sifted
½ l	water or stock
1	clove of garlic, whole
1	egg, beaten, to taste
	Caraway
	Salt

Soak the mushrooms in about ¼ litre of water and then cut into thin strips. Put the soup vegetable mix, the soaked mushrooms, sausage, streaky bacon, allspice and bay leaf in a pan with about 1 ½ litres of water, season to taste with soup powder and leave to simmer for c. 30–40 minutes.

Remove the sausage and vegetables from the soup, cut into small pieces and keep warm. Gradually mix in the sourdough or roux soup. Crush the garlic clove and add to the soup together with the horseradish. Season with salt, pepper and marjoram. Serve up with the sausage and vegetables back in the soup and with the solid soup ingredients.

Solid soup ingredients (potatoes with bacon)
Cut the bacon into small cubes and fry in a hot pan without any oil until golden brown. Peel the potatoes and boil in salted water, then mash and mix with the fried bacon bits. Add pepper to taste and the crushed garlic. You can also use roux soup instead of sourdough soup.

For the roux soup, make a roux from oil and flour and pour over half a litre of water (or stock). Add the salt, caraway and garlic and leave to boil for 30 minutes.

For the sourdough soup, ferment cracked rye bread in water a few days before preparing the soup. Adding the fermented bread to the soup results in a slightly sour taste.

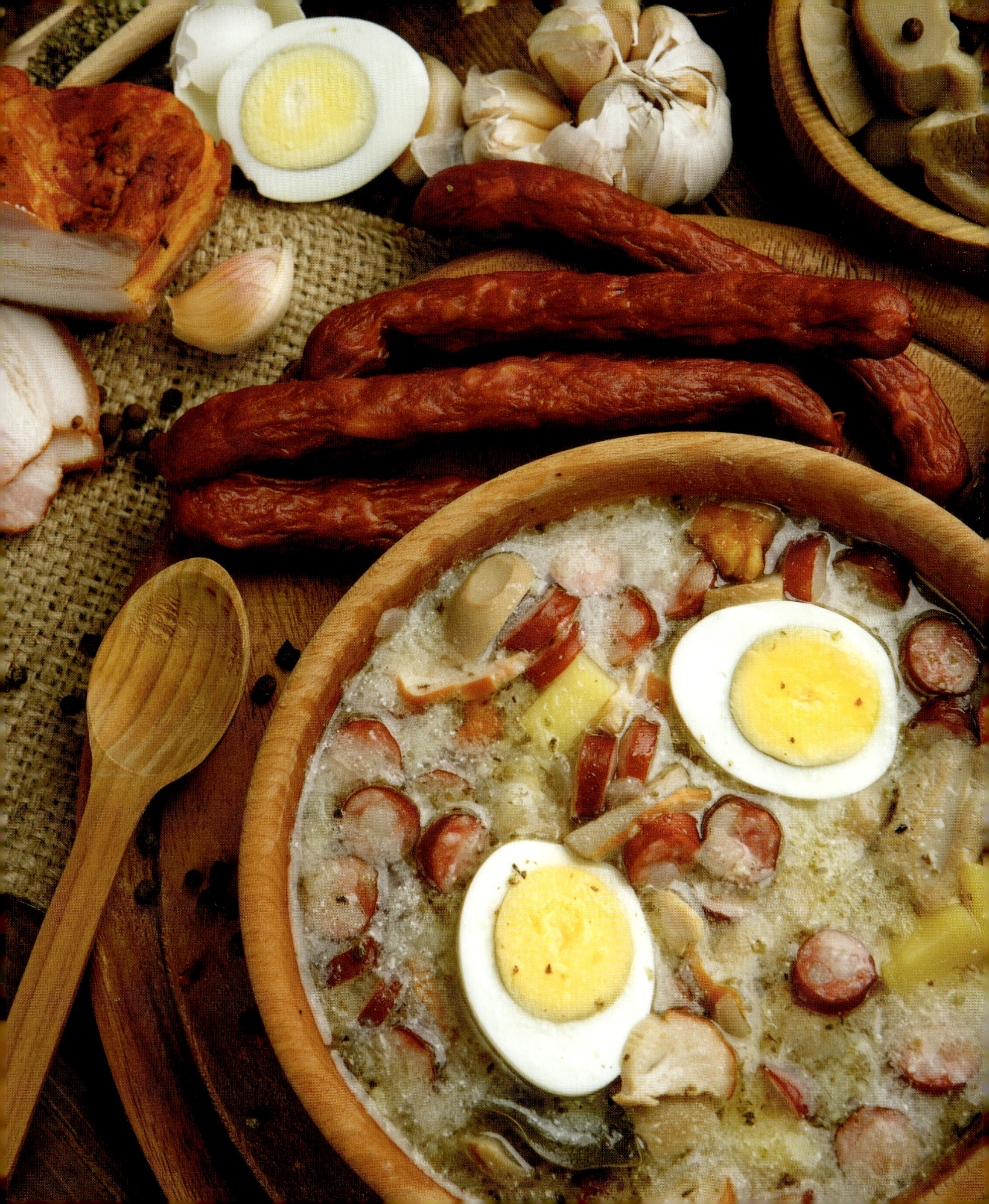

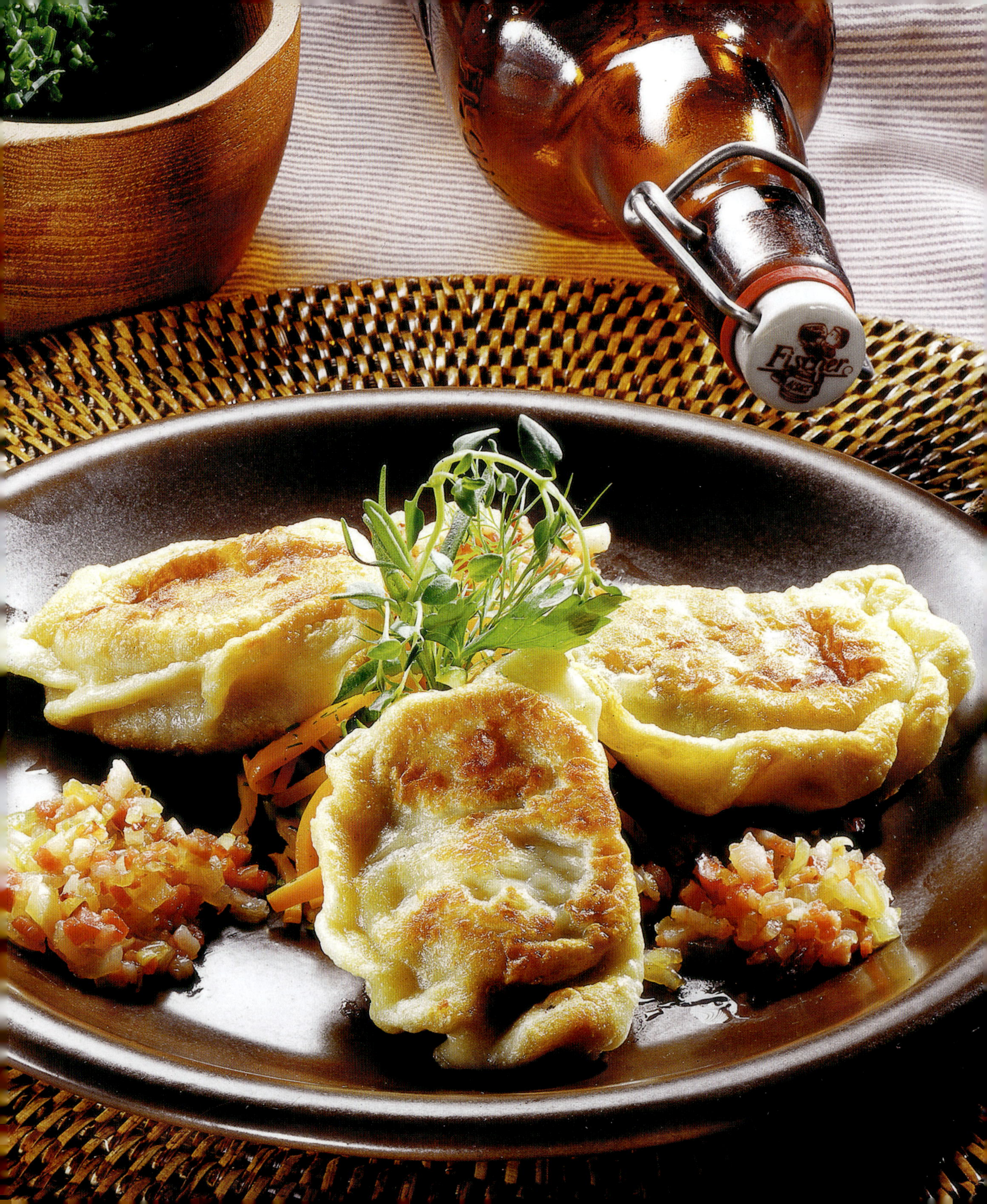
Fischer

Pierogi

(Pastry parcels with a sauerkraut and mushroom filling)

Pastry
375 g	flour
2	eggs
	Salt
	Oil

Filling
80 g	bacon, finely diced
1 tbsp	clarified butter
1	onion, finely diced
200 g	sauerkraut, well drained
	Cloves
	Juniper berries
	Bay leaf
	White wine
150 g	mushrooms, finely diced
	Butter
2	sprigs of thyme, picked
1	egg white
	Salt, ground pepper
	Butter for frying

Put the flour, the eggs, a little salt, some oil and 60 ml of water in a large bowl. Knead everything together to form a smooth dough. Cover and leave the dough to stand for 20 minutes.

For the filling, render the bacon in the clarified butter. Fry the onions lightly in the pan, add the sauerkraut and mix everything together well. Season to taste, stir in some white wine and leave to fry further for a few minutes. Then set aside.

Brown the mushrooms slightly in butter, season and add the thyme.

Remove the sauerkraut from the pan, leave to dry off and mix with the mushrooms in a bowl.

Thinly roll out the dough on a floured worktop and cut out 7–8cm circles. Brush the edges with a little egg white.

Put a heaped teaspoon of the filling in the middle of each circle of dough, fold over to make semi-circles and seal the edges together well.

Leave the Pierogi to simmer in boiling water. Stir carefully and, when they float to the surface, leave to cook for another 2–3 minutes. Fry the Pierogi in melted butter until golden brown and serve.

Poland

Sernik

(Cheesecake)

Shortcrust pastry base

250 g	flour
125 g	cold butter, cubed
75 g	(icing) sugar
1	egg
1 sachet	vanilla sugar
½	lemon, zested
	Salt
	Butter for the tin

Cheesecake filling

4	eggs, separated
100 g	butter
50 g	flour
400 g	sugar
1 sachet	vanilla sugar
500 g	quark, dry
3 tbsp	cornflour
100 g	candied orange peel
50 g	almonds, whole or julienned
50 g	raisins

For the shortcrust pastry base, mix together the butter, icing sugar, lemon zest and vanilla sugar and beat with a hand mixer until light and fluffy. Then quickly knead the flour in. Wrap the dough in cling film and leave to chill in the fridge for ½ hour.

Then roll the dough out flatly on the base of the buttered springform tin, turn up a small edge and prick with a fork a few times.

Blind bake for about 15 minutes at 180 °C (air circulation).

For the cheesecake filling, beat the butter until light and fluffy. Then gradually add the egg whites and mix well. Stir in the vanilla sugar and sugar and then also fold in the quark with the mix. Beat the egg whites with a little salt until they form stiff peaks and also fold into the cheesecake mixture. Then stir in the cornflour, adding a little extra flour if necessary. Then, add the raisins, almonds and candied orange peel.

Quickly put the filling on the blind baked base in the springform tin. Bake the Sernik at 200 °C (fan oven: 175 °C) for about 45 minutes.

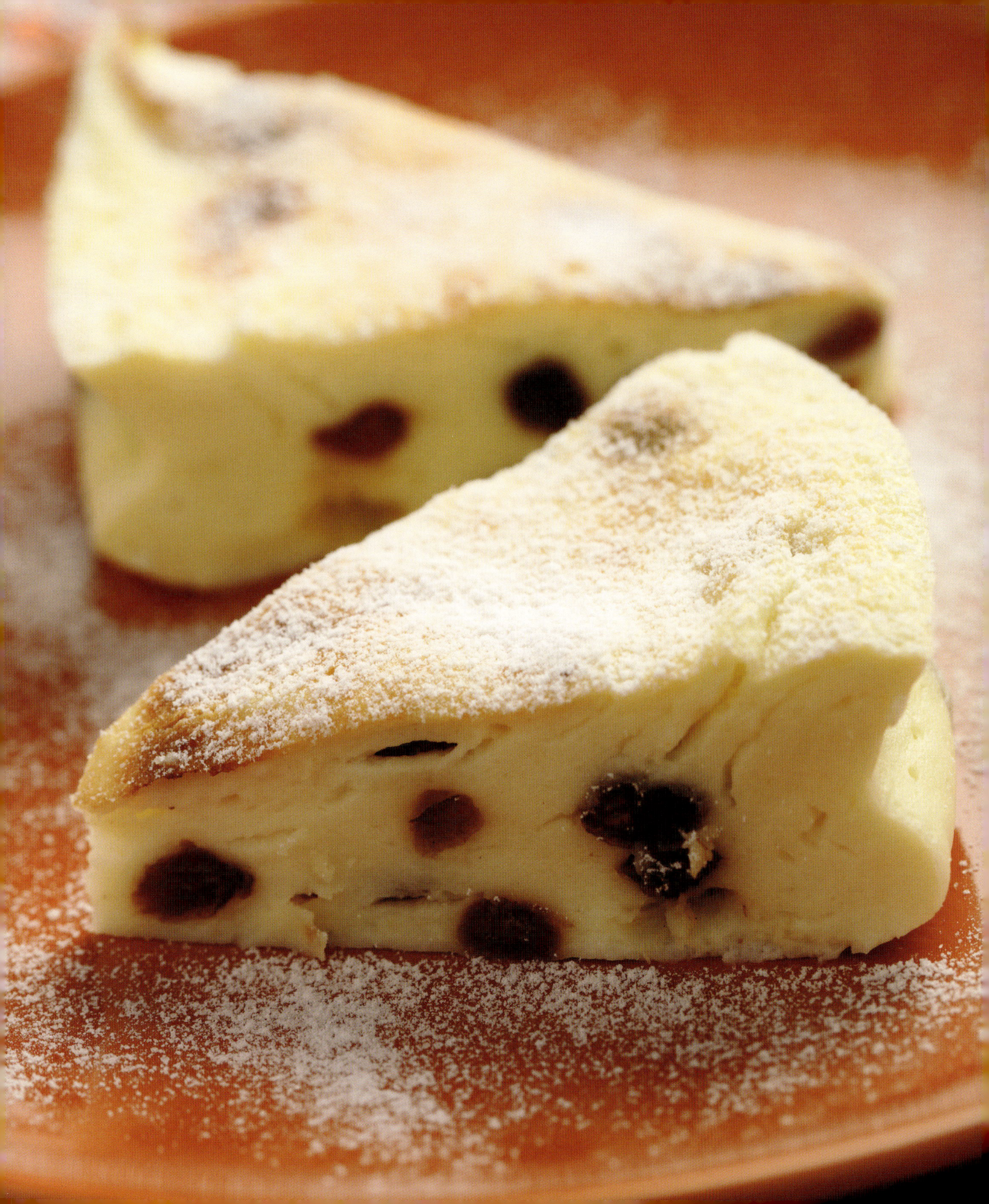

PORTUGAL

Feliz Natal e Próspero Ano Novo

Noite de paz, noite de amor

In Portugal, whole cities, not just houses and flats, are festively decorated for the entire duration of the Christmas period. Traditionally, the most important Christmas symbol is the manger with Baby Jesus. "Papa Christmas" brings the presents, or sometimes even Baby Jesus himself. And during the night of Epiphany, the Three Wise Men give out more presents. At midnight on Christmas Eve, the Portuguese attend "Rooster's Mass". They then sit down together for a proper meal a few hours later. The Christmas meal itself includes all manner of dishes, from fish to turkey to countless sweet biscuits. New Year's Eve is brimming with various traditions that are said to bring happiness and prosperity in the coming year. The Christmas period finally draws to a close on 6 January.

Contemporary Christmas celebrations in Portugal combine old Christian traditions with more recent rituals. As a Catholic country, Christmas is without a doubt the most important celebration of the year, with the central focus being the manger and Baby Jesus.

Right from the very start of the Advent period, many churches and buildings are festively decorated with colourful lights and other Christmas decorations. Christmas trees have also become increasingly popular in Portugal, but the most important element of Christmas for the Portuguese has always been, and will continue to be, the manger.

Noite de Natal, Christmas Eve on 24 December, is the high point of the Christmas celebrations, and it is predominantly a family affair. The festive cheer continues inside, with decorations on display in every room of the house. The manger and the Christmas tree, which has been a common feature in Portugal since the 19th Century, are put up.

For large families living in the countryside, Christmas is celebrated together with neighbours. Music plays a very important role for them. In many Portuguese families, Christmas songs are sung or played and poems along a similar theme are recited. In some regions, the people go from door to door playing flutes, guitars, accordions or mandolins and singing Christmas songs. The whole family attends midnight mass together and some people take along home-grown products from their gardens to place in the manger as a symbolic gift for Jesus. In many Portuguese villages, a tree trunk is then set alight in the church square so that the villagers can warm themselves around the fire after midnight mass.

After attending *Missa do Galo* (Rooster's Mass), there is *Ceia de Natal*, a late-night Christmas meal consisting of *Bacalhau* (salt cod) with potatoes and cabbage and *Bolo Rei*, the King's cake, made with candied fruits and nuts and other sweet dishes, always involving a lot of cinnamon and lemon.

In provincial regions, they perform traditional Christmas plays, but these nevertheless have a pagan origin. As part of

Bacalhau, Christmas salt cod dish

these, they satirise specific local events hoping to pillory social injustices, as is tradition. *Pai Natal* ("Papa Christmas" or Father Christmas) brings the presents, but sometimes this is left to *Menino Jesus* (Christ Child) himself. However, they traditionally only exchange gifts on Christmas morning, with each present symbolising the presents brought for Jesus by the shepherds.

On the first Christmas holiday, that is on 25 December, the whole family gathers for lunch.

The first course is usually *Farrapo velho*, fried and chopped left-overs from the previous evening's dinner, seasoned with a lot of garlic. *Cozido à Portuguesa* (Portuguese-style stew) is also very popular. This is often followed by a turkey dish or dried salt cod, but octopus also often crops up on the menu, along with various vegetables.

Arroz doce (sweet rice pudding) and pumpkin fried in a sweet pancake dough with sugar and cinnamon usually finish off the Christmas meal.

Sonhos de Natal (Christmas dream) features mostly in rural regions. This dish is made from wheat flour, milk, eggs, lemon zest and salt. *Fromigos* made of slices of white bread, eggs, pine nuts, port, sugar, milk and grated almonds are traditional sweet celebration day meals in northern Portugal. *Broa Castelar*, another speciality, is a dense maize and wheat flour cake with grated sweet potatoes, coconut and orange zest.

New Year's Eve traditions in Portugal are exceptionally varied. For example, if you find yourself holding a coin at midnight, you can be sure of prosperity in the coming year.

Similarly, at midnight, lots of people jump off a chair, "swinging" their way into the new year. But regardless of what custom you choose to follow, wearing new clothes is an absolute must for the turn of the year. In some regions, firework displays might may be replaced with smashing crockery and clanging pots and pans against one another, but this is certainly not the case in Madeira where their New Year's Eve fireworks are world famous thanks to their magnificence.

Christmas celebrations only end on 6 January, Epiphany. The Three Wise Men bring more presents for the children. In anticipation of this, the little ones stuff their shoes with carrots and straw the night before and leave them on the windowsill or outside the front door. They hope the Magi's horses will be tempted by the food and the Three Wise Men will leave them a present as a thank you.

Sopa de pedra
(Vegetable soup with bacon and sausage)

200 g	dried beans, soaked
3 tbsp	olive oil
2	cloves of garlic, finely chopped
2	onions, finely chopped
125 g	streaky bacon
125 g	spicy sausage (chorizo)
4	medium potatoes, peeled and diced
4	carrots, peeled, diced
2	small turnips, peeled and diced
1	small savoy cabbage, cut into thin slices
375 g	tomatoes, diced
1	bay leaf
2 l	chicken stock
20 g	fresh coriander, chopped
	Salt, pepper

Cover the beans in a pan with water and bring to the boil. Reduce the heat, put the lid on the pan, leave the beans until soft and drain. Finally, puree a part of them.

Meanwhile gently heat the olive oil in another pan and fry the onions and garlic in it. Add the bacon, sausage, vegetables, bay leaf and the chicken stock and bring everything to the boil. Remove the bay leaf, as well as the bacon and sausage, and cut into pieces about 1cm big. Put the pieces back in the pan, add the beans and heat everything quickly over medium heat. If needed, season with salt and pepper.

Serve on preheated plates, scattered with coriander. In some recipes, you can also find pigs' ear served on the side.

Bacalhau à Bras
(Salt cod with potatoes and egg)

500 g	salt cod
300 g	onions, cut into thin slices
500 g	potatoes, cut into the shape of chips
4	eggs, beaten
5 tbsp	oil
1	clove of garlic, crushed
½ bunch	flat leaf parsley
150 g	cherry tomatoes, halved
100 g	olives
	Salt, pepper

Cut the salt cod into pieces and soak well for 24 hours, changing the water regularly. Then pull the fish apart into small chunks.

Beat the eggs and season with salt and pepper.

Fry the potatoes in a pan with hot oil with the cloves of garlic, remove from the pan and then fry the onions. Add the salt cod and the fried potatoes and carefully mix.

When everything is hot and cooked, stir in the eggs and tomatoes and serve the whole thing with olives, before the eggs curdle. Finally, scatter with some more chopped parsley.

Bolo Rei
(King's cake)

1 kg	flour
100 g	sugar
200 g	butter
5	eggs
50 g	yeast
2 cl	port
250 ml	milk, lukewarm
50 g	each of pine nuts and walnuts, roughly chopped
50 g	currants
50 g	candied orange peel
50 g	sultanas (or raisins)
100 g	other dried fruits (plums, figs, apricots…)
	Icing sugar
50 g	cherries, glacé
1	egg, egg yolk
	Salt

Crumble the yeast in 3–4 tbsp milk with some sugar, stir and leave to stand in a warm place. Add the flour, the rest of the milk, sugar, butter, eggs, port and a little salt and knead to form a dough. Leave to rise for about half an hour.

Then add the fruit, knead well and leave to rise again. Shape the dough into a log so that it fits on a baking tray lined with baking paper as a wreath with a 30 cm diameter.

Tip: place a cup in the middle so that the dough does not become a round, flat cake during baking, or use a Bundt tin. Scatter some cherries and dried fruit on the dough and brush with egg yolk.

Bake for about 30 minutes at 180–200 °C. Leave to cool and dust with icing sugar.

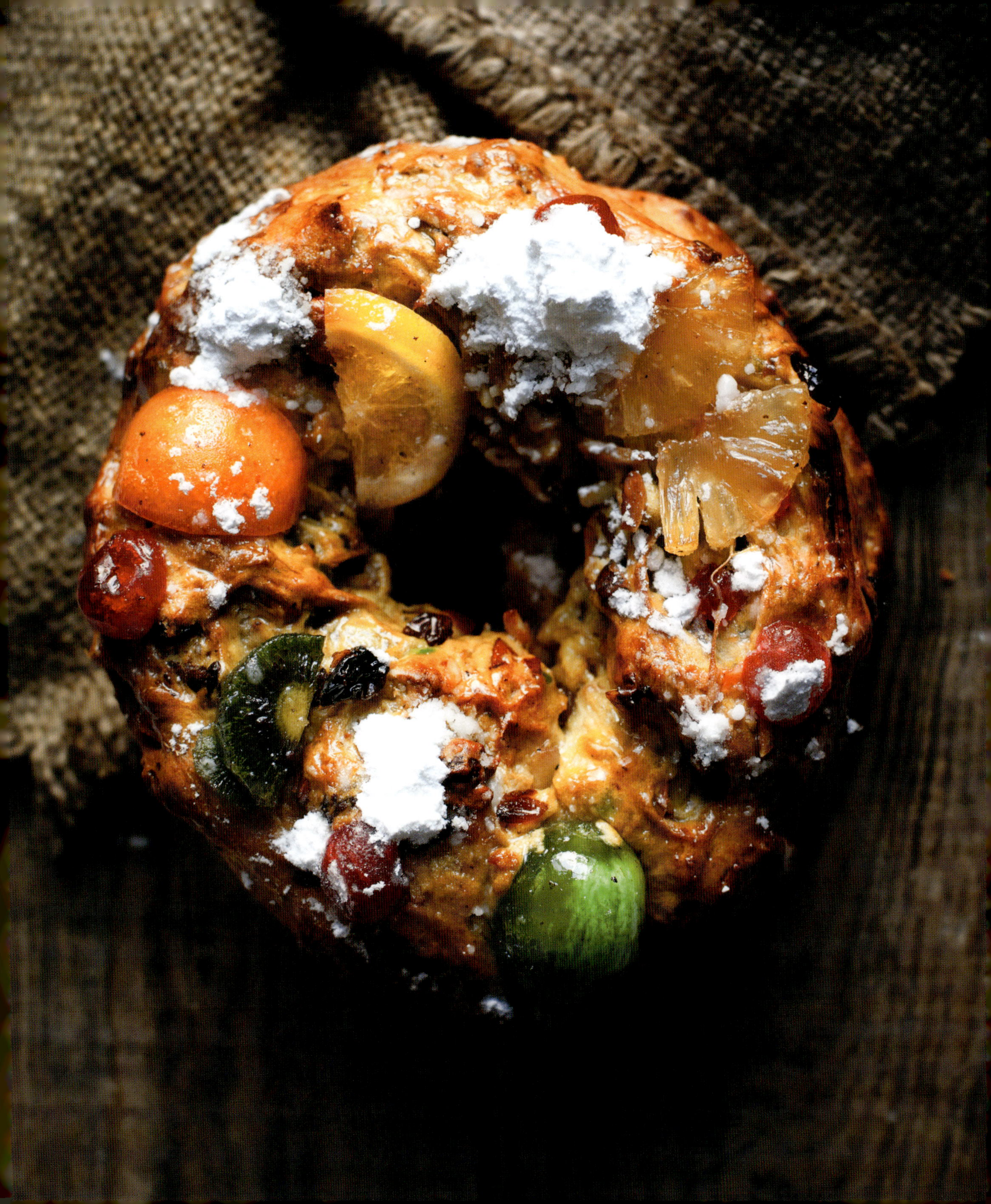

ROMANIA

Crăciun fericit și un An nou fericit **Noapte de vis, timp preasfânt**

In many parts of Romania, the fasting period is still strictly obeyed leading up to Christmas, which means there are intensive culinary preparations just before Christmas. In the meantime, St Nicholas brings presents for the children. The house and garden are given a thorough tidy in preparation for the celebrations. Before Christmas Eve, Christmas carollers go from house to house carrying a paper star. The Romanians celebrate the birth of Jesus with loud music and dancing. During midnight mass, scenic plays are performed. The following day there is the great exchange of presents and a hearty Christmas meal. On New Year's Eve, the Romanians wave lanterns which they hope will bring them happiness and they perform songs in exchange for food and entertainment.

Christmas tree in Brașov.

In Romania, the pre-Christmas period is a fasting period, which lasts up until Christmas Eve.

On 5 December, St Nicholas brings the first round of small presents for the children.

Slaughtering pigs and hens in preparation for the holidays starts about two weeks before Christmas. After this, everything is cleaned thoroughly so that it is all beautifully clean for the big celebrations.

All kinds of delights are baked and cooked up two days before Christmas. During the night from 23 to 24 December, children in the villages sing traditional Christmas songs and the group of singers is known as *Colindatori*. They carry round a star made of cardboard and paper, which is decorated with bells and colourful ribbons with scenes from the Bible depicted on it. In return, they receive all kinds of sweets, fruits and nut cakes.

Christmas Eve in Romania is known as *Moș Ajun*. They continue to fast until late in the evening. Presents only come after this. Traditionally, these are sweets, oranges and a plaited loaf of Christmas bread. Any bigger presents are only unwrapped on Christmas morning, which by eating breakfast together including stuffed eggs and cake. Later on in the day, the Romanians eat pork, enjoy Christmas cake,

Visinata, Romanian sour cherry liqueur

For New Year, the Romanians have various rituals which are said to promise happiness.

One example is stroking *Vasilica* (little lambs). They even receive a small payment for this pleasant task.

Groups of young people go from house to house seeking food and entertainment. Coffee, cake, wine and, of course, a strong, home-brewed brandy are often served. Then they wish each other "good health!" Otherwise, according to tradition, the house will be cursed.

Epiphany is also a bank holiday in Romania and rounds off the Christmas period.

known as *Cozonac*, which is a pound cake made with nuts or poppyseeds, and drink *Visinata* (sour cherry liqueur).

On Christmas Eve, the religious population of Romania carry an image of the saints from door to door and wish each other a merry Christmas. The birth of Jesus is celebrated with loud music and dancing.

At midnight, everyone goes to church to watch a special play, which is called *Wiflaem*. Many people get involved in this by donning various different costumes. They dress up as angels or devils, for example, and act out scenes with the Three Wise Men or the Virgin Mary and Jesus.

Typical Christmas dishes include *Salată de boeuf* (vegetable-beef salad), stuffed eggs with mayonnaise, *sărmale* (stuffed cabbage leaves), vegetable soup with meat (dumplings), meat patties, breaded schnitzel and biscuits. *Alba ca zăpadă* (layer cake), nut cream and strawberry biscuits are particularly popular pudding.

Stuffed tomatoes with mashed aubergine

Traditionally in winter, aubergines are put in the oven. The aubergine flesh is then mashed with oil, pepper, salt and an onion, which is then stuffed into cored tomatoes. After this, bake in the oven for about 30 minutes at 180 °C.

Romania

Sărmăluțe moldovenești with Mămăliga

(Moldovan stuffed cabbage leaves with polenta)

1	cabbage head
	Savoy

Filling
500 g	minced pork
500 g	minced beef
4 tbsp	rice
2	onions, chopped and steamed
	Lard or oil
	Dill, finely chopped
	Salt
	Ground pepper

Sauce
1 tbsp	lard
1 l	sauerkraut water, mixed with stock
100 g	tomato passata

Blanche the head of cabbage, then carefully remove the individual leaves.

For the filling, fry the onions in oil or lard, then add the minced meats and stir evenly until everything is well fried. Finally, mix in the rice and season. Then fill the cabbage leaves with the mixture and roll together.

Place the *Sărmălute* alternatingly with the rest of the finely chopped cabbage and savoy in oven-proof tins.

Pour over the sauce, until the *Sărmălute* are covered. Cook in the oven for about 1 to 2 hours. This will be quicker in a pressure cooker. Before eating, slide into the oven again to warm up. The stuffed cabbage leaves are eaten with mamaliga and crème fraiche.

Mămăliga

1 part	polenta (not cornmeal)
2 parts	water (or a mixture or water and whey)
	Salt
	Butter
	Yoghurt

Bring the water or the water-whey mixture to the boil with a little salt.

Gradually add the polenta and then remove the pan from the heat so that it doesn't catch on the bottom. Then it's just stir, stir, stir until the *Mămăliga* has the consistency of a thick pulp, which should happen quite quickly. Just before serving, stir through a knob of butter and yoghurt.

If needed, you can add more salt.

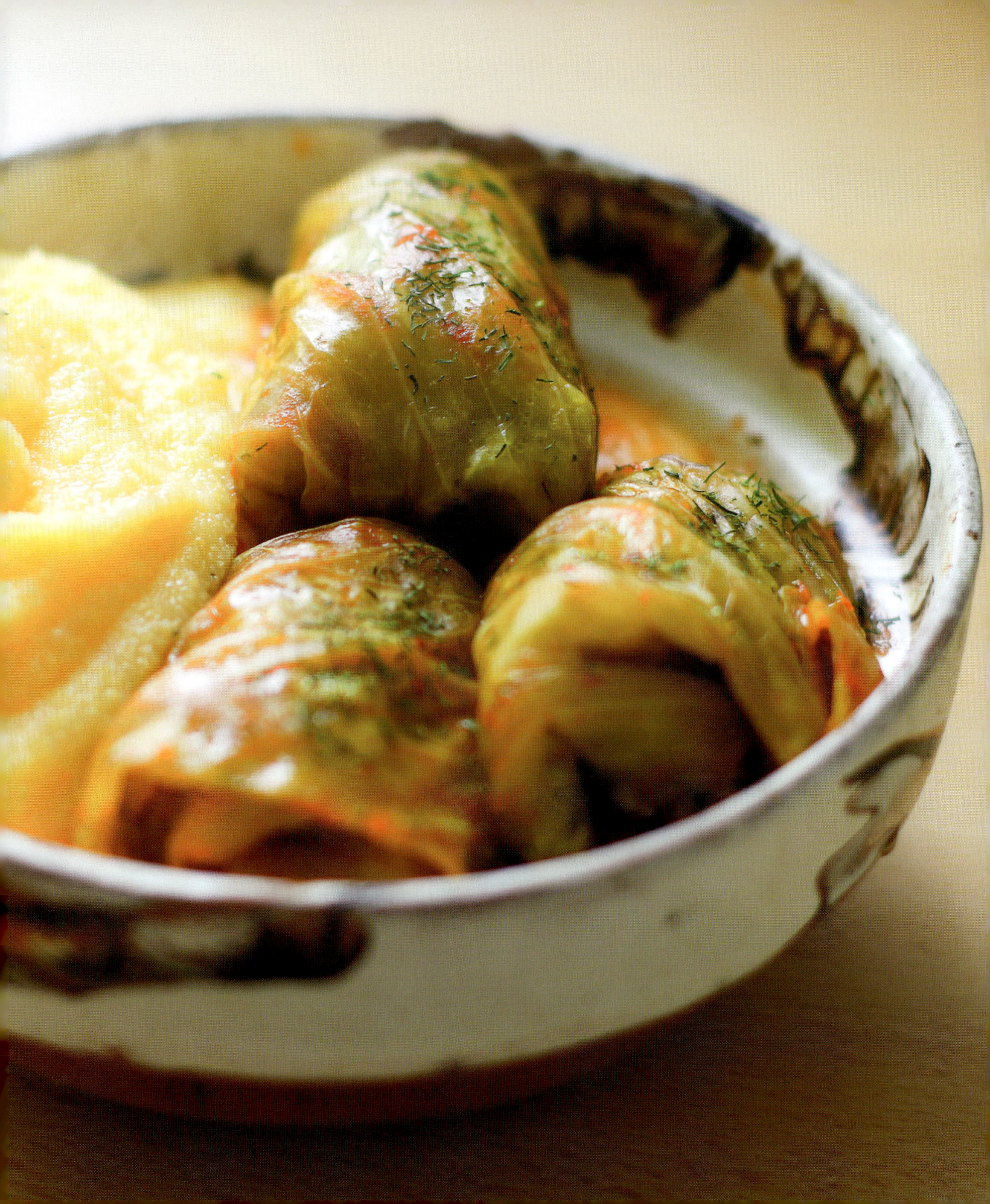

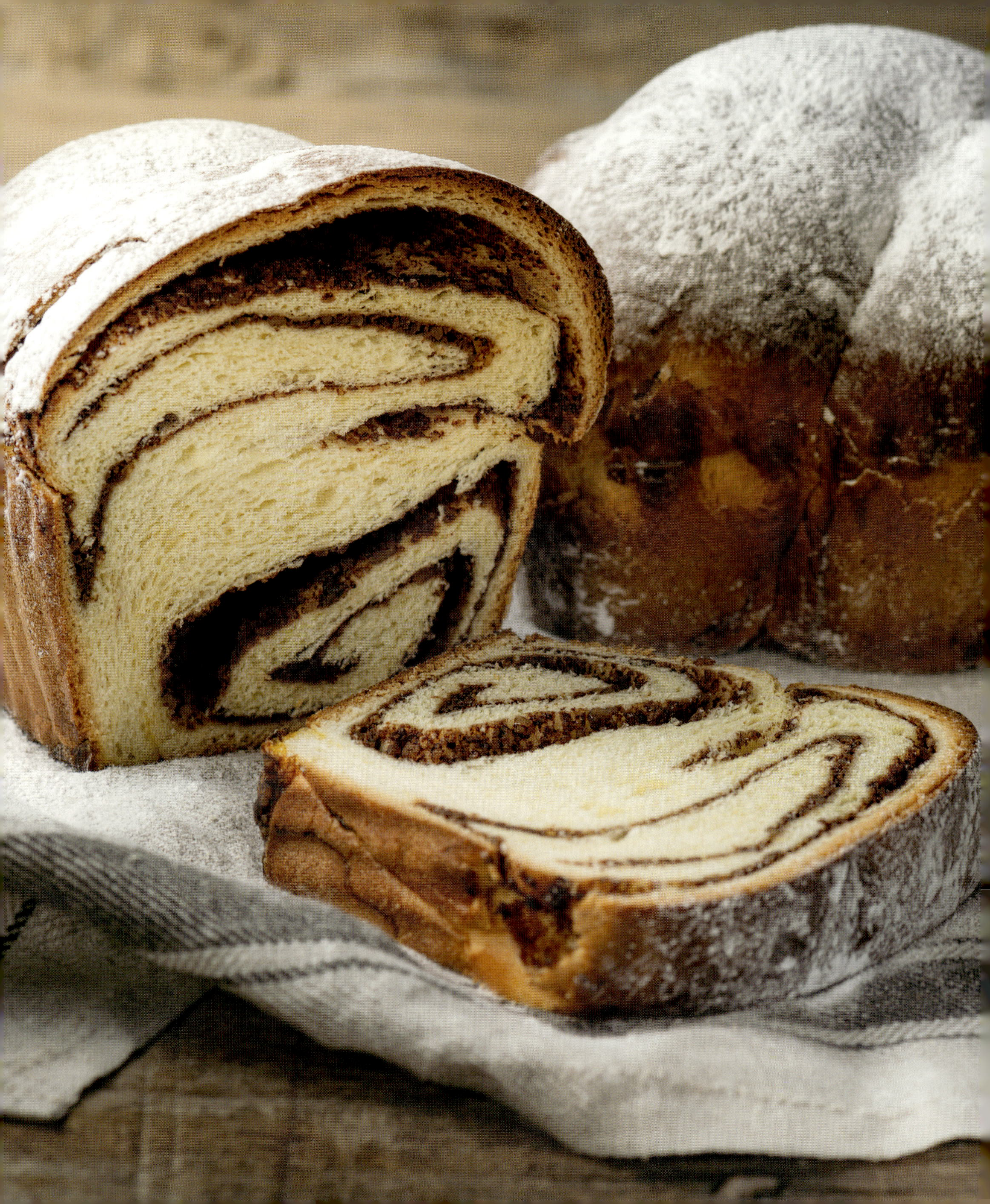

Cozonac

(Nut strudel)

Dough

600 g	flour
3 tbsp	sugar
1 cube	yeast
¼ l	milk, lukewarm
100 g	butter, melted
2	eggs
	Salt

Filling

2	eggs
300 g	sugar
400 g	walnuts, ground
100 g	raisins
	Milk
1	lemon, zest
1	egg, egg yolk for brushing

For the filling, mix together the eggs, sugar, lemon zest and raisins. Add enough milk to make a solid mixture. Then, for the starter, put the flour in a bowl, make a well in the middle and add the sugar and crumbled yeast. Add some milk, cover and leave the starter for 15 minutes.

Then mix in the rest of the milk, salt, butter and the eggs. Stir well with a wooden spoon and beat to form a smooth dough.

Roll out the dough, split into two, brush each half with the filling and roll up to make a strudel. Place both the strudels on a baking tray either buttered or lined with baking paper.

Leave to rise again for about 30 minutes.
Brush with egg yolk before baking and slide into the preheated oven for a good half an hour.

Romania

Russia · Ukraine · Belarus · Moldova

Russia

Pozdrevlyayu s prazdnikom Rozhdestva i s novim Godom

Tikhaya noch', divnaya noch'

The Russians celebrate Christmas only after New Year's Eve. As in some other Orthodox countries, Christmas in Russia falls on 7 January.

Ded Moros (Jack Frost) is the Russian equivalent of Father Christmas. He has a white beard and wears a red or blue gown. This figure emerged from St Nicholas. On 7 January, *Ded Moros*, along with his granddaughter *Snegurotschka* (Snowflake) brings presents for the children in a three-horse sleigh.

Christmas Eve, on 6 January, is preceded by a 40-day fasting period. Reminiscent of Jesus' twelve apostles, a twelve-course Christmas meal is served on this day.

After the Russian Revolution in 1917, Christmas was no longer officially celebrated; 7 January has only become a bank holiday again since 1991 with church services, which are celebrated with songs and light processions. Celebrating Christmas together with family and friends conjures up a festive culinary atmosphere. The main course is often goose or duck. Russian meat jelly is dished up as a starter with *oladji* (pancakes) for pudding.

A typical New Year's Eve meal is a layered salad, known as "herring in a fur coat". And of course, there's no shortage of vodka at such a happy and exuberant celebration.

Olivier, a beautifully decorated salad made of beef (but also often with crab meat), potatoes, carrots, peas and cucumbers, is served.

The celebration days in Russia end on 13 January, on the Orthodox New Year, which is traditionally celebrated exuberantly.

Ukraine

Z rizdvom Khrystovym i novym rokom

Tykha nich, svyata nich

Christmas celebrations in Ukraine can take place according to either the Roman Catholic calendar or the Orthodox one.

For Ukrainian children, St Nicholas' Day really is the most important day of the year since Saint Nick, who brings the presents, also happens to be the patron saint of children. It is also customary for every family member to receive a new piece of clothing as a Christmas present. In Ukraine, Christmas itself is a real family celebration. The Christmas period starts on Christmas Eve and ends with the celebrations for Epiphany.

On 24 December, the family gather together for dinner. *Sviata Vecheria* (the Christmas Eve meal) begins when the first star appears in the sky. This symbolises the Star of Bethlehem.

In Ukraine, the table is usually covered with two tablecloths, one for the ancestors and the other for the living members of the family. Hay is scattered under the table and under both tablecloths to be reminiscent of Jesus' birth in a stable.

There is a spare space at the table laid for dead family members. *Didukh* (stalks of straw) are placed below the house's icons. They also represent the family's ancestors.

Kolach (Christmas bread) lies in the middle of the dining table. *Kutia*, made of cooked wheat with poppyseed and honey, is traditionally always part of the festive meal. To go with "God's meal", they have uzvar, "God's drink" made of a blend of twelve different kinds of fruit juice.

The head of the family greets everyone with the phrase *Khrystos razhdaietsia* ("Christ is born"). Then, the family enjoy a vegetarian meal together that traditionally has twelve courses.

The sequence starts with *Borschtsch* (beetroot soup) followed by *Vushka* which are dumplings stuffed with mushrooms and onions, similar to tortellini in appearance. This is followed by fish courses and *Varenyky* (dumplings stuffed with cabbage, carrots, buckwheat or plums). The meal ends with Uzvar.

The following Christmas Days are then rather merry and exuberant. They dine sumptuously and sing a lot. The Ukrainians have their very own Christmas songs.

For New Year, they celebrate Jesus' circumcision and St Basil's Day. However, the celebrations for Epiphany are more important. On the evening before this celebration, the family gather together again for dinner.

Russian Matrjoschkas can also be found with festive painted decoration

Russia · Ukraine · Belarus · Moldova

175

Belarus

Z Kaliadami i novym godam

In Belarus, Christmas celebrations are based on an ancient holiday called *Koljady*, which marked the winter solstice. The majority of Eastern Orthodox Churches, as are found in Belarus, celebrate Christmas according to the Julian calendar, so on the night from 6 January to 7 January.

For *Koljady*, originally every family who could afford it would slaughter a pig and a deep clean was undertaken. You were expected, and would have wanted, to celebrate "cleanly", physically and spiritually.

During the *Koljady* period, fortune telling was commonplace between 6 and 14 January. There were many different ways that young girls could take a glimpse into their future, but only during this time, or so tradition has it. According to old tradition, there is a fasting period that

Cichaja noč, sviataja noč

lasts until 6 January. The Belarussians sit down for dinner only once the first star appears in the sky. According to traditional customs, there are certain things that are an absolute must, such as hay under the tablecloth and specific dishes on the table, such as *Kutja* (sweet corn dish) and *Uzwar* (a drink made from boiled dried apples and pears).

After the fasting period, the food at Christmas seems very rich. There are pancakes stuffed with meat and grilled sausages. Along with *Kutja*, other typical sweet dishes include "sugar kisses", little buns made of curd cheese dough, and apple cake. These are enjoyed with Russian spiced tea.

On the first Christmas day, that is on 7 January, the people of Belarus visit their godchildren laden with gifts.

Moldova

The languages spoken in Moldova are Russian, Romanian, Ukrainian and west-Turkish Gagauz. There is a Christmas greeting in each of these languages, as well as a version of the song "Silent Night".

Because many Moldovans work in Western Europe, they have picked up the holiday and celebration habits from there and like to celebrate Christmas twice – that is on 24/25 December and on 6/7 January.

Christmas traditions also include plays in local theatres which everyone gets involved in, even if that is helping behind the scenes with costumes, props and scenery.

In general, the customs are very similar to those in Russia. Father Christmas dresses in red, and they also have Mrs Christmas, who dresses head to toe in blue or white and in fur robes.

Moldovan cuisine is closely related to Romanian cuisine (particularly that from the Moldavian region). It is also influenced by Russian, Greek and Turkish food traditions.

There is always a lot of delicious food at any Moldovan celebration. At Christmas, this includes roast pork, meat patties, polenta, stuffed cabbage, salad with sweetcorn and eggs, carrot salad, pickled mushrooms, pasta, various kinds of fish, olives, meat and cheese platters, bread and roast chicken, just as an example!

Popular puddings include tiramisu, pralines, bananas and grapes.

They like to drink sect, wine, juice, coffee, tea and *Izvar* (mulled wine).

Here, they also welcome in the new year with champagne and fireworks.

Sweden

God jul och gott nytt år

Stilla natt, heliga natt

A lovely pre-Christmas celebration takes place in Sweden on 13 December, St Lucy's Day. *Tomte*, the Swedish house imp, and the *Julbock* made of straw play a big role in this. They dance in a circle around the Christmas tree. There is also more than enough food to go around. Many dishes and drinks have peculiar names, such as *Jansson's Temptation* or *Mumma*. There is, of course, also *Gjetost*, a cheese that tastes chocolatey. New Year's Eve is celebrated at home or with a lot of friends, and always with ferocious fireworks. Finally, the holiday's grand finale comes on *Tjudondag Knut*, 13 January.

The Swedes usually put up their Christmas decorations on the first Sunday of Advent, but the celebrations don't truly kick off in Sweden until 13 December, *St Lucy's Day*. On this day, it is tradition for the eldest daughter of the family to bring breakfast in bed to the rest of the family while wearing a white gown and a crown of lights on her head. They then spend the whole day celebrating with festive songs and saffron baking.

The *Tomte* (house imps) are supposed to help out with the Christmas preparations, and Christmas in Swedish is called *Jul*. These imps are also there to make sure that everything goes smoothly in the house and garden for the rest of the year.

On 23 December, the Swedes decorate their Christmas trees with more than a hint of patriotism since the trunk is traditionally adorned with small Swedish flags.

The most important Christmas day is 24 December. In the morning, they visit family and friends. However, before they leave the house, the Swedes leave a milk pudding outside the front door for the Tomte to encourage them to keep any evil spirits away from the house in the future. In the afternoon, many families watch old Disney films.

The presents only come after the obligatory dance around the Christmas tree when they sing Christmas songs. They are delivered by *Jultomte*, the Swedish name for Father Christmas, and he is usually related to the imps in some way.

The whole family goes to church on Christmas morning on 25 December. While they are away, *julbock*, a billy-goat made of straw, watches over the house and protects it from evil spirits.

There are, of course, traditional Swedish Christmas foods. *Julbord* is particularly popular, a Christmas buffet which includes many different hot and cold dishes. *Julbord* is common at office parties and social clubs leading up to Christmas.

In the evening on Christmas Day, the family eats a selection of dishes from *Svensk julbord* such as *julskinka* (Christmas ham), *Dopp I grytan* (rye bread which is dunked into the ham broth), *Vörtbröd* (raisin bread), brown and red cabbage, *Revbensspjäll* (ribs), *Köttbullar* (meatballs), *Prinskorv* (little sausages), *Kycklingleverpaté* (chicken liver pate) with Cumberland sauce, *Julkorv* (Christmas sausage), savoury jelly, *Rödbetssallad* (beetroot salad), smoked leg of lamb, brown cheese, crackers and fruit.

They drink *Julöl* (Christmas beer), *Julmust* (a non-alcoholic drink similar to malt beer), *Mumma* (a mixed drink made of port, Christmas beer, lemonade and vodka) and *Snaps* (schnapps, in particular Aquavit).

A typical Swedish Christmas menu is made up of the following dishes, to name but a few: *Ärter med fläsk* (pea soup with pork) *Julskinka* (Christmas ham), *Köttbullar* (meatballs), lasagne made with gravlax and white toast, cloud berry mustard sauce, *Pytti panna* (leftovers made of potatoes, meat and onions), reindeer goulash, *Plättar* (Swedish pancakes), Swedish pancake tart with *Gjetost* (goat's milk brown cheese).

New Year's Eve in Sweden is celebrated with raucous parties at home or in the local pub. Fireworks and a delicious New Year's Eve feast are also part of the celebrations. Here, festive clothing is particularly important to the Swedes. When celebrating with friends, one member of the group will traditionally give a New Year's speech.

The fireworks from the *Skansen* in Stockholm, the oldest outdoor museum in the world, are also sometimes broadcast live on Swedish TV. Malmö is also known for its impressive firework display. There they even have a display in the afternoon for the children.

6 January, *Trettondedag jul* (the 13th day of Christmas) is a bank holiday which is, however, celebrated without carollers.

The Christmas period in Sweden ends on 13 January, *Tjugondag Knut* (Knut's Day). On this date, it is quite common to just throw the pine tree into the streets once the decorations have been taken down.

Ärter med Fläsk
(Yellow pea soup with pork)

500 g	peas
1 ½ l	stock
2	onions, finely chopped
400 g	pork neck or belly, cured
	Root vegetables (1 carrot, ¼ stick of celery, ½ leek), finely diced
1	small bulb of ginger, finely chopped
½ bunch	of parsley, finely chopped
1	garlic clove, finely chopped
	Knob of butter
	Sweet mustard
1 tbsp	each of marjoram, thyme
	Salt, freshly ground pepper

Simmer the peas in salted water until al dente, drain and keep warm.

Brown the onions, the garlic, the ginger and the root vegetables in melted butter and fry the peas with them quickly. Fill with the stock, add the marjoram, thyme and meat. Leave everything to boil and simmer gently for 1 ½–2 hours. Take the pork neck or belly out of the soup and cut into slices.

Finally, season the soup to taste, scatter over the parsley and serve together with the meat and a little mustard.

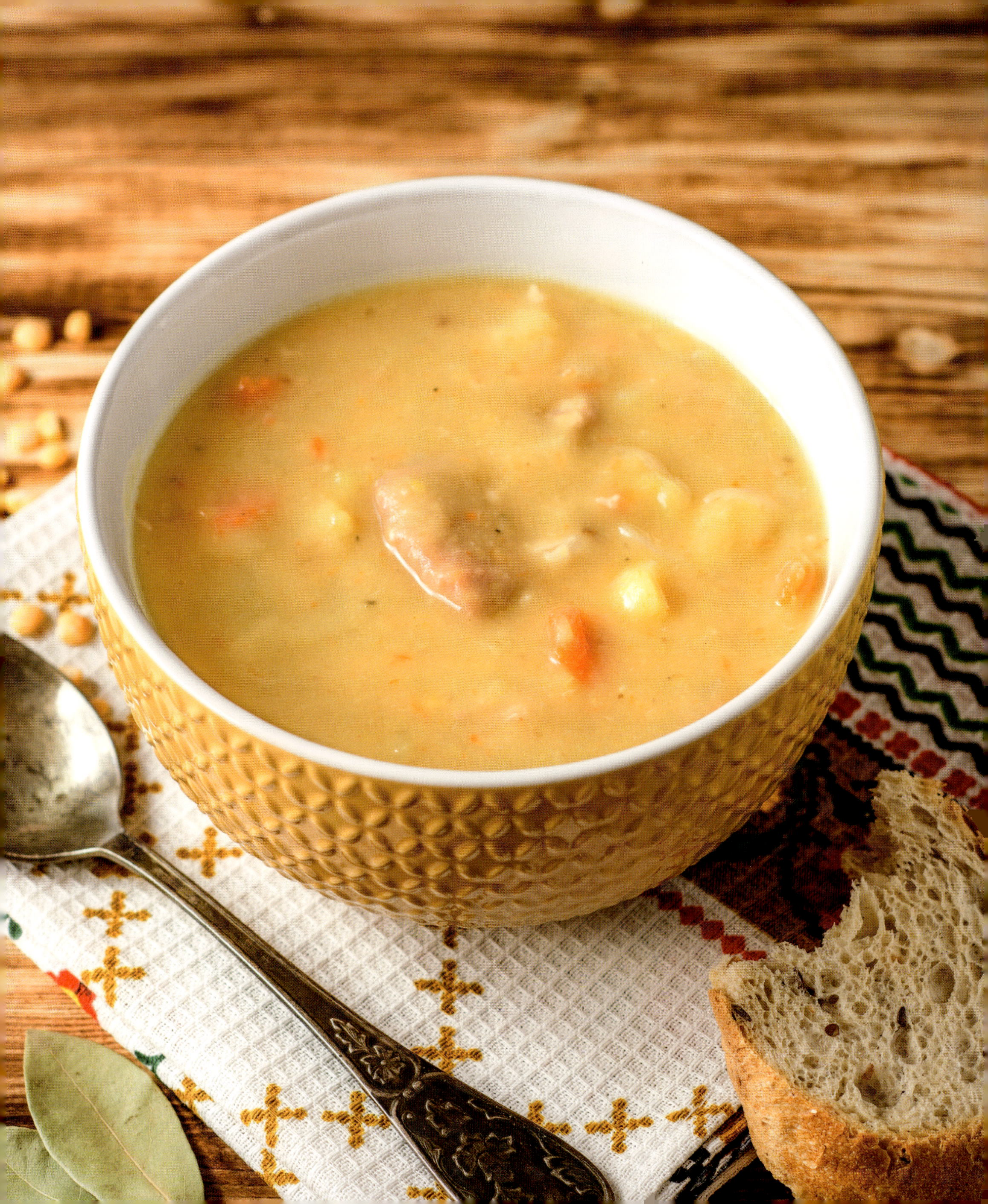

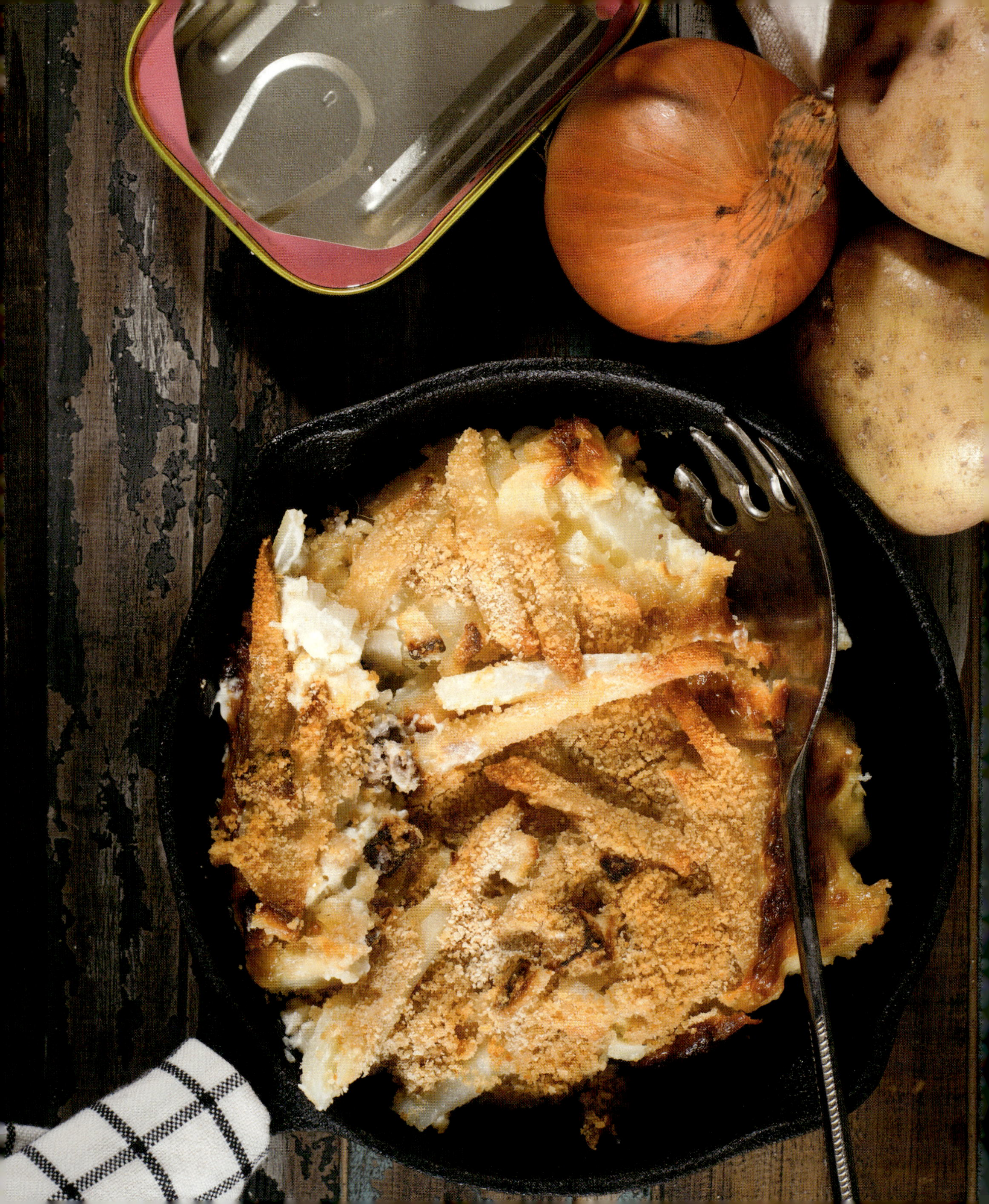

Janssons Frestelse
(Jansson's Temptation)

12	medium potatoes, peeled and cut into thin slices
4	large onions, cut into thin slices
250 g	herring filet, marinated or even pickled, boned
4 tbsp	butter
400 ml	double cream
2 cups	breadcrumbs
	Salt, pepper
	Butter for greasing the tin
3	onions, finely chopped
½ l	vinegar
3–4 tbsp	sugar
5	cloves
10	peppercorns
1	bay leaf
1	cinnamon stick

Put half the potatoes in a buttered tin. Cover with the onions, the place the herring on top, reserving the herring marinade. Place the remaining potatoes on top of the fish fillets, scatter over the breadcrumbs and dot some flakes of butter over the top. Pour over the marinade and half of the double cream. Season with salt and pepper. Put the tin in a preheated oven at 200 °C and bake for about one hour.

Depending on the oven, cover with aluminium foil at the start. After half of the cooking time, add the remaining double cream. Serve hot. I recommend using marinated herring since, on one hand, the marinade has a very strong flavour and, on the other hand, it uses up the inconvenient water from salted herring. Whether to use a vinegary marinade (rounded off with sugar) or the oil the herring has been pickled in is purely a matter of taste.

Ris à la Malta
(Maltese rice)

200 g	pudding rice
400 ml	water
	Salt
1 l	milk
200 ml	double cream
50 g	icing sugar
1 tbsp	vanilla sugar or seeds scraped from one vanilla pod
2	oranges or mandarins

Boil the pudding rice with the water and a little salt for about 10 minutes.

Then add the milk and leave to simmer away gently over a low heat for 45 minutes. Stir often so that the rice does not stick to the pan.

In the meantime, beat the double cream until stiff, then carefully fold into the cooled pudding rice. Afterwards, season the rice with the icing sugar and the vanilla pod or sugar, to taste.

Finally, stir two filleted, finely chopped oranges or mandarins into the rice mixture. This gives the ris à la Malta its festive flavour.

SWITZERLAND

Schöne Weihnachten und ein gutes neues Jahr
Schöni Wiënacht und es Guets Neus
Joyeux Noël et Bonne Année
Bon Natale e Felice Anno Nuovo
Bella Festas daz Nadal ed in Ventiravel Onn Nov

Stille Nacht, heilige Nacht
Nuit de Paix, sainte Nuit
Astro del ciel, pargol divin

Swiss Christmas traditions are very similar to those in other central European countries. Advent wreaths, church services, biscuits, Christmas trees and festive food are all part of the celebrations. The customs and specialities at this time of year are quite different from anything else. Whether it's the *Klausjagen* with *Samichlaus* and *Schmutzli*, the witch *Befana*, the *Archetringele*, the *Hinnerefürfraueli* or *Pastetli*, *Schüfeli* and *Rollschinkli*, *Fondue Chinoise*, *Panettone* or the *Nidlekuchen*: every region has its own specific peculiarities. At the end of the festive period on 6 January, the Swiss celebrate with the "Kings' cake lucky fellow".

Christmas in Switzerland is traditionally divided into three parts, a pre-Christmas penance and fasting period, the Advent period and finally a time for Christmas joy and celebration.

The children's long wait for Christmas is sweetened by Advent calendars brimming with chocolate. In the past, pious images could be found behind the small windows. There are smaller and larger Christmas markets across Switzerland, each selling mulled wine, grilled meats and various Christmas trinkets.

During the pre-Christmas period, the custom of *Klausjagen* is internationally famous and takes place in Küssnacht every year in 5 December. As part of this, they hold a large procession. *Geislechlepfer* go at the front, cracking their whips incessantly. They are followed by participants wearing large *Iffelen* (colourful lanterns) made of tissue paper and carboard on their heads, which are evocative of church windows. These are then joined by *Samichlaus* (comparable to Nicholas) and *Schmutzli* (similar to Knecht Ruprecht or Krampus). They throw nuts and sweets into the crowds of spectators. *Trychler* make up the largest part of the procession rhythmically chiming cowbells. Brass players come right at the end.

Samichlaus then visits Swiss children on 6 December and brings small presents for them in exchange for recited poems. In some regions he is still accompanied by *Schmutzli*.

In Ticino, it is *Befana*, a generous witch, who is responsible for presents at Christmas. As in Italy, she only comes in the night from 5 to 6 January.

In French speaking Romandy, they generally have *Chauche-Vieille*, as well as a female counterpart to St Nicholas.

The traditional exchange of gifts and Christmas trees decorated with baubles and candles found in the bigger cities have only become popular in villages in the 20th Century. In Ticino, according to an old custom, a manger with many figures is put up in many houses as well as a decorated pine tree in the village square. In the past, the Christmas tree was still brought by *Samichlaus*. However, since the 1860s, he has been regularly replaced by *Christkindli* – often the figure of a young girl dressed in white, who brought the children little trees decorated with lights in the evening on Christmas Day.

Music and singing are certainly also important parts of the Christmas period, whether that be playing music at home, church concerts, brass bands in towers, children's choirs, open singing or songs by Salvation Army choirs. "Silent night", "Oh du Fröhliche" ("O how joyful!") and "Oh Tannenbaum" (O Christmas Tree) are some of the most popular songs.

Depending on the region, different festive food is served for the family. In French-speaking Switzerland, this is often poultry with Foie, in Aargau *Pastetli mit Milke* (porridge) for example, and *Chügelipastete* (pastries stuffed with meat) in Lucerne. The Bernese tend to enjoy a platter of meat, sauerkraut and potatoes. Traditionally they also have ham like Schüfeli and Rollischinkli. Violet potatoes and carrots are almost always dished up with these.

A classic front runner, above all in southern Switzerland, is *Fondue Chinoise* or *Bourgignonne*. *Raclette* and other cheese fondues are also typical.

In the Italian-speaking part of Switzerland, *pasta* is predominantly served over Christmas. *Panetonne* is also a firm feature of the celebratory menu – above all in Ticino.

Across the whole of Switzerland it is traditional for family and friends to come together to eat. Guests often bring starters or pudding.

Christmas baking with cinnamon, cloves, star anise, ginger or cardamom can be found in every region, if only because the results make great gifts or can be taken home as *Bhaltis* (favours). Lebkuchen, currant buns and *Chüechli* (fritters) or pear buns and *Nidlekuchen* (cream yeasted cake) are typical Christmas baking projects.

In Switzerland, it's not only corks that go bang at midnight on New Year's Eve. There are also spectacular firework displays and noisy parades with masked figures, drums, bells and whips – supposedly to protect against evil spirits and daemons.

Archetringele (ringing down) is the name of a New Year's Eve custom, which is common in Laupen, for example, in the Mittelland. Here, a local resident dressed as an

Typically Swiss: cheese raclette.

Es (donkey) symbolises the old year. He is beaten by the "donkey leader" as punishment for everything bad that has happened in the previous twelve months. The donkey is driven out by the bride and groom, representing the new year, the devil, a vicar and the *Hinnerefürfraueli* who has two faces. This female figure takes a friendly look into the coming year with the beautiful half of her face.

The Christmas holidays then come to an end on 6 January, Epiphany, which is celebrated with the King's Cake in which a small figurine has been baked. Whoever finds this becomes "King" for the day and thus enjoys certain privileges.

This custom is relatively new and actually has nothing to do with religion. The King Cake was part of an elaborate media campaign by the association of Swiss bakers and master confectioners in the 1950s, which explains its popularity. Since then, the cake, a yeast dough wreath with balls, has obtained enormous importance. For Epiphany, several hundreds of thousands of this royal cake are said to be sold in Switzerland.

Switzerland

Pastetli with veal and mushroom filling

16	vol-au-vent shells made of puff pastry, pre-made or made from puff pastry
300 g	chicken, cut into cubes
300 g	veal, cut into cubes
300 g	mushrooms, cut into slices
2	shallots, chopped
200 ml	double cream
100 ml	chicken stock
100 ml	dry white wine
3 tbsp	freshly chopped herbs (e.g. tarragon, parsley, rosemary)
	Knob of butter
	A little olive oil
	A little flour
	Salt, pepper

Lightly fry the shallots in butter, add the mushrooms and herbs and put to one side.

Fry the meat in a mixture of oil and butter until golden brown, season with salt and pepper, if necessary, dust with a little flour, fry for a little longer and pour over the white wine and stock.
Reduce the liquid by half, add the mushrooms and double cream, bring to the boil.
Warm the pastry shells in the oven, then fill with the meat mixture and serve.

Vegetables such as peas, carrots or mashed potato go well with these.

Rollschinkli with sauerkraut and violet potatoes

1	rolled smoked ham (rolled roast, rolled shoulder), c. 600 g
300 g	violet potatoes
100 ml	stock
100 ml	white wine or diluted white wine vinegar
1 tbsp	flour
2	bay leaves
	Allspice kernels
	Salt, whole peppercorns

Sauerkraut

2–3 tbsp	clarified butter
1	small onion, finely sliced
2	garlic cloves, finely chopped
100 g	bacon, chopped into cubes
1–2 tbsp	flour
500 g	sauerkraut
1 l	stock
2	bay leaves
	Juniper berries

Fill a pan with water and the spices, put the rolled ham into the pan and boil until soft, usually a good hour.

Peel the potatoes and boil until soft. Melt the clarified butter in a pan, fry the onions and garlic, add the bacon after a little while. If the bacon is crispy and the onions are translucent, dust over a little flour, stir well and then gradually stir in the herbs.
Pour over the stock, add the bay leaves and juniper berries and season with salt and pepper. Stew the sauerkraut for about an hour until it has a soft, creamy consistency. Stir constantly so that it doesn't stick to the base of the pan.

Cut the rolled ham into slices and serve together with the sauerkraut and potatoes.

Switzerland

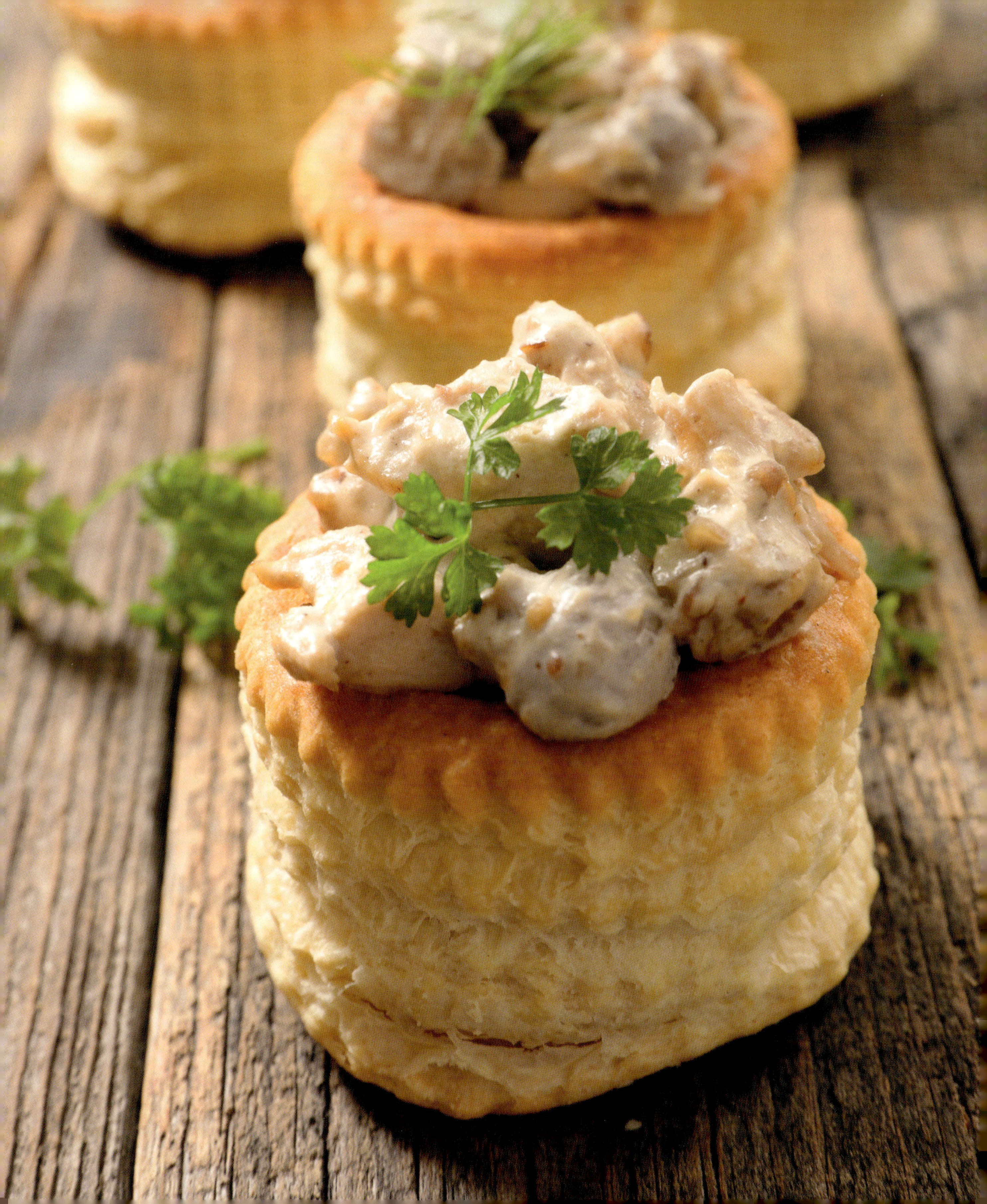

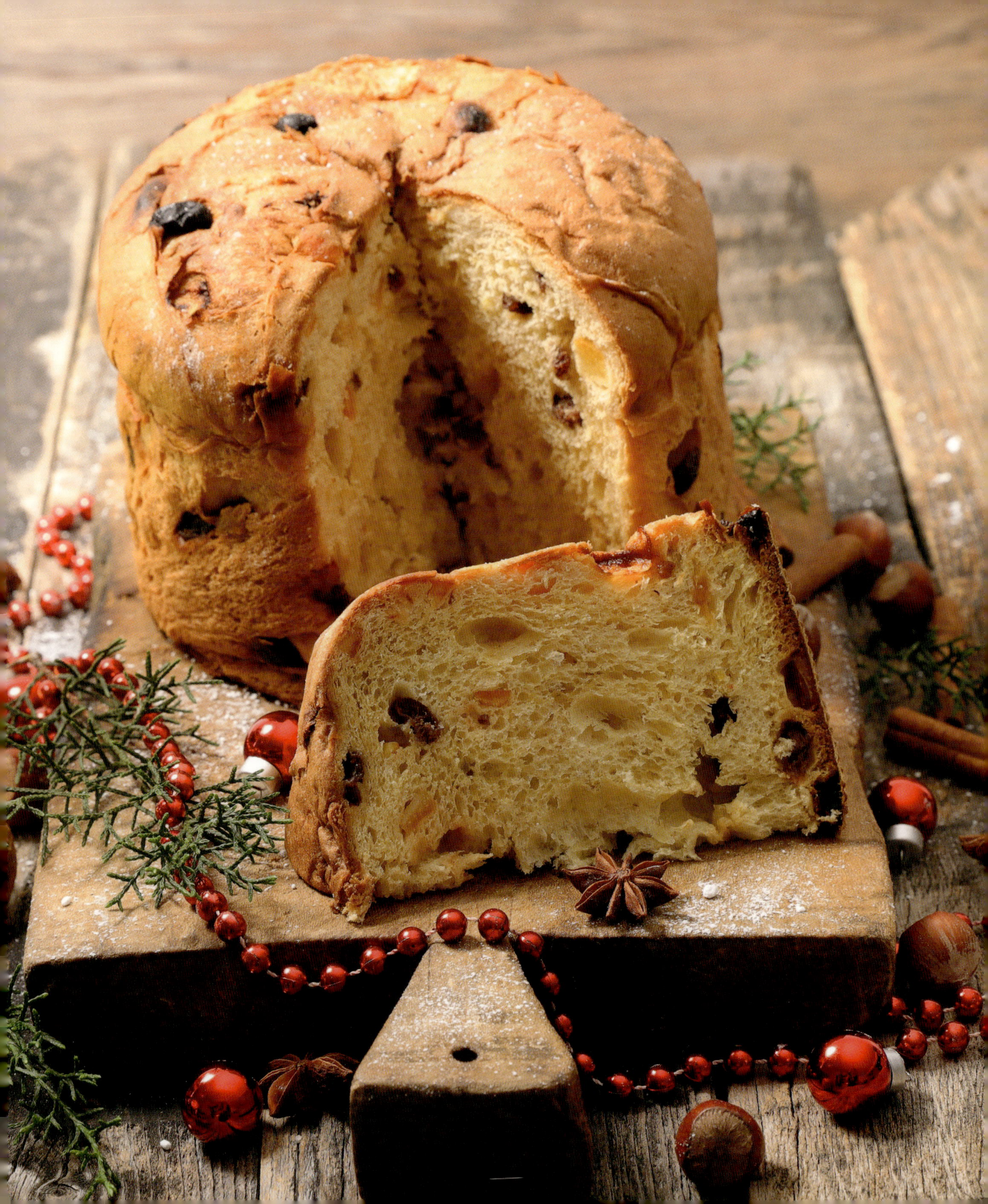

Panettone

(Yeasted cake with fruit; serves 8-10)

1	panettone mould of 3 l volume
	or springform tin about 18–20 cm in diameter
	Greaseproof paper to line the base and
	edges of the panettone
1	cube yeast
5 tbsp	sugar
150 ml	lukewarm milk
500 g	flour
Sugar	
1	lemon, zested
3	eggs, room temperature
150 g	butter, room temperature
	Pinch of salt
100 g	dried fruit
50 g	sultanas
	Icing sugar
	Vanilla sugar

Starter: stir the yeast together in a bowl with 1tbsp sugar and some warm milk, leave to stand for a little while. Then, add 200 g flour and mix everything together. Cover and leave to rise at room temperature.

Then, mix the rest of the sugar, lemon zest, eggs, salt, the rest of the milk and butter into the starter. Add the rest of the flour. Knead for about 10 minutes – this is easier using the dough hook of a hand mixer.

Preheat the oven to 50 °C and switch off. Cover the dough, put in the oven and leave until it has doubled in size.

Then add the dried fruits and sultanas to the dough and knead this for a further five minutes. Line the base of the tin with greaseproof paper. Fold the greaseproof paper arc longitudinally and place in the tin so that the paper protrudes over the edge. If necessary, stick the pieces of paper together with paperclips so that the paper mould holds up better.

Now place the dough in the prepared tin and leave to rise again in the oven. Turn the oven up to 160 °C for a conventional oven or 150 °C for a fan oven and bake the tin for about one hour.

Take out of the oven, carefully remove the cake from the tin after about 10 minutes and leave to cool on a cooling rack. Dust with icing sugar, if preferred with mixed with vanilla sugar.

SLOVAKIA

Veselé Vianoce a šťastný nový rok **Tichá noc, svätá noc**

Celebrating Slovakian Christmas basically means celebrating individually and traditionally. For women hoping to marry, the Advent period is brightened by the Barbara tradition, and they also set out to scare the men of this world on 12 December. Nobody leaves their house or flat on Christmas Eve. Christmas trees grown specifically for this occasion are decorated, and the Christmas table strains under the weight of cabbage and fish dishes, dried and fresh fruit, yeasted bakes and many other flour dishes. *Ježiško* brings the Christmas presents. Girls peel apples hoping for a glimpse into the future and some even take part in a New Year's Eve run across Bratislava's bridges, also hoping for a similar outcome.

The Slovakians have some very interesting traditions that take place between Christmas and New Year. Many of these can be traced back to pagan ceremonies to celebrate the winter solstice.

As in most countries, the Slovakians like going to the numerous Christmas markets during the four-week Advent period. The most popular one can be found in Bratislava. They also like to marvel at performances of old Christmas customs in outdoor museums.

On 4 December, the Slovakians celebrate St Barbara's Day in a very specific way. Young girls put fresh cherry branches in glasses of water. Come Christmas Eve, if these have blossomed, they will be lucky in love in the following year. However, the male population should not get too haughty and holier-than-thou since, on 12 December, groups of women go from house to house intending to scare the men and to teach them the meaning of fear.

Vianoce (Christmas) is very special and traditional for Slovakian Catholics. *Štědrý večer*, on Christmas Eve on 24 December, tradition has it that the Slovakians stay at home. They even say, "If you leave home on Christmas, you won't be home all year!" *Ježiško* (Baby Jesus) brings the Christmas presents on Christmas Eve. However, more recently, in some families Father Christmas dressed in red has also been known to come. Since the 16th Century it has become common to give children a little something to mark this celebration. The customary Christmas trees with Christmas decorations and candles only rose to prominence in the 19th Century, originating in Germany. For a number of years now, only certain nurseries that have been created especially to grow these Christmas trees are allowed to sell them.

The traditional "Light of Bethlehem", which, since 1990, has been organised by the Slovakian Scouting association, has also become an important part of Christmas for many people.

The Slovakians have another interesting Christmas tradition which involves girls peeling apples, keeping the skin in one piece, and throwing this over their shoulder. The letter which the shape of the peel resembles represents the first letter of the name of their (future) admirer.

Christmas dinner usually starts at sunset, after a prayer in Christian families. Sometimes, they use a garlic clove to draw a cross on their foreheads so that they are healthy throughout the whole of the coming year.

Money is placed in prayer books with the hope of ensuring enough money for the coming year. Everyone receives a wafer with honey and poppyseeds on top, which is reminiscent of the Eucharistic. Then, specific dishes are eaten. The main course of Christmas dinner usually consists of a sauerkraut soup, fish and potato salad. *Loke*, a traditional dish made of yeast dough with raisins and poppyseeds or stuffed yeast doughnuts with poppyseeds and honey as well as cheese, such as sheep's cheese, are served after dinner. Various fruits, such as dried plums and apples, oranges, pineapple as well as nuts and cakes are very common on this occasion.

In other regions, the menu includes a fish dish and a thick *kapustnica* (cabbage soup) with sausage, meat and dried mushrooms. Sweet Christmas biscuits, such as vanilla crescents, are very important. The oldest forms of Christmas baking are flat breads made of unfermented dough, which the typical Christmas wafers I mention above developed from. Furthermore, different types of cakes and pastries are typical which are also given to carollers, shepherds and even the cattle.

They celebrate with family on 25 December and with friends and acquaintances on 26 December. More recently, it has become commonplace for the adults to also exchange presents.

Good luck charms are exchanged on New Year's Eve, "Dinner for One" is watched on TV, fondue is served, lead is poured and, of course, they raise a toast with a glass of bubbly.

As in many cities around the world, there is also a 10km New Year's Eve run in Bratislava across the city's bridges which many sport enthusiasts take part year on year.

In Slovakia, Epiphany is a recognised public holiday and marks the end of a Christmas period steeped in tradition.

The Christmas market in Bratislava draws thousands of visitors to the city every year.

Seared trout with potato salad

4	rainbow trout, pre-prepared
1	lemon
Knob of	butter

Filling

400 g	button mushrooms
	(or other type of mushroom), sliced
1	onion
100 g	smoky bacon, diced
	Breadcrumbs
A little	parsley, finely chopped
A little	thyme, finely chopped
A little	caraway
	Lard
	Salt, ground pepper

Potato salad

400 g	potatoes, boiled, peeled, cut into slices
1	large onion, finely sliced
100 g	gherkins, finely sliced
100 ml	stock
	Vinegar, oil
	Salt, pepper
1 bunch	of chives, finely chopped

For the filling, fry the onions in the lard until translucent, add the bacon, fry together for a little while and then add the mushrooms. Season with salt, pepper and caraway and cook for about 10 minutes. Then add the parsley and thyme and scatter the breadcrumbs over the top. Cook for a further few minutes then leave to cool.

Wash and dry the trout, salt from the inside out, add the filling and place in a fish roasting pan. Add the rest of the filling.

Sprinkle the fish and filling with the lemon zest, place flecks of butter on the trout and bake in a preheated oven at 180 °C for c. 10 minutes. Then, you can increase the temperature and cook for a further 5 minutes.

For the potato salad, mix all ingredients together and finally scatter over the chopped chives.

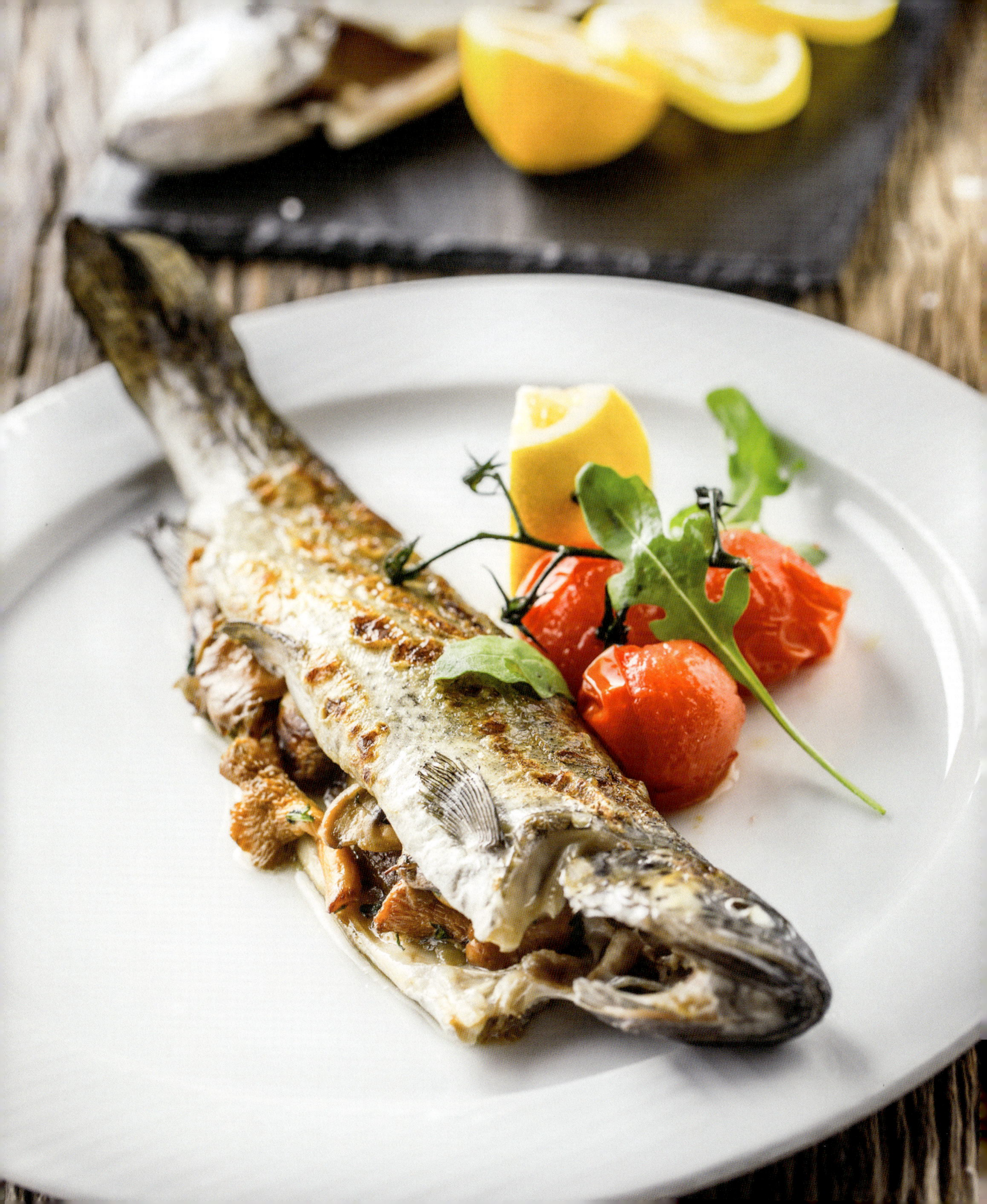

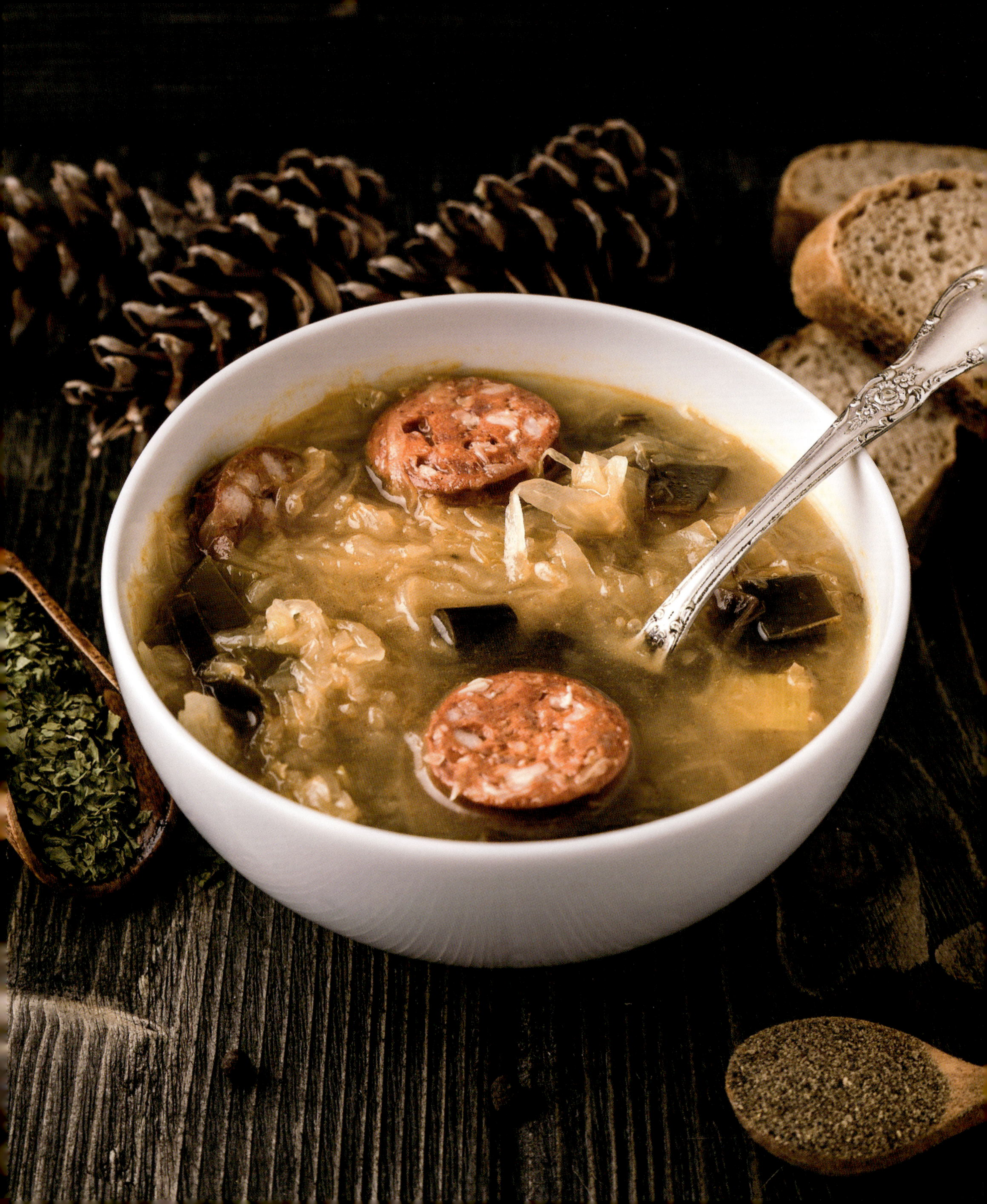

Kapustnica
(Sauerkraut soup)

300 g	sauerkraut
100 g	bacon, diced
200 g	smoked sausage
200 g	boiled sausage
1	large onion, finely diced
100 g	dried mushrooms
100 g	dried plums
50 g	ground paprika, sweet
	Thyme, fresh or dried
	Caraway, fresh or dried
2 l	vegetable stock
	Sour cream
	Olive oil
	Salt, pepper

Quickly fry the onion and bacon in the olive oil in a large pan, add both the smoked and boiled sausage whole and fry everything for c. 5 minutes.

Then add the mushrooms, dried plums and paprika powder. Stir quickly, pouring over the stock at the same time.

Finally, put the sauerkraut and the herbs in the soup to taste and season as necessary. Leave to simmer over a low heat for about three hours.

Just before the soup is ready, remove the sausages from the soup, cut into slices and return to the soup.

Kapustnica is served with sour cream.

Bobalky
(Yeasted noodles with poppyseed and honey)

Dough

250 ml	water-milk mixture (1:1)
120 g	butter
500 g	wheat flour
100 g	sugar
2 sachets	of dried yeast
2	eggs
	Salt

Icing

Butter, honey/sugar, poppyseeds

Make a yeasted dough from the ingredients, then shape into a log about 4 cm in diameter and cut into slices 2 cm thick.

Then boil these in a milk-water mixture. Finally, roll the Bobalky in a butter, poppyseed, sugar/honey mixture and serve immediately.

Spain

Feliz Navidad y próspero Año nuevo

Noche de paz, noche de amor

Traditionally, there is no Advent period in Spain and no special pre-Christmas customs. Christmas itself starts with a great Christmas lottery on 22 December. After this, nativity scenes with all the important characters start to appear, which also feature a certain someone known as the *Caganers*, or the "crapper". Christmas Eve is celebrated after work with family. There is a vast selection of different foods, including stews as well as fish and meat dishes with vegetables. *Turrón*, a sweet dish made from roasted almonds, sugar, honey and eggs, is undoubtedly also very popular. There is also the "urn of destiny", either before or after midnight mass. On New Year's Eve, the Spanish eat twelve grapes and they finally get round to their presents on 6 January.

St Nicholas, Advent calendars and wreaths, in fact Advent at all – none of these things are particularly important in Spain. However, there has been a noticeable increase in traditions such as Christmas trees or Santa Claus since the 1980s, which is down to the influence of central European and Anglo Saxon traditions.

As a result, the pre-Christmas period starts on 8 December, i.e. with the Immaculate Conception, and, since 1786, there has been a market in Barcelona on 13 December to celebrate St Lucy's Day. There are over 300 stalls selling the classic handmade *Figuritas de belén* (nativity figures).

The Christmas period really gets going on 22 December – and that is with the eminently popular Christmas lottery, *Sorteo de Navidad*, which has taken place every year since 1812. Fittingly, this lottery is also called *El gordo*, the "fat one".

The individual nativity scene, sometimes even homemade, is central to the familial Christmas celebration. Nativity scenes are also displayed in many shop windows, cafes or in public squares. In Catalonia, living nativity scenes are also common, which involve amateur actors wandering around the towns.

A surprising feature of these scenes, if a little peculiar, is the little figurines squatting with their trousers round their ankles. This figure is called the *Caganer* ("crapper"). Nowadays, these are often caricatures of famous people.

Festive 'Three Kings Parade'.

Spanish nativity scene.

These outlandish nativity figures have emerged from Catalonian culture and allegedly originate from as early as the 17th Century. *Caganer* was initially the figural caricature of a small country boy doing his business on the way to visit Jesus in the stable. This figure is not supposed to be evil or derisive, but simply and amusingly show us that we are all human – and small before God.

Noche Buena is the evening of 24 December. After a "normal" working day, the whole family eventually all gathers together for a festive meal with traditional stews and meat dishes from the local region. A small aperitif to start is followed by Iberian sausages and hams, soups, various vegetables, seafood, fish (bass, oysters, glass eel) or roast turkey or lamb. Of course they drink Spanish wine with all of these. *Turrón* is very typical for Christmas dinner. This sweet nougaty dream is made of roasted almonds, sugar, honey and eggs, while Marzipan and *Polvorones* (cinnamon biscuits) are also a must.

After eating, the "urn of destiny" is placed on the table. Inside there are small presents, but also "rivets".

The Spanish actually exchange gifts on 6 January. However, *Tió de Nadal* is a specific present tradition from Catalonia, which is common on Christmas Eve.

A wooden log is prepared a few weeks before Christmas with two legs, a smiling face and a red headpiece.

Once dressed up, the tree trunk is covered by a cloth and the parents place sweets underneath it. The children "feed" the smiling log with apples daily between the Immaculate Conception on 8 December until Christmas. On Christmas Eve, the little ones then "harvest" the small presents. However before they do this, they have to hit the trunk with sticks and sing a song.

In many places, there is a firework display before midnight mass. Midnight mass is then celebrated at 12am. In Spain, this church service is known as *Misa del Gallo* (hen's mass) because tradition has it that a hen is said to have been the first to proclaim the birth of Jesus.

After mass, the people often gather in large squares to sing Christmas songs together. The celebrations, including Christmas plays, continue until 6 January.

One special Spanish, in particular Basque, Christmas custom is the appearance of the *Olentzero* (coal burner), who comes into the village from the mountains to announce the good news about the birth of Jesus. The *Olentzero* who looks quite earthy and rustic is carried around sitting on a chair accompanied by flute. The meaning behind this puzzling figure is not that clear. It could be that it originally symbolised the return of the sun in the evening of winter solstice.

On 28 December, the day of the "innocent children", the Spanish remember the infanticide organised by Herod. However, the course of this day is more comparable to April's Fool Day for us, since this is when, up and down the country, they play tricks on one another and tease people.

Fiesta de la Coretta takes place from 30 December to 1 January. This is a procession with a decorated pine tree, which is then consecrated afterwards. Firewood is also collected. This custom possibly stems from Celtic culture, according to which the spirit of the wood is revealed in the smoke of the fire.

A propitious ceremony involves eating a certain number of grapes. Shortly before midnight, Spanish people meet in the town hall square and, on the strike of the twelve chimes that welcome in the new year, they eat an equivalent number of *Uvas de la suerte* (happiness grapes).

Also on the subject of happiness, another New Year's Eve tradition involves wearing old or borrowed clothing on this day and the following day, which, in any case has to be red. This is also supposed to bring joy and happiness.

5 and 6 January are high points of the festive season across all of Spain. The actual exchange of gifts as we know it only takes place in Spain on *Día de los Reyes Magos*, for the celebration of Epiphany on 6 January.

On 5 January, the "Three Wise Men" arrive in Spanish villages. When they get there, they are welcomed by a large procession and numerous biblical plays. Children receive sweets from the Kings.

In the evening, the children then place their squeaky clean shoes in front of their bedroom doors, as well as straw and water for the camels and, in doing so, hope to receive the presents they wished for. On 6 January, Spanish children look forward to the long-awaited present exchange, except naughty children only receive lumps of coal – but there's no such thing as a naughty child, right?

The day comes to an end with a feast, which also brings Christmas to a close. As part of this, *Rosco de Reyes* (King's ring cake) plays a significant role. A small porcelain figure and a bean are hidden in the dough of the cake. Whoever discovers the bean has bad luck and has to pay for the cake. However, whoever finds the figure is crowned King for the day and is said to have particularly good luck in the new year.

Prawn cocktail

350 g	crab and/or prawns and/or shrimp, ready to eat
2 tbsp	double cream
1 tbsp	sherry, medium dry
4 tbsp	mayonnaise
2 tbsp	tomato puree
½	lemon, juice
½	lemon, cut into slices
½	bunch of dill
	Tabasco
	Iceberg lettuce, if liked, finely sliced
	Salt, pepper

For the cocktail sauce, mix the mayonnaise, tomato puree, double cream, a splash of tabasco, sherry and lemon juice well. Season with salt and pepper.

Share the lettuce between the plates, place the prawns/crab or shrimps on top and pour over the sauce. Garnish with dill and the rest of the lemon.

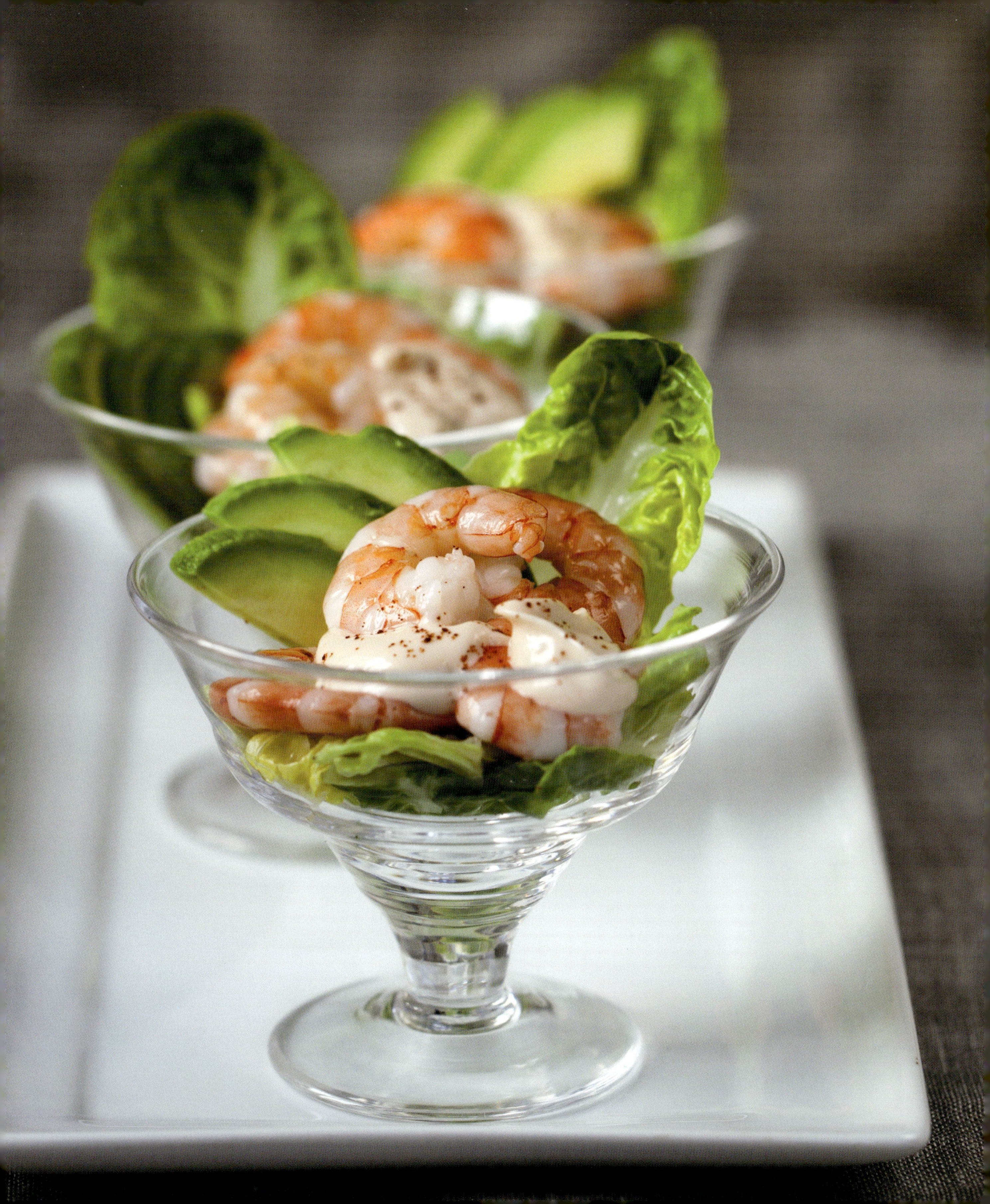

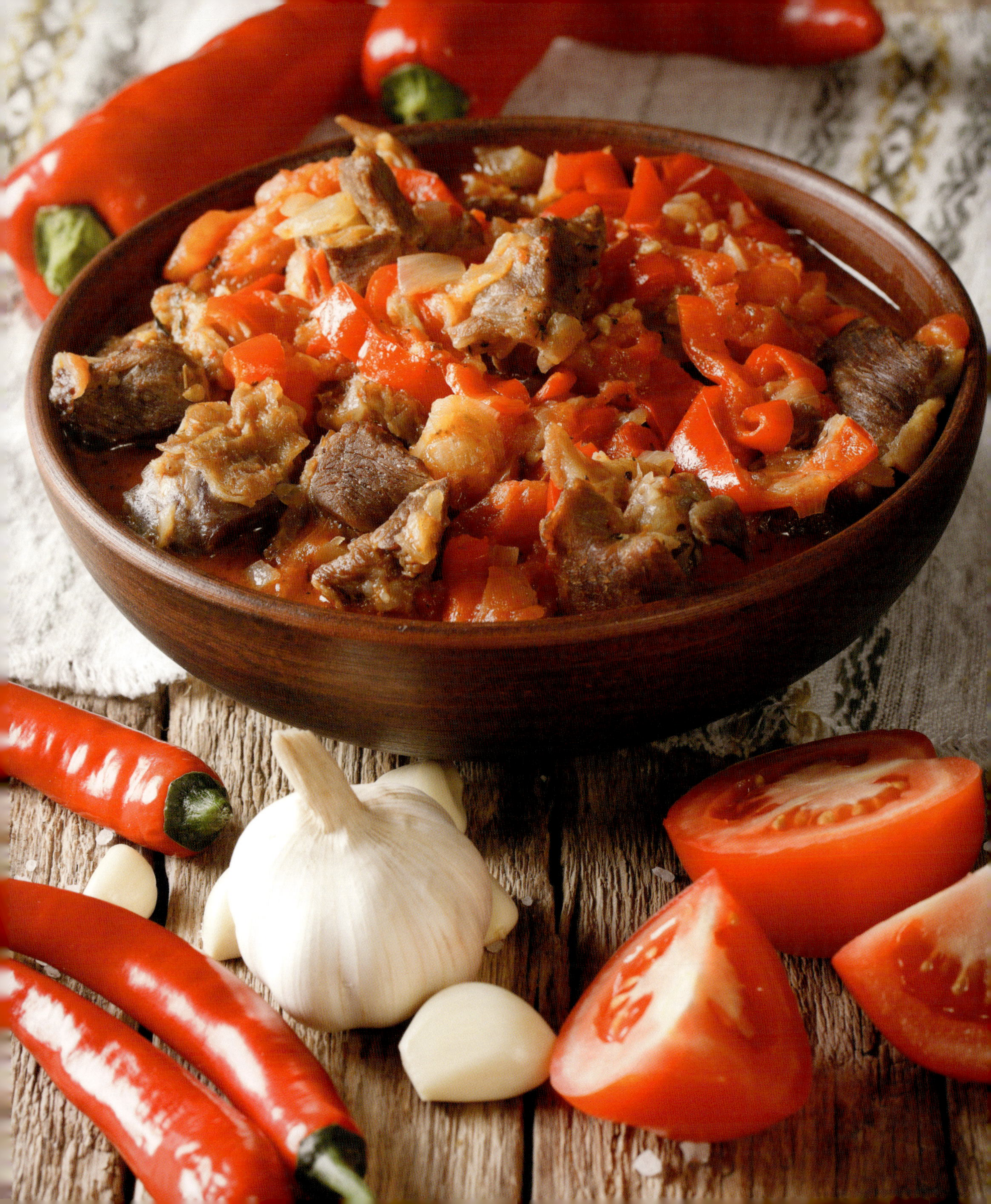

Cordero en chilindrón

(Moorish lamb stew with tomatoes and pepper)

500 g	lamb, cut into 3 cm cubes
2	onions, roughly sliced
100 g	Serrano ham, finely diced
500 ml	lamb stock or clear soup
500 g	tomatoes, quartered
4	red peppers, cut into strips
3	cloves of garlic, finely chopped
1 bunch	parsley, roughly chopped
1 tbsp	thyme
1 tbsp	rosemary
1 tbsp	sage
1 pinch	of cayenne pepper
1 pinch	sweet ground paprika
1 tbsp	almonds, roughly chopped
½ tsp	ground cinnamon
½ tsp	ground caraway
	Lard
	Oil
	Salt, pepper

Quickly fry the onions with the tomatoes, peppers, garlic and parsley in oil. Pour over the stock or soup, season lightly and leave to simmer over a low heat for a while.

Fry the ham and the lamb in lard, add the stock and season with salt and pepper.

Add the rest of the herbs and leave to simmer over a low heat for a further 20 minutes. Potatoes, rice and green beans make good accompaniments.

Roscón de reyes

(Three Kings' Cake)

400 g	wheat flour
1 cube of	yeast
150 ml	milk
120 g	butter
2	eggs
100 g	sugar
1	lemon, zest
1	orange, zest
3–4	candied orange slices
3–4	candied lemon slices
100 g	almonds, grated
	A little rum (flavouring)
1	egg, egg yolk
	Sugar crystals for scattering
	Double cream or chocolate cream, beaten, as preferred

Prepare a starter in a bowl with lukewarm milk, 1 spoonful of sugar and the crumbled yeast. Leave to rise in a warm place. Then, knead with the rest of the flour and sugar, eggs, butter, lemon and orange zest, rum, almonds and the remaining milk to form a smooth dough. Leave to rise again for about an hour, preferably covered with a tea towel.

Then, knead well, roll out into an even roll and place in a circle on a buttered baking tray. Leave to stand again for a good quarter of an hour.

In Spain, a nativity figure and a bean are traditionally hidden in the dough.
Now, brush the dough with egg yolk, coat with the candied fruits and finally scatter over the sugar crystals. Bake in the oven at 200 °C for about 25 to 30 minutes until golden brown.

Tip: after cooling you can split the wreath in the middle and fill with double cream or chocolate cream.

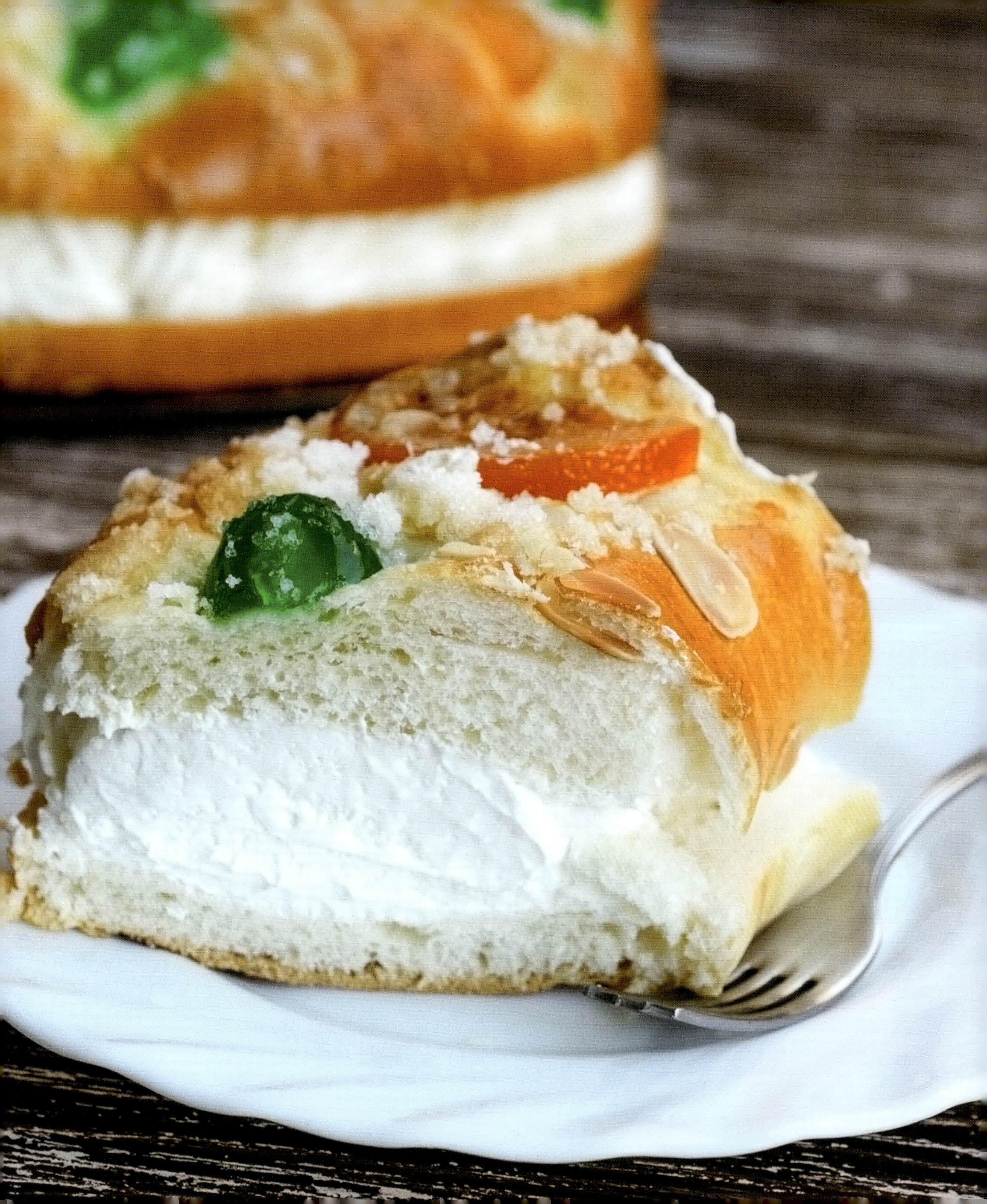

Czech Republic

Veselé Vánoce a šťastný nový rok **Tichá Noc, svatá Noc**

In the Czech Republic, Christmas celebrations revolve around culinary enjoyment and traditional customs, which are supposed to promise health, prosperity and happiness in the coming year. St Nicholas is called *Mikuláš* and is accompanied by angels and devils. On 4 December, the *Barborky* are cut and later used as Christmas decorations. The children often decorate the Christmas tree which Baby Jesus then places the presents under. They definitely make up for the pre-Christmas fasting period, feasting for several days from Christmas Eve. They also have unusual Christmas rules for the duration of the Christmas meal itself.

There are very old customs that start as early as 30 November, St Andrew's Day, which marks the start of the Advent period. These include many hoping to look into the future. On this day, girls pour out molten lead and, from the shape of the cooled lead, try to figure out how their future husband will look.

In other regions, the girls hope to uncover some indication about their future husband from the appearance of ice holes or, with the same intention, they might knock on the door of the chicken coops. If the hear the cockerel first, this is said to suggest there will be a wedding on the horizon in the next year. If a hen clucks first, the girls have to wait another year to find a man willing to get married.

Even Barbara blossoms can indicate a forthcoming wedding. On St Barbara's Day, 4 December, the *Barborky* (Barbara branches) are cut and placed in water. If they start to blossom by Christmas Eve, this means that the girl will find a bridegroom in the coming year. Today, Barborky are predominantly used as Christmas decorations.

The most popular of the Advent days is and remains *Mikuláš* (St Nicholas), which is celebrated on 5 December. In the late afternoon, after dusk, *Mikuláš* goes through the streets, accompanied by *Andel* and *Cert* (angel and devil). These two are symbolic of the good and evil in the world.

Most children sing a song for *Mikuláš* or read out a poem and are rewarded with sweets or other trinkets. Naughty children receive a sack of potatoes or coal as an allegory for the devil's bag in which, according to old beliefs, evil people are hidden and are thus brought to hell.

Numerous concerts with Advent and Christmas music take place across the whole country and there is a typical Czech nativity scene in many houses with *Ježísek* (Baby Jesus), the Virgin Mary with Joseph, the Angel of the Annunciation, the Three Kings and musicians. Of course, the shepherds with their sheep and the ox and donkey are also always there.

In the afternoon on Christmas Eve, the children often decorate the Christmas tree, preferably with edible goodies. Red apples, nuts, lebkuchen and sweets hang on the branches, and the Christmas star is resplendent at the top of the tree.

Many Czechs fast for the whole day on 24 December. Only when they spot the first star in the sky does the family gather together for Christmas dinner. Traditionally, there is carp, potato salad and braided Christmas bread. Typical Czech dishes for the Christmas holiday are: *Vanocka*, a Czech yeasted plait with raisins and almonds, Czech Christmas salad made from celery, Bohemian-style sauerkraut with potatoes and junipers, turkey with a Bohemian filling (eggs,

In the Czech Republic, Christmas trees are also traditionally decorated.

rolls, almonds, raisins), Bohemian apricot rings and delicious homemade Christmas biscuits and pastries.

They have a number of peculiar rules, often dictated by superstition: the table must be laid for an even number of guests. An odd number would bring bad luck, or even death. For the same reason, the Christmas meal has to have nine courses. If the table legs are knotted together with ropes, the house is protected from thieves and burglars for the coming year. In order to avoid bad luck, no-one is allowed to sit with their back to the door. All the food has to be eaten and no-one is allowed to get down from the table until the meal has ended.

Nevertheless, if there are leftovers, these should be buried under the trees in the garden so that there is a rich harvest of fruit the following year.

After eating, all the animals in the house must receive their food since no creature is allowed to go hungry on Christmas Eve.

On Christmas Eve there are also various customs relating to the future. Whoever finds a fish scale tucked under their plate will be granted happiness and riches for the entirety of the next year.

Of course, at Christmas girls can also venture a glimpse into the future world of relationships by throwing their shoes over their shoulders, which will reveal if a wedding is on the cards. The answer is "yes" if the toe is pointing towards the door.

Presents are unwrapped after eating, which *Ježíšek* has placed under the Christmas tree.

Late in the evening, most Czechs go to midnight mass, where, in some places, Christmas plays are also performed. In many regions, they go from house to house very late in the evening, preferably singing Christmas songs. In return, the singers receive a little something to eat or a glass of schnapps.

25 and 26 December are very significant holidays, which are all about family visits with festive meals for lunch and dinner. They also traditionally sing Christmas songs together.

Many of the customs that are common on Christmas Eve, usually the ones focussing on the future, are also practised on New Year's Eve. Furthermore, the change of the year is celebrated much like in most other countries in Central and South Europe.

The Christmas meal has to be eaten all up.

Czech Republic

Bohemian game soup

500 g	game meat (venison, deer etc.), cut into c. 2 cm cubes
200 g	prunes
2	onions, roughly cubed
75 g	bacon, finely diced
125 ml	condensed milk
1 ½ l	game or vegetable stock, clear
1	lemon, zest and juice
⅛ l	red wine or diluted balsamic vinegar
1 tbsp	redcurrant jelly or Powidl
	Oil or lard
	A little tomato puree, mustard
1 pinch	of sugar
	A few juniper berries
	Salt, pepper

Fry the bacon in a pan, possibly adding a little oil or lard, mix in the onions and leave to fry lightly together with the game. Then, season with salt and pepper and fry for a little while longer.

When everything is slightly brown, add the tomato puree, a few crushed juniper berries, red wine and a little sugar and stir well.

Now, top up with stock or water and cook slowly for a bit longer. Then, stir in the mustard and jelly and put in the stock that is no longer boiling. Stew the prunes with the lemon juice and some of the grated lemon zest and add to the soup.

Boiled carp in marinade

800 g	carp in bite-sized chunks (scored, that is cut down to the skin at 4–5 mm intervals)
250 g	root vegetable soup greens (carrots, parsley root and celery) washed, scrubbed, roughly chopped
250 g	mayonnaise
1	gherkin, finely sliced
25 g	capers, finely chopped
½ l	water, mixed with ¼ litre vinegar
2	medium onions, cut into slices
1	bay leaf
3	allspice kernels
6	peppercorns
	Juice of one lemon
	Fish stock
	Sugar, salt
	Pepper
	White bread

Put the onions, root vegetables and bay leaf, allspice and peppercorns in the warmed vinegar water, bring to the boil and then leave to simmer slowly until cooked. Then, remove the vegetables from the soup and keep warm.

Place the prepared pieces of carp in the soup and cook over a low heat for about 15 minutes. Being careful not to break the pieces up, remove from the soup. Now, if possible, remove the backbones and any other large bones.

Stir together the mayonnaise with 1 tbsp cold fish stock, lemon juice, sugar, salt and pepper. Stir in the gherkin and capers and season to taste.

Serve the pieces of carp on a deep plate, pour over the marinade and add the vegetables. Leave to stand in the fridge for several hours. Can be served warm or cold with white bread.

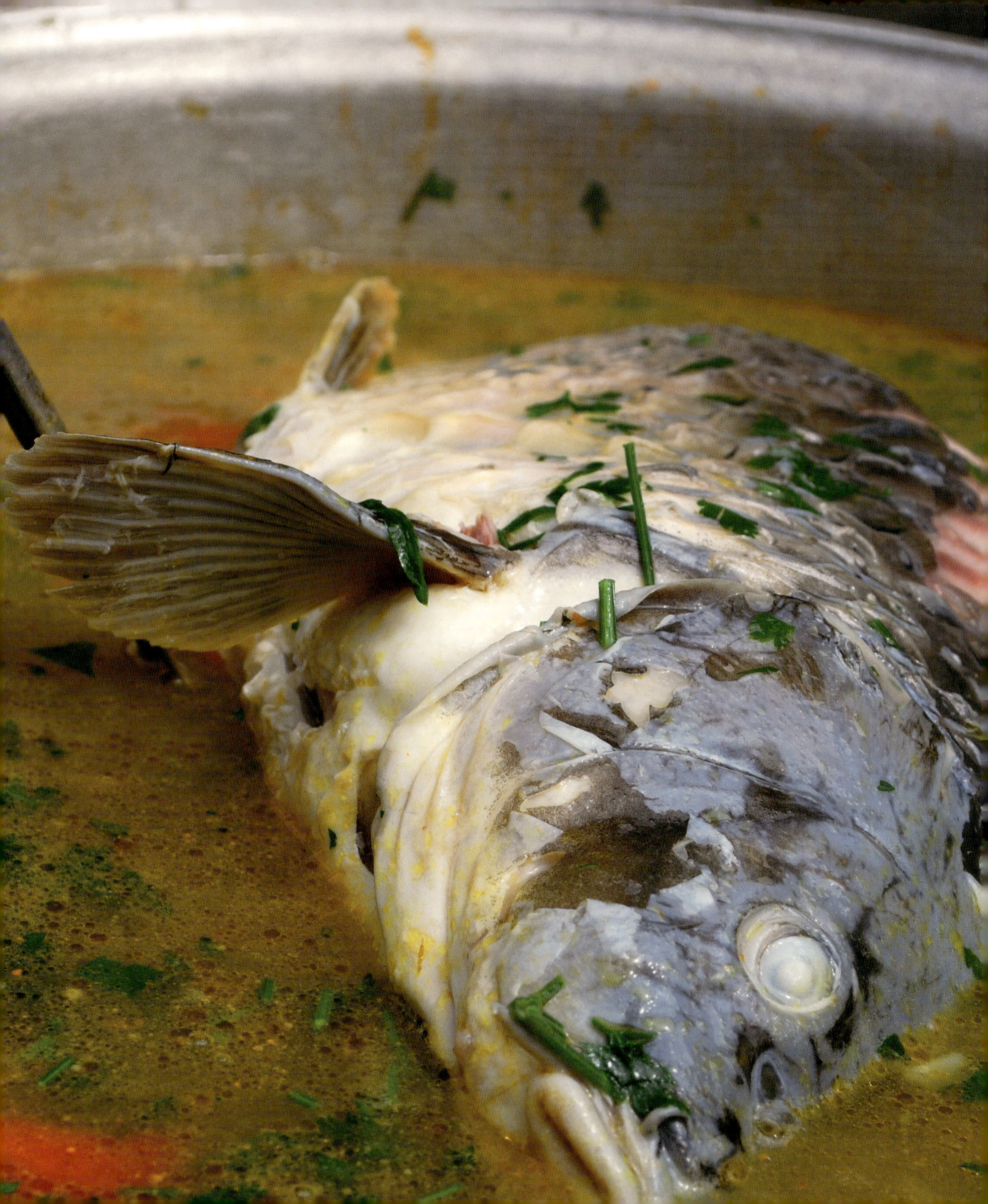

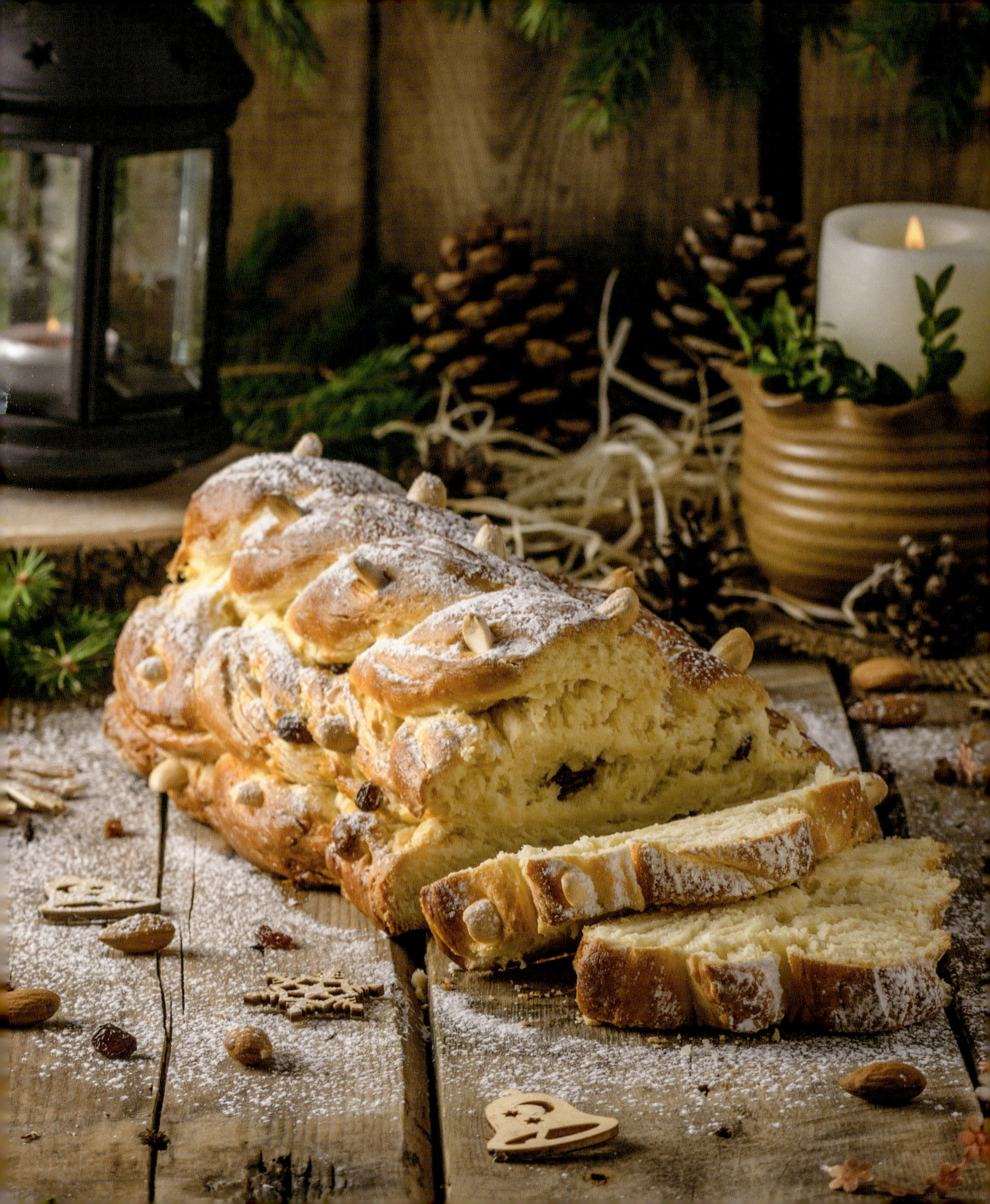

Vánočka

(Braided Christmas loaf)

400 g	flour
125 g	melted butter
1	cube of yeast
100 ml	lukewarm milk
100 g	sugar
1	egg, egg yolk
	Vanilla sugar
1	lemon, zest
	Nutmeg
60 g	raisins
60 g	blanched almonds, finely chopped
1	egg for brushing
	Salt

Prepare a starter with some milk, yeast, a little flour and one tbsp of sugar and leave to stand in a warm place. Put the rest of the flour, the rest of the sugar, vanilla sugar, a little salt, the lemon flavouring, grated nutmeg and egg yolk in a mixing bowl.

Then pour in the starter and finally add the butter, kneading well to form a dough. Fold in the raisins and almonds. Shape the dough into a loaf, cover and leave in a warm place again until doubled in size.
Split the mixture into nine equal long strips and braid plaits out of 4 or 3 or 2 of these strips. Starting with the largest, place the individual parts of the Christmas braided loaf one on top of the other on a baking tray lined with greaseproof paper and leave to rise again. Brush with egg yolk, scatter over some almonds and bake at 170 °C for three quarters of an hour.

Tip: so that the layers of the dough do not warp during cooking, stick a cocktail stick on each of the ends and in the middle.

Bohemian apricot rings

(Christmas biscuits from Bohemia, makes about 60)

(Shortcrust) pastry

500 g	flour
125 g	sugar
1	egg
1 ½ tbsp	ground hazelnuts
1	unwaxed lemon, zest
	Seeds scraped from ½ vanilla pod
	(or vanilla sugar or vanilla extract)
2 cl	rum (or 1 vial of rum flavouring)
250 g	butter
	Salt

Filling
200 g	apricot jam
	Icing sugar for dusting

For the dough, knead the ingredients together to form a shortcrust pastry, wrap in cling film and leave in the fridge for a good hour. Then roll the dough out on a lightly floured surface to about 3 mm thick and cut out round biscuits, about 6cm in diameter. Cut out the same number of rings which have the same diameter and are 1cm wide.

Bake all the shapes on the middle shelf of a preheated oven on a baking tray at 180 °C until golden brown. Brush the solid circle biscuits with jam while still hot and place the rings on top. Put a little more jam in the middle of the ring and dust with icing sugar once cool.

Czech Republic

Hungary

Kellemes karácsonyi ünnepeket és boldog új évet

Csendes éj, szentséges éj

Christmas customs and ceremonies in Hungary are shaped by Central European and Christian traditions, but are also influenced by Pagan times. *Mikulás* comes on 6 December. The women do not work on *Luca Napja*, but they can consult the future while the men start to build a special wooden chair. Angels bring the Christmas tree, a nativity scene and the presents. Classic Hungarian Christmas dishes include fish soup, fried fish or turkey, cabbage roulade, as well as game and beef in the Pustza region. On the first Christmas holiday, there are pastoral plays and, on 27 December, the wine is consecrated. On New Year's Day, tradition has it that the man should be first to wish everyone a happy new year.

In Hungary on 6 December, Mikulás (St Nicholas) comes, accompanied by two small "evil guys", the Krampusses, and places the presents into the children's shoes they have left for them.

During the Hungarian pre-Christmas period, the next celebration comes seven days later. In the past, *Luca Napja* (St Lucy's Day) on 13 December was observed in a very peculiar manner. Even today, St Lucy's Day is still celebrated. At one time, it was forbidden for women to work on this day for religious reasons otherwise they believed this could have a negative effect on the productivity of their chickens.

In contrast, according to old tradition, on 13 December, the men start constructing the *Luca széke* (Lucas chair) from seven different kinds of wood, which, according to traditional beliefs, each has its own magical power. If you sit on the finished chair on 24 December, specifically during midnight mass, you can supposedly tell if there is a witch or wizard present.

When blowing lead on St Lucy's Day, the girls also try to figure out the occupation of their future life partner. And some turn their hand to the "Thirteen Slip Oracle" every day until Christmas. Every day, a piece of paper with men's names is thrown away unread and whatever is left on the last slip is thought to be an indication of the future.

The Christmas tree has also made its way into many Hungarian families. The Austro-Hungarian Countess, Therese of Brunswick, is said to have brought the tree with her from the Tirol in 1824.

On 24 December, the parents traditionally prepare the celebratory meal, usually with fish. The "little angels" or the children set up the Nativity scene and decorate the Christmas tree with baubles, lights, tinsel and chocolates. And with every Hungarian Christmas tree, there is also heaps of *Szaloncukor* (parlour sweets) under the sweet Christmas decorations, sweets wrapped in twinkling paper stuffed with marzipan, fruit jelly or chocolate cream.

Originally, *Szaloncukor* was understood to be classic sweets, later chocolates with umpteen different fillings – from marzipan to fruit jelly. They are called "parlour sweets" because, by the end of the 18th Century, they

Hungarian cabbage roulades

Baked fish

would enjoy these sweet titbits in the parlours of "higher society". The individual parlour sweets were also always hung on the Christmas tree.

After the tree has been decorated, they exchange gifts and the family sings Christmas songs. However, the presents are usually not brought by Baby Jesus or Father Christmas, but by angels.

Fish soup, baked fish or turkey, cabbage roulade and game or beef in the Pannonian Steppe are typical Christmas dishes. However, nutty croissants or poppyseed croissants can be found everywhere.

At midnight or on the first Christmas day most families go to a Christmas church service.

On the first Christmas day, young men go from house to house dressed up as shepherds with a manger under their arms. They put on small theatrical plays about the Christmas story and the Three Wise Men. In return for this, they receive sweets or other trinkets.

In Hungary, 25 and 26 December are otherwise reserved for visiting family. On 27 December, some wine producers have their very best wine consecrated, which in doing so are said to develop magical healing powers for sick animals and people.

On 28 December, the day of the "innocent children", the little ones go to their neighbours and acquaintances with a twig and hit them lightly. In doing so, they wish them good health for the coming year, as they also do in some parts of Austria.

On New Year's Eve, many stands selling masks, fancy dress costumes, trumpets and firecrackers can be found, even first thing in the morning. A large number of musicians bustle through the streets. In the evenings they then celebrate privately, but also often in restaurants. The most beautiful firework display can be seen in Budapest by the chain bridge.

On New Year's Day, according to old customs, the husband utters the first greetings, followed his wife. The man "gives out luck" and the woman "takes it with her". However, this custom is slowly dying out.

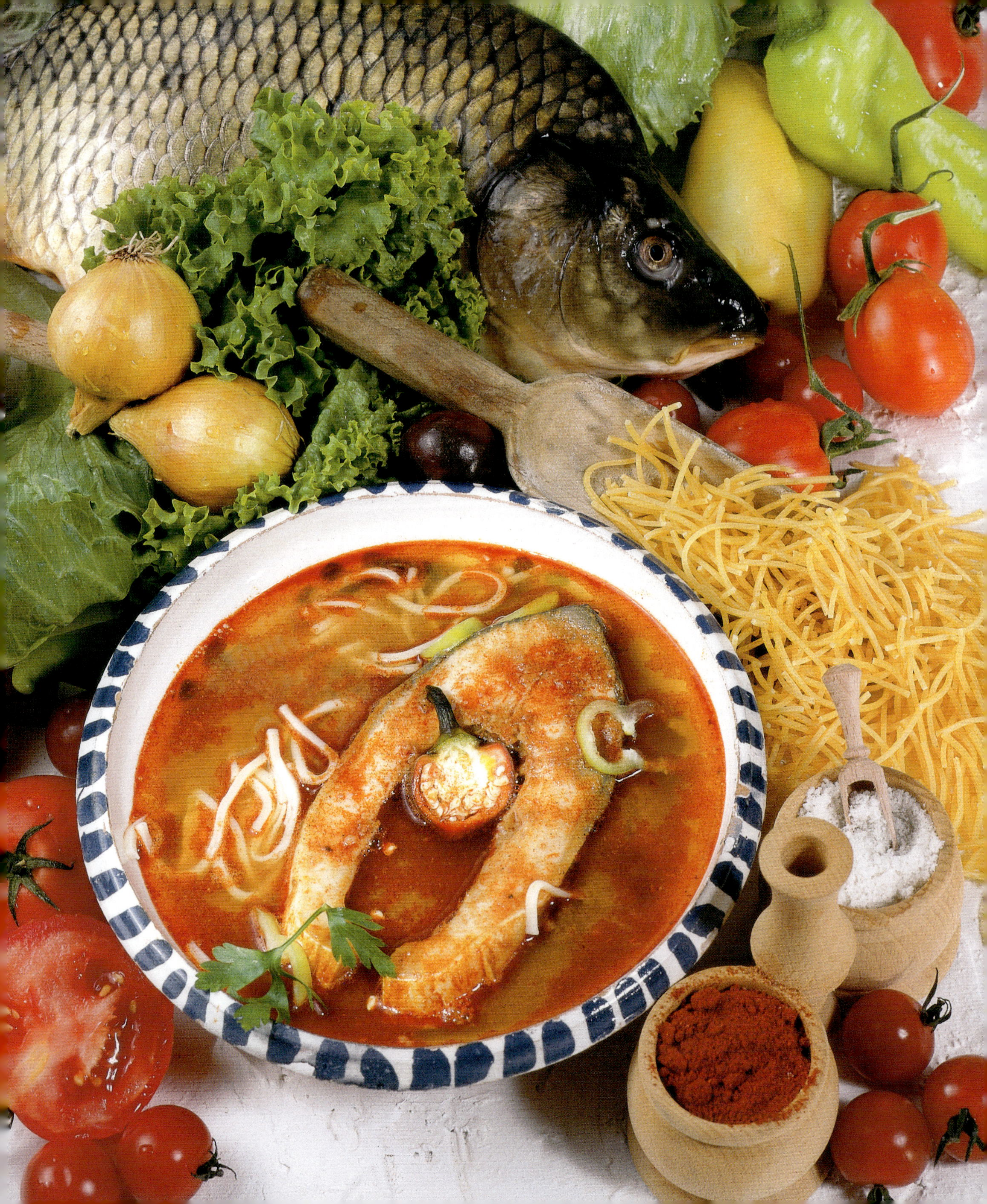

Halászlé

(Fish soup)

500 g	small fry, cleaned and prepared
1 kg	carp (or pike, bass etc.), filleted, bled, cut into chunks, keep the carcasses
1	large onion, finely chopped
1 tbsp	sweet paprika powder
1	tomato, diced
1	pimiento, hot
1	pointed pepper, green, hot, cut into rings
	Salt, pepper

Put the small fry and the carcasses into a pan together with the onions, fill up with water so that that the fish are just covered and simmer over a low heat for about 1 hour.

Then, pass everything through a sieve and leave to simmer further with another litre of water.

Add the paprika powder, tomatoes and the hot pimiento. Now, add only the chopped salted carp pieces. Leave the soup to cook over a medium heat for about 15 minutes.
Serve the finished soup in deep bowls and finish with rings of green pepper.

Tip: if the soup is a little too spicy, under no circumstances should you drink water to take the edge off, instead eat a slice of black bread.

Esterházy rostélyos

(Esterházy-style roast joint)

4	pieces roast joint
400 g	mixed vegetables (carrots, parsnips, kohlrabi, celery), cut into thin strips
1	large onion, cut into rings
200 ml	white wine
200 ml	sour cream
1	lemon, zest
½ bunch	parsley, finely chopped
A little	flour
	Butter
1	bay leaf
	A few capers
	Mustard
	Sugar cubes
	Salt, pepper

Wash the meat, pat dry, season with salt and pepper and coat in flour.

Quickly fry in hot oil and put to one side.

Fry the onions and half the vegetables with a bay leaf in the same pan with the oil and thicken slightly. Then add the wine and a little water. Season and bring to the boil. Now add the meat, cover and leave to cook further over a low heat, not stirring but shaking slightly.

Sauté the vegetables in butter, infuse a little and cook until al dente with the finely chopped parsley.
Season the now soft meat with capers, mustard, sugar, lemon juice, sour cream and add the vegetables. Reheat the meat fully with the sauce while covered.

Serve with rice or tagliatelle.

Hungary

Beigli
(Yeasted bakes)

400 g	flour
200 g	butter, room temperature
2	egg
1	egg, egg white
1	cube of yeast
100 ml	lukewarm milk

Filling

150 ml	lukewarm milk
200 g	icing sugar
200 g	walnuts, ground
100 g	ladyfingers, crumbled
150 g	raisins
1	lemon, zest
200 g	poppyseeds
50 g	semolina
	Salt

Prepare a "starter" from the yeast, a little lukewarm milk and some icing sugar and leave to stand. Then, add flour, the soft butter, eggs and a little salt, knead well, cover and leave to stand for about 2 hours.

Then split into two parts and roll each one out into rectangles about ½ cm thick.

Spread one rectangle with the nutty filling and one with the poppyseed filling, roll together lengthways and place on a baking tray lined with greaseproof paper. Brush with egg and leave to rise again for a while, lightly prick the dough with a fork several times.

Bake until golden brown at 200 °C in a preheated oven for about half an hour to three quarters or an hour. Dust with icing sugar before serving.

For the nut filling, boil ¼ l with 100 g icing sugar and add the ground nuts. Take the pan off the heat and add the ladyfinger crumbs, 50 g raisins and half the lemon zest and leave to cool.

For the poppyseed filling, mix the poppyseeds with the semolina and 150 ml boiled milk. Then add 100 g icing sugar, the remaining zest and 100 g raisins. Also leave the mixture to cool.

Parlour sweets

1 kg	sugar
300 ml	water
	(Raspberry, orange etc.) syrup, nuts, poppyseeds, almonds, raisins and other ingredients depending on your taste

Stir the sugar and water in a pan over a low heat until the sugar has dissolved. Then, boil with the fruit syrup, stirring constantly, over a high heat until the liquid is bubbling and you can blow bubbles when a wire ring is submerged in it. Now stir in the roughly chopped nuts, almonds, ground poppyseeds, raisins (and other ingredients to taste).

Grease a square baking tin with butter and pour the mixture in until about 2–3 cm deep. Leave to cool slowly and until hard. Then, cut into pieces 3–4 cm long, 2 cm wide and wrap in gold or silver foil.

Tip: you can also dunk the sweets in chocolate before wrapping.

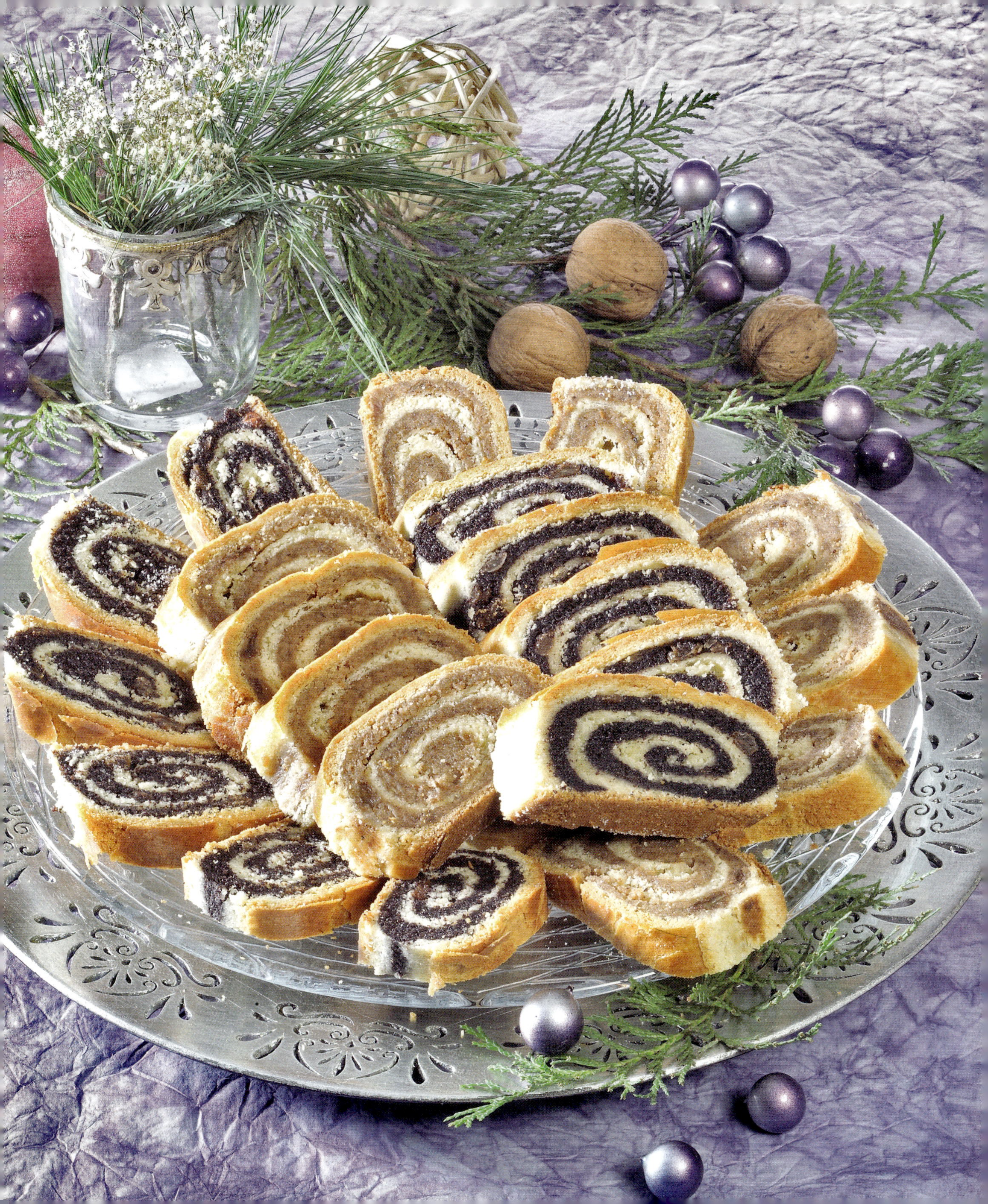

Cyprus

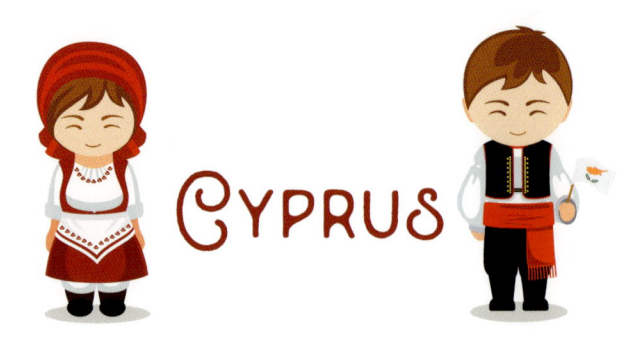

Kalá khristúyenna kai eftikhisméno to néo étos   **Ágia nýchta, se prosménoun**

Cyprus, at least the Greek part of the island, celebrates Christmas according to Orthodox tradition, but on the Gregorian date. The Christmas customs common here are partly British. In terms of food, Christmas Eve is still part of the fasting period, so meat is avoided. The children go through the streets singing and making music. The twelve-day Christmas fire, the gift-giver *Vissilios*, who only comes on New Year's Eve, and the Three Kings are festive "cornerstones" in Cyprus. The Christmas meal varies from turkey to fish, even extending to classically Arabic sweet dishes.

Unlike the large majority of Orthodox Christians, the Cypriots celebrate Christmas at the same time as Catholics and Protestants. In 1923, the Greek, the Cypriot, the Bulgarian, the Romanian and the Syrian Orthodox churches introduced the Gregorian calendar, which corresponds to our time reckoning.

In Cyprus, there are also festive decorations, and Christmas songs can be heard everywhere. With temperatures of over 20°C, blaring "White Christmas" out the speakers does seem a little peculiar.

On Christmas Eve, the children go through the streets and sing *Kalanda*. These are beautiful Christmas songs which the children play along to with bells and drums. Christmas Eve is still part of the fasting period which is why no meat is served up. There are plenty of sweets, such as *Baklava*, for example.

However, the presents only come on New Year's Eve, but, according to traditional custom, on Christmas Eve everyone is allowed to make a wish while they throw a piece of wood into the fire. The Christmas fire burns for twelve days from then and is said to banish goblins.

Many families also put their Christmas tree and nativity scene up on 24 December. Then on 25 December turkey stuffed with chestnuts is often eaten. This and numerous other Christmas traditions can be traced back to the British colonial period.

Agios Vassilios, a combination of St Nicholas and Father Christmas, only comes on New Year's Eve and places presents for the children under their beds.

For New Year, the old and young in Cyprus like to play gambling games to have fun and to sometimes get an insight into their future. On New Year's Day, they eat *Vasilopita*. A coin is baked into this large sweet bread. The finder is allegedly blessed with a whole year full of luck.

The most important part of the Christmas celebration from a religious point of view is *Epiphania* or Epiphany on 6 January. The churches are then decorated with palm leaves and the water is consecrated against evil spirits, in remembrance of the baptism of Christ.

Halloumi goujons

500 g	halloumi cheese, washed, cut into strips
750 g	Chinese cabbage
2	red peppers
2	green peppers
250 g	mushrooms
2	onions, finely chopped
2	garlic cloves, finely chopped
1	piece ginger, the size of a walnut, grated or finely chopped
300 ml	white wine, semi-dry
5 tbsp	oil
	Dried mushrooms
1–2 tbsp	cornflour, whisked in a little water
1 sprig	of rosemary
2 stalks	of thyme
	Salt, pepper

Fry the cheese in a pan with heat oil for 5–7 minutes until brown all over, then remove.

Then, fry the Chinese cabbage in the pan while stirring and remove. Add another 1 tbsp of oil into the pan and add the peppers and mushrooms. Fry for c. 5 minutes and remove. Fry the onions, garlic and ginger in the remaining oil until transparent.

Now, put all the vegetables back into the pan and fry for a further 5 minutes while stirring. Add the wine and mushrooms and fry for a further five minutes.

Bind together with the cornflour and season with pepper and salt, then add the cheese back to the pan and heat up. Finally, pluck the herbs and scatter over the finished dish. Rice or even crusty white bread go well with this.

Calamari with onions

1 kg	calamari, prepared, cut into small pieces
500 g	carrots, cut into small pieces
500 g	celery stalks, cut into small pieces
500 g	onions, cut into small pieces
200 ml	dry white wine
200 ml	olive oil
	Tomato puree
	Salt, peppercorns
	Bouquet of cloves, cinnamon sticks, bay leaves, all bound together in a linen bag

Put the calamari in a hot pan without fat (!) and fry until the liquid that appears has evaporated. Then add the vegetables, tomato puree, spices to taste and the wine and stir well.

Then add the oil, peppercorns and spice bag, cover and leave to simmer over a medium heat for c. 2 hours. Finally, remove the spice bag and serve hot. Potatoes go well with this.

Cyprus

Baklava

(Sweet flaky pastry bake)

500 g	filo pastry/flaky pastry
1 kg	almonds, peeled and finely chopped
250 g	butter
3 tsp	ground cinnamon
600 g	sugar
1	orange, zest
	Cloves
1	cinnamon stick
125 g	honey
1 tbsp	rosewater

Mix together the almonds, cinnamon and a third of the sugar.

Grease a baking tin or a high baking tray with melted butter, line with a first layer of pastry and brush this with butter.

Then, layer the almond mixture and pastry sheets alternately one on top of the other.

On the top, butter the final pastry layer as well and also sprinkle over a little water. Put the baklava in the oven for c. 45 minutes.

Boil the remaining sugar with the orange zest, a few cloves and cinnamon in 400 ml water for 15 minutes, then drain. Before it cools, add the honey and rosewater.

Then pour this syrup over the cooled baklava and leave to soak in overnight. To serve, cut into small portions.

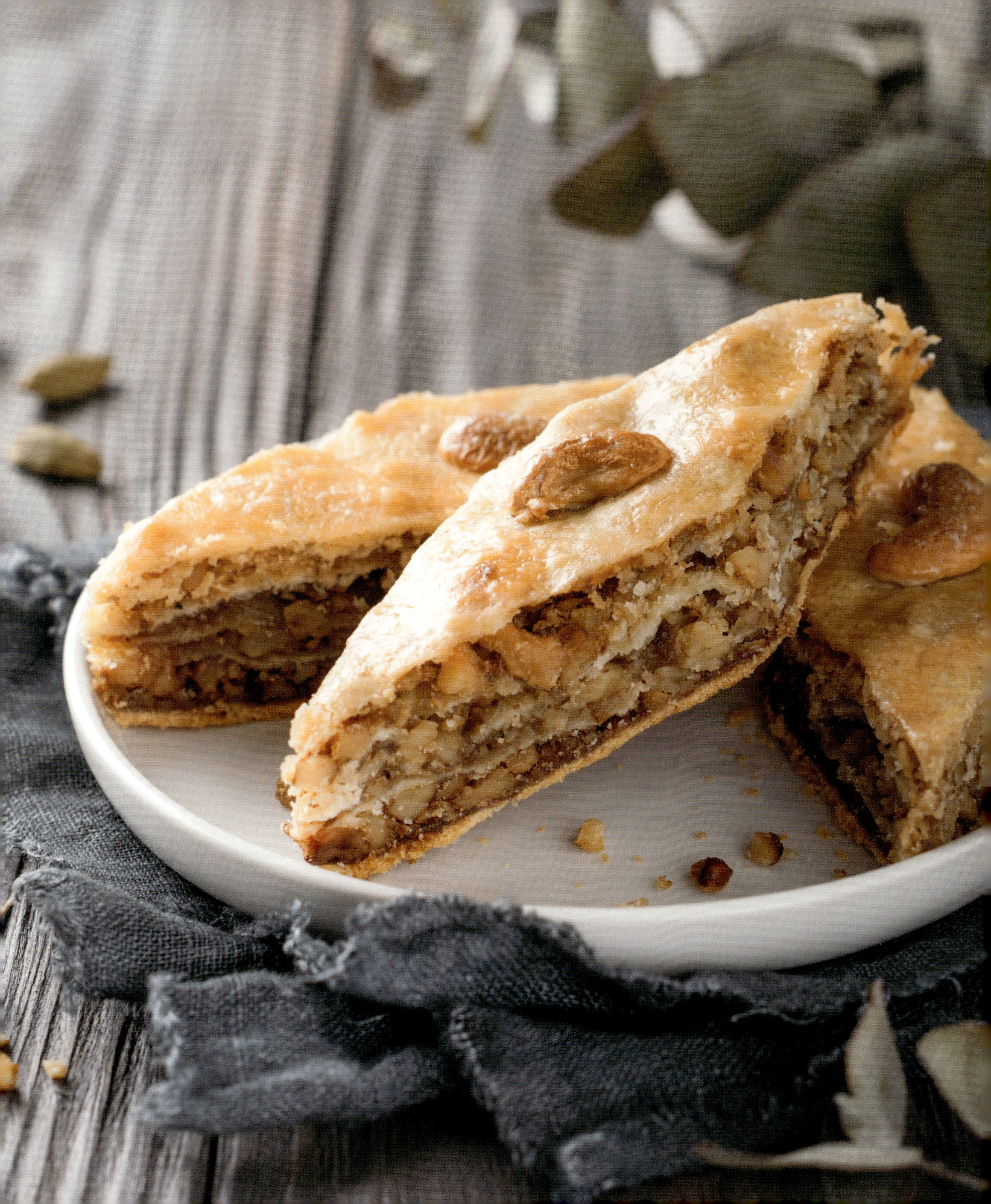

Acknowledgements

It is an extraordinary feat that the parish of Wagrain, together with the "Kulturverein Blaues Fenster", the mountain railways and the tourism association in Wagrain and Kleinarl, has decided to jointly undertake such a large and magnificent project.

Accordingly, I would like to thank the mayor, Eugen Grader, as well as the teachers at Neuen Mittelschule Wagrain (previously Hauptschule), in particular Irene Aster and the home economics teachers Greti El Makarim, Rosmarie Langeder, Anita Moser and Monika Huber.

A big thank you also goes to the heads of the tourism associations in Wagrain/Kleinarl, Stefan Paßrugger and his team as well as to Sonja Holzer who has worked on the project for many long years.

I would also like to thank "Kulturverein Blaues Fenster" with Mag. Carola Schmidt, and Maria Walchhofer for her numerous roles on site and with this project.

A posthumous thank you is also due to the former head of the cultural association, Mag. Elisabeth Kornhofer, whose enthusiastic support, in particular at the start of the project, I will always be grateful for, and another posthumous thank you to our tireless culture consultant, Bertl Emberger.

I must not forget Dr Eva Kreissl, cultural anthropologist and exhibition organiser, who first came up with the idea for this project and suggested I bring it to life.

A special thank you goes to the students who have slaved away over a hot stove for this project.

In 2010, Italy/Trieste, Czech Republic and Serbia was cooked by Berner Bastian, Fritzenwallner Malina, Gruber Elisabeth, Haitzmann Anna, Kreuzsaler Stefan, Payrich Julia, Pelzmann Samuel, Pfeiffenberger Sonja C., Rölle Örum Danel, Schartner Elisabeth, Thurner Karin, Winter Andreas, Winter Marlene C., Zuparic Marija and Aksic Miljana, Baldauf Theresa, Bjelic Andreas, Egger Alexandra, Gasser Helmut, Höller Sarah, Höller Simon, Kaml Katharina, Maier Daniel P., Paßrugger Andrea, Pröll Nathalie, Sendlhofer Gerhard, Stajkovic Dejan, Steinbacher Birgit, Thurner Alica S.

In 2011, Germany/Ore Mountains and Hungary (as well as Armenia, outaide the normal range of events) was cooked by: Aichhorn Simon, Berner Niklas, Đekic Miso, Ellmer Thomas, Fritzenwallner Katharina, Hagenhofer Anna, Hausbacher Laura, Höller Alina, Höller Lena, Kammerlander Christian, Palle Philipp, Pelzmann Samuel, Radauer Lea, Simovic Ivana, Stonig Hanna, Fritzenwallner Fabian, Fritzenwallner Theresa, Gwehenberger Matthias Huber Bernhard, Huber Sabrina, Keil Evelyn, Ortner Carina, Ortner Marion, Pichler Dominik, Rußegger Fabian, Schaidreiter Martin, Schaidreiter Thomas, Schwaiger Sabrina, Schwaiger Susanne, Schwarzenbacher Robin, Stramitzer Julia, Weiß Tobias.

In 2012, Denmark, Greee and Sweden were cooked by Ellmer Daniel, Haitzmann Josef, Islitzer Andre, Islitzer Pascal, Kaswurm Florian, Koblinger Samuel, Kramer Fabian, Kreuzsaler Lisa, Nikolic Andrija, Peric Zoran, Pronebner Kevin, Schartner Michaela, Simovic Tea, Thurner Sarah, Vasilic Darko, Aksic Anica, Aster Sophia, De Almeida Cardoso Tiago, Fritzenwallner Andreas, Fritzenwallner Ben, Fritzenwallner Lorenz, Hotter Christian, Huber Katharina, Kaml Theresa, Loipold Kevin, Paßrugger Lukas, Rettenbacher Marion, Soacaci Romina, Winter Julia.

In 2013, Belgium, Portugal and Slovenia were cooked by: Aichhorn Stefanie, Fritzenwallner Benjamin, Ganschitter Erik L., Hausbacher Hermann L., Höll Stefanie, Höller Marlene, Janjic Ivan, Janjic Lucia, Pichler Patrick, Rehrl Sarah, Riepler Martina, Soacaci Samir F., Thurner Lucas J., Unteregger Felix A., Viehhauser Judith.

In 2014, Estonia, the Ntherlands and Romania were cooked by: Birnbacher Andreas, Fritzenwallner Annalena, Fritzenwallner Elisabeth, Herzmaier Florian, Höller Mario, Kammerlander Bernhard J., Kramer Lisa-Maria, Kreuzsaler Thomas H., Nienhuis Carsten R., Pichler Manuel, Scharfetter Laura M., Schartner Jonas, Schwarzenbacher Florian, Silbergasser Laura.

In 2015, Norway, Poland and Spain were cooked by: Andexer Nina M., Berger Julia K., Berner Aliya , Demir Büsra, Devos Justin, Emberger Michael, Fritzenwallner Anna-Sophie, Fritzenwallner Rupert, Ganschitter Anja , Gasser Luca, Glatzhofer Nico , Gordon Elisa M. , Grabner Manuel, Gratz Lea, Gruber Selina , Grünwald Christina, Hagenhofer Claudia, Höller Ines, Höller Samuel, Holzer Theresa, Huber Klara, Kalchschmid Nico A., Knjeginjic Dimitrije, Miskovic Patricia, Ober Laura, Oberauer Nina, Pröll Fabian, Riepler Alexander, Schaidreiter Roland, Schaidreiter Stefan, Schartner Jakob, Schartner Marina, Schlögel Jakob, Soacaci Rafaela S., Stramitzer Stefan, Viehhauser Michaela. Viehhauser Theresa, Zuparic Ivan

In 2016, France/Alsace, Ireland and Malta were cooked by: Aichhorn Raphael, Berner Christina, Deseife Tobias, Emberger Vitus, Friedler Daniel, Fritzenwallner Nick, Gruber Tobias, Gsenger Julia, Heiss Stefan , Hettegger Luca, Höller Lea K., Höller Marlen, Höller Thomas, Kaswurm Anna S., Kössler Florian, Neumayr Lisa, Nienhuis Akke Brecht, Oberbichter Leon, Obermoser Anna-Lena, Oebster Elisabeth, Ortner Marcel, Paßrugger Tobias, Roe Noah C., Schachtner Leon, Schaidreiter Anna Lena, Schartner Sandra, Schönberger Felix, Schwarzenbacher Sophie, Schwarzenbacher Valentina, Stanovici Dalia, Stonig Sara, Takacs Emese, Taxer Kerstin M., Thurner Emma L., Wallner Lisa, Winter Verena L.

In 2017, Switzerland, Great Britain and Bulgaria were cooked by: Aksic Mihajlo, Althuber Ronja, Arentsen Yannik, Berner Emily, Emberger Christian, Erlandsson Lena, Feldbacher Elenor, Frank Ann-Sophie, Fritzenwallner Alexander, Gordon Eva, Gruber Martina, Haitzmann Mirjam, Hettegger Sarah, Hirner Johanna, Hörmannseder Philipp, Huber Maria, Janjic Dario, Junger Alexander, Knjeginjic Marija, Paßrugger Jakob, Paßrugger Maximilian, Pichler Matheo, Pichler Sebastian, Pichler Valentin, Rathgeb Nina, Reiter Selina, Riepler Laura, Riepler Marie, Schachtner Ben, Schartner Kevin, Schartner Lara, Schiestl Alexander, Thurner Julia, Thurner Michael, Viehhauser Johanna, Winter-Ebster Katharina, Zeferer Johann.

A heartfelt thanks to my personal consultant and collocutor, Hannes Kugler.

Thanks also to Verlag Anton Pustet in Salzburg for publishing this book.

Finally, I would like to thank the agencies and tourism organisations stated below, as well as the individual people from many different countries in Europe who have provided us with images for this book. Here, I would like to highlight the role of the flower chef and food stylist Monika Halmos and her photographer András Vass, for donating photos.

Thanks to the following organisations

**Netherlands Board
of Tourism and Conventions**
Natalie Poloczek, Intern. Marketing
Alexandra Johnen, PR-Manager
c/o Regus
Richmodstr. 6, 50667 Cologne
Postfach 270580, 50511 Cologne
www.holland.com, www.nbtc.nl
yourmediakit.com/login/Holland

Romanian Cultural Institute, Vienna
Alexandra PANICAN
Project coordination
Argentinierstrasse 39, 1040 Vienna
Tel. + 43 (0) 131 910 81
www.rkiwien.at
http://www.transylvaniancookbook.com/

**Consulatul onorific al României
în Landul Styria**
Honorary consulate Mag. Andreas Bardeau
Mag. Diana BilĐog,
Secretary and Public Relations Office
Mariatrosterstr. 211, 8044 Graz
Tel./Fax +43 316 39 21 56
Mobil +43 664 73 65 97 15
konsulat.romania@bardeau.ro

Intercultural Association of "Doina" Graz
Emanuel Viorel Deliu
Stela Maria Michl-Lukacs
Wielandgasse 23, 8010 Graz
Tel. 0677 / 624 631 44
verein.doina@gmail.com

Finnish Embassy
Petra Hedman
Gonzagagasse 16, 1010 Wien
Petra.Hedman@formin.fi
www.finland.at, www.visitfinland.com
imagebank.visitfinland.com

Tourist Information Office Malta
Corinna Ziegler
Marketing Manager
Office: +43-1-585 37 70
corinna.ziegler@urlaubmalta.com
www.visitmalta.com

Luxembourg City Tourist Office a.s.b.l.
Cathy Giorgetti
Marketing, Public Relations
Tel. +352/4796-4722
Cell +352/691 984722
30, Place Guillaume II L-1648 Luxembourg
P.O. Box 181 L-2011 Luxembourg
N TVA: LU 1562 1823 • R.C.S. Luxembourg F 754
www.lcto.lu

Embassy of the Republic of Estonia
Wohllebengasse 9/12, 1040 Vienna
Tel. (+43/1) 503 77 61 11
Fax (+43/1) 503 77 61 20
Helen Galkan, Helen.Galkan@mfa.ee
embassy@estwien.at
www.estemb.at

Croatian Centre for Tourism
Bernarda Kuhne, informant/secretary
Liechtensteinstraße 22a, 1/1/7, 1090 Vienna
Tel. +43 1 585 3884
Fax +43 1 585 3884 20
bernarda.kuhne@kroatien.at
at.croatia.hr

**Czech Centre for Tourism – CzechTourism
Austria & Switzerland**
Mag. Susanne Jandrasits, assistant to the directors
CzechTourism Vienna
Penzingerstraße 11–13, A-1140 Vienna
Tel.: +43/1/89 202 99
wien@czechtourism.com
www.czechtourism.com

visitirland, das Irland Reiseportal
Patrick Schulz
Cunostr. 92, D-14199 Berlin
Tel. +49 (0)30-89735514
info@visitirland.de
www.visitirland.de

Tourismusverband Erzgebirge e. V.
Regional office Altenberg-Dippoldiswalde
Anke Eichler,
project management, marketing,
cuisine/outdoor activities regional operations
Markt 2, 01744 Dippoldiswalde
Tel. 03504 614877
Fax 03504 614878
a.eichler@erzgebirge-tourismus.de
www.erzgebirge-tourismus.de
www.facebook.com/Erzgebirge.DieErlebnisheimat

Rószakunyhó Monika Halmos, András Vass
1162 Budapest, Roszos U. 53
0036-30-9647 144
info@halmosmonika.hu
www.halmosmonika.hu

Tourism Ireland – Representation Austria
Simon Bopp
Untere Donaustrasse 11/3 OG, 1020 Vienna
Tel. +43 (0)1 581 89 22 70
Fax +43 (0)1 585 36 30-88
sbopp@tourismireland.com
www.ireland.com

Spanish tourism information offcie (Turespaña)
Spanish Embassy
Walfischgasse 8/14, A1010 Vienna
Alexander Meindl
Tel. +43 1 512 95 80 16
Fax +43 1 512 95 81
alexander.meindl@externos-tourspain.es
www.spain.info

Embassy for the Republic of Bulgaria
Mag.a Valeriya Hamp
Ambassador's Office
Schwindgasse 8, 1040 Vienna
Tel. 01-505 31 13
Fax 01-505 14 23
amboffice@embassybulgaria.at

Slovenian Tourist Board – I feel Slovenia
Mateja Bauman
Dimičeva ulica 13
SI-1000 Ljubljana, Slovenia
Marjan Zana, zana.marijan@slovenia.info
MatejaKraner, Mateja.Kraner@gov.si
info@slovenia.info
www.slovenia.info

Embassy for the Republic of Latvia
Mag. Dace Veidmane-Pundure, Erster Sekretär
Stefan-Esders-Platz 4, 1190 Vienna
Tel. +43 1 40 33 112
embassy.austria@mfa.gov.lv
www.mfa.gov.lv/austria

Consulate for the Republic of Latvia
Honorary consul Dr. Karl Winding
im Diakoniewerk Salzburg
Guggenbichler Straße 20, 5026 Salzburg
karl.winding@diakoniewerk.at
Tel. +43-662-6385-927

Polish Tourist Information Office
Mag. Bozenna Plusa
Fleschgasse 34/2A, 1130 Vienna
Tel. +43 (1) 524 71 91
Fax. +43 (1) 879 05 30
wien@pot.gov.pl
www.polen.travel/de-at

Bibliography

Schweiz Tourismus
Mag.(FH) Elisabeth Sommer-Weinhofer
Projekt Manager Österreich, Ungarn
Schwindgasse 20, 1040 Wien
Tel. +43 (0)1 513 26 40-13,
Fax +43 (0)1 513 26 40--19
Mobil +43 (0)699 13 699 550
elisabeth.sommer@switzerland.com
www.MySwitzerland.com

Ticino Turismo
Via C. Ghiringhelli 7, CH–6501 Bellinzona
Tel. +41 (0)91 825 70 56
Fax +41 (0)91 825 36 14
info@ticino.ch
www.ticino.ch

**Botschaft der Republik
Albanien Deutschland**
Dr. Irida Laci (Lika), Counsellor
Friedrichstrasse 231, 10969 Berlin
Tel. + 49 (0) 30 25 93 04 61
Fax. +49 (0) 30 25 93 18 90
irida.laci@mfa.gov.al

Visitflanders
Tourismuswerbung Flandern–Brüssel
Mariahilfer Straße 121b/6. Stock, 1060 Wien
Tel. +43 1 596 06 60
office.at@visitflanders.com
www.visitflanders.com

Kulturforum DanAustria
Marianne Aguilar, Leiterin
Keilgasse 12/7, A-1030 Wien
Tel./Fax: +43 1 408 67 90
office@danaustria.org
www.danaustria.org

Bildhauer
Günter Hauer
Triesterstraße 370, 8055 Graz
Tel. +43 316 291630
Mobil +43 664 2868664
office@bild-hauer.at
www.bild-hauer.at

Casparek-Türkkan, Erika: Weihnachtsbäckerei, Gräfe und Unzer Verlag, 2007
Das große Hausbuch zur Weihnachtszeit, Ars Edition, 2017
Das kleine Buch der Weihnachtsbräuche, Jan Thorbecke Verlag, 2008
Die klassische Weihnachtsküche – Die besten Rezepte für die Festtage, Verlag Thorbecke, 2011
Erne, Andrea: Wir feiern Weihnachten, Ravensburger, 2012
Forbes, Leslie: Die schönsten Feste in aller Welt, Wilhelm Heyne Verlag München, 1992
Helm, Eve Marie: Hasenörl und Kirmesfladen, BLV Verlagsgesellschaft, München, 1984
Hirscher, Petra: Weihnachten in Bayern – Von Martini bis Dreikönig, 2010
Hofmann-Stollberg, Alfred/Jostmann, Renate (Hrsg.): Geschichten über Weihnachtsbräuche aus aller Welt, Stuttgart, Hohenheim, 2005
Höller, Christa: Kulturgeschichten um Weihnachten, Edition Strahalm, Graz, 2006
Klauda, Manfred: Die Geschichte des Weihnachtsbaumes, ZAM, München 1993
Kriechbaum, Reinhard, Weihnachtsbräuche in Österreich, 2010
Kruse, Hanne: Christmas cooking: Rezepte und Geschichten aus aller Welt, Fona Verlag, 2006
Kügler-Anger, Heike: Vegetarisches fürs Fest: Weihnachtsrezepte aus aller Welt, pala Verlag, 2009
Lang, Friedrich: Kultbuch Weihnachten, Komet Verlag, Köln, 2009
Lehmann, Herbert: Das Bäuerinnen Weihnachtsbackbuch – alte & neue Lieblingsrezepte, Leopold Stocker Verlag, Graz, 2008
Lindner, Gert (Hrsg.): Krippe und Stern, Gütersloher Verlagshaus Gerd Mohn, Gütersloh, 1961
Mack, Cornelia (Hrsg.): Das große Buch von Weihnachten, Hänssler Verlag, Neuhausen/Stuttgart, 1996
Maier-Bruck, Franz: Vom Essen auf dem Lande, Verlag Kremayr und Scheriau, Wien, 1988
Nieschlag, Lisa: White Christmas: Rezepte & Geschichten für eine entspannte Weihnachtszeit, Hölker Verlag, 2017
Oliver, Jamie: Weihnachtskochbuch, Dorling Kindersley, München, 2016
Österreichische Bäuerinnen decken den Weihnachtstisch – 180 Back- und Kochrezepte aus allen neun Bundesländern, Löwenzahn-Verlag, Innsbruck, 2006
Pörtner, Rudolf: Weihnachten nach dem Krieg, 1995

Sachslehner, Johannes: Weihnachten im alten Österreich – eine nostalgische Zeitreise, Styria, Wien Graz, 2009
Schmidt-Chiari, Katharina: Weihnachten in Österreich, Erfurt, Sutton 2015
Schönfeldt, Sybil Gräfin: Das große Ravensburger Buch der Feste und Bräuche, Otto Meier Verlag Ravensburg, 1980
Schönfeldt, Sybil Gräfin: Weihnachten, Komet Verlag, Frechen, 2003
Schulze, Michael: Stollen, Geschichte und Gegenwart eines Weihnachtsgebäcks, Lehmstedt, Leipzig, 2009
Standl, Josef A.: Stille Nacht, Heilige Nacht, Verlag Dokumentation der Zeit, Oberndorf, 1997
Stolzenberger, Günter: Das große Weihnachtsbuch – Erzählungen und Gedichte aus fünf Jahrhunderten, Artemis & Winkler, Düsseldorf, 2001
The Latvian Institute, The Cuisine of Latvia, 2014
Treichl-Stürgkh, Desiree/Lafer, Johann: Fröhliche Weihnachten, Verlag Brandstätter, Wien, 2012
Weihnachten. Bräuche & Rezepte, Buchverlag für die Frau, 2012

Internet
When researching this book, which took several years, a number of different internet sources were also taken into consideration. For reasons of space and accuracy, the list of the corresponding links has been omitted from this page. Anyone interested can find the full list at the following link:

www.stillenacht-wagrain.com

Recipe index

A

Æblekage →*s. Danish apple cake* **32**
Aguony pienas →*s. Poppyseed milk* **126**
Albanian bean soup →*s. Pasul* **15**
Albanian doughnuts →*s. Petulla* **16**
Apple sauce **132**
Arnaki frikassee →*s. Lamb fricassee*
    with chicory salad and lemon sauce **69**
Ärter med Fläsk
    →*s. Yellow pea soup with pork* **178**

B

Bacalhau à Bras →*s. Salt cod*
    with potatoes and egg 164, **166**
Bacon pancakes **141**
Baked alphabet letters for names **142**
Baked apples **41**
Baked carp **37**
Baklava
    →*s. Sweet flaky pastry bake* 13, 214, **216**
Bean paste →*s. Bigilla* **135**
Bean soup →*s. Bob-Tschorb* **25**
Beigli →*s. Yeasted bakes* **212**
Belgian beef dish →*s. Stoofvlees* **20**
Belgian Christmas biscuits with meringue
    →*s. Nic Nac Guimauve* **21**
Bigilla →*s. Bean paste* **135**
Black pudding →*s. Verivorst*
    →*s. Träipen* 42, **45**, 118, 128, **132**
Black pudding with creamed potato
    and apple sauce →*s. Träipen* 128, **132**
Bobalky →*s. Yeasted noodles*
    with poppyseed and honey **193**
Bob-Tschorb →*s. Bean soup* **25**
Bohemian apricot rings **207**
Bohemian game soup **204**
Boiled carp in marinade **204**
Bolo Rei →*s. King's cake* **166**
Braided Christmas loaf →*s. Vánočka* **207**
Braised turkey with boiled soft quark strudel
    →*s. Christmas roast with Štrukli* **113**
Bûche de Noël →*s. Yule Log* 57, **63**
Buzara →*s. Seafood* **98**

C

Calamari with onions **215**
Cesnica →*s. Serbian Christmas cake* 104f, **109**
Cheesecake →*s. Sernik* **162**
Christmas biscuits →*s. Kuciukai*
    →*s. Piparkuka* 121, 126
Christmas borscht **124**
Christmas bread
    →*s. Pitka* →*s. Jõululaib* **26**, 42, **49**, 57, 104,
    105, 110, 116, 145, 175

Christmas cake **79**, 81
Christmas carp **152**
Christmas ham with turnip and carrot
    casserole →*s. Joulukinkku* **54**
Christmas Plumpudding **79**
Christmas roast with Štrukli
    →*s. Braised turkey with*
    boiled soft quark strudel **113**
Christmas stollen 128, 149, **155**
Corba od pasulja
    →*s. Serbian bean soup* **106**
Cordero en chilindrón
    →*s. Moorish lamb stew*
    with tomatoes and pepper **199**
Cozonac →*s. Nut strudel* 169, **173**
Curd cheese sweets
    →*s. Kodused kohukesed* **46**

D

Dalmatian crème caramel
    →*s. Dalmatinska Rožata* **102**
Dalmatinska Rožata
    →*s. Dalmatian crème caramel* **102**
Danish apple cake
    →*s. Æblekage* **32**
Danish Christmas almond rice pudding
    →*s. Ris à l'amande* **32**
Danish herring salad →*s. Sildesalat* **29**
Danish red cabbage **31**
Duck breast à l'orange **60**

E

Easted cake with fruit →*s. Panettone* **187**
Esterházy rostélyos
    →*s. Esterházy-style roast joint* **211**
Esterházy-style roast joint
    →*s. Esterházy rostélyos* **211**

F

Finnish herring salad →*s. Sillisalaatti* **53**
Fish soup →*s. Halászlé*
    →*s. s. Kakavia* 64, **66**, 123, 208f, **211**
Flæskesteg →*s. Roast pork with crackling,*
    with potatoes and Danish red cabbage **31**
Flemish poultry stew →*s. Waterzooi* **18**, 90
Friulian Reindling →*s. Gubana* **95**

G

Ginger biscuits **55**
Greek Christmas Turkey **66**
Greek fish soup →*s. Kakavia* **66**
Gromperekichelcher mat Ierbsebulli
    →*s. Mashed potato with pea soup* **131**
Gubana →*s. Friulian Reindling* **95**

H

Halászlé →*s. Fish soup* **211**
Halloumi goujons **215**
Honey macarons →*s. Melomakarona* **69**

I

Ierbsebulli 131

J

Janssons Frestelse
    →*s. Jansson's Temptation* **181**
Jansson's Temptation
    →*s. Janssons Frestelse* **181**
Joulukinkku →*s. Christmas ham*
    with turnip and carrot casserole **54**
Jõululaib →*s. Christmas bread* **49**

K

Kakavia →*s. Greek fish soup* **66**
Kapustnica →*s. Sauerkraut soup* **193**
Kepenimis įdaryta veršiena riešutų padaže
    s. → *Veal roulade stuffed with liver*
    in a nut sauce **125**
King's cake →*s. Bolo Rei* **166**
Kodused kohukesed
    →*s. Curd cheese sweets* **46**
Kransekake →*s. Wreath Cake* **147**
Kuciukai →*s. Christmas biscuits* **126**

L

Lamb fricassee with chicory salad and lemon
    sauce →*s. Arnaki frikassee* **69**
Lamb's lettuce with nutty vinaigrette
    and Gjetost-Knusti **146**
Laufabrauð →*s. Snowflake bread* 86, **88**
Lentil soup **37**

M

Maltese pastry ring
    →*s. Qaghaq tal-ghasel* 135, **138**
Maltese rice →*s. Ris à la Malta* **181**
Marinated pot roast à la Marianne **142**
Mashed potato with pea soup
    →*s. Gromperekichelcher mat Ierbsebulli* ... **131**
Meat dish with sauerkraut from the
    Mulgi region →*s. Mulgikapsad* **46**
Melomakarona →*s. Honey macarons* **69**
Mince Pies 70, **76**, 80f, **84**, 135
Moldovan stuffed cabbage leaves
    with polenta →*s. Sărmăluțe*
    moldovenești with Mămăliga **170**
Moorish lamb stew
    with tomatoes and pepper
    →*s. Cordero en chilindrón* **199**

Mulgikapsad →s. Meat dish with
 sauerkraut from the Mulgi region................ **46**

N
Nic Nac Guimauve →s. Belgian Christmas
 biscuits with meringue.................... **21**
Nut roulade →s. Potica **114**
Nut sauce.. **125**
Nut strudel →s. Cozonac **173**

O
Orange and rosemary chicken **136**

P
Palneni chushki s oriz
 →s. Stuffed peppers........................**25**
Panettone →s. Easted cake
 with fruit 90, **92**, 135, 182f **187**
Parlour sweets.. **212**
Pasta con scampi →s. Pasta with prawns.......... **91**
Pasta with prawns
 →s. Pasta con scampi........................ **91**
Pastetli with veal and mushroom filling **184**
Pašticada →s. Pot roast beef 97, **101**
Pastizzi →s. Stuffed puff pastry pockets......... **136**
Pastry parcels with a sauerkraut
 and mushroom filling →s. Pierogi............ **161**
Pasul →s. Albanian bean soup............. **15**
Petulla →s. Albanian doughnuts **16**
Pierogi →s. Pastry parcels with a
 sauerkraut and mushroom filling..........157, **161**
Piparkuka →s. Christmas biscuits **121**
Pírági.. **119**
Pitka →s. Christmas bread.......................... 22, **26**
Poached salmon fillet with hazelnut **88**
Poppyseed milk →s. Aguony pienas **126**
Potato cake **38**
Potato salad........................**38**, 110, 189, **190**, 202
Potica→s. Nut roulade **114**
Pot roast beef →s. Pašticada **101**
Prawn cocktail.................................... **196**
Preistamppot met paddestoelen
 →s. Roast beef with leek mash pot
 and mushrooms **141**
Puff pastry tarts with a chicken and
 ham filling →s. Vol-au-Vent........................ **72**

Q
Qaghaq tal-ghasel →s. Maltese pastry ring **138**

R
Remoulade sauce..................................... **75**
Ris à la Malta →s. Maltese rice **181**
Ris à l'amande →s. Danish Christmas
 almond rice pudding **32**
Roast beef with Brussel sprouts,
 roast potatoes and remoulade sauce **75**
Roast beef with leek mash pot and mushrooms
 →s. Preistamppot met paddestoelen **141**
Roast pork with crackling, with potatoes
 and Danish red cabbage →s. Flæskesteg **31**
Roast pork with sauerkraut and potatoes **120**
Rollschinkli with sauerkraut
 and violet potatoes..........................**184**
Roscón de reyes →s. Three Kings' Cake........**200**
Russian-style sausage stew →s. Seljanka.........**45**

S
Salmon with crab in a
 mascarpone sauce **92**
Salt cod with potatoes and egg
 →s. Bacalhau à Bras................................**166**
Šaltibarščiai
 →s. Christmas borscht 22, 97, 105, **124**
Sarma →s. Stuffed cabbage rolls...................**109**
Sărmăluțe moldovenești cu Mămăliga
 →s. Moldovan stuffed cabbage
 leaves with polenta................................**170**
Sauerkraut soup →s. Kapustnica................**193**
Seared trout with potato salad....................**190**
Seafood →s. Buzara **98**
Seljanka
 →s. Russian-style sausage stew...................**45**
Serbian bean soup
 →s. Corba od pasulja..................................**106**
Serbian Christmas cake
 →s. Cesnica 104f, **109**
Sernik →s. Cheesecake **162**
Shkodra Carp...**15**
Sildesalat →s. Danish herring salad **29**
Sillisalaatti →s. Finnish herring salad................**53**
Simple biscuits in the shape
 of snowflakes →s. Snowflakes..................**132**
Simple Spekulatius **143**
Smoked salmon salad **59**
Snowflake bread →s. Laufabrauð **88**
Snowflakes →s. Simple biscuits
 in the shape of snowflakes........................**132**
Sopa de pedra →s. Vegetable soup
 with bacon and sausage **165**
Sourdough or roux soup →s. Zurek **158**
Stoofvlees →s. Belgian beef dish....................**20**
Štrukli dough (Pasta dough) 112, 113
Stuffed cabbage rolls →s. Sarma **109**
Stuffed peppers
 →s. Palneni chushki s oriz **25**
Stuffed puff pastry pockets →s. Pastizzi........**136**
Sweet flaky pastry bake →s. Baklava **216**

T
Three Kings' Cake →s. Roscón de reyes 59,
 182f, **200**
Torsk (cod) in mustard sauce..........................**146**
Träipen →s. Black pudding 128, **132**

V
Vánočka →s. Braided christmas loaf 202, **207**
Veal roulade stuffed with liver in a nut sauce
 →s. Kepenimis įdaryta
 veršiena riešutų padaže..............................**125**
Vegetable soup with bacon and sausage
 →s. Sopa de pedra **165**
Vegetable soup with homemade pasta...........**112**
Verivorst →s. Black pudding **45**
Vol-au-Vent →s. Puff pastry tarts
 with a chicken and ham filling **72**

W
Wagrain sausage soup **152**
Waterzooi →s. Flemish poultry stew **18**
Wreath Cake →s. Kransekake..........................**147**

Y
Yeasted bakes →s. Beigli **212**
Yeasted noodles with poppyseed and honey
 →s. Bobalky..**193**
Yellow pea soup with pork
 →s. Ärter med Fläsk..................................**178**
Yule Log →s. Bûche de Noël.............................**63**

Z
Zurek →s. Sourdough or roux soup **158**

Recipe index

Picture credits

Albanian Embassy, Foto Tana 13, 14; Christoph Weber 129; David September 18; Dirk Rückschloss/BURWerbung 34; Dörte Saße/reisefeder.de 88; Eugen Grader 10, 11; Gergely Vass 138; Günter Hauer 153; Jaroslav Beran 203 (top); Croatian National Tourist Board, Danica Pecaric, 99, 100, 103; www.slovenia.info/Foto Matej Vranic 110, 111; Marcel Drechsler 39; Mari-Liis Ilover (Blogger) 48; Monika Halmos und András Vass 209f. Retseptisahtel 43; Simone Andress 35 (top left); tourspain/Miguel Raurich 194; tourspain 195; VdL 128; Vesely Kopac 203 (bottom)
©shutterstock.com: Aleksandar Blanusa 105, Alexander Hoffmann 90, Alexander Propenko 84, Alexey Fedorenko 71, alicja neumiler 169, alpenkoch 94, AmyLv 161, Andrea Leone 75, Anna Kucherova 54, Anastasia Boiko 12, 17, 22, 27, 34, 42, 51, 56, 64, 70, 80, 85, 89, 96, 104, 110, 116, 117, 118, 122, 128, 134, 139, 144, 148, 156, 164, 168, 174, 175, 176, 177, 182, 188, 194, 202, 208, 214, Anatolii Riepin 159, anitasstudio 41, AS Food studio 19, 190 Athina Psoma 68, Avdeyukphoto 87, A. Zhuravleva 53, beta7 29, Bochkarev Photography 83, CatchaSnap 180, cge2010 168, cristi180884 106, Christian Jung 154, Cristina Arbunescu 172, Danilova Janna 6, 149, Dani Vincek 115, Danler 193, Diana Taliun 102, DigitalMammoth 145, Ekaterina Provsky 58, Egor Rodynchenko 95, f11photo 86, Fabio Balbi 93 , Fanfo 44, 47, 87, 145, 164, Foodio 91, Foxys Forest Manufacture 137, freeskyline 108, Galembeck 67, gresei 46, Gtranquillity 140, Harry studio 23, Heather Baird 147, Heidi Becker 77, irin-k 173, Ivana Lalicki 104, Jacob Lund 28, Jiri Hera 114, 143, Kamil Jany 192, Kiian sana 130, KMNPhoto 4, 7, 9, 218, 219, Kristina Loz 135, Laura Stone 175, LeventeGyori 200, Liv friis-larsen 30, Magdanatka 74, Mapics 189, MaraZe 101, 216, marchevcabogdan 171, margouillat photo 57, 185, 186, MariaKovaleva 149, Marian Weyo 191, Miha Travnik 107, mjols84 123, milart 97, Moving Moment 112, Muellek Josef 151, Nadezhda Nesterova 124, Nataliya Druchkova 217, Natali Zakharova 167, Nataly Studio 126, Natasha Breen 21, 32, 33, nathanipha99 25, Nattika 152, nesavinov 179, Nikola Bilic 63, Nida Degutiene 127, NoirChocolate 62, Olesia Reshetnikova 78, PinkPueblo 11, 15, 16, 18, 20, 21, 26, 29, 31, 32, 37, 45, 49, 53, 60, 66, 69, 76, 79, 88, 92, 109, 113, 119, 120, 125, 132, 136, 138, 141, 142, 146, 147, 155, 158, 162, 165, 166, 170, 181, 184, 187, 193, 196, 199, 204, 207, 211, 212, 215, PitK 65, plamens art 26, Rudnev 133, sana2010 98, sana.perkins 24, Sergiy Kuzmin 131, spaxiax 82, Stefano_Valeri 50, Stepanek Photography 206, stockcreations 183, StockphotoVideo 36, 163, stuar 71, Studio 37 169, Sunny Forest 40, Suzanne Tucker 140, Tatiana Trifan 205, Tommy Alven 177, vasanty 201, VICUSCHKA 61, viennetta 81, Wolna 38, Yasonya 72, Yellowj 190, Yulia Furman 157, zi3000 119, zoryanchik 73; Maria Kravets VS/NS.

Double page 10/11: picture 1: Alina Höller, Hannah Stonig; picture 2: Theresa Kaml, Sophia Aster, Tiago De Almeida Cardoso; picture 3: Nico Glatzhofer, Stefan Stramitzer, Dimitrije Knjeginjic, Jakob Schartner; picture 4: Luca Hettegger; picture 5: Stefan Schaidreiter; picture 6: Noah Roe, Tobias Paßrugger; picture 7: Gerhard Sendlhofer, Simon Höller, Bastian Berner; picture 8: Christian Hotter, Lisa Kreuzsaler, Andreas Fritzenwallner, Lorenz Fritzenwallner; picture 9: Andre Islitzer; picture 10: Martina Gruber, Nina Ratgeb, Johanna Hirner.

Bibliographic information of the German National Library
The German National Library has registered this publication in the German National Bibliography: detailed bibliographic data can be found online at http://dnb.d-nb.de.

© 2019 Verlag Anton Pustet
5020 Salzburg, Bergstraße 12, AUSTRIA
All rights reserved.

Cover image: Tanja Kühnel using graphics
©Anastasia Boiko/shutterstock.com

Graphics, setting and cover: Tanja Kühnel
Production: Hannah Meierhofer
Editing: Renate Emminger, Beatrix Binder
English Translation: Quarto Translations, UK
Printing: Christian Theiss GmbH, St. Stefan im Lavanttal
Printed in Austria

ISBN 978-3-7025-0941-5

www.pustet.at